Beacham's Encyclopedia of Social Change

AMERICA
in the
TWENTIETH CENTURY

REF
306
B
vol.2

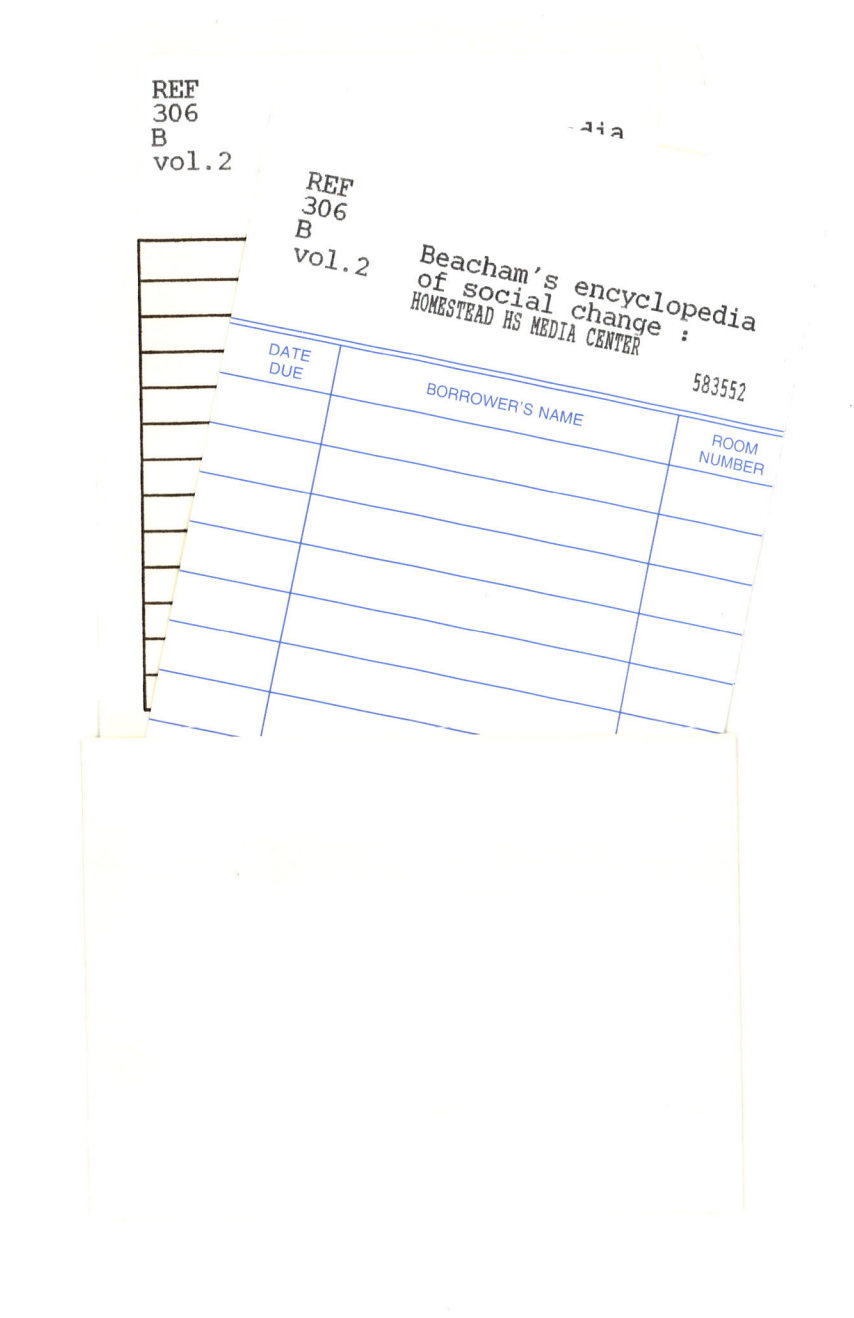

Beacham's encyclopedia
of social change :
HOMESTEAD HS MEDIA CENTER

583552

DATE DUE	BORROWER'S NAME	ROOM NUMBER

BEACHAM'S ENCYCLOPEDIA OF SOCIAL CHANGE

AMERICA *in the* TWENTIETH CENTURY

Edited by Veryan B. Khan

VOLUME 2: PAGES 499–1036

Published by
The Beacham Group LLC

Beacham's Encyclopedia of Social Change: America in the Twentieth Century

Veryan B. Khan, Editor
Walton Beacham, Project Director
Deborah Beacham, Production Manager

While every effort has been made to ensure the reliability of the information presented in this publication, The Beacham Group LLC neither guarantees the accuracy of the data contained herein nor assumes any responsibility for errors, omissions or discrepancies. Errors brought to the attention of the publisher and verified to the satisfaction of the publisher will be corrected in future editions.

This publication is a creative work fully protected by all applicable copyright laws, as well as by misappropriation, trade secret, unfair competition, and other applicable laws. The authors and editors of this work have added value to the underlying factual material herein through one or more of the following: unique and original selection, coordination, expression, arrangement, and classification of the information. All rights to this publication will be vigorously defended.

Copyright © 2001
The Beacham Group LLC
P. O. Box 1810
Nokomis, FL 34274-1810

All rights reserved including the right of reproduction in whole or in part in any form.

Distributed worldwide exclusively by The Gale Group

Book Design by Jill Dible

Library of Congress Cataloging-in-Publication Data

Beacham's encyclopedia of social change: America in the twentieth century / edited by Veryan B. Khan.
    p. cm.
    Includes bibliographical references and index.
    Summary: Traces the evolution of social ideas and values in the United States during the twentieth century, using such indicators as advertising, crime and justice, family life, fashion, music, race and class, sex and gender, and work.
    ISBN 0-933833-62-8 (set: alk. paper)
    ISBN 0-933833-64-4 (v. 1: ak. Paper)
    ISBN 0-933833-65-2 (v. 2: alk. paper)
    ISBN 0-933833-66-0 (v. 3: alk. paper)
    ISBN 0-933833-67-9 (v. 4: alk. paper)

    1. United States—Social conditions—20th century—Encyclopedias, Juvenile. [1. United States—Social conditions—20th century—Encyclopedias.] I. Title: Encyclopedia of social change. II. Khan, Veryan B., 1970-

HN59.2 .B43 2001
306'.0973Bdc21
                                                                           2001043141

Printed in the United States of America
10 9 8 7 6 5 4 3 2 1

Comments and Suggestions are Welcome

The editors invite comments and suggestions from users of *Beacham's Encyclopedia of Social Change: America in the Twentieth Century*. You may contact us by mail at: The Beacham Group LLC, P. O. Box 1810, Nokomis, FL 34274-1810; by telephone at (941) 480-9644 or (800) 466-9644; or by facsimile at (941) 485-5322. Our email address is beachamgroup@aol.com

Photo Acknowledgments

These photos are on the covers of all four volumes of *Beacham's Encyclopedia of Social Change: America in the Twentieth Century*: *U.S.S. Shaw*, Pearl Harbor, Hawaii, December 7, 1941, photograph. National Archives and Records Administration; Dr. Martin Luther King, photograph. The Library of Congress; Children in a parade of suffragettes, May 1913, Long Island, New York, photograph. The Library of Congress, George Grantham Bain Collection; Jim Thorpe, photograph. National Archives and Records Administration; Anti-Vietnam War protest at the Pentagon, Washington, D.C., photograph. National Archives and Records Administration; Dust bowl farm, parts of wagon wheels visible above sand, photograph. National Archives and Records Administration; President Franklin Delano Roosevelt shaking hands with Chief Noal Bad Wound, circa 1936, photograph. Hulton/Archive. Reproduced by permission; Laptop computer, Copyright © 2000 PhotoDisc, Inc. All rights reserved; Hindenberg flying over city, photograph. Archive Photos/Lambert. Reproduced by permission; Dorothy Dandridge, photograph. AP/Wide World Photos. Reproduced by permission; The Beatles wave to a crowd at an airport as they arrive in the U.S. for concerts and television appearances, photograph. Hulton/Archive. Reproduced by permission; Ulysses spacecraft in orbit, illustration. National Aeronautics and Space Administration (NASA). Reproduced by permission. All photos throughout the text are reproduced by permission from Hulton Archive/Getty Images.

Contents

Introduction ix
Contributors xiii

Advertising and Consumerism 1:1
American Expansion 1:47
Automobiles and Highways 1:107
Business and Labor 1:127
Cities 1:163
Crime and Justice 1:195
Death 1:227
Economy 1:273
Education and Literacy 1:411
Emotional Change 1:443
Environment 1:471
Ethnic Minority Groups 2:499
Family Life 2:541
Farming 2:577
Fashion 2:619
Food 2:651
Health and Medicine 2:705
Housing and Architecture 2:745
Immigration 2:831
Individual Prosperity and the American Dream 2:869
Inventions 2:897
Law Enforcement 2:929
Laws and the U.S. Legal System 2:955
Leisure 2:985
Morality 3:1037
Music 3:1089
Occupations 3:1135
The Press and Democracy 3:1155
Race and Class 3:1189
Race and Minorities 3:1261
Radio and Television 3:1311
Religion and American Life 3:1351
Retirement 4:1507
Science 4:1533
Sex and Gender 4:1579
Soldiering: Life in Combat 4:1615
Towns 4:1667
Transportation 4:1699
Travel 4:1749
War and the U.S. Military: Drivers of Social Change 4:1779
Work and the Workplace 4:1857

Timeline 4:1907
Index 4:1947

INTRODUCTION

It is a time for reflection as America steps into the twenty-first century, a century which in some ways resembles the transition from the Dark Ages to the Renaissance, a century of excitement and turmoil, of hope and resignation, in which perceptions about humankind's significance was constantly changing through booms, depressions, and wars.

Perhaps as never before, the delineation between two centuries can be seen through the terrorists' attacks on the World Trade Center and the Pentagon on September 11, 2001. Rarely has a single event established such a clear differentiation between centuries; ironically, the Spanish-American War (1898-1902), which marked the end of U.S. territorial imperialism, ushered in a new century that would demand a completely new role for American leadership, just as the terrorists' attacks on September 11 a century later forces new directions for the United States for the twenty-first century in which world interests take precedence over the ambitions of individual countries. As the United States achieved a position of world dominance at the end of the twentieth century, it renewed some of the same social arguments that prevailed during the period of American imperialism a hundred years before.

The evolution of the century provides fascinating insight into the spirit, values, and ingenuity of the American people. From our roots as outcasts and nonconformists, we developed instincts for survival, respect for social order, and a passion for independence and personal freedom. From the bounty of our land we learned the potential of natural resources and the possibility of abusing them. And from our naiveté we blundered into wars that secured our independence, turned our nation against itself, liberated Europe from tyranny, forced generations to reject each other's values, and established the United States as the most powerful nation.

America is the story of slaves, immigrants, Native Americans, and a European ancestry that created paradox and energy. America in the twentieth century has not been so much a "melting pot" as a nuclear reactor. To understand and appreciate the road from Kitty Hawk to Cape Canaveral, from Jamestown to Montgomery, from barley soup to Lean Cuisine®, *Beacham's Encyclopedia of Social Change: America in the Twentieth Century* traces American history through forty-one key indicators of social change. Each of the chapters—"Advertising and Consumerism" to "Work and the Workplace"—explains the progress of American culture each step of the way. Through our journey we see how Americans made their own history.

In a traditional sense, this encyclopedia is a history book with the usual timelines and statistical charts, but we prefer to think of it as a story book in which ordinary people struggle, suffer, strive toward great accomplishment, and change. What does food or fashion, family life or morality tell us about American values? Plenty. In 1909, as the suffragette movement gained strength, designers abandoned the corset and created the freedom of the Gibson Girl look; in the 1920s, when the proliferation of automobiles provided young people with privacy to pursue their own lives, women wore scandalous clothing, only to retreat to practical clothing during the Depression and World War II years. In the prim and proper 50s women wore tailored clothes and pillbox hats, and in their rebellion against their prim and proper mothers, the 70s women burned their bras and adorned baggy, tie-dyed pants. The fitness generation of the 80s wore her Calvins and in the 90s her spandex running shorts. The times they were a-changing, and what people wore tells us something about their times.

Rather than approaching history from a universal perspective, we look at it piece-by-piece, decade-by-decade, from a human perspective. We attempt to place readers *in* the historical moment, not above it looking down. How did American soldiers during World War I spend their countless miserable hours in the trenches? How did World War II women on the home front contribute to the war? What was life like without men? How did African Americans contribute to the war effort? Prisoners? Native Americans? You'll experience immigration through Mary Hagen's first Christmas after leaving Ellis Island twelve hours earlier; you'll discover that Thomas Edison had a dispute with an employee that forever changed the use of electricity; you'll learn that the bikini is named from an atoll in the Pacific Ocean that the Allies used for testing the atomic bomb during World War II. The fascinating facts, the photos, the timelines, and the sidebars help the reader experience life during a different time.

HOW TO USE THIS ENCYCLOPEDIA • We think of this encyclopedia as comparative history. Each chapter presents a separate key indicator of social change, but they are all interlocked and together complete a picture puzzle of American culture. Fashion alone reflects something about society; when compared to the same timeframes for other key indicators, we begin to see the whole of American society.

To facilitate studying American social history through comparison, we present each key indicator in small units with associated dates. Using the margin date to generally locate a timeframe and the subhead dates to narrow the time period, researchers can compare what was happening across key indicators, and thus see the influence of one on the other. The timeline at the beginning of each key indicator is divided into two parts: the top section list events related to the key indicator while "Milestones" lists other interesting events during the same time period.

Other study features include a composite timeline, which is useful in seeing connections across key indicators, and for generating ideas for research projects. Most of the references in the composite timeline are discussed in the encyclopedia, so that research on any one of them can begin here, then continue through the bibliographies and Internet resources. The comprehensive index provides the gateway for researchers.

The story behind many key indicators begins before the twentieth century opens, and our authors provide the background as far back as necessary to understand the twentieth century. Business and labor practices, for example, established their roots in the 1800s, while modern warfare begins with the Civil War, and modern economy begins with the development of the corporation and industrialization after the Civil War. Other key indicators—modern farming, health care, leisure, and retirement, for example—did not begin until the turn of the century, and thus our story begins there.

Social history is different from the history of great moments. Famous people or intensive events tell only one side of a story—an extreme side. Most people did not fly solo across the Atlantic Ocean or create great wealth by mining gold in California. Most of us who have flown the Atlantic were taking vacations to Europe; most of the miners who rushed to California panned a lifetime without finding an ounce of gold. To identify with these people is to be aware of who Americans are. To appreciate the plights of peoples past is a signpost as to where we might be going. Customs, traditions and behaviors have evolved dramatically in the hundred years of this past century. Following these changes is exciting, fascinating, and fun.

We think that the key indicators provide a personal approach to learning about history and culture. Whether or not readers are concerned about the larger historical picture, they are certainly interested in specific topics: how did Barbie contribute to the women's liberation movement (Sex and Gender); who did the Ku Klux Klan persecute before it turned its wrath on African Americans (Crime and Justice); and most important—a subject that touches on every aspect of American culture—what part have immigrants played in our evolving country (every article).

Usually, social changes occur over a slow, evolutionary process in which history, years later, reveals the gradual development and discernible changes between past and present. However, with a single event, much like the Japanese attack on Pearl Harbor, the twenty-first century has already become unique; we know, without the benefit of history, that America is a different society. Modern-day terrorism, domestic and foreign, began its infancy in the late twentieth century through horrific attacks on American soil and against civilians; the utter destruction of the twin towers in New York City will lead to many changes during the opening years of the twentieth-first century, and the clues to where America will refocus society for a strangely different century are embedded in the key indicators in this encyclopedia.

Veryan B. Khan

Contributors

Kenneth Adderley
Upper Iowa University

James F. Adomanis
Maryland Center for the Study of History

Cara Anzilotti
Loyola Marymount University

Brian Black
Pennsylvania State University, Altoona

Benita Blessing
Fellow, Institute of European History, Mainz

Stephen Burwood
SUNY, Geneseo

Peter Cole
Western Illinois University

Joel S. Franks
San Jose State University

Richard A. Garcia
California State University, Hayward

Jennifer Hamil-Luker
University of North Carolina, Chapel Hill

R. Steven Jones
Southwestern Adventist University
Keene, Texas

Veryan B. Khan

Judy Kutulas
St. Olaf College

R. A. Lawson
Vanderbilt University

Joan D. Laxson

Christina Lindholm
Virginia Commonwealth University

Mark Malvasi
Randolph-Macon College

Greg Moore
Notre Dame College, South Euclid, Ohio

Marie Marmo Mullaney
Caldwell College, New Jersey

Don Muhm

Michael V. Namorato
University of Mississippi

Karen S. Oakes

Paul Ortiz
University of California, Santa Cruz

Diane N. Palmer

Judith Reynolds

Elizabeth D. Schafer

Peter N. Stearns
George Mason University

Kathleen A. Tobin

Peter Uhlenberg
University of North Carolina, Chapel Hill

Christopher Waldrep
San Francisco State University

James D. Watkinson
Randolph-Macon College

The publisher wishes to thank the contributors for their outstanding contribution to this project.

Walton Beacham

Ethnic Minority Groups

~

(circa 1945) A man joining the NAACP (National Association for the Advancement of Colored People). The NAACP was founded in 1909 on Abraham Lincoln's birthday after a riot had broken out the year before in his home town of Springfield, Illinois.

TIMELINE

1619-1800 ~ Slaves and Native Americans

First slaves arrive in America at Jamestown, Virginia (1619) / House of Burgess in Virginia passes laws making the child of a black woman a slave for life and the child of a white woman free-born (1662) / King Philip of the Wampanoags destroys 20 New England towns killing more than 3,000 whites (1675) / Colonial army wipes out the Wampanoags and opens New England to white settlers. (1675-1678) / French and Indian Wars (1689-1763) / U.S. signs treaties with several Indian nations (1784-1794)

MILESTONES: John Winthrop lectures Puritans on board ship about model behavior before arriving in America (1630) • Early American cities established: Jamestown (1607), Santa Fe (1610), Boston (1630) • Constitutional Convention ratifies the Constitution for the new republic (1787) • Congress authorizes recruitment of marshals to serve warrants and subpoenas (1789) • Naturalization Law excludes non-whites from citizenship (1790) • Edward Jenner develops smallpox vaccination in England (1796)

1800-1849 ~ Claiming the Frontier

Andrew Jackson's troops kill 800 Creek Indians, including women and children (1814) / Indian Removal Act authorizes relocating Indian nations west of the Mississippi (1830) / Thousands of Indians die during forced relocation on the "trail of tears" (1831-1838) / Mass migration to western lands (1840s) / United States annexes Texas (1845) / War with Mexico (1846)

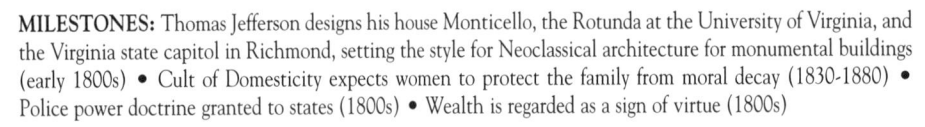

MILESTONES: Thomas Jefferson designs his house Monticello, the Rotunda at the University of Virginia, and the Virginia state capitol in Richmond, setting the style for Neoclassical architecture for monumental buildings (early 1800s) • Cult of Domesticity expects women to protect the family from moral decay (1830-1880) • Police power doctrine granted to states (1800s) • Wealth is regarded as a sign of virtue (1800s)

1850-1900 ~ The Debate over Slavery

Fugitive Slave Law requires whites to return runaway slaves (1850) / *Dred Scott* case makes slavery legal in the territories (1857) / Land Act gives whites in California control over Mexican property (1851) / Oregon Bill of Rights contains a Negro Exclusion Law that remains on the state's law books until 1926 (1859) / The American Civil War (1860-1864) / Chinese laborers build transcontinental railroad across the U.S. (1862-1869) / Chinese workers comprise one-fourth the population of Hawaii (1864) / Fourteenth Amendment declares that all persons born or naturalized in America are citizens (1866) / "Memphis Race Riot (1866)" Irish Policemen destroy Black township in South Memphis killing 46 people, burning 91 homes, 12 schools and 4 churches, raping 6 women, and robbing thousands of dollars from the wives of black soldiers / Fifteenth Amendment declares all men eligible to vote without regard to color (1870) / Indian Appropriation Act permits railroads to lay tracks across Indian lands (1871) / Chinese Exclusion Act restricts immigrant workers (1882 and 1884) / *Plessy v. Ferguson* declares it illegal for African Americans to ride in the same railroad car as whites (1896)

MILESTONES: Charles Darwin's *Origins of the Species* theorizes that man is descended from apes (1859) • Gerrit Miller Smith, a seventeen-year-old college student, establishes the first official football organization in the United States, the Oneida Football Club of Boston (1862) • Ku Klux Klan formed December 24, 1865 in Pulaski, Tennessee (1865) • Freed slaves elect sharecropper farming over paid wages (1867-1868) • Florida passes state law banning convicted felons, aimed at African Americans, from voting (1868) • Interracial alliances of workers and farmers forge national organization, the Knights of Labor (1880s-1890s) • City Beautiful movement advocates wide boulevards and classical architecture (1893-1910) • Capture of Geronimo ends formal warfare between whites and Native Americans (1886)

1900-1919 ~ Fighting for Rights and Freedom

Non-whites excluded from union membership (1900) / Chinese immigration banned except for diplomats, students, and merchants (1900) / W.E.B. Dubois opposes racial discrimination in *The Souls of Black Folk* (1903) / Mexicans strike against the Pacific Electric Railway company for equal wages and parity (1903) / National Association for the Advancement of Colored People founded (1909) / Ku Klux Klan revives (1915-1925) / More than 12,000 Native Americans join the U.S. Army and Navy during World War I and serve with distinction (1918) / Anti-black race riots break out in Elaine, Arkansas as African Americans attempt to earn higher wages, and to live outside of the segregated ghettos of North Chicago (Summer 1919)

MILESTONES: Social protest novels and essays are published that deal with relationships of racial and class oppression (early 1900s) • Social gospel requires churches to deal with social injustice (1900-1920) • Last yellow fever epidemic in the U.S. strikes New Orleans (1905) • Jack Johnson becomes first African American heavyweight boxing champion (1910) • Standardized tests developed to determine racial intelligence (1910s) • Eugenics movement declares that one's destiny is determined by one's genes (1910s) • Native American Jim Thorpe relinquishes his gold medals in the pentathlon and decathlon in the Stockholm Games when officials learn he had played professional baseball and football (1912)

1920-1939 ~ The Seeds of Rebellion

Japanese and Filipino farm workers strike against Hawaiian plantation owners (1920 and 1924) / Filipino immigration is restricted to 50 people a year (1934) / United Mine Workers of America (UMW), one of the nation's few interracial organizations, provides the organizational foundation for the emergence of industrial unionism (1935-1939) / African American Jesse Owens wins three gold medals at the Olympic Games in Berlin, dispelling Hilter's theory of Aryan superiority (1936)

MILESTONES: Harlem Renaissance produces renowned African American writers, artists and musicians (1920s) • J. Edgar Hoover becomes director of the FBI (1924) • John T. Scopes, a schoolteacher in Tennessee, is arrested for teaching evolution to his students (1925) • Supreme Court decision, *Buck v. Bell*, rules that involuntary sterilization for eugenic purposes is constitutional (1927)

1940-1959 ~ The Beginning of the End of Discrimination

President Roosevelt is forced to end racial discrimination in war production facilities (1941) / Executive Order 9066 requires internment of Japanese Americans living on the West Coast (1942) / Repeal of the Chinese exclusion law (1943) / McCarran-Walter Act permits Japanese to apply for citizenship (1952) / *Brown vs. Board of Education* rules that school segregation is unconstitutional (1954) / Montgomery Bus Boycott propels Martin Luther King, Jr. into national prominence (1955)

MILESTONES: 25,000 Native Americans join the Army, Navy or Marine Corps; another 40,000 support the war industries at home (1941-1945) • 3,600 Navajos recruited in the 382nd Platoon serve as "code talkers," using phrases from the Navajo language to transmit intelligence data over the airwaves (1942-1945) • Madame Chiang Kai-Shek visits the United States (1943) • Veterans Emergency Housing Program provides subsidies to create housing (1945) • "Ghetto," once referred to a broad range of ethnic residential enclaves, is now almost exclusively applied to African American and Latino neighborhoods. "Urban renewal" is openly referred to as "Negro removal" (1945-1970) • Housing Act provides for slum clearance and community redevelopment (1949) • Asian intellectual immigration permitted (1950-1980) • President Truman ends racial discrimination in government (1953)

1960-2000 ~ Age of Civil Rights

Freedom Riders firebombed on buses in Anniston, Alabama (1961) / Executive order bars discrimination in the sale, lease or occupancy of residential property owned or operated by the federal government (1964) / Freedom Riders firebombed on buses (1965) / Immigration and Nationality Act removes Japanese quota restriction (1965) / Cuban refugee immigration permitted (1975-1990) / U.S. restores sovereignty to Indian nations (1982) / Some Native American economies prosper from casino gambling (1982-2000) / Amnesty granted to illegal immigrants in the U.S. (1996 and 2001) / Hispanic population equals African American population for the first time (2000)

MILESTONES: Betty Friedan's *The Feminine Mystique* attributes women's problems to a sex-based society and not the personal failure of women, starting the women's liberation movement (1963) • After New York City police raid a gay bar, a riot ensues, and groups form to work for the repeal of laws that prohibit homosexual conduct (1969) • Pruitt-Igoe public housing project in St. Louis, built in 1955, is demolished (1972) • Rodney King is videotaped being clubbed and kicked by Los Angeles police (1991) • Michael Jordan leads the NBA in scoring ten times during his career, averaging 31.5 points per game (1984-1993; 1995-1998) • African American football superstar O.J. Simpson acquitted of charges of murdering his white wife (1995)

INTRODUCTION

*"We hold these truths to be self-evident that all men
were created equal and endowed with inalienable rights . . ."*
Declaration of Independence

In the United States today there are many ethnic groups with different customs, histories, and cultural backgrounds. These groups came to America from many different countries for a variety of reasons. But whatever their background, all those who came after the first English settlers arrived in 1607 were expected to conform to Anglo standards: to speak English and be assimilated into the prevailing culture. Consequently, people from different backgrounds merged into a mainstream culture, and, over time, began to think of themselves as "Americans." For most of the immigrants from Northern and Western Europe this soon became a reality; but by the end of the nineteenth century, there were some groups who stood out as minorities because they refused to relinquish their language, unique cultures and ethnic identities.

Ethnic minorities face many problems in America. What are these problems? How do they differ from one another? How do they relate to the dominant Anglo-American group (white Americans), and how are the prevailing relationships changing? What strategies are being used to bring about social change in America? Before attempting to answer these questions, it is necessary to consider the historical background of the four largest ethnic minority groups in the United States: Native Americans, Hispanic Americans (Mexicans & Latinos), African Americans and Asian Americans.

In the early seventeenth century, the first Europeans arrived in Jamestown, Virginia with the idea of possessing land and gaining wealth for themselves and the English crown. Within a few decades, the prevailing philosophy of the times came to be expressed in what is now known as a "three generational contract." This unwritten contract presupposed that a man was duty-bound to leave his land at his death to his son, who would in turn leave it to his unborn grandson, and so on. Property (land) in Europe was the expression of freedom. A man was free if he owned land, which, when passed down from father to son and to each succeeding generation, provided wealth for the family.

This thirst for land had been the dream of both rich and poor in London. Conditions in sixteenth-century England were so bad that London's poor preferred to sleep outdoors than to live in one of the poor houses. Also, Englishmen had learned the lessons of feudalism so well that "freedom" was expressed in terms of land ownership, since only landholders were allowed to vote. An example of this prevailing philosophy is clearly seen from the practice of the twelfth and thirteenth centuries when absentee English landlords, having control of huge tracts of land in Ireland, leased the land to middlemen who in turn charged the Irish peasants high rents, and also demanded a portion of the crops produced as well. Thus, the Irish people were left with very little land to farm for themselves or leave to their children. The time came between 1815 and 1848 when millions of Irish were forced to emigrate in order to avoid starving to death because of the Great Potato Famine. For several decades they came to America in droves looking for land and a better life, so that between 1815 and 1920 some five and a half million Irish had emigrated to America.

NATIVE AMERICANS

PRE-1500 • HISTORICAL POPULATIONS ~ Before the coming of the Europeans, and before the discovery of the "New World" the Native American population was estimated to be around five million persons belonging to more than five hundred tribes that lived in seven major regions: the northeastern woodlands, the southeastern forests, the Great Basin, the Great Plains, the northern plateau, the southwestern desert and the Pacific coast. By 2000, some statistics suggest that they number about only two million.

The nations in the Northeast included the Pequots, Pennacooks, Narragansetts, Mohegans, Massachusetts and Wampanoags. Five nations of the Iroquois Confederacy included the Mohawks, Oneidas, Onondagas, Cayugas, and Senecas. With the exception of the Oneidas, they all supported the British in the French and Indian War (1754-1763). These nations lived in the Hudson River Valley, while between the Great Lakes and the Ohio River the territory was controlled by the Sauk, Conestoga, Ottawa, Kickapoo, Erie, Chippewa, Shawnee, Menominee, Miami, Fox and Peoria nations. Most of these settled in permanent agricultural villages and hunted game for food and clothing.

The nations in the southeast between the Atlantic Coast and the Mississippi south of the Ohio included the Cherokees of North Carolina and Tennessee; the Seminoles and Calusas of Florida; and the Choctaws, Chickasaws, Creeks and Alabamas on the Gulf Coast.

In the Great Basin between the Rockies and the Sierra Nevadas the Ute, Mono, Paiute Shoshone and other nations roved from place to place with no agriculture or permanent villages and small groups of extended families subsisting on small game, berries, nuts and roots. By contrast the plateau Indians, which included the Flatheads, Yakimas, Nez Perces, Chinnooks and Spokanes, lived between the Rockies and the Cascades, hunted small game, and gathered berries and roots, but also fished for the giant salmon. They lived in semi-permanent villages along the rivers where the salmon spawned.

Two different cultures populated the Southwest: one group of nomadic hunters, and another group of sedentary urban dwellers. The first, fierce warrior hunters dominant in Arizona and New Mexico were the Navajos and the Apaches. They lived in tepees and often raided neighboring tribes. The second culture was comprised of the Hopi, Zuni and Pueblo Indians of Arizona and New Mexico. They planted corn, beans and squash; raised sheep, poultry and cattle, and lived in multilevel adobe buildings.

On the Pacific Coast in southern California more than a hundred tribes including the Yuroks, Salinas, Miwoks and Chumosh lived in nomadic villages and gathered seeds, berries, roots and shellfish. In northern California, Oregon and Washington the Coos, Chinooks and Tolowas built homes of wood and lived off an abundant supply of fish.

1500s-1600s • NATIVE AMERICAN/ EUROPEAN RELATIONSHIP ~ At first, the Native Americans and the Europeans enjoyed a rather peaceful relationship, and intermarriage between white men and Native American women was even encouraged. Even several decades after independence, no less a person than Thomas Jefferson pleaded that the Native Americans should intermarry with the whites and let both bloods fuse through their veins. If they refused to be civilized

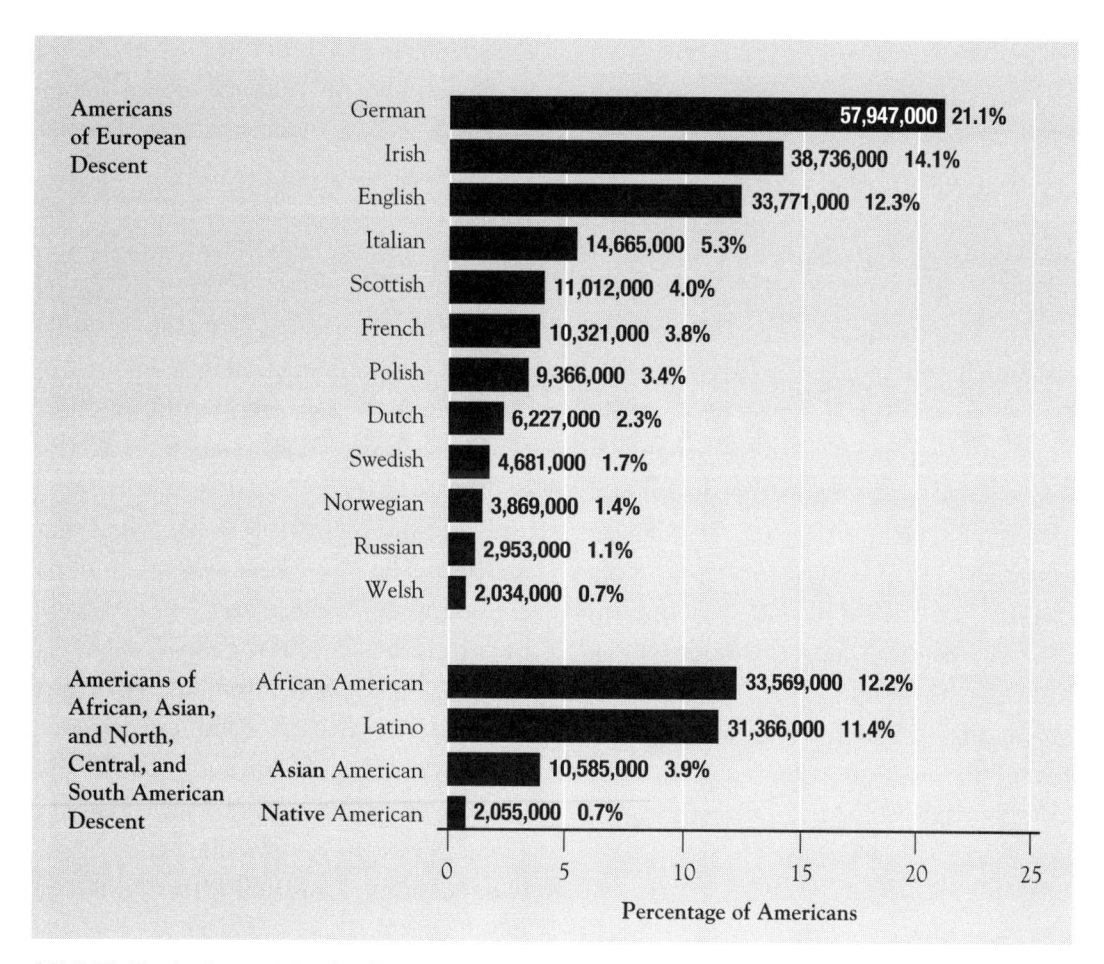

Americans of European Descent	German	57,947,000	21.1%
	Irish	38,736,000	14.1%
	English	33,771,000	12.3%
	Italian	14,665,000	5.3%
	Scottish	11,012,000	4.0%
	French	10,321,000	3.8%
	Polish	9,366,000	3.4%
	Dutch	6,227,000	2.3%
	Swedish	4,681,000	1.7%
	Norwegian	3,869,000	1.4%
	Russian	2,953,000	1.1%
	Welsh	2,034,000	0.7%
Americans of African, Asian, and North, Central, and South American Descent	African American	33,569,000	12.2%
	Latino	31,366,000	11.4%
	Asian American	10,585,000	3.9%
	Native American	2,055,000	0.7%

Percentage of Americans

SOURCE: Henslin, James M. *Social Problems*, 5th ed. Prentice Hall, 2000

by white blood, he told the Congress, they would be driven into the forests like the beasts. But friction and controversy escalated between the two groups; as more Europeans arrived they began a relentless push to make a better life for themselves, and white settlers, backed by the government, encroached more and more on Native American land.

The use and ownership of the land was at the core of conflict between the Native Americans and the white settlers. Whites considered Indian land-use wasteful and inefficient, which fact justified them in taking the land by force if necessary. On the other hand, the Native Americans viewed the land as a gift from the gods, and that their obligation was to protect, preserve and worship the land which provided for all living creatures. Thus, they believed in using resources without exhausting them or destroying the environment for others.

Historical accounts of the ways in which the Native Americans were subjected to intentional genocide stated that British General Amherst deliberately gave them blankets contaminated with smallpox as peace offerings. However, it was not only the Anglo-European of the eighteenth century that sought to decimate the Native Americans, but also nativist Americans, who, born many decades later, applied various methods in a systematic way to divest the Native Americans of their ancestral lands.

1633-1678 • WAR AND RESISTANCE

~ After the Puritans landed in America, they began to build the Kingdom of God in the New World on the belief that God had given them this land in their escape from the evils of the Old World, and when a smallpox epidemic wiped out thousands of Native Americans in 1633 and 1634, the Puritans interpreted this as an act of God and proof that Christianity would triumph in the New World. Acts of sporadic violence occurred between the Pequots of New England and the Puritans until around 1637 when the white settlers retaliated for the alleged killing of several whites by the planned massacre of 600 Pequots on Long Island Sound. On July 4, 1675, King Philip of the Wampanoags destroyed some twenty or more New England towns, killing more than 3,000 whites. In retaliation, a colonial army wiped out the nation and by 1678 the New England territory was opened to white settlers.

1689-1763 • French and Indian Wars

The French and the English engaged in four colonial wars in North America between 1689 and 1763. The English, with the help of the Iroquois, defeated the French and other Indian nations. Thousands of English, Germans and Scotch-Irish rushed in to take the lands of the defeated Native tribes after the French surrendered in 1763 and were forced to cede Canada to the English. The Ottawas, joined by the Delawares, Shawnees and Miamis, followed their chief Pontiac in resisting the settlers. To bring about better relations with the Indians, the British Parliament issued the Proclamation of 1763, which prohibited settlement and expansion west of the Appalachians. Pontiac kept fighting, but after three years of hostilities, he was forced to sign a peace treaty.

For a decade relations between the English and the Native Americans improved, while that with the colonists declined. Thus, by the American Revolution of 1776, most of the Native American tribes sided with the British. Native Americans had resisted in every way the advance of the white colonists, but they were soon to be on the losing end. Thus, while the white population increased as more and more settlers arrived, the Native Americans decreased in numbers because of war and European diseases.

1784-1794 • Treaties

After the Revolution, the Continental government stopped attempts by white settlers to take Indian lands in the Ohio valley, but it was cautious of its Native American policies. The fear was that conflict with Native American tribes might divide the states of the fledgling republic. The government wanted to conciliate the Native Americans and bring about better understanding. However, the lust for land by whites and the idea that America would be a land of farmers justified all attempts to wrest the land from the "uncivilized" savages. They were stereotyped as lacking intellect and culture, and caused whites to regard them as uncivilized. It was in this vein that Thomas Jefferson urged amalgamation so that the Native American could become "civilized."

The new revolutionary government recognized that the Native American nations along the frontier would be a never-ending problem, especially if the British in the Ohio River Valley assisted them in hostilities. Thus, when many argued that the sovereign claims of Native American lands could only be satisfied with Indian consent, American leaders decided to make treaties with the nations.

In 1784, the Treaty of Fort Stanwix brought about peace with the Iroquois, and a treaty guaranteeing that Cherokee lands would not be invaded was signed in 1785. Furthermore, the Cherokees were invited to send a representative to Congress. In 1787, Congress passed the Northwest Ordinance, which promised to respect the rights of Native Americans in the Ohio Valley. But when several thousand white settlers overran Kentucky and Ohio, Native Americans went on the attack. The settlers demanded governmental assistance, and Washington dispatched troops. In a surprise attack, the Shawnees killed more than 600 soldiers and the settlers screamed for retribution. Three years later in 1794, General "Mad" Anthony Wayne defeated the Shawnee nation at the Battle of Fallen Timbers. The following year, the Treaty of Greenville drove the Shawnees out of Ohio altogether. Thus began a spate of treaties, negotiated by the American government, broken by the white settlers, backed by the force of the U.S. army and ending with the surrender of ancestral Indian lands after military defeats or bloody massacres.

1800s • CHRISTIANIZING THE SAVAGES ~ The westward expansion beyond the Appalachian mountains brought to a crescendo the cry that God had given a superior white civilization a destiny to control the continent and civilize the savages. Thus, as the white farmers cleared the land and built their farms, Native Americans faced greater difficulties to survive.

Missionaries and white idealists launched crusades to convert the Native Americans to Christianity. Envisioning Indian farmers who worshiped in church on Sunday mornings in American villages, the missionaries preached love and friendship. However, most Native Americans resisted this cultural change because they believed that the Great Spirit had granted each race its own customs and land. Some Native Americans received the message, wore European clothes and tried their hands at farming. But caught between two cultures, and always exploited by white land speculators, many returned to their own ways. Ironically, all attempts to create a unified Indian nation failed because of centuries of tribal conflict. So they continued to resist western expansion by the only way they knew. However, when they tried to stop this expansion, tens of thousands of Native Americans were slaughtered in a policy called "pacification."

1800s • INDIAN REMOVAL POLICY ~ Beginning in 1789 during the ratification of the U.S. Constitution, American leaders Thomas Jefferson and George Washington advocated that the Native Americans should be evicted to lands west of the Mississippi. On February 16, 1803, President Thomas Jefferson wrote to Andrew Jackson of Tennessee advocating that the Native Americans sell their "useless" forests and become farmers. Twenty-five years later, when Andrew Jackson became president, he trumpeted the idea of Indian sale or removal. He had made his reputation as an Indian fighter, and easily persuaded white Americans that Indians should be removed so that white Americans could get their land. He repeatedly dehumanized the Native Americans as "savage bloodhounds" or "blood thirsty barbarians."

At the Battle of Horse Bend in March 1814, Jackson and his troops surrounded 800 Creeks and mowed them down, including women and children. Afterwards, as historian Ronald Takaki graphically expressed it, "his soldiers made bridle reins from strips of skin taken from the corpses; they also cut off the tip of each dead Indian's nose for body count." Calling the Indian lands "valuable country" Jackson constantly boasted of his massacres as victories, while he sought moral justification saying that Providence is pleased that these " . . . fiends . . . will no longer murder our women and children, or disturb our quiet borders."

In 1805, the Choctaw Treaty legalized the land-allotment program instituted by Thomas Jefferson. By this treaty the federal government reserved certain tracts of land for Choctaw families. He encouraged Native Americans to become farmers, build houses and leave them to the wives and children upon death. Clearly this program was to make European-styled farmers of the Choctaws. Perhaps unknown to him was the fact that the Choctaws had been farmers long before the whites came to America. As farmers they had a organized community, established a common granary, and had progressed to raising cattle and domesticated animals. Some of them even had owned hundreds of acres worked by black slaves. Despite all of this, however, even after they were forced to shoot their last arrow and become property owners in accordance with the law, the Choctaws were not allowed to remain on their land. They had come face to face with the dominant attitude of white society in nineteenth century America, which could not tolerate social interaction with people of color. Thus in January of 1830, the government of the state of Mississippi abolished the sovereignty of the Choctaw nation and took the remaining lands by intimidation and forced them to sign a treaty.

1831-1838 • THE TRAIL OF TEARS: FORCED EXTRADITION TO THE WEST

By 1830, around ten million Native Americans were still settled on a domain of about twenty-five million acres east of the Mississippi in North Carolina, Tennessee, eastern Alabama and northern Mississippi. Within this domain, nearly 60,000 Cherokees, Choctaws, Chickasaws and Creek Indians lived everyday with broken treaties and white hostility. Desperately desiring to remove the Native American tribes from proximity to white settlements, President Andrew Jackson, on December 8, 1829, demanded that Congress authorize him to remove the tribes living east of the Mississippi River to a western location in order that superior Anglo-American farming culture, civilization and religion could replace the "strange and barbarous way of the red man." Congress complied with Jackson's request, passing the Removal Act in May 1830. In order to justify this action, white Americans promptly stereotyped all Native Americans as "savages" who needed to be conquered, christianized and civilized. To this end, the idea of a God-ordained mandate for America was born.

In one of the most despicable acts in American history, one hundred thousand Native Americans were marched across the Mississippi on the Trail of Tears to Oklahoma. The Choctaws were the first to be moved in 1831, and many died of hunger and disease on the way. In 1832, the Cherokees took their case to the federal courts and the U.S. Supreme Court upheld their claims; but Jackson refused to abide by the court decision in flagrant disobedience to his own court's ruling. The Cherokees resisted for a few years more before being evicted by the U.S. Army in 1838. Four thousand died on the march to the West. In 1835, in similar fashion, the Creeks were moved from Georgia and Alabama; and in 1837 the

U.S. Army removed the Chickasaws as well. The removal treaties negotiated by the federal government supposedly guaranteed perpetual ownership to the new lands, but it soon became clear that this was not so as white settlers continued to flood the new areas..

The Sauk and Fox were transferred to their new home on "neutral ground" in Iowa. However, most of the land given them did not meet their needs for survival. Thus hungry and desperate to feed their women and children, a thousand Indians under the leadership of the proud warrior Big Black Bird Hawk crossed the Mississippi to return to their old homeland on the Rock River in search of food. They also wanted to protest the treatment they had received at the hands of the white settlers in Iowa. When news of the Indian incursion into Illinois was heard, mass hysteria broke out, prompting Governor John Reynolds to call out the state militia in order to repel the Indian invasion. Despite the fact that it was evident that Black Hawk and his followers were not a war party, Reynolds initiated a bloody conflict which forced Black Hawk and his party to fight for their lives. Drunken militiamen hounded them, and although Black Hawk successfully fought them off, he faced an even harder conflict when federal troops led by General Henry Atkinson joined the fray. At the Battle of Bad Axe along the Mississippi River, more than two hundred of his people were killed, including women and children. This ended the four months of Black Hawk's resistance to white domination. Immediately, all lands held by the Sauk and Fox were confiscated as indemnity for the war. This suppression of so-called "Indian hostilities" led the federal government to seize lands belonging to neighboring tribes in Wisconsin in 1832; and one by one they were all forced to relocate in order to provide land for white settlers.

1833-1845 • MASS MIGRATION AND MANIFEST DESTINY ~ In 1833 the *Christian Advocate and Herald*, a Methodist journal, published a letter written by an educated Native American. The letter stated that western tribes wanted the "Book of Heaven" and missionaries to instruct them. Thus, by the late 1830s, spurred by the Panic of 1837, immigrants were moving westward in droves and soon "Oregon Fever," as it became known, was spreading throughout migrant communities in the East. By 1843 the movement westward had become a mass migration, and the lust for land had stirred the blood of new adventurers. In an attempt to encourage this mass migrant movement in 1845, John Louis O'Sullivan, editor of *the United States Magazine and Democratic*

> In 1804, Governor William Henry Harrison – by trickery and intimidation – forced three Sauk and Fox chiefs to sell all the lands in western Illinois without tribal approval. History records that Harrison had gotten the Indian chiefs drunk. At Shallow Water (St. Louis), Harrison met with a Sauk chief named Kwaskwami in the winter of 1804. Kwaskwami had gone to a trading post to spend the winter near Shallow Water so he could sell his pelts. Tribal rumors told of how he hunted there and "hobnobbed" with the big official, and that he drank with him a great deal. Later, government officials came to the Sauk and Fox in the Spring and told them that according to a treaty signed by the Governor and Kwaskwami the people had to move as soon as possible across to the west bank of the Mississippi.

1870s-1880s

Review, wrote: "Our Manifest Destiny is to overspread the continent allotted by Providence for the free development of our yearly multiplying millions." Quite innocently, O'Sullivan had coined the phrase "Manifest Destiny," not knowing that it would ring throughout American history for centuries.

1870s-1880s • CONFISCATING INDIAN TERRITORY ~ From the time of the War of Independence, because each tribe was different, the government had dealt with it as a separate nation when signing treaties. However, by the time Congress authorized President Jackson to remove the five nations from the Southeast, the government reserved large tracts of land for the exclusive use of the various tribes out of the way of white frontiersmen. A Bureau of Indian Affairs was created to provide goods and services as needed, and to mediate conflicts between Native Americans and the white settlers. But these treaties were systematically broken and Native American rights violated as the government consistently backed the Anglo settlers who continually demanded more land. Many atrocious acts were perpetrated upon the Native Americans; and in order to justify these inhumane actions, the Anglo settlers used stereotypes that described the Native Americans as pagan savages who were thieves and murderers. A large number of the Bureau agents were also corrupt besides being lax in their responsibilities to the tribes. Consequently, when the United States Army engaged in the systematic murder of women and children there was very lit-

(1927) The attorneys and witnesses for the Yankton Sioux, who are supporting the tribe's legitimate claim to the Red Pipestone Quarry in Minnesota. White settlers had begun to exploit both the quarry and the surrounding land, ignoring the treaty of 1858 which deeded them to the Yankton, and a bitter court battle ensued.

tle public outcry. Most of the white settlers and many army officers contended that the only solution to the Indian problem was to remove them altogether from the lands whites wanted to inhabit. The Anglos were "settling" the land, according to John O'Sullivan, and it was their "Manifest Destiny."

In 1853, a newspaper editor praised the advent of the railroad and its contribution to American society. From that time onward, The Irish crews of the Union Pacific and the Chinese crews of the Central Pacific were driven to complete the transcontinental railroad. But while this proved to be a boon for the white American settlers, it ended the Native American fight to keep their homeland. Railroad corporate interests pushed for passage of the 1871 Indian Appropriation Act, which declared that no Indian nation or tribe shall be acknowledged or recognized "with whom the United States may contract by treaty." With this act as justification, the railroad companies laid rails all across America and opened the west for new settlement, and thousands of white Europeans crossed the Mississippi in search of their own wealth and prosperity.

Anglo reformers, under the guise of being friendly to the Indians, proposed that title deeds be given to each head of family who would denounce tribal traditions and become assimilated as farmers. With little opposition, Congress acquiesced when it became aware that if land was thus distributed, a large surplus would be left that could be added to public lands and sold to raise revenue. Thus, in 1887 Congress passed the Dawes Act allotting title to 160 acres to each family head, and smaller allotments to single members of tribes who shot a "last arrow" and were willing to become farmers. The title, however, would be held in trust for 25 years by the government, and the Native Americans were to be recognized as U.S. citizens. With this action, the conquest of Native America was complete.

This meant that with the growth of the Indian population, the 160-acre plots would have to be subdivided more and more into smaller plots, and the descendants of each generation would have to farm under worse conditions than the whites. Thus, in 1902, realizing the stark reality, Congress allowed them to sell their parcels of land before the 25 years had expired. Within three years, hungry and confused, Native Americans sold their land, amounting to more than 250,000 acres, to white speculators for a few dollars. Congress passed the Burke Act in 1906, which empowered the Bureau of Indian Affairs to decide when Indians were capable of handling their own affairs, at which time he could sell to the highest bidder. Bureau agents and their friends, like Governor Harrison, used trickery and liquor to defraud the Native Americans of their lands.

1918-1945 • THE ROLE OF INDIANS DURING WORLD WARS I AND II ~ On October 12, 1911, about fifty Native Americans assembled in Columbus, Ohio and formed the Society of American Indians. Most of them, like Dr. Charles A. Eastman, were graduates of industrial or boarding schools. Dr. Eastman, who was raised on the Santee Sioux Reservation, was a graduate of Dartmouth. These new representatives provided the impetus for a generation of new Native Americans who would challenge the U.S. government according to law. Consequently, when WWI began and Native Americans were among the first to volunteer, the Society was quick to object to U.S. government's policy that Indian soldiers be segregated like the African Americans who had also volunteered. More than 12,000 Native Americans joined the U.S. Army and Navy, and served with distinction. At home, some ten thousand women and men served as Red Cross personnel, and Native Americans purchased $25 million of war bonds, a far higher percentage for their level of income than many Americans.

On the battlefield, Native Americans established themselves as brave soldiers, three of them single-handedly capturing 171 German prisoners and 50 machine guns. For this they were awarded the highest French honor, the *Croix de Guerre*. They served as the best and most effective scouts because they communicated in their tribal languages, which could not be deciphered by German experts. In spite of all this brave contribution to the war effort, Native American servicemen returned to the U.S. only to find that the democracy for which they fought still denied them the right to vote.

At the outbreak of WWII, 25,000 Native Americans joined the Army, Navy or Marine Corps. Another 40,000 supported the war industries at home. Some 3,600 Navajos recruited in the 382nd Platoon served as communication experts or "code talkers." Using phrases from the Navajo language, they transmitted intelligence over the airwaves that frustrated Japanese eavesdroppers. At home some were decorated with the Congressional Medal of Honor.

When these veterans returned after the war, they were men who had proved their bravery and their courage, and felt that they were equal to the white American men. They knew that they had a stake in America because some 10,000 of them had died in the war. Like the African Americans, they had fought for Democracy but were all too eager to forget that America was a segregated place that allowed first-class citizenship to only white men. Unable to vote in a few states, and unable to get G.I. loans, they smarted under the discrimination of second-class citizenship. Desirous of merging into American society as equals, they became cognizant that they did not possess the skills necessary to compete in the American marketplace. Many became discouraged wanderers, while others eked out a living wherever they could on the reservations.

It was not until Dillon S. Meyer was appointed Commissioner of Indian Affairs in 1950 that relief came to Native Americans. Meyer argued that the reservations were concentration camps from which Indians must be freed as soon as possible. The word "termination" described his new policy; and he stated that government had to terminate the ward status and trust responsibilities for Indian lands. Thus, in 1954 of the ten bills summarizing the plight of Native Americans submitted to Congress, six passed, which persuaded Native Americans to move to the big cities and use their lands as collateral for small businesses. With a new word, "Relocation," on their lips, the Bureau planned to help Native Americans find apartments, jobs and schools for their children. But the word "Relocation," just like the word "Removal," struck fear and resentment in the hearts and minds of Native Americans until the words "Employment Assistance" produced a milder response.

1982 • RESTORATION OF INDIAN SOVEREIGNTY

Today the crippling effects of the American government's "Indian policy" of the nineteenth century can still be seen. Native Americans have the lowest median family income of the

(1939) No Beer To Indians. Indian policy and social stigma can be seen here. A sign in the window of a tavern on the Sisseton Indian Reservation forbidding the sale of alcohol to Native Americans.

ethnic minorities; the lowest percentage of college educated persons; and the highest percentage among those groups who live below the poverty level. About 27 percent of all Native American families list females as head of households, and more than half of these are poor.

However, since the restoration of Indian sovereignty by the federal government in 1982, several Native American economies have prospered from casino gambling. After the federal government allowed tribal groups to control reservation lands, some tribes discovered natural resources on their land. A number of other reservations established casino and bingo operations; and casino gambling became the major employer, providing jobs for as many as 300,000 Native Americans. One small tribe, the Mdewakanton Dakota in Minnesota, operates a casino near Minneapolis-St. Paul which nets over $600,000 a year for each man, woman and child of the 270-member tribe. The Oneida tribe of New York employs 3,000 people in their casinos, hotels, restaurants and gas stations, and produces such a high income level for a few hundred families that their Anglo neighbors are extremely resentful. Although many other tribes are not so fortunate, present treaties exempt Indian reservation lands from state and federal regulations, including sales taxes on cigarettes and gasoline.

1990s • Improved Quality of Life

~ With this windfall and change of governmental attitude, Native American education improved significantly, and by 1999 two-thirds of all adults were high school graduates or better. Nevertheless, different educational levels separate city dwellers

1990s from those who still reside on reservation lands. On the other hand, however, Native Americans have achieved a higher percentage of high school graduates than Hispanic Americans. However, the present reality of this ethnic minority is still somewhat uncertain. Although there is a revival of Native American culture, a large majority of middle-class Native Americans have assimilated into Anglo-American culture by marriage and lifestyle, and tribal leaders continue to worry that Native American culture will be lost.

While Anglo Americans view the distinctly 500 different Native American cultures as "one people," the tribes still see themselves as many nations. Since the federal government has never had to deal with a united Native American nation, a modern movement has brought Pan-Indianism to the forefront and has encouraged Native American lawsuits for the benefit of those below the poverty level.

HISPANIC AMERICANS

The 2000 census revealed that in the 1990s the Hispanic population in the U.S. grew by 35 percent to about 27 million, making it equal to the African American population. During the next decade, Hispanics will be the largest ethnic minority group in the United States because of two main factors. First, the average Hispanic age is between 26 and 27, which means that they are, in the main, some nine to ten years younger than white Americans. Secondly, because of religious beliefs and family lifestyle, Hispanic fertility produces more childbirths than white Americans. Since 1975, Hispanic births in California have more than doubled, and the minority group is growing at a rate of about four times faster than the national population. But, in order to understand this ethnic group, one needs to know that Hispanics are divided into two main classifications in America: *Chicanos* and *Latinos*.

1990s • MEXICAN (CHICANO) AMERICAN POPULATION ~ Hispanic Americans originate from many different countries and represent a wide range of social classes. Mexicans (*Chicanos*) represent 64 percent of the entire U.S. Hispanic population, while *Latinos* comprise the other 36 percent with 13 percent coming from Central or South America (Nicaragua, Peru, Columbia, Argentina, Panama, etc), 11 percent from Puerto Rico, five percent from Cuba and seven percent from other areas. Hispanic Americans are concentrated in four states: California, Texas, New York and Florida. However, more than 50 percent of them live in California and Texas, most of them coming from Mexico and Central America. Two million others who live in New York are from Puerto Rico, and some one million Cubans reside in Florida.

1841-1845 • U.S. RELATIONS WITH MEXICO ~ During the nineteenth century the American lust for land was clear-

Major Hispanic Populations in the U.S.

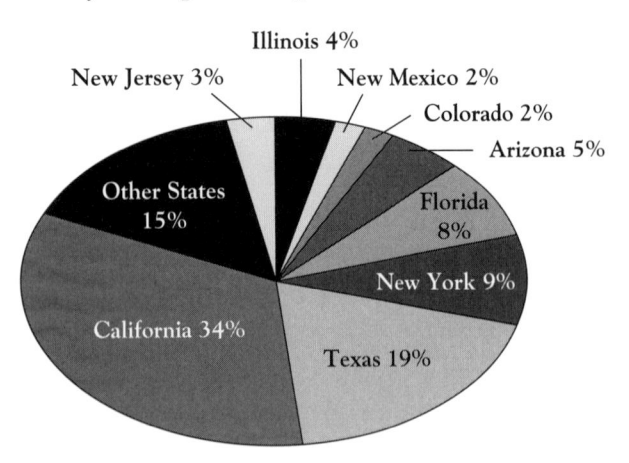

- Illinois 4%
- New Mexico 2%
- Colorado 2%
- Arizona 5%
- Florida 8%
- New York 9%
- Texas 19%
- California 34%
- Other States 15%
- New Jersey 3%

SOURCE: Henslin, James M. *Social Problems*, 5th ed. Prentice Hall, 2000.

ly demonstrated in the annexation of Texas, and the acquisition of California and Arizona. The Mexican government, after its independence from Spain in 1821, had invited Anglo-Americans to settle in the Mexican territory now known as Texas. Many southerners responded to the opportunity to acquire land and migrated into the territory carrying black slaves as their property.

In 1830, however, the Mexican government outlawed slavery, and made it clear that further American immigration into Texas was not allowed. The American foreigners balked at the new laws; and many who were slaveholders were determined to keep blacks working for them in defiance of the new policy. As word spread, many Americans crossed the border illegally, even bringing their families to settle. However, they did not settle with the hope of becoming future Mexicans; their clear intent was to make the territory American land. Thus by 1835, Americans outnumbered the Mexicans by a ratio of five to one—20,000 to 4,000—making the Mexicans minorities in their own land.

Although the Mexicans complained about the Americans from time to time, historical records reveal that there was never any hope for redress, especially since Mexico had refused an offer of one million dollars to sell Texas in 1826 during the administration of John Quincy Adams. All was quiet for a few years; but when the Mexican government decreed that there would be no slaves in Mexican territories, the American foreigners felt that they could no longer live under laws made by what they called "an arbitrary" Mexican government, and a movement began to take control of Texas. Not opposed to the idea, the United States annexed Texas in 1845 and Mexico immediately broke off diplomatic relations.

1846 • WAR WITH MEXICO ~ By 1846, the Mexicans were complaining about the "hordes of Yankee immigrants" they could not arrest, who would not abide by the laws of the country. Determined to wrest Texas and California from Mexico, President James K. Polk manipulated American opinion with propaganda that increased American desire for Mexican territory. Early in 1846, under orders from Polk, the army invaded Mexican territory and blockaded the mouth of the Rio Grande in an act of aggression defiant of international law. When the Mexicans tried to defend their territorial rights, Polk, in a declaration of war, told the American people that Mexico had invaded U.S. territory and shed American blood on American soil. The result was an outraged clamor for war. This clamor provoked the U.S. Army to commit such atrocities against the Mexican people that General Winfield Scott lamented, "....Heaven weep and every American of Christian morals blush for his country."

On June 6, 1846, thirty armed American rebels awakened General Mariano Vallejo before daylight in the first action to establish control of California. Rough and uncouth frontiersmen, these rebels had crossed the border after the Mexican government had banned further immigration. Thus, the first illegal aliens into California were not Mexicans, but Americans who had been in the territory for less than a year. Placing the image of a grizzly bear and a lone star on a homemade flag, they claimed the land as their own. To the Mexicans, the bear was a thief, and was considered a fitting symbol for these American plunderers who, by establishing the Texas Republic, made the Mexican a minority in his native land. Thus, while the original Mexicans

1870s-1890s

never crossed the border into America, the American border, pushed by illegal American aliens, crossed over Mexican homelands and set up its own boundaries.

A few months after General Winfield Scott occupied Mexico City in 1848, the treaty of Guadalupe Hidalgo forced Mexico to accept the Rio Grande as the Texas border and cede the remainder of the Southwest territory to the United States for $15 million. That territory included the present-day states of New Mexico, Nevada and California, as well as parts of Arizona, Colorado and Utah. The border crossed Mexicans already living in this territory; but the treaty permitted them to remain in the United States or to move across the border into Mexico. If they chose to remain, they were guaranteed all the rights of United States citizens in accordance with the principles of the Constitution. Most of them remained in their homes, but soon came to realize that they were "foreigners in their own land."

1870s • RESTRICTIONS AGAINST MEXICANS

As the Americans increased in numbers, they controlled the politics of California and Texas, and everywhere the Mexicans became foreigners in the places of their birth. Mexicans lost their homes despite the various treaties and guarantees of the U. S. government.

By 1873, as whites flocked to Santa Barbara, Mexican voters were outnumbered at the polls. Since they dominated the state legislature, the white Americans passed several laws that served to restrict the Mexicans in all areas of life. The "Greaser Act" defined as vagrants "all persons commonly known as 'Greasers'" or those people who contained Spanish or Indian blood. The Mexican Miners' Tax demanded tax from those who spoke Spanish or those Americans who had Mexican ancestry. Even though Mexican miners showed Anglo miners how to extract gold from the mines, the whites regarded everyone who was not white as an interloper, and defended the right to the gold as their own. All foreigners were evicted because they had no right to mine gold in America. Attacked by more than a hundred whites in Coronel, Mexicans were forced to abandon their claims and flee for their lives.

In the 1890s, Anglo Americans established "white primaries" to disenfranchise Mexicans and blacks, and they passed laws like the poll tax to restrict Mexican political participation. The prevailing feeling was that superior white Americans should not allow ignorant Mexicans to vote on questions that might affect white lives. Such political restrictions did not only affect Mexican ability to utilize the rights guaranteed them as "citizens" (if the remained in their homes), but also it affected their ability to protect themselves as landowners.

1851 • U.S. LAND ACT

The original version of the treaty of Guadalupe Hidalgo had guaranteed Mexican titles to

---

One note to the Mexican-American war in the 1840s, was that the United States army included a number of Irish immigrants. They had been pushed out of their ancestral homeland by the British, and had migrated to America looking for land and new opportunities. Now, by an ironic quirk of fate, they were affirming themselves as Americans by pushing the Mexicans and Native Americans off their ancestral lands, under the banner of Manifest Destiny.

"property of every description." But, when the U.S. Senate ratified the treaty, this article was omitted. The American government issued a "Statement of Protocol" instead, which stated that by suppressing Article X, the American government "did not in any way intend to annul the grants of lands made by Mexico in the ceded territories." Consequently, numerous Mexican families lost their lands. Anglos rushed by the thousands into California and poor whites began squatting on Mexican property. When the Mexican authorities tried to remove them, they protested to Congress, which passed the Land Act of 1851.

This act created the Board of Land Commissioners and gave it authority to resolve confusing titles. White Americans controlling the Board conducted hearings in English and ruled in favor of the squatters. If a decision was given in favor of a Mexican claim, the cases were appealed to federal courts, which took as many as seventeen years for completion. In the meantime, court costs and attorney fees drove the ranchero and Mexican landowner to the place where he had to mortgage his land and sell livestock in order to pay legal expenses and other fees. Victimized by tax laws aimed at them, they eventually lost their property for unpaid taxes or mortgage foreclosure, and the land was made available for Anglo squatters to purchase for one-fifth the price.

Unable to compete with unjust laws and the political system supplanted upon them, Californios (Mexican landholders in California) were forced to sell their land and join the laboring class. Whites then segregated Mexican American children in schools as they did the blacks, and discouraged the use of Spanish. The Mexican Americans were now a suppressed ethnic minority in a secular industrial society without resources or the wherewithal to compete with American expansion. The Mexican was systematically relegated to peon status, and stereotyped as lazy, docile and ignorant.

1880-1900 • LABOR AND ECONOMICS
∼ The expanding American control in the Southwest not only appropriated the land, but also Mexican labor. Before Texan independence, Mexican farm laborers using a Mexican system of irrigation had transformed the Texas landscape from dry scrubs to green fields. But during the 1880s, after the Chinese Exclusion Act of 1882, Mexicans comprised the majority of workers contracted to lay tracks for the Texas and Mexican Railroad.

Thus by the 1900, Mexicans were farm laborers, cotton pickers and railroad workers in the mining industries of California, and the copper mines of Arizona, Utah and Nevada, where they mined copper for the manufacture of electrical wires. Even though Mexican miners in the copper mines of Arizona, Utah and Nevada, have played an important role in making possible the illumination of America by electricity, the Mexican laborer has always been degraded by Americans, and seen as one who begs and steals rather than one who has made a contribution to the country.

Mexicans were the original cowboys who taught the Anglos techniques of roping and branding cattle and Mexican agricultural workers cultivated the fields. Everywhere they performed the same work as Anglo Americans, they were vilified and paid less than half what the others received. Anglo employers likened Mexican laborers to the black slaves of the South and labeled them with stereotypes of Sambo—possessing a kind of happy docility but being ignorantly obsequious.

Hispanic Ancestry

At the end of the twentieth century, two-thirds of Hispanics were Mexican Americans. There is, however, much disagreement among them as to whether Mexican Americans should be considered a racial group or cultural group. In addition, many Mexican Americans reject the thought that they are an ethnic minority. Because of their history, the Mexican Americans divide themselves into three categories that are readily accepted by white Americans. These categories include: (1) the original "Spanish" landowners who lived in California, Texas and New Mexico before these areas became part of the United States; (2) those born in the United States of earlier immigrants; and (3) first generation immigrants (legal and undocumented).

The first group is seen as those of elite Spanish "pure-blood" ancestry, who were undefiled by an Indian mixture. These are usually represented as the dons and caballeros of the Hollywood *Zorro* movies. The second group is a burgeoning middle class born in America who may or may not identify themselves as Hispanic. The term *Chicanos* is usually used to identify members of this group. The third group includes those who worked in the lowest paying jobs, possessed the least education and demonstrated the least skills. The people in this group are immigrants from Mexico, (*Mexicanos*) whether they are legal residents or undocumented aliens. The present reality is that while elite Mexican Americans may be accepted into Anglo-conformity, the *Mexicanos* are discriminated against at every level of American society.

It is generally accepted that the words *Latino* and *Hispanic* do not refer to race, but to ethnic groups. While some 19 million *Chicanos* claim Mexico as their country of origin, eight million *Latinos* originate from several different countries: three

(1960) Portrait of a group of young Hispanic children posing for the camera on a sidewalk on the Lower East Side, New York City.

million from Puerto Rico, one million from Cuba and four million from Central and South America. Almost 80 percent of these are concentrated in four states—California, Texas, New York, and Florida.

1990s • EDUCATION OF LATINOS

According to 1998 statistics of the Department of Education, 40 percent of all Hispanics have less than a high school education. Among Mexican Americans, less than 47 percent of adults between 25-34 have a high school diploma. One reason for this can be attributed to the discrimination Mexican Americans endure unless they are in that small group of elite of "pure blood" Spanish ancestry. The average Mexican child hears Spanish at home from parents and grandparents, who desire above all else for him/her to retain the cultural heritage. Spanish is also the language of the *barrios*, but the Mexican student is expected to learn English quickly (a foreign language to him) and master it immediately to be able to excel in America. The irony here is that in the late 1840s California and Texas were taken from Mexico, but within a few years, a *Chicano* majority may take them back and gain political control because they would be an English-speaking majority.

Although some *Latinos* do not speak Spanish, it is the main factor that distinguishes this ethnic group from the other minorities. And while a large number speak both languages, it is a severe handicap for those who speak only Spanish in an English dominant society. More and more Latino households are emphasizing the need to retain their cultural heritage, and the growing use of Spanish has become a grave social issue. In 1981, Senator S.I. Hayawaka of Hawaii initiated an "English-only" movement; but ever since that time, the City of Miami has become a battleground for the more than one million *Latinos* from Cuba and Central and South America, who prefer Spanish as their native tongue.

1990s • ASSIMILATION

The median income of *Latinos* is only three-fifths that of Anglo Americans. Only one out of every ten *Latinos* is a college graduate; and the unemployment rate is double that of whites. Moreover, at every educational level, whites are paid more. This forces Latinos to reject assimilation and a movement has begun to retain Hispanic culture at all costs. However, although they earn less than Anglo Americans, on the average, there is a great disparity between the income levels of the educated *Latino* and those comprising the 90 percent on the lower educational level.

In the 1998 *Statistical Abstract*, although *Latinos* comprised 11 percent of the population, they had only 17 representatives of 435 in the House of Representatives, and no senators of 100 in the U.S. Senate. However, it is a certainty that they will hold great political power shortly because the four states in which they are concentrated hold one fourth of the electoral college votes: Florida (21), New York (36), Texas (29) and California (47). Latino political power has been seriously compromised, however, because of strong class divisions. For example, almost all of the 500,000 Cubans who fled to Miami when Fidel Castro overthrew dictator Fulgencio Batista in 1959 were well-educated professional people. Two decades later, more than 100,000 "boat people" from Mariel were from the lower class and very poorly educated. In addition, *Latinos* from Puerto Rico seem to have very little in common with those from Columbia,

Nicaragua or Venezuela. Consequently, while the educated have assimilated and been accepted into Anglo-conformity, a large majority continues to vacillate between Anglo and Latino culture.

African Americans

1600s • Fate of Slaves Born in America ~ In 1619, one year before the importation of white women into the Virginian colony, Africans were brought to Jamestown, Virginia on a Dutch-owned ship and forced to work as slaves. For more than forty years, they worked the land for the benefit of white Anglo colonists without receiving much in return, but without the brutality that would surface in subsequent years. However, in 1662, concerned that the children of black slave women fathered by white men would eventually acquire property, the House of Burgess in Virginia passed laws which made the child of a black woman a slave for life, and the child of a white woman free-born. Thus began the awful condition of racial apartheid that plagued America for two hundred more years until the Civil War.

1830-1930 • Changing Definitions of "Negro" ~ Although white Anglo American males continued to engage in the practice of fathering offspring with black women, by the 1830s there was enough flexibility in the laws of Virginia to allow some Negroes (Mulattoes) to legally change from being black to being classified as white. The constant changing of the laws demonstrate the attitudes of white Americans towards the people of African descent who were building America's economy. Although the change did not take place all at once, by 1930 the racial definitions had changed to where a "single drop" of "Negro blood" was sufficient to classify a person as Negro. Portions of the laws are as follows:

1833 (Chapter 80)- "A court upon satisfactory proof, by a white person of the fact, may grant any free person of mixed blood a certificate that he is not a Negro, which certificate shall protect such person against the penalties and disabilities to which free Negroes are subject."

1833 (Chapter 243)- "Certain parties . . . who heretofore were held in slavery and acquired their freedom since 1806 are not Negroes or Mulattoes but white persons, although remotely descended from a colored woman, and are hereby released from all penalties whatever . . . ."

1866 (Chapter 17)- "Every person having one-fourth or more Negro blood shall be deemed a colored person. . . ."

1910 (Chapter 357)- "Every person having one-sixteenth or more Negro blood shall be deemed a colored person . . . ."

1930 (Chapter 85)- "Every person in whom there is ascertainable any Negro blood should be deemed a colored person. . . ."

(J. John Palen, *Social Problems for the Twenty-First Century*, 64)

1850s • Restricting Freedom for Slaves ~ African Americans suffered the indignity of slavery in the southern states, but free Negroes in the North were subjected to discrimination and many indignities even though they had opportunities for education and mobility that the former did not enjoy. Although free, many of them faced great peril during the years when the Congress passed the Fugitive Slave Laws of 1795 and 1850. In addition, the greatest deterrent to African American freedom from slavery at that time was the U.S. Supreme Court decision in the *Dred Scott* case in 1857, making slavery legal in the territories, and the prevailing attitudes of Anglo Americans against African Americans. Bartered and sold like cattle and bred like horses, African Americans endured untold abuse even while they produced huge economic profits for the southern states.

1861-1865 • BLACK SOLDIERS DURING THE CIVIL WAR ~ When hostilities began between the North and the South in 1861, Free African Americans in the North, and some in the South as well, volunteered in large numbers to fight for the Union Army. However, those who responded to Abraham Lincoln's call discovered that they were not wanted. The racist attitudes of northern whites mirrored that of the federal government which felt that under no circumstances should blacks be trained to use arms in a "white man's war." After a while, Union Army officers decided that blacks should have the opportunity to fight since they sought freedom for the slaves. However, by the time the War Department recognized the black regiments in August 1862, that had assembled voluntarily, black soldiers had already seen combat against the Confederacy. It was not until the North was losing the war, and the first draft call was made, that black regiments were officially raised. Even though this allowed the U.S. army to raise black units, it did not reduce white prejudice. What it did do was allow white men to send black men to fight in their place, and many noted that it was better for a black man to die as a substitute for a white man.

African Americans fought bravely and proved white opinion wrong on every count. They comprised ten percent of the Union's total fighting force but they suffered 45 percent casualties by war's end. However, they also endured much discrimination and degradation. When Governor Andrew was given permission to raise the 54th Massachusetts black regiment, he was told to offer $13 per month, plus rations and clothing. In addition, the soldiers were to receive a signing bonus of $50 and were promised $100 when they were mustered out of the army. However, in June 1863, the War Department decided to pay the black troops only $10 per month, $3 of which would be deducted for their clothing. The white soldiers were to receive the full $13 per month pay. Citing a principle from which there was no retreat, the entire 54th Massachusetts regiment refused to accept anything less than the same pay as whites and they maintained their stand for more than a year. By doing so they displayed higher moral behavior than the leaders of the U.S. Army, and eventually won their protest.

1861-1866 • GRANTING CITIZENSHIP TO SLAVES ~ After the Civil War began, the slaves, realizing that they would not be given their freedom unless they acted, walked off the plantations in huge numbers and rallied behind the Union Army lines. They became "contraband of war" in accordance with the 1861 Confiscation Act, which declared all slaves owned by Confederate sympathizers to be free. Many of them served as spies for the North, passing themselves off as slaves since they knew the countryside. These black soldiers built fortifications, grew food, and cared for the animals, making a great contribution in the "fight for their freedom." Ironically, the

Southern rebels also used black slaves and free southern blacks as soldiers in the Confederate army. They even promised slaves their freedom if they would fight for the South. This callous attitude demonstrated that they had no concern for blacks, and certainly would not set free the slaves unless they were forced to do so.

Finally, after a hard-fought struggle, the South surrendered; but the question that confronted Abraham Lincoln and Congress was: "What will be the status of four million freed slaves?" Before his assassination Lincoln wanted to find a country that would take the blacks and send them out of the United States, even without regard for all the work that they had done to build America. In retrospect, historians have calculated that American slave owners owed African Americans more than 13 billion dollars plus interest by the time of the Civil War. However, rather than pay African Americans for their labor in building the Southern states and maintaining its economy, Abraham Lincoln and other influential people in Congress favored paying reparations to the former slaveholders. Consequently, although the Thirteenth Amendment abolished slavery legally, the continuing injustice placed more emphasis on the loss of white-owned property than on the freedom of black people.

Fearing that all the efforts of the abolitionists and moral thinkers in America would be lost in President Andrew Johnson's pardons of Confederate leaders, and that grave injustice would be done to the freed slaves of America, a handful of Radical Republicans in Congress lobbied for a Constitutional Amendment that would grant citizenship to blacks born in America. There was no sympathy for this measure neither in Congress nor among Northern whites; but President Johnson's vetoes and antagonism pushed moderate Republicans into the camp of the radicals and the Fourteenth Amendment, passed in 1866, declared that all persons born or naturalized in America were citizens of the United States of America, and subject to due process of law. Reconstructed Southern states refused to ratify this amendment, and demanded payment for their lost slave property. This sentiment, which viewed African Americans as property akin to horses and cattle, would deny African Americans the "due process of law" as guaranteed by the Fourteenth Amendment for more than one hundred years.

1870 • THE RIGHT TO VOTE ~ In the late 1860s, the fact that African Americans outnumbered Anglo Americans in many states gave rise to the Fifteenth Amendment that sought to use the black vote to keep control of those states. Consequently, it was for political reasons that the amendment, ratified in 1870, provided that all men were eligible to vote without regard to color. In this way, Reconstruction laid the foundations for equality; but the failure of the Republicans to enforce the Fourteenth Amendment, and provide economic help to the freedmen by granting them the right to own property, forced them to submit to their old masters in a new pernicious system based on white supremacy. The worse irony of all was that although black labor had produced untold wealth for whites in both the South and the North, Congress preferred to give them the right to vote rather than grant them land in order to feed themselves.

Benjamin Montgomery had worked as the business manager for the Davis plantations before the war, and he had operated the plantation store at Hurricane on his own. After the war, when Joseph Davis returned, he discovered that the federal government was leasing the land in the area to blacks, and that Montgomery had become the leader of the African American community. But in 1866, President Andrew Johnson restored the property to Davis. Realizing that at 80 he lacked the will to rebuild his plantation, he sold it to his former slave, and only when the law prohibiting black ownership was overturned in 1867 did he publicize the sale.

Even though there were many difficulties to overcome, floods, droughts and declining cotton prices, the African Americans who farmed at Davis Bend, Mississippi produced 2,500 bales of cotton, and went on to produce more than two-thirds of the state's crop in subsequent years. Benjamin Montgomery and his sons acquired another plantation and became the third largest planters in the state, owning some 5,500 acres of land. They won national and international awards for producing a better quality of cotton. By their success, the Montgomerys demonstrated what African Americans would have been able to achieve if given the chance. Blacks needed their own land and economic power after emancipation, but the Republicans only gave them the vote, which vote was soon taken away systematically by the various tests and clauses and laws of disfranchisement. For more than 200 years African Americans had been denied land ownership, and today this fact is at the core of the cry for reparations.

1870-1877 • DEMOCRATS REGAIN CONTROL AFTER RECONSTRUCTION

∼ Between 1870 and 1877, Reconstruction in the South produced many black legislators, U.S. senators and lieutenant governors. These men, by and large,

> Joseph Davis had been financially ruined by the war, so in November 1866 he sold his Mississippi plantations Hurricane and Brierfield to his slave Benjamin Montgomery. Joseph was the elder brother of Jefferson Davis, who, before the war had operated the Brierfield plantation as his own even though Joseph held the title deed to it. Such a sale would have attracted much attention so it was decided to keep it a secret, since Mississippi law prohibited African Americans from owning land.

voted along conservative lines, and helped to pass laws that benefited the states. Emphasis was given to education. However, in the few places where integrated schools were allowed, they were still administered on a segregated basis. This segregation deepened after the Compromise of 1877. In the 1876 presidential campaign, the Democratic candidate, Samuel J. Tilden of New York, won a clear majority of 250,000 votes over Ohio Governor Republican Rutherford B. Hayes.

The outcome in the electoral college was in doubt because both parties claimed victory in three disputed states. Votes from South Carolina, Florida and Louisiana, the only reconstructed states still controlled by the Republicans were still in dispute. Hayes needed all the votes from those three states to be elected; but Tilden, who had already gained 184 electoral votes, needed only one more to have a two-thirds majority. The Republican canvassing boards systematically disqualified enough Democratic votes to give Hayes the election.

Congress decided to arbitrate and created an electoral commission of 15 to

1870-1877

solve the problem: five members each from the Senate, the House, and the Supreme Court—a total of seven Republicans, seven Democrats and one independent. But when the one independent had to withdraw due to illness, the Republican who replaced him cast the deciding vote that followed a straight party line. Thus, by an eight to seven vote, the electoral commission gave the election to Hayes. The Democrats threatened a filibuster designed to prevent the counting of the electoral votes; and in the ensuing compromise on February 26 at a hotel in Washington, the Republicans abandoned their fight for the civil rights of African Americans, gave back control of the southern states, and promised to recall the Union soldiers still garrisoned in the South in exchange for the presidency.

Promising to respect the rights of black people, the Democrats assumed control of the former Confederate states.

Following this compromise, the entire South was back in the hands of the "Redeemers," as they were called, who would be honored for a hundred years by the *Ku Klux Klan* for having redeemed the South. Immediately, they passed laws which seriously restricted the lives of African Americans and which contradicted in every way imaginable the Fourteenth Amendment. Subsequent decisions by the Supreme Court would frustrate all efforts by African Americans to achieve their rights under the Constitution for another one hundred years. For example, in 1883 the Supreme Court held that the Civil Rights Act of 1875 was unconstitutional. Then in 1896

(1961) Separate but equal was not an accurate description of what was happening to African Americans. Seen here an African-American woman is being shown where her "rest rooms" were for she could not use the bathroom in an area marked for "white people".

(1966) African-American children stand in the grass by a dirt road, watching people marching to Jackson to encourage the African-American vote in Mississippi. The marchers continued the mission of James H. Meredith, the first African-American student admitted into the University of Mississippi, who was shot by a white man near Hernando, Mississippi as he led the march for voting rights.

in *Plessy v. Ferguson*, the court upheld a lower court's decision, which segregated railroad cars, making it illegal for African Americans to ride in the same railroad car as whites. This enunciated the "separate-but-equal" doctrine, which effectively locked African Americans out of the mainstream of American life, because the whites applied this decision to every area of life.

1954 • Overturning "Separate but Equal"

For 58 years, African Americans worked as sharecroppers in the main, unless they found employment in the most menial jobs as washers, day laborers, janitors or housekeepers for white families. A few established themselves in service occupations as barbers, beauticians and carpenters in the African American communities. Subjected to poorer education than whites, or that available to new European immigrants, African Americans were forced to establish organizations and institutions that provided for their needs. Churches, burial societies, schools and fraternal organizations provided educational and occupational opportunities until in 1954 the U.S. Supreme Court ruled in *Brown vs. Board of Education*, Topeka, Kansas, that segregation was unconstitutional. African Americans immediately applied this decision to every area of life, just as the whites had done, and began to challenge segregation everywhere. But strong white resistance to desegregation sparked the Civil Rights Movement, student sit-ins at lunch counters, the jail-ins for sitting in southern bus and train station waiting rooms, bus rides which challenged segregated seating arrangements and demonstrations against segregated restaurant service.

1955-1990s

1955 • DR. KING COMES INTO NATIONAL PROMINENCE ~ The Montgomery Bus Boycott of 1955 in Montgomery Alabama started by the Women's Political Council of Montgomery against the atrocities perpetrated on African Americans brought into national prominence Civil Rights leader Martin Luther King, Jr. King would later be assassinated in April 1968 in Memphis, Tennessee, and African Americans across the country believed that the time for more radical action had come. Consequently, a younger group of black activists, with slogans of "Black Power" sought to sensitize America to the injustice and hypocrisy of democracy.

1970s-1990s • CLASSES AMONG AFRICAN AMERICANS ~ By the end of the century, there was much ambivalence among African Americans. While there appears to be social acceptance in U.S. society, African Americans are acutely aware of the rising specter of racism, which has changed its face from hooded white sheets to the business suits of bankers and the camouflaged green of paramilitary zealots. Ever since they were refused the promise of "forty acres and a mule" by Congress, African Americans have systematically been denied the right to buy property wherever they so desired. They have suffered "redlining," particularly when applying for mortgages or finance capital to start local businesses (see entry on Housing). Until the Fair Housing Act of 1968, African Americans were restricted to black-only neighborhoods. Federal and municipal governments used restrictive covenants to enforce segregated housing patterns.

By contrast, a small black elite has always existed. When referred to, they have been used as tokens of success to prove that America is open to anyone who has the work ethic and determination to succeed according to the laws. Some white Americans, by pointing to conservative elite African Americans like Secretary of State General Colin Powell and Supreme Court Justice Clarence Thomas, imply that African Americans who are not successful are lazy, dishonest or desirous of "something-for-nothing" as welfare recipients. In the words of Henry Louis Gates, Jr., an African American scholar from Harvard: "There are . . . two nations in America . . . one hopeless and one full of hope . . . and both are black."

1975-PRESENT • PROGRESS ~ In the main, however, African Americans are making progress. The percentage of African Americans matriculating to college after high school increased from 25 percent in 1975 to 31 percent in 1998. College enrollment is up due to the increased numbers of African American women enrolled. Between 1976 and 1994 there was only a 20 percent increase in bachelor degrees for black men while black women increased by 55 percent. This disparity has social as well as economic consequences. However, there is still no study that considers the extent of white male corporate help toward black women as opposed to white male-black male antagonisms.

For most affluent whites, wealth is derived from property passed down from father to son to unborn grandson. Until the last two decades, African Americans had very few assets to pass on to their offspring, because before the Fair Housing Act the majority of African Americans possessed little real property to leave as an inheritance to their children.

Of significant interest is the fact that the African American middle class has expanded to such an extent that one of

(circa 1938) A flag hanging outside the headquarters of the NAACP (National Association for the Advancement of Colored People).

every four families earns more than $50,000 per year. On the other hand, one of five African American families earns less than $10,000 per year, thus dividing African Americans into "haves" and "have-nots."

The future outlook is mixed. The old segregation based on the color line is gone. Restrictions to educational opportunities are also gone. Grants and educational loans make it possible for African Americans to excel in education as never before. Degreed African Americans are succeeding in occupational opportunities as equally as white in mid-level positions, even though the communal consensus is that whites always earn more in similar occupations for the same jobs. In addition, there are signs of rising racism among this generation of young whites. Born after 1970, white youth are duped into joining the *Ku Klux Klan* and other white supremacy hate groups in huge numbers through their websites on the Internet.

1980s-1990s • HATE GROUPS ~ In its 1997 annual report, the Intelligence Project of the Southern Poverty Law Center, which has been tracking U.S. hate groups since 1981, released statistics indicating that the number of hate groups increased by 20 percent that year, and numbered 474 such groups. Of the 474 hate groups, 127 were *Ku Klux Klan* organizations; 42 were skinhead; 100 were neo-Nazi; and 81 were of the Christian Identity religion.

Of the 474 organized hate groups, 48 were in Florida; 35 in California; 26 in Illinois; Louisiana, North Carolina, and Pennsylvania, 21 each; Ohio, 19; Alabama and Texas, 18 each; Kentucky, 12; Oregon, 11; Indiana, Maryland, Tennessee, Washington, and Wisconsin, 10 each; New York, nine; Arkansas, Idaho, Massachusetts, Minnesota, Oklahoma, and South Carolina, eight each; Arizona, seven; Colorado, New Jersey, and West Virginia, five each; Kansas and Montana,

Asian Americans in the U.S.

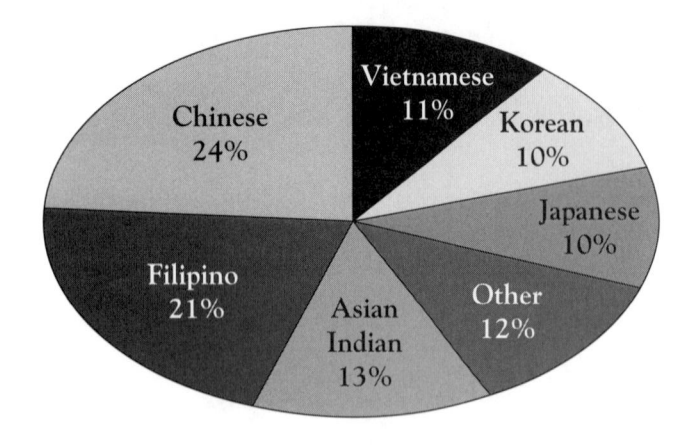

Pie chart:
- Chinese 24%
- Vietnamese 11%
- Korean 10%
- Japanese 10%
- Other 12%
- Asian Indian 13%
- Filipino 21%

SOURCE: Henslin, James M. *Social Problems*, 5th ed. Prentice Hall, 2000.

1820-1860 four each; Nebraska and Nevada, three each; Alaska and Utah, two each; Connecticut, Delaware, Hawaii, New Mexico, South Dakota, and Vermont, one each.

Upper-middle-class teenagers, who may not have considered attending a Klan rally before, are exposed to "at least 163 hate sites on the internet" and are targets for recruitment. Reportedly, while two neo-Nazi organizations—the World Church of the Creator and the National Alliance—mushroomed because of the *Turner Diaries* (1980), a novel that served as a blueprint for the Oklahoma City federal building bombing, the *Ku Klux Klan* organizations grew from one to 12 chapters in 1997.

Proof of the rising tide of hate, in an article published by *U.S.News & World Report*, April 2, 2001, the hate groups total more than 600. In order to combat white hate groups, black separatist groups now number 48. Thus the United States, according to the Southern Poverty Law Center, has seen a rise of 10 percent more groups than 1999. Included in the list are Neo-Nazi, 180; *Ku Klux Klan*, 110; Neo-Confederate, 88; Black Separatist, 48; Racist Skinhead, 39; and Christian Identity, such as the World Church of the Creator, 32."

Also, African Americans still face greater discrimination than Hispanics or Asians.

But as African Americans are gaining success and respect in white America, they are also losing their cultural identity as the black middle class may soon be assimilated into Anglo-conformity. This not only causes a loss of cultural identity for African Americans but also widens the gap between those who have and those who have not.

ASIAN AMERICANS

The Asian population in the United States increased by more than 40 percent since 1990, from about four million in 1980 to 12.1 million as of 2000. Estimates forecast a population of more than 17 million by 2010. Most Asian Americans are immigrants or children of immigrants, and most of them are foreign-born. About 40 percent live in California, with more than one million residing in Los Angeles. Although Asian Americans are treated as one group, there are many different cultures and ethnic populations. The largest group is Chinese (24 percent), followed by Filipinos (21 percent), Japanese (10 percent), Koreans (10 percent) and others including Vietnam, Malaysia and Thailand (35 percent).

1820-1860 • CHINESE IMMIGRANTS
In 1820, the U.S. government initiated the practice of keeping immigration records, but by 1849 there were only 43 Chinese on record. By January 1850, however, the Chinese population of San Francisco was recorded as 787 men and

two women. For more than 200 years, the Chinese had been restricted to travel by the ruling Qing dynasty because they feared the influences of rebels in exile abroad. Consequently, laws were passed that promised execution or 100 lashes for anyone who was caught after leaving the country.

Two years after gold was discovered in California, food shortages, brought about by floods and natural disasters, caused rebellion and the social unrest of some 430 million Chinese. Many young men between the ages of 15 and 40 risked the prescribed punishment to travel abroad in search of economic opportunities. For three years before, in 1847, American and Portuguese businessmen had started an illicit trade in cheap Chinese labor, recruiting "coolies" to work in the pits of Peru, or the plantations of Cuba. Several thousand Chinese were transported by Henry Chauncey, an American, to build a railroad from Panama to Colon. By 1859 American shippers had carried an average of more than 6,000 Chinese workers to Cuba per year. U.S. Congressional records reveal that American shippers had carried more than 50,000 men between 1847 and 1859.

Shortly after the Treaty of Guadalupe, Hidalgo gave California to the Americans in 1848, Aaron H. Palmer proposed to Congress that Chinese laborers be imported to build the transcontinental railroad and to cultivate the fertile lands of California. The fact that they were experienced farmers was well known. A year later, Chinese workers began to migrate to America on their own trying to escape harsh economic conditions and high taxes. They came to *Gum Sann*, or the "Gold Mountain" of California, drawn by the possibility of making a living. By 1870, there were 63,000 Chinese in America; but they were ineligible for citizenship. A 1790 federal law had reserved naturalized citizenship for white persons.

1860S • LABOR AND ECONOMY ~ During the 1860s, between 24,000 Chinese were laboring in the California mines of Mariposa, Placer and Pine Tree, even though most of the white miners had left the dried up claims. They also worked mines in Oregon, Montana and Idaho. However, the census of 1870 showed only a little more than 17,000 still mining the Placer mines. Chinese miners were constantly attacked by lawless men, and they were also subjected to gross discrimination, unfair taxes and other legal obstructions even though the U.S. commissioner responsible for mining statistics reported that the Chinese were the most faithful and earnest workers of all. In his conclusion, he emphasized that they were not "coolies" and predicted that their labor would be of great value to America.

1862-1869 • BUILDING THE TRANSCONTINENTAL RAILROAD ~ In 1862, Congress, by official act, asked the Central Pacific and the Union Pacific to build the first American transcontinental railroad with the former laying tracks east starting in Sacramento and the latter going west from Omaha. Two years went by and the Central Pacific had only gone about 50 miles. A decision was made to hire Chinese workers; but some protested that they were too small and frail for such heavy construction. Those who protested were reminded that the Chinese had built the Great Wall of China, the biggest masonry structure in the world. They also had invented gunpowder and showed Europeans how to use it. By 1869 when the railroad was completed, between 12,000 and 14,000 Chinese were employed by the Central Pacific. Although it was generally agreed that they were better workers than the whites, they were given less pay. On average, a white worker earned $35 a month plus room and board; a Chinese worker, on the other hand, received between $26 and $35 a month and had to pay for his own food and lodging. The work was hard and dangerous; and many Chinese died in the explosions in the High Sierras. In addition, extremely harsh winter conditions and blizzards killed untold numbers.

1870s • Chinese Workers Challenge Freed Slaves ~ During Reconstruction, some white Southerners brought Chinese workers into the Mississippi Delta to replace black workers because they wanted to break the growing political power that the freed slaves were developing. African Americans engaged in sharecropping were constantly complaining about the quasi-slave conditions and low pay. Planters used the Chinese as models for black workers in order to force the African Americans to forget their gripes for "forty acres and a mule." The Chinese, although despised socially, had been recognized as the providers of good cheap labor; and even the most prejudiced employers hired Chinese workers. Because of the social prejudice they faced, many Chinese workers left the southern fields to settle in large cities in Mississippi, Louisiana, Texas and Arkansas.

1820-1884 • Chinese Workers in Hawaii ~ Beginning in 1820, American plantation owners brought Chinese workers to Hawaii to labor on their sugar plantations. By 1850, sugar had become the number one product in the Island's economy. Because of the shortage of satisfactory labor, the Americans looked to China for cheap labor. They had found that the Chinese were quiet, peaceful and willing workers; and until the influx of Japanese workers in the 1890s, the Chinese comprised the main labor force. By 1884, there were more than 18,000 Chinese workers in Hawaii, and they comprised almost a quarter of the population. Some married Hawaiian women and settled in the islands. However, by the time the U.S. annexed Hawaii in 1898 some 46,000 Chinese contract laborers had been brought to the islands. Almost immediately U.S. law outlawed contract labor and stopped the importation of Chinese workers.

1868-1876 • Opportunities for Chinese Workers ~ In 1868, Chinese labor was essential for California wheat farmers. Without these workers there was no crop for market; but by the end of the year they had harvested wheat valued at $20 million. After the completion of the railroad, California farmers, with easier access to the markets of the East Coast, gradually switched from wheat to fruit, a more profitable crop. Grapes, oranges and vegetables, which were more perishable before, were also now more profitable. Thus the railroad had solved the problem of spoilage. By the thousands, Chinese laborers drained swamps, built dikes, dug canals and tamed the lands of the Sacramento-San Joaquin Delta. But while working for white employers, several leased ranches and grew vegetables for themselves. Hundreds of these Chinese farmers used their experience to create successful farming operations; they also shared that expertise with white employers. Within a decade, they had contributed to making California into the orchard capital of the United States. The value of farmland rose from $28 per acre in 1875 to $100 per acre by 1877.

Not all the former railroad workers turned to agricultural work. Many went to work in the factories of California. More than 12,000 of them worked in the shoe, clothing and cigar factories. About ten percent of them were tailors earning about $50 per month. The other 90 percent were low wage earners who earned only $24 a month; but as was the case with the other minority workers, they were always paid less than white workers who did the same jobs. In each case they were segregated, and the competition in the manufacturing industries often created white hostility against the Chinese workers. They were often used as strike breakers, which the whites resented. By 1873, Chinese laborers were producing more than 50 percent of the boots and shoes of California, but they were blamed for causing the loss of jobs, as the depression of 1873 got worse. This gave rise to a clamor that resulted in the exclusion of Chinese workers from America.

Reports of the cigar and tobacco industries show that Chinese income increased significantly because many workers owned the factories themselves. Almost 70 Chinese merchants owned cigar factories between 1860 and 1870. In 1876, some 7,500 Chinese workers were employed in the cigar and tobacco industry, and the value of cigars manufactured increased three times within a decade to $107 million in 1879.

1880s • RESTRICTIONS AND MIGRATION TO THE CITIES ~ Although white hostility had been directed against the Chinese in earlier years, it wasn't until the 1880s that it reached serious proportions. Numerous attacks against this ethnic minority took place, and Chinese were harassed, attacked or expelled from California, Washington, Oregon and Nevada towns. Millions of dollars of their property was destroyed. As resistance to the Chinese increased, they moved for safety from the rural to urban areas; but this urban population found it more difficult to find manufacturing jobs and they had no land on which to farm. Consequently, fearing racial violence, and having very little capital, they congregated in Chinatowns and engaged in small-scale commerce or worked as cooks, domestic servants and laborers. Chinese workers were systematically excluded from society, so that Chinatown became their safety net; but it also became the barrier to acculturation and assimilation, and, at the same time, perpetuated strong cultural ties to their ancestral homeland.

In 1882 President Chester A. Arthur signed the Chinese Exclusion Act, which restricted Chinese immigration and seriously reduced the number of farm laborers imported. Congress had passed the Act to placate white worker demands and maintain white "racial purity." The Act stated that the suspension was for ten years. Between 1849 and 1882 some 250,000 Chinese laborers had come to America to strike it rich and return home. But in 1882 only 39,579 Chinese entered the United States while 102,991 were admitted from Great Britain and 250,630 from Germany. Chinese workers in the United States challenged the constitutionality of the act but their efforts failed, and the act was renewed for another ten years in 1892. In 1884 a more restrictive law suspended for ten years the entry of Chinese laborers from any foreign country. In 1902 Chinese immigration to the United States was made permanently illegal. The Chinese government, however, did not investigate the reasons for the restriction, and those allowed to remain in the United States had to keep silent until they were eligible for citizenship in 1943.

1937-1945 • IMPROVING THEIR STATUS ~ In July 1937, a full-scale war broke out between China and Japan. The Chinese people in America immediately made financial contributions to aid China in the fight for its survival, and American sympathy increased. American newspapers reported Chinese life, philosophy and social traditions in contrast to the atrocities committed by invading Japanese soldiers in China. When Japan bombed Pearl Harbor, China and the United States became allies, and Chinese American support increased with the encouragement of the American government. They bought large quantities of war bonds issued directly by the Central Bank of China.

By invitation of President Franklin D. Roosevelt, Madame Chiang Kai-Shek visited the United States in 1943. Madame Chiang had been educated in America as a teenager and spoke very good English. Beautiful and gracious, she proved to be an excellent "good-will ambassador." In order to counteract Japanese propaganda, which charged the U.S. with treating the Chinese as inferior minorities, Congress, at the instigation of President Roosevelt passed a bill to lift the ban on Chinese immigration. Roosevelt signed the bill on December 17, 1943, which allowed a yearly quota of 105 Chinese immigrants, regardless of their place of birth. While this was highly discriminatory in comparison to European quotas, the bill neutralized the opposition of veteran and labor organizations that feared an influx of cheap Chinese labor.

1868-1924 • JAPANESE IMMIGRANTS ~ The second wave of Asian migration to the United States began in 1868, when Japanese workers went to Hawaii. The partition of China by the western powers worried that they might also be dominated by foreigners. They restored the emperor and made efforts to establish a strong central government backed by a more powerful military. To accomplish this, heavy taxes were imposed on the people, and the farmers suffered severe hardships. Stories that a plantation laborer in Hawaii could earn in three years the equivalent of ten years in Japan produced emigration fever. More than 28,000 applications were received in response to the Japanese government's request for 600 emigrant workers. Thus, between 1885 and 1924, 200,000 Japanese workers crossed the Pacific to work in Hawaii, and 180,000 came to the United States. The difference between the Japanese worker immigration and that of the Chinese was the fact that a significant number of women were included, who were more receptive to travel overseas. A Hawaiian report of 1886 stated that Japanese men were better plantation workers when they had wives. Consequently, after the annexation of Hawaii to the United States in 1898, Japanese women were welcomed to Hawaii by U.S. planters.

1875-1910 • JAPANESE LABORERS ~ Between 1875 and 1910, Japanese workers cultivated lands that jumped from 12,000 to 214,000 acres. The planters continuously imported more workers from Japan. In order to control the huge Japanese work force, planters purposefully created divisions by importing Filipino, Portuguese and Chinese workers. They believed that to avert strikes a variety of ethnic workers was required. In 1903 they imported Korean workers to pit against the Japanese. Because the planters were aware of the antagonism between these two peoples, they believed that any organized Japanese strike would fail. The Korean supply of workers was cut off in 1905, so they turned to Filipino laborers. In order to maintain control over the workers, the Hawaiian Sugar Planter's Association passed a resolution in 1904 that restricted skilled positions to U.S. citizens or those eligible for citizenship. Asian workers were excluded because they were ineligible due to the federal law mentioned above.

"Work gangs" were comprised of 20 to 30 workers with a large percentage of female workers. Each gang had a supervisor who was almost always a white man; but Japanese workers feared the Portuguese overseer who carried a whip and was often brutal. Work gangs sometimes constituted one nationality of workers, but more often than not were comprised of a mixture of nationalities. Treated badly, Japanese workers resisted exploitation, and in 1909 organized a strike because they made up 70 percent of the work force. The Japanese Federation of Labor demanded higher wages, an eight-hour work day, paid maternity for expectant mothers and an insurance retiree fund.

Children of immigrant workers posed a problem for the planters, who did not want to educate them beyond the sixth grade. They wanted to keep the second generation as agricultural workers, and this would not be possible if they aspired to higher education. In school, these children were learning about freedom, American democracy and equality, which were all bad things to know for those who were to become future plantation workers. They saw whites on the top and Asians at the bottom of society. They saw that their parents were paid low wages, and each family decided to give their children every possible economic and educational advantage, especially since they had built the canefield economy.

1880s-1920s • Continuing Hostilities toward Japanese Workers

In America, anti-Japanese hostility was puzzling to visitors from Hawaii. There they represented more than forty percent of the population; but in America they were only a very small minority. They were scorned by white Americans, and were often attacked by hostile white workers. Denied opportunities, many of the Japanese workers sought to become entrepreneurs, while others made arrangements to work as sharecroppers. At the time they became farmers in California, the system of irrigation had transformed farming, and this aided the Japanese significantly. They produced strawberries, tomatoes, onions and other vegetables, and by 1920 were cultivating more than 458,000 acres.

Initially, the majority of Japanese came to America in the hope of making money and returning to Japan. Because they felt that this was a temporary sojourn, they felt no desire to contribute to American society or to assimilate. In turn, this brought about a clamor for exclusion from anti-Japanese groups. However, in 1906 a few Japanese families settled in California and planted grapevines—a crop which takes four years to mature. By 1918, they were shipping 260 carloads of fruit to market, and were hoping that they could become naturalized citizens.

1942-1945 • Internment of Japanese Americans

In 1924, Congress passed a law that prohibited the entry of

1942-1980s

aliens who were ineligible for citizenship. This was based on a 1790 law that allowed only white persons to become citizens. By the time World War II began, sixty-three percent of all Japanese Americans had been born in America. Called the "Nisei" the second generation Japanese had been schooled in America, and had been raised under American customs and language. The first generation, "Issei" reminded their children that they were Americans and had opportunities that had been denied them. But although they had been schooled in America, the Nisei found it difficult to get employment due to racial discrimination. They felt trapped between two cultures and were powerless to change ethnic appearances. Thus when Japan bombed Pearl Harbor on December 7, 1941, all their fears would be realized to the fullest in internment camps.

The Chamber of Commerce, the American Legion, and the Veterans of Foreign Wars demanded the arrest of all the 125,000 Japanese living in America; and through Executive Order 9066, the President authorized the removal of all Japanese Americans from the West Coast and confined in inland internment camps. The Federal Bureau of Investigation arrested nearly 2,000 people of Japanese descent, including Issei and Nisei businessmen, teachers, editors and priests. Although thousands of German and Italian aliens were arrested, there was no general concern about these ethnic groups because they were "white."

1942-1952 • LOYAL JAPANESE ~
Nearly 18,000 Nisei served in the U.S. army and fought in Europe but were not allowed to fight in the Pacific. They sustained thousands of casualties and won thousands of Purple Hearts, hundreds of Bronze Stars, Silver Stars, Distinguished Service Crosses and divisional citations. On December 18, 1944, a Sacramento court decided that it was unconstitutional to incarcerate law-abiding American citizens. In 1952, the McCarran-Walter Act permitted Issei to apply for citizenship, and the Immigration and Nationality Act passed in 1965 removed the Japanese quota restriction. In the 1980s, Congress began paying damages of more than $1 billion to those who suffered incarceration.

1980s • JAPANESE MOVE INTO MAINSTREAM AMERICAN SOCIETY ~
In the 1980s, Japanese students poured into colleges and universities, and remembering their grandparents' legacy of internment camps, protested discrimination and stereotyping. They demanded Japanese studies in the schools and colleges, and militant Japanese called for "yellow pride" and "yellow power." Because so many Japanese were educated and enjoying middle-class status, the new attitudes brought about the end of isolation and submission.

The extraordinary success of the Japanese economy during the 1980s, combined with the recession in the United States that occurred during the Reagan Presidency (1980-1988), much animosity arose from Americans whose jobs were threatened by Japanese imports. When the U.S. auto industry was experiencing a slump because Americans were buying more Japanese cars than American, some parking lots in Detroit restricted parking to American cars only, and many companies in Michigan required their employees to drive American models.

The political and economic prosperity that Japan fostered after the war kept emigration to America at a minimum. This decline in Japanese immigration fostered an acceleration of the assimilation of Japanese Americans into American society; and by the early 1990s, the large majority of Japanese Americans were marrying persons of non-Japanese extraction.

1909-1920 • FILIPINO AMERICANS IN HAWAII ~ After the Japanese worker strike of 1909 in Hawaii was broken, the Hawaiian Sugar Planters Association imported large numbers of Filipino laborers. By 1920, the Japanese work force had dropped from 70 percent to 44 percent, and the Filipino had increased from less than one percent to 30 percent. They organized their own "blood" union, but soon realized that there would have to be interethnic cooperation. When the Japanese demands of an eight-hour work day and paid maternity leaves were rejected by the planters association, the Filipinos struck and invited the Japanese to join them. Three thousand Filipinos set up picket lines and agitated for worker solidarity. Joined by Spanish, Portuguese and Chinese workers, the Filipino and Japanese laborers recognized for the first time the contributions that they had made to the Hawaiian economy, which was all for the benefit of American entrepreneurs. The planters struck back with the divide and conquer rule by fomenting distrust between the union leaders. They bribed the Filipino leader who suddenly called off the strike citing it as a Japanese action designed to cripple the economy.

1925-1966 • STRIKES AND UNIONS ~ Like other ethnic groups, Filipinos became politically active, and this activism surfaced as a workers' movement. After white growers cut the wages of asparagus workers in 1925, the Filipinos organized an Agricultural Labor Association and won several strikes in the 1930s and 1940s. In 1966, Filipino unions joined the Mexican American labor union founded by Cesar Chavez in creating the United Farm Workers Organizing Committee. Chavez was named the head of the union, and Philip Vera Cruz, a Filipino, was named the vice-chairman.

The Filipino communities in California continued to grow in the 1980s, but eradicating poverty was difficult. As large numbers of Filipinos with extremely limited resources entered America, without the ethnic institutions and financial resources like the other Asian groups, they found it difficult to succeed. They had come from an island nation where hundreds of languages and linguistic differences divided them. Thus, by the early 1990s, most Filipinos were unskilled workers with incomes at the lowest levels.

1965-1991 • LARGE NUMBER OF FILIPINOS IMMIGRATE ~ The passage of the Immigration and Nationality Act of 1965 accelerated immigration from the Philippines. America's military presence in the islands from 1898, and the fact that American servicemen had married many Filipino women bringing them to the United States, set the stage for their entry into America. By 1991, Filipino Americans, who constituted 20 percent of all Asian Americans in the United States, numbered more than 1.4 million.

1990S • SUCCESS OF ASIAN AMERICANS ~ Asian Americans are more affluent than Native Americans, Hispanic

1990s

Americans or African Americans. More than nine out ten Asian Americans aged 25 or over have completed high school. They outnumber white college graduates by a ratio of more than two to one; and 46 percent of adult Asian American males and 37 percent of the females are college graduates. The Asian American family income is more than $18,000 above the average for Hispanic families, and $20,000 above the average for African American families. This figure is probably due to the fact that there are several working family members in the household. However, as of 1998 Asian Americans below the poverty line comprised 14 percent as compared to 13 percent of the entire U. S. population. The economic success of this ethnic group is directly related to strong family support systems, value on education, and a pooling of family resources.

In recent years open hostility has been directed against Asian Americans, who are seen as a "superior minority" clannish, and set apart in their own ethnic conclaves. They are often viewed as receiving special treatment by other ethnic minorities because of Japan's global economic leadership, and their hard work and ingenuity is often not considered. It is predicted that the Asian American minority status may disappear within a few decades, and full assimilation be achieved.

CONCLUSION

Because the number of African Americans increased dramatically in post-war America, they gained political strength and tended to vote mainly for the Democratic Party. Following the Baton Rouge Bus Boycott and the Montgomery Bus Boycott in 1955, African Americans, led by Martin Luther King, Jr., used direct political action to challenge discrimination in America. Joined by Native Americans, Mexican Americans, Puerto Ricans and Liberal Whites, the Civil Rights Movement pressured Congress to pass the Civil Rights Acts of 1964 and 1968 and the Voting Rights Act of 1965. Since that time, using the watchdog system employed by the NAACP, African Americans remain guarded to challenge discrimination and white supremacy wherever these ideas are found.

Throughout the 1960s and 1970s, African Americans, Mexican Americans and Puerto Rican Americans took to the streets in challenge of unequal economic and educational opportunities. Against the background of the Vietnam War, poverty and other economic downturns, they demonstrated and rioted trying to win equality in a plural society while white leaders continued to drag their feet. By the end of the Nixon Administration, however, it was clear and the world saw that government in America was less than perfect and that American society was fraught with many social problems. Nevertheless, in spite of all this, immigrants continued to come to America in search of a better way of life.

In the 1980s, 29 percent of the immigrants came from Asia, with a majority of them being the boatpeople of Vietnam, while 56 percent of the rest came from Canada, Mexico, Central America and the Caribbean. Also, by 1992, there were some three million undocumented immigrants living in the United States with an estimated annual increase of some 250,000 people. In order to address this situation, Congress passed the Immigration Reform Control Act of 1986, which granted resident alien status to any individual who proved continual residence since 1982. Then in the Immigration Act of 1990, Congress tried to attract wealthy and well-educated immigrants by offering residence to 10,000 people annually who would invest at least $1 million in an American business able to employ a minimum of ten people. Thus, the United States became a salad bowl with mixtures of languages, cultures, ethnic backgrounds and faces.

At the present time, however, because of the increasing need for global cooperation, all of these ethnic minority groups seemed poised to take advantage of opportunities in the United States, and have opted for educational excellence, economic action and political participation. Powerful lobbyists in Washington support each group, recognizing that they have great voting potential. They are aware that if these ethnic minority groups would combine their voting strength, they could decide a presidential election. Perhaps that is why the electoral votes in Florida and California were so important in the recent presidential election of 2000. A question of great importance is whether a voting alliance of these ethnic minorities would ever come about. For the moment, divided by class, education and religious background, these ethnic minorities fall under the domination of one of the two parties in America. However, from recent population statistics it can be shown that the mushrooming Hispanic presence in the State of California is growing so fast that they may recapture all the high offices by ethnic votes within a decade.

BIBLIOGRAPHY

Camarillo, Albert. *Chicanos in a Changing Society*. Cambridge: Harvard University Press, 1979.

D'Angelo, Raymond. *The American Civil Rights Movement*. New York: McGraw-Hill, 2001.

Franklin, John Hope. *From Slavery to Freedom: A History of African Americans*. New York: McGraw-Hill, 2000.

Henslin, James, M. *Social Problems*. Upper Saddle River, NJ: Prentice Hall, Inc., 2000.

Miller, Kerby A. *Emigrants and Exiles: Ireland and the Irish Exodus to North America*. New York: Oxford University Press, 1985.

Nabokov, Peter. *Native American Testimony*. New York: Penguin Books USA Inc., 1991.

Oslon, James S. *Ethnic Dimension in American History*. New York: St. Martin's Press, 1994.

Palen, John J. *Social Problems for the Twenty-First Century*. New York: McGraw-Hill, 2001.

Reimers, David M. *Still the Golden Door: the Third World Comes to America*. New York: Columbia University Press, 1985.

Takaki, Ronald. *A Different Mirror: A History of Multicultural America*. New York: Little, Brown and Company, 1993.

Tsai, Shih-Shan Henry. *The Chinese Experience in America*. Bloomington: Indiana University Press, 1986.

Young, Mary E. "Indian Removal and Land Allotment: The Civilized Tribes and Jacksonian Justice." *The American Historical Review*, 6, 1 (Oct-Jan, 1958-1959.

Weber, David, ed. *Foreigners in Their Native Land*. Albuquerque: University of New Mexico Press, 1973.

Internet Resources

Racial and Ethnic Minorities
The purpose of this site is to encourage research, theory, and teaching concerning the relation between socially defined racial and ethnic groups.
http://www.asanet.org/sections/raceeth.html

Race Relations
http://racerelations.about.com/index.htm

Race and Ethnicity
Published by the Section on Race, Ethnicity and Politics, in the American Political Science Association. Resources for the study of racial and ethnic politics, especially in the United States.
http://www.providence.edu/polisci/rep

The Movies, Race, and Ethnicity
Provides a broad sampling of ethnic and racial representations in the movies over the last century. These films include works of mainstream Hollywood, as well as historical and current movies by filmmakers of color.
http://www.lib.berkeley.edu/MRC/EthnicImagesVid.html

The Race and Ethnicity collection, one of over forty literary collections on the Eserver. Consists of reference material, essays, and other works addressing issues of race and ethnicity in the United States.
http://eserver.org/race

Center for the Study of Race and Ethnicity
The Center for the Study of Race and Ethnicity at Brown University is an interdisciplinary organization that develops and promotes research and programs on Race and Ethnicity.
http://www.brown.edu/Departments/Race_Ethnicity

Race Ethnicity Sociology Teaching Resources
A selection of online resources for teaching a variety of courses and issues in the areas of race and ethnicity.
http://sociology.about.com/cs/teachingrace/index.htm (About Sociology)

Race ethnicity online museums
Visit a selection of the best online museum exhibits dealing with race and ethnicity.
http://sociology.about.com/library/weekly/aa081601d.htm (About Sociology)

Race and Ethnicity
A focus on the social significance of racial and ethnic groups, relations between dominant and minority groups, and the ways the social constructs of race and ethnicity impact our lives.
http://sociology.about.com/cs/raceethnicity/index.htm

Indigenous Peoples of Alaska
Links to information sources on Alaska's original peoples.
http://arcticculture.about.com/cs/indigenouspeoples1/index_2.htm

Native American Indians and Crime

American Indians and Crime - The rate of violence against American Indians is more than twice the national average

http://nativeamculture.about.com/library/weekly/aa052301a.htm

Native American Religion

Spirituality and faiths of the many tribes and nations native to the North American continent.

http://altreligion.about.com/cs/nativeamerican/index_2.htm
(About Alternative Religions)

Native American History - Native Americans and the United States

Many people including the United States government have treated Native Americans poorly throughout American History. These resources explore the information available about the different groups of Native Americans from the past and the present.

http://americanhistory.about.com/cs/nativeamericans/index_2.htm

Red Feather Development Group is a national nonprofit housing and community development organization that works with American Indian nations to find solutions for the lack of proper housing and poverty that continue to plague many of these communities.

http://www.redfeather.org

Cuban History

The History of Cuba and Cuban-Americans.

http://latinoculture.about.com/cs/cubanhistory/index.htm

African-American People

The very rich history of the infinite contributions and contributors made to this country from African-Americans.

http://americanhistory.about.com/cs/afamerpeople/index.htm

Tobacco Use Among U.S. Racial/Ethnic Minority Groups

Statistics outlining trends in tobacco use by African Americans, Asians, Hispanics, and American Indians.

http://www.cdc.gov/nccdphp/osh/sgr-minorities.htm

Ethnic Minorities at Greater Risk for Stroke Deaths

According to the Centers for Disease Control and Prevention, African Americans, American Indians and Alaska Natives, Asian and Pacific Islanders, and Hispanic adults are all more likely to die from stroke than white adults.

http://cardiology.medscape.com/reuters/prof/2000/02/02.14/ep02140f.html

Kenneth Adderley
Upper Iowa University

FAMILY LIFE

~

(circa 1953) A young couple smile as they wheel a baby carriage on a neighborhood sidewalk.

TIMELINE

1850-1919 ~ The "Cult of Domesticity"

"Cult of domesticity" advocates that women belong in the home (1850-1900) / One-fourth of pregnancies end in abortion (1850s) / Proliferation of birth control devices (1880-1900) / Marriage rates steadily decline (1850-1900); by 1900 ten percent of marriageable women choose to remain single / Middle class family symbolizes the ideal family (1900) / Consumer goods help free women from housekeeping to devote more time to children (1900) / Working-class families in cities live in terrible conditions (1870-1900) / Children under the age of 15 produce 20% of the family income (1860-1900) / Homestead Act attracts farm families to inhospitable living conditions on the prairie (1862-1880) / Women on the prairie perform many men's tasks (1860-1900) / Husbands and wives become companions and sexual partners (early 1900s) / Education dramatically changes the role of women in society (1900-1920)

MILESTONES: Widespread use of child labor (1870) • Passionless marriages control birth rate (1870s-1880s) • Women's enrollment in college rises from 20 percent in 1870 to 40 percent in 1910 • Women begin to express favorable opinions about sex but in moderation (1890s) • Electrolux and Hoover introduce the first vacuum cleaners (1901) • U.S. Census Bureau reports the divorce rate at one in fifteen marriages (1906) • Margaret Sanger risks arrest by opening up birth control clinics and importing and distributing contraceptives illegally (1914) • Child labor abuse made a federal crime (1916) • The United States fights in World War I (1917-1918)

1920-1929 ~ The Companionate Family and Rise of the "New Woman"

"Flappers" symbolize the new role of women in society (1920s) / Proliferation of automobiles engenders the emergence of a youth culture (1920s) / Congress passes legislation for child labor laws, compulsory education, juvenile justice systems, and health care programs (1920s) / Older workers are forced out of the labor system, leading to pension plans (1920s)

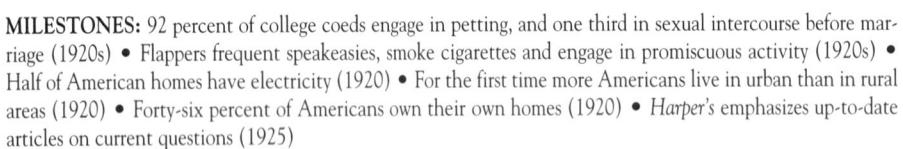

MILESTONES: 92 percent of college coeds engage in petting, and one third in sexual intercourse before marriage (1920s) • Flappers frequent speakeasies, smoke cigarettes and engage in promiscuous activity (1920s) • Half of American homes have electricity (1920) • For the first time more Americans live in urban than in rural areas (1920) • Forty-six percent of Americans own their own homes (1920) • *Harper's* emphasizes up-to-date articles on current questions (1925)

1930-1949 ~ Crisis Years

Decline in marriages/divorces/childbearing as a result of the Depression (1930-1935) / Many men unable to support their families desert them (1932-1935) / Family of four survives on $25 a week (1930s) / Percentage of teenagers finishing high school increases from 50% in 1930 to 75% in 1940 / New Deal programs offer government assistance to families for the first time (1932-1938) / Five million women enter the labor force (1940-1945) / Teenagers leave school to fill job vacancies during WWII (1941-1945) / Divorce occurs in 25% of marriages made during WWII (1946-1949)

MILESTONES: Under pressure, the movie industry enacts the Production Code, addressing crime, sex, vulgarity, obscenity, profanity, costumes, dancing and religion (1930) • Women dominate the professions of teaching, nursing, and social work (1930) • One-third of college professors are women (1930) • Working wives are publicly criticized as selfish and "a menace to society" (1930) • Charities and churches are permitted to hold bingo games legally in Massachusetts (1931) and Rhode Island (1937) • One quarter of the work force is unemployed (1932) • Economy Act stipulates that married women be discharged from their jobs (1932) • *Reader's Digest* has a circulation of over 1,000,000 readers (1935) • Christian Dior introduces his "New Look" for American women (1947)

1950-1965 ~ The Golden Age of Family Life

Marriage rates are at an all-time high and the marriage age at an all-time low (early 1950s) / 70% of American women are married by the age of 24 (early 1950s) / Young brides and women in their 30s began having post-war babies (1946-1952) / Two thirds of college women drop out to marry or to make themselves more eligible for marriage (1955) / Church membership rises from 50% in 1940 to 75% in 1955 / Dr. Spock raises awareness of child-rearing practices (mid-1950s) / Disillusionment for the ideal family begins to erode family unity (late 1950s) / 90% of the 1950s housewives hope their daughters will lead different lives (late 1950s) / Family income triples between 1950 and 1970 / Women's liberation movement is primarily confined to white, middle class women (1960s) / Poverty rate declines from 20% in 1960 to 12% in 1969 because of government assistance programs

MILESTONES: Housing starts reach 1.7 million (1950) • Federal home loan programs discriminate against minorities (1950s-1960s) • Decade of "correct" fashions and complicated rules of behavior (1950s) • Barbie doll creates public debate about her unattainable body standard (1959) • Women's liberation movement encourages smaller families and free access to the birth control pill (1960s) • Oral contraceptive pills approved (1960) • New fertility drug, Pergonal, introduced, resulting in multiple births (1964) • Enactment of Medicare and Medicaid reduce death in the elderly (1965)

1966-1979 ~ The "Me Generation"

Sexual Revolution brings equivalency to some women regarding family choices (mid 1960s-) / Proliferation of the birth control pill reduces forced marriages and abortions (1960s-) / Rise in cohabitation challenges traditional moral values (1960s) / Sharp divisions between the younger generation and their parents over the Vietnam War lead to the breakdown of some family unity (1968-1972) / Greater financial independence for women and the rapid rise in rate of working mothers contribute to the increase in the divorce rate (1970s)

MILESTONES: *Woman's Day* adds articles on health and money management to help working women (1966) • California is the first state to permit "irreconcilable differences" divorce, leading the way to no-fault divorce (1969) • *Sesame Street* premieres (1969) • Women make up 40 percent of the overall labor force and represent a substantial increase in married women who work (1970) • White flight to the suburbs increases urban deterioration (1970s) • Supreme Court rules in *Roe v. Wade* on the constitutionality of abortion rights (1973)

1980-2000 ~ Seeking a return to the "Golden Age"

Number of working mothers increases from 12% in 1950 to 60% in 1990 / 25% of teens do not graduate from high school (1990s) / Family and Medical Leave Act provides worker security during family emergencies (1993) / Politicians embrace "family values" as a political issue (1990s) / Pro-life advocates bomb birth control clinics and attack some doctors (1990s) / Episcopal Diocese of Newark, NJ declares there is nothing in the scriptures to preclude the homosexual relationship to become a holy union (1994)

MILESTONES: Sally Ride is the first woman in space (1983) • Housing and Community Act establishes a housing voucher program (1987) • Rampage killing by students in their own schools raises questions about family responsibilities (late-1990s) • Successful heart surgery performed on a fetus in the womb (1991) • ATF assaults the Branch Davidian Compound in Waco, Texas, leading to a 51 day stand off and the deaths of all the inhabitants, many women and children (1993) • Many companies permit employees to work from their homes (1995-1999) • Introduction of Viagra — a drug to treat sexual dysfunction in men (1997)

INTRODUCTION

Many Americans are concerned over the loss of the traditional American family, focusing on the fact that fewer than ten percent of American households resemble the commonly accepted definition of a family: breadwinner father, stay-at-home mother and children who work only to supplement their allowance. Care must be taken when talking about the traditional family, because in reality there has never been a standard, unchanging family form in America. The family has always been a dynamic institution, changing in response to social, cultural and economic pressures. There is a great deal of discussion about "family values," but care should be taken to qualify this phrase. Exactly what is meant by family and which values are Americans interested in preserving?

Most Americans likely define family by identifying the typical nuclear family of husband, wife and children. But this family form does not represent the traditional family for many Americans, and in fact is not necessarily traditional at all. For example, during the colonial period, a family might consist of a married couple, their children, apprentices, servants and (in the Southern colonies) slaves. Many households also included grandparents and grandchildren, step- and half-siblings, step-parents, aunts, uncles, cousins and occasionally various "fictive" kin (people unrelated by blood or marriage, but considered relatives). By the end of the twentieth century, a growing number of families consisted of childless couples, same sex couples, single parent households and individuals living alone. The tidy mental image of the suburban family "Ward, June, Wally and the Beaver" (as depicted in the popular 1950s TV show "Leave it to Beaver") has never been truly typical or representative of the way most Americans have lived. The 1950s family was in many ways an anomaly, as it was not a continuation of what had come before it, and was quickly replaced as the family as an institution changed with the times. Preconceived notions aside, the American family has always been a dynamic institution.

1850-1900 • THE IMPACT OF INDUSTRIALIZATION ON AMERICAN FAMILIES

∾ The years immediately following the Civil War saw profound changes in American family life. By the middle of the nineteenth century, the family became far less rigidly patriarchal than it had been during the colonial period, where households had functioned as little commonwealths, and wives and children were expected to be obedient to the patriarch—the husband and father. Instead, American families were much more companionate by the nineteenth century, with husbands and wives viewed more as partners and children as individuals to be nurtured. But this companionate family was largely confined to the urban middle class. And while the middle class family came to represent the domestic ideal in America, many families exhibited very different characteristics.

Until the middle of the nineteenth century, most American families lived on farms in rural communities. But as the United States industrialized following the Civil War, more and more Americans migrated to cities to take part in the country's rapid economic transformation. This process of industrialization and urbanization had a powerful impact on American family life. Rather than a collection of producers all engaged in a family economic enterprise (the farm), urban middle class families became instead primarily consumers, and most family members were disconnected from economic endeavors. One of the hallmarks of middle class status was the fact that only the husband and father worked for wages outside the home. He was employed in one of the new "white collar" jobs—where the employee wore a dress shirt rather than a work shirt—available in the industrial economy. His was the aggressive world of business. His wife devoted herself to household responsibilities. Hers was the private world of domesticity. For American couples, two distinct spheres emerged, male and female, public and private, and the lives of men and women began to sharply diverge. The home came to be regarded as a "haven in a heartless world," made so through the efforts of the housewife, whose job it was to provide a nurturing, harmonious and beautiful environment for her husband and children. Her greatest strength was her virtue and piety, and her greatest fulfillment would be found in the domestic sphere, or so she was told. The middle class domestic ideal insisted that a woman's true place was in the home. This "cult of domesticity" came to dominate middle class family life until the end of the nineteenth century.

A Woman's Place

Her assumed natural proclivity for morality and virtue gave a woman a great deal of influence in American society. And it led to important changes in gender relations as well. Married women saw their legal status improve in some crucial areas, as they gained the right to own property in their own names, to enter into contracts independent of their husbands, to control their own income and to seek a divorce. But custom still dictated that women were seen as subordinate to men, the junior partner in marriage. Though acknowledged for her piety, a middle class housewife was still expected to defer to her husband, as she was understood to be his intellectual inferior. Her mind was best suited to make her the companion or ornamental appendage to man.

Though she was in essence barred by convention from seeking outside employment, the middle class housewife had a wide array of consumer goods and small appliances available to make the job of housekeeping easier, such as ready-made clothing and canned and packaged foods. She most likely employed at least one servant, a black woman if she lived in the South, an Irish immigrant if she lived in the Northeast. But as household conveniences like washing machines reduced some of the labor required of home making, new attitudes about the quality of housekeeping ensured that a woman's

Percentage of mothers in the workforce

Year	Percentage
1900	6 percent
1920	9 percent
1930	12 percent
1945	25 percent
1950	12 percent
1970	30 percent
1980	45 percent
2000	50 percent

SOURCE: Compiled from *Women and the American Experience* (2000), *Domestic Revolutions* (1998), *The Way We Never Were* (1992) and *Divided Lives* (1992).

(1900) A monkey dressed in butler's uniform admires its reflection in the bottom of a saucepan. An advertisement for 'Monkey Brand,' a soap for cleaning metal, mirrors and crockery made by Lever Brothers.

1900 work was never done. Standards of cleanliness changed to extend the efforts required to maintain a middle class household. Still, consumer goods and domestic help freed the housewife from much of the drudgery of housekeeping, and gave her more time to devote to one of her principle responsibilities, child rearing. It was her responsibility to see to the proper moral training of the young, to nurture them and to inculcate in them the morality and the piety so highly valued by American society.

1800-1900 • CHILDREN IN THE NINETEENTH CENTURY ~

Until the middle of the nineteenth century, children had predominantly been viewed as an economic asset, their labor a valuable commodity on the family farm or in their father's workshop. But as middle class families increasingly became consumers rather than producers, large families were no longer desirable. Instead, they were seen as a liability, as parents understood that they could best help their children succeed in the competitive world of the middle class by reducing the size of their families in order to provide more guidance and material assistance to their offspring. Over the course of the nineteenth century, the size of middle class families fell by half, from an average of seven or eight children per couple in 1800 to about four children per couple in 1900.

Family size	
1800	7-8
1850	5-6
1900	3.6
1929	2.4
1933	1.8
1957	3.8
1990	1.8

SOURCE: Compiled from *Women and the American Experience* (2000), *Domestic Revolutions* (1998), *The Way We Never Were* (1992) and *Divided Lives* (1992).

1880-1900 • SEXUAL PRACTICES ~

Middle class couples turned to various forms of birth control to limit family size. By the second half of the nineteenth century, condoms, diaphrams, sponges and douches were available, though many couples were reluctant to employ the use of condoms because of their association with prostitution and the prevention of venereal disease. More often, couples relied on the rhythm method (avoiding intercourse during a woman's fertile period), coitus interruptus (withdrawal) or abstinence. Some doctors advised that couples end their sexual relationship once they determined not to have more children. Others insisted that women were responsible for controlling the sexual appetites of their husbands, as they had little interest in sex themselves. As one expert insisted "the majority of women (happily for society) are not very much troubled by sexual feeling of any kind." This notion that women were "passionless" provided them with a scientific justification for refusing their husbands' sexual advances in order to avoid unwanted pregnancies, though it did not in fact reflect the reality of married couples' sexuality. When various forms of contraception failed, women turned to abortion as a means of birth control. Sources indicate that during the middle of the nineteenth century, 25 percent of pregnancies were ended intentionally.

1850 • CHILD-REARING PRACTICES ~ With the advent of industrialization, fathers spent much of their time away from home, and unlike their pre-industrial predecessors, they did not play an active role in the day-to-day rearing of their children. Mothers were the main source of moral and physical well-being for the young. According to the experts, mothers were precisely the right source to provide the upbringing necessary for the children of the middle class. Society believed women to be the moral superiors of men, so it was only natural that women were deemed best suited to rear the next generation of middle class Americans. Women, therefore, were serving society by shaping their children's character and instilling virtue in the next generation of American citizens. Child rearing was a responsibility for which women were thought to be uniquely qualified.

This shift from father to mother as primary parent came with the new understanding that children were governed more effectively by coercion than by force. Women could persuade their children to act responsibly through their own good example. Virtue could be learned from the virtuous. By the middle of the nineteenth century, too, children were staying at home under parental supervision longer than they had in the past, certainly into their teens but sometimes into their early twenties. Adolescence was a newly identified life stage, and experts warned that it was a particularly unsettling time in a young person's life. "Early departure from the homestead," wrote one, "is a moral crisis that many of our youth do not show themselves able to meet. It comes at a tender age, when judgment is weakest and passion and impulse strongest." This was certainly not a time to trust young people to venture out on their own. Instead, it was precisely the time for close parental supervision to ensure that members of the next generation made a smooth transition from child to adult.

1850-1900 • EDUCATION ~ This prolonged period of childhood sometimes generated tension between the generations as young people sought independence from parental control. But there were real benefits to this change as well.

1850-1900

In particular, the children of the middle class had an unprecedented opportunity to receive an education, allowing them some measure of assurance that as adults they would be able to maintain their middle class status. In fact, education became another important hallmark of middle class status, as parents now had the economic resources to educate all of their children, daughters as well as sons. Access to higher education provided young women with a degree of independence that had been unknown to previous generations. Armed with high school, and increasingly with college, diplomas, the daughters of the middle class were able to take up leadership roles in the charity and reform organizations to which they committed their time and energy. In addition, those who chose to could seek employment in a slowly widening field of women's occupations, including teaching, nursing and social work. In accepting paid employment, though, these young women had to overcome the social stigma of working for wages. "Working girl" was a term generally used to describe a prostitute, and young women worried about the negative connotation of the phrase. Middle class sensibilities dictated that true "ladies" remained at home.

1850-1900 • MARRIAGE ~ Armed with an education and presented with a slowly widening variety of occupations, the daughters of the middle class began to reconsider their options, and many re-evaluated their beliefs about marriage. Courting was still carried out within the confines of the home and under parents' watchful eyes, but the choice of a spouse was considered a personal one, and love was regarded as a central element in the decision. Still, during the second half of the nineteenth century, the marriage rate in the United States declined steadily. Fully 10 percent of the young women old enough to marry chose to remain single. For many, marriage was viewed negatively, as they worried about the loss of independence this change in status would bring. They hesitated to take on the responsibilities of wife and mother at the same time that they resisted entering into the isolated world of the domestic sphere. In addition, the generation of American women who came of age at the end of the nineteenth century had come to expect more from marriage than their mothers did. They sought a new level of emotional satisfaction from marriage and a greater degree of equality with their spouses. But these rising expectations for self-fulfillment were often unmet, and led to feelings of isolation and unhappiness, and a steady rise in the divorce rate. Despite the stigma attached, increasing numbers of American couples sought to dissolve their marriages during the second half of the nineteenth century. In addition to the customary reasons for taking such action (desertion, abuse), women began to cite personal unhappiness as their justification. Still, divorce remained relatively rare, while large numbers of women were treated for classic female afflictions like hysteria and depression.

1870-1900 • LIVING CONDITIONS ~ Women were not alone in lamenting the isolation of the middle class family. Industrialization saw an important shift in urban demography that resulted in the creation of middle class enclaves (suburbs) on the fringes of American cities. Those who could afford to actively sought to relocate from the city centers. The middle class embraced the suburbs as a

(1908) At Home. Life in these middle class suburban communities came with a social cost, isolating families from kin and community. The middle class family, nuclear in its structure, found itself increasingly detached from external supports at the same time that it was expected to meet both the economic and emotional needs of all its members.

healthy environment, both physically and morally. "Streetcar suburbs" became an important part of the urban landscape, and were specifically designed to conjure up notions of a rural ideal. Residence in such communities became a badge of class affiliation. The further a family lived from the city center, the higher its status in the hierarchy of urban communities. Those with the highest incomes could afford the cost of transit to downtown jobs. In addition to status, members of the middle class relocated to the suburbs in search of cleaner air, greater privacy and more amenities. Indoor toilets, central heating and electricity came to be regarded as basic commodities by suburbanites. But life in these middle class communities came with a social cost, isolating families from kin and community. The middle class family, nuclear in its structure, found itself increasingly detached from external supports at the same time that it was expected to meet both the economic and emotional needs of all its members. The result was not always successful. Still, the middle class family came to be regarded as the domestic ideal, despite the fact that large numbers of Americans defined family in very different terms.

1870-1900 • THE WORKING CLASS FAMILY ~ Suburbs provided the middle class with the opportunity to escape from rapidly growing urban centers with their racially and ethnically mixed populations. By moving to the suburbs middle class families could distinguish themselves from the ever-growing throng of working class men and women crowding into the cities (see the entries on Cities and Immigration). Industrialization and urbanization had a profound influence on working class families during the second half of the nineteenth century. New working and living conditions, triggered by the economic revolution, led to the adoption of new strategies for survival. By the end of the century, working class Americans had developed family forms that were often significantly different from that favored by the middle class. Attitudes towards courtship and marriage, gender roles, child rearing and kinship all separated the working class family from its more affluent contemporaries.

Child Labor

At the turn of the century, children made up a significant proportion of America's workforce. Of all the children under the age of sixteen, one in five was at work. Children as young as nine or ten entered the workforce by the millions. As many as four million children worked for wages in America's coal mines, textile mills, canneries and farm fields. Employers valued them as a supply of cheap labor, as children could be hired to perform a variety of manufacturing tasks at a fraction of the wages paid to adults. But their parents valued these working children as well. One immigrant father referred to his children as his "savings bank." For many working class families, the income provided by their children was essential for survival.

As early as the 1870s, reformers sought to curtail the use of child labor in America's factories, mines and mills. Many states passed laws limiting the hours children could work, and some mandated that those under the age of fourteen spend a stipulated number of days per year in school. By the end of the century, reformers worked to end the exploitation of children. But their efforts were opposed not only by employers, but by working class families who relied on the wages their children contributed to the family economy. The reformers, who were known as the "child savers," publicized the plight of working children, and succeeded in generating support for a national child labor law. In 1916, Congress passed the Keating-Owen Bill prohibiting employers from engaging workers younger than sixteen. But this victory was short-lived, as the bill was struck down by the United States Supreme Court only two years after its enactment. The court supported business interests in its ruling that Congress could not regulate manufacturing practices within the states. Employers regained the right to hire children, and young laborers had their "constitutional right" to work restored.

It was the Great Depression of the 1930s that finally ended the use of child labor in the United States. In keeping with its goal to provide American workers with a decent standard of living, Congress passed the Fair Labor Standards Act in the summer of 1938. The bill called for a national minimum wage (twenty-five cents an hour) and a maximum work week of forty-four hours. It also put restrictions on the employment of children, thereby shrinking the pool of laborers competing for scarce jobs. By establishing a minimum pay rate for employees in many fields, this New Deal legislation was an important step toward ending poverty, and it also finally freed children from the drudgery and danger of full time employment.

1870-1900 • LIVING CONDITIONS ~ America's working class was a relatively transient population, due in large part to the vagaries of the industrial economy. Full time, year round employment was the exception, not the rule. Because of this and the fact that wages did not keep pace with prices, most families required the income from several wage earners. Where the middle class enjoyed a marked improvement in their standard of living, the working class saw no such change. Poverty kept them trapped in the decaying city centers with overcrowded and unsanitary conditions. Tenement housing was poorly constructed, cramped and dark. Most families lived in tiny airless apartments with no plumbing. Water was carried in from faucets in the hallway or spigots in the street. Communal toilet facilities consisted of crude outhouses either in the basement or in the yard. The streets were filled with garbage and sewage, and the occasional dead carthorse cut from its traces and left where it fell. These streets and buildings were the playground for neighborhood children. No parks, few schools, no streetlights and an abundance of saloons marked most working class neighborhoods. Middle class observers worried that working class families would disintegrate under the stress of their situation, but to the contrary, in some ways the working class found their families strengthened and their communities enriched by their condition.

The working class clung to more traditional familial patterns, looking to mutual assistance and extended kinship ties to see them through. This was particularly true of recently arrived immigrants, for whom family, kin and community remained vital connections. The assumption has been that migration destroyed kinship ties as people moved from countryside to city or from Europe, Asia or Latin America to the United States. However, members of the working class, taking their places in America's industrial economy, found that family connections were crucial resources, providing not only a source of information about jobs and housing, but also as a source of assistance with child care or temporary emotional and physical shelter in case of accident or illness. Kin and community also provided individuals with access to capital through loans or even with cash gifts for newlyweds or to cover funeral expenses. Such mutual assistance remained an important component of working class life as it was understood to be essential for survival in the cutthroat world of industrial capitalism.

1870-1900 • INCOME ~ Contemporaries estimated that in the middle of the nineteenth century, a working class family required an income of about $10.00 per week in order to cover the basic expenses of food, rent and clothing. This left no surplus for extras or emergencies and most working class families found even this modest goal impossible to meet on a father's income alone. Men turned to child labor and the ingenuity of their wives to make up the shortfall. In fact, though few of them were engaged in paid labor outside their homes, working class wives contributed significantly to their families' economic well being. They took in piecework that they could complete at home, such as finishing hems on ready-made garments, making paper flowers, rolling cigars or stringing beads, they took in laundry, or they took in boarders who supplemented the family's rent in exchange for a bed and meals. Still, women were primarily concerned with their domestic responsibilities, and it was left to their husbands and children to bring in the bulk of the family's income. Child labor was so crucial to the economic well-being of working class families that it is estimated that children under the age of 15 supplied nearly 20 percent of their families' incomes. These children were expected to postpone marriage in order to continue contributing to their families' financial resources. Children recognized their obligation to assist their parents, particularly as their fathers and mothers aged and needed additional care, both monetary and physical.

1870-1900 • MARRIAGE ~ For immigrants in particular, marriage was entered into after much deliberation and careful long-term planning. Still, for the working class, all expected to marry. Some groups, like Southern Italians and Jews, made use of matchmakers to orchestrate a suitable match. Unlike their middle class counterparts, love was regarded as the least important criteria for a successful union. The Irish immigrant community had a saying for it – "Beauty don't boil the pot." Once wed, women took on the role of homemaker, but also the role of family matriarch. Whereas many middle class housewives found the domestic sphere stifling, working class women were in general satisfied with their situation—for them marriage meant an exit from the factories. Because they saw their children as economic assets, working class families remained relatively large through the end of the nineteenth century. A high child mortality rate (in some communities two out of three children did not survive past their second birthday) made a high birth rate imperative for the working class.

Generational conflict marred the relationship between parents and children among America's industrial poor. This was especially evident among immigrants and their native-born children. While parents wanted their children to succeed in America's industrial economy, they also expected adherence to traditional cultural values. Children, on the other hand, felt tremendous pressure to assimilate and rebelled against the traditionalism forced upon them by their parents. For working class Americans, community, not the individual, was preeminent. Personal wants, needs and desires were to be subordinated. This was the recipe for survival for the working class. Yet it sharply divided the working class family from its middle class contemporary, for whom individualism and self-reliance were the key watchwords.

1860-1900 • FAMILIES ON THE WESTERN FRONTIER ~ Despite the nation's rapid industrialization following the Civil War, in the decades from 1860 to 1900 the majority of American families still lived on farms. After the federal government passed the Homestead Act in 1862, would-be farmers flocked to western lands to make their fortunes. They were told that "rain follows the plow," meaning that the semi-arid west would become verdant farmland following cultivation. Instead, periodic droughts drove many settlers from their farms in defeat. In the west, the notion of rugged individualism persisted despite the reality that farmers, ranchers, miners and lumbermen were inextricably tied to eastern markets. Without urban demands for food (wheat, corn, beef) to supply a growing population, western farmers and ranchers would have had little more than subsistence as the reward for their labors. But the rapidly increasing eastern market provided the promise of economic success for families in the West. Still, success was far from assured for those who sought their fortunes on the farming and ranching frontier.

1860-1900 • LIVING CONDITIONS

The vagaries of farming in an inhospitable region where droughts, blizzards, prairie fires and grasshoppers threatened the best-laid plans, were coupled with the personal hardships faced by frontier families. Hard work, primitive conditions and isolation made life in the west particularly difficult. Many families were forced to improvise as they made their homes on the arid, treeless plains. They built houses from sod or dug caves into hillsides. These dirt dwellings were in fact a clever innovation, as they were very cheap to construct, relatively cool in summer and warm in winter, but they had their own peculiar drawbacks. When it did rain, these dirt houses quickly turned muddy. In addition, all manner of prairie fauna lived in the walls and the roof, so that snakes, lizards, rats, mice, spiders, fleas, flies and others were constant visitors. Just as they had in building their homes, frontier families had to improvise to heat them and to fuel the fires to cook their meals and perform many other chores, like washing clothes. Again, the prairie provided what was necessary, in the form of dried cow and buffalo manure.

Life on the plains required resilience, but also a reliance on kin and community. Family members and neighbors relieved the boredom of farm life and were crucial in helping to complete the never-ending round of arduous chores. Though the nuclear family had become the norm among the urban middle class, extended kinship networks and close ties with the community allowed western farmers to prosper. Likewise, children remained an economic asset on family farms, as their labor was crucial to the success of the family economic enterprise. Even young children could carry out a variety of daily tasks including feeding chickens, milking cows, fetching water from wells or streams and carrying eggs or butter to neighboring farms as part of the barter economy.

1860-1900 • ROLE OF WOMEN

Despite the hardships, a degree of gender equality prevailed in the West that was largely missing in the East. On farms, women routinely carried out a variety of tasks that would have been considered men's work in the East. They butchered livestock, drove wagons and plows, chopped wood and carried guns. They also engaged in a local market network, trading the goods they raised or produced with other farm wives. And they took up homesteads themselves when widowed or deserted. Still, farm families were generally eager to embrace some of the social and cultural refinements of the East. In farming communities and cattle towns, women pressed for the establishment of schools and churches, lobbied to close saloons and brothels, and sought to recreate some of the social stratification they had left behind in more settled regions of

Women as a percentage of the work force

1900	18 percent
1920	21 percent
1930	25 percent
1945	50 percent
1950	25 percent
1960	35 percent
1980	50 percent
2000	50 percent

SOURCE: Compiled from *Women and the American Experience* (2000), *Domestic Revolutions* (1998), *The Way We Never Were* (1992) and *Divided Lives* (1992).

1900-1920

the country. So even in the Wild West, middle-class notions of family and society were beginning to make inroads by the end of the nineteenth century.

1900 • THE COMPANIONATE IDEAL: INTO THE TWENTIETH CENTURY

By the early years of the twentieth century, Americans were redefining family and placing new expectations on familial relations. Gone were the presumptions that the family alone was responsible for the physical and material well-being of its members. In the past, Americans had looked to the family as the primary source of education, job training, health care and poor relief. But one-by-one people outside the family had assumed these roles, including doctors, teachers and social workers. It was left to the family to see to the emotional needs of its members. The key goal of family life was now emotional fulfillment.

The companionate family was united by mutual affection. The companionate ideal in marriage assumed sexual attraction, equality and companionship. The key to achieving it was communication between partners. This ideal represented a powerful change in the way Americans viewed marriage and family. Nineteenth century sentimentalism that had focused on stern fathers, virtuous mothers and innocent children was replaced by more democratic notions of familial relations, including greater freedom from parental control for children. Rather than glorifying the family as a haven from a corrupt world, Americans began to view the family in more concrete terms as a source of psychological and emotional fulfillment for all its members.

1900-1920 • ROLE OF WOMEN

This change in the perspective on the family can be attributed in large part to changes in women's lives. By the early twentieth century, young women were realizing new possibilities for themselves. Access to education gave them heightened expectations of equality and a widening arena of public action gave them an opportunity to exercise influence outside the home. The daughters of the middle class were reaping the benefits of their parents' financial security by graduating from high school and going on to college in record numbers. These young women postponed marriage and entered the workforce as teachers, nurses, social workers, librarians and occasionally as doctors and lawyers, and offered their skills to a wide variety of charitable and reform organizations, seeking to do something meaningful with their lives. Many of these young women expressed the desire to remain in the workforce even after they married (although almost all of them did expect to marry). They were not satisfied with the traditional female role of homemaker. And yet while these young women tended to express liberal attitudes, they acted in a much more traditional fashion, seeking "man, marriage and domestic life." But the marriage they sought embraced a new ideal. They were seeking a "romantic-sexual union" in which spouses were lovers and companions and wives experienced a greater degree of equality than had been the case for previous generations of married women. But equality and companionship were sometimes at odds with one another, as many young men rejected the idea of working wives and young women came to understand that "companionate potential could best be realized if she was willing to assume a subordinate role, and preferably a domestic one." Still, these wives-in-waiting had high expectations.

They understood that marriage should provide more than just economic security, and they openly favored divorce if marriage failed to provide sexual satisfaction and emotional intimacy.

THE FLAPPER SOCIETY: WOMEN IN THE 1920S

By the 1920s, on college campuses and in the workplace, young women began to adopt a new persona reflecting this ideal of companionship and equality between the sexes. The Flapper, so called because of the flapping sound caused by leaving the tops of her galoshes unbuckled, came to represent a new female identity, a young woman who embraced sexual freedom and economic independence. With her bobbed hair, short skirt, stockings rolled down to her knees and face made up with rouge and lipstick, the flapper epitomized a profound change in American popular culture as well as a widening generational divide. She smoked, drank, danced provocatively, dated and engaged in sexual relations, making use of the automobile to seek greater freedom from parental authority. In fact, critics began to refer to cars as "houses of prostitution on wheels." Dating completely replaced courting by the 1920s. Young women no longer received callers at home. Instead, they ventured into public, into a social realm that emphasized paired activities and prepared them for their new role of romantic partner. The Flapper was at once a sexual temptress and a pal – the equal of her male companion in intellect, ambition and sexual desire. Gone was the nineteenth century's notion of passionlessness. Instead, the new woman of the early twentieth century demanded liberation from the social constraints of her mother's generation. Women born after 1900 were much more likely to engage in sex outside of marriage than had been true of women born before the turn of the century. Their male contemporaries did not experience any significant change in their sexual behavior, except that their partners were now much less often prostitutes.

1920S • EMERGENCE OF A YOUTH CULTURE ∼

Young men likewise resisted traditional domestic roles and responsibilities. As they spent an increasingly large amount of time away from home in pursuit of success in the business world, they began to identify with popular cul-

(1921) Margaret Gorman from Washington D.C. wearing a large Statue of Liberty crown and a striped cape, as the first Miss America, Atlantic City, New Jersey. The Miss America Pageant was first devised as a way to extend the summer tourist season in the beach-front town.

ture's glorification of the independent man, the one who turned his back on domesticity. In literature, particularly westerns and adventure novels, this rugged individual demonstrated that personal fulfillment could only come in the world outside the home.

By the 1920s, the generational divide had given rise to a distinct youth culture, complete with its own brand of popular culture, including activities, clothing, speech patterns and sexual behavior. Because young people were spending an increasing amount of time in school, they were also spending an increasing amount of time with people their own age. Their peers came to play an important role in their lives, as it was through the influence of their friends, not their parents, that adolescents came to develop their ideas and attitudes. The emergence of this youth culture ultimately led to concerns about the decline of parental control. The field of child psychology was developed to help establish guidelines for effective parenting, and experts concluded that "scientific mothering" could improve child rearing and contribute to the development of well-adjusted youth. Mothers were held responsible for their children's emotional development, and were taught the proper way to mold the young mind while furnishing each child with a loving environment.

It was the emphasis on emotional fulfillment that ultimately led to fractures in the family. Men and women sought a greater degree of personal satisfaction in marriage, which made their unions more fragile. During the first decades of the twentieth century, the divorce rate climbed at a rapid rate, leading some Americans to express their fear that the family was in crisis. One expert put that fear into words when he wrote that "in fifty years there will be no such thing as marriage." In fact, by the 1920s, the United States had the highest divorce rate in the world. One marriage in seven failed. Legislators responded by tightening up divorce statutes, but to little effect. And while divorce was on the rise, the birth rate was continuing its century old decline. Native-born, middle-class Americans were not producing enough children to replace themselves, leading to fears that they were inadvertently committing "race suicide."

1920s • LEGISLATION ~ The early twentieth century saw a dramatic increase in activism on the part of the federal government where families were concerned. Legislators joined with middle class reformers to implement a host of programs and legal remedies to address society's concerns about the family. Child labor laws, compulsory education, a juvenile justice system, health care clinics and milk programs all found support from Congress. In addition, legislators sought to provide assistance to the elderly, with the understanding that they were the victims of changes in family form and function.

By the 1920s, as the birthrate fell, the elderly were becoming proportionately a larger cohort of the population, and their needs were coming to the attention of reformers. Left with no pensions and few resources as they were pushed from the labor force through mandatory retirements, the elderly became a conspicuous population of the poor, leading most states to establish a program of old age pensions (see Retirement). This was an important starting point. But government agencies, at both the state and federal level, dramatically increased their direct involvement in the lives of American families as a response to the economic

(1925) Conference Delegates - 25th March 1925. Even before the problems of the Depression, there were great debates about birth control. Shown here are representatives at a Birth Control Conference (from left) Professor Di Lapouge, Norman Have, Thit Jensen, Dr. V.C. Drysdale, Margaret Sanger, Juliet Barrett Rublee and Gabriel Hardy outside Mrs. Rublee's house in New York.

and social catastrophe unleashed by the Great Depression.

1930-1939 • CRISIS FOR AMERICAN FAMILIES ～ The Depression of the 1930s was unprecedented in its scope and duration. The United States had seen sharp economic downturns before, but the economic impact of this episode triggered far-reaching social consequences as well. By 1932, nearly one quarter of the work force was unemployed, and many of those who still had jobs saw their pay or their hours reduced. More devastating was the fact that the economic crisis hit not only the working class, accustomed to feeling the effects of economic boom and bust, but likewise the middle class, creating a new category of the poor. Families that had been spared the effects of other economic downturns suddenly faced real hardship for the first time. Many dealt with the emergency by struggling to keep up appearances. Families used up savings, borrowed against life insurance policies, and left bills and mortgages unpaid rather than cut back on expenditures and risk loss of status.

An unanticipated benefit of the Depression was that it led families to reconnect with an extended kinship network. Americans found that it was important to seek out others for support, pool resources and turn inward. At the same time, the economic crisis intensified tensions within families, as unemployment led to a decline in living standards. Marriage and birth rates plummeted, as couples found that they could not afford to marry and start families. Married couples put off having additional children. During the 1930s, the birth rate in the United States was so low that the country was at risk of losing population. Because so many couples sought to limit the size of their families, sales of condoms remained strong, and the public's acceptance of birth control increased markedly. Laws that had prohibited the dissemination of birth control information were repealed. Abortions, though illegal, increased, but because they were often performed under clandestine, unsanitary conditions, they claimed the lives of as many as 10,000 women a year.

1930s • FAMILY FINANCES ~ Not surprisingly, divorce rates fell, while rates of desertion increased. Few couples could afford to divorce and maintain separate households, so the logical way to escape an unhappy marriage was simply to walk away. Men who lost their jobs suffered a powerful blow to their self esteem as they were no longer able to provide for their families. Women found their influence within their families increasing as it was now up to them to generate income and see to the distribution of limited resources. Married women entered the work force during the Depression because they found that those jobs traditionally labeled as "women's work" were sometimes available when jobs for men were not. The industries hardest hit, like steel, were those that hired predominantly men. Housewives also adopted all manner of money-saving techniques, including sewing their own clothes and growing and canning their own food. One of the few industries to thrive during the Depression was the manufacture of glass jars. Sales of glass jars soared as housewives turned to home production rather than spending precious family resources on prepared foods. As annual income declined, the average housewife had to feed and clothe her average family of four on less than $25 a week. Deflation helped somewhat, as the price of bread dropped to seven cents and milk sold for ten cents a quart. Still, every penny counted.

Children were also enlisted to supplement their families' incomes. They earned extra money by running errands or recycling glass bottles for the two cent deposit. Because job opportunities were scarce, some young people stayed in school longer than they might have in a better economic climate. In 1930, only about 50 percent of the teenagers in the United States attended high school. By 1940, that number had increased to 75 percent. But in poorer communities, children were forced to suspend their education either because their schools were closed due to lack of funds or because their families needed them to enter the workforce. Real destitution for some families meant that there was not always adequate food or clothing for all family members. When a teacher in West Virginia told a student to go home and get some food, the girl replied "I can't. This is my sister's day to eat." Though there were few cases of absolute starvation, chronic malnutrition became a pressing problem.

1930s • GOVERNMENT ASSISTANCE TO FAMILIES ~ Initially, relief efforts were left in the hands of private charities. But such organizations were quickly overwhelmed with the demand. Americans therefore turned to the federal government to step in and provide assistance to families to save them from destitution. This marked a turning point in public attitudes about the role of government in everyday life. Until the 1930s, many Americans felt that the federal government should not directly intervene in the day to day affairs of American families. Most middle-class Americans had held the belief that the poor were responsible for their own condition, and that little effort should be exerted to assist them, as this would only reward them for their lack of industry. But once the middle class found itself affected by poverty, too, attitudes towards the poor quickly changed. Americans were now convinced that it was the responsibility of the federal government to safeguard savings, provide jobs for those who were unemployed and support those who could not help themselves. Because of this change in attitude, the New Deal marked a major shift in perspective as the federal government now played a direct role in the public's welfare. A host of programs were enacted that directly affected American families, from the Federal Emergency Relief Administration (FERA) to Social Security, to federally insured bank deposits (FDIC) to rural electrification. Along with the New Deal's specific programs, the Depression called forth a shift in philosophy. Americans were forced to acknowledge that individuals could not effectively protect themselves and their families from severe economic crises, that they must rely on the federal government for assistance. For the first time, Americans came to expect the government to take an active role in their daily lives and their well-being.

1941-1945 • WORLD WAR II AND THE FAMILY ~ The Great Depression proved to be a catalyst for significant changes in family life in the United States. But just as profound were the effects of World War II. When the nation went to war, society underwent further transformation, beginning with a rebound for the economy. The return of prosperity led to a sudden sharp jump in the marriage rate as couples who had postponed weddings rushed to the altar. As young men entered military service, their families felt the effects of prolonged separation. In addition, the rapid expansion of the wartime economy created a highly mobile population as families relocated to take advantage of war industry jobs. The result was a disruption of the kinship network that had sustained many Americans through the lean years of the Depression. In addition, in the communities suddenly experiencing a population boom as a result of the war, housing shortages posed a real problem, and schools and child care facilities could not meet the demand. As women entered the work force in record numbers, they experienced a dramatic shift in self-perception.

As a result of the war, unemployment virtually disappeared in the United States. But while family incomes rose, the standard of living did not appreciably change due to wartime shortages of all types of consumer goods from food and clothing to gas and electricity. The government ordered a halt in production of many consumer goods, including automobiles, refrigerators, radios and sewing machines. When the government rationed rubber, American car owners, unable to buy tires, put their cars up on blocks and walked. But as Americans walked, they wore out their shoes. The government began to ration shoes—two pairs per person per year. But people adjusted to the hardships, and overall society did benefit from a dramatic decrease in income disparity. The United States became a middle-class nation as more than half of all American families attained middle-class status.

1941-1945

WORKING WOMEN DURING THE WAR

Public attitudes about working women changed virtually in an instant, fueled by the need for workers to replace the men in uniform. Before the war, most of the women in the work force were young and single. But married women were increasingly recruited by war industries to meet the shortage of workers. "Womanpower" was understood to be essential to the war effort, so war industries enticed them with calls to their patriotism and with reassurances that they were equal to the task. One advertisement insisted that "If you've used an electric mixer in your kitchen, you can learn to run a drill press." Women responded in large numbers. During the war years, more than half of all women in the workforce were married, and four million of these women workers had young children at home. But these women were not interested in overturning society's beliefs about women's proper place. They still defined themselves primarily as wives and mothers assisting their men abroad. But that did not diminish their sense of pride in their accomplishments.

Still, there was some anxiety surrounding the entrance of so many women into the workforce. People worried that it would lead to marital strife by disrupting gender roles. There was concern that women would lose their femininity as a result of their employment. Experts warned of the negative consequences for children left without parental supervision when their mothers took jobs. Finding adequate child care was a serious dilemma for working women. Many relied upon relatives and friends to watch their children, but significant numbers of boys and girls became "latchkey kids," left to care for themselves until their mothers returned home from work. Teenagers in large numbers quit school to take advantage of the availability of jobs. As they entered the labor force or the armed services, they became more independent, less subject to parental control, raising public fears of juvenile delinquency.

With the prosperity generated by the war, Americans began to spend money on the medical and dental care that they had put off for lack of resources. As a result, overall health began to improve, and the rate of infection from communicable diseases like typhoid fever, tuberculosis and diphtheria dropped significantly. The mortality rate among infants dropped by a third and life expectancy for all Americans increased by three years.

(circa 1945) Family Christmas. The post-war years saw Americans rush to create a domestic ideal. Shown here is the mid-century ideal of a family Christmas.

The powerful changes sweeping American society as a result of the war produced stresses that eventually took their toll on families. For example, the divorce rate shot upward during the 1940s, so that by 1946, one in four marriages ended. The failure rate can be attributed to the fact that many couples married after very brief courtships at the outbreak of the war, then experienced long separations. In addition, many wives who became accustomed to a great degree of independence were reluctant to resume a subordinate role in their households once their husbands returned home. Their self-sufficiency had led them to expect more equality in their marriages, and when expectations were not met, dissatisfaction often set in. Nonetheless, the post-war years saw Americans rush to create a domestic ideal.

1950s • THE SEARCH FOR STABILITY ~ Most Americans regard the 1950s as the "golden age" of the family, and gauge recent changes in society and family life against this ideal. The truth is that the 1950s family was something of an anomaly. In other words, family life in the fifties was a real departure from anything that has occurred either before or since. On the surface, the family was more stable during the immediate postwar period. Marriage rates were at an all time high, marriage age was at an unprecedented low, the divorce rate grew at a much slower pace than it had since the early twentieth century, and family size was twice what it is today. But all of these factors were out of step with long-term trends.

During the 1950s, 95 percent of all Americans of marriageable age were making the trip to the altar. Brides and grooms were younger than they had been since the turn of the century. In 1900, the average American woman was 23 on her wedding day, and her spouse was 26 (roughly the same as couples at the end of the twentieth century). Young men and women who married in the 1940s and 1950s deviated sharply from this practice and married unprecedentedly early, at age 22 and 20 respectively. In fact, 70 percent of American women were married by age 24 (as compared with 50 percent of American women at the end of the century), and a third of all brides were teenagers. These couples were reacting against nearly two decades of national emergency, depression and world war, and the new uncertainties presented by the Cold War and the atomic age. For them, marriage and family represented security and a retreat from a threatening world.

1950s • BIRTHRATES ~ The Americans who married during the 1940s and 1950s expected to have children—child rearing was regarded almost as a patriotic duty. The birth rate in the United States had been steadily declining since 1800, but it began a meteoric rise in 1946, generating a "baby boom" that lasted until the 1960s. Four million babies a year were born to American couples from the mid-1950s until the mid-1960s. This dramatic upsurge in births can be explained by the fact that two cohorts of American women were having children at the same time. Women who had postponed marriage and family during the Depression and the war, and who were now in their thirties, were having children for the first time. In addition, as the marriage age fell, and as newlyweds began producing children immediately, a second group of American women was having children very early. Family size was also on the rise, though the baby boom did not see a shift to very large families. The average American family consisted of 3.2 children, so the increase was really rep-

1950s

resented by many women producing at least one additional child. The birthrate for third children doubled, and that for fourth children tripled, but there were few very small or very large families.

1950s • STABILITY THROUGH MARRIAGE AND RELIGION ~ Couples who married during the 1950s also tended to stay married. The divorce rate, which had been climbing at a consistent rate since

Dr. Spock's Baby and Child Care

~

Following World War II, as Americans retreated to the suburbs, they began to place new emphasis on children. Child rearing took on new importance as women embraced the new ideal that motherhood was their most important responsibility and that raising healthy, well adjusted children should be their primary goal. For assistance mothers turned increasingly to the experts, in particular to Dr. Benjamin Spock, whose advice manual, *Baby and Child Care*, became an indispensable tool in many American households. First published in 1946, Spock's book went through a number of subsequent editions reflecting changing social patterns and attitudes toward child rearing. But his underlying message remained the same. He constantly reassured women that "you know more than you think you do."

Early editions of *Baby and Child Care* urged women to put the needs of their children first, particularly by staying home rather than seeking employment. The working mother, according to Spock and others, was rejecting her children, leading them to feel abandoned and putting them at risk of juvenile delinquency. But just as dangerous was the overprotective mother who crippled her children by sheltering them too much. Experts had identified the effects of this suffocating parenting during World War II. They noted that many young soldiers suffered from a condition psychologists identified as "Momism" that had left them so dependent that they could not function independently. Mothers were urged to find a balance between the two extremes, to be a constant presence while allowing their children to become independent.

Spock instructed parents to be flexible in raising their children, to forego a rigid schedule for feedings, naps and baths in favor of allowing infants to set their own schedules. Though he insisted that children needed firm guidelines and flourished with parental leadership, Spock wrote that the most important element in successful child rearing was a mother's love. He insisted that "children raised in loving families want to learn, want to conform, want to grow up. If the relationships are good, they don't have to be forced to eat, forced to learn to use the toilet." It was up to mothers to mold their children through their good example and to meet their physical and emotional needs. Their reward would be more than well adjusted children; they would also find a sense of personal fulfillment.

Subsequent editions of *Baby and Child Care* reflected changing attitudes. Spock came to embrace greater structure and less permissiveness in the parent-child relationship. He wrote in the 1968 edition that "nowadays there seems to be more chance of a conscientious parent's getting into trouble with permissiveness than with strictness." Further, Spock came to recognize the importance of a father's role in parenting. By 1976, fathers held a vital place in the parent-child relationship. He recognized that caregivers might be mothers, fathers, baby sitters or day care centers. Spock explained that the criticisms of feminists and his own conversations with young people led him to reevaluate the centrality of mothers in child rearing. Parenting was reevaluated as a dual responsibility.

the middle of the nineteenth century, leveled off. Roughly the same proportion of couples divorced in 1960 as had been the case in 1940. The vast majority of Americans viewed marriage as central to a happy, stable life, and believed that a single person simply could not be satisfied. The media reinforced these ideas. Central to the image of the stable family was the happy housewife. Experts insisted that a woman's primary responsibility was to manage her house and care for her children. In fact, it was widely believed that she could only find true happiness in the role of wife and mother.

During the forties and fifties, growing numbers of American women gave up personal goals of education and career in order to fulfill what they believed to be their destiny. Homemaking would be their career. Two thirds of all the young women who entered college during the 1950s dropped out, either to get married, or because they worried that a college degree would make them unattractive to men. *The New York Times* reported in 1955 that "girls feel hopeless if they haven't a marriage at least in sight by commencement time." But under the surface there was a conflict between these traditional roles and young women's inclinations. Told that they should strive for nothing more than the satisfaction of caring for their homes and families, and worried that they would be less successful in that venture if they tried to juggle home and career, most young women opted for domesticity.

The postwar period saw another powerful change for American families. Religion came increasingly to symbolize security and stability in uncertain times. Nearly 75 percent of the people in the United States belonged to a specific religious group in the mid 1950s, whereas less than half had been church members in 1940. Congress reinforced this upsurge in religious identity by adding the phrase "under God" to the *Pledge of Allegiance* that children recited daily in school.

1950s • HOUSING ~ Along with this resurgence of religious affiliation came an exodus of families from American cities to the suburbs. Prosperity for many Americans was represented by home ownership, and the housing boom was taking place on the outskirts of major cities (due as much to many people's fear of nuclear attacks on heavily populated urban areas as to the availability of cheap land for new communities). Developers like William J. Levitt created new towns almost over night using mass production techniques. He established the first of several Levittowns on Long Island. Construction began in 1947, and by 1951 the community contained 17,000 homes, as well as a town hall, shopping centers, parks, playgrounds, community swimming pools and bowling alleys.

1950s • CHILD-REARING PRACTICES ~ The rush to the suburbs cemented the family orientation of American society. In their new communities, families devoted an unprecedented amount of time to child-oriented activities and relied on experts to instruct them in the details of "scientific" child rearing. Parents came to rely on experts like Dr. Benjamin Spock to help them raise their children properly. Spock's book, *Baby and Child Care*, became an instant best seller. Concerns focused not only on children's physical well-being, but also on their psychological development. Mothers were warned alternately not to smother their children with too much attention or to abandon them to pursue jobs and interests of their own.

1950s

Spock urged women to seek counseling to combat the urge to escape their parental responsibilities by seeking jobs. To do so, he warned, would leave their children emotionally as well as physically abandoned and could lead to delinquency. Mothers should not be overly protective of their children, and he urged fathers not to take too active a role in the household, as this would be confusing to young children. "Live your gender," advised one manual, because it was crucial for children to have "manly men and womanly women" as their role models (see Emotions).

1950s • Dissatisfaction with Roles ~ In part this concern stemmed from anxiety about American "teenagers," a term that came into use at the end of World War II. Young people were differentiated from children and adults and viewed as a group with a distinctive identity. But Americans were anxious about that identity, about trends in hairstyles, clothing, music and activities, and about the fact that teenagers were now relatively free from adult supervision. This was in part the result of the expansion of higher education. As young people spent more time in school, they found themselves increasingly in the company of people their own age. At the same time, many became alienated from their parents and rebelled against the idea of social conformity. Adults saw teenagers as irresponsible and aimless, and viewed youth culture as a serious social threat to the stability of postwar society, as personified in the film *Rebel without a Cause* (1955).

But teenagers were not the only Americans to feel disaffected by the domestic ideal. The popular image of the fifties family was something of a myth, because it hid a great deal of dissatisfaction. The discontent was identified first among housewives, those women the experts described as happiest of all. But women felt frustrated and trapped by the mystique that the role of housewife was the source of their greatest fulfillment. As young women they had enjoyed access to higher education and jobs, but as wives and mothers they were told to content themselves with homemaking and to sacrifice their own ambitions for the good of their families. The media emphasized women's domestic role, and sent a powerful message to society that homemaking was the highest calling to which women should aspire. Many women masked their unhappiness with alcohol or tranquilizers.

Men, too, felt dissatisfied. They faced the stress of supporting a wife and children and maintaining the middle class ideal, and worried that their role within their families was weakened by the fact that they spent so much time away from home. They were distant figures to their families, and their function was increasingly simply that of wage earner. "Careerism" became the malady of middle-class men, as they focused on work to the exclusion of all else and in the process suffered a host of physical ailments from ulcers to heart attacks.

While the media continued to extol the virtues of family life, and warned women of the dire consequences to their children and to their own identities if they went to work, in fact married women were entering the workforce in record numbers during the 1950s. The booming economy beckoned, and by 1960, one third of American wives were in the labor force. Most of these women were in their mid-thirties with school-age children. They held traditionally female jobs as sales clerks, secretaries and teachers. They were also very careful to explain their decision in terms of family priorities. Their incomes were earmarked for paying off mortgages or putting children through college. Working mothers never described their jobs as a route to personal fulfillment. In fact, many felt guilty about their decision to work, as child-care experts warned of the consequences of abandoning their children to enter the labor force.

Because American women during the 1950s married young and had children immediately, they also ceased child bearing at a relatively young age. This meant that they had longer periods of their lives free from child-care responsibilities than had been the case for women in the past. In addition, there was the economic reality that it was becoming increasingly difficult for American families to maintain a middle class lifestyle on one income alone. While American housewives still insisted that they were very happy with their lives, 90 percent of those who responded to a Saturday Evening Post Magazine poll stated that they hoped their daughters would not "lead the same kind of life they did."

1960s • FAMILIES IN TURMOIL ~ For most Americans the 1950s represent the norm for American culture and society. Changes that have taken place since the early 1960s are generally viewed as backward steps, retreats from this ideal. But the reality is that the fifties were unique, a break with long-term trends in American social history. The baby boom temporarily reversed a steady decline in family size that had begun in 1800. Likewise, early age marriages for American couples and a stabilization in the divorce rate ran counter to long-standing social trends. The difficulties of depression and world war, coupled with the insecurity of the atomic age, led Americans to crave conformity and

(1963) A sign advertising The Little Chapel of the Flowers in Las Vegas, where couples could get married for $15.

domesticity and the security it represented. But their children entered adulthood with a very different world view. Young people who grew up in prosperous, stable families rebelled against the conformity their parents prized. By the mid-1960s, the pro-family orientation of the postwar years was giving way to a return to individualism.

The 1960s marked a dramatic shift in American culture. Rather than consensus, Americans came to embrace the ideals of personal growth and self-fulfillment. This change can be explained in part by the affluence of the era. Couples who married and raised families in the postwar years had grown up during the Depression. They enjoyed the prosperity of the postwar economic boom, but while they engaged in the consumer culture of the 1940s and 1950s, they had relatively modest ideas about money. Their children, on the other hand, grew up in an era of unprecedented affluence. Between 1950 and 1970, median family income in the United States tripled. Those children born during the baby boom had opportunities that had not been available to young people in previous generations, and those opportunities led to heightened expectations of financial and emotional well-being and a revolt against their parents' values.

1960s • GENERATIONAL CONFLICT ∼ Generational conflict became widespread during the 1960s, sparked by the disaffection of young people and growing opposition to the war in Vietnam. Across the country students on college campuses demonstrated against the war and for greater freedom for themselves both academically and personally. Many universities responded by rescinding the longstanding policy *in loco parentis* (in the place of parents) and gave students a powerful measure of independence. The rebellion against their parents' generation also swelled the ranks of those who joined the counterculture and chose to "tune in, turn on and drop out," embracing a lifestyle of sex, drugs and rock and roll. One of the greatest sources of conflict between parents and children was a dramatic shift in sexual behavior. Casual sexual encounters came to reflect the new emphasis on self-awareness and personal fulfillment. A new singles culture emerged, highlighted by a new standard of morality. The sexual revolution competed with more traditional goals of marriage and family, emphasizing relationships rather than commitment and competition among young women for the attention of men.

Though the number of Americans who rejected traditional society in favor of the counterculture was quite small, their influence was felt on a large scale. Their attitudes affected large segments of American society, giving rise to permissive attitudes regarding sexuality. The sexual revolution had far reaching repercussions for American society and for the family, because it signaled a move away from marriage and towards a singles culture. The trend towards postponement of marriage was coupled with a dramatic rise in extramarital sexual relations and a jump in the divorce rate. American society gradually became more tolerant of such previously proscribed behavior as cohabitation, homosexuality and abortion.

As social attitudes changed, the family began to change, too. The baby boom was over by the mid-1960s, and family size began to shrink. The introduction of the birth control pill in 1960 helped women limit their fertility. Couples had fewer children, and because life expectancies were rising, parents spent a smaller portion of their lives devoted to child rearing. The average American woman could expect to live to the age of 75 in 1970, as compared to a life span of 54 years in 1920. In addition, attitudes towards child rearing were changing. Parents sought to establish close emotional bonds with their children, and yet a majority admitted that they were less inclined to make sacrifices for their children than their parents had been.

1960s • WORKING WOMEN ∼ As women entered the work force in increasing numbers, they no longer felt the need to justify their actions by citing family need. However, while working mothers had expected increased equality both at work and at home, most working mothers found that they were still handling most domestic responsibilities as well. The "superwoman syndrome" told them that they could have it all – career, family and romance. The reality was often growing disillusionment. The Women's Liberation Movement had made some significant changes in women's lives, particularly in opening up the professions to female workers. But Women's Lib also sharply divided women along class lines. Those who embraced the call for gender equality tended to be white and middle class, women who could take advantage of access to higher education and good jobs. For working class women, the issue was more complex. While many were forced to work to help their families make ends meet, and therefore suffered due to the pay inequity between men and women in the workforce, many blue collar working women resented the fact that they were in the workplace at all. When given the opportunity, they gladly stayed home and embraced the identity of homemaker. As one woman put it, "When your husband is a tugboat operator or garbage collector, you don't want his job."

1960s • AFRICAN AMERICAN FAMILIES
~ As middle class white families were experiencing new pressures and adopting new values, black families were likewise experiencing profound changes. Poor African Americans found themselves facing economic decline and increasing social instability during the 1960s and 1970s. Concerned about the impact of poverty on the black family, the U.S. Department of Labor issued a report written by Daniel Patrick Moynihan entitled "The Negro Family: The Case for National Action." Moynihan argued that the fundamental problem facing African Americans was a breakdown in the black family. "The evidence—not final, but powerfully persuasive," he wrote, "is that the Negro family in the urban ghettos is crumbling."

Moynihan's report provided statistics to back up his assertion that the "fabric of conventional social relationships" within the urban black community had collapsed. He noted the rise in the number of black families headed by women and the rising rate of illegitimacy to bolster his contention that the family was breaking down and that the breakdown in turn led to sharp increases in reliance on government aid, unemployment, delinquency, drug use and school dropout rates. The rise in female headed households, according to Moynihan, had powerful negative consequences for children, who were raised without the influence of a male role model. The lack of an authority figure was cited as a major contributing factor for the overall failure to achieve among poor blacks.

Moynihan was correct in addressing poverty and single parent families as key sources of instability in the poor black community. But he overestimated in his calculations, failing to take note of the fact that six out of ten black families contained both parents. The difference in black and white rates of illegitimacy can be explained by the fact that white women are far more likely to seek an abortion or put their babies up for adoption than are black women. Moynihan also overlooked the fact that poverty was responsible for the differences between black and white families. When African American households are compared to white households within the same socio-economic status, the differences disappear.

The greatest flaw in the Moynihan report was his assessment that because black families did not embrace the middle-class ideal, they were crumbling. When he looked at poor black families,

1960s

(1960s) As middle class white families were experiencing new pressures and adopting new values, black families were likewise experiencing profound changes. Poor African Americans found themselves facing economic decline and increasing social instability during the 1960s and 1970s. However, when one looks at middle class white families and middle class black families the differences between white and black disappear.

he did not see the nuclear family so prevalent among the white middle class, and he assumed this to be evidence of collapse. Instead, poor black families adopted coping strategies honed over generations of living with poverty and instability. Black men, discouraged by low wages and few employment options, found it difficult to carry out the role of stable husband and father. The welfare system inadvertently contributed to the pattern of female-headed households by insisting that women could not collect benefits for their families unless their partners had deserted them. But through an effective informal network of kin and community members, black women were able to successfully support their children. Within poor black communities, "domestic networks" made up of friends and relatives came to replace the nuclear family as a highly successful unit of social organization. In fact, it is not the structure of the family but poverty that is responsible for the problems facing poor African Americans. Contrary to Moynihan's assertions, the black family was not collapsing. It had never resembled the white family to begin with. What Moynihan's report uncovered was a very different family form among poor black Americans, and his study underscored the point that poverty causes dysfunction, not the other way around.

In 1964, President Lyndon Johnson unveiled his War on Poverty. Central to this program was the federal government's pledge to strengthen the American family. He made issues including income, jobs,

568 ~ FAMILY LIFE

housing and health care the responsibility of the federal government. Johnson's Great Society committed federal resources to assisting poor families by establishing Medicaid and Head Start, and expanding governmental programs like Aid to Families with Dependent Children (AFDC), food stamps, subsidized housing and school lunch programs. Such federal intervention made significant improvements in the lives of poor families. Poverty rates declined during the 1960s, with the number of families classified as poor falling from 20 percent in 1960 to 12 percent in 1969. Infant mortality rates among the poor also dropped significantly as a result of the government's medical and nutritional programs. And yet federal assistance to the poor generated powerful criticism, including the conservative argument that government welfare programs contributed to dependence on federal handouts and the weakening of the family.

In 1971, Congress passed a measure providing for a national system of day care centers and after school programs. President Nixon vetoed the measure in part because he viewed it as damaging to American families. Nixon argued that the bill would hinder parental authority and would involve the national government in communal child rearing, thereby lessening the "family centered approach." The reality was that despite the failure of a national child care system, the number of children in group day care centers or nursery schools rose substantially as more and more mothers entered the workforce. At the beginning of the twenty-first century, more than two thirds of all three- and four-year-olds were enrolled in such a program.

1980s • "Delayed" Families

Beginning in the 1960s, Americans began to focus on the effects of social change on the family. By the 1980s, age at marriage had risen sharply, so that by 1985, almost 60 percent of American women were still single at age 24. This was in part a result of the increase in cohabitation among unwed couples, a trend begun in the 1960s. Delayed marriages gave rise to concerns that some women would find themselves left out of the marriage market altogether. In the 1980s social scientists at Harvard and Yale examined census data and suggested that women who were still single in their late thirties were more likely to be struck by lightning or kidnapped by terrorists than they were to find husbands. Women responded to the study by arguing that men had not become more scarce. Rather, women had become more selective.

Along with delayed marriage came delayed parenting, as couples waited longer to start families. Older mothers represent a distinct break from the 1950s pattern. An increasing number of couples opted to forego parenting. As many as one fifth of young single women expected to remain childless. Marriage itself failed to provide the stability many sought, as the divorce rate increased dramatically. By the 1980s, most states instituted "no-fault" divorce statutes, making it easier for couples to dissolve their marriages. At the end of the century, about 50 percent of all marriages ended in divorce. The average union lasted 10 years, meaning that marriages are no more durable today than they were in the colonial period where the early death of one spouse kept marriages short. Men tend to fare much better following divorce. One study, analyzing divorced couples in Los Angeles, found that men's incomes rose 42 percent in the first year, while that of their ex-wives dropped by 73 percent.

1990s • Family Concerns Today

Changes in the family, like the rising divorce rate, have generated a great deal of concern about the welfare of children. One expert has observed that "children are becoming less and less of a deterrent to divorce." Single parent, female headed households have increased sharply, as have dual income households in which both parents work for wages outside the home, and these changes, too, have caused alarm. In 1950, about 12 percent of married women with young children worked for wages outside the home. By 1990, that figure had grown to 60 percent.

In addition, families have grown increasingly isolated as career mobility has led couples to relocate and move away from relatives and friends. One study has indicated that only five percent of American children have regular contact with a grandparent. The decline in parental involvement has been cited as a grave threat to children and the family. Television and day care centers provide busy parents with some relief from child care responsibilities. But there are concerns about the consequences. In fact, children spend an average of twenty-five to thirty hours a week watching television. Two thirds of all three- and four-year-olds are in some form of day care. There is a fear that the lack of parental supervision and the fact that parents too often fail to exercise authority in the home will leave their children maladjusted.

The facts are alarming. One in four students do not graduate from high school. Teen suicide rates have risen sharply, as have rates of juvenile delinquency and juvenile violence. Eating disorders, teen pregnancy and drug abuse all have increased. All these indicators lead Americans to believe that society is failing in its task of preparing young people for adulthood. But the movement to identify and support children's rights have hindered parents' ability to exercise authority. In some communities, discipline, like spanking, is equated with criminal behavior. The courts have increasingly upheld individual rights at the risk of diminishing family cohesiveness.

Divorce rate

1900	1 in 8
1920	1 in 7
1930	1 in 6
1950	1 in 4
1980	1 in 2
1990	1 in 2
2000	1 in 2

(In 2000, 50 percent of first marriages and 60 percent of second marriages fail.)

SOURCE: Compiled from *Women and the American Experience* (2000), *Domestic Revolutions* (1998), *The Way We Never Were* (1992) and *Divided Lives* (1992).

The 2000 Census

The 2000 census revealed that for the first time less than a quarter (23.5 percent) of U.S. households are comprised of married couples with children compared to 45 percent in 1960. The rate has steadily declined, with the rate of single-parent families growing faster than the rate of married couples. During the 1990s, the number of families headed by women grew five times faster than the number of married couples having children. The number of unmarried couples grew from 3.1 million in 1990 to 5.5 million in 2000.

Reasons for the decline include people waiting longer to marry and couples

The Divorce Debate

One of the most hotly debated issues facing the American family today is the effect of divorce on children. With the dramatic rise in the divorce rate since the 1960s, more and more children are experiencing the breakup of their families. But what, if any, are the lasting consequences of this difficult experience?

Sociologists and psychologists have debated the impact of divorce on children, and their findings offer a mixed message. Most experts who have studied the topic acknowledge that among children whose parents divorce there is a greater percentage who experience difficulties like behavior problems and academic problems than is the case for children whose parents remain together. Children whose families are disrupted experience higher rates of emotional problems, drug and alcohol abuse, and trouble with the law than do their peers from stable families. There are potential long term effects as well, including emotional distress and insecurity that can affect an individual's personal relationships later in life. But those who study these children are quick to point out that the majority do not experience severe consequences, and that divorce does not explain many social ills, like teen pregnancy. About 10 percent of children from two parent families experience behavior problems, while the rate is 20 to 25 percent for children from disrupted families. But as one experts notes, "You can say, 'Wow, that's terrible,' but it means that 75 to 80 percent of kids from divorced families aren't having problems, that the vast majority are doing perfectly well." And studies note that it is children whose families have been disrupted more than once by divorce, remarriage and subsequent divorce that have the most difficult time making an adjustment.

It is the loss of stability that often accompanies divorce that plays the more important role in determining a child's response to this life change. Family breakup is often accompanied by relocation, financial loss and loss of contact with the non-custodial parent. In the 1970s, state legislatures began enacting sweeping changes in the divorce law that allowed couples to dissolve their marriages at will. One important effect of this change was the elimination of alimony. As a result, some men find that their standard of living increases following divorce, while their ex-wives and children experience a downturn in their living standard. In addition, children must adjust to the fact that their mothers may have less time and energy to devote to parenting as they take on the added responsibility of sole financial supporter. Divorce often entails relocation, which can be an emotional process for young people. But more troubling is the sense of abandonment many children feel following breakup of their family. In more than 90 percent of divorces, custody of children is awarded to mothers. Within a very short time (as little as two months) fewer than half of these children see their fathers once a week. Within three years, half of these young people do not see their fathers at all. This can trigger additional trauma for children as well as additional conflict for divorcing parents. Post-divorce strife has been identified as the primary factor responsible for poor adjustment in children whose parents divorce.

In fact, it is conflict in their parents' marriages, whether the family remains intact or not, that has the most lasting impact on children. One study has found that children in families that suffer from high levels of discord have a more difficult time coping than children whose parents divorce. According to the researchers, these children "were more depressed, impulsive, and hyperactive" than children in more stable family settings.

simply living together; unmarried couples represent nine percent of all permanent relationships, up from six percent in 1990. The number of households in which people live alone or live with non-family members comprise a third of all households. The median age of the first marriage for men has increased to 27 years old in 2000 up from 22 years old in 1960; for women, it has increased to 25 years old from 20 in 1960.

The booming economy allowed younger people to leave home and live on their own, and a bulging portfolio combined with medical advances permitted many elderly people to live independently longer. And the divorce rate, while it leveled off, created a large group of middle age people living alone. Reasons why married couples have fewer children include both partners working or nurturing careers, the higher costs of caring for children, children being exposed to violence in contemporary society and the poor condition of school systems in may parts of the country.

CONCLUSION

The "crisis of the family" that many Americans lament masks a much larger issue —the breakdown of social obligations and the loss of community. While individualism is still the cultural watchword, many Americans seek ways to restore a sense of social cohesion and inclusiveness beyond the family. When asked, most Americans express a desire to return to a more traditional ideal of family. But care must be taken in defining family, and in identifying exactly whose values are considered traditional. Where do single parents, childless couples, gays and lesbians fit into the portrait of family in America? The family is in a state of transition, just as it has always been. Family has been constantly redefined as it has adapted to changing social and economic circumstances. So what is really meant by "family values"? That concept is not as straightforward as it seems, because family means something different to everyone. More importantly, it is not the attitudes and behaviors of individual families that is crucial to a stable society, but rather families working together despite their social and cultural differences to create a stable community that will produce lasting improvements.

BIBLIOGRAPHY

Armitage, Susan, Ruth B. Moynihan and Christiane Fischer Dichamp, eds. *So Much to be Done: Women Settlers on the Mining and Ranching Frontier.* Lincoln: University of Nebraska Press, 1990

Bailey, Beth L. *From Front Porch to Back Seat: Courtship in Twentieth Century America.* Baltimore: Johns Hopkins University Press, 1988.

Bane, Mary Jo. *Here to Stay: Families in the Twentieth Century.* New York: Basic Books, 1976.

Barnouw, Erik. *Tube of Plenty.* New York: Oxford University Press, 1975.

Barrett, James R. *Work and Community in the Jungle.* Urbana: University of Illinois Press, 1987.

Breines, Wini. *Young, White, and Miserable: Growing Up Female in the Fifties.* Boston: Beacon Press, 1992.

Carroll, Peter N. *It Seemed Like Nothing Happened : The Tragedy and Promise of America in the 1970s.* New York: Holt, Rinehart and Winston, 1983.

Coben, Stanley. *Rebellion against Victorianism: The Impetus for Cultural Change in 1920s America*. New York: Oxford University Press, 1991.

Coontz, Stephanie. *The Way We Never Were. American Families and the Nostalgia Trap*. New York: Basic Books, 1992.

Coontz, Stephanie. *The Way We Really Are. Coming to Terms with America's Changing Families*. New York: Basic Books, 1997.

Cowan, Ruth Schwartz. *More Work for Mother : The Ironies of Household Technology From the Open Hearth to the Microwave*. New York: Basic Books, 1983.

Degler, Carl N. *At Odds. Women and the Family in America from the Revolution to the Present* (1980).

D'Emilio, John and Estelle B. Freedman. *Intimate Matters: A History of Sexuality in America*. New York: Harper & Row, 1988.

Douglas, Susan J. *Where the Girls Are: Growing Up Female with the Mass Media*. New York: Times Books, 1994

Ehrenreich, Barbara. *The Hearts of Men: American Dreams and the Flight From Commitment*. Garden City, NY: Anchor Press/Doubleday, 1983.

———. *Fear of Falling: The Inner Life of the Middle Class*. New York : Pantheon Books, 1989.

Eisler, Benita. *Private Lives: Men and Women of the Fifties*. New York: Franklin Watts, 1986.

Evans, Sara M. *Born for Liberty: A History of Women in America*. New York: Free Press, 1989.

Fass, Paula S. *The Damned and the Beautiful: American Youth in the 1920s*. New York: Oxford University Press, 1977.

Gans, Herbert. *The Levittowners: Ways of Life and Politics in a New Suburban Community*. New York: Vintage Books, 1982.

Gerson, Kathleen. *Hard Choices: How Women Decide About Work, Career and Motherhood*. Berkeley: University of California Press, 1985.

Gilbert, James Burkhart. *A Cycle of Outrage: America's Reaction to the Juvenile Delinquent in the 1950s*. New York: Oxford University Press, 1986.

Gluck, Sherna Berger. *Rosie the Riveter Revisited: Women, the War, and Social Change*. Boston: Twayne Publishers, 1987.

Graebner, William. *Coming of Age in Buffalo: Youth and Authority in the Postwar Era*. Philadelphia: Temple University Press, 1990.

Hochschild, Arlie. *The Second Shift: Working Parents and the Revolution at Home*. New York: Avon Books, 1989.

Hunter, James D. *Culture Wars: The Struggle to Define America*. New York: BasicBooks, 1991.

Jones, Jacqueline. *Labor of Love, Labor of Sorrow: Black Women, Work, and the Family From Slavery to the Present*. New York: Basic Books, 1985.

———. *The Dispossessed: America's Underclasses from the Civil War to the Present*. New York: Basic Books, 1992.

Kasson, John F. *Rudeness and Civility: Manners in Nineteenth Century America*. New York: Hill and Wang, 1990.

Kennedy, Susan Estabrook. *If All We Did Was to Weep at Home: A History of White Working Class Women in America*. Bloomington: Indiana University Press, 1979.

Lasch, Christopher. *Haven in a Heartless World*. New York: Basic Books, 1977.

Lystra, Karen. *The Searching Heart: Women, Men and Romantic Love in Nineteenth Century America*. New York: Oxford University Press, 1989.

Marc, David. *Demographic Vistas: Television and American Culture*. Philadelphia: University of Pennsylvania Press, 1984.

Marsh, Margaret. *Suburban Lives*. New Brunswick, NJ: Rutgers University Press, 1990.

May, Elaine Tyler. *Homeward Bound: American Families in the Cold War*. New York: Basic Books, 1988.

Meyerowitz, Joanne, ed. *Not June Cleaver: Women and Gender in Postwar America, 1945-1960*. Philadelphia: Temple University Press, 1994.

Mintz, Steven and Susan Kellogg. *Domestic Revolutions. A Social History of American Family Life*. New York: Free Press, 1988.

Modell, John L. *Into One's Own: From Youth to Adulthood in the United States, 1920-1975*. Berkeley: University of California Press, 1989.

Polenberg, Richard. *War and Society: The United States, 1941-1945*. Philadelphia: Lippincott, 1972.

Rosenberg, Rosalind. *Divided Lives. American Women in the Twentieth Century*. New York: Farrar, Straus, & Giroux, 1992.

Salamon, Sonya. *Prairie Patrimony: Family, Farming and Community in the Midwest*. Chapel Hill, NC: University of North Carolina Press, 1992.

Scharf, Lois. *To Work and to Wed: Female Employment, Feminism, and the Great Depression*. Westport, CT: Greenwood Press, 1980.

Schur, Edwin. *The Awareness Trap: Self Absorption Instead of Social Change*. New York: Quadrangle/New York Times Book Co., 1976.

Skolnick, Arlene. *Embattled Paradise: The American Family in an Age of Uncertainty*. New York: Basic Books, 1991.

Strasser, Susan. *Never Done: A History of American Housework*. New York: Pantheon Books, 1982.

Taylor, Ella. *Prime-time Families: Television Culture in Postwar America*. Berkeley: University of California Press, 1989.

Tuttle, William M., Jr. *"Daddy's Gone to War": The Second World War in the Lives of America's Children*. New York: Oxford University Press, 1993.

Wandersee, Winifred D. *Women's Work and Family Values: 1920-1940*. Cambridge: Harvard University Press, 1981.

Weitzman, Lenore J. *The Divorce Revolution: The Unexpected Social and Economic Consequences for Women and Children in America*. New York: Free Press, 1985.

Woloch, Nancy. *Women and the American Experience: A Concise History*. 2nd Ed. New York: McGraw-Hill, 2001.

INTERNET RESOURCES

GENERAL

U.S. Department of State generated site covering the entirety of the United States' history by chapter and then topic.
http://usinfo.state.gov/usa/infousa/facts/

A list of events categorized by decade and year.
http://www.yale.edu/amstud/formac/amst191b/timeline.html

An odd assortment of original texts and analysis of them by the Library of Congress; covers all of U.S. history.
http://lcweb2.loc.gov/ammem/mcchtml/corlst.html

The directory page of online exhibits furnished by the Library of Congress, which often include text and pictorial explanations of a variety of topics.
http://memory.loc.gov/ammem/collections/finder.html

www.historychannel.com is a good general site and worth exploring and searching.

http://www.historychannel.com

This web site has an interesting collection of various events and topics in U.S. history interpreted though pictures.
http://www.historyplace.com/

RESOURCE GUIDES
These pages are directories to a vast amount of information on the internet and are divided into historical topics and chronological periods.
http://www.ukans.edu/history/VL/USA/index.html

Web guides on the decades of the twentieth century
http://www.nhmccd.edu/contracts/lrc/kc/decades.html

http://www.myhistory.org/history_files/index.html

http://www.looksmart.com>library>humanities > history > U.S. history

SPECIFIC CATEGORIES
Culture/ Domestic Life/ Labor
http://www.as.ysu.edu/~cwcs/Exhibit1.html (Nostalgia about family life)

http://www.hartford-hwp.com/archives/45b (Working Class)

http://www.hartford-hwp.com/archives/45/index-b.html (Society)

http://www.fordham.edu/halsall/pwh/index-am.html
(Lesbian, Gay, Bisexual, Trans)

Ethnic Groups
http://www.lib.washington.edu/exhibits/harmony/exhibit/default.htm (Japanese Americas /WWII Internment)

http://www.io.com/~segreta/index.html (Italian Americans/WWII Internment)

http://wlc.ushmm.org (Jewish Americans / Jews / U.S. Holocaust Museum)

http://www.stanford.edu/group/King (African Americans / Martin Luther King, Jr.)

http://www.civilrightsphotos.com (African Americans / Civil Rights / Photography)

http://www.airpi.org/history.html (Native American Indians)

http://www.tolatsga.org/Compacts.html (Native American Indians)

TIME PERIOD
http://www.fiftiesweb.com (1950's)

http://www.sixties.net (1960's)

HUMAN DEVELOPMENT & FAMILY LIFE EDUCATION RESOURCE CENTER
Child development, adolescence, parents, families, child care, divorce, urban issues, poverty
http://www.hec.ohio-state.edu/famlife/

FAMILY LIFE ~ 575

Kearl's Guide to the Sociology of the Family
Political significance of the family.
http://www.trinity.edu/~mkearl/family.html [more from this site]

Sex, Etc. — A Website by Teens for Teens
Network for Family Life Education from Rutgers University
http://www.sxetc.org/

Teen love
Answers to common questions about love. How can you tell if you are really in love, and what does it mean.
http://teenadvice.about.com/cs/whatislove/index.htm

Family Life in the 1920s
http://hometown.aol.com/roeyroad/myhomepageindex.html

Family History
Links to sites related to the importance of family history to a marriage
http://marriage.about.com/library/weekly/aa042097.htm

Marriage
Links to many sites addressing various aspects of marriage.
http://marriage.about.com/index.htm

Divorce Support Site
Even the most amicable divorce can be difficult. Learn from and talk with others who know what it's like.
http://divorcesupport.about.com/index.htm

Divorce
Becoming a single parent as a result of divorce can be a trying time—find ideas on coping and managing as a new single parent
http://singleparents.about.com/cs/divorce/index.htm

Cara Anzilotti
Loyola Marymount University

Farming

(1915) The automobile and the mechanization of farming would drastically change the face of America during the twentieth century.

TIMELINE

1900-1919 ~ Migration of the Farm Population

Pure Food and Drug Act sets standards for food and drug control (1906) / Mass migration of workers across the nation depletes the farm population (1915-1919) / African Americans comprise more than 20% of the workers in the Chicago stockyards (1917) / Eighteenth Amendment outlawing the sale of alcoholic beverages begins prohibition era (1919)

MILESTONES: Formation of the Ford Motor Company (1903) • Wright brothers' gasoline engine aircraft successfully flies at Kitty Hawk (1903) • World War I provides new roles and opportunities for women (1917-1919) • Great flu epidemic begins in U.S. (1918)

1920-1929 ~ Beginning the Farming Revolution

Farm tractor begins the farming revolution (1920s) / For the first time more Americans live in urban than in rural areas (1920) / Pig Stand in Dallas is the first drive-in restaurant (1921) / Japanese and Filipino farm workers strike against Hawaiian plantation owners (1920 and 1924)

MILESTONES: Women's right to vote enacted (19th amendment, 1919) • Route 66 beginning in Chicago and ending in Santa Monica, CA is begun; by 1937 it is fully paved, crossing 8 states and 3 time zones (1926) • Stock market crash propels economy into the worst economic depression in American history (1929)

1930-1939 ~ Dust Bowl Misery and Federal Assistance to Farmers

Hog and corn subsidy programs enacted (1933) / Rural Electrification Act brings electricity to rural areas (1935) / Soil and Water Conservation Act provides government assistance for soil-saving efforts (1936) / Hybridization yields significantly better seeds and harvests (1930s-1940s)

MILESTONES: Unemployment is 24.9%; 9,000 banks fail; 100,000 businesses fail (1932-1933) • Twin engine Boeing 247, the first modern commercial aircraft, put into service (1933) • Germany invades Poland, starting WWII (1939)

1940-1949 ～ The Beginning of Commercial Farms

Commercial fertilizers introduced (1940s) / Farmers dramatically increase food production for the war (1942-1945) / Massey-Ferguson introduces the first combine (1944) / The beginning of commercial farms (1946)

MILESTONES: Japanese attack American ships at Pearl Harbor, forcing the U.S. into WWII (1941) • Executive Order 9066 requires internment of Japanese Americans living on the West Coast (1942) • Women, blacks and immigrants increase the work force from 46 million in 1940 to 60 million in 1945 • General Agreement on Tariffs and Trade expands trade opportunities (1947-1948)

1950-1979 ～ Food Safety and the U.S. Farm Commerce

First McDonald's opens (1952) / Poultry Inspection Act regulates poultry commerce (1957) / Federal Food, Drug and Cosmetic Act prohibits cancer causing additives (1958) / Soviet Union purchases $1 billion of U.S. wheat (1972) / President Nixon imposes soybean embargo (1973) / President Nixon orders a ceiling price on both beef and pork, the first time such price controls have been put in place in peacetime (1973) / Fair Packaging and Labeling Act sets standards for labeling additives to food (1975) / Vegetarian movement advocates eliminating meat products from the diet (1976)

MILESTONES: 33,600 American combat deaths and 20,600 non-combat deaths in the Korean War (1950-1953) • *Brown v. Board of Education* ends "separate but equal" school segregation (1954) • Race riots across America start with MLK's assassination (1968) • Neil Armstrong becomes the first person to walk on the moon's surface (July 20, 1969) • Hostages taken from the U.S. embassy in Teheran (1979)

1980-1999 ～ The Era of Big Farms

President Carter imposes grain embargo against the Soviet Union (1980) / Country singer Willie Nelson hosts the first Farm Aid benefit (1985) / Immigration Reform Act makes it illegal for employers to hire undocumented workers (1987) / North American Free Trade Agreement opens trade borders to Mexico and Canada (1993) / Number of farm workers declines from 13.6 million in 1915 to 2.85 million in 1995 / Scottish doctors report the cloning of a sheep, Dolly (1996) / *e. Coli* bacteria in contaminated hamburgers kills several people (1998)

MILESTONES: First space shuttle, *Columbia*, is launched (1981) • Northeast and Midwest lose 1.5 million manufacturing jobs while the South and West gain 450,000 jobs (1980-1990) • Amnesty granted for illegal immigrants in the U.S. (1986) • Dissolution of the Soviet Union ends the Cold War (1991) • Smoking banned on all U.S. domestic flights of less than 6 hours (1990)

INTRODUCTION

Each year thousands of interstate travelers visit Living History Farms—a 600-acre tract dedicated to helping educate people about the nation's agricultural legacy—which straddles Interstates 80-35 in the heart of Iowa. The "living" historical farms offers the opportunity for people to become better acquainted with some of the many significant changes that have taken place in American farming during the twentieth century. For some with agrarian roots, it is like a visit to "grandfather's farm." But Living History Farms isn't a theme park with rides and glitter. Quite the opposite: about the only "ride" available to the public is on a hayrack pulled by a typical farm tractor or a team of draft horses.

In a few hours the visitor is exposed to agriculture-past, providing a grass-roots look at farming as it existed at the turn of the century—the era just before the 1920s when the farming revolution began full-steam ahead due to the row-crop type tractor. It was just a few years ahead of the debut of hybrid seed corn that entered the farm picture in the early 1930s, followed by commercial fertilizer in the 1940s and then chemical weed-killers after World War II. These elements changed farming forever and represented the key ingredients in what turned out to be a progressive half-century when American agriculture developed into a food-producing industry unlike any the world has ever seen.

This technology, coupled with other innovations such as artificial insemination, hormones and feed additives, and improved veterinary medicine produced a surplus flow of food that at times overwhelmed domestic markets and caused economic problems for farmers and growers, while simultaneously providing an abundance of American food for export.

The nostalgic centerpiece unit at Living History Farms is its Farm of 1900, replete with the traditional red barn, white farm house, windmill, large garden and featuring livestock and real "horse-power." It is an operating farm where chores are done the way they were a century ago and where a woman posing as the old-time farm wife cooks without any of the modern conveniences, including electricity or gas. She draws any water she needs with a hand-pump from a shallow well. Her pots and pans are antiques, too.

For a few hours, visitors at Living History Farms at the northwest edge of Des Moines are given a look back in time to the farm life of 100 years ago, and the way food for the tables of America was produced back then—before the advent of the revolutionary hybrid seeds, farm chemicals, modern tillage and harvesting machines—before modern devices like microwave ovens, deep-fat fryers, dish-washers and electric clothes-dryers eased the chores of the farm wife.

The concept of Living History Farms was the idea of an Iowa State University economics professor, William G. Murray, an educator who accurately foresaw two things happening in farming: fewer and fewer farms producing food and fiber, and consequently, fewer and fewer people understanding—or, indeed, appreciating—where and how food is produced. There would be a shrinking percentage of Americans who would have an appreciation for the skills that modern agriculture and farming required, and especially have an appreciation for the fact that the United States in general has never lacked food, not even during the Depression of the 1930s. Famine and starvation, which have ravaged other portions of the world, have never been a real fear in

America. Instead our nation has served in part as a food merchant to the world and also a benevolent Food for Peace provider during times when hunger and famine erupted half a world away.

Rather than establish just another museum of farm tools and implements to reflect progress in food production, Dr. Murray wanted something that would be "alive" and growing and also blend fun and education. The result is a special place devoted to providing an opportunity to quickly grasp an understanding of—and an appreciation for—farming history and the progress this industry represents—a good place to examine a way of life that by the end of the twentieth century had become almost unrecognizable.

1915-1995 • FARM NUMBERS REFLECT CHANGE ~ As technology and inventions came to the farm, not nearly as many people were needed to do the farming chores, in the field or elsewhere in agriculture. Records provided by the U.S. Department of Agriculture's National Agricultural Statistics Service show how dramatically fewer workers are needed to grow, care for and harvest crops. The total number of farm workers has declined from its peak of 13.6 million in 1915 to 2.85 million in 1995. At the same time, the number of farms in the United States has also declined from 6.8 million in 1935 to 2.2 million in 1999. The U.S. population in 1910 was 92 million, or roughly 200 million fewer than at the end of the century, so the ratio of farmers to the general population was significantly higher during the first decades of the century.

Consequently there has been a significant population shift off the farm, beginning in the 1930s and continuing through

(1905) A farmer plows a field with a team, Watertown, Massachusetts.

1930s

the rest of the century. More and more people left the farm and sought work elsewhere, including some who became part-time or weekend small farmers. Off-farm incomes supplemented the income of many farm families.

It took only 2.2 million farms to produce most of the food needed by 280 million Americans in 1999, with enough left over to export billions of bushels of produce, corn, wheat and soybeans. This bountiful production existed even though the U.S. Government for two-thirds of the century had in place crop-idling, federal farm programs designed basically to do two things: curb excessive farm output and price-depressing crop surpluses while at the same time buoying up farm income through a complicated system of quotas, allotments, commodity loans and direct payments to farmers.

What happened in the twentieth century was simple: although U.S. farm numbers declined by two-thirds from their high in the 1930s in roughly two generations of time during which the number of American consumers more than doubled, the farming industry produced plenty of food for the nation. The increased productivity of each farmer resulted from a combination of factors, including superior seeds and crop-growing technology, tools, techniques and equipment. In a generation, from the 1930s to the 1960s, the output per farm virtually doubled. This trend in efficiency translated into fewer farmers and increased competition for farmable land.

Bullishness about farming prospects soared during World War I, as a wartime economy boom took place. Demand for farmland pushed land values to record levels, with the peak in values coming in 1920. After that, land values—the best barometer of the farm economy—were to decline for almost a half-century, from 1920 until the 1970s. The wartime boom and the high price for wheat caused thousands of acres of prairie and grassland to be plowed and brought into production, thus sowing the seeds that created the environment that spawned the Dust Bowl phenomenon of the 1930s drought.

1930s • AN OLD-FASHION FARM

It helps to understand the dramatic change in farming by looking back to the stereotypical image of a farm. In the 1930s farms were much smaller than they are today. Usually one family had all the work it could handle on a quarter-section 160 acres. In northern Iowa for example, it was common to find four families living on four 160 acre farmsteads, or on each of the four corners of a section of land (640 acres).

One-room country public schools were found every two miles or so. A single teacher taught all eight grades. The nearest town was small, and located about a half-day's ride by horse-drawn wagon or buggy from the next nearest small town, with most hamlets located near or on a railroad spur. The location of county seat towns were geographically the distance a person could conveniently travel by a horse rig or on horseback to do his business and be back home in time for the evening chores.

The principal crops grown on this 1930s farm included hay, oats, perhaps some flax, a few acres of soybeans (then a new crop with an uncertain future), pasture grass for grazing and, of course, the crop stalwart of middle America, corn. Most farms back then were fully diversified, with small herds of milk or beef cattle, hogs and possibly a small flock of sheep. Many farm units had a flock of hens that provided eggs for the family plus enough to trade or barter for store-bought groceries in town. Baby chicks were delivered to the farm via the rural mail carrier. There also might be a few domestic geese or ducks as well.

The dairy cows were milked by hand until the rural cooperative brought electrical power to the farm and a milking machine could be utilized. The "cash cows" represented another important and steady source of cash income. Their cream was separated from the skim milk and then hauled in stainless steel milk cans to the local creamery for cash. What milk was left was either consumed by the family or utilized in the rations of livestock at the farm.

While you could find a small herd of milk cows on nearly every farm a generation or two ago, and a butter plant or creamery in many country towns and hamlets, at the end of the twentieth century one would not find a single milk cow or processing market for milk in most Iowa counties. In the 1930s, the two biggest local businesses were usually the farmers' cooperative grain elevator, the local livestock sales barn and the implement dealer. The most important local business establishment was the bank and the banker who knew everyone and, indeed, their financial condition as well.

1930s • GIVING FARMERS A CHANCE
~ In the height of the 1930s Great Depression era a small cluster of nearly 50 one-family frame houses were built at the edge of Granger in central Iowa. These dwellings were located on small acreages of land. These new units were occupied by the impoverished families of out-of-work coal miners who moved into what became known as "The Homestead." Everything was financed and built with U.S. Government funds as a pilot project that would be copied nationally.

Behind this scheme, backed by First Lady Eleanor Roosevelt, was an Italian-born country parish priest, Luigi Ligutti, who lived in the Granger community just northwest of Des Moines. Ligutti was motivated by the severe depression, which hit that area particularly hard when the demand for soft-coal mined in that locality waned and miners lost their jobs. This pioneering Homestead project involved loans, not grants; participating families had 30-year mortgages.

It was Ligutti who supported his argument for such family assistance by preaching a social-economic doctrine related to the existing times when anti-democracy forces preyed on the ill fortunes of the American people. Ligutti's litany was based on this philosophy: "Give a man a cow and he doesn't become a communist; give him land and he becomes a capitalist...." Privately in interviews with media and elsewhere, Ligutti preached the same gospel—have governments and the church help people to achieve the essentials of farming—"a plow, a sow and a cow." This saying reflected a social philosophy of providing land on which a farmer could plow and plant crops, including a big garden that he could use to help feed his family. The sow represented a future supply of meat, while the cow, of course, promised milk.

Ligutti, the Granger priest behind the plow-sow-cow strategy, pictured a national public program sponsored by the government. Years later, after he became the chief agricultural advisor to the Pope stationed in Vatican City, he urged this same plan world-wide to combat hunger, and to help poor families feed themselves and improve their economic plight.

Ligutti's dream of more people becoming small family farmers with his "plow, sow and a cow" program didn't gain the support he hoped it would, despite the fact the First Lady helped the Iowa Homestead become a reality.

Political Symbolism of Farming

The long-held public image of a "family farm" is the big, hip-roofed red barn surrounded by farm animals in a pleasant country setting. To many, the farmer is pictured as a strong, hard-working, God-fearing man who battles weather, insects and other elements. The family farmer is a political symbol, and almost every presidential candidate makes at least one "farm speech" during a presidential campaign, including a photo opportunity in a rustic rural setting, surrounded by bales of hay; he cuddles a baby pig or poses with some other farm animal. Presidential candidate Jesse Jackson went so far as to locate his national presidential headquarters in the little county seat town of Greenfield, Iowa in 1988, announcing his candidacy in the dairy barn of Dixon Terry where he milked a cow mainly for the benefit of the cameras. Farm states, especially Iowa, have more political influence during elections years than their small populations would normally justify because voters respect the image and importance of the family farmer.

~

According to the U.S. Department of Agriculture's Census of Agriculture definition, a "farm" is any unit from which $1,000 worth of "agricultural products" has been marketed in a year.

~

1997 • Commodity Markets ~ American commodity markets can and have been buffeted by government-imposed grain embargoes in modern times, ordered by Presidents Nixon, Ford and Carter. Such developments impact directly on the farm economy and the family farm.

Top 10 States in Total Acres of Land Being Farmed

State	Acres of Farmland
1. Texas	130.5 million acres
2. Montana	57 million acres
3. Kansas	47.5 million acres
4. Nebraska	46.4 million acres
5. New Mexico	44.7 million acres
6. South Dakota	44 million acres
7. North Dakota	39.4 million acres
8. Wyoming	34.6 million acres
9. Oklahoma	34 million acres
10. Iowa	33 million acres

SOURCE: USDA, 1997

1860s-1930s • The Origin of American Grain Surpluses ~ The seeds of American grain surpluses of the 1970s were sown over a century earlier. Indeed, President Lincoln's Secretary of Agriculture in 1862 reported that the farm economy then was suffering from what would become a common, almost chronic ailment—an oversupply of crops.

Government involvement since the mid-1800s has evolved into a myriad of attempts to help the farm economy through federal farm programs. In the early 1920s, during the post-World War I era when farm prices collapsed, the Capper-Volstead Act opened the door

(circa 1973) Labor rights leader Cesar Chavez (third from right) and Coretta Scott King (fourth from right) leading a lettuce boycott march down a street in New York City.

for formation of modern farm cooperatives and guaranteeing these units full antitrust exemption in their efforts to help farmers prosper.

During the Depression, President Hoover created a national farm board that was to figure out how to bolster the sagging agricultural economy. Then, after Franklin D. Roosevelt took office in 1933, a series of historic New Deal executive orders began to permanently change the face of rural America. With the leadership of his Secretary of Agriculture, a gifted agricultural journalist named Henry A. Wallace, the Roosevelt-style farm programs debuted.

Overnight the brand-new FDR-Wallace "corn-hog" program augmented the farm economy. First, it provided a base support price for corn (which had been worth only a few pennies per bushel in the marketplace if sold as grain). Second, it provided fed for hogs through a new corn loan program that in essence guaranteed a

1860-1930

Farm Numbers By Selected Years

1910*	6,406,200
1930	6,545,600
1935	6,813,700
1960	3,962,520
1990	2,145,820
1999	2,194,070

SOURCE: USDA, National Agricultural Statistics Service

* 1910 was the first year the U. S. Department of Agriculture estimated the number of farms in the nation.

1860-1930

States with the Most Farms/Ranches

1.	Texas	227,000
2.	Missouri	110,000
3.	Iowa	96,000
4.	Tennessee	91,000
5.	Kentucky	91,000
6.	California	89,000
7.	Oklahoma	84,000
8.	Minnesota	81,000
9.	Ohio	80,000
10.	Illinois	79,000

SOURCE: USDA, Census of Agriculture, 1997

---

minimum price for this feed grain. This innovative concept was to endure, with modifications by ensuing administrations, until the "Freedom-to-Farm" program was passed 60 years later in 1996.

GOVERNMENT ASSISTANCE TO FARMERS ~ Government payments continued after the 1996 Farm Act was passed, through which $28 billion in direct financial assistance was provided to farmers in 2000, with $8 billion parceled out to nearly 1.4 million farmers, and another $5.5 billion paid for emergency relief. In addition, $8 billion was paid in "loan deficiency payments" which resulted when market prices dropped below target levels and $11 billion was given in supplemental income assistance.

U.S. Agriculture Secretary Dan Glickman had this comment about the $28 billion provided to farmers: "I remain concerned that the 1996 farm bill has left farmers without an adequate (economic) safety net in tough times. Emergency assistance while helpful in the short term does not address the long-term structural problems of the 1996 Farm Bill."

1860-1983 • THE AMERICAN SURPLUS FOOD PRODUCTION STRUGGLE ~

The age of agricultural super-abundance just didn't happen, and it didn't happen over night. No single event was responsible, but rather, agricultural super-abundance was the result of a series of events occurring over years: the Homestead Act of 1862 (which provided 160 acres of public lands free to encourage land-hungry European immigrants and others to settle the prairies and high plains of the west and Midwest); the creation of land-grant education which focused on agricultural and mechanical arts; the discovery of hybridization, or how to harness heterosis, and the introduction of hybrid seeds; the invention and manufacture of machines and equipment that would allow one farmer to do faster and better what a dozen of his predecessors were able to do.

The twentieth century agricultural revolution was put into a brief perspective by a journalist born in 1928 and who grew up on a Midwest farm: "I remember when I was a kid growing up there were twice as many farmers producing about half as much; now we have half as many farmers producing more than twice as much."

Such developments in farming enhanced the American farmer's offering for the tables of his country and then beyond its borders to other parts of the world. Efficient farming led to record, bin-busting harvests, bothersome surpluses and depressed markets. This bountiful scenario resulted in government action.

For 60 years, beginning with the Roosevelt Administration in the 1930s, there were a wide variety of U.S. government programs designed to hold down the production of food and feed crops. These measures had many different names. In the Eisenhower years of the 1950s, there was the "soil bank" program in which cornfields were plowed up or left fallow in order to bolster prices.

The effort by the U.S. Government to throttle food harvests hit its peak during the Reagan Administration when a mammoth cropland retirement program was enacted. Whole farms could be idled in 1983; participants were paid either in dollars or "payment-in-kind" ("PIK") in what President Reagan called a "crop-swap." Farmers had the option of getting paid in government grain, which they could sell, or getting a government check for not planting crops. There was a limit that no more than a fourth of crop acres could be idled in any one county. Several southern Iowa counties reached that maximum with 25 percent of their crop acres left fallow in 1983. Somewhat ironically, a late-season drought occurred that same year, when a record acreage of cropland was idled, wiping out what had been record grain surpluses.

1930s • COMBATING THE DEPRESSION IN RURAL AMERICA

President Roosevelt knew of the plight of rural people in part through his farm chief, Henry Wallace. He also became acquainted with rural conditions because of his frequent vacation trips to Warm Springs in rural Georgia. In addition, the FDR Administration was aware of subversive activities by some interests preying on the dire economic plight of rural Americans to foster anti-government sentiments, and to create more unrest and discontent.

Economists and social historians were concerned that the confiscation of private property in communist Russia (the USSR) was occurring in a different guise in farmland America. R.M. Evans, an Iowa agricultural official, wrote in 1936:

> We have all been concerned about the confiscation of private property in Russia, but in the severe depression from which we are just emerging, farm property in Iowa in reality has been confiscated by the taxing bodies because the earning power of the land was barely adequate to pay the taxes and the insurance on the buildings, leaving practically nothing for the farmer's wages or for a return on any capital invested in the farm.

Evans pointed out how the FDR-Wallace emergency measures had helped

---

Farm Organizations

The long-standing logo of the National Farmers Union (which will be 100 years old in 2002) features a trilogy that represents readily identifiable symbols of American farming and agriculture—the plow, the hoe and the rake. Although the Farmers Union is not really a "union" in the organized labor union sense, it has, from its beginning in Texas in 1902, battled for the family farmer and for the farm family. Its main quest is to lobby for government programs, direct aid and protection of family agriculture.

The largest farm organization is the American Farm Bureau Federation with 5 million members. It has generally opposed what some of its leaders have described as government involvement in agriculture, and has championed independence for farmers in a "free market" absent of government controls, quotas and allotment programs.

farm people. "Three years ago (1933) farmers faced the planting season very uncertain as to just where they would be one year later. Banks had failed on every hand. Prices were abnormally low and despair was everywhere evident...." The new corn-hog farm program developed by Wallace brought $74 million in government payments to Iowa farmers in 1934 and another $42 million the following year. The great gain economically, Evans added, occurred because of increased prices for corn and hogs brought about largely by the innovative government programs hastily enacted to bolster farmers' markets. One measure was the new corn loan (45 cents a bushel) program that set a "floor price" for this commodity.

1933 • Hog Subsidies ~ Another Depression program was the government's emergency hog-buying subsidy, through which it bought 6 million young pigs and hogs, as well as 220,000 pregnant sows to aid farmers encountering historically low swine animal prices. These animals were then slaughtered for food or fertilizer. Expectant sows were made into salted pork meat and given to families on relief. Young pigs were turned into fertilizer substances. This activity bolstered the hog market, but the killing of "piggy sows" brought much criticism from the public.

The emergency financial aid was all a part of the Agricultural Adjustment Act passed by Congress in May 1933. The first hogs were bought by the government at markets in Omaha, St. Paul,

(1936) A family of migrant workers fleeing from the drought in Oklahoma camp by the roadside in Blythe, California.

Chicago, Kansas City, St. Joseph, Missouri and Sioux City, Iowa. Swine weighing 80 pounds or more were converted into dry salted pork (100 million pounds were distributed by the Federal Emergency Relief Administration). Lighter pigs were tanked and rendered into grease (21 million pounds), with the bulk of the residue (5,043 tons) converted into fertilizer tankage.

1930s • OTHER HISTORIC FARM PROGRAMS ~ The FDR-Wallace political partnership introduced the nation's first corn loan program in the fall of 1934. That historic price support loan went to a Pocahontas County, Iowa farmer at the introductory rate of 45 cents a bushel. The farmer had to seal the corn in approved storage bins on his farm. At some future time he had the option of repaying the loan and marketing the corn, or forfeiting the grain to the government and collecting 45 cents per bushel, whichever was most profitable for him.

In addition to the guaranteed price for corn, the new administration introduced the reduction/payment program, in which farmers who agreed to idle one-fifth of their corn acreage would receive a government payment. Nationally, the acreage reduction program involved $350 million in "reduction payments," with $75 million paid to Iowa participants. Cooperating farmers were paid a rate of 30 cents a bushel for every bushel they did not plant (based on their historical yields).

Hog farmers also had a "reduction" program, with payments of $5 for each hog they didn't raise in line with normal production. There was a limit on the cutback in hog herds. Pork producers could not reduce their hog numbers by more than 75 percent of the average number marketed in the past.

> The "piggy sow" subsidy was a government program that was never tried again, despite the fact that the market for hogs became severely depressed and unprofitable several other times in later years. There was a dairy herd program enacted in the 1980s when dairy surpluses accumulated where producers could send mature animals to slaughter and receive government payments. The dairy farmer had to agree not to engage in dairy farming for at least five years.

This FDR New Deal era gave birth to broad scale farm commodity support programs and other significant, enduring programs, ranging from the establishment of farm and cooperative credit and land banks to rural electrification cooperatives and pioneering soil conservation districts. The impact on rural America as a result was historic, and elevated the standard of living closer to what it was in urban America.

1935 • RURAL ELECTRIFICATION COOPERATIVES ~ Perhaps the most dramatic achievement occurred in rural American as a result of regional electrical cooperatives organized to provide electricity to country folks for the first time. Farmers had been ignored by the private power companies because of the tremendous cost per customer required to provide electricity to remote and sparsely populated regions of the country. The Rural Electrification Act (1935) provided low-interest loans and grants to cooperatives, which brought to much of rural America the magic spark of electricity in a relatively short time between 1935 and the beginning of World War II.

1930s-1940s

When the USDA observed the 65th anniversary of the REA in 2000, the agency pointed out that this legislation was responsible for installing nearly one-half of all electric lines in the United States. Agriculture Secretary Dan Glickman said, "Bringing modern electrical service to rural America was one of the nation's most important achievements during the twentieth century. The challenge for us in the twenty-first century is to ensure that America's rural utility infrastructure keeps pace with increasing demand of rural power users."

1936 • SOIL AND WATER CONSERVATION ~ Another major effort with far-reaching and permanent impact nationally, spawned by the Roosevelt Administration, was the soil and water conservation movement. The seeds for this campaign were planted during the sky-darkened days of the Dust Bowl in the early 1930s when red clouds of dust blew from Oklahoma and coated the steps of the nation's capitol half a continent away.

The debut of the conservation program called attention to a special impetus for the creation of self-governing county soil conservation districts. The concept for self-government came from Roosevelt's Secretary of Agriculture Henry A. Wallace in the form of a model soil district plan formulated and then sent to officials in every state in early 1937. Wallace believed strongly that people should be able to work "collectively through government" to improve things and better their lot in life.

Wallace was the author of, and successfully lobbied Congress in 1936 to pass the Soil Conservation and Domestic Allotment Act which made it possible for local farmers and land-owners to organize soil conservation districts and invite the federal government to provide trained technicians to help implement soil-saving practices and programs. It was a pioneering effort based on one of the first and most significant pieces of national environmental legislation ever enacted. It established a foundation for future conservation programs.

An example of the effectiveness and acceptance of the conservation act was the fact that in some states every acre of land was enrolled in a conservation district within a dozen years after the passage of the historic conservation law in 1936.

1930s-1940s • IMPROVED SEEDS ~ One of agriculture's biggest success stories in the twentieth century undoubtedly is the hybridization of corn, the most important feed and food grain raised in the United States. Secretary of Agriculture Henry Wallace was one of the early proponents and a major figure in the development of hybrid corn and was one of the chief founders of a successful company that pioneered the production of this improved seed. His Iowa-based firm later became the world's largest producer and marketer of hybrid seed corn.

A similar rural movement had its birth some time after the severe drought of the mid-1950s when the first rural water districts were organized. These units were patterned after the successful electric cooperatives in water-short sections of the nation in order to bring a wholesome, reliable supply of water to the farm areas for human, animal and agricultural uses. The federal government aided this development through a system of low-interest loans and grants authorized by Congress.

The immediate bonus of heterosis, or hybridization, was an increase in yields—a boost of anywhere from 15 percent to 30 percent in general, according to *The Hybrid-Corn Makers*, a book published in 1947. A plot of corn planted in a University of Illinois experiment in McLean County, Illinois in 1936 showed that three hybrid fields averaged 101.3 bushels per acre compared to less than 25 bushels per acre in plots planted with conventional seed corn. It was a hot, dry summer with temperatures over 100 degrees in early July and no rain for a week. A hundred and ten bushels per acre were harvested in fields where conventional open-pollinated seed corn was planted. The news of such amazing results caught the attention of farmers nationally. That one experiment demonstrated that not only did hybrid corn outyield regular seed, but hybrid plants performed better in a severe drought year like 1936 which was extremely hot and dry, with temperatures ranging from 102 to 111 degrees in central Illinois where the university yield test was conducted.

Because hybridization brought immediate increases in corn yields, the advent facilitated the farmer's acceptance of a new marketing plan where farmer-dealers sold the improved seeds, which were very expensive and in limited supply. The first corn seed company executives believed that farmer-selling-to-farmer was the best way to market the hybrid seed. This marketing strategy worked well and corn yields increased steadily in following years, ascending far beyond what early hybrid promoters had anticipated.

In the 1930s when the first hybrid seed became commercially available, the average corn yield was about 35 bushels per acre. Since then, corn yields have continued to increase because of commercial fertilizers, insect and weed control and better farm management. By 1950 the U.S. average yield of corn was 38.2 bushels per acre. The first time corn yields nationally topped 100 bushels per acre was in 1978 when farmers nationally averaged 101 bushels per acre. The record corn yield was 138.6 bushels per acre harvested in 1994.

> An Iowa corn grower epitomizes this remarkable increased productivity, harvesting nearly 400 bushels per acre to win the individual Iowa corn-growing championship—a title Francis Childs of Manchester in northeast Iowa has won for a half-dozen consecutive years.
>
> This farmer annually shoots for the highest possible yield in his cornfield, planting seed at abnormally high rates while pouring on fertilizer as well. Childs loves to win contests, which might explain his mastery of yields in corn growing circles.

1930s-1970

1950-1970 • IMPROVING SEED STOCK

Over time there have been other genetic changes in corn that have brought both higher yields and questionable changes. Scientists and plant breeders have successfully introduced traits which, for example, discourage insect damage. Losses to the once costly European corn borer have been reduced by development of seeds which produce a plant that is resistant to or discourages infestation by the gnawing insect that earlier caused extensive economic losses to the nation's corn crop. Losses caused by the corn borer were particularly costly in the post-World War II era into the early 1950s before seed companies developed varieties that could better withstand attacks by the insect.

1950-1970

Some other examples of genetic engineering of crops include herbicide resistance, increased protein and oil content in grains and oilseeds, and the development of "organic" specialty food and feed crops for niche markets, such as tofu or edible soybeans.

On the other hand, a costly experience resulted in 1970 after scientists developed a male-sterile type corn, which eliminated the expense of detasseling (the removal of the tassel in the male corn plant) of seed fields. Detasseling by hand was commonplace, and represented a major expense in producing hybrid seed. However, this new male-sterile type of corn proved very vulnerable to the southern corn leaf blight, which shriveled the size of the nation's corn crop in 1970.

1910-1950s • LEAVING THE FARM
In John Steinbeck's epic 1939 novel *The Grapes of Wrath*, uprooted Okies (Oklahoma residents) put the blame of their hopeless economic plight on being "tractored off the land" during the Dust Bowl days. While their generation may have represented the first mass exodus from farming, mechanization may not have been the sole reason. But clearly mechanical technology and the ability of one person to farm more land and produce as much or more per acre than his predecessor has been a definite, major and prolonged factor in the out-migration from the land.

Some observers think that the nearly century-long industrialization trend in American agriculture, which has sounded the death knell for thousands of so-called "family farmers," had its beginning with the introduction of the tractor. Others trace this trend back even further to the invention and development of the world's first practical working steel moldboard plow by John Deere in 1836. His plow helped open up the virgin prairie

(1938) Dustbowl Colorado.

sod more efficiently to be planted by the pioneers. Another development, which allowed the pioneers to drain marshes and create a new source of fertile farmland, was the introduction of drainage tile and drainage district systems, which added thousands of acres that had been too wet and boggy to farm earlier.

Then followed the first generation of "tractors" (that name has its origin in the fact some of the early machines had extensive treads or traction devices), which were king-sized, heavyweight, clumsy behemoths. These machines representing the first farm mechanical "horsepower" were destined to gain great momentum in replacing the real-life horsepower on the farm fields of America. Evidence of this trend is reflected in government records.

The USDA estimated there were 26.5 million horses and mules on the nation's farms in 1915, just prior to the widespread use of tractors. Forty-two years later, in 1957, there were only 3.9 million head of horses and mules. Tractor numbers mushroomed during the World War II era, going from 1.7 million in 1941 to 4.1 million 10 years later.

The USDA counted only 120,000 mechanical corn pickers on the nation's farms in 1941; by 1951 this number had quadrupled to 500,000.

When the USDA first began counting the number of farms in 1910, there were 6.4 million farms in the nation. This number was to grow to a record 6.8 million farms in 1935. Then the number of farms began a steady decline, which continues today for various reasons, including weather, surplus output and increased production per farmer. No matter what farm policy or program was provided, or what political administration was in power, and no matter what the farm economy, farm numbers have continually and steadily declined since the mid-1930s. By the end of the twentieth century the number of farms in the United States was estimated at 2.2 million; two-thirds of the farm units present in the mid-1930s had vanished.

1941-1945 • FARMERS AND THE WAR EFFORT ~ At no other time during the past century was food production more important than during the duration of World War II and immediately after the Allied victory in 1945. American farmers were urged to go all out to produce food "to help win the war." Despite wartime rationing of gasoline, farmers could get all of the gasoline they needed.

The farm tractor and implement companies were directed by the federal government to help farmers produce more food, but at the same time not interfere with the building of a bigger war machine. The farm firms thus became bound by a "limitation order" issued by the U.S. Government in December 1940, before the U.S. was officially at war. The Office of Production Management ordered a limit on all farm implement manufacturers to 80 percent of what they produced in new farm machines in 1940, and 150 percent of repair and maintenance parts.

Plants were converted to war production, too. Army tank transmissions and power drive units for M-3 medium tanks were built by Deere & Co. at a Canadian factory beginning in March 1941. Ford-Ferguson executives proposed a plan to the War Production Board in 1942 that stepped up production of the company's lighter-weight tractors, replacing the wartime quota of pre-depression era heavyweight tractors. The Ford-Ferguson people argued for this plan by saying it would "save" enough steel to build 42 battleships.

1941-1945

Symbolic of the nation's drive to boost production was the goal announced by the War Food Administration in the spring of 1944 to have farmers step up wheat harvest by a billion bushels. This led Massey-Ferguson to lobby the government to allow increased manufacturing limits for its new small self-propelled combine to help harvest the hoped-for bigger wheat crop. The firm also argued that the combine would help offset the shortage of farm workers caused by the military draft.

But there were suspicions that the farm companies were preparing for the boom in post-war tractor and implement sales while helping with the war effort. The U.S. Justice Department threatened a

---

Deere & Company's Wartime Activity

In a special report made to presidential assistant Donald M. Nelson at the White House in February 1945, Deere & Co. President C.D. Wiman outlined how this Midwest-based farm equipment manufacturer did double-duty during World War II.

Its 9,000 workers wore two hats—first as a supplier of farm machinery needed to help "food win the war," but also as a source of essential and strategic military equipment for the War Production Board. Deere worked to fill 1,098 war contracts producing $36 million worth of airplane parts alone, along with varied items ranging from shells to transmissions for the General Grant tank.

Deere actually began its wartime role as a military materials supplier ahead of the official beginning of World War II when the Army Ordnance Department contracted in March 1941 for the company to begin building tank transmissions for Great Britain at its Waterloo, Iowa tractor and transmission subsidiary. There were 22,000 tank transmissions made there, each weighing 7,600 pounds, and valued in total at more than $100 million.

In addition, Deere began manufacturing its first crawler-type tractors under government contracts totaling $18 million. The "military tractor" was symbolic of the war effort, because no fewer than 11 Deere factories had a hand in making the parts and shipping them to the factory where the final crawler was assembled. It was, Deere said, "a family job" making the MG-1 and MG-2 machines.

At the same time it geared up to help win the war, Deere had to keep up the supply of repairs and parts as well as other machinery and equipment on the farm front. The bottom line was that during WWII, Deere & Co. produced $200 million worth of war goods, including machines, parts and materials, while also turning out war food equipment permitted under the War Production Board limitations.

In his report to The White House, Deere president Wiman summarized, "The combined manufacture of war goods and implements has brought new production records for the company in spite of a constantly critical shortage of labor."

The first of five war citations was awarded to Deere & Co. On August 20, 1942, when the Army-Navy "E" (for Excellence) Award was given to the John Deere Waterloo Tractor Works and its subsidiary, Iowa Transmission Co., for the quality and quantity of the production of transmissions for the U.S. Army's medium tanks. At its peak the Waterloo Deere workers were making a thousand tank transmissions per month. Deere was the first in Iowa to earn the Army-Navy "E" award.

grand jury examination if some farm firms were building up inventories for civilian needs at the same time they were directed to augment wartime materiel needs.

Ammunition was produced at the Ankeny Ordnance Plant northwest of Des Moines, Iowa in a facility where Deere & Co. now produces cotton-pickers and other farm items.

Consumers encountered all kinds of rationing, from sugar and meat to coffee and other items put into short supply by the war. Hoarding was discouraged and so-called "Victory Gardens" were encouraged. Americans planted more gardens to help conserve farm-produced food for the military. Metal scrap drives took place, with a farm an excellent source of old, unused or broken equipment and steel items that could during the emergency be transformed into weapons and ammunition.

Hog farmers were encouraged by the government to produce more and fatter pigs, because the fat and grease yielded by the porkers could be used to manufacture munitions and explosives.

1941-1945 • CHANGE FOR WOMEN DURING THE WAR

The novelty of such things as planting a Victory Garden, the hemp crop harvest, metal scrap drives, food and gas rationing, all seemed to bring the wartime effort closer to the people in the rural regions of middle America. It was a time of change, and that change was coming to the farm. One of the major changes pertained to women. During the wartime emergency, many did much more than keep the home fires burning and raise Victory Gardens. They shed their traditional homemaking role and took strategic jobs temporarily to help fill the labor void created by the men going off to serve in the

> For three years the U.S. Government encouraged farmers to grow hemp for use in making ropes. The government subsidized the planting of thousands of acres of the new crop and issued an emergency call for farmers to raise hemp. It simultaneously ordered a network of hemp plants to be built in the Midwest to process the hemp into the rope-making fiber material needed for the war effort. Farmers were guaranteed a price and schools permitted students to take two weeks off to help with the harvest, which required much hand labor. One of the hemp plants was built in the small farm community of Britt in northern Iowa. German prisoners of war imprisoned at nearby Algona provided a source of manpower at this rope-making facility.

war. After the wartime period ended, some of these workers never really returned to their pre-war domestic status, and in a way charted a new vocational course for more and more women in the nation's work force.

1940s • FARMS BEGIN TO CHANGE

Even during World War II, when manpower for farm power was as scarce as it had ever been, the farming job got done. The nation's warriors had C-rations and were fed. And despite food rationing at home, America had something to eat.

Eventually over time, farms would increase in size with fewer and fewer workers needed because of the trend toward more and more mechanization. At the same time, operations would become more concentrated and more specialized, with farmers focusing their talents and labor on only a few enterprises like the production of crops, livestock or poultry.

1940s

The average farm size has grown dramatically, from the day when 160 acres was commonplace and sufficient to keep a family busy, to the point where at the beginning of the twenty-first century thousands of acres were needed to justify expensive, high-powered equipment.

Statistics tell the story. The average size of an Iowa farm in 1938 was 168 acres. In 1999, the average size had grown to 343 acres. Iowa State University records show that the average farm size nationally increased from 332 acres in 1964 to 461 acres in 1990. In Iowa, the increase was from 214 acres in 1964 to 322 in 1990.

(1953) Matthew Black (aged 17), a member of the Mormon sect, driving a tractor at Short Creek, Arizona (a Mormon community). He is one of the young men left to tend the farmlands after a mass police arrest of Mormon men for suspected polygamy.

1946 • THE BIRTH OF "COMMERCIAL" FARMS ~ Farming structure began to change in the days after World War II in several significant ways. First, there was the flow of new machinery from the wartime factories that produced military equipment to the peacetime manufacture of equipment that in many instances was vastly different from pre-war products. For example, farm tractors were improved, becoming bigger and more diversified. The comfort and safety of the tractor operator became important—cabs for drivers appeared, followed by air-conditioning. The tractor-testing facility at the University of Nebraska gained national attention as it compared tractors for efficiency and safety.

After World War II, weed-killing sprays and granular products became commercially available for the first time. Instead of cultivation as the chief weed-control measure, farmers began to use herbicides—a few ounces per acre would keep crop fields free of certain weed invaders that threatened to reduce yields.

Insecticides combated corn rootworms; new and more powerful insecticides were developed, as farm pests became immune to old poisons. The individual farmer could do more, and more quickly and more efficiently than ever before. But everything cost more and the family farmer needed more land to farm to make the new equipment pay for itself.

Old-time farmers who grew up behind a team of horses shook their heads in disbelief at what was happening. The 160-acre farm they spent a quarter-century farming now wasn't big enough to support a family like it did. The farm magazines called it "a farming revolution," but some old-timers felt it was a revolution from which no one emerged a winner. The bottom line for agriculture at mid-century was that a single farmer using modern machinery could easily plant or harvest in a day more acreage than his predecessors could harvest in a season.

1930-1960s • Tough Times Out On The Farm

History shows that difficult times for rural people seem to develop in almost every generation or so, despite what's happening elsewhere in the nation's economy.

In 1928, C.F. Curtiss, the Dean of Agriculture at Iowa State College, observed: "The world war (I) not only changed the map of the world—it changed the economic conditions of the world as well. The American farmer is confronted with permanent higher production costs and higher marketing costs. American agriculture has been depressed since the close of the war; while European agriculture, with the exception of one or two countries, has been prosperous…the American farmer has not shared in the post-war period of prosperity in the United States. There can be no permanent national prosperity in which all important industries do not share alike…." Dean Curtiss called for a national policy for agriculture where efforts would be made to promote and protect the domestic agriculture of the United States to make it the "cheap food supplier of the world."

The depressed farm picture Dean Curtiss saw in 1928 turned into the Great Depression when most Americans suffered. However, it was not the final farm depression of the century, despite all of the new programs that emerged from the 1930s to help stabilize farming. A post-Korean War period saw depressed livestock prices in the mid-1950s, followed by a two-year drought in the Midwest.

In the 1960s, small groups of angry farmers engaged in public protest demonstrations at livestock markets in the Midwest. They belonged to the National Farmers Organization (NFO), a group that sought a collective bargaining program for agriculture. It ordered farmers to boycott markets rather than sell at what it considered unfair prices. In 1968, the NFO staged thirty-one public hog-killing protests in eleven states when it couldn't get the prices it sought for its members. The protesters shot and buried 14,083 hogs.

1960s-1970s • Alternative Jobs for Farmers

The number of farm operators declined by 17 percent from 1964 to 1987 in Iowa, while the average age of a farmer held fairly steady at 48-49 for that same period. And the number of farmers with off-farm income from non-farm jobs has increased by a third.

Some moonlighted at small seasonal businesses, like farm supply firms that, during the winter months, hire temporary employees to build up or restore inventories. One example is a Mississippi firm, Marting Manufacturing Co., which hires farmers during the winter to make livestock feeders and other equipment. Many of these temporary employees are grain farmers who are under-employed during the winter season.

Other seasonal off-farm jobs include employment at meat-packing plants, recreational vehicle factories, the local grain elevator and other local businesses which have seasonal fluctuations in sales activity, and farm supply concerns providing products needed for spring planting and harvesting.

1972 • Food Shortages in the Soviet Union

America's full granaries and overall surplus opened new markets, at least temporarily, to American farmers. In 1972 the Soviet Union was so

1972

short of food that it acknowledged to the world its agricultural shortcomings. The Soviets had to shop on the global market for one of the most basic foods—wheat. Eventually, the Soviets wound up buying a billion dollars worth of wheat from American farmers. This Soviet food shortfall resulted even though there had been an agricultural exchange between the two world powers. This international farm exchange had its roots in Iowa in 1955, and included the importation of hybrid seed corn from the U.S., as well as food counseling and advice on boosting food production.

In 1959 Soviet Premier Nikita Khrushchev visited the Iowa farm of Roswell "Bob" Garst, a seed corn promoter and farmer who had exported some of his hybrid seed to the Soviets at a time when many Americans regarded the Russians as an enemy. The idea for a farm exchange originated in an editorial penned in 1955 by Lauren K. Soth of the *Des Moines Register* whose editorial won the Pulitzer Prize the following year.

The U.S./Soviet relationship developed despite the international tensions of the Cold War that existed then between the two world powers. The United States, where some so feared a World War III that they built personal backyard bomb shelters, also was the same country which sent farm representatives to Russia to help them farm better. However, some critics thought that unless the Soviet leaders became committed to investing more resources in the nation's food production plant and spending less on military matters, their hopes of achieving greater food self-sufficiency would fall short.

The exchange also provoked comparisons in lifestyles between a democracy and a dictatorship. American farmers argued that they stood to gain or lose personally in their farming efforts while this incentive was non-existent in Russia. An Iowa agriculturalist who took part in the exchange told how he would not hesitate to get up in the middle of the night to baby-sit an expectant sow, adding, "I can't see a Russian farm worker doing the same thing with a communist sow that he doesn't own and which really belongs to the state."

In short, what took place between the two countries really was not a farm exchange in its truest sense, because the Soviets had little they could put on their side of the international table in exchange for the American help in attempting to create bigger Soviet harvests.

However, the contrasting picture between the pair of world powers and their food harvests was clear. On one hand you had the Soviet Union which obviously couldn't feed itself sufficiently; on the other hand there was the United States which for much of the past century had been struggling under the American farmer's tendency to over-produce the market because of the increasing ability to produce food despite the use of massive, complicated and expensive government programs designed to throttle food output and reduce the chance of price-depressing surpluses. In short, this all represented a problem of plenty, something many other nations, including Russia, never confronted.

Following the historic Soviet Union wheat purchase in 1972, farmers pocketed record prices for all major commodities. Farmland prices quadrupled in Iowa and zoomed upward elsewhere in the farming regions of the country as farm indebtedness grew to record proportions.

1973-1980 • GRAIN EMBARGOES AND PRICE CONTROLS ~ Two grain embargoes were ordered by U.S. Presidents in one decade. The first embargo resulted from a directive issued by Richard Nixon within a year of the Soviet grain purchase. It had been a wild spring for the grain trade in 1973 with soybeans advancing to historic high market levels. "Beans in the Teens" was the bullish quote of the times, as the cash price in the Midwest Soybean Belt moved up to $12 a bushel for the first time ever and appeared to be on the march even higher. A newspaper reporter spent a day at a central Iowa grain elevator waiting to interview soybean growers who were cashing in on the record market. But none showed that day. "No one has any left to sell," the cooperative elevator manager explained. "The ones who had any to sell already sold them."

President Nixon had demonstrated a high-level interest in commodity prices. In March 1973, Nixon made history when he issued a directive putting a ceiling price on both beef and pork at the wholesale level. It was the first time such price controls had been put in place in peacetime. Then in June 1973, President Nixon ordered a halt to all soybean exports. It was a demand reflecting a "feed America first" mentality that existed in some circles, including the presidency. Hardest hit by Nixon's directive was the biggest U.S. foreign farm customer, Japan. "They want soybeans," the U.S. Agricultural attaché stationed in Japan said. "And, they want them at any price because they need them."

In January 1980, President Jimmy Carter ordered a grain embargo in response to Soviet military activity in Afghanistan. This action was extremely unpopular in rural America where farmers depended on grain and soybean exports for a substantial share of their income, particularly after the Soviet Union's historic grain purchases beginning in July 1972.

Some farm leaders questioned the use of food in foreign policy matters, especially after the United States for many years had made food products the centerpiece of several international programs such as P.L. 480 (enacted by Congress during the Eisenhower Administration), which provided food shipments of tons of grain and other products to combat hunger and famine around the globe, and the Food For Peace program which originated in the Kennedy Administration.

1980s • COMMUNITY RURAL BANKS GO BROKE ~ In the 1980s the worst economic crunch occurred in rural America since the 1930s. Land prices fell by 62 percent in Iowa, and thousands of farmers went bankrupt. Special bankruptcy laws were passed to help people restructure and reorganize debts and a system of arbitration was established. Iowa State University started a hotline telephone where troubled people could call toll-free and talk confidentially to an expert in legal, financial and family matters. Hundreds called for advice and counseling.

Almost unbelievably, the once-thriving specialized farm credit bank system encountered severe, historic losses and federal laws were passed to save them. Several of the farm credit banks had to be reorganized. Millions of dollars of farm debt had to be written off. This financial upheaval emphasized just how unsuspecting so many had been of the difficult economic times ahead. Indeed most people in rural America were unprepared for what eventually happened. It was like rural America had forgotten the basic economic lessons taught so harshly by the Great Depression experience.

1980s

In addition to the collapse of several farm credit banks, dozens of small, hometown commercial country banks in the Midwest closed their doors, including 38 in Iowa (however, all but one of the Iowa banks reopened later under new ownership). The procedure for a bank closing was repeated—the Iowa Superintendent of Banking would announce bank closings on Friday afternoons, thus giving the local community a weekend to digest the bad news. Then by Monday morning, new owners would open for business as usual. As farmland values tumbled, as they did year after year, and net worths continued to erode, more and more farmers and small-town businesses in rural America quit or shut down.

Troubled farmers organized new farm organizations called "alliances" and "coalitions" to join together and focus their resources and efforts on coping with the difficult times. The Farm Unity Coalition, Prairiefire, the Center for Rural Affairs and other groups sponsored demonstrations hoping to stall or prevent farm foreclosures. They erected small, white wooden crosses on the lawns of county courthouses. Each cross was to mark the "death" of a family farm operation. While some efforts were made to stage "penny auctions" at farm closing sales like those that took place in the 1930s, such low-price bidding to discourage farm foreclosure activity was at a minimum in the 1980s. Special treatment was available, including a provision where farmstead exemptions allowed bankruptcy proceedings to leave a farmer a place for him and his family to live while they tried to work out their financial problems.

One financially stressed farmer in southeast Iowa went on a one-morning rampage. He shot to death his wife, his banker and a neighbor before killing himself. Also, there were several suicides blamed on the hard times faced by some, but not all, of the farmers. Those who hadn't borrowed money and gone heavily into debt survived. And some of these people disliked and criticized openly the financial write-offs and emergency aid given to many of those who encountered severe money problems. Especially critical of special financial aid were those out-bid by their neighbors on farmland both parties wanted to buy when times were good and land prices were booming.

During the height of the Farm Crisis of the 1980s, U.S. Agriculture Secretary John R. Block issued an order that the USDA's lender of last resort, the Farmers Home Administration, "go the extra mile" in its lending to those facing financial hardship. The agency ordered farm debts restructured, debts forgiven, and in some instances, lent more money to the same troubled borrower.

1985 • FARM AID BENEFIT CONCERTS

~ Rallies were held to call attention to the troubles of rural people, including a national meeting attended by thousands held in the basketball coliseum on the campus of Iowa State University. One event that attracted much publicity and attention was called "The Farm Aid Concert." Hosted by entertainer Willie Nelson, people filled the University of Illinois football stadium one Sunday in September 1985. The Beach Boys, John Denver and other stars performed during a noon-to-midnight program that raised millions of dollars for farm financial assistance. People across the nation telephoned in pledges and donations that were later distributed through various farm groups. That first concert ended at 1:30 a.m. the following Monday morning

(1986) Farmers in Kansas attending an auction of farm equipment after a family decided to sell out.

with fireworks shot off from the stadium.

Despite improved economic conditions in the years that followed, a "Farm Aid" concert has been held annually, ever since that highly-publicized and nationally-televised initial event in 1985 before thousands in the Illinois football stadium. But none has matched the dimension of that first concert.

The Des Moines Register organized a "Farm Aid Express" chartered train trip to the first Farm Aid Concert, set up by Northwestern Railway. Five hundred people boarded at several locations across the state, including Iowa Governor Terry E. Branstad, presidential hopeful Howard Baker, U.S. Senator Tom Harkin of Iowa and others invited to make the trip as guests of the newspaper and the railroad company. Dozens of people gathered along the rail route to greet the Farm Aid Express train as it traveled across Iowa, stopping at railroad depots and country crossroads. Some on-lookers held banners and signs proclaiming support of the event, while others simply waved as the train went by. The passengers on the train wore special "Farm Aid" sweatshirts and farmers' hats, which added color to the occasion. This public demonstration of a cause seemed unusual in farm country. It was unlike any other time when so many people at the grassroots were bonded for a cause.

1990s • MODERN FARMING ~ The farmer of the 1990s concentrates only on producing crops, and having available the machinery and equipment to plant, care for and harvest his acreage of soybeans and corn in a timely and efficient manner—using mostly family labor. Once his harvesting rigs are in motion, the machines never stop rolling—grain pours into wagons that keep up with the combine. When full, workers empty their bounty into one of the three semi-trucks the farmer owns. These trucks wait at the edge of the field, and are used to transport the newly-harvested crop to the cooperative which will either buy the grain outright or store the corn and soybeans for the farmer to sell when he wants.

This farmer may own only a small portion of the 3,000 acres he farms. The bulk of his land is obtained by paying rent to the landowners. Much of the farmland is farmed under such an arrangement today in the Midwest as contrasted to a landlord-tenant, or sharecropping type of operation commonly used earlier in the century.

The bulk of the food produced in the United States comes from a fourth of the nation's farms. Eighty-five percent of all of the nation's livestock and crops comes from only a half-million farm operations, or only about a third of the farms in the United States.

Consolidation has occurred at both ends of the nation's food chain—at the farm level and at the processing and retailing sectors as well. One out of every four farms has been "merged" with existing farm units, and there has been the consolidation of major meat packers as well as big food conglomerates such as Kellogg merging with Keebler, General Mills with Pillsbury, and Pepsi with Quaker Oats. What these changes mean to consumers remains to be seen.

Family farms continue to be dominant in crop farming, while conglomerates control livestock and poultry production, products that lend themselves well toward industrialization. The 1997 agricultural census showed 86 percent of the 2.2 million farms nationally were categorized as family farms.

Combines: A Symbol of Modern Farming

Today, handling the chores and hard work once done either by human hand or in combination with draft animals is now performed by mammoth, expensive, efficient machines. The harvesting rigs are called generically "combines," a name derived from the fact they "combine" two or more harvesting operations which early in the twentieth century were separate, laborious tasks.

It is the combine (used to harvest grain crops) that is the symbol of modern farming more than anything else. It represents "bigness"—an implement designed for large farms and huge acreages with bigger crop yields, thanks to improved seeds and growing practices and methods. There was nothing like these mechanical behemoths in the farming of yesteryear, not before what is now called the agricultural revolution of the twentieth century.

A single combine can harvest easily in a day what it took the pioneer farmer a full season to accomplish. At the same time much more grain is grown per acre, and the harvest features a greater flow of crops. For example, the average corn yield was 127 bushels per acre in 1997 when farmers in the United States harvested 73.7 million acres. By comparison, the total U.S. corn crop averaged only 38.2 bushels per acre in 1950.

SEED-TO-PLATE CONTROL BY FOOD CONGLOMERATES

One organization strongly opposed to corporate farm development and corporate mergers and consolidations, which result in fewer markets for farm produce, is the National Farmers Union. This group, which was organized nearly a century ago, steadfastly opposes the emergence of firms having "oligopoly-like power" in the nation's food industry. "The consolidated control by these large conglomerates in the food system is diluting the power of both consumers and farmers," the organization said in a 2000 report.

There has been "an acceleration toward seed-to-plate, market-wide control" in retail food and dairy industries in recent years, which represents a loss of competition. The organization urged a Congressional investigation into how recent consolidation and concentration in the food industry is affecting family farmers and consumers. It charged (but did not identify) that the five biggest food retailers in the U.S. marketed 45 percent of all retail food sales in 2000. That is compared to 24 percent only three years earlier, according to the Farmers Union study.

Concern from local groups about competition from "corporate farm" or mega-farm operations has resulted in restrictive laws enacted in some Midwest states over the years. In Iowa for example, it is illegal for a meat packer to either own or feed livestock. Also, foreign ownership of land is confined to no more than one square mile.

In addition, some states like Iowa have enacted laws that prohibit anything seen as being in competition with farmers through ownership or other corporate

States Specializing in Various Commodities

ARKANSAS: rice
CALIFORNIA: 25 vegetables, garden and fruit crops, from apricots to winter potatoes
COLORADO: summer potatoes
FLORIDA: sugar cane, all oranges, grapefruit, limes and tangerines
GEORGIA: peanuts, pecans and rye
HAWAII: bananas, pineapple, papaya, macadamia nuts, coffee and taro
IDAHO: all potatoes, and white, pink and small beans
IOWA: corn and soybeans
KANSAS: wheat, grain sorghum and silage sorghum
LOUISIANA: all sugar cane
MICHIGAN: cultivated blueberries, tart cherries, navy beans and cranberry beans
MINNESOTA: sugar beets and dark red kidney beans
NEBRASKA: Great northern beans and light red kidney beans
NORTH DAKOTA: Durum wheat, barley, spring wheat, flax seed, sunflower seed and pinto beans
OREGON: cultivated blackberries, black raspberries, loganberries and peppermint
TEXAS: cotton and hay
VERMONT: maple syrup
WASHINGTON: commercial apples, pears, red raspberries, lentils, hops and dry edible beans

1990s

activity related to farming. Anti-corporate farm laws, for example, have been enacted in some states, such as Minnesota, Nebraska and South Dakota. Also, some states have enacted new laws providing cooperatives more protection from possible antitrust action.

1997-1999 • NO STATE LIKE CALIFORNIA ~ When it comes to being number one in providing food for the table, California is clearly at the top of the list in many major and minor food crops. The state ranks first in the production of large lima beans, baby lima beans, black eye (peas) beans, garbanzo beans, and in other dry edible beans, according to the USDA in its 1997 summary of where our food comes from.

California also ranks first in the harvest of prunes and grapes, apricots, nectarines, kiwi fruit, dates and figs, olives, all raspberries, almonds, walnuts, Pistachio nuts, plus both winter and spring potatoes (ninth, though, in the category of "all potatoes" where Idaho leads with production of 135.4 million hundredweight in 1997).

California ranks first nationally in the production of alfalfa hay (7 million tons). It is second in all hay (8.6 million tons), behind Texas (10.8 million tons) and in "all cotton" (2.6 million bales) trailing Texas (5.3 million bales), and is second also in acreage of corn harvested for silage (8.2 million tons) behind Wisconsin (10.9 million tons).

California is second in "all oranges" with a total harvest of 68 million boxes (Florida led with 226 million boxes in 1997).

California leads in the value of agricultural produce, with $23 billion in farm production sales in 1997. This represented about 12 percent of the nation's total supply of agricultural marketings that year. Texas was second, with $13.8 bil-

(circa 1935) Workers kneeling down amongst crates in a field picking carrots, Imperial Valley, California.

Top 10 States in Market Value of Agricultural Products Sold

State	1999	1997	1992
1. California	$24.1 billion	$23 billion	$17 billion
2. Texas	$13.2 billion	$13.8 billion	$12 billion
3. Iowa	$9.8 billion	$12 billion	$10 billion
4. Nebraska	$8.7 billion	$9.8 billion	$8.2 billion
5. Kansas	$7.5 billion	$9.2 billion	$8.3 billion
6. Minnesota	$7 billion	$8.3 billion	$6.4 billion
7. Florida	$6.9 billion	$6 billion	$5.3 billion
8. Illinois	$$6.8 billion	$8.6 billion	$7.3 billion
9. North Carolina	$6.4 billion	$7.7 billion	$4.8 billion
10. Wisconsin	$5.9 billion	$5.6 billion	$5.3 billion

SOURCE: USDA: National Agricultural Statistics Service

lion in sales or about 9 percent, followed by Iowa which had $12 billion worth of agricultural products sold in 1997.

California's sale of agricultural products increased by $6 billion from 1992 to 1997, according to government estimates. Nationally, the value of farm products marketed increased by $17 billion during that 5-year period when the agricultural census was taken.

1982-1997 • THE NUMBER OF HOG FARMS DECLINES SHARPLY ~ Evidence of a trend to "industrialized" operations is found in pork production alone. The number of farms reporting hog or pork-producing operations declined sharply from 1980 to the turn of the century, when nearly 60 percent of one-family pork operations discontinued raising swine because of unprofitable returns. However, despite this sharp reduction in the number of hog operations and the number of hogs slaughtered, the amount of pork produced for consumers remained virtually unchanged.

In short, while the number of farms on which hogs are raised has declined sharply from 1982 to 1997, there has been no corresponding drop in the amount of pork produced. In fact, a record supply of pork was produced in 1998, forcing prices to modern historic lows.

Top 10 States in Net Farm Income

State	Net Farm Income
1. California	$5.4 billion
2. Texas	$3.1 billion
3. North Carolina	$2.4 billion
4. Iowa	$2.3 billion
5. Florida	$2.2 billion
6. Georgia	$1.9 billion
7. Nebraska	$1.8 billion
8. Arkansas	$1.6 billion
9. Kansas	$1.5 billion
10. Illinois	$1.48 billion

SOURCE: USDA, 1999

1982-1997

Top 10 States in Milk Production

State	Pounds of Milk/Year
1. California	30.5 million lbs.
2. Wisconsin	23 million lbs.
3. New York	12 million lbs.
4. Pennsylvania	10.9 million lbs.
5. Minnesota	9.5 million lbs.
6. Idaho	6.5 million lbs.
7. Texas	5.6 million lbs.
8. Washington	5.5 million lbs.
9. Michigan	5.4 million lbs.
10. New Mexico	4.7 million lbs.

SOURCE: USDA, 1997

Top 10 States in the Production of Freestone Peaches

1. California	739 million pounds
2. Georgia	160 million pounds
3. South Carolina	160 million ponds
4. Pennsylvania	75 million pounds
5. New Jersey	65 million pounds
6. Michigan	61 million pounds
7. Washington	45 million pounds
8. Alabama	29 million pounds
9. Texas	20 million pounds
10. Arkansas	14.3 million pounds

SOURCE: USDA, 1997

From 1974 to 1987, the number of Iowa farms reporting pigs or hogs declined by 38.4 percent; however, the number of hogs increased by 13.1 percent during that period. Further, the average herd size increased by 83.8 percent, which means those still in the business have bigger and bigger pork operations.

Oddly, the nation's biggest pork-producer is no longer a Midwest Corn Belt state. It is North Carolina, the state that late in the twentieth century threatened to oust long-time pork leader Iowa as the No. 1 pork state. Iowa farmers had marketed more hogs than any other state for more than a century, beginning in the early 1880s, according to census figures. Illinois, thanks to the famous Chicago stockyards, was the nation's No. 2 pork producer for many years.

It seemed only a natural development that the two Corn Belt states, Iowa and Illinois, would double as the nation's top producing states in both corn and pork. This was the case for many years until the industrialization of the pork industry entered the picture. Hog production units grew in size and the number of farms where hogs were raised began to decline sharply. However, at the same time the trend became fewer and bigger pork production units, the nation's supply of pork has in general increased.

Iowa reflects this significant change. The number of farms marketing hogs has dropped by 62.5 percent in this state during a 15-year period. Where there were 49,012 hog farms in Iowa in 1982, the number of pork units dropped to 18,370 in 1997. However, the number of hogs produced and raised in Iowa increased, from 23 million head marketed in 1982 to 27.5 million 15 years later.

1906-2000 • FOOD SAFETY, A GROWING CONCERN

Food safety is not really a new issue. It had become a major public concern in the United States early in the twentieth century, thanks largely to the writings of author Upton Sinclair. He wrote articles that exposed adverse business and working conditions in the Chicago stockyards and meat packing industries.

Sinclair's book, *The Jungle* (1906), led to the passage of the nation's federal pure food laws and the creation of what today is the U.S. Food and Drug Administration. In 1968 *The Des Moines Register* won a Pulitzer Prize for a series of articles focusing on unsanitary conditions in non-federally inspected meatpacking plants in Iowa. The newspaper articles resulted in a statewide meat inspection program for plants not subject to federal meat inspection.

Over the years other developments have created public awareness about food safety, including the controversial use of growth-boosting additives fed to livestock, poultry and dairy animals. Concern also has been exhibited because of the use of agricultural chemicals such as pesticides and herbicides on fruits, vegetables and cereal crops.

There have been incidents where substances identified as carcinogenic (cancer-causing) brought national publicity. One situation in the late 1950s involved a herbicide used in cranberry bogs. Another pertained to a chemical sprayed on apple orchards in the 1980s. A third episode related to a growth-boosting additive fed by many farmers to beef cattle, sheep and poultry after its discovery in 1954 and its banning in the 1970s. These matters created a public awareness and concern about the presence of suspected cancer-causing substances in common food items.

This interest in the basic wholesomeness of food spawned the development of "organic food" outlets, with special stores, and organic farmers' markets. This movement was accompanied by interest in labeling or identifying truly organically-grown, chemical-free food products ranging from vegetables and fruits to meat and meat products. After years of squabbling over the definition of "organic," the FDA

Top 10 States in Pork Production

State	Hog Farms	Number of hogs sold
1. North Carolina	2,666	36.4 million
2. Iowa	18,370	27.5 million
3. Minnesota	7,717	13 million
4. Missouri	5,183	8.5 million
5. Nebraska	6,296	7.6 million
6. Indiana	6,623	7.6 million
7. Ohio	5,938	3.5 million
8. Kansas	2,873	3.2 million
9. Pennsylvania	2,971	2.5 million
10. Michigan	2,690	2.2 million

SOURCE: USDA Census of Agriculture, 1997

Commercial Hog Slaughter

1. Iowa	29.6 million
2. North Carolina	10 million
3. Illinois	9.5 million
4. Minnesota	8.4 million
5. Nebraska	6.4 million
6. Indiana	6.2 million
7. Oklahoma	4.5 million
8. South Dakota	4.1 million
9. Missouri	4 million
10. Virginia	3.9 million

SOURCE: USDA, 1999

(Note: The difference between hogs sold and hogs slaughtered is the fact that some hogs are butchered at non-commercial or federally-inspected plants or local meat lockers. Also, some hogs are marketed as "feeder pigs," and fed to market/slaughter weights elsewhere. Missouri and Wisconsin export young feeder pigs to Iowa buyers, for example)

Top 10 States in Tobacco Production

1. North Carolina	714 million pounds
2. Kentucky	427.7 million pounds
3. Rhode Island	125 million pounds
4. Virginia	111.1 million pounds
5. Tennessee	104.5 million pounds
6. Georgia	89.3 million pounds
7. Florida	19.6 million pounds
8. Indiana	18.7 million pounds
9. Ohio	18.6 million pounds
10. Pennsylvania	15.4 million pounds

SOURCE: USDA, 1997

Top 10 States in Cotton Production

1. Texas	5.3 million bales
2. California	2.6 million bales
3. Georgia	1.9 million bales
4. Mississippi	1.8 million bales
5. Arkansas	1.7 million bales
6. Louisiana	1.1 million bales
7. North Carolina	930,000 bales
8. Arizona	865,000 bales
9. Tennessee	656,000 bales
10. Missouri	580,000 bales

SOURCE: USDA, 1997

Top 10 Beef Cattle States

State	Number of Cattle
1. Texas	13.9 million head
2. Nebraska	6.5 million head
3. Kansas	6.5 million head
4. Oklahoma	5.2 million head
5. California	5.1 million head
6. Missouri	4.4 million head
7. South Dakota	3.9 million head
8. Iowa	3.7 million head
9. Wisconsin	3.4 million head
10. Colorado	3.2 million head

SOURCE: USDA, 1997

adopted guidelines in 2001 for truth in labeling and marketing organic foods.

In addition, the public became concerned about water and air pollution related to or linked to industrial or agricultural accidental spills. Efforts have begun to create conservation zones through the use of "green belts" or buffer strips that are seeded with native grasses to filter runoff water so it doesn't contaminate ground or surface water. In some cases wetlands that were drained to grow crops are now being restored to help absorb runoff water that might damage or pollute the natural environment, and to filter out undesirable elements that might affect water quality.

As a result of such environmental concerns, several states have enacted laws requiring large livestock, poultry or dairy operators to obtain permits from state regulatory agencies in order to stay in business or to build new facilities. These permits are issued only after the parties involved file an acceptable manure disposal plan. To date such restrictions have been in effect only at the state levels, although interest has existed in possibly seeking federal standards concerning the size and management requirements of large livestock, poultry or dairy enterprises.

Some conservation-minded farmers began to champion what became known as "sustainable agriculture," where more attention was given to preserving the inherent fertility of existing natural resources as contrasted to intensive farm-

Top 10 Sheep States

State	Number of Sheep
1. Texas	1.2 million head
2. California	800,000 head
3. Wyoming	570,000 head
4. Colorado	440,000 head
5. South Dakota	420,000 head
6. Utah	400,000 head
7. Montana	370,000 head
8. New Mexico	290,000 head
9. Idaho	275,000 head
10. Iowa	265,000 head

SOURCE: USDA, 1997

Top 10 States for Red Meat Production (Dressed weight)

State	Pounds of Meat/Year
1. Nebraska	6.9 million lbs.
2. Iowa	6.3 million lbs.
3. Kansas	6.2 million lbs.
4. Texas	4.9 million lbs.
5. Illinois	2.6 million lbs.
6. Colorado	2.1 million lbs.
7. Minnesota	2 million lbs.
8. North Carolina	1.9 million lbs.
9. Wisconsin	1.3 million lbs.
10. Indiana	1.2 million lbs.

SOURCE: USDA, 1997

ing practices. In hopes that this movement would become adopted widely, a center for sustainable agriculture was established at Iowa State University to help educate farmers concerning different farming systems.

1990s • CONTAMINATED CORN ~ In the 1990s, when borer-resistant and higher protein corn varieties were developed, questions arose in some sectors and some nations about the human safety of genetically-modified food and feed crops. One genetically-modified crop was a variety of corn which yields a protein that kills the European corn borer but at the same time can be toxic to some humans. The U.S. Food and Drug Administration (FDA) approved this type of corn marketed under the brand name StarLink for livestock feeding only, and not for human use.

1990s • MAD COW AND OTHER DEADLY DISEASES ~ British health authorities directed an extensive and costly campaign to combat an out-break of mad cow disease in 2000. The United States and other nations imposed embargoes on any importation of meat and meat products from England, while suspect herds of cattle were destroyed. The U.S. also issued a feed ban on all rations containing animal parts from sheep, goats or cattle.

In addition to the "mad cow" disease, which has never been found in the United States, there are other highly

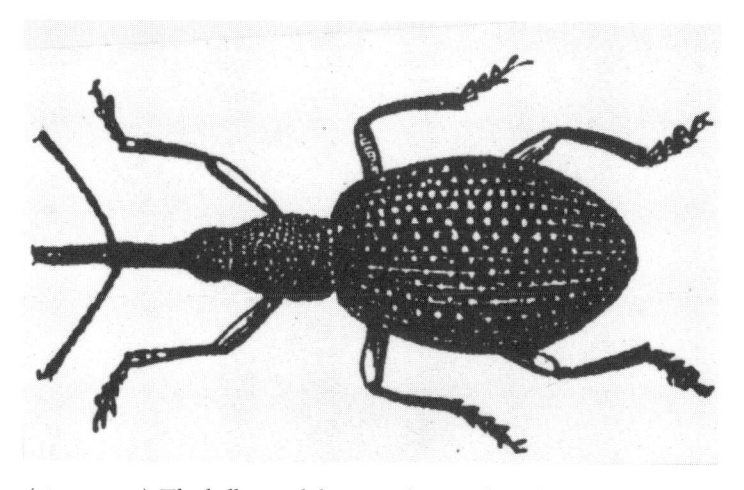

(circa 1900) The boll weevil devastated crops throughout the southern states of America.

1990s

infectious livestock diseases in the world for which there is no cure. The list includes African Swine Fever and foot and mouth disease, which affects cloven-footed animals (cattle, hogs, sheep and goats). An outbreak of any of these three dread diseases would represent a serious threat to the nation's food supply.

1998-2000 • BREEDING PRACTICES AND LIVESTOCK CLONING ~ The use of artificial insemination in farm animals, particularly in dairy cattle breeding, became commonplace in mid-century after its commercial introduction before World War II. Farmers who once maintained their own bulls, which at times became unruly and dangerous, quickly adopted the use of commercial studs, which often represented improved genetic potential that upgraded their herds for beef or dairy purposes.

The use of superior sires available through breeding cooperatives became popular, and milk production per cow greatly increased. Then followed efforts to increase the progeny prolificacy of farm animals through the use of fertility drugs and surrogate or host mothers for fertilized eggs and embryos. The offspring of prized animals greatly increased as a result.

Late in the century cloning became a distinct possibility, and then a reality. It represents an exciting genetic breakthrough with all kinds of potential to enhance future food supplies by improved performances in meat and dairy animals. The cloning activity on the heels of basic gene-splicing and gene-engineering in laboratory conditions opens up a new era of biotechnology, but at the same time raises many ethical and other questions.

Other questions beyond breeding and cloning arose in the food safety arena in the United States when there were isolated outbreaks of *e. Coli*, a human pathogen which can prove fatal to the very young, elderly or those whose immune systems are weakened. In 1998 *e. Coli* bacteria found in contaminated hamburgers served in some fast food chains killed several people and made many others sick. As a result, millions of pounds of hamburger were recalled after discovery of contamination following an illness outbreak in Nebraska.

In 2000 the USDA developed new rapid tests which detect *e. Coli* and salmonella pathogens much faster than previous inspection systems. The government agency reported that in 1996 as many as 5 million illnesses and 4,500 deaths in the United States had been caused by unsafe

---

Foot and mouth disease poses no danger to humans. "Mad cow" disease is known as "bovine spongiform encephalopathy" and is linked with a deadly human disease called "Creutzfeldt-Jakob Disease," which comes from eating infected meat from animals afflicted with "mad cow" disease.

A ban on the importation of livestock and fresh or frozen meat products from the European Union was ordered in mid-March 2001 by the U.S. Government as a precautionary measure after an outbreak of foot and mouth disease occurred in Britain. The last outbreak of this virulent disease in the U.S. was in 1929 in California. In 1924-25 in California the disease resulted in 58,791 head of cattle, 58,791 swine, 28,382 sheep, and 1,391 goats being destroyed because of infection or exposure. Also, 22,214 deer in the Stanislaus National Forest in California were killed.

The worst outbreak took place in 1914-15 when the disease was found in 26 states, the District of Columbia and the Union Stock Yards in Chicago.

Genetic Engineering and Growth Hormones

In March 2001 the USDA agreed to pay $20 million to purchase genetically-engineered corn seed. The American Seed Trade Association estimated that only one percent of the 40 million bags of seed corn to be sold to farmers in 2001 by the nation's 250 seed firms contained biotech seeds. A bag contained 80,000 kernels and sold for about $75 to $80. The National Corn Growers Association has warned farmers to buy only seed certified free of StarLink in order to encourage genetic research for alternative products.

Controversy developed after StarLink-tainted corn was found in food items such as fast-food tacos produced by Taco Bell. The grain trade theorized that the contaminated corn may have come from fields that naturally cross-pollinated with StarLink corn, or from the mere accidental co-mingling of grain in transit.

A great deal of financial risk was involved in the case of contaminated corn causing the marketer to later agree to reimburse farmers and others who sustained losses because this type of corn entered the food chain. The firm paid 25 cents per bushel of contaminated grain, and estimated that farmers and grain firms in 17 states could collect up to a billion dollars in cash payments, based on company records. Of this total, it was predicted that 40 percent of the contaminated crop cases originated in the nation's No. 1 corn state, Iowa.

Criticism of the food supply isn't new, although the most recent publicity about genetically-modified food and feed products demonstrates modern concerns about basic food-related illnesses as well as genuine fear of new bio-tech food items. The current debate overshadows the public concern that earlier existed because of the widespread use of growth hormones and substances used widely by American livestock, poultry and dairy producers and feeders. Some of the critics of biotechnology and genetic engineering warned of the possible creation of what they call "Frankenfoods," a term linked to the mythical man-created monster Frankenstein.

In the wake of controversy that followed the discovery of banned products in common food products, mainly traces of StarLink corn substances found in common food products, the Food and Drug Administration announced a plan where food companies would consult with the agency before marketing modified food items. Under the plan, firms would notify the FDA at least four months before new modified products would be available to consumers. At the same time the agency chose not to require special labels on food products that contain genetically modified substances. Another critic of the government's failure to regulate genetically-modified foods, Rebecca Goldburg, a scientist representing a group called Environmental Defense, urged immediate action to establish guidelines for the food industry regarding any genetically-altered food item.

However, the most opposition to the new family of genetically-modified food-crops so far has originated in Europe. This in turn has affected grain exports from the United States. Many questions have been raised by Europeans concerning such controversial matters related to American exports because of the use of such products as growth-boosters, hormones and drugs in rations fed to livestock and poultry in the U.S. Food safety concerns have grown in the wake of the "mad cow" epidemic in England and France, as well as the outbreak of foot and mouth disease in early 2001 in the United Kingdom and later in other European countries.

1990s

meat, poultry and egg products. The USDA said that by 1999 there had been between 22 percent and 70 percent reduction in food borne illnesses caused by common pathogens on meat and poultry. In addition, the USDA in February 2000, began using irradiation on raw meat products such as ground beef and steaks to significantly reduce or eliminate *e. Coli* and other hazardous microorganisms.

The USDA also announced a plan to improve the safety of eggs and to reduce salmonella-related illnesses. It involves on-farm inspections coupled with an in-shell pasteurization of eggs. The new Salmonella program is expected to cut illnesses in half by 2005.

1990s • Cruelty to Animals Issues

~ The food safety controversy was extended by groups concerned about the treatment and care of animals and poultry. One of these organizations, PETA (People for the Ethical Treatment of Animals), frequently staged public demonstrations with its members dressed up in costumes resembling animals or vegetables and parading in public at livestock meetings and other events. PETA also published newspaper advertisements condemning the consumption of meat, and comparing meat packing plant operations to human cannibalism.

Other organizations more traditionally involved in environmental than agricultural issues, such as the Green Party, Sierra Club and Environmental Defense Fund added animal and agricultural concerns to their list of causes.

1970-2000 • Finding New Uses for Old Crops and for Land

~ Over the many years of surplus production of grains, farmers and agricultural interests have urged efforts to discover new uses for old crops like corn and new crops like soybeans. One highly touted use of corn is as a source of ethanol, a fuel additive for motor vehicles. "Make my cornfield your oil field" was a slogan developed in Iowa in the 1970s when the first alternative fuel was being touted. A major energy crunch was in effect that put the nation's focus on American dependence on foreign oil.

Ethanol remains somewhat controversial. One criticism relates to the tax break ethanol enjoys compared to other fuels, and whether it is just another form of pork barrel subsidy to farmers. While there is some interest among farmers in building cooperative ethanol plants, the major ethanol supplier is ADM, an agribusiness conglomerate based in Minneapolis, with ethanol plants in Illinois and Iowa.

Soybean growers promoted a new product, a soy-based bio-diesel fuel. This

(circa 1945) A health worker for the U.S. Food and Drug Administration checks on a sample in a laboratory to ensure that it is safe for human consumption.

bio-diesel fuel, said to help protect the environment, also represents a potential new market for this crop. Interestingly, the great American industrialist Henry Ford was an early proponent of the soybean, and at one time his research scientists unsuccessfully tried to build an entire car out of the versatile soybean. The auto industry, however, put the soybean to good use in a variety of plastic trim products in several lines of new cars.

In October 2000, U.S. Secretary of Agriculture Dan Glickman announced a $300-million bio-energy program designed to expand the production of "environmentally friendly fuels" made from corn, soybeans and other crops. This program promotes bio-fuels like ethanol (made from corn) and bio-diesel (made from soybeans). The government will make payments to firms that increase their purchases of crops to expand production of ethanol and other bio-fuels.

The USDA also begin solicitation of proposals for pilot projects where vegetation like switchgrass would be harvested and then burned to produce energy. In the 1980s scientists developed a new soybean product, a hard, plywood-like wall board that is used in the production of furniture.

The government also encouraged the development of energy-producing wind-powered generators as a modern source of electricity and other energy. Clusters of windmill-generators have begun to emerge in certain areas of the nation, from California to the prairies of the Great Plains and the Midwest, thanks to legislation which provides financial incentives.

1980-2000 • NEW TYPES OF CROPS
~ Interest in finding a new, more profitable crop to grow on the fertile plains of the Midwest included some exotic crops. In the 1980s, on the heels of a farm economic crisis period, a new group organized and began promoting the Jerusalem artichoke as an alternative to the common corn-soybean crop rotation used by most Midwest farmers.

The Jerusalem artichoke was advertised as "the best thing in farming since soybeans" to hit the Corn Belt. "It's food, feed and fuel all combined into one," the promoters added. They urged the planting of the Jerusalem artichoke because the roots supposedly yielded a healthy human food, while the bushy leafy portion could be used for either livestock feed or biomass for fuel or energy production purposes.

What the proponents didn't explain was the fact that there was no realistic market for any of the crop parts, and that the Jerusalem artichoke also has weed-like potential. This plant can be extremely difficult to remove if a farmer decides to go back to raising corn and soybeans.

In 2000, the USDA made botanical history by introducing the "cuke-melon," a first-ever cross of a cucumber with a melon. This new "cuke-melon" serves as a genetic bridge, the USDA scientists said, to allow the shuffling of useful genes, especially those boasting resistance traits that thwart diseases and pests, between both crops—cukes and melons.

At the same time the USDA scientists developed a space age-remedy for an old potato foe, the fungus which caused the great Irish potato famine of the 1840s. The researchers discovered a means to identify the fungus pathogens early enough to give the growers a timely start on curbing the disease before it impacts potato crop yields.

1996-2000 • EXPORT MARKETS IMPORTANT TO FARM ECONOMY ~ Foreign markets represent an important element in the nation's balance of trade as well as

1996-2000

a vital part of the nation's farm economy. The record export of agricultural products was set in 1996 when nearly $60 billion worth of U.S. farm commodities and related products were exported.

The major buyer in 1996 was a quartet of markets known in the export/import trade as "the Big Four" (Japan, China, Taiwan and Hong Kong). This foursome bought nearly one-third of the total farm exports that year, with $19 billion worth of purchases. NAFTA (a trade agreement uniting the U.S., Canada and Mexico—the North American Free Trade Agreement) was the second biggest market ($16 billion).

In 1997 Asia (including the Big Four) represented the most important regional market for America's farmers, with $23.9 billion of agricultural products shipped to that part of the world from the U.S. The European Union ranked second, with nearly $9 billion in purchases that year.

Individually in 1997, Japan was the biggest single customer for the American farmer, with purchases totaling $10.7 billion; second that year was Canada ($6.6 billion), followed by Mexico ($5 billion) and South Korea ($3.3 billion). The former Soviet Union bought only $1.3 billion worth of agricultural products.

Grains and feeds represented the biggest category of farm exports ($16.5 billion) followed by oilseeds (soybeans and other commodities) and oilseed products ($11.5 billion), horticultural products such as fruits, vegetables, and nuts ($10.6 billion), livestock and meat products ($7.7 billion), and poultry and poultry products ($2.9 billion). Tobacco exports totaled $1.6 billion.

Corn topped the list of commodities shipped to overseas markets, with 46.6 million metric tons exported in 1997. Wheat was the second biggest, at 24.9 million metric tons, followed closely by soybeans at 24.1 million metric tons. The export totals also included 6.3 million metric tons of soybean oil meal that is an important feed ingredient for livestock and poultry.

At the same time agricultural products are imported into the U.S. The USDA reported agricultural imports totaled $38.9 billion in 2000, a year when exports of farm commodities and related products were estimated at $50.9 billion. That left a favorable trade balance of $12 billion, the smallest favorable trade balance in several years, according to the USDA.

1997-2000 • CORN AND SOYBEAN PRODUCTION

While corn is used for other things, its chief use is as a feed grain for livestock, dairy cows and poultry. For many years the acreage devoted to corn production has surpassed that of any other commercial crop grown in the U.S. In 2000 Iowa farmers harvested 1.74 billion bushels of corn to continue to reign in as the number one corn state, as tradi-

Top 10 Top Corn-producing States

State	Bushels of Corn/Year
1. Iowa	1.74 million bu.
2. Illinois	1.67 billion bu.
3. Nebraska	1.01 million bu.
4. Minnesota	957 million bu.
5. Indiana	816 million bu.
6. Ohio	485 million bu.
7. South Dakota	431 million bu.
8. Kansas	420 million bu.
9. Wisconsin	408 million bu.
10. Michigan	254 million bu.

SOURCE: USDA, Crop Year 2000

tionally is the case. Illinois ranked second with 1.67 billion bushels.

Nebraska, which is called "the Cornhusker State," was third, thanks to irrigation development. The record corn crop nationally was 10.1 billion bushels harvested in 1994. The record yield per acre was 138.6 bushels in 1994.

Top 10 States in the Production of Corn for Silage

1. Wisconsin	10.9 million tons
2. California	8.2 million tons
3. New York	8.2 million tons
4. Pennsylvania	7.6 million tons
5. Minnesota	6.5 million tons
6. Michigan	4.7 million tons
7. South Dakota	4.1 million tons
8. Iowa	3.4 million tons
9. Nebraska	3.0 million tons
10. Colorado	2.5 million tons

SOURCE: USDA, 1997

The honor of being the nation's top soybean-producer is a title that generally alternates between two Midwest states, Iowa and Illinois. While soybeans represent an age-old staple in the Far East, soybeans are relatively new in the United States, introduced here in the twentieth century.

Over the years soybean acreage has increased steadily with a significant portion of the crop exported. The record harvest of 2.77 billion bushels was harvested in 2000 when Illinois ranked as the nation's biggest soybean-producing state (460 million bushels). The record yield was 41.4 bushels per acre harvested in 1994. The upturn in soybean yields has not been as dramatic as that for corn. Where the average yield nationally in 2000 was 38.1 bushels per acre, the yield in 1950 was 21.7 bushels per acre. The first published yield estimates for soybeans compiled by the USDA came in 1924 when the then new crop averaged only 11 bushels per acre.

Only a small portion of the soybean crop is utilized as food in this country, with the bulk of the crop processed into soy oil and feedstuffs for livestock and poultry, or marketed to foreign buyers.

Top 10 States in Soybean Production

State	Bushels of Soybeans
1. Illinois	460 million bu.
2. Iowa	459 million bu.
3. Minnesota	293 million bu.
4. Indiana	259 million bu.
5. Ohio	186 million bu.
6. Nebraska	181 million bu.
7. Missouri	175 million bu.
8. Kansas	174 million bu.
9. South Dakota	153 million bu.
10. Arkansas	94 million bu.

SOURCE: USDA, 2000 Crop Year

1894-1999 • AGRICULTURAL PIONEERS ~ There have been some remarkably talented people in American agriculture during the twentieth century. One of these gifted persons is Dr. Norman E. Borlaug, an Iowa native who won the Nobel Peace Prize in 1970 for his discovery of the high-yielding miracle "dwarf" wheat. Called "the father of the Green Revolution," Borlaug saved millions from starvation and famine with his discovery while working at the Rockefeller International Wheat and Maize Center near Mexico City.

Borlaug described himself as "the first person with dirt under his fingernails" to earn the world peace prize. And, as the first person with agriculture credentials to win the Peace Prize, Borlaug stressed in media interviews that his Green Revolution research only bought time, and that unless steps were taken to make more countries self-sufficient in food production, the specter of starvation and famine was a distinct possibility in the future.

At the World Food Summit held in 1996 U.S. Agriculture Secretary Dan Glickman said the United States "as the world's most wealthy and agriculturally abundant nation is uniquely positioned to lead the world 'war on hunger'." The nations assembled entered into an agreement to reduce world hunger by 50 percent by 2015.

In 1999 the U.S. provided about 9.5 million metric tons of commodities to needy countries, including North Korea and Saharan Africa. This aid included nearly 2 million metric tons of wheat, corn, rice and other commodities shipped to regions of Africa stricken with drought. Secretary Glickman accompanied a shipment of humanitarian food aid to Nigeria.

Another agricultural leader was Hugh Hammond Bennett, a North Carolina native who was the nation's first soil conservation chief with the U.S. government. Bennett was in the forefront of the soil and water conservation movement in its formative years.

Certainly the contributions of Henry A. Wallace make him one of the most prominent agricultural figures. He was a journalist (editor of *Wallaces Farmer*), hybrid seed corn pioneer (he was a co-founder of the company that became the world's largest hybrid seed corn producer), and politician (FDR's Secretary of Agriculture, then his vice-president, and finally a third party presidential candidate in 1948). His handprint exists on some of the most far-reaching federal farm and rural programs ever developed, from farm credit and rural elec-

U.S. Secretaries of Agriculture

(D) Democrat (R) Republican

1889 Norman J. Coleman, Missouri (D)
1889 J. M. Rusk, Wisconsin (R)
1893 J. S. Morton, Nebraska (D)
1897 James Wilson, Iowa (R)
1913 David F. Houston, Missouri (D)
1920 E. T. Meredith, Iowa (D)
1921 Henry C. Wallace, Iowa (R)
1924 Howard M. Gore, West Virginia (R)
1925 William M. Jardine, Kansas (R)
1929 Arthur M. Hyde, Missouri (R)
1933 Henry A. Wallace, Iowa (D) *
1939 Claude R. Wickard, Indiana (D)
1945 Clinton P. Anderson, New Mexico (D)
1948 Charles F. Brannan, Colorado (D)
1953 Ezra Taft Benson, Utah (R)
1961 Orville L. Freeman, Minnesota (D)
1969 Clifford M. Hardin, Indiana (R)
1971 Earl L. Butz, Indiana (R)
1976 John A. Kneble, Virginia (R)
1977 Bob Bergland, Minnesota (D)
1981 John R. Block, Illinois (R)
1986 Richard E. Lyng, California (R)
1989 Clayton Yeutter, Nebraska (R)
1992 Edward F. Madigan, Illinois (R)
1993 Mike Espy, Mississippi (D) **
1995 Dan Glickman, Kansas (D)
2001 Ann Veneman, California (R) ***

* Son of Henry C. Wallace, 1921 Secretary of Agriculture.
** First African-American to be appointed Secretary of Agriculture.
*** First woman to be named Secretary of Agriculture.

trification to soil and water conservation and price support measures.

Another outstanding agricultural figure was George Washington Carver. Born of slave parents in Missouri, he studied with Wallace at Iowa State College. After graduation in 1894, Carver became a noted researcher at what is now Tuskegee Institute in Alabama. He developed 300 products from the peanut, 110 items from the sweet potato, and created a new type of cotton named Carver's Hybrid. Wallace hired Carver as collaborator of the USDA's plant mycology and disease division in 1935.

CONCLUSION

There are several significant highlights in farming during the twentieth century, ranging from improved seeds and huge advances in mechanization to fewer farms and fewer workers needed to grow, care for and harvest the crops, livestock and poultry. The bottom line: never have so few fed so many so well and so widespread on the face of the globe.

The biggest change? Easily, it is the promise of the ability to feed growing multitudes through developments such as Henry Wallace's hybrid seed, Borlaug's "Green Revolution," and President Kennedy's Food For Peace program. Today the specter of genetic engineering, cloning and modifications are at the roots of the basic essence of life itself.

The only clouds on the agricultural horizon are those relating to food safety—the presence of disturbing and threatening elements like *e. Coli* bacteria, the mad cow phenomenon and the periodic eruption of the dreaded foot and mouth disease and African Swine Fever. These things add uncertainty about the ability of farmers and food producers to provide safe, nourishing food in adequate, sustaining amounts in the future for all of humanity. The burgeoning world populations indeed pose a challenge.

However, in addition to the new technology in agriculture, perhaps some of the future food production pioneering efforts may center on efforts to learn how to better "farm" the oceans and seas of the world and produce a greater portion of the sustenance tomorrow's growing world populations will need for survival.

BIBLIOGRAPHY

Bickel, Lennard. *Facing Starvation*. Pleasantville, NY: Reader's Digest Press, 1974.

Broehl, Wayne G. Jr. *John Deere's Company*. New York: Doubleday & Co., 1984.

Crabb, Richard. *The Hybrid-Corn Makers*. New Brunswick: Rutgers University Press, 1947.

Culver, John C. and John Hyde. *American Dreamer*. New York: W.W. Norton & Co., 2000.

Dyson, Lowell K., and Red Harvest. *The Communist Party and American Farmers*. Omaha: University of Nebraska Press, 1982.

Freeman, Orville L. *World Without Hunger*. New York: Frederick A. Praeger, 1968.

Garst, Jonathan. *No Need For Hunger*. New York: Random House, 1963.

Harl, Neil E. *The Farm Debt Crisis of the 1980s*. Ames: Iowa State University Press, 1990.

Heady, Earl O. *Roots of the Farm Problem*. Ames: Iowa State University, 1965.

Hurt, R. Douglas. *The Dust Bowl: An Agricultural and Social History*. Chicago: Nelson-Hall, Inc., 1981.

Kirkendall, Richard S. *The Annals of Iowa*. Vol. 47, No. 2, Iowa State Historical Society, 1983.

Muhm, Don. *The NFO, A Farm Belt Rebel*. Red Wing, MN: Lone Oak Press, Ltd., 1999.

Paarlberg, Don. *The Agricultural Revolution of the Twentieth Century*. Ames: Iowa State University Press, 1999.

Plambeck, Herb. *Corporate Farming and The Family Farm*. Ames: Iowa State University Press, 1970.

Saloutos, Theodore. *The American Farmer and The New Deal*. Ames: Iowa State University, 1982.

Spitzer, Robert R. *No Need For Hunger: How the U.S. Can Help the World's Hungry to Help Themselves*. Danville, IL: Interstate Printers & Publishers, 1981.

Woods, Thomas A. *Knights of the Plow*. Ames: Iowa State University Press, 1991.

INTERNET RESOURCES

PRODUCE FARMING AND MARKETING
Links to seeding, planting, growing, producing and marketing commercial vegetable and other produce operations.
http://agriculture.about.com/cs/produce/index.htm

SOYBEAN FARMING AND MARKETING
Information about the growth, harvesting, production and marketing of soybeans.
http://agriculture.about.com/cs/soybean1/index.htm

ORGANIC AND HERBAL FARMING
Information about techniques, trends, how-to's and conditioning.
http://agriculture.about.com/cs/organicandherbal1/index.htm (About Agriculture)

ORGANIC GARDENING AND FARMING IN THE UNITED STATES
Practical and legal information, plus links to organic associations.
http://environment.about.com/cs/organicgardening/index.htm

POULTRY FARMING
A resource center for poultry raisers and farmers. Links to topics about feeding, caring, marketing and profiting in the poultry industry.
http://agriculture.about.com/cs/poultry/index.htm

Careers in agriculture, farming, ranching, and horticulture.
http://votech.about.com/library/weekly/aa062101a.htm

Crop raising careers in agriculture and farming.
http://votech.about.com/library/blpages/blfarmcrop.htm

Animal related careers in agriculture, farming, and ranching.
http://votech.about.com/library/blpages/blfarmanimal.htm

CORN GROWING AND PRODUCTION
A resource center for links to information, issues, news, trends and methods of successful corn farming and production.
http://agriculture.about.com/cs/corn1/index.htm

WOMEN IN AGRICULTURE
Women currently operate 8.6 percent of all working farms in America, according to the 1997 Census of Agriculture.
http://usgovinfo.about.com/library/weekly/aa010101a.htm

Don Muhm

Fashion

~

(circa 1934) Thelma Todd (1905 - 1935), the perky American leading lady and heroine of many two-reel comedies, influenced the fashion world of the 1920s, along with other movie stars of her day.

TIMELINE

1990-1919 ~ Discarding the Corset

Paul Poiret discards corsets (1909) / Gibson Girl anticipates modern woman's wardrobe (1909) / First publicly advertised maternity wear (1911) / Blouses are mass produced in sweatshops (1910s) / Comfortable clothes created for wartime working women (1917-1918)

MILESTONES: Color photo reproduction provides cheap, eye-catching images for ads (1900) • Queen Victoria dies, ending the Victorian era; Edwardian era begins (1901) • Andrew Carnegie gives $350 million for social causes (1900-1919) • World War I provides new roles and opportunities for women (1917-1919) • Workers demand and receive an eight-hour day and equal pay for women (1918)

1920-1929 ~ Flapper Fashion and the New Woman

Helena Rubinstein and Elizabeth Arden start the cosmetics business (early 1920s) / First shopping mall opens in Kansas City (1922) / Federal Trade Commission officially recognizes manmade textile filaments (1925) / Mail order catalogues and magazines bring fashion awareness to every household (1925-1929)

MILESTONES: Flappers frequent speakeasies, smoke cigarettes and engage in promiscuous activity • Harlem Renaissance produces renowned African American writers, artists, and musicians • *Harper's* emphasizes up-to-date articles on current questions (1925)

1930-1949 ~ Depression, Wartime and Movie-Star Fashion

Conservative attire reemerges (1930-1935) / Development of nylon (1938) / Claire McCardell designs clothes for the American career woman (early 1940s) / Wartime restrictions on goods cause fashion to be more austere (1942-1944) / Christian Dior introduces his "New Look" to American women (1947) / Dior becomes the first designer to license his name for ready-to-wear clothing (1948)

MILESTONES: Under pressure, the movie industry enacts the Production Code, addressing crime, sex, vulgarity, obscenity, profanity, costumes, dancing, and religion (1930) • One-third of college professors are women (1930) • Five million women enter the labor force (1940-1944) • *Seventeen Magazine* is founded (1944) • *Women's Day*, *Family Circle*, and *Better Living* become actively engaged in social issues (1940s)

1950-1959 ~ Expanding the Rules of Decorum

Decade of "correct" fashions and complicated rules of behavior (1950s) / First fully enclosed shopping center opens in Minnesota (1956) / Italian influence in design comes to America (1958) / Baby boomer children inspire diversity in clothing (1950-1959) / Barbie creates public debate about her unattainable body standard (1959)

MILESTONES: Kinsey reports that more than 50% of American women are not virgins when they marry (1953) • Elvis Presley releases first single (1956) • Supreme Court rules that a literary work containing explicit materials must be judged as a whole and not by its parts (1957)

1960-1979 ~ Women's Liberation

Jackie Kennedy sets standards for elegance (1960) / Mary Quant creates the miniskirt (early 1960s) / Bra burning protests symbolize women's liberation and have tremendous impact on the fit of clothing and the undergarment industry (1963) / The Gap opens, catering to "generation gap" buyers (1969) / Political rebellion causes anti-establishment dress codes (1968-1975) / *Dress for Success* becomes a bible for corporate America (1975) / Disco has profound impact on fashion (1977)

MILESTONES: Women's liberation movement encourages smaller families and free access to the birth control pill • Oral contraceptive pills approved (1960) • Surgeon General declares cigarette smoking a health hazard (1964) • Ms. magazine reflects a revolution in women's thinking • *Woman's Day* adds articles on health and money management to help working women (1966) • Magazine advertisers begin profiling and segmenting readers (1970s)

1980-2000 ~ The Youth Culture

Fashion industry creates Supermodels to conceal the fact that fashion is in a slump (1985-1987) / Top clothes designers cross over to the home decoration market (1990s) / Internet/Casual workplace dress is accepted (1990s)

MILESTONES: Public's insatiability for intimate details about celebrities gives rise to paparazzi journalists (1980s-1990s) • Women's magazines focus on questions of dating, sex, gays/lesbians, mental health, and health problems as well as fashion (1990s) • Trendy teen glossies, *Teen Vogue, Cosmogirl, Teen People, Teen*, and *Elle Girl*, publish frank articles about self-empowerment, racism, eating disorders, rape, sexual diseases, pregnancy, and depression (1995-2000)

INTRODUCTION

Human beings have covered their bodies for longer than history records. Along with food and shelter, clothing is considered by social scientists to be one of the essential elements for survival. Clothing has been common to all people throughout all times. As part of the material culture, it reflects the social, psychological, technical, physical and aesthetic components of the culture that produced it. It also serves as an unspoken communication system that can indicate the status or rank, group membership, occupation, age, gender and spiritual affiliation of an individual.

Though the terms "clothing" and "fashion" have come to be used interchangeably, this is a twentieth century concept. Prior to the Industrial Revolution, the material and labor requirements for garments meant that most people only possessed one set of clothing. This outfit was generally made of plain cloth as cheaply as possible. It was worn constantly and expected to last for years, with little concern given to style or appearance. Fashionable clothing differed between countries and social classes. Styles changed gently over decades, rather than seasons. The Industrial Revolution changed the status quo through the development of new machines and processes that took manufacturing from small, labor intensive shops to large-scale businesses capable of massive output in short periods of time. An enormous range of goods was suddenly available in greater quantities, at more affordable prices than ever before. Previously, men set fashion trends and women followed suit. Elaborate dress was impractical for the industrialist, so his attire evolved into the forerunner of the businessman's suit that is worn today. Eager to display his success, he purchased a lavish home and beautiful clothes for his wife and children. Since the only thing a woman was allowed to own was her wardrobe, most women were interested in clothing.

New wealth did not arrive with good taste or knowledge of proper etiquette. Englishman Charles Worth created an entire industry by assuming the role of guide through the murky waters of polite society. He opened an atelier in Paris in 1858 and in contrast to the practice of the day, imposed his artistic ideas on design and dictated what his customers wore. He used his impeccable taste to advise the nouveau rich in developing an image appropriate to their financial position. He signed his work and presented a new collection every year, thereby introducing the factor of annual change into fashion. Other couturiers opened around him and the haute couture was born. Their clientele was wealthy and wanted to live and dress in the same style as the aristocracy. Garments were individual and made to measure. The fit was perfect, and each gown was a small work of art. All ladies of means sought the excellence of the haute couture, making Paris the center of world fashion.

The twentieth century witnessed the evolution, automation and democratization of fashion. In America, the anonymous little dressmakers and tailors who served the working classes evolved into a powerful industry with labor concerns and political clout. New technologies impacted textile development, manufacturing processes, information management, communication, distribution, advertising and consumer research. During the two World Wars, women assumed new roles requiring drastic change in their attire and redefining their traditional roles. The middle class expanded to a significant portion of the population, creating a large consumer market.

Reacting to this, clothing was produced in greater abundance and at more affordable costs than at anytime in history. Dirty and ragged clothing virtually disappeared from all but the very poorest. Once a precious commodity that was included in wills, clothing became plentiful and disposable.

Several themes reoccur during the last century. Industrialization led to increased production of consumer goods and rising birth rates contributed to greater demand. Technology and invention literally changed the way people lived, and medical advancements heightened the quality of life. There were two World Wars, though the aftermath from each was markedly different. Class distinctions became blurred as education and income allowed people to climb the social ladder. There were periods when the young were the prevalent trendsetters and other times when maturity reigned supreme. At no other time in history has so much occurred in such a short period of time. In one hundred years, humans went from riding in horse drawn carriages, to walking on the moon, from pen and ink to email. The century that began with Queen Victoria ended with Victoria's Secret.

1900 • WEALTH AND PLENTY...FOR THE FEW ∼ The new century brought a "try everything" attitude. Queen Victoria's 60-year reign was over and the rigidly proper repression that identified the era seemed to die with her. Optimism abounded as new inventions continued to make fortunes for entrepreneurs and life easier for consumers. Millionaires built mansions and sailed to Europe to have their wardrobes made by the French couture. The styles were copied in New York, Philadelphia and Chicago, but it was not the same as coming from the masters. Henry Ford revolutionized manufacturing with his automobile assembly line, and railroads spread across America. Everything from the permanent hair wave to the telephone, electric light and the automobile gained acceptance and changed the way people lived. Immigrants flocked to America, providing a cheap labor source.

Edward ascended the British throne in 1901. Though nearly 60 years old, he was the leading male fashion figure and widely copied and quoted. As a mature gentleman, he preferred a full figured lady, so a rounded silhouette became the desired look. The "Health" corset of the prior decade was often laced too tightly, causing the top half of the body to jut forward and the lower half to be thrust back. If nature had not sufficiently endowed a woman's bosom, ruffles could be sewn inside her bodice for a more impressive display. The resulting 'S' curve shape was alluring, if not practical. The restrictive nature of the garment prevented ladies from engaging in any strenuous activities, rendering her useless for anything resembling work. Her social position and wealth were further advertised by the quality of her garments and accessories, and the number of servants employed to attend to the family needs.

Life was peaceful and pleasant for those who had money, and there was no shortage of social events. Etiquette books were published for the industrial millionaires, and their wives were determined to present fashionable figures, at any cost. Ladies traveled with multiple trunks and a weekend away could require as many as sixteen complete changes of clothing, including hats, gloves, shoes and jewelry.

(1902) America's leading corset, the Erect Form, follows the natural outlines of the form and does not compress the figure into a graceless illogical shape.

1909

There were garments for the morning, for luncheon, for strolling in the garden, for receiving guests and for dinner. Naturally, all of these ensembles required the assistance of another person to don, as well as complicated care and maintenance.

1909 • THE DEMISE OF CORSETS
Alongside the mature woman, a new type of young woman was emerging. Depicted by the artist Charles Dana Gibson, and dubbed the "Gibson Girl," she was strong, self-confident and independent. Able to make her living as a shop assistant, typist or governess, she was the forerunner of the modern working woman. Her participation in sports, especially bicycling, gave her freedom and took her away from the watchful eyes of a chaperone. Though Amelia Bloomer advocated a two-legged costume for riding, it was generally not embraced. The Gibson Girl favored a "tailor made" suit that consisted of a long skirt, a matching fitted jacket, and a shirtwaist blouse. Many of the blouses were made at home, but by 1909, 600 sewing shops employing 30,000 workers were manufacturing blouses in the U.S. Standard sizing became a necessity, as these garments were not made to measure.

Automobiles became more prevalent and Americans purchased ten million of them in the second decade. Motoring required a special set of clothing. The costume consisted of a long linen coat, known as a "duster," huge scarves to tie hats on, dust proof veils, high button boots (for pushing the vehicle out of the mud when it got stuck), and goggles to protect the eyes. The outfit did as much to advertise affluence as the actual automobile. Once the automatic ignition was developed, driving would provide women with the freedom to go where they pleased, much as the bicycle had.

The popularity of the matronly figure died with King Edward. Primed by the youth of the Gibson Girl, the public was receptive to a new ideal. French couturier Paul Poiret provided an exotic vision with his designs. His muse was a vamp and a seductress and with her, he would shatter tradition. Inspired by the Ballet Russes, Arabian Nights and the Orient, he was known as the Sultan of Fashion. His fascination with the East resulted in kimonos, harem pants, caftans and turbans made from exotic silks and fabulous brocades inspired by artists Leon Bakst, Pablo Picasso, Gustav Klimt and Paul Duffy. Famous for his parties, his designs worked as well as costumes as they did for dress. His styles allowed for a natural posture and underneath it was a slim, attractive figure clearly without a corset. His new designs had a V-neck, raised waistline and soft skirt flowing to the ankles. His dresses gave women a taste of freedom and comfort, but by 1911 his skirts had narrowed to the point of inhibiting stride. Women rejected the "hobble" skirt, but loved his bright colors after the pale pastels and overbearing black of the Victorian and Edwardian eras. He was the first designer to introduce perfume in an era where it was considered "fast." Scandalized by the obvious decline in morality, ministers denounced the new neckline as vixenish and doctors warned of pneumonia, but women sat for hours with lemon soaked cloths around their necks to make their skin creamy white to accentuate the risqué necklines.

Poiret's designs caused women to discard the corset. The ability to move, eat and breathe opened the possibilities for other freedoms. His clothing signaled the deliberate rejection of Victorian reserve and the enthusiastic embrace of the seductive Eastern trend. Makeup, previously not worn by "nice" women, became fashionable, resulting in a blurring of social lines. It was difficult to tell definitively what social group a person belonged to, and, in fact, ceased to matter in the pursuit of pleasure.

1911-1916 • EMERGING SEXUALITY

A clear sign of the change in attitude was a 1911 Lane Bryant advertisement. Though the *New York Herald* chose to

The Little Black Dress

Look in the closet of any American woman and you are sure to find at least one, if not several simple, black dresses. Produced in endless fabrics and variations, the "Little Black Dress" arguably has been the most constant item of women's apparel for nearly 100 years.

As early as 1915, Coco Chanel was promoting a simple, elegant black dress for both day and evening. Her early versions used traditional fabrics of lace, silk, tulle and embroideries, but her ingenious cutting made the garments masterpieces of understatement. With World War I on the horizon, overdressing was considered gauche. Chanel's concern for comfort and practicality ensured that her designs would be adopted during the busy war years, as women embraced new and ever more active roles.

After the war, women savored their newly found freedom and continued their appreciation of the garment. Chanel worked closely with models to develop dresses of beauty, comfort and ease of wear. The Little Black Dress survived the Depression, World War II and continues today as the most dependably "right" thing to wear for almost every occasion. Though now produced under many labels, fabrications and at virtually every price point, the little black dress remains the standard of sexy good taste and elegance.

1910-1918

place it in the back pages, it was the first time maternity wear was publicly advertised for sale. Such things were not acknowledged in Victorian times, much less in an open forum. Like the shirtwaist, the simple fit of the garment made it appropriate for mass manufacture. Birth control became available in 1913 with the introduction of the diaphragm and obtainable when Margaret Sanger opened the first birth control clinic in 1916. These three events indicate a new attitude toward sexuality and women's activities. Though marriage and family would remain the only option for most women for several more decades, the diaphragm would give her control over biology.

1910s • Mass Production in Sweatshops ~ The sewing machine was invented in the mid-1800s and gained immediate approval for its speed and evenness of stitch. It was adopted for producing uniforms quickly in the American Civil War. After that conflict, it was largely used to produce prison uniforms and garments for stevedores. Machine sewn clothing was not desirable, but demand for ready-made clothing increased steadily after the turn of the century. The success and convenience of purchasing simple garments that didn't require elaborate fitting encouraged more people to buy things not specifically made for them. In the U.S., sweatshops continued to spring up to meet the demand, often taking advantage of new immigrants who came from Europe with sewing skills.

Working conditions in the garment industry were far less than optimum. Low pay, long hours with no breaks, poor light, little to no ventilation, and overcrowding were tolerated only because it was better than what many left behind. The concept of ergonomics would not arrive until well after the Second World War. After several years of struggle for a decent workplace, the terrible conditions were brought to public attention in 1911 when the Triangle Shirtwaist Factory caught fire. The factory was the largest blouse manufacturer in the country and one of the strongest voices against unions. Located in three floors of an old building, most of the doors were locked and the exits blocked by fabric awaiting construction. The sole fire escape was a deathtrap that ended in midair leaving only the windows as an escape route. One hundred and forty-six women perished in fifteen minutes. The ensuing public outrage gave impetus to a movement for legislation that would protect workers. Thirty-six new laws were enacted during the following three years addressing working conditions, vacations, sick leave, wage and hour standards. Although the International Ladies Garment Women's Union (ILGWU) had been founded in 1900, this tragedy gave it sufficient publicity to make headway in their pursuit for fair labor practices. By 1915, clothing was the third largest industry in the United States, following steel and oil. While the upper class still had their garments custom made, this was a clear indication that the lower and middle classes were growing in economic strength.

1917-1918 • The Effects of War ~ The outbreak of World War I brought women into the workplace on a large scale. With most men at the front, women took over the bulk of their jobs, working in farming, munitions factories, as drivers and as postal carriers. Many entered military service and wore uniforms for the first time. For those running family businesses, clothing took on an austere style. Leisure was considered unpatriotic and everyone found a way to contribute to the war effort. Seductive and sumptuous clothing and jewelry were put away in favor of more functional styles. Skirts became shorter and fuller for easy movement, and jackets took on a decidedly military flair. Their new roles as managers and decision-makers required clothing that was comfortable and practical and women liked the fact that the styles made them look serious and competent. Women's suffrage was won in the U.S. in 1920, but in truth, was in practice during the war years.

1920 • LETTING GO ~ Tremendous changes occurred after the war. It was a time of defiance and instant gratification, of crime and glamour. Called the Era of Wonderful Nonsense, it was also a time of hope, idealism and a passion for life. Innovations brought new wealth and conveniences. Penicillin was discovered, as was King Tut's tomb, and radio went commercial. Music gained wider audiences and public dancing was popular, if not exactly proper. Art Deco style gave everything a sleek modern look.

Disillusioned by the war and tired of hard work and deprivation, people wanted to have fun. Jazz was a new sound from America and the Harlem clubs where it was played were all the more attractive because of Prohibition. The young women who frequented the clubs were known as Jazz Babies or Flappers. Loath to give up the freedom women won during the war, they imitated a boyish look with cropped hair, flattened bust, and short, straight, drop waist dresses. Shoes were designed with dancing in mind, so most had ankle straps and were cut in such a way that they would stay on during even the wildest Charleston. Women smoked and they dieted to stay thin. Many of these young women worked and lived away from home, having no desire to be under parental supervision. With reliable birth control and the cure for venereal disease at hand, the flapper was able to indulge in free love. She sported red lips, dark kohl lines around her eyes, and darkened her brows with burnt matches. Seeing a potential market, Helena Rubinstein and Elizabeth Arden started the cosmetics business and by 1925 most women were using at least some makeup.

Artificial silk, later renamed rayon, was adopted for dresses, blouses, stockings and the skimpy undergarments beneath. The fiber was affordable, washable, comfortable and best of all, nearly weightless. It allowed a freedom of movement previously unknown so that unfettered young women could literally dance until they dropped. Fashion was now being dictated by fun rather than by function or style.

1920s • OLDER WOMEN ~ The reaction to the Roaring 20s by older women was mixed. Some followed the styles set by their daughters and nieces, while others clung to conservative prewar fashions and complained about the young driving, smoking and living on their own. In an attempt to return to propriety, Marshall Fields in Chicago wouldn't hire women with shorter than shoulder-length hair, and there are stories of young women being suspended or fired for cutting their tresses. Men generally didn't like the crop style so many women pretended that their hair was accidentally burned by a candle or oil lamp and thus had to be cut.

DAPPER DAN AND WOMEN IN PANTS

Men became quite dapper during the 20s. Accustomed to the relative ease and comfort of uniforms, they rejected the

1920s

stiff Victorian style clothing in favor of softer fabrics and looser cuts. As university education became more prevalent, young men in Ivy League schools contributed new fashion trends like "plus four" golf knickers and wide legged Oxford bags (loose pants worn over athletic shorts) visually bragging about their sports ability. They brought European styles home from their vacations and sports competitions and followed what the handsome Prince of Wales wore. Like him, they required silk pajamas, brown suede shoes, red ties, knitted Fair Isle vests, Panama hats and Windsor knots for ties. Unlike their sporty counterparts, female university students often wore Dutch boy haircuts, berets and smocks and frequented the Left Bank in Paris or Greenwich Village in New York.

It was common for women to wear pants during the war for functional reasons. Afterward, they were largely abandoned though a small group of Paris intellectuals, including Colette, Gertrude Stein and Alice B. Toklas, occasionally sported clothing worn previously only by men: blazers, shirts and ties with cufflinks, lounging robes and dinner jackets.

There was a population shift after the war as farm machinery replaced some of the need for manual labor. People moved to the East Coast cities looking for manufacturing work, and by the mid-1920s, the population in cities was larger than that in the farmlands. Having been away from home to serve in the war made moving to the city more acceptable as families had become accustomed to being separated. It was the beginning of the mobile society. Long factory hours created pale white skin, once the sign of a genteel person, so tanning became a sign of leisure, travel and class.

(circa 1927) A man and woman arm in arm, both wearing knee length trousers or knickerbockers. A referendum in Reedy, West Virginia had come out in favor of women wearing knickerbockers in public but an ordinance was issued, forbidding them to do so. The women appealed to the Attorney General with the result of a majority of one vote in favor of overturning the ban.

1925-1929 • ASSEMBLY-LINE PRODUCTION ~ The horror of the war, the booming economy, the emphasis on youth and the newfound independence of women contributed to a frenzied pace. Fashion reflected this with an abundance of clothing available for immediate purchase. Factories set up to produce uniforms switched to fashion clothing after the war. The new straight shaped styles made for much easier manufacturing so ready to wear clothing was increasingly accepted. Machinery and the small electric motor helped in mass production.

Cutting knives, ironing and pressing machines and plentiful labor increased the speed. By the 1930s, assembly lines had streamlined production and engineering and efficient management meant that clothing was sold in ever growing numbers to department stores, offering all prices and styles to customers of all ages and tastes. Mail order catalogues and magazines brought fashion awareness to every household, no matter how remote. Store-bought clothing offered the cache of being modern, so the independent seamstress gradually lost popularity. France was the only country that retained its couture industry and it remained the center of the fashion world.

1930-1935 • THE DEPRESSION YEARS ~ The United States stock market crash and ensuing depression affected the entire world. Foreign businesses catering to American buyers suffered as their markets dried up. As many as 10,000 people were unemployed from the French fashion industry. Many people found they had lost everything in an instant. One fourth of the American labor force was jobless and thirty billion dollars was wiped from the U.S. economy. American fashion came to a screeching halt as attention turned to the grave matters of mass unemployment and financial ruin. The flapper dress disappeared and was replaced by conservative adult clothing. The decade long party was over and it was time to grow up. Security and maturity were equated in the public mind and people were anxious for safety. Skirt lengths dipped below the knee and garments had classic styling designed with years of wear in mind. If new clothing was not affordable, old ones were lengthened. Insets of lace, ribbon or other trims conquered a shortage of fabric. The ideal look was a slim, feminine figure, which was sporty and had a natural beauty. The hips were slim and the bust line natural, if a little on the low side. This was a step toward the feminine by no longer flattening the bosom, but not yet emphasizing it either. Comfort and movement were important because working outside the home was common, even if it was volunteer work.

Shoes, hats and costume jewelry became the major accessories and a way of updating appearance for those who could afford little else. Shoes tended to be a focal point because of the longer length of the skirt. Hats could be somewhat silly, perhaps as a gesture of humor in otherwise grim circumstances. Elsa Schiaparelli produced hats that literally looked like upside down shoes or a pork chop perched on the head. These surreal hats are an example of determined optimism that better times were just around the corner. Since even those who still had money considered extravagance in poor taste, costume jewelry was accepted and worn in great abundance.

Those who managed to retain their wealth had the good taste not to flaunt it. They frequented resorts like Palm Beach and Monte Carlo where the sporty clothes they wore were the first to combine comfort with style. Some entertained in private homes where they enjoyed modern art and furniture inspired by Art Deco and the Cubist movement. Their clothing was long, sleek and cut on the bias grain to conform to the body.

1930s • MOVIE STARS ~ Movies provided an escape from the deprivation of the Depression. As many as 85,000 Americans attended theaters every week. It was the beginning of a love affair that

(1930) Showing Some Flare. American actress Joan Crawford (1908 - 1977), the stage name of Lucille Fay LeSueur, wearing a flared dress. Many department stores had "Cinema" departments that sold reproductions of movie clothes at reasonable prices, so women were able to buy exotic beachwear like Dorothy Lamour's sarong and Lana Turner's sweaters. Macy's sold 500,000 copies of the dress Joan Crawford wore in the 1932 film Letty Lynton.

1920s would last for decades. Actors provided their own wardrobe in 1920s films, and searched endlessly for slim lines to counteract the ten pounds added by the camera. As the movies grew in popularity, major stars were clothed by the Paris couture, though they would hire inhouse designers like Travis Banton, Edith Head and Adrian after the 1929 stock market crash. Hollywood stars became the American royalty and what they wore, how they lived and every detail of their personal lives provided escape from the harsh reality of hard times.

Clothing became more casual in general, in the style of Katharine Hepburn and Greta Garbo. The down side of movie impact occurred when Clark Gable revealed that he wore nothing under his shirt in *It Happened One Night* (1933), and men's undershirt sales took an immediate dive. But, Marlon Brando revived T-shirts and made them a hot outerwear item in the 1951 movie *A Streetcar Named Desire*. Movie stars were not the only fashion role models. Notorious Bonnie Parker, of Bonnie and Clyde fame was known for her sweaters, skirts and beret.

1930s • SPORTS ~ As the depression lifted, sports became a major part of life. Cycling, tennis and golf were popular, while the well heeled enjoyed motoring and aerial sports. Particular clothing was designed for each activity and the freedom and comfort of sports clothing pervaded the haute couture. Lighter weight fabrics and comfortable knits that were produced for the playing fields became popular for casual wear, and design houses offered fashionable clothing with a decided sporty feel.

1935-1939 • COPYING COUTURE ~ In the later part of the 1930s Americans once again looked to Paris for fashion. Manufacturers sailed to France on the *Normandie* so often that it was nicknamed the 7th Avenue shuttle. Department store buyers would pay a deposit in order to gain entrance to the collection presentations. This amount was deducted once they purchased either a finished design or a pattern with complete directions for fabrics and construction details. This way, American stores were able to offer customers "original copies." As often as not, though, groups of store representatives would examine a garment repeatedly, each one memorizing a specific area. Later, they would work together to recreate the design and produce it without permission. These copies were in turn copied, so the finest couture style eventually was produced in a watered down version in cheap fabric for the lowest end of the market.

1925-1950 • SYNTHETIC FIBERS: STOCKINGS AND POLYESTER ~ The Federal Trade Commission in 1925 officially recognized manmade textile filaments. Originally an effort to produce artificial silk, there were as many as four varieties of manmade fibers on the market. Confusion developed among both garment manufacturers and consumers about the different properties of each. Some ironed easily, while others melted upon contact with the iron. Some faded faster than others did and some dried quickly. In the 1950s, the nomenclature separated the fibers into rayon, defined as 100 percent cellulose, which had a cottony feel and could be washed and ironed, and acetate, defined as a cellulose compound, which was silkier and required dry cleaning.

Recognizing that new development would contribute to company growth, DuPont supported Dr. Wallace H. Carothers in a long-term research project. While working in the lab, one of the lab assistants grabbed a stir stick out of a thick molasses-like mixture of liquefied chemicals. Clinging to the stick, it followed him across the room in a long fiber. Once cooled, the filament could be drawn out to several times its original length and possessed remarkable strength and sheen. Though Carothers concentrated on nylon, others would take some of his work on polymers and develop it into polyester in the next couple decades.

Within a few years, the new fiber, nylon, had been manufactured into ladies stockings. They were an immediate success with supposedly, 780,000 pair sold the first day they were available. Unfortunately, they went off the market almost immediately as the U.S. entered World War II and it was discovered that nylon was a suitable replacement for silk in parachutes. After the war, nylon was used for men's shirts, but the dense weave made them unbearably hot, and they were widely discarded.

1935-1939 • SOCIETY IN FLUX ~ Political upheaval in the mid-1930s made for uncertain times. Fascism was rising in Italy, Stalin was making waves in Russia, and there were rumors of coming war in Europe. In the U.S., a high school teacher was put on trial for teaching the theory of evolution and Washington was rocked by scandals. Fashion was mixed, with no clear direction. Men's clothing was still inspired by the Prince of Wales and the preferred suit was one with a nipped-in waist to show off his athletic physique. Those associated with criminal activity felt compelled to look tough, so their suits were exaggerated, with broader shoulders and even narrower waists.

Jazz musicians influenced African American men by developing individual styles, from the impeccably dressed Louis Armstrong to the beret-wearing Dizzy Gillespie. As early as 1934 women's clothing took a turn to the severe. The shoulders became increasingly wide, either with added shoulder pads, or puffy sleeves and these were worn with shorter, full skirts. The feminine lower half was somewhat contradicted by the strong, broad-shouldered upper half, indicating that women were shouldering more responsibilities and burdens. By the time World War II was declared, women's dress seemed uniform-like.

1941-1945

1941-1945 • WORLD WAR II ~ Before the war, American designers worked for manufacturers who produced clothing under a company name. Paris styles had been their major source of inspiration, so once World War II broke out and France was occupied, the U.S. designers were forced to look at home for ideas. Several couturiers fled Europe and opened up shop in New York bringing an international flavor, though the industry would embrace one of its own as the reigning queen. Hailed as the Mother of American Fashion, Claire McCardell designed clothes intelligently for the American career woman. Recognizing that life was different in the U.S. than in Europe, her garments were practical and comfortable. Easily packed mix-and-match separates solved travel problems by reducing the number of outfits required to look acceptable. They were characterized by affordability, freedom of movement and comfort. She used common fabrics in new ways, cutting pillow ticking into dresses and using gray flannel for evening gowns. McCardell was the first designer to prove that clothing didn't have to be expensive to be fashionable and attractive. Her concept of designing clothing for the way people really lived was the defining moment of the American Fashion Industry, and Americans would never look to Paris in quite the same way.

Directed by the Germans to continue, the French couture industry struggled to produce new creations. Those who offended the Germans were closed down. Shortages of materials, as well as money to purchase and occasion to wear further stymied their efforts. Gallows humor prevailed as they named their garments "False Alarm," "Offensive," and "Occupation Evening Gown." The French later explained that these extreme clothes were their effort to make the women of the victors look ridiculous.

1941-1945 • WAR-TIME RESTRICTIONS ~ With all goods and resources in the rest of the western world being funneled into the war effort, fashion once again came to a halt. The British Board of Trade went so far as to bring out regulations for "Utility Clothes." Manufacturers were forbidden to use more than a stated amount of fabric, or to produce more than a specified number of new styles each year. In the U.S., cuffs, vests, a second pair of suit pants (the two pant suit was common prior to the war as pants always wore out faster than jackets) and evening clothes were forbidden for men by Law 85. Women were not allowed evening clothes, hoods, shawls, patch pockets, cloth belts, pleats, long or full skirts, deep hems or complicated garment backs. The restrictions resulted in shorter wool sox for men, and shorter, narrower skirts, small, close-fitting sweaters, three-quarter length coats and bobby sox for women. People were urged to mend, patch and make do. Old clothes were recut and even blankets were made into coats. Popular styles included berets because they didn't require elastic, wooden soled wedgies, gabardine shoes and handbags and shoulder bags so emergency medical supplies could be carried. Hair was one of the few things not in short supply, so women copied the Veronica Lake style of shoulder-length hair falling provocatively over one eye.

Noncompliance was seen as a lack of patriotism and sparked conflict when suits with exaggerated proportions were worn in Harlem and Los Angeles. Sported by young black and Hispanic men, the "Zoot" suit had baggy cuffed pants, an overly long jacket and wide shoulders that seemed to make a mockery of the wartime restrictions. The overt machismo may have been a blustery insistence that the wearer was still manly, despite not being enlisted. The War Production Board banned the garments.

A strong military flavor pervaded even civilian clothing, making everyone feel part of the war effort. Women returned to work in droves and adopted pants for factory work. Hoping to impress the women they worked with, men adopted sport shirts and slacks for work, rather than their customary work shirts or coveralls. Though fashion per se was out, styles worn by military heroes became popular. The down-filled jacket designed for aviators by Eddie Bauer is still today a fashionable item. General Eisenhower popularized a short belted jacket with a turned down collar, while the British favored General Montgomery's knee-length duffel coat with wooden toggles and windbreakers copied from the British Royal Air Force. Designers supplied new markets by working on uniforms for women in the military, coveralls for defense factory workers, and costumes for patriotic Broadway shows.

The war touched everything and would forever change the way people lived. In Europe, the wealthy were deprived of servants as the working class was either drafted or enlisted. Those not in military service engaged in work connected with the war effort. Many of these occupations provided uniforms, and vast numbers of lower class people experienced relatively good clothing for the first time. The uniforms erased all mark of background, education and former occupation, blurring the line between the classes. Once peace returned many of these former servants entered new occupations and the tradition of families being in service for generations came to an end, making society even more cognizant of a changing civilization.

1947 • DIOR'S REVOLUTIONARY DESIGNS ~ Though the war ended in 1945, the shortages did not. Everything was at a premium, from clothing to gasoline and restrictions were not lifted in the U.S. until 1946 and in Britain until 1949. Tired of wartime deprivations, Christian Dior, a young French designer introduced his "New Look" in 1947. The style could not have been more different from the efficient suits and dresses worn at the time. Dior's designs emphasized a rounded, feminine shoulder, plunging V neckline, full bust, tiny waist and long full skirt. Complicated undergarments were required to give the silhouette the proper shape,

---

The famous "Ike" jacket, attributed to General Dwight Eisenhower was actually modeled after a British battle dress jacket. At the time the U.S. entered World War II, there was very little consistency in military attire. The U.S. Army uniform had changed with nearly every campaign since the Revolution, loosely following British and Prussian uniforms and civilian fashions. Without a uniform policy, many variations had evolved and bits and pieces were still in use. This changed in 1942 when the Research and Development staff of the Office of the Quartermaster General commenced a program to standardize the Army uniform.

1947

from pushup or padded bras to corsets that cruelly cinched the waist. The garment itself emphasized the small waist either by padding out the hip line or using petticoats under the skirt. The look was completed with small flowered veiled hats, high-heeled shoes and matching bags, colored gloves and pearl necklaces. Some of the skirts required as much as 20 or 25 yards of fabric, which was attributed to Dior's backing by a textile company. The reaction was mixed. Some women loved the femininity while the blatant excess outraged others. There were reported stoning incidents, while 1,300 women in Dallas, Texas formed the Little Below the Knee Club, and 700 women in Louisville, Kentucky signed a petition against the New Look. In Britain, women felt it was an obvious move to reclaim the seat of fashion power, since they were still operating under wartime restrictions.

Neiman Marcus bestowed upon Christian Dior their prestigious Oscar of Couture award and invited him to the U.S. While visiting in 1947, Dior was so appalled by the copies of his designs that he agreed to produce a ready-to-wear line for the store. This was significant because it was the first time authentic designer clothing was available off the rack. He opened a boutique in New York and when he introduced hosiery in 1948, he became the first designer to license his name.

Out of uniform and back in the work force, men returned to wearing suits. They celebrated the end of cloth rationing by adopting rather excessive styles. The double-breasted suit was popular, with broad shoulders and wide, peaked lapels. Trousers were cut with full legs and cuffs returned.

Whether for or against the New Look, it did clearly signal that the war was over and it was time to get back to living. The overtly feminine shape was a renunciation of the male role women had assumed during the war. With a shortage of marriageable men, the shapely style likely played a part in the mating rituals that were the precursors to the Baby Boom of the following years.

1950s • THE NEW, POST-WAR SOCIETY

~ As the soldiers returned home and picked up the pieces of their lives, it was obvious they were not returning to the world they left. Too much had changed. The world was ready for restoration and

---

The "bikini" swimsuit, first designed in 1946, was named for the Bikini atoll in the Pacific Ocean, where the United States conducted atomic testing in the late 1940s and early 1950s, which says something of the cultural connections between "explosives" and sex.

(circa 1946) A woman wearing a leopardskin bikini and sunglasses.

people were eager for a return to sanity, when roles were clearly defined and everyone knew what was expected of them. They were anxious to marry, settle down and find happiness. Only now, they also wanted a share of the good life and to enjoy the same things as the upper class. Having seen the world, many soldiers were determined to improve their station in life. The G.I. Bill helped countless veterans go to college and buy homes. Suburban developments offered amenities like driveways, yards, and built-in closets and families left city neighborhoods in droves. Single family home ownership in the 1950s was at an all time high.

The 50s, called "Everyman's Decade," marked the beginning of mass consumerism. As wartime factories converted to peacetime output, all things seemed within reach. Manufacturing increased 60 percent between 1945 and 1958. Luxuries like vacuum cleaners, refrigerators and washing machines, were easily available. Mass manufactured ready-to-wear garments, synthetic fabrics, and department stores made it possible for the masses to copy the styles of the wealthy.

Most women left their wartime jobs, willingly or not and assumed the roles of wife, mother and homemaker. Having time and money, new events and activities like bowling, cocktail parties, coffee klatches, and barbecues became part of their lifestyle. Clothing specially designed for each activity was required and women were expected to be attired immaculately at all times. Many a wife rose before her husband to dress, arrange her hair and apply make-up, lest he should have to see what she really looked like. Reminiscent of the late 1800s, women were once again visible proof of their husbands' success. Throughout the day, she might change several times, depending on her agenda. Insecure and self conscious, people were willing to conform in order to be accepted.

The rules of right and wrong were pivotal to social advancement. Magazines provided "help" by dictating long lists of "correct" fashions as well as complicated rules of behavior and social interaction. Movies and television contributed to the perfection fantasy by portraying women managing homes and caring for children in pearls and heels with never a hair out of place. Few women were able to accomplish this without some level of stress and anxiety. This was the façade that would shatter and lead to the women's movement in the 60s.

For men, the 50s businessman became the Man in the Grey Flannel suit. The look started by Ivy League graduates was a suit that had natural shoulders, three buttons and narrow lapels. It was soon adopted by working men trying to fit in and work their way up the corporate ladder. Dubbed the "sack suit," it reflected the conservative and narrow thinking of the day. His female counterpart was also conservative and likely to wear a cashmere twin set, tweed skirt, pearls and gold circle pin. With Senator Joseph McCarthy's Red Scare raging, patriotism was vital and conformity was a requirement.

1945-1962 • SHOPPING CENTERS
The growing population led to a growth in retail. The booming economy, expansion of manufacturing and the availability of merchandise allowed stores to open new branches and merge with other stores, creating conglomerates. There were about 1,000 department stores in 1899, and more than 4,000 by 1950. The first mall opened in 1924 in Kansas City, and as downtown shopping areas became clogged

1950s

with traffic and parking became a problem, businesses moved out into strip malls. Sears, Roebuck and Montgomery Ward opened free standing branch stores outside of downtown areas in the 30s and 40s, and joined other retailers in the mall setting in the 50s. In 1956, Victor Gruen built the first fully enclosed shopping center in Minnesota. Offering year round comfort, department stores as anchors and a center court, it was the birth of the modern mall. It replaced downtown as the place to shop, meet, browse and socialize.

Though discount stores had been in existence since Edward Filene opened a basement to sell his father's off price goods in 1908, discount stores came into their own after World War II. Ben Franklin was Samuel Moore Walton's first store in 1945, followed by the Walton 5&10 in 1950. He and his brother J.L. "Bud" Walton opened WalMart in 1962 and it is now the world's largest retailer. Mass manufacture and discount outlets led to a visual improvement among the lower classes. Clothing was so available and affordable that dirty, torn garments all but vanished except among the very poor. Many companies provided lockers at work, so people commuted back and forth in more acceptable street clothes.

1958-1959 • THE ITALIAN INFLUENCE ~ Italy emerged as a fashion force at the end of the 50s. Long known for beautiful fabrics, the postwar Italian government focused on free trade and their new film industry. Sophia Loren helped promote the sultry Italian look and American women clamored for sandals, Capri pants and sunglasses. Travel was affordable and Italian shoes, bags and gloves were a bargain for tourists. An advance in steel technology allowed for a narrow, yet strong spike to be installed in a shoe. The stiletto heel was responsible for ruining countless floors and carpets, not to mention feet. The high thin heel forced the wearer up on the ball of her foot and caused the calf muscle to tighten. As she tottered along, her hips swayed from side to side, presenting a sultry figure. The Italian men's suit was adopted by "Rat Pack," actors Frank Sinatra, Peter Lawford, Sammy Davis, Jr. and Dean Martin and parlayed into the continental look. This shapely suit would battle the Ivy League sack suit as the most popular style for several years.

1950-1959 • CLOTHES FOR CHILDREN AND TEENS ~ Manufacturers expanded their range of clothing categories to address the needs of the vast numbers of children. Previously sold in infant or children's departments, fashion for the young expanded into ranges that included newborns, infants, the more mobile toddlers, preteens and teenagers. Families were large and hand-me-downs were common.

As the first wave of the baby boom generation approached teenage years, marketers realized that between their allowance and part-time jobs, young shoppers had a considerable amount of disposable income and composed an increasing segment of the market. Teenagers became a recognized consumer group and there was a mad scramble to provide goods designed with them in mind. Saddle shoes were popular for the teen girl, as was the poodle skirt. Interest in ballet made dancewear a popular look. Television also provided fashion news with the smash hit "American Bandstand" influencing a generation of teens.

A growing number of dissatisfied teens chafed against the conformist and unimaginative setting of the 50s. Influenced by music, movies and the free and easy lifestyle documented by Beat generation writers Allen Ginsberg and Jack Kerouac, they deliberately rejected the era's consumerism. They dressed in the jeans, white T-shirts and black leather jackets like James Dean in *Rebel Without a Cause* (1955) and Marlon Brando in *The Wild One* (1954). An alternative persona was the Beatnik who dressed in black; berets, bulky pullovers, tights and lots of eye makeup for her, and leather jacket, jeans, work shirts and black clothes for him. They hung out in coffee shops, smoked and read existential literature and fancied themselves above the constrictive lifestyle of their parents. As children of affluence, it was easy to sneer at society's efforts at better living standards. They had never endured war, shortages or been hungry.

The 1959 introduction of the Barbie doll created a public debate that is still going on. While detractors criticized Mattel for presenting an unattainable body standard, supporters pointed out that Barbie was the first grown up image for little girls to play with. Before her, dolls were babies or little girls, putting the child in the mothering role. Barbie was an adult who represented what a girl might strive to become. She had her own car and house and a wardrobe that included professional outfits for being a fashion designer or nightclub singer. Later ensembles showed her as pilot and NASCAR driver. While Barbie has had numerous wedding dresses, Mattel has never manufactured children for her.

1960s • SOCIETY IN TURMOIL ~ The 1960s brought more upheaval and change than any other decade of the century. John F. Kennedy would not live long enough to see how correct he was in his inaugural speech when he spoke of the new "frontier of the Sixties, a frontier of unknown opportunities and perils, a frontier of unfulfilled hopes and threat." The country enjoyed a strong economy, but was torn apart by political strife and the assassinations of John F. Kennedy, Robert Kennedy and Martin Luther King, Jr. Space exploration resulted in the first walk on the moon only a few years after minorities marched to Selma, Alabama demanding equal rights. Young people protested the war in Vietnam, and showed up a million strong at Woodstock, a music festival held in upstate New York in 1969. The introduction of the birth control pill allowed sexual freedom at the same time pantyhose allowed hemlines to

Barbie's Vital Stats

Although there has been some dispute about the exact dimensions of Barbie's body, the generally-accepted estimates of what she would look like if she were life-size are that she would stand 5 feet 10 inches tall and measure 35-20-32, although some argue her bust would be larger and her waist still smaller. Over the years, her career wardrobe has included fashion model, ballerina, flight attendant, medical doctor, Olympic athlete, TV news reporter, dentist, and most recently, president.

1961-1965

rise high above the knee. The sheer numbers of the young made them a force with which to be reckoned.

As the youngest president and first lady in history, the Kennedys were sophisticated and elegant. Jackie symbolized style with her simple suits, Halston pillbox hats, pearls, low-heeled shoes, gold chain bags and large sunglasses. Anything she wore became fashionable, from sleeveless dresses to Pucci prints. Though a lover of French couture, it was a political necessity to designate American Oleg Cassini as her official designer. She instructed him to make sure all her dresses were original so no one would have exactly the same dress as she. Countless women around the world copied her style.

(circa 1966) Married American pop/rock singing duo Sonny Bono (1935 - 1998) and Cher walk arm-in-arm down the street, New York City. They wear herringbone tweed jackets and slacks. Bono wears a floral peasant shirt.

There have always been clashes between generations as the young seek to establish their own identity. As the baby boomers came of age, one-third of Great Britain was under 20 and one-half of the U.S. was under 25 years old. They looked to one another for inspiration and ideas, while rejecting materialism, the gray flannel authority figure, and the restrictive and conformist 50s. They lived by the pleasure principle and wanted to try everything. While united in a general departure from their parents' lifestyles, their search for new identities had several outcomes.

1961-1965 • ANTI-ESTABLISHMENT CLOTHING: FROM THE BEATLES TO TWIGGY ~ The popularity of the Beatles brought the international spotlight to England and many adopted the Mod style of mop hair and Edwardian cut jackets, while the Rolling Stones presented an edgier street chic. Londoner Mary Quant had opened her boutique Bazaar in the 50s, and started designing clothing in the 60s when she couldn't find what she wanted to appeal to the young. She is credited with creating the miniskirt, which was an instant hit with girls who didn't want to dress like their mothers. The flapper dress of the 20s is somewhat similar to the 60s mini. Both garments skimmed the body, without revealing the underlying curves, and both were youthful fashions that would be adopted by older women. But the flapper wanted a boyish figure and male privileges, while the 60s girl was rejecting the conformity of her corset-clad mother. Sixteen-year-old, ninety pound model Twiggy epitomized the new ideal of youthful innocence. The simplicity of the mini dress was in direct contrast to the constructed dresses, body shaping underwear and spike heels of the 50s.

The strong influence of British music and fashion was known as the "British Invasion" and the "Youthquake."

1965-1969 • PROTEST AND FASHION
~ Those who were politically motivated embraced the faded and worn denim of workers and cowboys as a symbol that they were concerned with issues more important than appearance. There was tremendous rage against The Establishment as the young protested politics, lack of civil rights and women's rights. "Black is Beautiful" became a statement of ethnic pride and Afro hairstyles became popular, as did dashikis, wide collarless shirts and caftans, a trend that would continue into the 70s. Black models like Naomi Sims gained acceptance in Paris and New York.

The protest against the war in Vietnam moved from the fringe to the mainstream in just a few years, and wanting to fit in, the demand for denim far outpaced the supply. Since old was better than new, people went to great lengths to make their jeans look as though they had been worn for years. They were washed repeatedly, beaten with rocks, dragged behind cars, pelleted with shotgun fire and even buried for short periods.

Hippies were social dropouts who rejected commercialism and espoused a return to nature. Some did overindulge in marijuana and LSD, but others banded together to live peacefully in communes, largely abandoning modern conveniences. There was a desire to wear as little clothing, underwear or makeup as possible. Both men and women let their hair grow long, and the men often grew beards. Clothing was frequently unisex, and from the back, it was often not possible to discern gender. Ethnic clothing, love beads, handmade tie-dyed shirts and hip-hugging bell-bottomed blue jeans were almost a uniform. Dressing alike was more about identification with each other than rejection of identity. "Flower Power" and "Make Love, not War" was the sentiment of this peaceful group.

1963-1969 • WOMEN'S LIBERATION
~ Betty Friedan's book *The Feminine Mystique* (1963) struck a chord with many dissatisfied women. Frustrated and exhausted by the demands of 50s perfectionism, a growing number of older women rejected the confines of society and started demanding equal rights. The younger generation had no desire to follow their mothers' path into subservience. The 50s bra became the symbol of male dominance and many young women burned or discarded their bras in the 1960s. This had a tremendous impact on the fit of clothing, as well as on the sales of the undergarment industry. In an effort to provide a compromise, some manufacturers offered a lightweight, stretchy garment that gave breasts a natural look. Some women expressed their freedom by wearing "see-through" blouses with (or without) a bra. No longer supported, the bust line dropped and the lack of underclothing became clearly evident. By the decade's end, even store mannequins had a natural bust and erect nipples.

1969-1974 • FASHION REBELLION
~ In 1969, The Gap opened. The name referred to the generation gap and the store catered to the baby boomers, offering Levi's and records for sale. It launched its own jeans line in 1974, but continued to carry Levi's for several years. The owner recognized that the young did not want to shop in the same stores as their parents, or dress the same way. Numerous other clothing manufac-

1968-1975

turing chains for the youth market would follow the Gap. The highly successful company now owns Gap Kids, Baby Gap, Banana Republic and Old Navy.

The youthful styles were adopted by nearly all ages. Even grandmothers shortened their skirts and selected less constructed clothing. Since this was the opposite of elaborately built Parisian garments, haute couture lost many customers and would flounder for several years. Reluctantly accepting reality, several couturiers opened ready-to-wear lines and offered accessories for sale. Others refused to accept the trends. The beloved Balenciaga declared that "Fashion has become vulgar" and closed his French and Spanish salons.

Fashion went through many incarnations and wild swings in the 1970s. Lacking any clear profile, the fragmented looks caused it to be labeled the "decade that taste forgot." Music was responsible for much of the visual clamor as David Bowie strutted his stuff as Ziggy Stardust, Elton John sported wacky glasses and wild costumes and Kiss and Alice Cooper took stage makeup to the extreme. At the decade's end, a wave of rap and hiphop developed in the South Bronx with the B boys and the Fly Girls, who popularized athletic clothes, track suits, gold jewelry and chunky gold necklaces called "dukie ropes." Tom Wolfe called it the "Me" decade referring to its excess, hedonism and self-indulgence. The birth control pill allowed sexual freedom and the drug culture became a mass phenomena. Taste and propriety were deliberately defied as people wore garish colors and extreme styles and rejected classic clothing.

The hippie lifestyle became more mainstream with the "granny" look. Sporting long hair, little round wire frame glasses and beautiful lace trimmed long dresses, these garments were either dug out of attics, found in vintage stores, or lovingly recreated. Health food, back to nature, vegetarianism, and world peace was part of their ideology.

1968-1975 • EXPRESSING IDEOLOGY
Anti-fashion was still a strong message for those involved in political struggles. The Vietnam war, civil rights and the women's movement concerned them more than their appearance. Unfortunately, as the issues gained widespread support, people attracted to the popularity of the causes, rather than the causes themselves, joined the protesters. A social conscience was a requirement and those lacking one were made to feel shallow and selfish. Consequently, second hand jeans, the preferred uniform, became scarce and more expensive than new jeans. Textile manufacturers developed processes for stone washing, acid washing and otherwise making new jeans look acceptably used, as though the wearer had been protesting for years rather than weeks.

T-shirts became the top counterculture status symbol. They were billboards for logos, political slogans, jokes and brand names. The Watergate crisis inspired "Don't Bug Me." Parisians preferred T-shirts with American university names and crests, while people from Los Angeles liked rhinestone encrusted shirts for the dance floor and New Yorkers liked hot dogs from Nathan's. "Keep on Truckin" was one of the most famous. T-shirts from concert tours advertised one's taste in music.

The emphasis on youth continued and people strove to look young and be young. Considered trashy and low-class in the 50s, the use of hair dye increased from 7 percent to 70 percent in ten years, as Clairol bragged on the naturalness of its color with the advertisement "Does she or

1970s

doesn't she? Only her hairdresser knows for sure." Diets and exercise became increasingly important as most women wore styles like ultra short hotpants and bikinis. The undergarment industry was dealt a further blow when pantyhose replaced girdles. Football quarterback Joe Namath appeared in a TV commercial wearing a pair, convincing women that if Hanes can make his legs look good, just think what it would do for theirs.

MID-1970S • MANMADE FABRICS ~ The oil crisis in 1973-74 caused the economy to drop. There was a real concern that this would cause a shortage of the oil-based polyester fiber. It was popular because it did not shrink, fade or require ironing. Manmade fibers accounted for almost half of manufacturer consumption. Inflation and rising costs caused garment manufacturers to seek production facilities in Third World countries and free trade zones. This triggered unemployment in the American textile and garment factories. Imported goods were boycotted, but most people couldn't resist the lure of cheap goods. Popular looks included turtlenecks, Halston sweater dresses, blouses with neckties, wide collars, clingy mid-length shirtdresses belted at the waist, gaucho pants with boots, neutral tones, crocheted bags, hats and scarves for women and the now despised leisure suit for men. Both genders wore tight printed unisex shirts and tight flare bottom pants that evolved to skintight, tapered styles later.

MID-1970S • WHO WEARS THE PANTS? ~ Hem lines dropped, as skirts really couldn't get any shorter. The calf length midi and the floor length maxi length fought with mini until women abandoned skirts altogether. Pant sales increased as dress sales decreased. Pantsuits became accepted in the workplace and androgyny helped blur the line between men and women. Television's "Charlie's Angels" became the symbol of liberated women in a traditionally male role. The show reinforced the braless look and hair stylists everywhere copied Farrah Fawcett's close fitting feathered hair.

Young men growing up as baby boomers were so confused about what to wear that John Malloy published *Dress for Success* in 1975. This became a bible for those interested in working for corporate America and advised men how to shop so they would present a serious business image. Like the "how to" books of the late 1800s and the 1950s, the formula was widely adopted and created an era of look-alikes reminiscent of 50s conformity. He later published a companion book for corporate women, though it did not enjoy the popularity of the male version.

Yves St. Laurent is considered the designer of the decade for his work in presenting the mindset of the day. He produced day clothes with a masculine quality that coincided with women's rising power in the work force. He also designed fantasy collections like his Ballet Russes of 1976 and the Chinese collection in 1977. He is credited with making the gypsy and peasant look popular. YSL was one of the first couturiers to introduce a ready-to-wear line and take inspiration from street clothing. Along with several other women's designers, he began to design for men in the 70s.

1970S • MOVIE-STAR FASHIONS, JEANS, AND PUNK ~ Movies defined the decade. *Saturday Night Fever* (1977) made disco clothes popular, and sequined, sparkly, attention grabbing body conscious clothing was the rage. It

1970s

had a profound impact on fashion, so by the decade's end, even Barbie was wearing slinky disco duds, hot pants or granny dresses. American designers like Betsey Johnson, Stephen Sprouse, Stephen Burrows and Norma Kamali helped push the disco rage.

Other movie fashions included the crocheted hat and scarf from *Love Story* (1970), the funk (enormously flared pants and shirts open to the navel) look from *Shaft* (1971) and *Superfly* (1972), cornrow braids from *10* (1979), and the *Annie Hall* (1977) oversized shirts under vests and neckties, loose skirts, baggy khakis and men's hats. *American Graffiti* (1973) and *Grease* (1978) triggered a brief 50s revival. Dapper James Bond remains one of the most popular movie icons, from the stylish Sean Connery to the handsome Pierce Brosnan, influencing generations of hopeful Don Juans with his designer suits and sportswear that seems to go "everywhere."

Calvin Klein revolutionized jeans by reshaping the cut, putting his name on the back pocket, using dark, crisp denim and charging the outrageous sum of $48. They were an instant craze. Worn so tight that it took two sales clerks to zip them, many women literally could not sit down in them. Since the cost was common knowledge, they conferred immediate status on anyone willing to spend that much on jeans. Sexy advertising showed models proclaiming "me and my Calvins." It was the start of the designer craze for the masses and became the most sought after garment of the season. Other designers followed with high fashion jeans, but none gained the prestige of Calvins.

(1977) Disco dancers performing in costume at the opening of Studio 54, New York City.

Toward the end of the decade, the Sex Pistols brought the Punk rock movement from London. Their look of bondage pants, kilts, spider web sweaters and T-shirts with offensive messages, Doc Marten boots, ripped army surplus clothes, safety pins, multiple piercing and lots of metal spikes, chains and studs expressed their desire to shock, and replaced hippie love and peace with sex and violence. As the look was adopted in Great Britain and the U.S. by rebellious youth, it advertised their poverty, aggression and leisure. The look ultimately spread to the mainstream though and made black leather popular again.

The decade ended with a plethora of styles in everyone's closet. Like the chameleon, people changed their look as it suited their mood and for the first time had a mixed wardrobe. No longer willing to follow Paris' dictates, America and Italy challenged France in design. Fashionable people around the world appreciated the clean simple sportswear of Ralph Lauren, Anne Klein, and Perry Ellis. Bill Blass, Oscar de la Renta, and Geoffrey Beene dressed the "ladies who lunched," while Dianne Von Furstenberg's wrap dress landed her on the cover of Newsweek. Halston's customers loved the liquid jersey and cashmere he used in his unconstructed separates.

A major shift began in the fashion industry in the 70s as large companies bought out smaller ones. Family-owned concerns became part of conglomerates and profit demand soared to the detriment of the consumer. The trend continued into the next decade and over borrowing and spending caused the demise of several venerable department store chains like B. Altman and Bonwit Teller.

1980s • GLAMOUR FOR THE REAGAN YEARS ~ An obvious sign that the population was aging was the 1980 election of Ronald Reagan. Twenty years after electing the youngest president, America elected the oldest. The Reagans ushered in an era of conservative elegance and the message that wealth and consumption were once again acceptable. A size six, former actress Nancy Reagan was a clothes horse and loved designer clothes and black tie events. Glamour was back, and black was touted as one of the top three colors for daywear (Mrs. Reagan preferred red) and one of the top ten colors for evening wear.

Romanticism reemerged when Diana Spencer and Prince Charles were married in 1981. Their fairy tale wedding was the dream of all young girls and her dress was the most popular design to sell for the next several years. As a public figure, everything Diana wore was photographed, discussed and ultimately copied. Her untimely death in 1997 raised her to near sainthood, causing the prices of her auctioned clothing to bring astronomical prices.

The "Dress for Success" practice of the 70s became the "Dress to Impress" look of the 80s. Power dressing and appearance were so important that politicians and industrialists hired consultants to help them achieve the proper image. Department stores created the personal shopper to assist their customers and manuals like The Preppy Handbook and Dress for Excellence were the 80s versions of the proper "how to" guides.

While manufacture and consumerism have largely defined the twentieth century, the 80s were the true decade of the designer. Consumption was conspicuous and logos and labels were worn on everything from underwear to coats. People lived lavishly and spent money on clothing like never before. Sophisticated marketing put designers in front of the public and their

1980s

names became household words. They became recognizable celebrities, much photographed and followed. With so much to choose from, clothes were often discarded before they were barely worn. Resale shops offered gently worn clothes and new houses boasted walk-in closets.

Personified by the yuppie (young urban professional), the successful 80s businessperson, of either gender, favored the suit. For men, the shoulders were broad, but made of soft fabrics that gave a nod to femininity. Female yuppies wore both skirt suits and pantsuits. They were sharply tailored and used enormous shoulder pads in the early 80s, though they adopted a more natural shoulder line later in the decade. This established them as serious and competent, much like the tailored clothes worn by working women in the World War I. Sexy and beautiful underwear was popular as a way to remind themselves of their femininity. Garter belts and stockings returned, but were soon relegated to the boudoir because of the discomfort and inconvenience for daytime.

1980s • FILM AND ORIENTAL INFLUENCES ~ Movies continued to influence fashion. *Flash Dance* (1983), *Perfect* (1985) and *Rocky IV* (1985) sent the entire generation to the gym seeking to get in shape. Athletic clothes became fashion statements and were worn on the street as often as they were working out. *Out of Africa* (1985) spawned safari wear, *Top Gun* (1986) popularized Ray-Ban sunglasses and reinforced the cachet of the leather flight jacket and *Crocodile Dundee* (1986) introduced the Aussie outback hat. Michael Douglas in *Wall Street* (1987) was the role model for the successful yuppie trader, while TV's "Miami Vice" created a demand for casual T-shirts and unstructured jackets. "Dallas" and "Dynasty" provided a glimpse into the exclusive lifestyle of millionaires.

Presenting fashion in an entirely different way, Japanese designers gained popularity in the 80s. Using the body as a base, they moved interesting and textured fabrics around it, creating a new silhouette. Though Kenzo and Hanae Mori appeared in Paris in the 70s they were somewhat traditional. Issey Miyake, Rei Kawakubo, Yohji Yamamoto and several others offered an alternative to western fashion and created the first major departure in fashion in decades.

(circa 1924) Jean Wilson gives the Easter parade on Fifth Avenue a novel touch, appearing in her modified Japanese pajamas.

644 ~ FASHION

1980s • GENDER BLENDING ~ Gender roles blurred again as rock stars like Boy George, Prince and Michael Jackson proved that vanity was not restricted to women. The movies *Victor/Victoria* (1982) and *Tootsie* (1982) begged the question of what was masculine, what was feminine and where was the line between? The dominant female star was Madonna and there was no doubt about her gender. Though she wore men's boxer shorts in *Desperately Seeking Susan* (1985) and changed personas like most people changed socks, she was thoroughly female. By adopting a shifting image, she showed women that they could be who or whatever they wanted to be with (or without) clothing and makeup.

In search of the perfect body, plastic surgery became an accepted beauty-enhancing practice. Breasts and lips were enlarged and waists, hips and thighs were reduced. Circles and lines were erased and noses, ears and chins were reshaped. Eyeliner could be tattooed on and eyelashes could be dyed for a more permanent solution. The cosmetic industry provided creams, lotions and elixirs to rejuvenate, conceal and improve ones appearance. Department stores provided professional makeup artists to demonstrate how to use their products, as makeup changed from enhancing appearance to designing faces and creating a variety of "looks."

1980s • THE INFLUENCE OF BLACK CULTURE ~ An important part of 80s fashion was the contribution by the black youth culture. Rap and hiphop led to the emergence of break dancing. In the consumer spirit, break-dancers favored comfortable sportswear and brand name athletic shoes. The dance style and the homeboy style of baggy pants gained popularity across all classes; suburban white kids quickly imitated by wearing their baseball caps backwards and shoeing up in Reeboks, Nikes or Adidas.

1985-1989 • AIDS AND SUPERMODELS ~ In 1985, the World Health Organization declared AIDS an epidemic. Fashion designers and illustrators died in large numbers and the industry would be decimated before safe sex practices slowed the spread of the disease. A crossed red ribbon became the symbol of the fight against AIDS and a memorial for those who died.

With the 1987 stock market crash, the high flying, free spending 80s were over and high end fashion houses were some of the first places to feel it. The supermodel phenomenon was the creation of clever marketing to try to disguise the fact that the luxury market was in trouble. Basically anonymous until Twiggy in the 60s, media hype allowed models to attain celebrity status and command enormous fees. They virtually overshadowed the clothes they were supposed to be showing. Replacing reclusive Hollywood actresses as objects of fascination, the models kept glamour alive and helped hide the fact that fashion was in a slump. Rumors of inflated egos and non-cooperation, along with cutbacks put many of the models out of work in the early 90s.

1980s • FASHION SHOWS AND PROFESSIONAL MODELS ~ It's hard to imagine anonymous models after the media blitz of Naomi (Campbell), Christy (Turlington) and Linda (Evangelista), but models were not always familiar faces. Fashion photography appeared toward the end of the nineteenth century and actresses, dancers and society ladies were featured in magazines modeling fashions. At the couturier salons, it was usually

1990s

shop assistants or occasionally the designer's wife who showed the clothing. In the mid 1890s, English designer Lucille (Lady Duff-Gordon) was the first couturier to hold a live model show, the forerunner of what is done today. No lady would parade herself in public, so Lucille hired six girls from middle- and lower-class London to wear her dresses. Runway presentations became popular, though the models were said to have questionable reputations and were even compared to prostitutes.

French designer Jean Patou created a public relations furor in 1925 when he auditioned 500 American women looking for professional models. With the help of a panel of *Vogue* magazine associates, Patou selected six women to take back to France with him. The models were dressed in capes with a large initial P on the back, using designer initials for the first time. The modeling career has evolved since then. *Vogue* magazine has used primarily professional models since World War II and there are several well-established agencies that train, schedule and promote models.

The growth of the advertising industry has put models in front of the public, selling everything from cosmetics to cars. The models have become media personalities, often generating more press coverage than the clothing they wear. Along with the fame, came exorbitant paychecks and in some cases, difficult attitudes. Once the free spending 1980s were over, elaborate fashion shows and high priced models became a thing of the past in the U.S. In Paris, the haute couture shows are just that—elaborate performances that draw full houses. Though it is estimated that there are fewer than 500 regular couture customers, the shows are still well attended. Touted as a place for experimentation and a vehicle for promoting fragrance and ready-to-wear, the twice-yearly Paris shows amaze and delight.

As showy designs were again frowned on, basics became acceptable and fashion pared down for good value in classic, conservatively cut clothing. Technology had improved rapid information flow, so designer clothes could be copied and made available faster than ever before, making fashion very uniform across all price lines. The more basic designer-level clothing was, the easier it was to replicate, the main difference being the quality of the fabrics used. Even jewelry, hair, and makeup became very minimalist. Black and gray were the predominant colors, in keeping with an atmosphere of sobriety. "Less is more" defined the mood. Naturally, the slow-down in consumer spending served to make designers more cautious in their styles. In a downward spiral, people bought less, designers offered increasingly conservative styles, which consumers already owned, so they bought less. The young, relating to grunge music from Seattle, adopted an anti-fashion look of sloppy, frumpy clothes, clunky boots, and greasy hair.

1990s • Bulging Waistlines

Major changes occurred in mid-decade as several couture houses changed ownership. In efforts to rejuvenate the haute couture, young new designers took the helm of Gucci, Lanvin, YSL and Dior who brought out clothing with a strong youth message. Realizing that another large generation was on the way to maturity, American design also became more youth conscious, producing small, fitted clothes. A baby doll look was largely rejected, but many women did accept the body shaping and smoothing undergarments that made the closer cut fashions more attractive. At the same time, Lycra has been introduced into almost all clothing for a comfort factor.

Running counter to the youth and small clothing trend is the fact that 68 percent of Americans are overweight and becoming more so. In the ten years between 1980 and 1990, the average man at 5'9" tall went from 173 pounds to 180. His female counterpart at 5'4" tall weighed 144 pounds in 1980 and 153 in 1990. The demand for plus size clothing geared to all ages and price ranges is a continuing challenge.

Politics was not removed from fashion in the 90s. Much of the discussion around trade concerned import/export regulations, tariffs and quotas specifically aimed at the textile trade status with China, sweatshop labor, and child labor issues abroad. And anyone who endured months of the Clinton impeachment news will never look at blue dresses or berets in the same way.

Textile technology has played an enormously important role in the last decade. Smart fabrics provide comfort through stretch, breathability, shape and appearance retention and ease of care. They can lift, shape and support and are flameproof and anti-microbial when necessary. They can keep one warm, cool or dry and protect from the sun, or tan through, if desired.

1990s • Home Decoration Fashion

~ Sobered by the 1987 stock market crash and the spread of AIDS, the 90s came in quietly. The home became the center of security and comfort and people turned their resources into building cozy nests. Ralph Lauren and Laura Ashley had been in the home fashion arena since the 70s, and others followed, recognizing the trend. Whether involved in the actual design and manufacture or licensing, several familiar apparel names like Calvin Klein, Donna Karan and Tommy Hilfiger crossed over to capture the lucrative market.

Conclusion

Communication technology has simply changed the way we live. Home offices allow employees to stay home and teleconference, fax or email their work. The impact of this on the consumption of work clothing remains to be seen. But many companies have agreed to loosen their traditional dress codes, with Casual Fridays. Some companies have adopted a daily casual policy. While useful for communicating with the office, the Internet has become a major player in retail sales. The concerns that "e-tail" would replace brick and mortar establishments have not proven to be founded. Yet, sales using the Internet went up 200 percent in the second half of 1998. Details regarding credit card number theft, returns, shipping times and garment fit still need to be addressed. Or, the convenience of ordering from a company across the world at midnight, in one's pajamas, may train the consumer to deal with the problems much like consumers learned to fight for mall parking places during the Christmas rush.

Starting in the 90s, fashion for the masses has become less about a designer's artistic ideas than about a company's desire to manufacture goods that the public will buy. Consumers are carefully divided into markets and studied to better understand what products appeal to them. Their age, education, income and lifestyle are only a few of the characteristics that market research firms view. Through a process that includes surveys, consumer focus groups and instore interviews, researchers provide manufacturers and retailers with information about their different segments of society. Using that information and the services of trend forecasters, color companies and collection reports, they try to provide items that will sell to their customers.

The prevailing major change of fashion in the twentieth century is its move to the masses. High fashion and haute couture will always belong to the wealthy, but technology has allowed every person to adopt whatever appearance they choose. It is the eternal struggle between craving social acceptance and security and retaining individual liberty and self-expression.

BIBLIOGRAPHY

Anspach, Karlyne. *The Why of Fashion*. Ames: Iowa State University Press, 1967.

Ash, Juliet and Elizabeth Wilson. *Chic Thrills: A Fashion Reader*. Berkeley and Los Angeles: University of California Press, 1993.

Batterberry, Michael and Ariane. *Mirror, Mirror*. New York: Holt, Rinehart and Winston, 1977.

Black, J. Anderson and Madge Garland. *A History of Fashion*. New York: William Morrow and Company, 1980.

Calasibetta, Charlotte. *Fairchild's Dictionary of Fashion*. New York: Fairchild Publications, 1975.

Corbman, Bernard. *Textiles Fibers to Fabric*. 6th ed. New York: McGrawHill, 1983.

de la Haye, Amy. *Fashion Source Book*. Secaucus, NJ: Wellfleet Press, 1988.

Etherington-Smith, Meredith. *Patou*. London: Hutchinson & Co., 1983.

Frings, Gini Stephens. *Fashion: From Concept to Consumer*. Upper Saddle River, NJ: Prentice-Hall, 1999.

Horn, Marilyn J. *The Second Skin: an Interdisciplinary Study of Clothing*, 2nd ed. Boston: Houghton Mifflin Company, 1975.

Kaiser, Susan B. *The Social Psychology of Clothing*. New York: Macmillan Publishing, 1985.

Lohrer, Robert, ed. "Century: One Hundred Years of Fashion." In *Daily News Record* 29, 57 (May 14, 1999) New York: Fairchild.

Lurie, Alison. *The Language of Clothes*. New York: Random House, 1981.

Melinkoff, Ellen. *What We Wore. An Offbeat Social History of Women's Clothing from 1950-1980*. New York: Quill, 1984.

Milbank, Caroline. *Rennolds Couture: The Great Designers*. New York: Stewart, Tabori & Chang, 1985.

Murray, Maggie Pexton. *Changing Styles in Fashion*. New York: Fairchild Publications, 1989.

Schnurnberger, Lynn. *Let There Be Clothes*. New York: Workman, 1991.

Seeling, Charlotte. *Fashion the Century of the Designer*. Cologne, Germany: Konnemann, 2000.

Stein, Leon ed. *Out of the Sweatshop*. New York: Quadrangle/The New York Times Book Co., 1977.

Vreeland, Diana. *Inventive Paris Clothes 1909-1939*. New York: Viking, 1977.

Walkley, Christina. *The Ghost in the Looking Glass: The Victorian Seamstress*. London: Peter Owen, 1981.

The Fashion Book. (no author listed) London: Phaidin Press, 1998.

WWD "Century: One Hundred Years of Fashion." *Women's Wear Daily* supplement (September 1998).

INTERNET RESOURCES

First resource for links to any subject related to fashion
http://www.fashionangel.com/linkpages/

A site for links to libraries, listservers, usenet groups, and other costume resources
http://www.library.ubc.ca/finearts/COSTUME.html

Reproductions of plates from this nineteenth-century publication
http://www.siue.edu/COSTUMES/history.html

A time line of fashion history.
http://www.costumes.org/pages/timelinepages/timeline.htm

A history of fabrics used in fashion design
http://www.fabriclink.com/History.html

A history of fashion from ancient fashion to the twentieth century
http://www.geocities.com/Heartland/Acres/7631/costume.html

A listing of fashion books
http://good-books-bad-books.com/d-books/fashion.html

Sponsored by the National Gallery of Art, this site is a good place to begin any search on period dress in the U.S. Especially useful for hard-to-find info on period accessories.
http://www.nga.gov/home.htm

Christina Lindholm
Virginia Commonwealth University

Food

~

(circa 1947) A salesperson shows an array of Westinghouse electric kitchen appliances, including a waffle-iron, egg-beater and iron, to two women who look surprised, at a 'big dividend sale,' from an advertisement in the late 1940s.

TIMELINE

1700-1859 ~ Early American Eating

African slaves adopt New World foods to African cuisine (1700s) / Vegetables and fruits are an important part of the American diet (1700s) / Americans eat seven times more meat than bread (1790s) / Spanish recipes are adopted as Americans occupy the Southwest (1830s) / William Graham, father of the Graham cracker, crusades for eating brown bread (1830s) / Mechanization of tin can production inaugurates factory canning (1849) / Children's Aid Society of New York begins a school meals program (1853) / Borden invents canned milk (1856) / Mason and Bell jars improve canning (1858) / Great American Tea Company pioneers supermarkets (1859)

MILESTONES: Eli Whitney invents interchangeable parts, making mass production possible (early 1800s) • Cult of Domesticity inspires women to protect the family from moral decay (1830-1880) • First use of anesthetic (ether) on humans in the U.S. (1842) • Women hold first Women's Right Convention in Seneca Falls (1848)

1860-1879 ~ New Food Preservation Methods and Products

Improved meat packing plants and railroads make meat more accessible (1860s) / Ice making machines come into production by 1865 / Refrigerated railcars permit long-range shipment of meats, fruits and vegetables (1870s) / Henry Heinz invents new methods of packing under steam to make large scale production of pickling possible (1870s) / Henry Nestle introduces milk chocolate (1875) / First national restaurant chain, Harvey House, is founded (1876)

MILESTONES: Children under the age of 15 produce 20% of the family income (1860-1900) • Irish and Chinese laborers build transcontinental railroad across the U.S., connecting it at Promontory Point, Utah (1862-1869) • The great cattle drives from Texas northward occur (1865-1870) • Introduction of electricity for streetlights and factories (1870-1900)

1880-1899 ~ Industrialization of Food

Coffee roasting technique is developed (1880) / Cafeterias become popular in large cities (1880s) / Coca Cola is developed (1886) / Biardot family begins the first commercial canned soup operation (1887) / Federal meat inspection laws are enacted (1891) / Milton Hershey begins his chocolate empire (1893) / Fanny Farmer publishes her first cookbook (1896) / John Torrance invents condensed soup (1897) / C.W. Post invents Grapenuts cereal (1898) / The term "home economics" is first used and leads to academic study (1899)

MILESTONES: Proliferation of birth control devices (1880-1900) • New Wave immigration, mainly from Southern and Eastern Europe (1880-1920) • German physician Robert Koch discovers tuberculosis bacterium (1882) • Louis Pasteur first demonstrates use of antibiotics, France (1887) • Development of diphtheria antitoxin in Germany (1890) • Wilhelm K. Roentgen discovers X-rays, in Germany (1895) • Spoiled food and yellow fever kill U.S. troops in Cuba (1898-1899)

1900-1919 ~ Food Safety and Awareness

Robert Hunter's book *Poverty* leads to the awareness of hungry school children (1904) / Pure Food and Drug Act passed (1906) / First compulsory pasteurization law enacted, in Chicago (1908) / Three billion cans of food are produced (1910) / Polish chemist Casimir Funk uncovers knowledge of vitamins (1911) / White Castle chain invents the hamburger steak (1916) / U.S. Food Administration alters Americans' diet to conserve food for soldiers in WWI (1917) / A million acres of vacant city lots are turned into gardens to support the war effort (1917) / National Restaurant Association is begun (1919)

MILESTONES: Only effective drugs available for treating disease are digitalis, quinine, and opium (1900) • U.S. Army Yellow Fever Commission confirms mosquitoes as the disease carrier of malaria (1900) • 20% of Americans die before reaching age 5; less than half survive to age 60 (1900) • Crowded unsanitary tenements and undernourished people plague the cities (1900-1910) • Hybrid corn is the United States' most valuable crop, adding $1.6 billion to the economy (1908) • Introduction of water chlorination for water purification in the U.S. (1913) • Discovery of Vitamin D (1917) • 675,000 Americans die during the influenza epidemic, far more deadly than World War I (1918)

1920-1929 ~ Commercialization of Food

Prohibition causes changes in diets and food consumption (1920-1934) / Proliferation of food advertising (1920s) / Charles Birdseye develops a quick-freeze technique, making frozen foods possible (1924) / Campaign begins to encourage children to drink milk (1922) / Diets rich in liver control pernicious anemia, usually a fatal disease (1926) / A&P supermarket has 4,621 stores nationwide (1929)

MILESTONES: Infant death rates fall by 20 percent (1920) • Discovery of Vitamin E (1921) • Discovery of the human growth hormone (1922) • Development of whooping cough (pertussis) vaccine (1923) • Discovery of iron as a major factor in the formation of red blood cells (1925) • Coca Cola is sold in sixty-six countries (1929)

1930-1939 ~ Depression Years

Synthesized vitamins are sold as pills without prescription (late 1930s) / "Hollywood Diet" consisting of a few select vegetables, protein, and grapefruits becomes the prototype for fat-burning diets (1930s) / First personalized lunch box, with a likeness of Mickey Mouse, is introduced (1935) / McDonald Bothers open their first drive-in restaurant (1937) / Fifteen states have school lunchrooms (1937) / Earl Tupper begins producing plastic gas masks and signal lamps for the military (1938), the catalyst for his kitchen wares empire / First experimental food stamp program initiated, in Rochester, New York (1939)

MILESTONES: Common cold virus is discovered (1930) • Women dominate the professions of teaching, nursing, and social work (1930) • Infant mortality rates decline by 25 percent between 1930-1939 • Alka-Seltzer becomes widely used (1931) • Discovery of Vitamin C and Riboflavin (1932) • Studies relate fluoride and reduction of tooth decay (1933) • Pellagra treated with niacin (1938) • Discovery of Vitamin K (1939)

1940-1945 ~ Food for the War Effort

National Research Council advises government on dietary standards (1940-1943) / Howard Johnson's obtains a monopoly for food service on the first interstate highway, the Pennsylvania Turnpike (1940) / M&M's candy distributed to soldiers in cardboard tubes (1942) / *Gourmet Magazine* begins, reflecting trends in upscale cooking (1941) / Victory gardens supply vegetables for millions of families at home, freeing farm produce for military use (1942-1945) / Farmers dramatically increase crop production for the war effort (1942-1945)

MILESTONES: Development of new vaccines against typhus and tetanus (1940s) • Development of chemical sprays to control diseases spread by insects (1940s) • Development of penicillin, erythromycin, tetracycline, and other antibiotics (1940s) • World War II restricts production of consumer goods and controls agricultural production (1941-1945) • Massey-Ferguson introduces the first combine farm machine (1944) • Isolation of DNA (1944) • American Cancer Society founded (1945) • Sickle-cell anemia, prevalent among African Americans, is described as a molecular disease (1949)

1946-1969 ~ Postwar Affluence

National School Lunch Act provides food for needy children (1946) / Pillsbury introduces cake mixes (1949) / Swanson introduces the TV dinner; powdered milk is created (1954) / Poultry Inspection Act regulates all poultry and poultry products (1957) / All-aluminum beer cans introduced (1962) / Julia Child pioneers a television food program "The French Chef" (1963) / Child Nutrition Act targets poor, undernourished children (1966) / Federal government forms agencies to study preventive nutrition (1968)

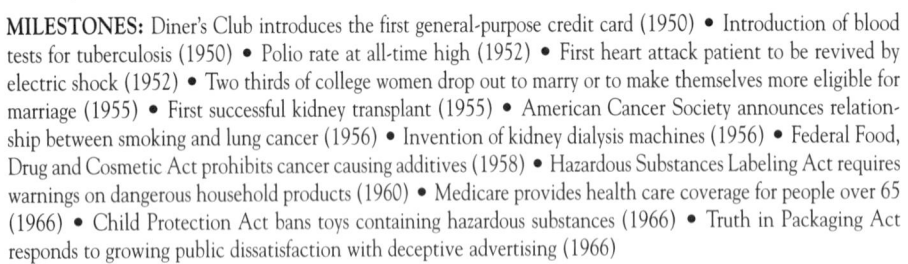

MILESTONES: Diner's Club introduces the first general-purpose credit card (1950) • Introduction of blood tests for tuberculosis (1950) • Polio rate at all-time high (1952) • First heart attack patient to be revived by electric shock (1952) • Two thirds of college women drop out to marry or to make themselves more eligible for marriage (1955) • First successful kidney transplant (1955) • American Cancer Society announces relationship between smoking and lung cancer (1956) • Invention of kidney dialysis machines (1956) • Federal Food, Drug and Cosmetic Act prohibits cancer causing additives (1958) • Hazardous Substances Labeling Act requires warnings on dangerous household products (1960) • Medicare provides health care coverage for people over 65 (1966) • Child Protection Act bans toys containing hazardous substances (1966) • Truth in Packaging Act responds to growing public dissatisfaction with deceptive advertising (1966)

1970-1989 ~ Becoming Aware of Dangerous Foods

Fair Packaging Labeling Act forces disclosure of a product's nutritional value (1975) / Artificial sweeteners introduced (early 1980s) / Microwave ovens become popular despite fears of causing radiation poisoning (1980s) / National Cancer Institute publishes dietary guidelines for reducing cancer risks (1982) / Five major fast food chains reduce their use of saturated fats (1986)

MILESTONES: Consumer Product Safety Commission provides a continuous review of consumer goods for risks (1972) • First "test-tube baby" born in England (1978) • Cardio-vascular disease falls 30 percent (1980-1989) • AIDS becomes the second leading cause of death (following accidents) among American men aged 25-34 (1989)

1990-2000 ~ Food for a Busy Culture

Nutritional Labeling and Education Act enables consumers to know about the fat, fiber, and caloric content of foods (1990) / Food Network pioneers avant-garde cooking programs (1993) / Food producers introduce products specifically for women (1996) / One of every four Americans is obese and 60% are overweight (2000) / Organic food industry grows to $6 billion annually (2000) / Average supermarket stocks over 24,000 items (2000) / Over half of all American meals are prepared by restaurants or delivery services (2000)

MILESTONES: Smoking banned on all U.S. domestic flights of less than six hours (1990) • Deaths by cancer decrease 8 percent (1990-1999) • Number of farm workers declines from 13.6 million in 1915 to 2.85 million in 1995 • Scottish doctors clone a sheep, Dolly (1996) • *e. Coli* bacteria in contaminated hamburgers in Jack-in-the-Box Franchise kills several people (1998) • Heart disease, cancer, and strokes account for 60 percent of all deaths (1999) • Mapping of the human genome, one of the twentieth century's most outstanding scientific accomplishments (2000)

INTRODUCTION

Is there a quintessential American diet? Soft drinks, hamburgers, and French fries may appear to be as American as apple pie, but this has not always been the case. The fast food industry that has popularized the burger as a lunchtime choice, the golden arches that dot our landscape, the familiar habits of eating out in restaurants, and taking out meals to eat at home are all products of the second half of the twentieth century. Whether we are taking about the fast food industry, the standardization of the American diet, increased nutritional awareness, the enormous variety of products available to us, the growth of such commercial interests as supermarkets, the application of high technology to food processing and cooking, the increased receptivity toward ethnic and exotic foods – each of these developments is rooted in a particular time and place.

ROOTS OF AMERICAN FOODWAYS, 1700s

Anthropologists use the term "foodways" to describe the eating habits and dietary customs of a group of people. American foodways of the twentieth century cannot be understood without an accompanying awareness of how those habits were made possible by nineteenth century developments. These include the standardization of food choices resulting from the invention, promotion, and use of packaged processed foods, changes in retailing and marketing operations, and the application of powerful advertising techniques to the food industry. Another extremely important development of the nineteenth century was changing immigration patterns that brought a new diversity to American eating habits. The melting pot metaphor certainly rings true when applied to food choices. Also true is the romanticized image of America as a land of plenty. The lure of a better life that drew many immigrants to these shores was reflected in the traditional American diet, abundant, calorie-laden, heavy in pork and subsequently beef. Substantial meals were the rule, even in colonial America. A visitor to Boston in 1740 remarked on the abundance of poultry, fish, and venison. As early as 1793, an impressed French traveler commented that Americans ate seven to eight times as much meat as bread, a tradition that would persist for generations.

COLONIAL AND EARLY NATIONAL PERIODS ~ Prior to the nineteenth century, it is fair to say that there was no American diet, but a combination of regional ones. Local availability as well as the ethnic makeup of the regional population determined what was eaten. Native peoples ate maize, beans, squash, fish, and game. The newly arriving British colonists brought with them a diet based on grains, meat, and milk products, and introduced chickens, hogs, and fruit trees into New England. What became known as New England cooking, which one food historian has called "one of the most austere" in the western world, combined indigenous new world foods with those brought from Europe: shellfish, clambakes, succotash (beans and corn) johnnycake (a baked or fried kind of cornbread), codfish balls or cakes, Indian pudding milk and molasses, cheese, salted fish, oatmeal, hard biscuit, raisins, prunes, and dates. Simplicity, frugality, and God-fearing customs all played a role in the New England diet. The Puritans adopted the Indian clambake technique and used it to make slow-simmered beans cooked in the Indian way – using a sealed bean pot buried overnight in a pit of embers. Baked beans, described by Lucy Larcom in a nineteenth century cookbook as the "canonical dish of our forefathers" was prepared in advance to avoid cooking on the strictly observed Sabbath. The famous New England boiled dinner, based on carrots, potatoes, cabbage and corned beef (meat corned with salt as a preservative), was also simple to prepare, with all ingredients boiled together in unseasoned water. Pies baked like bread were made from whatever fruit was seasonally available. They were so popular that a Yankee came to be defined as someone who ate pie for breakfast.

In the coastal regions, oysters were considered a poor man's dish. Lobsters were so abundant as to be practically valueless, and historians tell us that people were ashamed to eat them! Clams and cod went into pies or "cakes."

West African slaves adopted many New World foods to old ways of frying, stewing, and making sauces. Africans were responsible for introducing flavorful varieties of greens (collard, turnips, okra) to the European diet. They grilled meats, wrapped food in cabbage leaves, and turned many of their classic dishes like rice and black-eyed peas into traditional Southern favorites like Hoppin' John (blackeyed peas and hamhocks) and pilau, made with pork. The use of fatty rather than lean pork for slaves was justified by the conviction that fat provided energy needed for hard labor, and pork has remained a staple of traditional Southern "soul food" right up to the present day. The experience many house slaves acquired in food preparation enabled them to continue in such roles after the Civil War. One food historian has noted that modern brand names like Aunt Jemima and Uncle Ben appeal to this older tradition of the nurturing, food-serving African-American.

The Southern planter class demonstrated its status through conspicuous consumption and lavish dinner parties. Plantation dinners were elaborate, multi-course affairs. One of most extravagant examples of this was a Carolina wedding cake made in 1850. It was made from 20 pounds each of butter, sugar, flour, raisins, along with 20 nutmegs and 20 glasses of brandy. One author has estimated that it would have required 1500 eggs and probably weighed 900 pounds. One dinner on record featured ham, turkey, chicken, duck, corned beef, fish, sweet potatoes, "Irish" potatoes, cabbage, rice, beets, eight pies, jelly, and preserves, all washed down with peach brandy and corn whiskey.

In the backcountry areas, the mountainous regions west of the original coastal zones, frontier settlers relied on a diet of oats, pork, potatoes, and various sorts of unleavened flat cakes cooked on a griddle. There was a heavy reliance on game during the earliest stages of settlement, and deer, bear, squirrels, opossums, raccoons all appeared on frontier tables.

> One of the earliest African American Cookbooks was *Good Things to Eat: As Suggested by Rufus* (Estes), published in 1911.

Whiskey, first Scotch, then bourbon, was the beverage of choice.

Even in the eighteenth century, Americans seem to have enjoyed vegetables and fruits. Amelia Simmons, the author of an early American cookbook published in Hartford in 1796, assumed that any good meal included vegetables. Vegetables, however, were cooked for much longer periods than today, probably to accommodate those with few or no teeth.

One colonial cooking device can still be found in many of today's kitchens. This was a heavy, round cast-iron pot with a rim on the lid to hold coals. Called a "Dutch Oven," it was used to bake bread, roast meats, and make stews.

1800s • THE ROLE OF THE FRONTIER ~ The diet of farm and pioneer families was heavy and abundant. High-calorie diets were essential to generate the energy necessary for strenuous physical labor. The average male consumed about 4,000 calories per day, compared with a modern day recommendation of half that amount. John Mack Faragher in his *Women and Men on the Overland Trail* describes the daily regimen of a typical mid-nineteenth century farm family as follows: two kinds of meat, eggs, cheese, butter, cream, corn, bread, several vegetables, jellies, preserves, relishes, cake, pie, milk, coffee, tea. A staple of the plains pioneers was sourdough bread, leavened by a yeast starter that was kept active by periodic feedings of water and flour. Known from California to the Canadian wilderness, it formed the basis of loaves of bread, pancakes and sweet desserts.

Though corn and pork remained especially popular in the South, the midwestern production of beef and wheat changed the face of the American diet. Southwest cattle drives and the development of the Chicago stockyards made enormous quantities of beef available to the American consumer. Chicago's stockyards modernized in the 1860s and by 1875 manufacturers such as Swift and Armour boasted of the cleanliness of their production facilities. Railroads facilitated beef distribution to all parts of the country. Contemporaries were well aware of the changing nature of the American palate. One newspaper of the mid-nineteenth century proudly boasted: "We are essentially a hungry, beef-eating people who live by eating." Thus began the American taste for beef as a distinctive feature of the American diet, a penchant lampooned by one critic as "the great American steak religion."

As Americans expanded into the Southwest, Spanish recipes and traditions entered our culinary repertoire. By 1896 an Army cookbook included Spanish recipes that were actually Mexican in origin: tamales, tortillas, chiles rellenos and refried beans with cheese.

THE IMPACT OF THE INDUSTRIAL REVOLUTION, 1830-1900

This regional, localized diet began to change in the early nineteenth century, with the impact of the Industrial Revolution. Many technological inventions were responsible for revolutionizing the American diet. The cast-iron stove meant that women no longer needed open fires for cooking, making work in the kitchen safer for women who no longer had to worry about burns or even death from open flames. New mechanized roller mills manufactured white flour that was not only cheaper than

(1950) The perfect post-World War II housewife and children advertise this deluxe model refrigerator, complete with freezing compartment and crammed with an abundance of food.

brown flour, but also kept longer, made loaves of bread that rose higher, and was easier to digest. It also made better sauces and pastries.

Home canning of foods became safer and more reliable with the invention of screw-type Mason and Bell jars in 1858 and the Shriver pressure cooker (or "retort"), introduced in the nineteenth century. The first tin cans were handmade but the invention in 1849 of a machine that could produce them spurred the age of factory canning. The most significant food to be canned was milk, a process pioneered by Gail Borden and patented in 1856. His firm supplied large amounts of canned milk and juice to the Union Army during the Civil War.

1850–1900 • REFRIGERATION ~ By the 1830s, expanding railroad networks enabled easier and faster ways of carrying products from the country to the city, and opened regional and local markets to competition from producers all across the nation. The invention of the icebox (probably occurring in Maryland at the beginning of the century) enabled food to be kept safe for longer periods. While the ice had to be changed frequently, other innovations — the discovery of the vapor-refrigeration principle and the invention of various compression machines — were initial steps toward more permanent forms of refrigeration. By the end of the Civil War, ice-making machines existed, and by 1880

**LATE 1800S
EARLY 1900S**

some 3,000 patents related to the topic of refrigeration had been issued by the U.S. government.

The development of refrigerated railcars (and ships) in the 1870s and 1880s permitted the slaughter and processing of animals near where they had been raised. In 1879 Gustavus Swift developed a system that allowed beef to be fattened and slaughtered in Chicago and shipped east in refrigerated cars, a process that catapulted him to fame as a meat packing and processing giant. Fresh meat, much more nutritious than the salted and preserved meats of colonial days, became more widely available, as did fresh milk.

Refrigerated transport also allowed for the distribution of a wider variety of citrus fruits and vegetables. Such foods had until then played only a limited role in the American diet. Navel oranges from Bahia, Brazil were planted in Florida in 1870 and in California in 1873. In 1887 California shipped 2,212 railcar loads of citrus fruit, mostly oranges. By 1892, this number had risen to 5,871 carloads of oranges, and 65 of lemons. Grapefruits and bananas also became popular. In 1903, agricultural scientists developed iceberg lettuce which was very hardy and held up well in shipping and storage.

EARLY 1900S • AGRICULTURAL CHANGES ~ Mechanization and technology also effected changes on the American farm. Steam powered implements, used since the nineteenth century, were later replaced by gasoline powered vehicles. Although horses remained important, by the early 1900s engineers had designed powerful new tractors. These gasoline and steam-powered vehicles were capable of pulling 16 plows, four harrows, and a seed drill, simultaneously breaking and planting as much as 50 acres per day.

Overall, mechanization and new farming techniques—dry farming, the machine harvesting of wheat, the use of mechanical twine binders, threshing machines, and new and better plows—served to increase agricultural productivity.

MASS PRODUCTION AND STANDARDIZATION ~ The new machines of the nineteenth century provided the mechanical power necessary to produce new consumer goods in quantity, and mechanization brought widespread dietary changes. The period saw new manufactured products and services replace traditional domestic production. New processed foods were more convenient to use, especially for residents of America's growing cities. Some of the products developed by emerging food industry giants such as Heinz, Nabisco, Kellogg, and Campbell have remained staples of the American diet.

1870–1900 • CANNING AND CONDIMENTS ~ One of the first to realize the size of the potential market for preserved and canned food was Henry J. Heinz. By the late 1870s, new methods of packing under steam pressure greatly reduced heating time and made large scale production of glass jarred pickles possible. Through brilliant promotion, Heinz capitalized on the American taste for sweet and sour condiments by persuading American housewives that his pickles and other condiments were just as tasty, yet healthier and more convenient, than homemade.

Heinz had his competitors. The addition of pureed tomatoes to canned salt pork and beans soon made Van Camp's another market leader. In 1887 the Biardot family started the first commercial canned soup operation in Jersey City, New Jersey. Capitalizing on the newly elevated status of French cooking, they adopted the Franco-American label for their line of canned soups. Another giant of the canned food industry emerged in 1898. The Joseph P. Campbell Co. of Camden, New Jersey owed its success to chemist John T. Torrance, who in 1897 used his scientific knowledge to streamline bulky cans with his invention of condensed soup.

CRACKERS ~ New companies aiming for a nationwide market competed with local and regional providers. One of the most famous companies to emerge from the competitive scramble was the National Biscuit Company. Soda crackers and biscuits had a long history as American staples, with cracker barrels the traditional center of the oldtime general store. Most crackers had been supplied by wholesalers who distributed crackers and biscuits by region, but the railroads had opened these local providers to competition from biscuit bakers all across the country. The resulting competitive scramble resulted in a series of mergers by large manufacturers attempting to limit competition. The National Biscuit Company, one of the most famous examples of this trend, accounted for 70 percent of the entire industry's sales by the end of the nineteenth century.

1870–1900 • NEW "OLD FAVORITES"
~ Many other familiar products appeared in the late nineteenth century:

- Coca-Cola, one of the most ubiquitous symbols of the American diet, was developed in Atlanta in 1886. Devised by druggist John S. Pemberton from extracts of coca leaves and cola nuts, it was originally prescribed as a remedy for headaches and hangovers.

- By 1876 America was producing millions of pounds of "butterine" (or margarine), a new product made from waste animal fat. Crisco, a mixture of fats, became a highly popular product because it freed housewives from having to render or strain hot grease.

- A process for making granulated commercial gelatin was perfected by Charles Knox. Once again, the new powdered gelatin was a time saver, eliminating the labor of boiling calves feet.

1880–1915 • CANDY
~ Candymaking developed into a popular industry in the nineteenth century, with the discovery of sugar beet juice and the advance of mechanical appliances. The first candy machines displaced tedious mortar and pestle techniques for making lozenges. Combined with the spread of sugarcane cultivation to tropical areas, these mechanical innovations made candy available and affordably priced. Sales of sugar doubled between 1880 and 1915, and new sweets began to appear. By the late nineteenth century, lemon drops and peppermints were sold from glass cases in drugstores and markets. Chocolate was first made into candy in the second quarter of the nineteenth century. Milk chocolate was introduced in 1875, through the efforts of Henry Nestle, a maker of evaporated milk, and Daniel Peter, a chocolate maker. Fudge was invented by accident in 1886 when candymakers in Baltimore and Philadelphia made the mistake of allowing caramels to crystallize too early.

The most famous candymaker of them all was Milton S. Hershey, the inventor of the candy bar, who parlayed the emerging national taste for chocolate into a personal empire. Having first made his fortune in caramels, Hershey turned to chocolate making after having seen a chocolate making machine on display at the 1893 Columbian Exposition in Chicago. Installing similar machinery in his Lancaster, Pennsylvania factory, Hershey produced the first chocolate bar at the turn of the century.

Tootsie Rolls were America's first penny candy to be individually wrapped. In 1896, Austrian immigrant Leo Hirshfield brought his recipe for a chewy chocolate confection to the United States. Beginning production in a small New York shop, he named the new treat after his five-year-old daughter, nicknamed "Tootsie." Lollipops also owe their origin to an inventive immigrant. In 1916, Samuel Born, a Russian, invented a machine to mechanically insert sticks into hard candy, and the lollipop (allegedly named after the famous turn of the century racehorse Lolly Pop) was born.

A one-time soap salesman from Philadelphia named William Wrigley, Jr. promoted a candy-flavored novelty chewing gum in the last decades of the century. He attributed shrewd advertising to his success. "Tell 'em quick and tell 'em often," was the formula.

1880 • COFFEE ~ Until the last decades of the nineteenth century, coffee was usually made in the traditional way, by roasting beans over a fire or on the stove and grinding them at home. As with other foodstuffs in the era of industrialization, inventors turned their attention to improvements in coffee processing. In 1880, Joel Cheek of the Great Atlantic and Pacific Tea Company developed a coffee roaster that allowed less flavor to escape during the roasting process. He marketed the coffee produced by this new method in his company's stores, naming the brand after the Maxwell House Hotel in Nashville where it was first served.

By 1900 the American food processing industry had become a very big business, accounting for 20 percent of the nation's manufacturing. Its top four sectors were meat packing, flour milling, sugar refining, and baking.

LATE 1800s • FOOD AND ADVERTISING ~ By the late nineteenth century, giant food processors had begun to harness their power to the growing importance of advertising. Food advertising became increasingly central to the work of national advertising companies like N.W. Ayer. In 1877, food ads had represented less than one percent of the agency's business; by 1901 this had increased to almost 15 percent. Food remained the single most advertised class of commodity until overtaken by the automobile in the 1930s.

1880–1925 • ROLE OF IMMIGRANT GROUPS ~ Social historians speak of the changes wrought by the new immigration of the period 1880-1924, when new groups of Europeans, primarily from the Southern and Mediterranean regions, changed the face of American urban life. Before this, most immigrants had come from northern Europe, with the Irish and the Germans most prominent. Like the English, the Irish had little tradition of refined cuisine. The typical Irish diet consisted of up to 10 pounds of potatoes per day, often with little else but milk or cabbage. "Colcannon," a mixture of mashed potatoes, kale (or cabbage) and butter, was popular. German fare was also characterized by large quantities of potatoes and cabbage, along with other vegetables like beets and onions that kept well without refrigeration. Pork was the meat of choice.

What came to be known as Jewish cooking was actually a combination of various traditions brought by German, Romanian, Hungarian, and Slavic emigrants. Pastrami, corned beef, potato pancakes (latke), borscht (beet) soup and chicken soup remain popular in the delicatessen fare of today.

LATE 1800s • ITALIAN INFLUENCE ~ Although originally derided as "garlic eaters," Italians were along the most influential of the new immigrant groups in terms of their impact on the American diet. The tomato had first been introduced to Europe as a result of the Columbian exchange, and by the time of Jefferson, some Americans were growing tomatoes and cooking pasta. It is said that Jefferson brought a pasta-making machine back to Virginia from Italy. What differentiated Italians of Northern cities was the desire to continue reliance on the fresh vegetables of their homeland, especially tomatoes. Home gardening (along with canning) was common. During the depression of the early 1890s, the city of Detroit offered gardeners the use of vacant lots. By 1896 the practice had spread to some 20 other cities, notably New York, where reporters commented on the lavish plots of tomatoes, peppers, and eggplant grown by Italian migrants. Italians have also been credited with planting and cultivating the vineyards of California, where they were an identifiable presence since the time of the gold rush. There they also came to be involved in the restaurant business.

1830–1850 • NINETEENTH CENTURY FOOD REFORMERS ~ As is true with so many other aspects of modern life, the nutrition-mindedness of the last decades

(circa 1955) A scene of east meets west in San Francisco's Chinatown, where a poster advertising American cigarettes stands behind baskets of the traditional Chinese soup ingredients of kelp and white fruit nuts, on sale outside the Chong Kee Jan Company shop.

Chinese Restaurants

~

Along with Italians, the Chinese are usually credited with developing the first American restaurants. The first Chinese arrived in America in the 1820s, and their numbers accelerated during the California gold rush. Mostly Cantonese, they grew Asian vegetables in garden plots, introduced the use of new seasonings like ginger, and acquainted Americans with new cooking techniques like stir frying.

of the twentieth century also has its roots in the nineteenth century, which saw some celebrated and colorful challenges to the typical calorie-heavy diet. The first food reform movement began in the 1830s. Among the most famous and influential of reformers were:

- Presbyterian minister William Sylvester Graham (1794-1851), called the "prophet of brown bread and pumpkins" and the father of the Graham cracker. Stemming from "vitalist" theories then prevalent in France, his crusade was based on the idea that the nervous system contained a force on which all life depended. This force would be debased and debilitated by the consumption of meats and spices, by sexual activity, and by the use of stimulants like alcohol. Graham was also suspicious of any food that had been altered from its natural state. Critical of Americans for forsaking breads made of corn, rye, and whole wheat, he was best known for condemning the new white breads made from refined or "bolted" flours.
- John Harvey Kellogg (1852-1943) co-inventor with his brother William of cold breakfast cereal. The "cornflakes" for which he became famous were a staple at the famous sanatorium at Battle Creek, Michigan, which he directed. This was a vegetarian health resort founded by the Seventh Day Adventists, a Protestant sect originating in 1863 that made food reform part of their religious creed. Like Graham, Kellogg warned against eating foods that overstimulated the nervous system. Condemning meat, spices, tea, coffee, tobacco, and alcohol as unhealthy and immoral, he promoted "foods of vegetable origin" as those most likely to pave the way to salvation and "God-given health and happiness."
- C.W. Post (1854-1914), an early client of Kellogg and patron of Battle Creek. Another contributor to the new search for moral and healthy eating, Post developed "Postum," a coffee substitute, in 1895 and the more famous "grapenuts" flakes in 1898.
- Henry Perkey, an entrepreneur, who gave us Shredded Wheat, another healthy breakfast food, in 1891.
- Horace Fletcher, a wealthy American businessman and food faddist. Fletcher was an advocate of "thorough mastication," explaining that each mouthful of food should be chewed 100 times. He also promoted radical reduction of food intake, arguing that people should eat only when hungry and then only enough to satisfy that hunger.

INTO THE TWENTIETH CENTURY, 1900-1914

DIETARY HABITS ~ These nineteenth century developments continued to shape the American diet as the twentieth century opened. By 1900, the health and stature of Americans appeared to be improving as a result of these nineteenth century trends. The diets of ordinary people improved as more and more could afford to take advantage of the new products made available by advances in transportation, refrigeration, production, and processing. Improvements in canning techniques continued to increase the productivity of canners. By 1910, over three billion cans of foods were being produced annually by American plants.

This meant that many Americans were no longer restricted to eating seasonal fruits and vegetables. Grocery shops had grown enormously in number since the 1880s and in all but the most remote rural areas replaced the old general store.

Except for the very poor, most people probably ate more food than necessary. Obesity and digestive problems related to overeating were common. Affluence explained the overindulgence of the upper classes. In 1913 a New York dinner hosted by Frank Woolworth of dime store fame featured caviar, oysters, turtle soup, pompano with potatoes, guinea hen, terrapin, squab, grapefruit-walnut salad, ice cream, coffee, punch, and wine. The lower classes also relied on a calorie-heavy diet because of the hard physical labor they were expected to do. Bread, potatoes, cabbage, and onions were staples of the workingman's diet. In the early part of the century steelworkers in Pennsylvania ate a typical American supper of meat, beans, potatoes, fruit, beets, and pickles. First generation immigrants focused on food, because hunger and scarcity had been one of the prime factors encouraging their migration to America. Their diets tended to include more meat than they had been used to eating in their homelands. The new immigrants were also fond of one-dish items like stews, goulashes, and pasta with meat and

(circa 1955) A young girl licks frosting from a bowl as she helps her smiling mother frost a cake in the kitchen.

LATE 1800S EARLY 1900S

tomato sauces. Bread, usually purchased from ethnic bakeries, was a staple of importance. Pork was still the country's most popular meat.

The diets of skilled and semi-skilled workers were more varied, reflecting their economic situation and the good selection of products available. Common in the diets of the better off urban classes were fresh meat, eggs, white sauces, potatoes, fruits, vegetables, and desserts. While the more affluent families tended to use the new commercially canned fruits and vegetables (which became symbols of wealth, a progressive mindset, and status), immigrant women relied more on home canning.

The diets of rural Americans varied widely. Tenant farmers and sharecroppers, forced to rely on cash crops, usually had inadequate diets. Pellagra, a chronic disease causing digestive and nervous disturbances, was common. By contrast, more affluent farmers, especially those who had their own farms, tended to eat a wide variety of nutritious foods.

LATE 1800S • THE RISE OF THE RESTAURANT ~ Although inns and taverns had traditionally offered food since the colonial period, widespread restaurant eating is really a phenomenon of the twentieth century. In the early decades of the nineteenth century, virtually no restaurants existed outside eastern cities which had grand hotels. The most famous restaurant in the Northeast was Delmonico's, which opened in 1825 and served a Frenchified menu. The Chinese had pioneered restaurants on the west coast, specializing in Chinese-American dishes like chop suey and chow mein. Many Americans, however, were apprehensive about eating in these restaurants, affected by rumors accusing the Chinese of eating dogs and cats. Toward the end of the nineteenth century, some Italians had also begun opening restaurants in urban areas. The first national restaurant chain, Harvey House, was founded in 1876 and served standardized fare in locations along railway lines. Peter Luger's, the famous Brooklyn steakhouse, opened in 1887 and reflected the growing national appetite for beef. Until the onset of Prohibition, the most popular place for a free lunch in the early twentieth century was the saloon, which offered free food to customers who purchased alcohol.

EARLY 1900S • CAFETERIAS AND AUTOMATS ~ By the late nineteenth and early twentieth century, novel forms of serving food attracted new customers to eating establishments. Restaurants serving both male and female customers, especially the new urban middle classes seeking acceptable places to eat a noontime meal, became increasingly common. Cafeterias became very popular, tracing their origin to the Exchange Buffet which opened in the commercial district of New York in 1885. Patrons, men only, helped themselves and ate standing up. Several social and philanthropic organizations run by women established cafeterias in Chicago in the 1890s, and the concept of "see and select" your food became increasingly popular. By 1915, cafeterias existed in Los Angeles, San Francisco, and Washington D.C. Clean, respectable, fast, and convenient, cafeterias became even more attractive with the invention of steam tables that could provide the hot foods then considered necessary at midday.

Another new and popular development was the Automat, popularized by Horn and Hardart. A system of Swedish and German origin, the concept first

(circa 1935) Impoverished men eat a meal consisting of soup and a sandwich in a cafeteria-style restaurant on the Bowery in New York City.

appeared in Philadelphia in the years before the war. Open to both sexes, automats seemed at the time to embody the ultimate in hygienic, fast, and convenient service. Food was exposed behind glass openings, and a nickel dropped in the slot provided your selection.

In 1916, the "hamburger steak" that had first become popular in the nineteenth century was made into a sandwich by Billy Ingram and Walter Anderson, the founders of the White Castle chain. America's fascination with fast food had begun.

In March of 1919, Kansas City restauranteurs held the first meeting of what would become the National Restaurant Association. At that time, the fledgling organization represented an industry of 43,000 establishments.

1880–1920 • THE PROGRESSIVE MOVEMENT AND SAFETY CONCERNS

∼ The food industry was directly affected by the Progressive ethos of the time. Investigative journalists, the famous muckrakers of the day, drew public attention to a variety of social ills.

The U.S. government's interest in food safety and nutrition had been sparked by the "embalmed beef" scandal of the Spanish-American War, when charges arose that thousands of cans of rotten beef had been served to troops in Cuba. In response to the subsequent uproar, the government announced that a new emergency ration for men in the field had been developed. The 1902 announcement reflected the findings of a new, increasingly influential group of nutritionists. The new product, the army

EARLY 1900s

(1933) A typical 1920s kitchen with primitive furniture, sink and stove, and simple cooking utensils.

was proud to note, had been figured out by physiological mathematicians and carefully reduced "to grams and calories the protein, the fats, the carbohydrates, and fuel value of the ration."

As food processing, meatpacking, and commercial canning became more commonplace, growing attention came to be paid to the healthfulness of the new products. Concerns were raised about the conditions under which food was processed and marketed, the safety of ingredients, and the probability of spoilage. The drive for meat inspection, which had begun in the 1880s, led to passage of a federal meat inspection law in 1891. This was followed by a tougher Meat Inspection Act in 1906 and by one of the most famous of Progressive reforms, the Pure Food and Drug Act of 1906.

Although much credit for the latter is usually given to Upton Sinclair's muckraking novel *The Jungle* (1906), with its revolting description of conditions in Chicago's meatpacking plants, other publicists were also important. Dr. Harvey Wiley, chief chemist of the U.S. Department of Agriculture, was a leading crusader in the movement to obtain federal regulation of food additives and compulsory labeling of ingredients. In 1908, concern over the purity of milk led to enactment of the first compulsory pasteurization law in Chicago. By 1920, many similar laws had been passed on the local and state levels. Because many smaller companies often could not afford the investments necessary for the equipment and monitoring required to comply with the new laws, the period saw a continued trend toward merger and acquisition of these smaller companies by larger ones.

THE RISE OF SCIENTIFIC EATING AND THE NEW NUTRITION ~ The early decades of the twentieth century also saw a growing interest in home economics and nutrition, especially among the middle classes. Food historians have christened this period the age of "scientific eating" or the era of the "New Nutrition." The movement had several causative roots. Building on the activities of early food reformers, the new domestic science of the late nineteenth century was an attempt to apply science to the kitchen. The movement was attractive to middle class women anxious to gain a new professional status. In a period of increasing feminist agitation, domestic science was clearly a less radical and threatening way for such women to demonstrate their usefulness to society. Women like Catherine Beecher, author of a book on "frugal housewifery," urged women to take control of the household economy in order to save money on food and other expenses, and increasing numbers of women enrolled in cooking classes to learn the new methods.

HOME ECONOMICS ~ The newly christened "home economics" movement, a term first used in 1899, placed many women in university positions and cooking schools. Such schools originally aimed at providing working class girls with commercially and domestically useful skills, but soon grew popular among the middle class as well. One of the first of such schools was the Boston Cooking School, founded in 1879. Its most distinguished graduate was Fanny Farmer, whose *Boston Cooking School Cook Book*, first published in 1896, registered sales of over one-third of a million copies by the time of her death in 1915. Although recipe books had been in circulation since the colonial era, hers was the first to approach food preparation in a more practical, scientific way.

COOKBOOKS ~ The establishment of the International Bureau of Weights and Measures in 1875 contributed to the rise of "scientific eating" by the standardization of cup and spoon measures. Along with the production of machine made culinary tools, the nineteenth century had also seen improvements in the mechanization and automation of printing. Taken together, these developments made possible the success and popularity of cookbooks. Food historians consider the first quarter of the twentieth century to be the "golden age of cookbooks" as recipes became more standardized and reliable. Some have argued that during this period Americans relied on cookbooks more than ever before or after. They now had better resources for sharing methods of food preparation, while resources for avoiding cooking (microwaves, TV dinners, fast food joints) were not yet created.

Cookbooks of the first half of the twentieth century aimed to teach Americans the basics of food preparation. Works like *The Joy of Cooking* (1931) and the *Betty Crocker Picture Cookbook* (1950) became standards in American homes. Only later in the century would cookbooks reflect more sophisticated and upscale tastes. The mere ownership of such volumes, as opposed to their actual use, would become a mark of social status.

NUTRITION REFORMERS ~ Interest in the new nutrition also drew strength from Progressive concerns about social problems. Reformers investigating the lifestyles of new immigrants and the urban poor drew attention to the lack of milk, fruits, and vegetables in the diets of city dwellers. In 1904, a study of poverty in New York City (*Poverty*, by Robert Hunter) estimated that sixty to seventy thousand school-children went to school hungry each day. The book was a strong

1850s–1890s

influence on subsequent U.S. efforts to feed hungry and needy children in school. The famous muckraker John Spargo also drew attention to the undernourishment of thousands living in the New York slums. Attention was also drawn to the scarcity of milk among the city's children, and the problems of tuberculosis and rickets.

From the mid-nineteenth century, sporadic efforts to feed school-children were undertaken by private societies and associations interested in child welfare. In 1853, the Children's Aid Society of New York initiated a program to serve meals to children attending vocational schools. In 1894, the Starr Center Association of Philadelphia began serving penny lunches to school children, ultimately servicing nine schools in the city. By the first decade of the twentieth century, similar programs were established in Boston under the auspices of the Women's Educational and Industrial Union.

The diet reformers of the 1830s had first drawn attention to the relationship between food and health, but their contributions were hampered by the fact that they had little scientific data to substantiate their claims. Few Americans actually thought about the chemical composition of the foods they were eating until the last quarter of the nineteenth century, when European scientific knowledge concerning nutrition was accumulated by American chemists. By the late nineteenth century, chemists realized that food products consisted of three principal elements: protein, fats, and carbohydrates. The first American credited with making a careful analysis of food by European methods was Wilbur O. Atwater, a graduate of Wesleyan University who studied agricultural chemistry at Yale. In 1869 he received a Ph.D. after completing a thesis dealing with the chemical composition of maize. After studying at universities in Berlin and Leipzig, he became a professor of chemistry at Wesleyan where he remained until his death in 1907. Atwater's works remained the standard references on American nutrition for many years. His central argument was that Americans were extravagant in their food habits, i.e. that their diets were too reliant on high cost foods such as meat. Instead, they should aim to meet standard requirements at lower cost by filling their calorie needs with cheaper foods such as bread. In an increasingly competitive age, Atwater also took an international view of the food problem. He pointed out that international competition in industry and commerce was becoming stronger and America's population growing larger. Unless Americans reformed their diets by greater use of cheaper energy yielders, the future would bring loss instead of gain in material prosperity.

Atwater's most famous disciple was industrialist and economist Edward Atkinson who published his own book on "pecuniary economy" in food. Also relying on concepts of scientific eating exported from Germany, he deplored the fact that Americans of both the lower and middle classes spent too large a percentage of their household budgets on food. The remedy, he argued, was "to teach not only the working people but even the prosperous the right methods of obtaining a good and wholesome subsistence at less cost in money than they now spend for a poor and dyspeptic one." In 1893, Atkinson advocated the establishment of food laboratories in connection with Agricultural Experiment Stations set up under the Hatch Act of 1887. He urged government to make nutrition awareness a matter of national policy, encouraging Washington to spend a little money "for the prevention of waste of human energy, viz., the waste of our food supply." In 1895, Congress appropriated $10,000 to enable the Secretary of Agriculture to investigate and report upon the nutritive value of various articles and commodities used for human food. Special attention was to be paid to the identification of "wholesome, and edible rations less wasteful and more economical than those in common use." Atwater himself was appointed a special agent in charge of nutrition investigation.

Another notable nutritionist of the period was Professor Russell Henry Chittenden, physiological chemist and head of the Sheffield Scientific School at Yale. In a 1905 book, *Physiological Economy in Nutrition*, he too chided Americans for overconsumption, especially of meat. Arguing that an excess of protein was unnecessary and dangerous because it put a harmful strain on the kidneys, he advocated the benefits of a low protein diet.

In the opening decades of the twentieth century, funds appropriated for USDA education efforts increased. Home demonstration agents of the USDA were active in encouraging the production and consumption of nutritious foods. Government funds were also used for demonstration of improved agricultural techniques, and for publications in support of local home economics programs.

The urgings of the "new nutritionists" were heeded more by the middle classes than by the poor for whom they had originally been intended. Perhaps this was

(1930) The predominantly female workforce of a U.S. canning factory peels and cores ripe tomatoes prior to processing.

because certain tenets of the new nutritionists took sharp aim at the habits of immigrant groups. Nutritionists condemned one-pot meals such as stews, pasta dishes and goulashes as difficult to digest, expressed a preference for canned over fresh vegetables, and demonstrated a continued hostility toward spices and flavorings. Even the fresh hot bread so favored by immigrants was frowned upon by experts. Believing freshly made, hot bread to be indigestible, experts advised immigrant families to buy their breakfast bread and pastries during the evening **before** they were to be eaten so that these would cool and harden before meal time.

By contrast, the middle classes appeared to be more receptive to the teachings of the new nutritionists. After 1905 there was a definite trend among the middle classes toward eating smaller, less elaborate meals. Several factors may have been responsible for this: the warnings against overeating issued by nutritionists; the difficulty of obtaining satisfactory domestic service; and the desire of increasingly emancipated women to spend less time in the kitchen. Labor was saved by simpler menus, the use of fewer ingredients in dishes, fewer steps in food preparation, and the serving of fewer courses.

WORLD WAR I AND THE HOOVERIZATION OF THE AMERICAN DIET, 1914-1918

The rise of the new nutrition and the increasing involvement of government in the area of food and nutrition served the nation well as the crisis of war unfolded. Shortly after the United States entered the war in April 1917, Herbert Hoover was appointed to head the U.S. Food Administration (FA) and was given broad powers over the prices, production, and distribution of food. The central goal of the Food Administration was the voluntary restriction of certain key staples — white wheat flour, meat, sugar, and butter — that needed to be shipped overseas for use by fighting men. Here the work of Atwater and other nutritionists provided important inspiration for the goals of the FA, which encouraged Americans to consider more seriously how much and what they were eating. A major propaganda campaign was mounted to teach the rules of the new nutrition and to persuade Americans that they would not harm their health by eating less or by changing some of their food habits. Substitution along the lines recommended by Atwater was encouraged. To save meat, Americans were encouraged to eat protein rich foods like fish, eggs, cheese, and nuts. To save sugar, people ate more fresh and dried fruits. The battle to save wheat was especially important, as the FA opined that "the

(1943) Meat cuts with ceiling prices and point values per pound properly displayed in a butcher's case.

way in which the shortage of wheat is met may be the deciding factor in winning the war." Corn, barley, oats, rice, and rye were recommended cereal substitutes. Americans also substituted beans for meat, cornmeal and oats for wheat, and lard and vegetable oil for butter.

Home economists recruited by the FA devised recipes and menus employing such recommended substitutes. A typical recommended menu to spare meat was hardly austere. One daily menu called for fresh fruit juice, dry and hot cereal, fried, stewed or broiled oysters, grilled whitefish, broiled mackerel, or crabmeat au gratin. Women's magazines and the editors of women's pages in daily newspapers enthusiastically accepted FA material, usually at the rate of one article per week. The American Home Economics Association set up an Emergency Committee to turn out war recipes for the press, write pamphlets for women's clubs, and create course outlines for school home economics courses.

The FA also used posters and other visual propaganda to drive home its calls to observe Meatless Tuesdays, Wheatless Mondays and Wednesdays, and Porkless Thursdays and Saturdays. Such urgings combined patriotism with nutritional advice: "Feed a Fighter," urged one poster. "Eat Only What You Need/Waste Nothing/That He and His Family May Have Enough." "Lick the Plate and Lick the Kaiser" was another favorite FA slogan.

Because Italian food provided a ready-made example of dishes using little or no meat, Italian food became one of the first immigrant foods to gain widespread acceptance during this period. Since fruits and vegetables were too perishable to send to Europe, their consumption was encouraged, and this provided an unexpected nutritional boon to the American public. Americans were encouraged to plant Victory Gardens by the National Emergency Food Garden Commission. By the end of 1917, more than one million acres of city lots were in gardens, yielding about $350 million worth of garden produce.

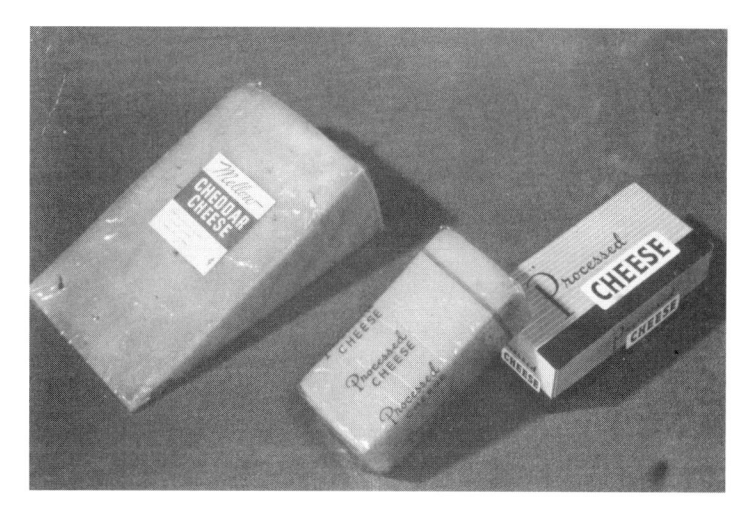

(circa 1941) A photo of three packages of cheddar and processed cheese, used for advertising.

It is common to speak of the American diet becoming "Hooverized" in these years. The war experience fostered new habits and attitudes, as Americans learned to get along on less food and to make better food choices.

POST WORLD WAR I AMERICA, 1918-1929

THE LEGACY OF WAR ~ Government-sponsored nutritional efforts continued on several fronts. The condition of children in war-torn countries re-directed attention to the longstanding problem of malnutrition in the U.S., a problem highlighted by numerous studies:

- In 1917, Dr. Josephine Baker of the New York City Department of Health estimated that 21 percent of the children in city schools were undernourished.

1915–1922

- In 1918, Dr. Thomas Wood set the national figure for undernourished schoolchildren at 15-25 percent.
- In a 1921 article in *The Annals of the American Academy*, well known nutritionist E.V. McCollum estimated that half the children in American cities had or had had rickets; 90 percent had decayed teeth; and more than 20 percent were seriously underweight.
- In 1929, a New York City Department of Health report indicated that 13.4 percent of new entrants into the public school system showed evidence of malnutrition.

Concern was also being expressed for farm families whose health may have suffered from greater use of processed food. By this period, nearly all farm families were buying commercially prepared cornmeal and flour, and less bread was being baked in farmhouses. Health concerns were raised as highly refined cereals replaced the less thoroughly milled products of local mills.

In response to such investigations, President Herbert Hoover convened a White House Conference on Child Health. Other agencies devoting themselves to the problem of malnutrition in the 1920s were the Child Health Association (known, after 1922, as the American Child Health Association) and the American Red Cross, which conducted specialized nutrition services throughout the decade.

One result of these activities was a concerted drive to encourage greater use of milk. The School Children's Welfare League, a New York City women's organization, conducted a drive in 1922 for funds to provide a million quarts of milk for undernourished children. "Milk weeks" were publicized by city officials and boxing bouts were held for the benefit of various milk funds. Following the tradition of the propaganda campaigns used by the FA in the Great War, the USDA distributed films showing a big league baseball pitcher in action to illustrate the power of milk.

1915–1917 • FOOD STANDARDS ~ The war had also encouraged a new attentiveness to national food standards and the establishment and enforcement of national grades. In the years immediately before the war, great progress had been made toward ensuring a more reliable fruit and vegetable supply. In 1915 the USDA established an Office of Markets which issued daily reports as to the movement of supplies toward city markets. In 1917 Congress established an inspection service which set up standards and graded shipments at terminals. During the war local food administrators appointed under the FA used a nationwide corps of inspectors to determine the quality of fruit and vegetable shipments.

One result of government inspection was the creation of regional cooperatives by fruit and vegetable growers, and later by dairymen. Such groups were different from the cooperatives formed by granges and farmers' alliances in the nineteenth century. While both aimed to reduce the middleman's margin and to bring about greater returns by curtailing production and/or price fixing, the new organizations also focused attention on advertising and merchandising methods as ways to increase profits. Two of the most effective leaders in the use and development of these new advertising and merchandising methods were the California Fruit Growers' Exchange and the Florida Citrus Exchange.

1750–1850 • ALCOHOL CONSUMPTION ~ From colonial times, drinking in

(1933) Bartenders at Sloppy Joe's bar pour a round of drinks on the house for a large group of smiling customers as it was announced that the Eighteenth Amendment had been repealed and Prohibition had been removed from the U.S. Constitution after 13 years, Chicago, Illinois.

America had centered on alcoholic beverages, with hard cider, some beer, whiskey, and rum the drinks of choice. According to food historians, the gentry of the Chesapeake region were voracious consumers of alcohol. When Virginia governor Lord Norborne Berkeley Botetourt died in 1770, he left behind more than 2,000 bottles of wine, brandy, ale, and many kegs of spirits. New types of lagered beers were introduced to America by German immigrants, and heavy drinking remained the norm in America until the mid-nineteenth century.

1918–1934 • Temperance and Prohibition

The temperance movement drew strength from that time, as advocates, acting from religious, humanitarian, and feminist impulses, encouraged the replacement of alcohol with tea, coffee, and pure water, then available for the first time in many American cities. A reaction to the endemic drunkenness and excessive alcohol consumption of the eighteenth and nineteenth centuries, the drive toward outright Prohibition was fed by a variety of forces and gained momentum during World War I.

Constitutionally in effect from January 1920 to January 1934, Prohibition led to a variety of changes in American habits of food consumption. Many restaurants, among them the legendary Delmonico's, were forced to close their doors, unable to sustain themselves without the high profit margins created by alcohol consumption. Certainly the free lunches of bars and saloons were no more, and Prohibition hastened the development of the lunchtime restaurant industry, spurring the conversion of bars to sandwich counters, luncheonettes, and other more novel establishments like hamburger chains. At least initially, Prohibition harmed the development of the young American wine industry, which had been developing in California since the late nineteenth century.

It resulted in a sharp decrease in alcohol consumption, at least in the early years, until new methods and means could be devised to subvert the law.

1920s • The "Newer Nutrition" ~ Food historians call the decades immediately following the Great War the age of the "newer nutrition." They use this term to distinguish the trends of this period from those of the prewar and wartime era. At that time, nutritionists focused on the economical and nutritional benefits of finding attractive substitutes for familiar foods. Vestiges of this thinking continued into the 1920s. Quaker Oats, for example, continued to advertise its products as an inexpensive source of calories, much more economical than beef or fish. California walnut growers said their "vital food" possessed "important heat and energy producing qualities," while raisin and prune producers stressed the value of their fruits as sources of energy-producing sugar.

The claims of the newer nutrition, however, were very different. Consumption and not substitution was now the issue. Food concerns came to realize that the American market was limited and that most Americans had enough to eat. Any increase in the consumption of one commodity would have to come at the expense of another. Hence, advertisers came to stress the unique benefits of their products, and encouraged Americans to buy them with so-called "eat more" campaigns.

1911–1922 • Vitamins ~ The age of newer nutrition was different in another way as well, focusing as it did on a new understanding of the role played by vitamins in human nutrition. The new nutritionists had generally been ignorant of vitamins and knew little of minerals, but the decade immediately before the war had seen important new developments in this area. The nutritional investigations of the Office of Experiment Stations resulted in a new understanding of the role of minerals like iron, calcium, and phosphorus. In 1911 Polish chemist Casimir Funk isolated a chemical substance of the class of chemical compounds called "amines." To it he added the prefix "vita", (Latin for life) and the knowledge of vitamins was born. Further work in this area was done by young Yale chemist Elmer Verner McCollum. By 1917, the U.S. Food Administration considered the value of these substances to have been so effectively demonstrated that it encouraged their use by the public. Official government manuals lectured that adequate supplies of vitamins A and B were "as necessary for health and growth as the better known constituents of food." At the close of the war, knowledge of Vitamin C was announced, followed, in 1922, by Vitamin D.

Media campaigns now informed the public that it was important to eat an abundance of foods rich in vitamins and minerals. The message appeared in nutrition textbooks, articles in women's magazines, home economics publications, and the medical advice columns of many periodicals.

1920s • Advertising Nutrition ~ New nutritional campaigns by advertisers and producers stressed, sometimes extravagantly, the benefits of their products. In the 1920s, Fleischmann's Yeast spent enormous amounts of money spreading the message that eating four of its yeast cakes daily would provide enough vitamin B to "rid the body of poisonous wastes," raise energy levels, and cure indigestion, constipation, acne, pimples, "fallen stomach," and "underfed blood." The subtle transition from the new to the newer nutrition can be seen in the changes in advertising campaigns utilized by the Campbell's Soup Company. In 1925 Campbell's Tomato Soup was advertised as the soup that "appetizes and invigorates." By 1926 advertising stressed that children should eat it because it contained the "growth" vitamins that were so beneficial in promoting sound and healthy development.

Dairy industries were also very successful in spreading vitamin awareness. Giant milk distributors formed a national organization to inform the public of milk's nutritional value. In the late 1920s a process was invented to irradiate canned milk with Vitamin D, and its use soon expanded to butter and fresh milk. Powerful producer cooperatives and giant dairy companies were then able to change the image of milk from a children's food to a perfect food for adults as well, one which contained virtually every nutrient essential for food health. These skillful advertising techniques helped reverse the trend toward reduced per capita consumption of milk which had prevailed from 1909. After the new ad campaigns of the 1920s, consumption of milk and milk products rose steadily. The tradition of promoting milk as a perfect food for those of all ages has continued into the twenty-first century. In recent years, America's Dairy Farmers and Milk Processors have waged celebrated "Got Milk?" campaigns featuring photographs of highly recognizable, white-mustached personalities.

(circa 1955) Actress Geene Courtney models a scarf, skirt, bracelets, and a crown made from hot dogs, frankfurters, and kielbasa in her role as Queen of National Hot Dog Week, as selected by the Zion Meat Products Company.

1920s

The era of newer nutrition also saw home economists become increasingly linked to food industries. Diet kitchens, manned by home economists, became almost universal in the big food companies. Some even developed prototypical home economists to lend a personal touch to the advertising of their products. The best known example of this trend was the invention of "Betty Crocker" by General Mills (formerly the Washburn-Crosby Flour Milling Co.). The invention of Betty Crocker reflected the pressure on processors to come up with catchy brand names and promotional gimmicks. In similar fashion, California raisin growers adopted the Sun Maid label to pitch the very successful slogan, "Had Your Iron Today?"

1920s

Shrewd advertising campaigns also introduced consumers to new products. Asparagus, for example, was practically unknown in the United States until the 1920s, when the asparagus section of the Canners League of California invested in a substantial promotional campaign.

Pop culture also helped to spread the new nutritional awareness. Comic strip hero Popeye performed amazing feats of strength after eating mouthfuls of spinach, a definite factor in encouraging children to eat spinach. A survey conducted in 1936 showed that the previously unpopular vegetable then ranked second among the vegetable choices of children.

By the late 1930s, most vitamins had been synthesized and were being produced commercially in the form of pills or tonics and sold without prescription. Food producers joined the medical profession in expressing alarm over this development. Doctors feared that people would seek nonmedical help when stricken with illness, while food producers were anxious to assure consumers that vitamin supplements were unnecessary because they could obtain more than enough nutrients to ensure good health simply by eating a balanced diet.

1920s • CONTINUED DEVELOPMENT OF NEW PRODUCTS ~ By the 1920s, new scientific knowledge, powerful advertising, new marketing strategies and the continued creation of new products made brand names increasingly attractive to consumers. These new products became fixed in the consumer mind as uniform, dependable, and reasonably priced. New innovations contributed to the continued standardization of the American diet. In the 1920s, Clarence Birdseye developed a method of quick freezing that allowed food to freeze and thaw within the same cardboard packaging, all the while retaining an attractive appearance. Ultimately purchased by General Foods, his company prospered even during the Depression as many American households acquired refrigerators with freezer compartments. Other new frozen confections of the decade included the Good Humor Bar (1920); the Eskimo Pie (1921); and the Popsicle (1924). By 1941, there were as many as 250 firms marketing frozen food.

1859–1929 • SUPERMARKETS ~ The growth of new products was matched by the creation of new methods to sell those products. Originally pioneered by the Great American Tea Company in 1859, supermarkets increasingly began to displace locally owned stores. By 1876, the re-christened Great Atlantic and Pacific Tea Company had 67 stores nationwide; by 1912 it had nearly 500. The first markets were called "groceterias" until the handier term was coined. National chains promised economy, convenience, and abundance. In 1920, A&P had 4,621 stores nationwide; by 1929, the total had grown to 15,418. Piggly Wiggly began the decade with 515 stores, and expanded to 2,500 by 1929. The grocery business was fiercely competitive. By 1928 the nation boasted 860 rival chains. Piggly Wiggly featured a method of operation new to the field. Under the proud slogan "scientific merchandising," it created a self-service system, with all its markets laid out according to a patented traffic pattern. The self-service format worked spectacularly well and was highly popular with consumers. The Piggly Wiggly grocery chain boasted the nation's highest average sales per customer. Larger purchasing power meant lower costs. In 1921 Piggly Wiggly offered three pounds of a

(1968) The diner became an American institution as the hub of small town social life, or the stopping off place in cities. This scene in Texas could be anywhere in rural America.

national brand coffee for $1.05, while a conventional service store charged $1.55. Even A&P, the biggest egg merchant of them all, could not match the Piggly Wiggly price of 36 cents per dozen.

1920s • NEW RESTAURANTS ～ The growth in new ways of selling food was paralleled by the rise in new ways of selling prepared foods. New kinds of restaurants appeared in the 1920s, continuing the progress made in this industry in the years before the war. The coming of Prohibition destroyed the lunchtime food business of older saloons and taverns, and created a need for new establishments to feed the growing numbers of lower middle class office and sales workers of both sexes. By the mid-1920s, cafeterias were beginning to give way to new luncheon restaurants featuring even lighter foods. " Newer" nutritionists de-

1920s

1920s

(circa 1930) 'The Brown Derby' a well known restaurant in Los Angeles patronized by members of the film world.

emphasized the traditional focus on the hot lunch, and salads, sandwiches, and other cold dishes became popular. Toasted bread was now more conveniently prepared with the recent invention of the electric toaster. New "luncheonettes" became popular, and drugstores also began to serve sandwiches and other food items at their soda fountains. In 1929, it was estimated that 61 percent of all drugstore sales took place at the soda fountain, 67 percent of this in food sales.

Although they had been in business before the war, tea rooms became extremely successful in the years after Prohibition. A new trade journal, *Tea Room Management*, reflected their popularity. Some tea rooms were opened by home economists determined to put their knowledge to profitable use. Tea rooms specialized in lighter fare thought to be both attractive and appropriate for women who, by the mid 1920s, accounted for 60 percent of restaurant patrons. The period witnessed a kind of sex stereotyping in eating. "Manly" meals of beans, potatoes, and beef were distinguished from proper female fare: salads, marshmallows stuffed with raisins, and "Dainty Desserts for Dainty People." While such stereotyping seems abhorrent to the egalitarian sensibilities of modern America, old traditions died hard. A brand of "Hungry Man" frozen dinners featuring large portions remained popular well into the last decades of the twentieth century.

The new eating establishments reflected other social trends. In the 1920s, Frank G. Shattuck capitalized on the declining interest in home cooking demonstrated by the newly emancipated "New Women" of the period. He promoted his chain of Schrafft's restaurants as places where one could get the "home cooking" which mothers no longer had the inclination to do. The Child's chain catered to the health conscious. Its menus were emblazoned with the slogan, "Watch Your Step: Go Vegetable-Wise." Also notable about its menus was the detailed tabulation of calories and protein requirements that accompanied food choices. Items rich in vitamins were demarcated with a (v).

Fast food chains first appeared in the 1920s, feeding the concurrent American fascination with other new developments like the automobile and the highway. The first hamburger chains were also products of the 1920s. White Tower and White Castle, with their focus on white, addressed the American concern with cleanliness. The owners of the White Castle operation, anxious to reassure customers concerned abut the safety of chopped meat, announced they had chosen "white for purity."

1937–1940 • MCDONALD'S AND HOWARD JOHNSON'S ~ In 1937, the McDonald Brothers opened their first drive-in restaurant near Pasadena, California, although it would be decades before the national mania for Big Macs really emerged.

In what may be considered to be the first example of food franchising, the Howard Johnson's chain obtained a monopoly for food service on the Pennsylvania Turnpike, which in 1940 opened as the nation's first interstate highway. HoJo's standardized architecture, notably its orange roofs, made it instantly recognizable.

1926–1932 • FOOD ON THE RADIO ~ Radio reflected the prosperity and seemingly boundless opportunity of the Roaring Twenties. The new medium also offered Americans an opportunity to bone up on their housekeeping and cooking skills. "Housekeeper's Chat", a radio show first broadcast on October 4, 1926, introduced Americans to Aunt Sammy, a character created by the USDA's Bureau of Home Economics and Radio Service. This mythical wife of Uncle Sam dispensed traditional wisdom on sewing, furniture, appliances, family issues, and cooking. Menus and recipe sharing were a highlight of the show. So many listeners requested copies of these features that the Bureau responded first with mimeographed samples and later with pamphlets. The demand for "Aunt Sammy's Radio Recipes" was so great that the pamphlet was revised and enlarged three times between 1927 and 1931. In 1932 it became the first cookbook published in Braille. The recipes give us insights into the kind of home cooking popular in the period. Many of the recipes are still beloved favorites – macaroni and cheese, Harvard beets, coleslaw, and corn fritters. A few, however, such as fried apples and bacon, scalloped onions and peanuts, and "rocks," a cookie made of brown sugar, cinnamon, and walnut meats, have faded

1920s

into obscurity. Like the rocks she taught about, Aunt Sammy herself was discontinued as a character in 1934; the show itself disappeared from the airwaves in 1946.

1890–1924 • THE AMERICAN DIET IN THE 1920S ∼ Because of all the factors enumerated above, the American diet continued its trend toward standardization. The Immigration Reform Act of 1924 further contributed to this standardization. Curtailing immigration as it did, it stopped the influx of new immigrants who would have brought with them reinforcement of old country traditions. First generation immigrants were further influenced by their children, who brought home American ideas. School lunch programs, women's magazines, the movies, and school home economics courses further contributed to the standardization and "Americanization" of the national diet. By the end of the decade, Americans ate about five percent fewer calories but consumed a wider variety of foods than had their counterparts in the 1890s. The average American ate more fruit (especially citrus), more vegetables (especially green ones), more milk and cheese, but fewer quantities of cereal, potatoes, and cornmeal. Even beef consumption had fallen from 72.4 lbs. per capita in 1899 to 55.3 lbs. per capita in 1930.

THE CRISIS YEARS: DEPRESSION AND WAR, 1929-1945

1920S • CRISIS ON THE FARMS ∼ The prosperity of the 1920s was not shared equally by all Americans. Even by the early 1920s, a crisis loomed on the American farm; prices for farm products fell about 40 percent in 1920 and 1921, and remained low throughout the decade.

(circa 1935) A row of men in overalls, and one girl, sit in front of an out-of-business cafe with soaped windows, during the Great Depression, United States.

Low prices for farm products drove many farmers to dump milk, shoot cattle, and burn grains rather than sell them for little or no return. Many farmers lost their farms through bankruptcy or were forced to become tenants or abandon farming. Severe droughts, dust storms, and erosion hit parts of the Midwest and Southwest in the 1930s, with the most severe droughts occurring in 1934 and 1936. Thousands of farmers were wiped out, and many migrated to the fertile agricultural areas of California hoping to find work.

1930S • DEPRESSION EATING ~ The crisis on the farms was exacerbated by the collapse of stock prices in 1929. Americans responded to resulting unemployment and economic insecurity in a variety of ways.

While the Depression did bring hunger, soup lines, hoboes, and beggars, starvation itself appears to have been unheard of. Persistent hunger, especially in localized areas, was more common. There appears to be no indication, in mortality or other statistics, of an overall deterioration in national health. Calorie consumption averaged over 3,000 calories per day for an adult male with a family income of over $3 per person per week. Those with incomes ranging from $2-$3 still averaged 2,800 calories, while only those at the very bottom of the income level lived near the margin of hunger, averaging 2,470 calories per day. Malnutrition remained a problem in the urban ghettoes, among the rural poor, migrant workers, and native Americans.

Falling food prices seem to have helped avert a larger tragedy, since surpluses, not shortages, were the immediate problem. The Depression itself seems to have made for improvement in the farm diet, as farmers turned to growing produce and other products for home use as they found other markets closed to them. Even in Southern mill-towns, where the Depression brought a reversion to the traditional "3M" diet of maize, meat, and molasses, poorer workers still ate better than their counterparts of 20 years earlier. While they did cut back on meat, fowl, fish, and fresh fruit, they still ate adequate amounts of vegetables, both fresh and canned. The Depression reinvigorated the teachings of Atwater and the substitutionists. Beans, peas, and cheaper cuts of meat were substituted for more expensive ones; thrifty homemakers returned to cooked cereals rather than use the more expensive dry, commercial brands. Home gardens and home canning played important roles in enhancing the food supply both during the Depression and World War II. Jello became very popular. Invented in 1897, it cost only pennies per package, yet added color and flavor to otherwise drab Depression tables. Jello was a versatile product. It could be mixed with mayonnaise and

(December 27, 1930) Dolly Gann (L), sister of U.S. vice president Charles Curtis, helps serve meals to the hungry at a Salvation Army soup kitchen during the Great Depression.

canned fruit or vegetables for a quick and easy salad, entrée, or dessert.

1930s • Government Relief Efforts ~ The government responded with numerous efforts both to safeguard the nation's agricultural base and to assist those in need. In an attempt to remedy the problem of surplus, the federal government authorized price supports and for the first time in history, began to buy farm products directly. Public Law 320, passed by the 74th Congress in 1935, authorized the Secretary of Agriculture to encourage domestic consumption of certain agricultural commodities by diverting them from the normal channels of trade and commerce. Surplus foods were supplied to needy families and school lunch programs.

Government relief operations helped to prevent any marked increase in malnutrition in the Depression and post-Depression years. The center of government activity was the Federal Surplus Commodities Corporation, which was active in distributing surplus products to relief agencies. Surplus commodities in distribution included canned meat and poultry, dried beans, canned fruits and vegetables, cooking fats, cornmeal, flour, nonfat dried milk, peanut butter, rice, rolled wheat, and other cereals.

The Depression years deepened concern over the malnourishment of school children. Many states and municipalities responded with legislation and funds enabling schools to serve noonday meals to children. By 1937, 15 states had passed laws specifically authorizing local school boards to operate lunchrooms.

The earliest federal aid came from the Reconstruction Finance Corporation (RFC) in 1932 and 1933, when it granted loans to several towns in Missouri to cover the cost of labor employed in preparing and serving school lunches. Federal assistance expanded to other areas in 1933 and 1934 under the operations of the Civil Works Administration and the Federal Emergency Relief Administration. The program ultimately reached into 39 states and employed over seven thousand women. In some large cities, central kitchens were established and WPA drivers delivered buckets of hot soup and fresh desserts to schools at lunchtime. Assistance in planning meals and creative use of recipes was given by dietitians who frequently used the publications of the Bureau of Home Economics as a guide. Lunch almost always meant a hot meal, and included milk, fresh fruits or vegetables, and sometimes soup and dessert.

1930s • Food Stamps and School Lunch Programs ~ Government lunch programs during the Depression years became the prototype and inspiration for the National School Lunch Act signed by President Harry Truman in 1946. The program provides nutritionally balanced, low cost or free lunches to needy children in public and nonprofit private schools as well as residential child care institutions. By century's end, the NSLP serviced nearly 27 million children in over 96,000 institutions each day.

In 1939 an Experimental Food Stamp Plan was put into effect in Rochester, New York. Stamps were used as if they were cash to purchase food. Grocers used the stamps to pay wholesalers, who in turn were reimbursed by the government. Two types of stamps were issued: orange and blue. Orange-colored stamps were sold to relief families in amounts proportionate to family size. For each $1 of stamps purchased, the recipient obtained 50 cents of blue stamps free. Recipients then went to various shops and used the orange stamps to make desired purchases. Blue stamps could be used only to make purchases from the surplus list: flour, cornmeal, dried beans, butter, eggs, and citrus fruits. Originally designed to dispose of agricultural surpluses, the stamp plan appears to have resulted in better balanced diets for those on relief.

Throughout the Depression years, home demonstration agents continued efforts to raise levels of nutritional awareness. Housewives, encouraged by extension agents, paid greater attention to home canning. In Texas alone, the number of glass and tin containers used in home canning rose from 11 million in 1930 to 50 million in 1932. Government agencies like the Tennessee Valley Authority (TVA) and Rural Electrification Commission (REC) facilitated the use of perishable food by spreading the use of refrigeration throughout more remote rural areas. The use of electrically serviced cold storage lockers expanded. By 1936, for example, 30,000 refrigerated lockers had been built in the creameries of the Northwest. Farmers made extensive use of these facilities to store meat and poultry for their own use and for keeping vegetables fresh.

1940–1943 • NUTRITION AND DEFENSE ~ As war threatened, government efforts extended to examining the relationship between diet and defense. In 1940, a Committee on Food Habits headed by anthropologist Margaret Mead was established under the aegis of the National Research Council to recommend ways in which national food habits could be altered in the face of expected wartime shortages. Harriet Elliott, consumer commissioner of the National Defense Advisory Commission created by FDR in 1940, drew further attention to the problem of malnutrition. Concerns were first raised by reports from the Selective Service Administration regarding recruit rejection. These reports revealed that 40 percent of men reporting for service were being turned down for physical reasons, and that one-third of these rejections were related directly or indirectly to poor nutrition.

These concerns prompted federal action and opened up a new era in nutritional science. The latest research into the biochemical functions and metabolism of essential nutrients was used by federal agencies to create practical dietary guidelines for consumers. In 1940, the Food and Nutrition Board (FNB) of the National Research Council was established to advise the federal gov-

(1943) Two young girls compare the point value of canned and bottled juices against values in their War Ration Books in a grocery store aisle during World War II.

ernment. Charged by FDR with the task of developing a set of dietary standards to serve as a norm for good nutrition, the FNB developed the first set of RDA's (recommended daily allowances) of vitamins and nutrients. Issued for the first time in 1943, the standards set recommended levels of intake for healthy adults of various ages. Home economists and nutritionists of the USDA developed a "Seven Group Plan" in 1943. Based on the RDA's published that same year, it served to assist consumers in making food choices, and was influential in developing the concept of a balanced meal.

Continuing concerns over nutrition led to other federal actions. Enrichment of bakers' bread with key ingredients (thiamine, riboflavin, niacin, iron, and calcium) became mandatory, legislation that resulted from concerns that key vitamins and minerals were being lost with the removal of cereal hulls during the milling and refining steps of processing. During the war years, the government required that oleomargarine be fortified with vitamin A and milk with vitamin D.

1941–1945 • Feeding the Fighting Man

Government involvement played a role in the continuing standardization of the American diet and in the further development of new products and processing methods. Research done by the Quartermaster Corps of the Department of Defense aimed at developing foods useful to fighting men under a variety of conditions. Just as Gail Borden had used his recently perfected condensed milk to supply Union forces during the Civil War, the demands of the U.S. military resulted in new methods of processing foods. Two of the most celebrated foods to have come out of the World War II experience were Spam, a canned pork product, and a specially formulated Hershey bar designed to provide sustenance and calories in emergency situations. Much work was done on dehydration techniques, since dehydrated foods do not require refrigeration, are lighter (with up to 99 percent of the water removed), and easier to transport. The fruits of this research were applied to domestic production in the postwar years.

Armour and Company proudly boasted that "not one man in ten ate as nourishing, well balanced meals at home as he gets in the Navy today." The typical Navy diet began with prunes, cornflakes, and one-fifth of a pound of bacon with fried scrapple. Lunch was usually cream of tomato soup, one-half pound of pot roast of beef with potatoes and spinach, and chocolate cake. Dinner was one-half a pound of ground hamburger, salad, and pudding. America's fascination with meat continued. "He's the greatest meat eater in the world," continued the folks at Armour, pointing out that the U.S. Navy ration mandated one pound of meat per man per day.

Other familiar American treats also emerged during the war years. M & M's, the bite-size chocolate candies, were first sold to the American public in 1941. On a trip to Spain, developer Forrest Mars, Sr. encountered soldiers who were eating pellets of chocolate that were encased in a hard sugary coating to keep them from melting. Packaged in cardboard tubes, M & M's were sold to the military as a convenient snack that traveled well in any climate, and the new candy soon became a favorite of GI's everywhere.

1941–1945 • The War on the Homefront

Government efforts also extended to the homefront. At the end of December 1941, USDA Secretary

Claude R. Wickard encouraged civilians to plant Victory Gardens since commercial farmers were busy feeding the men overseas. Millions responded by planting lettuce, tomatoes, beets, carrots, peas, radishes in a variety of locales, including such unlikely sites as the Portland (Oregon) zoo, Chicago's Arlington Racetrack, and the yard of the Cook County (Chicago) jail. Amateur farmers were guided by publications issued both by the USDA and seed companies.

Other campaigns prompted Americans to can foods. Pressure cookers were made available, often on loan from the government, with the average family putting up 165 jars of canned goods annually.

To deal with the problem of shortages, the Office of Price Administration created a rationing system. Sugar, fats, meats, canned fruits and vegetables were rationed. The OPA issued ration books of stamps with point values, and assigned specific point values to foods. Housewives were then required to pay grocers with stamps as well as cash. To replenish his stocks, the grocer sent the stamps to the wholesaler, who in turn redeemed the stamps at a local bank and got credit to buy more food. On average, grocers had to cope with about 14 billion points a month, actually handling about 3.5 billion tiny stamps. As in World War I, these restrictions indirectly encouraged the increased consumption of eggs, milk products, and fresh fruits by civilians.

The wartime U.S. appears to have been better fed than ever before. In 1945, the USDA reported that Americans ate more food and spent more money on food than at any other time in their history. In sum, the war years served as a tremendous catalyst to the further development of food science and the food and nutrition industry in general.

(circa 1945) A housewife bends down to pick up the newspaper and milk bottles at the front door of her house.

POSTWAR AFFLUENCE, 1945-1960

1950S

1950s • Producers, processors, and entrepreneurs developed an assortment of new methods for preserving, packaging, precooking, and serving food. Concerns about health and nutrition receded as Americans celebrated their prosperity, inventiveness, and affluence. In contrast to the decades immediately following and preceding this period, an assortment of experts ensured Americans that they were "the best fed people on earth." In 1955, a Food Consumption Survey issued by the USDA confirmed the abundance of the American food supply. While grocery stores in 1916 had carried only about 600 items, several thousand diverse products were now available. Improved air freight, packaging, and shipping conditions also added to the diversity of the food supply. It appears to be no accident that Vice-President Nixon's famous debate on the merits of American capitalism took place in a showcase kitchen, and that Soviet Premier Nikita Khrushchev toured a supermarket during his visit to America. Food had become a weapon in the Cold War.

1950s • THE NEW CONSUMERISM: TV DINNERS AND DRIED FOODS ~ The new consumer society was fascinated with novelty and convenience. Although frozen foods had been developed in the 1920s, their use accelerated in the 1950s with the growing proliferation of home food freezers. One of the most popular new products of the period was the packaged and frozen complete meal. Christened the TV dinner, it reflected Americans' fascination with another new marvel of the age.

In 1954, bacteriologist Betty Cronin was assigned by C.A. Swanson and Sons of Omaha, Nebraska to test a fried chicken dinner on her friends. The first ones sold for 98 cents in a package with a picture of a television set. Swanson sold 5,000 of the dinners in 1954; by 1955 annual sales were ten million. With the promise of more leisure time available for TV viewing and other recreational activities, other frozen packaged meals became popular: Banquet beef dinners, Morton Pot Pies, Quaker Oats, Aunt Jemima brand of frozen pancakes. Dishes such as Welsh rarebit were made easier with the introduction (in 1953) of Kraft's Cheese Whiz, a processed foamy cheese product sprayed from an aerosol can. Pillsbury and General Mills introduced cake mixes in 1949.

The research in dehydrated foods that had begun during the war years culminated in a number of new products. Powdered (instant) skim milk came on the market in 1954, and by 1958, orange and grapefruit juice powders were also available. Better technology also improved the quality of dried eggs, and dried "instant" mashed potatoes became a popular novelty. Both freeze and air-drying were used for such products as coffee, tea, meat, fish, fruits, and vegetables.

1930s • FOOD PACKAGING AND STORAGE ~ There were also advances in food packaging. These stemmed from the discovery of polyethylene and applications of polyvinylchloride in the late 1930s, coupled with the search for substitute materials during the war years. In addition to traditional packaging products like waxed paper and aluminum foil, housewives now enjoyed the use of flexible transparent plastic wraps to cover their food.

Another modern marvel to become an American icon was Tupperware, the brainchild of inventor Earl Tupper. Learning about plastics design and manufacturing while employed at DuPont, he formed his own company in 1938. During the war years, the Earl S. Tupper Company garnered several defense contracts, molding parts for gas masks and Navy signal lamps. After the war, he capitalized on the growing consumer market by designing plastics products for home use. Tupper succeeded in overcoming the popular perception that plastic was greasy, brittle, and unreliable. His greatest success came with the invention of an advanced seal mechanism known as the "Tupper seal." "The lids were their secret success," beamed one satisfied customer. "You could turn a bowl upside down and it wouldn't leak!" Tupper also capitalized on the period's celebration of the joys of domesticity. Teaming up with Brownie Wise, a marketing expert and motivator, he sold his kitchen cups, bowls, and containers in a unique way, the home "Tupperware" party.

1940s–1950s • OUTDOOR COOKING ~ Suburbanization also left its mark on American habits of preparing food, as the desire for suburban backyards and patios gave new uses to the previously regional barbecue. The fad for outdoor barbecues fed the American passion for steak. West Coast chef and author James Beard promoted this new passion with his popular books: *Cook It Outdoors* (1941); *Barbecue Cooking* (1954); *The Complete Book of Outdoor Cooking*, written with popular California author Helen Evans Brown (1955); and *James Beard's Treasury of Outdoor Cooking* (1960).

1930s–1950s • LUNCH BOXES ~ Other cultural fads also affected American foodways. TV, the cult of domesticity, and the affluence of the postwar years created a new childhood craze – the character lunchbox. Plain metal lunch kits were first mass produced in the late nineteenth century for use by factory workers and field hands. Metal lunch kits for children first appeared in the early twentieth century. In 1935, the Milwaukee company of Gender, Paeschke and Frey pioneered the character lunch box when it printed a likeness of Mickey Mouse on the lid of a tin carryall. It was the power of television, however, that opened up a wealth of ever-changing character possibilities. Credit for the new phenomenon belongs to character artist Robert O. Burton who in 1949 pasted a sketch of Hopalong Cassidy on a standard metal lunch box and presented the idea to Alladin Industries of Nashville, Tennessee. After the product was introduced in 1950, it spawned other competitors, notably the American Thermos Company of Norwich, Connecticut which began producing its popular Roy Rogers and Dale Evans lunch kits in 1953. In subsequent years, character lunch boxes celebrated TV stars, toys, sports, musicians, and superheros. In the 1980s, collectors paid high prices for the vintage kits, with the original Mickey Mouse kits selling for prices of $2,000 and up.

1940s-1960s • DIETARY CONSUMPTION ~ Despite the immense variety of new foods available in the immediate postwar years, Americans' actual eating preferences appear to have changed little from previous decades. Animal meat was still considered to be an essential part of the average diet, augmented by fruits, potatoes, and vegetables. Sales of fresh fruit dropped from 140 pounds per person in the 1940s to 90 pounds per person by the 1960s. Sales of preserved fruit (loaded with sugar), as well as soft drinks, increased. Intensive marketing of soft

---

With 11 million employees, the restaurant industry was the nation's largest private-sector employer in the year 2000. In 2000, Americans spent more than 45% of their food dollar at eating and drinking establishments, up from 25% in 1955.

SOURCE: National Restaurant Association

1940s–1950s

drinks resulted in an average annual rise in consumption from 90 servings per capita in 1939 to 500 in 1969.

1940s–1950s • THE FAST-FOOD INDUSTRY ~ Although the fast food industry can trace its roots to the White Castle and White Tower chains of earlier decades, no phenomenon so captured the American imagination (and came to symbolize American foodways) as did the postwar achievement of Ray Kroc and the McDonald Brothers. The original McDonald's was a drive-in establishment operated by Richard (Dick) and Maurice (Mac) McDonald near Pasadena, California. Its specialty was hotdogs. This was followed by the establishment of a much larger restaurant near San Bernardino in the 1940s. In 1948, the McDonald brothers totally redesigned their image in the hope of attracting a more family-oriented clientele. Aiming to deliver the fastest possible service at the lowest possible cost, they replaced silverware and dishes with cardboard and paper plates, and began to focus solely on hamburgers, selling them for as little as a nickel. Ray Kroc was a kitchen equipment salesman who had supplied the McDonald brothers with mixers. Possessed of talents and a vision that the McDonald brothers lacked, he purchased the right to sell and manage McDonald franchises in 1954. Ruthless about quality control, and realizing that cleanliness and hygiene were important to his customers, he saw to it that all franchised restaurants met the standards established by the McDonald's. Standardization ensured uniform quality. French fries, for example, were made from Russet Burbank potatoes of uniform size and aged for a predetermined period.

Other chains like Burger King and Kentucky Fried Chicken soon emerged. In the 1950s one of the McDonald's neighbors in San Bernardino adapted their technique to serving Mexican food, and Taco Bell, the first of other ethnic chains, was born. On the West Coast the

(1942) A waiter serving food to motorists at a Hot Shoppe in Chevy Chase, Maryland.

pizza business had been pioneered by Greek Americans who developed a new technique for making pizza. Instead of rolling and kneading the dough just before baking, the dough was prepared in advance, stored in metal containers, refrigerated, then popped into the oven directly from the freezer. The Wichita-based Pizza Hut chain perfected this technique and transformed pizza into another fast food.

1940s–1950s • ROOTS OF UPSCALE COOKING ~ Although it was not apparent at the time, what would become a more upscale approach to home cooking also had its roots in this postwar period of affluence and consumerism. *Gourmet Magazine* appeared in 1941, the first of what—over the next decades — would become many glossy and high-priced magazines dedicated to the preparation of fine food. Its most famous contributor was James Beard, who would go on to become known as the dean of American cooking. In the early 1950s, Bazar Français, a French restaurant supply business in the garment manufacturing district of New York City, was discovered by avant garde New Yorkers. The store supplied copper pots, pans, molds, bakeware, and other tools of the trade for the haute cuisine French restaurants that were becoming the chic dining experience among the upper middle class. Bloomingdales, the New York based retailer, recognized the interest in French cooking and transformed a corner of its housewares department into a haven for Francophiles. In 1953, Chuck Williams bought an old hardware store in Sonoma, California and opened the first Williams-Sonoma, the cooking store of choice for the yuppies of the 1980s and 1990s. 1959 saw the publication of Joseph Donon's

(1976) Nathan's Famous restaurant on Coney Island, New York, which is recognized as selling the City's finest hot dog, as well as catering for other tastes.

Classic French Cuisine, one of the best books ever written on French cuisine for the American cook.

1950s–1960s

THE AGE OF NEGATIVE NUTRITION, 1960-1980

1960s • Throughout the 1960s and 1970s, the food industry continued to grow, building on trends established in the immediate post World War II years. By 1960, the food industry had grown at a rate faster than the general economy. The 1960s saw dramatic growth in home delivery systems (especially in pizza and Chinese food), the popularity of drive-through windows in fast-food restaurants (popularized by Wendy's in the 1970s), and continued advances in food packaging. These new developments included:

- Plastic tubs for cottage and cream cheeses (1969)
- High-density polyethylene gallon milk jugs (1961)
- All-aluminum beer cans (1962)

> ## The American Sweet Tooth
>
> Satisfying the American sweet tooth became a bigger and bigger business as the 20th century unfolded. By century's end, Americans consumed 26.2 pounds of candy per year, split between sweet confections and chocolate. Below, the birthdays of some of our favorite treats:
>
> 1893 Juicy Fruit gum and Wrigley's Spearmint gum
> 1896 Tootsie Rolls
> 1898 Candy Corn
> 1901 NECCO wafers
> 1902 NECCO Conversation Hearts
> 1906 Hershey's Kisses
> 1912 Life Savers
> 1913 Goo Goo Clusters
> 1920 Baby Ruth
> 1921 Chuckles
> 1923 Mounds
> 1924 Milky Way
> 1925 Bit-O-Honey
> 1926 Milk Duds
>
> 1928 Reese's Peanut Butter Cups
> 1929 Snickers
> 1931 Tootsie Roll Pops
> 1932 Red Hots
> 1933 3 Musketeers Bar
> 1936 5th Avenue Bar
> 1939 Hershey's Miniatures chocolate bar
> 1940 M & M's Plain Chocolate Candies
> 1949 Junior Mints
> 1954 Marshmallow Peeps
> 1960 Starburst Fruit Chews
> 1963 SweeTarts
> 1974 Skittles
>
> SOURCE: Chocolate Manufacturers Association; National Confectioners Association
> http://www.candyusa.org/milleniumlist.html

1960s

- Polyethylene-coated milk cartons (1962)
- Easy-open aluminum tabs for beer cans (1964)
- Screw-off closures for beer bottles (1965)
- Plastic foam egg cartons (1968)
- Large bottles for soft drinks (1970)
- Bag-in-box for wine (1976)

1960s • THE AGRICULTURAL AND GREEN REVOLUTIONS ~ The productivity of farms continued to increase dramatically as a result of a variety of changes heralded as the "second Agricultural Revolution." These factors included the expansion of the rural electrification programs of previous decades, dramatic increases in the use of commercial fertilizers, insecticides, and herbicides, improvements in farm equipment, better nutrition and veterinary care of farm animals and dramatic advances in crop breeding. The so-called Green Revolution saw scientists, along with U.S. governmental and international agencies, working together to improve agricultural productivity in the Third World.

1960s–1970s • THE WAR ON POVERTY ~ Despite these developments, however, challenges began to be posed to the image of a prosperous and complacent America. Beginning with the publication of Michael Harrington's *The Other America* in 1962, social activists drew attention to continuing problems of poverty and malnutrition. Inspired both by Harrington and John F. Kennedy, President Lyndon Johnson formally launched the War on Poverty in 1964. This resulted in the expansion or initiation of a wide variety of programs designed to alleviate the social, cultural, educational, and medical condition of America's lower classes. The Food Stamp Program built on the relief programs of the New Deal. In 1972, Congress authorized a Special Supplemental Food Program for Women, Infants, and Children (WIC). The School Breakfast Program (SBP) was established under the Child Nutrition Act of 1966. First begun as a pilot project, the program targeted schools in poor, "nutritionally needy" areas. It aimed to ensure that all children had access to a healthy breakfast in order to promote learning readiness and healthy eating behaviors. The program became permanent in 1975, and by century's end, the SLP operated in more than 72,000 schools and institutions, providing nutritionally balanced, low cost, or free breakfasts to 7.4 million children each school day.

1960s • PREVENTIVE NUTRITION

The most important new trend of the period, however, was another new wave of nutritional awareness. In contrast to the ages of the New and Newer Nutrition, which had focused on the benefits of eating certain foods, this time nutritional advice focused on products to be avoided. Funding for health science research had increased since the late 1950s, and by the late1960s increasing sums were being allocated to studying the links between diet and health. Huge new nonprofit charities like the American Cancer Society and the American Heart Association subsidized research into the harmful effects of certain foods. The prime target was cholesterol, which since the late 1950s had been com-

(1968) A boy eats breakfast cereal next to a glass of juice and a small carton of milk in a school cafeteria under the USDA Child Nutrition Program, Gary, Indiana. The program provided cash and USDA donated food to public and private nonprofit agencies to help them provide nutritious meals to children.

1920s-1970s

ing under suspicion as a cause of heart disease and other ailments. Sugar also became a target, especially condemned for its addictive and otherwise deleterious effects on children. Poor eating habits were increasingly linked to a variety of chronic health conditions including obesity, hypertension, coronary heart disease, cancer, and diabetes, and these links were repeatedly emphasized by the American media. This interest in preventive nutrition led to the establishment of the Senate Select Committee on Nutrition and Human Needs in 1968. This was followed by a White House Conference on the topic in 1969.

Governmental attention led to the publication of a revised set of dietary goals and guidelines which highlighted the relationship between diet and health. The guidelines stressed the need to maintain ideal weight, to moderate salt, sugar, and alcoholic intake, and to eat a diet low in fats and cholesterol and rich in vegetables, fruits, and grain. Health concerns about the healthfulness of cholesterol-laden red meat led many Americans to increase their intake of plant foods. By the late 1970s, many Americans had begun to alter their eating habits by consuming more chicken, fish, and vegetables, and less red meat and butter.

1920s–Present • Dieting ~ Changing eating habits could also be attributed to a growing national obsession with slimness. Diet consciousness can trace its origins at least to the 1920s when the trend toward boyishly slim bodies made the flapper an American ideal. The 1930s saw the fascination with the so-called "Hollywood Diet" – which consisted of a few select vegetables, small amounts of protein, and grapefruits, believed to contain a special fat-burning enzyme. This Hollywood Diet became the prototype of more than a dozen grapefruit diets over the decades. Other popular diet programs emerged in the 1960s and 1970s, among them the Jenny Craig and Weight Watchers weight loss methods. In 1972, Dr. Robert C. Atkins penned his blockbuster bestseller, *Dr. Atkins Diet Revolution*. It argued that drastic cutbacks in carbohydrates forced the body to burn stored fat. Over the next few decades, hundreds of weight loss programs appeared on the market – high protein diets, liquid diets, grapefruit diets, juice or broth fasts, food combining diets, and "crazy for cabbage" diets. One of the most popular new fads at century's end was the Zone Diet, which promised to produce a metabolic state of optimal health where one's body works at peak efficiency. As the century ended, it was estimated that at any given time, one-third of American women were dieting. Although the feminist revolution decried such obsession with body image, old habits died hard. "Lite" beer and Lean Cuisine, however, were marketed to both sexes.

1950s • Keeping Food Safe ~ The counterculture mindset of the 1960s also focused suspicion on the tactics and techniques of food processing giants. Since the late 1950s, concerns had been raised about food additives, when scientists found that the hormones used to fatten chicken and cattle were carcinogenic. Congress responded with important legislation aimed at safeguarding the food supply. The Poultry Inspection Act of 1957 regulated all poultry and poultry products in interstate commerce. In 1958, the Food Additives Amendment was added to the Federal Food, Drug, and Cosmetic Act of 1938. This amendment contained the key Delaney or "cancer clause," which stipulated that no food additive would be deemed safe if it were found to induce cancer in humans or animals. The law allowed processors to continue using hundreds of chemicals then in use but they would be required to obtain government approval before introducing any new ones. In 1977, the government directed the Food and Drug Administration to re-evaluate all of the substances that had previously been "generally recognized as safe" (GRAS).

Tougher food labeling standards also resulted from federal action. In 1966, Congress authorized the FDA to set up requirements for fair disclosure information in labeling and packaging. The Fair Packaging and Labeling Act went into effect in July 1975. It set standards for the labeling of any food to which a nutrient had been added or for which a claim was being made regarding nutritional value.

1970s • THE POLITICS OF EATING

As was the case with many other aspects of life in a period when the personal was deemed political, dietary habits became mired in politics. Social critics denounced American business as a part of the military-industrial-complex responsible for Vietnam, and large corporations were attacked for the immense resources at their command to coerce Americans into eating overprocessed, unhealthy, and environmentally hazardous products. Concern over the purity of food prompted a return to earlier reformist traditions. As had their nineteenth century predecessors, the most radical food reformers drew connections between eating and spiritual, holistic well-being. Rural agrarian communes formed to pursue alternative spiritual ways of life. Some published their own recipe books, touting the value of soybeans and whole grains. Vegetarianism became increasingly popular, inspired by animal rights ideas. Vegetarians drew heavily on the influential work of Adelle Davis and Frances Moore Lappe, authors of *Diet for a Small Planet* (1971), which advocated replacing meat protein with the "complementary" proteins found in grains and beans. The most famous vegetarian cookbook was *Laurel's Kitchen* (1976), complied by members of a vegetarian collective in Berkeley, California. Like the food reformers of the nineteenth century, its authors shunned spices, meat, and white flour.

Food co-ops, the most famous of which was the Berkeley (Calif.) Food Conspiracy, provided members with access to unusual foreign and organic foods. As organic, unprocessed, natural foods came into vogue, cynics responded that the new craze simply gave American business another opportunity. Soon food producers came to emblazon a variety of foods with labels such as "natural," "Nature's Own," "Fresh," "Farm," and "Mountain Valley." Pet owners could even buy natural dog food.

Food became associated with politics in other ways as well. Feminists helped focus attention on the physical and psychological dimensions of women's health. They decried the undue focus on body image perpetuated by American culture, an obsession with thinness that resulted in a variety of eating disorders among young women. Boycotts of grapes, lettuce and other crops were organized in protest against the living and working conditions of migrant farm workers. American corporations were condemned for their sale of infant formulas in Third World nations, a practice that exploited a fascination with American culture at the expense of infants for whom, it was argued, mothers' milk was the healthier alternative.

Politics was also in part responsible for a rebirth of interest in soul food. The

1960s–1970s

"Roots" phenomenon and a resurgence of racial pride rekindled an interest in traditional African-American cuisine.

At the same time, Americans seemed to become more interested in the history of their own indigenous cuisine. The desire to record regional traditions and old family recipes was reflected in the publication of *The American Heritage Cookbook*, 1964. In 1972, James Beard published his celebrated *American Cookery*. Its more than 1,500 recipes focused on ingredients native to America: corn, beans, squash, nuts, berries, and domestic fish and game.

1960s • Food and Status ∼ An appreciation for fine food increasingly became a mark of social status. The early 1960s saw a new interest in French food, attributable, at least in part, to Jackie Kennedy's decision to import a French chef to supervise the White House kitchen. A key role in popularizing French fare was also played by Julia Child, the wife of a Foreign Service officer stationed in France, who was one of the first to use television to explain the techniques of food preparation. Her pioneering program, "The French Chef," appeared on Boston educational station WGBH in 1963. Child also authored an immensely successful two-volume cookbook, *Mastering the Art of French Cooking*, that introduced French creations to middle class Americans. By 1974, the first volume had sold over 1.25 million copies, a total exceeded by only a few other standard texts like *The Joy of Cooking* (1931). New magazines like *Bon Appetit* and *Food and Wine* joined the long-established *Gourmet*. There were new shops and mail order catalogs designed for an upscale audience of both male and female cooks. Among the most acclaimed was the famous Manhattan gourmet shop, The Silver Palate, whose owners Julee Rosso and Sheila Lukins collaborated to produce two of the trendiest cookbooks of the period, *The Silver Palate Cookbook* (1979) and *The Silver Palate Good Times Cookbook* (1985). In 1979, Nina and Tim Zagat created a new standard for the restaurant and travel guide business with the introduction of their first *Zagat New York City Restaurant Survey*, which used customer satisfaction as a new standard in the restaurant rating business.

In sum, food habits reflected the narcissism characteristic of the "me decade" of the 1970s. In the opinion of food historians, a trend toward "dietary individualism" marked these years.

Ethnic and Regional Diversity

∼

Changing immigration patterns were also responsible for diversifying the American palate. New legislative enactments in 1965 led to increases in the number of immigrants from Southeast Asia, Latin America, and the Caribbean, cultures where vegetables occupy a large part of the diet. New varieties of Chinese regional cooking, especially Szechuan and Hunan, began to replace the long established Cantonese and Chinese-American dishes. Other cuisines—northern Italian, regional Mexican, Vietnamese, and Cajun became trendy.

DIVERSITY AND CONTRADICTION, 1980-2000

Scientific breakthroughs, abundance, diversity, and contradiction appeared to be hallmarks of the American diet as the century came to a close.

1980s • BIOTECHNOLOGY, GENETIC ENGINEERING, AND THE COMPUTER REVOLUTION ~ Scientific and technological breakthroughs once again altered and held the potential to further alter American eating habits. Biotechnology enabled the use of living organisms or processes to make or modify products, to improve plants or animals, and to develop microorganisms for specific uses. Improvements in the yield of plant products have resulted, as scientists have developed disease-resistant, herbicide tolerant, and insect-or-virus resistant plant varieties.

Science also responded to the American quest for thinness. The consumption of artificial sweeteners has increased as new, better tasting options have become available. Aspartame, commonly known by the brand name Nutrasweet, has been widely available since the early 1980s. The food industry also responded to the demand for low-calorie, fat-free, and cholesterol-free foods by developing an assortment of fat replacements and fat substitutes like Simplesse (introduced by the Nutrasweet Company of Skokie, Illinois) and Olestra (produced by Proctor and Gamble). In 1984, almost 20 percent of the $290 billion spent on retail foods in the United States went for special "light" or diet foods.

Technology also affected not only which foods were available for Americans to buy, but also how Americans shopped for food. Grocery picking or selection services as conveniences for harried consumers began to emerge in the late 1980s, expanding steadily through the 1990s and moving to the Internet. As the twentieth century closed, on-line food shopping accounted for less than one percent of total U.S. supermarket sales, but predictions called for web-based grocery sales to reach $18.5 billion in 2005.

1980s • HEALTHY EATING ~ The emphasis on healthy eating and preventive nutrition begun in the 1960s has continued. In 1982 the National Cancer Institute published a report containing guidelines for reducing cancer risks, and consumers have become increasingly educated with respect to the dietary intake of fat, fiber, and alcohol. Americans have also been urged to limit their use of foods preserved by salt curing, i.e. salt pickling, smoking, or nitrite curing. The Nutrition Labeling and Education Act of 1990 called for packaging to provide consumers with information enabling them to reduce consumption of total and saturat-

Average Per Person Weekly Grocery Expenses — 2000

TOTAL	$35
GENDER	
Men	$39
Women	$33
TYPE OF HOUSEHOLD	
Children	$27
No Children	$40

SOURCE: Food Marketing Institute, *Trends in the United States: Consumer Attitudes and the Supermarket*, 2000, p. 44
http://www.fmi.og/facts_figs/keyfacts/grcryexpenses.htm

1980s–1990s

ed fat, increase fiber intake, and reduce overall caloric intake.

Yet despite this focus on healthy eating, obesity remains a national problem. According to the Centers for Disease Control and Prevention, one out of four Americans was obese in the year 2000, and more than 60 percent were overweight. Fast-food items (soft-drinks, shakes, hamburgers, and fries) with their high calorie, fat, sodium, and cholesterol content remain very popular. Americans spent more than $110 billion in fast food restaurants in the year 2000.

Beginning in the 1980s, the industry attempted to address concerns about the nutritional value of their products, and healthier choices like prepared salads, grilled chicken, and baked potatoes were added to fast-food menus. McDonald's introduced Chicken McNuggets in 1983 as a response to concerns about Americans' continued overconsumption of red meat. In 1986 at least five major chains decreased their use of saturated fat, switching from an animal-vegetable shortening to an all-vegetable product for all purpose frying.

Surveys conducted in the 1990s indicate that at least two million Americans consider themselves vegetarians, while perhaps 10 million more avoid red meat. A growing trend is the number of "vegans," those who eat no foods of animal origin, such as milk, eggs, or honey. Other dietary fads became popular in avant garde communities.

One was macrobiotics, invented by George Ohsawa in Paris. Based on Zen monastic cooking from Japan, macrobiotics was based on a series of progressively restrictive diets, beginning with fish, noodles, clam sauce, and vegetables.

The interest in organic foods has continued. Domestic sales of organic foods increased more than 20 percent annually each year since 1990, and reached total sales of $6 billion in the year 2000. Proponents argue that organic foods are better looking, better tasting, and naturally more nutritious. At the end of the year 2000, the USDA issued national standards to govern the production and marketing of foods labeled organic. In the making for ten years, the standards ban the use of irradiation, biotechnology, and sewer-sludge fertilizer for any food labeled organic. The standards also ban synthetic pesticides and fertilizers in the growing of organic food, and the use of antibiotics in any meat labeled organic.

1990s • DIVERSITY AND ABUNDANCE

By the end of the century, Americans were exposed to an unprecedented variety of food choices, with the average supermarket stocking well over 24,000 items. Affluence, immigration, and an exploding interest in travel contributed to the fascination with diverse and exotic food choices like Thai lemongrass, sundried toma-

Food and Drink in the U.S.
1970 – 2001
(Billions of Current Dollars)

1970	$ 42.8
1980	$119.6
1990	$239.3
2001*	$399.2

*Projected

SOURCE: National Restaurant Association
http://www.restaurant.org/research/ind_glance.html

toes, Jerusalem artichokes, and varieties of hummus. Diversity was also encouraged by the trend-setting habits of "young urban professionals" (christened "yuppies" by the media), who tended to define people by their consumption habits.

Ethnic foods exploded into the mainstream in the last two decades of the century. Chili peppers became highly popular, and catalogs listed hundreds of varieties from which to choose. Hot sauces figured prominently in a variety of trendy new specialties: Mexican, Tex-Mex, Cajun, and some variations of Asian cuisine. Burritos, tacos, and salsa became available in supermarkets everywhere, and by the 1990s sales of salsa had exceeded those of catsup. A fad for stir-frying caused supermarkets to carry Oriental vegetables, bean sprouts, and soy sauces, and woks and Chinese steamers appeared in gourmet food stores. What the yuppies called "grazing," eating small portions of a variety of foods, encouraged an interest in Asian "Dim Sum," and Japanese-inspired sushi bars proliferated.

The interest in French cooking has continued, but the "nouvelle cuisine" is of the healthier "minimalist," variety first pioneered in France in the 1970s. Served not with the traditional flour thickened sauces but with reduced stocks, it also includes a new emphasis on fresh ingredients. Al dente vegetables and pasta are featured prominently in the newly popular northern Italian cuisine, with its diminished focus on traditional tomato sauces. The interest in regional cooking is probably more pronounced in the South than elsewhere, popularized by chains such as Stuckey's, Po' Folks, and Cracker Barrel, and re-defined and "yuppified" in publications like *Southern Living* Magazine.

Although alcohol consumption has dropped significantly, sales of beer and wine have increased. There is a new interest in novelty and variety here as well, with a resurgence of interest in local beers and new microbrewed beers reminiscent of the beers of yesteryear brewed in taverns and private homes. Regional wineries are also increasingly popular.

Another new trend emerging at century's end was the marketing of certain foods specifically to women. Spurred by a 1996 USDA survey that found more than half of adult women failing to meet recommended dietary allowances for six essential nutrients, new gender specific products have been developed. These include: Harmony, a new General Mills cereal that calls itself a "low-fat" nutritional cereal for women," pumped up with calcium, antioxidants, soy, iron, and folic acid; Quaker Oatmeal Nutrition for Women, which adds calcium, iron, folic acid, and B vitamins; and lines of vitamin and herb drinks such as Femme Vitale which contain calcium, iron, and folic acid. Production of such products is likely to continue, as food companies recognize that women buy 80 percent of the groceries sold in the United States and that they like having products pitched specifically to them.

1990s • KITCHENS WITHOUT COOKS

∼ According to some indicators, the last decades of the century appear to have witnessed a new interest in cooking. What one food historian has termed a "tidal wave of interest in food" appears to be reflected in architectural and retailing trends: gourmet kitchens equipped with restaurant grade stoves, sub-zero refrigerators, cooking islands, double sinks to facilitate food preparation, a whole array of high priced food processors, blenders, choppers, bread and pasta making machines. An interest in the preparation of fine food has been popularized by the cable TV industry, which has presented an

1980s–1990s

exploding number of cooking shows. The Food Network, which pioneered in 1993, has been amazingly successful, with revenues jumping at about 60 percent per year through the last decade of the century. Since 1998, the number of homes where the Food Network could be seen nearly doubled to 54 million, and primetime viewership more than doubled to 295,000, according to Nielsen Media Research. Professional Chefs Emeril Lagasse, Mario Battali, and Ming Tsai were among the best known TV chefs of the 1990s. Another fascinating exemplar of social trends was entrepreneur Martha Stewart, the Westport, Connecticut caterer who parlayed an interest in food preparation and presentation into a one-woman industry celebrating the joys of domesticity.

Ironically, however, fewer and fewer meals are actually cooked and eaten at home. In the 1990s, it was estimated that only about 15 percent of American households regularly cooked and ate three meals per day at home. The fast-food industry remained a multibillion dollar per year phenomenon, accounting for at least 40 percent of monies spent on meals eaten away from home. Experts say that the percentage of food dollars spent away from home should continue to increase. Projections place this figure at 53 percent in 2010, up from 27percent in 1955.

In New Jersey alone, the number of restaurants grew 28 percent in the period 1990-1998, from 12,500 to 16,000. One new trend of the 1990s was the increase in take-home meals from table service restaurants. The National Restaurant Association reported that in 2000, 52 percent of all meals were being taken out or delivered from the nation's mid-price, table service restaurants, surpassing for the first time the number of meals eaten on the premises. Increasingly affluent Americans appear to want the convenience and quality of restaurant-cooked meals without the nutritional pitfalls of fast-food.

1980s • HEAT AND EAT FOODS

Consumers have also demanded a larger variety of heat and eat foods, a trend made possible by the increasing availability of the microwave oven. Such ovens first became popular in the1980s, despite the misconception that they emitted dangerous radiation and made food radioactive. At least 90 percent of American homes were equipped with microwave ovens by century's end. The main advantage of the microwave is that it makes quick re-heating possible, a big convenience for families with different schedules. New products are catering to consumer desires for fostering illusions of domesticity without expending the time and effort that would otherwise be involved. Stouffer's "Oven Sensations," dinner meals in a bag that pour into a baking dish, bubble in the oven and are table ready after 25 minutes.

1990s • BRINGING HOME THE DINNER

The frenzied pace of life at the turn of the twentieth century explains these new variations in American eating habits. Affluence, along with the increase in the number of working mothers, has resulted in new ways to answer the question, "What's for Dinner?" More meals are eaten in restaurants, more meals are eaten at home that have been cooked elsewhere, the use of take-out foods has increased, there has been an increase in the number of meals delivered from restaurants, there is a greater use of convenience items, and even supermarkets now routinely offer a large assortment of high-quality, store-cooked, take-out items.

One of the newest solutions to the American dinner-time dilemma has been the emergence of personal chefs. In-home chef services as replacements for takeout and processed foods first came to national attention in the mid-1990s. Although a luxury first reserved to affluent couples with children, by century's end such services had filtered into the mainstream. The U.S. Professional Chefs Association, one of the industry's largest training and certifying organizations, placed the number of full-time in-home chefs at 6,000, and customers using them at 100,000 or more.

CONCLUSION

In 1949 the Pillsbury Company pioneered the Pillsbury Bake Off, one of the oldest and most prestigious of American cooking contests. Designed to celebrate women's return to the home after World War II, the contest attracted such participants as First Ladies Eleanor Roosevelt, Mamie Eisenhower, and Pat Nixon, along with first daughter Margaret Truman and the Duke and Duchess of Windsor. A review of prizewinning recipes over the decades provides fascinating insights into the changing American diet. While a hearty veal casserole took the title in the 1950, by the 1970s a whole wheat raisin loaf was the grand prize winner. The 1980s brought Italian zucchini crescent pie, while the 1990s celebrated chicken fajita pizza and couscous served with chicken thighs cooked in salsa. Contestants in the year 2000 made use of tofu, lemon grass, and hoisin sauce. Pillsbury publishes a trends report, predicting the continuing influence of ethnic influences and ingredients. Recipes using lemon grass, hoisin sauce, and tofu are expected to become popular.

So what does the future hold for the American diet? There appears to be no indication that the trends of this century – new products, diversity amidst standardization, the search for convenience – will abate any time soon. More and more processed foods of every kind, including foods altered by biotechnology and genetic engineering, will confront the American consumer. Yet it is heartening to know that some traces of regional idiosyncrasy do persist. Scarcely known outside its native city, a "transcultural mishmash" known as Cincinnati chili has retained its hold on the local palate since the 1920s. Invented by a Bulgarian immigrant named To Kiradjieff, the dish combines hamburger and stew meat, herbs, spices, and cinnamon. The novelty of the concoction, however, lies in the variety of ingredients that can be added. The basic version comes on a bed of spaghetti and is called "chili spaghetti." "Three-way" chili adds a layer of cheese, "four-way" chili boasts chopped white onions, while "five-way" chili is complete with a layer of beans. Served in fast food chains, local restaurants, and prepared at home, Cincinnati chili adds special meaning to the concept of the American melting pot.

BIBLIOGRAPHY

Aronowitz, Stanley. *Food, Shelter and the American Dream.* New York: Seabury Press, 1974.

Barer-Stein, Thelma. *You Eat What You Are: People, Culture and Food Traditions.* Buffalo, NY: Firefly Books, 1999.

Belasco, Warren J. *Appetite for Change: How the Counterculture Took on the Food Industry, 1966-1988.* New York: Pantheon Books, 1989.

Brenner, Leslie. *American Appetite: The Coming of Age of a Cuisine.* New York: Avon Books, 1999.

Brewster, Letitia and Michael F. Jacobson. *The Changing American Diet*. Washington, DC: Center for Science in the Public Interest, 1978.

Brown, Dale. *American Cooking*. New York: Time-Life Books, 1968.

Camp, Charles. *American Foodways: What, When, Why and How We Eat in America*. Little Rock: August House, 1989.

Collins, Douglas. *America's Favorite Food: The Story of Campbell Soup Company*. New York: Harry N. Abrams, 1994.

Cummings, Richard Osborn. *The American and His Food*. New York: Arno Press, 1970.

Germov, John and Lauren Williams, eds. *A Sociology of Food and Nutrition*. South Melbourne, Australia: Oxford University Press, 1999.

Kiple, Kenneth F. and Kriemhild Conee Ornelos. *The Cambridge World History of Food*. 2 vols. Cambridge: Cambridge University Press, 2000.

Lager, Fred. "Chico." *Ben and Jerry's: The Inside Scoop*. New York: Crown Publishers, 1994.

Levenstein, Harvey A. *Paradox of Plenty: A Social History of Eating in Modern America*. New York: Oxford University Press, 1993.

Levenstein, Harvey A. *Revolution at the Table: The Transformation of the American Diet*. New York: Oxford University Press, 1988.

McIntosh, Elaine N. *American Food Habits in Historical Perspective*. Westport, CT: Praeger Publishers, 1995.

Mogelonsky, Marcia. *Everybody Eats: Supermarket Consumers in the 1990s*. Ithaca, NY: American Demographics, 1995.

Root, Waverly, and Rochemont, Richard De. *Eating in America: A History*. Hopewell, NJ: Ecco Press, 1981.

Schlosser, Eric. *Fast Food Nation: The Dark Side of the All American Meal*. New York: Houghton Mifflin, 2001.

Shenton, James P., et al. *American Cooking: The Melting Pot*. New York: Time-Life Books, 1971.

Sonnenfeld, Albert. *Food: A Culinary History*. New York: Columbia University Press, 1999.

Tannahill, Reay. *Food in History*. New York: Crown Publishers, 1989.

Ward, Susie, Claire Clifton, and Jenny Stacey. *The Gourmet Atlas*. New York: Macmillan, 1997.

Walker, Eugene. *American Cooking: Southern Style*. New York: Time-Life Books, 1971.

Williams, Peter W. "Foodways." In *Encyclopedia of American Social History*, pp. 1331-1344. Edited by Mary Kupiec Cayton, Elliott J. Gorn, and Peter W. Williams. New York: Charles Scribner's Sons, 1993.

INTERNET RESOURCES

FirstGov
Centralized directory provides access to all federal U.S. government web sites and documents. Key in "Food" to go to associated government links.

Milestones in U.S. Food and Drug Law History
http://www.fda.gov/opacom/backgrounders/miles.html

Center for Food Safety & Applied Nutrition offers consumer advice on additives, product labeling, nutrition, and foodborne illness.
http://vm.cfsan.fda.gov/list.html

Environmental Protection Agency: Food Safety. Key in "Food" to find associated sites.
http://www.epa.gov/history/topics/food

History of Kosher Food in the USA
http://www.koshertodayonline.com/history.htm

FOOD TIMELINE
Find out when chickens where domesticated or when coffee came to Europe using this food timeline that begins in BC 17,000.
http://www.gti.net/mocolib1/kid/food.html

THE HISTORY OF FOOD IRRADIATION
1920s French scientists discovered that irradiation preserves foods. 1940s U.S. Army began testing irradiation of common foods.
http://www.exnet.iastate.edu/Pages/families/fs/rad/irhistory.html

History of Rations
http://www.qmfound.com/history_of_rations.html

FOOD SECURITY
History of the federal food security measure. Go to the bottom of the home page to select key topics related to food and agriculture.
http://www.ers.usda.gov/briefing/foodsecurity/history

ALHN Food Page
Everything you wanted to know about food, from recipes to history.
http://www.usroots.org/~genranch/food/

History of Soul Food
http://www.foxhome.com/soulfood/htmls/soulfood.html

Teacher resources for food history lessons
http://www.gti.net/mocolib1/kid/food2.html

Marie Marmo Mullaney
Caldwell College, NJ

HEALTH AND MEDICINE

(1972) Serpent handler Bill Haast charming a cobra. He makes his living by extracting venom for medical use at his laboratory in Miami, Florida.

TIMELINE

1600-1899 ~ Breaking Ground

William Harvey describes the circulation of blood in England (1628) / Edward Jenner develops smallpox vaccination in England (1796) / First use of anesthetic (ether) on humans in U.S. (1842) / Louis Pasteur first demonstrates use of antibiotics in France (1887) / Wilhelm K. Roentgen discovers X-rays in Germany (1895)

MILESTONES: Isaac Newton makes significant contributions to mathematics, physics, astronomy, and optics (1600s) • Oliver Evans builds the first steam-powered motor vehicle in the U.S. (1805) • Bessemer steel process invented (1850s) • George Eastman invents celluloid rolls of film for use in Kodak cameras (1888)

1900-1909 ~ Institutional Involvement

U.S. Army Yellow Fever Commission shows mosquitoes as the disease carrier of malaria (1900) / U.S. Public Health Service identifies the hookworm parasite devastating the Southern population (1902) / Pure Food and Drug Act sets standards for food and drug control (1906) / First mental health organization is the Connecticut Society for Mental Hygiene (1908) / Karl Landsteiner classifies blood groups in Austria (1909)

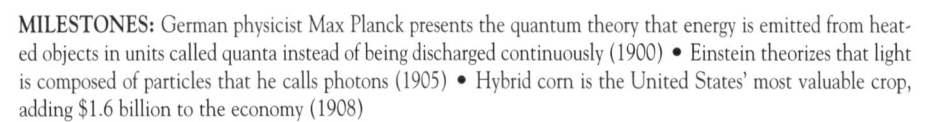

MILESTONES: German physicist Max Planck presents the quantum theory that energy is emitted from heated objects in units called quanta instead of being discharged continuously (1900) • Einstein theorizes that light is composed of particles that he calls photons (1905) • Hybrid corn is the United States' most valuable crop, adding $1.6 billion to the economy (1908)

1910-1919 ~ Broadening Health Care Concerns

Salvarsan used against syphilis (1910) / Measles discovered to be a viral infection (1911) / Congress creates United States Public Health Service (1912) / Vitamin A discovered (1912), Vitamin D (1917) / American Cancer Society founded (1913) / Water chlorination for purification is initiated in the United States (1913) / Mammography developed to detect breast cancer (1913) / Pasteurization of milk begins in large cities (1914) / Curative effect of sunlight on rickets is discovered (1919)

MILESTONES: Einstein develops his theory of relativity (1910) • Theodore W. Richards becomes the first American to win a Nobel for chemistry for his work with atomic weights (1914) • George Hale constructs a 254 centimeter telescope and learns that galaxies other than the Earth's Milky Way exist (1917) • Worldwide flu pandemic arrives in U.S. (1918)

1920-1929 ~ Exploring the Causes of Diseases

Inkblot test introduced by Hermann Rorschach for psychoanalysis (1921) / Vitamin E discovered (1921) / Insulin used to treat diabetes (1922) / Invention of electrocardiograph (1923) / Alexander Fleming discovers penicillin in molds (1928) / George Papanicolaou develops the Pap test for diagnosing uterine cancer (1928) / Iron-lung respirator invented (1928) / Electroencephalograph (EEG) invented (1929)

MILESTONES: Listerine advertising creates fear of bad breath (1922) • Robert A. Millikan wins a Nobel Prize for his work with electrons (1923) • Charles Birdseye develops a quick-freeze technique, making frozen foods possible (1924) • John T. Scopes, a teacher in Tennessee, is arrested for teaching evolution to his students (1925) • Supreme Court decision, *Buck v. Bell*, rules that involuntary sterilization for eugenic purposes is constitutional (1927)

1930-1935 ~ Health Research

National Institute of Health established (1930) / Common cold virus discovered (1930) / Vitamin C discovered (1932) / Blue Cross hospital insurance program created (1933) / First successful lung surgery removes cancerous lung (1933) / First use of electric shock to reverse potentially fatal ventricular fibrillation of the heart (1933) / Studies relate fluoride and reduction in tooth decay (1933) / First wearable hearing aid is produced (1935)

MILESTONES: Ernest O. Lawrence's use of a cyclotron accelerates nuclear particles to smash atoms and release energy from matter (1930) • The Nobel Prize winning geneticist, Hermann J. Muller, attacks the eugenics movement for "lending a false appearance of scientific basis to advocates of race and class prejudice" (1930s) • Thomas Hunt Morgan becomes the first American to win a Nobel Prize in medicine and physiology (1933) • 1.5 million latex condoms are being produced in the U.S. each day (1935)

1936-1939 ~ Vitamins

Sulfa drugs introduced to U.S. (1936) / Vitamin B synthesized (1936), Vitamin B12 isolated (1937), Vitamin K discovered (1939) / First successful treatment of bacterial infection with sulfanilamide (1937) / Angiocardiography introduced (1937) / Electroconvulsive therapy, ECT or "shock" therapy, is used to treat mental illness (1938)

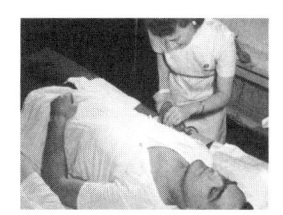

MILESTONES: Infant mortality rates decline by 25 percent between 1930-1939 • Euthanasia Society of America is established (1938) • Heart disease, cancer, and stroke replace contagious diseases as leading causes of death (1939) • Wallace H. Carothers at the E.I. Dupont chemical company develops the synthetic fiber, nylon (1938)

1940-1945 ~ Miracle Drugs

Plasma discovered to substitute for whole blood in transfusions (1940) / Treatment of pneumonia with sulfanilamide (1941) / Discovery of streptomycin, a new antibiotic (1943) / Isolation of DNA (1944) / Aureomycin antibiotic introduced to attack a broad range of viruses (1944) / Oral penicillin introduced (1945)

MILESTONES: Westinghouse Science Talent Search (later sponsored by Intel) is organized to identify high school students who have extraordinary scientific potential (1941) • Military leaders regard venereal disease prevention as a major priority (1942-1945) • Availability of the new drug penicillin to treat venereal disease changes attitudes and caution about intercourse (1943)

1946-1949 ~ Treating Diseases

Synthetic penicillin produced (1946) / Prefrontal lobotomy brain surgery used to treat schizophrenia (1947) / Sickle-cell anemia described as molecular disease (1949) / Lithium used to treat psychiatric disease (1949)

MILESTONES: Kinsey report on sexual behavior of the human male published (1948) • National Institute of Mental Health established (1949)

1950-1954 ～ Tuberculosis, Heart Disease, and Polio

Introduction of blood tests for tuberculosis (1950) / Heart-lung machine developed (1952) / Heart attack patient revived by electric shock (1952) / Artificial pacemaker regulates heart rhythm (1952) / Introduction of open-heart surgery (1954) / Mass trials of Salk polio vaccine begin (1954)

MILESTONES: Polio rate at all-time high (1952) • National Educational Television launched (1952) • Kinsey reports that more than half of the nation's women are not virgins when they marry (1953) • Swanson introduces the TV dinner (1954)

1955-1959 ～ Organ Transplants, Ultrasound, and Vaccines

First successful kidney transplant (1955) / Live polio vaccine introduced (1955) / Kidney dialysis machine invented (1956) / Ultrasound examination of fetuses in the womb (1958) / First coronary artery cauterization (1958) / Combined vaccine for whooping cough, diphtheria, and polio released (1959)

MILESTONES: Relationship between smoking and lung cancer announced (1956) • First National Conference on Air Pollution (1958) • Pressure test for eye disease, glaucoma, developed (1959)

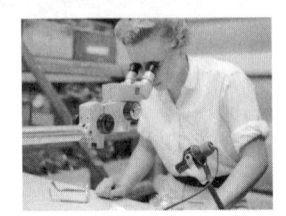

1960-1963 ～ Birth Control and Transplant Advances

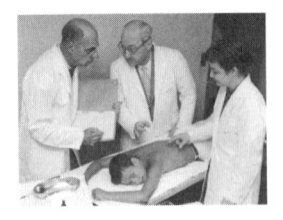

Oral contraceptive pills (1960) and intrauterine contraceptive devices developed (1961) / Vaccination for Rh-negative mothers prevents their antibodies from affecting future pregnancies (1961) / First successful reattachment of a severed arm (1962) / Rubella (measles) virus isolated (1962) / Valium introduced (1963) / First human liver transplant (1963) / First human lung transplant (1963)

MILESTONES: Hazardous Substances Labeling Act requires warnings on dangerous household products (1960) • John H. Glenn, Jr., becomes the first American to orbit the Earth (February 20, 1962) • Rachel Carson's *Silent Spring* calls attention to pollution (1962) • Boston Strangler murders thirteen women (1962-1964) • Number of deaths due to automobile accidents increases 46 percent (1960s)

1964-1969 ～ Women's Health and Heart Transplants

New fertility drug, Pergonal, introduced, resulting in an increase in multiple births (1964) / Female hormone estrogen discovered to prevent osteoporosis (1965) / Meningitis vaccine introduced (1968) / First artificial heart transplant (1969)

MILESTONES: Surgeon general declares cigarette smoking a health hazard (1964) • Child Protection Act bans toys containing hazardous substances (1966) • Truth in Packaging Act responds to growing public dissatisfaction with deceptive advertising (1966) • Clean Air Act sets pollution guidelines (1967)

1970-1979 ~ Space Age Diagnostic Techniques

First nerve transplant (1970) / First dual heart and lung transplants (1971) / Ultrasound diagnostic techniques developed (1974) / Legionnaires' disease outbreak (1976) / Balloon angioplasty reopens diseased arteries (1977) / Magnetic resonance imaging (MRI) scanner developed (1977) / First test-tube baby born in England (1978)

MILESTONES: Norman E. Borlaug, a plant pathologist, receives the Nobel Prize for genetically creating a strain of high yield dwarf spring wheat that had sufficient protein and calories to alleviate malnourishment, and is credited with saving millions from dying of starvation (1970) • Environmental Protection Agency is created to restrict pollution (1970) • Clean Air Act attempts to minimize vehicle produced pollution (1970) • Occupational Safety and Health Act sets safety standards in the workplace (1970)

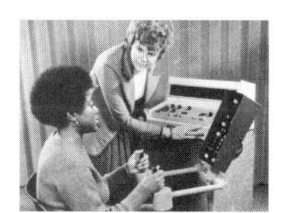

1980-1989 ~ AIDS Epidemic

World Health Organization (WHO) announces worldwide eradication of smallpox (1980) / AIDS recognized as beginning a worldwide death toll (1981) / First successful surgery performed on a fetus (1981) / First permanent artificial heart used in a human (1982) / First baby born from a donated embryo to an infertile mother (1984) / First dual heart and liver transplant (1984) / First U.S. liver transplant using a living donor (1989)

MILESTONES: Barbara McClintock becomes the first woman to win a Nobel Prize as an individual, for her work in gene behavior (1983) • Russell Higuchi becomes the first scientist to clone an extinct animal's DNA segment (1983) • The Human Genome Organization is organized (1988) • AIDS becomes the second leading cause of death (following accidents) among American men aged 25-34 (1989)

1990-2000 ~ Cloning and Genome Mapping

First gene therapy performed on a human to treat an immune deficiency (1990) / Norplant implantable contraceptive approved for women (1990) / Successful heart surgery performed on a fetus in the womb (1991) / First significant decline in AIDS deaths is attributed to new protease inhibitors (1997) / First mapping of an entire human genome (2000)

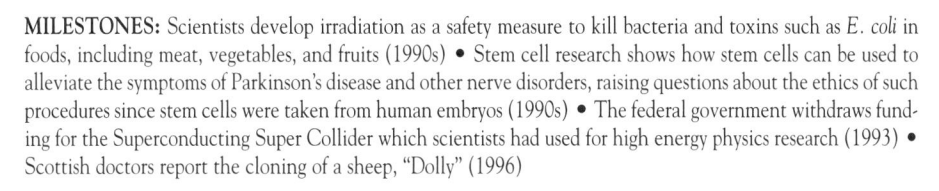

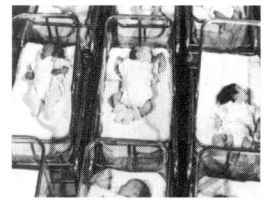

MILESTONES: Scientists develop irradiation as a safety measure to kill bacteria and toxins such as *E. coli* in foods, including meat, vegetables, and fruits (1990s) • Stem cell research shows how stem cells can be used to alleviate the symptoms of Parkinson's disease and other nerve disorders, raising questions about the ethics of such procedures since stem cells were taken from human embryos (1990s) • The federal government withdraws funding for the Superconducting Super Collider which scientists had used for high energy physics research (1993) • Scottish doctors report the cloning of a sheep, "Dolly" (1996)

INTRODUCTION

When the clock struck midnight on December 31, 1899, a major landmark in the history of medicine already existed—the discovery of disease-causing microorganisms. This revolutionary discovery would influence both American medical practice and the health of Americans throughout the twentieth century. Prior to the mid-nineteenth century, physicians blamed illnesses on such things as the weather or topographical conditions, the decaying of local organic matter, or "bad air" or miasma from other sources; and there was much uncertainty about how to prevent or control the great epidemics. Proofs of the germ theory of disease causation, as advanced by Robert Koch, Louis Pasteur, and their followers in the decades after 1870, radically changed the practice and belief system of American medicine, bringing new forms of relief to the ill, influencing new technologies, and altering the earlier, more holistic, focus of medicine from the sick person as an individual to his disease process.

Before the advent of the germ theory, medical practice paid attention to a broad range of biological, psychological, and social processes in explaining and treating disease. Since disease concepts focused on the relationship of the individual to his environment, treatment often consisted of the manipulation of the environment. Effective public health measures were developed during the nineteenth century, even without any knowledge about the causes of the diseases. By the late nineteenth century most

(1966) Microscopes are given one last inspection before they are cleared for distribution and use.

large cities' established departments of public health with responsibilities for epidemic control and sanitary water supplies. Almshouses began to be transformed into hospitals for the needy. They did not greatly reduce mortality because earlier advances in public health already fulfilled this role. But they did mark the beginnings of the modern hospital movement. Medical schools proliferated, but the twentieth century would see drastic changes in the training and practice of medicine.

As the twentieth century approached, medical concerns began to narrow to the pathologic and physiologic processes of disease, and the mission and training of physicians shifted from the care of sick people to the diagnosis and cure of disease. American medicine is traditionally aggressive. The thinking throughout much of the century was that disease could be conquered. This American medical focus on diagnosis and the aggressive treatment and cure of acute diseases rather than on prevention would lead to major changes in health care policies throughout the century, and ultimately prove unsatisfactory by the year 2000 as deaths due to acute disease declined but chronic diseases increased. As doubts arose by the end of the twentieth century about the ultimate conquest of disease, and bureaucratic forms of managed care took over medical practice, medical practitioners and patients alike became increasingly alienated from medicine.

1900-1999 • THE HEALTH CENTURY

∼ The twentieth century was truly "the health century." From 1900 to 1999, Americans saw their life expectancy increase by 29 years; a remarkable increase in a short time in light of the fact that it took 4,500 years—from the Bronze Age to 1900—to bring the last life span increase of at least 27 years.

Declining infant mortality, control of infectious and nutritional diseases via public health advances, including improvements in sanitation, general access to clean water, fresh food and the discovery

Life Expectancy at Birth, 1900-1998

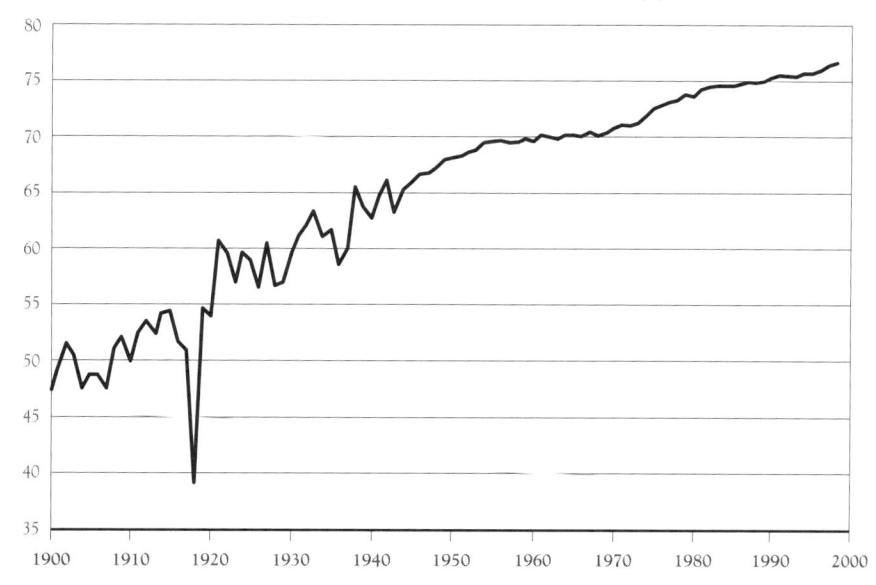

The dramatic rise in the death rate in 1918-1919 reflects the great influenza pandemic of 1918-1919, which resulted in over a half-million deaths in the United States.
SOURCE: Compiled from *World Almanac and Book of Facts*, 2001 and other 20th century issues.

Death Rate per 1,000 Population

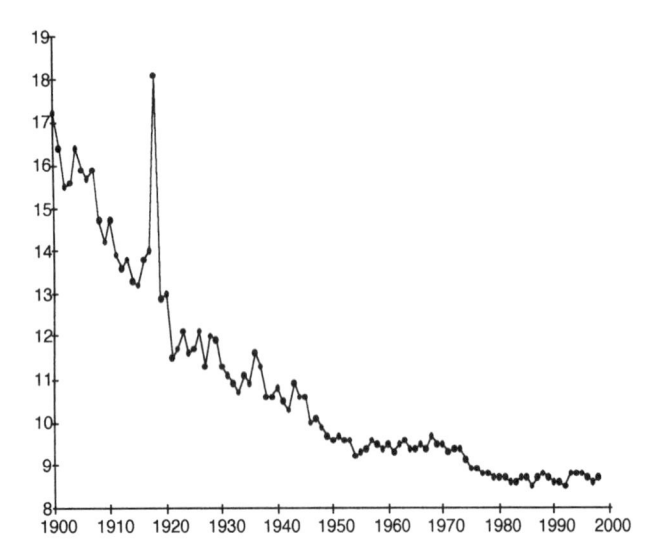

SOURCE: Compiled from *World Almanac and Book of Facts*, 2001 and other 20th Century Issues.

1900-1930s • THE NATION'S HEALTH: LIFE EXPECTANCY, SMALLPOX, DIET, ANESTHESIA, DRUG REGULATION

A baby born after the stroke of midnight on January 1, 1900, had an average life expectancy of 47 years. Life expectancy is not to be confused with length of life, the maximum possible length of a human life. It represents the number of years, based on known statistics, to which any person of a given age may reasonably expect to live. Saving an infant or child from death by infectious disease, who may then survive to age 70, gives a larger gain in life expectancy than saving a 70-year-old from heart disease, who may then survive for another decade. At the beginning of the century, Americans died at younger ages than they did by century's end. In 1900 only 19 percent of individuals who died were over age 65, compared to the end of the century when 72 percent of all deaths occurred in those over 65. The three leading causes of death in 1999 were diseases more likely to be associated with advanced age than were influenza and pneumonia, tuberculosis, and gastroenteritis, the three leading causes of death in 1900.

1900-1930s

of vitamins; better pre- and post-natal care; new immunizations and antibiotics; and important advances against modern-day killers such as cancer and coronary artery disease all contributed to this remarkable change. Twentieth century scientific advances and space-age technology led to such inventions as new imaging techniques which rendered some surgeries obsolete, computerized medicine, successful organ transplants, and amazing surgeries even on the unborn.

With these medical advances came changes in the practice of medicine and the training of those who administer medical care. Medical practice changed from an "art" to a "science" with these scientific advances and improvements in medical education. But by 1999, the United States still lagged behind other nations in life expectancy and infant mortality, and the spiraling costs of medical care, access to medical care for all Americans, and the management of bureaucratic health care systems had become the major medical concerns of the nation.

The Ten Leading Causes of Death in the United States, 1900

Influenza and pneumonia
Tuberculosis
Gastroenteritis
Heart disease
Cerebral hemorrhage
Chronic nephritis
Accidents
Cancer
Diseases of early infancy
Diphtheria

SOURCE: *Historical Statistics of the United States, Colonial Times to 1970.*

A low life expectancy reflects a high death rate especially among infants and young children. Infant and maternal mortality rates were still high in 1900. If a baby born in 1900 survived infancy, diseases that flourished in more crowded populations, such as polio, smallpox, yellow fever, typhoid fever, and deadly pneumonia, might take him or her in childhood or adulthood. Children suffered and sometimes died from measles, whooping cough, and scarlet fever. Bacterial infections raged through neighborhoods and doctors were helpless against most of them. Pellagra and hookworm were problems, especially in the rural South. Tuberculosis (TB) caused many deaths. Fresh air, nutrition, and rest were the only treatments for TB, and often available only to the wealthy.

Smallpox vaccine was available in 1900, but diphtheria, typhoid, or scarlet fever could not be prevented. By 1900 more effective patient care and better general public health had already begun to make inroads into the health of Americans. Ironically, a great growth in products for self-dosage took place with the scientific advances in medicine, with quackery taking advantage of conventional medicine's promises as well as its weaknesses. There were few doctors, especially in rural areas, and mail-order cures were substituted for physician care. Many of these were aimed at treating children and sold as teething "syrups," sweet powders, cough killers, and "babies' friends." They depended for their effectiveness on alcohol, opium, morphine, and/or chloroform. Used to excess on a fussy child, they could kill; but even in moderation they could gradually become addictive.

Urbanization during the nineteenth century brought changes in disease patterns and a corresponding rise in mortality. City eating habits aggravated health problems, especially among the urban poor. Quantity, not quality of food was stressed and over-eating was a national habit. The diet stressed starchy diets, salt-cured meats, and fat-fried foods. Especially missing in urban diets were fresh fruits and vegetables and milk, which contained important vitamins for resisting diseases.

A number of advances in patient care were in place by 1900. Anesthesia was available in the form of ether and chloroform gases for pain-free surgery. Patients' fears of painful operations were greatly reduced and prescriptions of narcotics made the pain more bearable. The widespread adoption of the antiseptic methods of Englishman Joseph Lister in the 1870s led to sterile conditions in operating rooms, and cleaner treatment techniques helped patients in surviving their medical treatments. Physicians began to wash their hands and sterilize their instruments before touching their patients.

The Pure Food and Drug Act of 1906 was an example of early twentieth century expansion of federal protection over the health of Americans. It led to both better foods manufactured under more sanitary conditions and a war on drugs. The widespread sale of addictive substances such as opium and morphine in unregulated pharmacies resulted in a high number of drug addicts. Some were hooked on opium or morphine and had little difficulty buying these addictive substances at unregulated pharmacies. Others were addicted to the ingredients in many of the various patent medicines advertising themselves as cure-alls. The Pure Food and Drug Act regulated the patent medicine business with its restriction on the use of addictive drugs and required labeling of ingredients.

1918: What to Do About the Flu

In 1918 the United States suffered the worst epidemic in its history, the so-called "Spanish Influenza," which led to the death of a half million Americans. With "the 'influence' in influenza...still veiled in mystery," public health departments such as the one in New York City could do little else than give the following advice:

"If you feel sick all over, with chilliness or aching of the bones, and with feverishness and headache, perhaps with a cold in the head or throat, you are probably getting influenza.
Go to bed and, until you can get a doctor, do these things:

- Take castor-oil or a dose of salts to move the bowels.
- Keep reasonably but not too well covered, and keep fresh air in the room, best by opening a window at the top.
- Take only simple, plain food, such as milk, milk-soups, gruels, or porridge, or any cereals, and bread and butter, and any kind of broth, or mashed potatoes; also eggs, but not more than two a day. Do not take any meat, or any wine, beer, whisky, or other spirits, unless you are ordered to by the doctor.
- Do not get up, unless it is absolutely necessary, and then do not walk about and expose yourself to cold, and do not go about in bare feet. In this way you will avoid getting pneumonia or bronchitis.
- Do not take any medicine unless ordered by the doctor.
- You should drink plenty of plain water all through the sickness.
- Stay in bed until you have no fever and are feeling much better. Stay in the house two or three days longer.
- If you are not much better, or practically well in two or three days, call a doctor, if you have not done so already, or ask the nearest hospital for help, or call the nearest nursing center, or notify the nearest Board of Health Clinic."

SOURCE: "Advice of the New York Health Department to Persons with Influenza." *Literary Digest* Vol. 59: 20. November 2, 1918.

1918-1919

1918-1919 • THE GREATEST EPIDEMIC ~ By the end of the twentieth century, young Americans viewed AIDS as the last major epidemic to be solved by medical science, while their parents remembered the great polio epidemics of the 1950s. Yet the greatest of all American epidemics, a terrible pandemic popularly known as "Spanish influenza," has all but been forgotten. At the beginning of the century influenza epidemics were familiar to Americans and were the leading cause of death, but the "Spanish flu" developed into pneumonia and secondary complications with astonishing rapidity during 1918-1919. Nearly one out of every four Americans was affected by it, and more than 550,000 Americans died out of a population of 103,208,000 (July 1, 1918, population estimate). Its primary victims were infants, young adults, and the elderly, and its deadliness and speed were

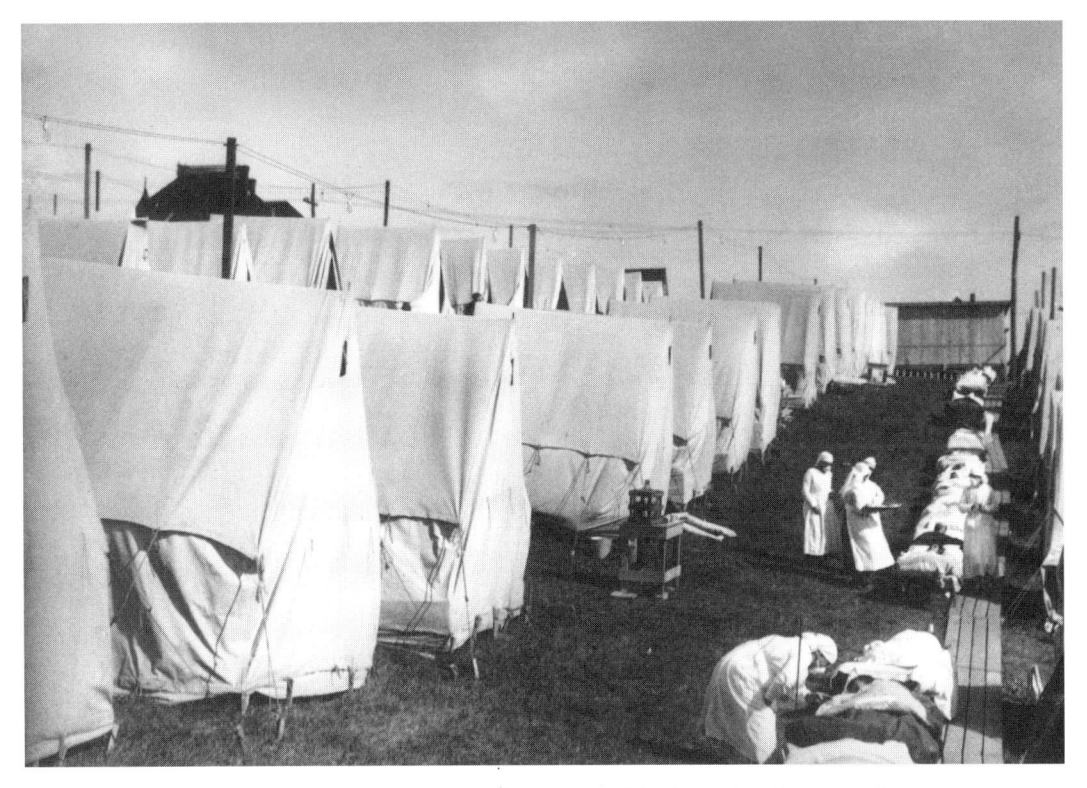

(1918) Lawrence, Massachusetts. Nurses care for victims of the Spanish influenza epidemic in a makeshift hospital because of over crowded conditions.

unprecedented. Nothing else has ever killed so many in such a short time. Hospitals and coffin supplies were rapidly exhausted and emergency tent hospitals were set up everywhere. The "Spanish flu" was a worldwide pandemic that devastated not only World War I troops who were still in uniform but the civilian populations as well. The leaders of scientific medicine and pubic health were virtually helpless to combat it. The disease had to be left to run its short course, ultimately killing 21.64 million people throughout the world, more than one percent of the world's population.

1900-1941 • PHYSICIANS ~ At the beginning of the twentieth century, there were approximately 121,000 physicians in the United States, about 1.8 doctors per 1,000 Americans. Medicine was still a rich brew of science, folk medicine, and outright quackery, and physicians were not sought out. Since there was a relatively low demand for their services and a relatively large number of physicians, they often resorted to competitive maneuvers to attract patients. Among the means they sometimes used was the sale of wonder medicines, later declared to be worthless and sometimes dangerous nostrums. The physician's role was largely that of sage and comforter since there were few effective drugs or equipment beyond the microscope, stethoscope, laryngoscope, medical thermometer, and x-rays available for diagnosis. The superior education of doctors often led to common sense solutions to problems of illness, but they often could do little beyond offer comfort to the sick and infirm. There were few hospitals, which were largely in urban areas and served mostly the poor. Most minor surgeries were still performed in the home.

While the more traditional form of fee-for-service solo practice was still common, organized group practice in which a number of physicians practiced medicine in a single location was becoming more common. The founding of the Mayo Clinic in Rochester, Minnesota, at the end of the nineteenth century began organized group practice as it exists today. This was the forerunner of the HMOs and other managed care organizations of the later part of the century. Initially, the American Medical Association (AMA) was ambivalent about group practice, and expressed concern about the quality of care as well as the competition from lower fees sometimes charged by the groups. These concerns came to a head in 1933 when the AMA charged that groups of physicians in salaried practice were considered unethical. Questions about the AMA's role in regulating medicine gained publicity in 1941 when the AMA and the District of Columbia Medical Society were found guilty on the charges of restraint of trade and for having conspired to monopolize medical practice.

EARLY 1900S • MEDICAL TRAINING ~ In the early 1900s, it was easy to become a doctor. In 1756, the first medical school, the College of Philadelphia, opened in the colonies. At the time of the Revolutionary War there were only some 3,500 medical practitioners in the country, and only about 200 of them held medical school degrees. During the nineteenth century the United States saw the emergence of some four hundred proprietary medical schools owned by physicians who operated them for profit. The quality of the schools was mixed, as was the quality of medical practice.

Standards of admission varied, as did standards of instruction. Most of these medical "schools" had no libraries or laboratories, nor did they provide much clinical experience. In many of the private proprietary schools, degrees were granted after one year of courses that consisted mostly of listening to lectures. Most physicians were trained through apprenticeships (working physicians teaching part time). One could become a physician with little more than the purchase of a few pills and instruments and a bag. Old ways were passed down informally since there was no mechanism for new knowledge to enter educational programs. In 1900 fewer than 10 percent of practicing physicians were graduates of qualified medical schools, and 20 percent had never attended a lecture.

Ironically, this type of medical education resulted in opportunities for women and African Americans to train as doctors in significant numbers. Because of stringent segregation laws, blacks had had to create their own medical schools and hospitals. In 1900 a dozen colleges in Washington, D.C., Louisiana, Tennessee, North Carolina, Kentucky, Maryland, and Pennsylvania existed to train black physicians. By 1900 many medical schools admitted women with men, and only two of the nineteenth-century medical colleges for women were still open. In 1900 there were over 7,000 women physicians representing five percent of all doctors. This percentage remained constant until the 1960s when it began increasing.

By 1910 the modern medical school and teaching hospital in the United States had been created, and the first revolution in American medical education was complete. However, the quality of training in medical schools was poor, and a report on the state of medical education conducted by Abraham Flexner published in 1910 led to these sweeping changes. Flexner's report brought the inadequacy of American medical schools and the poor training of physicians to the attention of the U.S. legislators and public, and resulted in major reforms. The AMA (established in 1847), which was relatively powerless and represented only a small number of physicians who were found predominantly in the East and Northeast, took on the task of defining the blueprint of an approved, adequate, qualified, or upgraded school, thus giving the AMA an effective monopoly on the control of educational regulation. The AMA now had the power of accreditation and the ability to define the curriculum, establish policies, and determine teacher-student ratios for medical colleges.

The immediate result was the upgrading of the education of physicians, and the limitation of the number of physicians relative to the population, causing competition for clients to decrease. As the AMA pushed through its demands, medical schools became university-based, faculty were engaged in original research, and students participated in "active" learning through laboratory study and real clinical work in hospitals.

An unexpected result of the Flexner revolution was the closure of many of the poorest equipped and staffed schools that trained women and African American physicians at a time when discrimination prevented them from being admitted to

---

Should Doctors Tell the Truth?

Only in recent decades in American medicine have doctors begun to lose what many see as their traditional attitude of omnipotence and patriarchy. In 1927 one particular physician defensively answered the question, "Should doctors tell patients the truth?" with a resounding, "No!"

Dr. Joseph Collins felt that telling his patient "the whole truth" was often crueler than to withhold it. "The physician," he reported, "soon learns that the art of medicine consists largely in skillfully mixing falsehood and truth [to] keep men from being poor shrunken things, full of melancholy and indisposition, unpleasing to themselves and to those who love them."

Collins saw his stance as based more on a practical, rather than moral standpoint, and firmly believed that patients did not really want to know the truth about their condition. If patients knew the "gravity of their diagnosis," Collins believed they would be "so apprehensive and depressed" as to interfere with their seeking further treatment which might cure them.

Dr. Collins argued that "every physician should cultivate lying as a fine art," backing up his conviction with stories of patients who had been spared months of anxiety by the deception, and by telling of a patient with a terminal condition who, "buoyed by the hope that his health was not beyond recovery," was able to continue to work and provide for his family until his death.

A personal experience of truth telling that led to a patient's suicide, the culture of medical practice at the time, and the uncertainty of medicine in 1927 no doubt underlay this physician's attitude. But it would be foreign indeed to most American patients today who have come to regard full medical revelation and information from their physicians as a basic human right.

SOURCE: Joseph Collins, M.D. "Should Doctors tell the Truth?" *Harper's Monthly Magazine*. Vol.155: 320-326. August 1927.

1880-1915

mainstream schools. Medical education became increasingly expensive and the profession became increasingly dominated by the middle and upper classes.

American medical schools have always had three missions: education, research, and patient care. Early twentieth-century medical schools understood teaching to be their most important function, and patient care was used primarily as a teaching device rather than an end in itself. As medical faculties taught, they also participated in research. By the 1930s, the United States was the primary nation in medical research, but medical schools would not begin to see research as their primary function until after World War II.

Another major change occurring in medical practice and education during this early period was specialization or the development of sub-occupations within the occupation of medicine. Each specialty contains only a portion of the knowledge and tasks of the total field. As early as the mid-nineteenth century, occasional medical specialties began to appear. In the larger cities, some physicians began focusing on eye and ear diseases, mental illness, and lung ailments. By the 1930s, male physicians had taken over much of the obstetrical practice from female midwives among northern upper-class and middle-class women.

With the growth of medical knowledge and the increasingly technical natures of certain areas of practice in the early twentieth century, many physicians began to focus on a single medical specialty. Others were drawn by the shorter hours, fewer house calls, higher income, and greater prestige. During World War I medical educators began to worry that the United States was becoming overpopulated with specialists. The general practitioner in the form of the "country doctor" was fast becoming a vanishing species, large numbers having already moved to the cities after World War I to become specialists. One important implication of this trend was that medical care became more fragmented from the patient's perspective, and more costly as increasing numbers of people were involved in patient care.

1880-1915 • HOSPITALS ~ Medical practice changed as hospital use increased. In the late nineteenth and early twentieth centuries, the number of hospitals grew rapidly as hospital sanitation improved, hospital infections decreased, and antiseptic surgery was introduced. By the twentieth century, every community, no matter how small, seemed to believe that it must have its own hospital. As hospitals became more common, doctors increasingly sought access to them, to admit their patients, and to continue treatment. In 1914, the Council on Medical Education of the American Medical Association published its first list of approved hospitals, thus encouraging the standardization of hospitals. To be accredited by the AMA, a hospital had to have a clinically competent staff organized to provide a planned educational program; a well-equipped medical library; a competent case history program for all patients; adequate laboratories and X-ray equipment; and the services of a pathologist to perform autopsies.

These hospital standards controlled a number of practices that were ethically questionable, such as ghost surgery and illicit fee splitting. General practitioners uncomfortable with the rigors of surgery, but unwilling to disclose that fact to their patients, would hire another doctor to perform surgery while their patients were under anesthesia, thus giving rise to the term "ghost surgery." Fee splitting involved the surgeon's dividing the fee with other physicians without the patient's knowledge. In its worst form it was a kickback from the surgeon to the referring physician as a payment for the referral. The AMA's code of ethics prohibits fee splitting, but the practice was widespread until the Second World War.

The refinement of anesthesia and improvements in hospital diet, lighting, ventilation, and supplies of medication and instruments, as well as the introduction of the X-ray at the turn of the century, led to the increasing reliance on hospitals by the upper and middle classes who were becoming persuaded that hospitals were as adequate for them as for the poor. In particular, women of the upper classes began to accept the idea of giving birth in the hospital. Nevertheless, even the best hospitals in the United States did not play much of a role in reducing mortality until almost the end of the late 1930s when sulfa drugs began to be available.

1870-1920 • NURSES ~ During the early decades of the twentieth century, patients were already getting steadily improved care, largely because of the reform of nursing. The history of nursing parallels the history of war. The English pioneer and founder of modern nursing, Florence Nightingale, was known as "the lady with a lamp" in the Crimean War in 1854; and during the American Civil War, such women as Clara Barton greatly influenced nursing. The efforts of women such as these helped lead to the establishment of formal training schools for nurses.

Nursing began as a helping profession in the United States with training programs associated with general hospitals. One of the earliest was formed at New York's Bellevue Hospital in the early 1870s; and by 1900 over 400 such institutions had been created. These hospital diploma school programs weighted their training in favor of on-the-job training rather than academic programs and much of a student's time was spent in the

(circa 1915) Ambulance Women. Nursing was not the only occupation for women in the early teens. With the invention of the automobile, ambulance drivers became a premium at hospitals, too. Here, four workers in uniform pose in front of four ambulances with drivers sitting behind the wheels. The ambulances bear the logos for the Motor Corps of America, New York Corps.

wards, nursing patients. These nursing students received room and board but no other compensation. By 1910 steps to upgrade nursing were initiated, including the formation of professional societies, the creation of journals, and a new insistence on cleanliness in the wards.

World War I increased the number of nurses and dramatized the role played by them and the need for more and better prepared nurses. During the war, a number of college and university nursing programs developed that granted baccalaureate degrees instead of a diploma. On passing the same state licensing examination taken by the diploma school graduates, the baccalaureate graduate also became an RN (Registered Nurse). After the war, many RNs became involved in maternal and child health programs. In 1923, the first major American study of nursing and nursing education recommended that nurses be prepared in universities instead of in the more apprentice-like programs found in hospitals.

1930-1938 • ADVANCES DURING THE DEPRESSION YEARS ~ During the Great Depression of the late 1920s and 1930s, acute (quickly acquired, quickly treated, and of short duration) diseases began to decrease as chronic (prolonged, lingering) diseases increased; and polio was a major concern in the nation. Although it was generally unknown to the American public, even President Franklin D. Roosevelt was a crippled polio victim. Venereal disease afflicted as much as 10 percent of the population. In this preantibiotic age, the mortality rate of pulmonary tuberculosis was 70 deaths per one hundred thousand population per year. It took more lives than any other contagious disease. Still, mortality from "the Great White Plague" or TB had declined from the 200 TB deaths per one hundred thousand population per year in 1900. By the 1930s, scientific advances, such as a better knowledge of the spread of the disease, as well as earlier and better diagnosis, prevented the spread of the more serious forms of the disease, and the pasteurization of milk reduced infections in children. Treatment still consisted of a period of confinement in special TB sanatoria for those who could afford it.

Medical science continued to make major improvements in the nation's health. In 1936 President Roosevelt's son was successfully treated for a life-threatening streptococcal infection with a new sulfa drug. Only twelve years before, the son of another president, Calvin Coolidge, had died of "blood poisoning" (streptococcal infection) from a tennis blister on his foot.

In the 1930s, the biggest concern was how to pay for medical care. Because of the Depression, many Americans had to go without health care and others could not pay their medical bills. Planners who joined Roosevelt in fashioning the New Deal made medical and public health relief a significant part of their economic relief and recovery agencies, and significantly expanded the federal government's permanent role in medicine and health.

Congress debated creating a government funded national health insurance plan but did not pass it into law. Instead, the 1930s saw the creation of a major private voluntary health insurance in the emergence of the Blue Cross-Blue Shield plans. In 1933 the American Hospital Association created the Blue Cross plan for hospital costs. In 1939 the Blue Shield program was created to cover medical and surgical costs. Thus, instead of a single health insurance system for the entire country, the United States would evolve a system of private insurance for those who could afford it and publicly funded services for those who could not.

1920-1940 • HEALTH AWARENESS
~ In the first decade of the century, successful campaigns were waged against yellow fever, pellagra, and hookworm, and there were public education crusades against tuberculosis. By 1920, the urban population outnumbered the rural population, giving Americans better access to medical care.

After women gained the right to vote in 1920, activists persuaded Congress to pass the Sheppard-Towner Act in 1921 to provide matching funds for states for prenatal and children's health centers to reduce the still-high rates of maternal and infant mortality. But in 1927, the American Medical Association, fearing competition from these free health centers, persuaded the government to withdraw support for these programs. The efforts of advocates for birth control led to the passage of federal laws to recognize the right of the medical profession to provide contraceptive information and services. By 1938 contraception was legal under state laws in all but three states: Connecticut, Mississippi, and Massachusetts.

New impetus to more healthful eating came through several discoveries. Researchers discovered vitamin A in 1913 and vitamins, B, C, D, and E in the 1920s. During the same decades, a large Public Health Service study established pellagra as a food deficiency disease. Caloric tables were widely distributed and used by the new professional nutritionists in schools, hospitals, and other institutions. Pasteurization, which eliminated harmful bacteria in milk, became widespread during World War I.

America's involvement in World War I reflected the new complexity of twentieth century medicine. War-time innovations and health-care organization in the field meant that, for the first time in the country's history, there were fewer deaths from diseases than from battle wounds. Physical examinations and newly invented IQ tests found startling numbers of young men with disqualifying physical or mental conditions that increased the medical practice's awareness of the country's health problems. In the military hospitals, surgeons saved and restored many seriously wounded patients with a greater variety of operations using asepsis, anesthetics, and other still newer techniques such as plastic surgery. The lessons learned in surgery, in X-ray work, in the treatment of poison gas victims, and in the serum treatments used for such diseases as typhoid fever, lockjaw, pneumonia, and meningitis were some of the outcomes of the war years.

After the war, research by Frederick Banting and others created insulin used to treat diabetes, and immunizations and antitoxins brought scarlet fever under control. Philip Drinker invented an iron lung mechanical respirator that breathed for the polio patient and saved many lives. The increasing unrest in Europe in the 1930s greatly influenced American psychology and psychiatry as many Freudian practitioners fled Austria and Germany, contributing to the growth of a more influential psychiatric profession in the United States.

By the 1930s many of the old health problems, such as diphtheria and typhoid, were controlled by public health and medical measures, but vaccines and cures for such diseases as polio and tuberculosis were still in the future. Even with the many new scientific advances and public and private public agencies, public health and the ideal of preventive medicine

1940-1960

failed to take hold in the United States because of the medical culture's focus on the diagnosis and cure of acute disease processes. The country's individualistic social and economic traditions conflicted with a more collective emphasis on preventive medicine, but the greatest opponent was the opposition of the conservative medical establishment. Physicians were in great demand as health officers, but they continued to choose better paying careers in private practice. The American Medical Association was actively against preventive and public medicine. It strongly opposed compulsory health insurance, fought against government-supported clinics, and resisted proposals for both group medical care and prepaid-medical care as being "socialistic" in nature. For many years the AMA advocated privately funded health care and research in order to avoid government intervention or regulation.

1940-1960 • THE NATION'S HEALTH

∼ As the decade of the 1940s began, American governments—federal, state, and local—were much more involved in medical affairs than in previous decades. American citizens were more confident in physicians and other health professionals than at any other time in the nation's history, and many utilized modern mainline medicine regularly. However, the Depression caused a decline in both physicians and hospitals, and World War II made the situation even worse. By 1944, with so many doctors in the military, civilian doctors saw an average of 1,700 people a year. Before the war, Americans viewed syphilis as their most serous public-health problem; and during the decade of the 1940s, polio epidemics raged, affecting not only children, but military troops as well.

The demands of the war led to a coordination of financing and teamwork in medical research and development. The groundwork in medical science and research in the first four decades of the century and the needs of the war combined to produce new miracle antibiotics such as penicillin and the sulfa drugs, improved treatment of trauma shock, and uses of blood plasma, DDT, better vaccines, and improved hygiene.

During the mid-century decades, both the medical community and Americans felt they were in a Golden Age of Medicine. It seemed that medical science had an unlimited potential to cure disease. By 1945, a significant number of the worst diseases had nearly disappeared from the American scene, including yellow fever, scurvy, cholera, pellagra, malaria, smallpox, and some of the ordinary childhood diseases. However, epidemic diseases still threatened the population with outbreaks of potent new epidemic diseases or unpredictable modifications of old ones. These included several damaging pandemics of influenza in its various forms—Asian flu in 1957 and Hong Kong flu in 1968.

The Ten Leading Causes of Death in the United States, 1950

Heart disease
Cancer
Cerebrovascular diseases
Accidents
Diseases of early infancy
Pneumonia and influenza
Tuberculosis
General arteriosclerosis
Chronic nephritis
Diabetes mellitus

SOURCE: *Historical Statistics of the United States, Colonial Times to 1970.*

Protection against measles, pioneered by Francis Home in the 18th century, became routine after the development of an effective vaccine by John Enders almost 200 years later. Enders, along with Thomas Weller and Frederick Robbins, also had a pivotal role in developing the poliomyelitis vaccine, which was perfected as an oral preparation of live attenuated virus by Albert Sabin and as a killed-virus vaccine by Jonas Salk in the 1950s. In 1952 the incidence rate of new polio cases was 37.2 per hundred thousand population. By 1960 it fell to 1.8 per one hundred thousand population; by the 1980s there were fewer than ten new cases a year; and in 1999 the World Health Organization began to voice hopes that polio, like smallpox, could be eradicated from the world. The continued discovery of these new medications and the increasing quality of medical care significantly reduced additional major diseases such as polio, tuberculosis, pneumonia, influenza, childbed fever, mental disease, infant diarrhea, venereal disease, and others.

Life expectancy in the mid-century in 1950 was 20 years longer than in 1900. Cancer was the most feared disease in mid century, although heart disease was now the number one killer of Americans with one half of all deaths attributable to heart disease. American Cancer Society campaigns and fund raising heightened public optimism that cancer was curable, and concentrated the attention of the public on early detection, and provided much-needed

1955: Beyond Polio

One of modern medicine's greatest victories occurred at mid-century when, "The world rejoiced. Everywhere, churches held special thanksgiving services, and everywhere parents echoed. . .a Detroit mother of five, who said simply, 'God bless Dr. Salk!' In Syracuse, N.Y., the traffic light went red and traffic came to a dead halt, while bells rang and sirens screamed. In Franklin Lakes, N.J., where all the schools had been closed, and all public gatherings banned...because of a polio epidemic, a terror was lifted." For the first time in human history, the world could face a future unmarred by the specter of polio. Dr. Jonas E. Salk's vaccine for polio worked.

But in the midst of all the rejoicing in 1955, science sounded a sober note. The fight against disease still had many battles to be won. While important progress had been made in heart and blood-vessel surgery, the cause and cure for arteriosclerosis, responsible for half of all heart disease deaths remained a mystery. For the number two killer, cancer, science hoped to develop chemicals, taken by mouth or injection that would kill cancer cells anywhere in the body. More than half of all U.S hospital beds were being occupied by the mentally ill, but the "causes and mechanics of the mind's malfunctions" were still unknown.

By 1955 the "arsenal of medicine" had become more effective against many diseases, and optimistic Americans hoped that, like the Salk polio vaccine, other medicines would "light up the long road ahead."

SOURCE: "Beyond Polio: A Great Task." *Newsweek* Vol. 45: 31-32. April 25, 1955.

1941-1949

money for government research. Surgery, radiotherapy and X-ray therapy were available cancer treatments in the 1950s, and chemotherapy was beginning to be developed. In 1955, President Eisenhower's heart attack focused the nation's attention on heart disease. The decade saw many advances in the treatment of this problem. The electronic pacemaker was developed in 1952 to control heart rhythms, and by 1953 heart-lung machines took over the function of the beating heart during cardiac surgery. By the end of the decade, open-heart surgery was commonly performed.

Americans' fears of cancer and heart disease ironically reflected the successes of science, medicine, and the affluent society in mid-century America that led to a rapid rise in the numbers of the aged in the population. This increase in elderly Americans meant a rise in the incidence of the degenerative diseases of old age: cancer, heart and vascular system diseases, kidney disorders, stroke, and other organ failures. It also meant large new demands on hospital facilities, health insurance systems, and welfare programs.

1941-1945 • WAR-TIME MEDICINE ~

Wartime needs stimulated medical and scientific advances and coordinated financing and teamwork in medical research and development. During the war, research efforts combined with the biomedical scientific advances of the first four decades of the twentieth century produced the miracle drugs penicillin and the sulfonamides, the insecticide DDT, new medical technologies, vaccines, and improved hygienic measures. After the war these new medical accomplishments became available for civilian as well as military use.

Mental-health issues in the military changed the public image of psychiatry, as it made the nation recognize a great, unmet need for psychiatric services. Following the war, the government created the National Institute of Mental Health (NIMH), and mental health treatment began to shift away from the warehousing of the mentally disabled to more proactive prevention and treatment.

1945-1949 • PHYSICIANS AND MEDICAL TRAINING ~

After World War II, the family doctor was no longer the only provider of medical care. Physicians still made house calls and treated an average of 26 office patients a day. The average wait to see a doctor was one to two hours.

Physicians were well paid by the standards of the time in 1949. The average salary for a physician was $11,058 ($77,400 in 1999 dollars) as compared to

Physician Earnings for 1949 as reported by the Department of Commerce

Specialty	Salary	(Salary in 1999 dollars)
Neuro-surgery	$28,628	$200,396
Pathology	$22,284	$155,988
Obstetrics and Gynecology	$19,283	$134,981
General Practitioner	$8,835	$61,845

SOURCE: *Time.* July 30, 1951.

(1928) Special Hospitals to fight specific diseases were created. Seen here the newly built tuberculosis sanatorium in Colorado, where every patient has a separate cottage.

the median family income in the United States of just under $3,400 ($23,800 in 1999 dollars), but a specialist's salary could vary dramatically compared to that of a general practitioner or family doctor. By the 1960s house calls became rare because a physician's time was limited, and routine diagnoses required medical tools that were not portable.

After World War II, research became the dominant activity of most medical faculties, replacing teaching. This was attributable to the expansion of the National Institutes of Health, which poured money into medical research and development. At nearly every medical school, the research program grew to an enormous size.

1950s • NURSING AND PHYSICIAN ASSISTANTS ~ During the 1950s, a new type of nurse training program began to develop in community colleges. These programs lasted about two years, and upon completion, the student was granted an associate degree. On passing the same state licensing examination taken by the diploma school and college or university graduate, the student became a registered nurse. The college or university approach is distinctive in that it alone has a public health nursing component. There is debate over which is the best program for training nurses, but regardless of their training, nurses have similar roles and functions in hospitals and generally receive the same salary. An expanded role for nurses was that of the nurse practitioner who was trained in a two-year master's degree program to provide extended nursing services generally in one of three types of care: infant and

1960s

child health care, maternity care/family planning, and adult health care.

In the mid-1960s, the physician assistant (PA) profession originated in response to a shortage of physicians. PAs are trained to extend doctors' services by performing comprehensive physical exams and simple laboratory procedures, and providing basic treatment for people with common illnesses. Almost 75 percent of all PAs work with physicians in primary care specialties.

There are differences between nurse practitioners and PAs. Training and orientation differ: PAs receive more medical education while nurse practitioners are taught patient education and wellness practices, such as disease prevention.

1960s • HEALTH ADVANCES ~ In the mid-1960s the Medicaid and Medicare programs of the Lyndon Johnson administration made good medical care available to the poor and elderly for the first time in American history. Medicare was a vast, government-financed program of social health insurance for the elderly, supplemented by the Medicaid program, which shared costs with the states. The decade after 1965 witnessed a sharp increase in the use of medical services by the poor. But as well intended as these social reform programs were, they contributed to the financial crisis that burdened the American health-care system by the end of the century.

Mid-century was a period of rapid and dramatic medical advances. The war years saw the discovery of revolutionary disease therapies in the new antibiotics and sulfa drugs. Rates of venereal disease quickly dropped, and many of the old TB sanatoriums closed since streptomycin, the post-war wonder drug, effectively eradicated tuberculosis. The 1950s saw advances in heart surgery. Fluoridation of the water supply by public health officials meant that generations of American children could escape the dentist's drill. The electric pacemaker was developed in 1952 to control heart rhythms, and by the end of the decade, open-heart surgery was commonly performed.

By the end of the 1960s, cryosurgery removed cancerous tumors by freezing the tissue. Home-dialysis machines were available for treating kidney failure. Doctors' offices had portable EKG machines that detected heart problems. Organ transplant surgery became available in 1963 with the first successful human liver transplant. In 1969 the FDA (Food and Drug Administration) approved a vaccine for rubella (measles). Measles could result in mental retardation for children and severe birth defects in the infants of women who contracted the disease while they were pregnant.

In 1960, the FDA approval of the first oral contraceptive (the birth control pill) for the general population revolutionized women's sexuality. By 1964 there were six versions of the "Pill" available.

1970-2000 • THE NATION'S HEALTH ~ In the decades after World War II, Americans had a relatively high quality of life, as seen by their declining morbidity rates and their increasing longevity. The life expectancy for a person born at the end of the century was 76.5 years, compared to 49.2 years in 1900. In the early part of the century, most deaths were from infectious respiratory diseases, such as pneumonia, influenza and tuberculosis. By 1910, heart disease had become the leading cause of death and remained so for most of the century. Pneumonia and influenza remained the second leading cause until 1933, when

The Ten Leading Causes of Death in the United States, 1999

Heart disease
Cancer
Cerebrovascular diseases
Chronic obstructive pulmonary diseases
Accidents
Pneumonia and influenza
Diabetes mellitus
Suicide
Chronic liver disease
Homicide

SOURCE: *Statistical Abstracts of the United States*, Chart No. 139

cancer replaced them. The age-adjusted death rate from cancer increased by about 55 percent from 1900 to 1998.

In 1915, approximately 100 white infants per 1,000 live births died in their first year of life, and the rate for black infants was nearly twice as high. In 1998, the infant mortality rate was 7.2 deaths per 1,000 live births—a decrease of 93 percent. Rates in 1998 were 6.0 for white infants and 14.3 for black infants. At the beginning of the century, most deaths among children over one year of age were caused by infectious diseases. By 1998, the percentage of these deaths declined from 61.6 percent to 2 percent. In the first part of the century, improvements in water and food safety and other environmental factors caused the decline. After World War II, new vaccines impressively reduced preventable diseases, and virtually eliminated deaths from diphtheria, pertussis (whooping cough), measles, tetanus, and polio.

Women in Medical School

American women have had a long history in medicine from the time that Elizabeth Blackwell became the first woman physician, graduating from the Geneva New York Medical College in 1849. But discrimination made it difficult for their numbers to expand until the 1970s when attitudes towards the role of women in American society began to undergo major changes.

During the 1970s, events of the 1960s and early 1970s had an impact on the medical arena. One of the last sturdy bastions of discrimination against American women began to crumble as they were admitted to medical schools in increasing numbers. During the early 1970s, enrollments doubled from 3,894 women in medical schools to 7,824. Their proportion of total enrollment rose from 9.6 percent to 15.4 percent and continued to rise.

In the fall of 1974, Harvard's entering class in its medical school had 33 percent women compared to eight percent three years before. Nor did women have to face some of the same admissions interview questions about managing career and marriage that earlier aspirants faced. Also changing were attitudes that barred women from certain medical specialties such as surgery. Yet certain aspects of American society's attitudes and expectations of women still held sway, as the article concluded, "And last, some feel that women's social conditioning will perhaps make medicine a more compassionate enterprise."

SOURCE: "Medical schools: The Female Influx." *U.S. News and World Report*. Vol. 106: 55 . July 27, 1974.

1970-1990

The maternal death rate dropped from 582 deaths per 100,000 live births in 1936 to 7.1 deaths in 1998 because of better prenatal care, more births in hospitals and better hospital care, establishment of blood banks, and the introduction of antibiotics.

1970s-Present • The Elderly
The elderly population increased dramatically during the century. In 1900 about six percent of the American population was over age 65. In 1999 about 13 percent or about 34.1 million people were 65 or older. Much of this increase is also attributable to public health advances, including general access to clean water, fresh food, better pre- and post-natal care, immunizations and improvements in sanitation. By 2000 even older Americans live longer. Those over age 75—or the "old-old"—represented the fastest growing segment of the population. Along with the changes in the population came changes in the scientific challenges confronting medicine. Life expectancy increased during the century, but people died from different diseases such as cancer, heart attacks or strokes, and suffered longer with chronic diseases to a greater extent than had earlier Americans. From the standpoint of research, these conditions were more difficult to understand and control than many infectious and nutritional diseases. Chronic diseases cannot be "cured" in the same way as acute disease. The focus of medicine must be more on their management than their eradication.

1970-1990 • Epidemic Diseases
A huge area of concern during the late century was the continuing threat of epidemic diseases, especially with the increase in world tourism and international trade that provided new possibilities for the contact and transmission of disease-causing organisms. Old diseases formerly thought to be under medical control reemerged. Influenza outbreaks continued to occur, resulting in widespread vaccination programs aimed at the elderly and other potentially vulnerable victims. The outbreak of Legionnaires' disease in 1976 proved that Americans were still under considerable threat from new and mysterious organisms. Named for its outbreak at an American Legion convention in Philadelphia, this unidentified, flu-like disease spread throughout nineteen states, killing about one out of every five people who caught it. It also highlighted the work of the "disease detectives," the Centers for Disease Control (CDC) in Atlanta, Georgia, and its hard-working epidemiologists who tracked the disease to its source, a previously unidentified bacterium traced to the air-conditioning systems of hotels.

The outbreak of Lyme disease, an infection caused by the corkscrew-shaped bacteria that are transmitted by the bite of deer ticks in the eastern part of the United States and western blacklegged ticks in the west, began in the northeastern states during the 1980s and steadily spread throughout the country. Lyme disease was another reminder of some of the limitations of modern medicine. While it was rarely fatal, it caused its sufferers flu-like symptoms, and included fatigue, headache, neck stiffness, jaw discomfort, pain or stiffness in muscles or joints, slight fever, and swollen glands. By the century's end, preventive vaccines were available as were treatments with antibiotics.

Alarming news also came of bacterial infections that seemed unresponsive to antibiotic therapy, including resistant strains of tuberculosis seen in immunosuppressed patients (especially those with

(1988) AIDS activists demonstrate at an Act Up Coalition To Unleash Power rally with signs which read 'silence = death,' New York City.

AIDS). Persistent infections that were previously easy to treat, were even more frightening. Strains of Streptococcus-A (promptly dubbed by the media as "flesh-eating bacteria) proved resistant to the usual antibiotic therapy. Many of these problems were attributed to the overuse and over-prescribing of antibiotics and failure of patients to complete courses of treatment, thus strengthening bacteria that adapted to the medications. Since both the American people and the medical profession have such a strong belief that germs are the cause of disease, too many American doctors prescribed antibiotics even if a bacterium was only possibly present, and many of their patients demanded antibiotics, even for many viral symptoms, which do not respond to antibiotics in the absence of bacterial infection. Antibiotic use in the United States was very high. One comparison found American doctors prescribed about twice as many antibiotics as Scottish doctors.

The most alarming of all the late-twentieth-century epidemics was the sudden and rapid ambush of AIDS, beginning in the 1980s. Not only was the diagnosis of AIDS an apparent death sentence; it carried a lot of social baggage as well. Its rapid spread among homosexuals and intravenous drug users and shocking rate of mortality led to the shunning of its victims, even those who were infected by transfusions from a tainted blood supply. The disease led to massive research programs in the country's laboratories and, by the mid-1990s, the mortality rate began to decline with the advent of new drugs such as reverse transcriptase and protease inhibitors which controlled the rapid

1970-1990

HEALTH AND MEDICINE ~ 729

spread of the disease throughout the body without curing it. Widespread public programs touting prevention also caused a decrease in the incidence of new cases so that AIDS fell from being the eighth leading cause of death in 1996 to the fourteenth in 1997. While the disease seemed to be temporarily under control in the United States at the close of the decade, it raged unchecked throughout many Third World countries.

1980s • Eating Disorders ~ Eating disorders, such as anorexia and bulimia, became a public issue in the 1980s; but the major health concern associated with eating disorders was the increasing epidemic of obesity. By the end of the twentieth century, over 55 percent of the total American population was overweight (defined as carrying about 20 to 40 extra pounds, depending on height and frame), and one out of four adults were obese (20 percent above desirable weight). All this extra weight had burdensome consequences and fueled a major diet industry. In the Nurses' Health Study, women who gained even 15 pounds in their middle years had a significantly increased risk for chronic diseases. Those Americans who were obese had higher rates of heart and cardiovascular disease, colon cancer, stroke, gallstones, and diabetes. Approximately 280,000 adult deaths in the United States each year are attributable to obesity. With their faith in medical "magic bullets," overweight Americans have had a hard time changing their eating habits and doing the recommended daily half-hour of exercise. Phentermine and fenfluramine (the Phen/Fen diet), an appetite suppressant and one of many supposed medical remedies for obesity was taken off the market in 1997 when it was discovered to lead to primary pulmonary hypertension and heart valve lesions in a small number of the millions of Americans who took the anti-obesity drug combination. By century's end, one fad diet after another marched across American tables with the popular, but controversial, high-protein, low-carbohydrate Atkins' and Eades' diets leading the way.

1965-2000 • Managed Care and the Health Bureaucracy ~ Economic factors increasingly determined the differences in health in different parts of the nation's populations during the twentieth century. Americans had to confront the soaring costs of medical services, and the poor health conditions of their fellow citizens who lived near or below the poverty level. By 1987, one in five American children were born into poor families. The mortality rate among American infants was the highest among twenty leading industrialized nations, especially among the non-white population. Fully 16 percent of American citizens lacked health insurance coverage, private or public by the end of the twentieth century.

By the mid-twentieth century, the federal government influenced much of American medical research and education, hospitals and health finance organizations, medications and foods, and other health matters. In the mid-1980s, a new health-care crisis came to the nation's attention, one not marked by epidemics but by a seemingly inexhaustible demand for expensive medical services. The American health care system is an economic contradiction. According to classic economic dictates, as demand goes up, supply rises to meet the demand, thus bringing prices down. But in medicine, as supply rose, so did the cost with expensive duplication of services, and systems that allowed for the seemingly inexhaustible demands for medical services at increasingly inflated prices.

This problem increased in severity during the early 1980s, when medical expenditures began growing approximately twice as fast as the Consumer Price Index (CPI). Numerous reasons exist for the faster growth of prices for medical services including:

1. Insurance coverage and premium subsidies (third-party payment);
2. Lack of price competition among providers;
3. Open-ended payment systems (fee-for-service);
4. Developments in technology;
5. Malpractice litigation;
6. Self-referral (many physicians own diagnostic equipment and labs to which they refer their patients to enhance income);
7. Expenses related to containment policies (cost-containment systems increase both payer and provider overhead); and
8. Increasing physician supply.

SOURCE: Health Care Financing Administration.

The American system of medical care stood alone in the developed world. Other nations such as Canada, Japan, and the western European nations all adopted universal, standard payment schedules set by direct negotiation with doctors and hospitals. Most have set an overall ceiling on national medical expenditures. As a result, only the United States spends more than ten percent of its gross national product on health care. In 2000, the U.S. was projected to spend 13.5 percent of its gross domestic product on health care, more than any other nation. In terms of health care expenditure per person, the U.S. ranks number one. In 1998, U.S. health expenditures totaled $1.15 trillion. But in its overall goal attainment, which measures factors in the level of health of its citizens, infant mortality, and the responsiveness to the needs of disadvantaged groups, the U.S. ranked number 15 among nations at the end of the century.

The arrival of Medicare in 1965 greatly contributed to this change. Under Medicare, all doctors were paid on the basis of their "usual and customary" fees for a given service. This approach permitted each physician to name his or her own price, and insurance companies honored this pricing system. Doctor's fees began a rapid upward climb with hospitals profiting as well since they could now include the cost of capital improvements into their rates.

In the 1970s and 1980s this situation started to change as managed care evolved. Managed care refers to a wide variety of payment plans that have third-party payers try to control costs by limiting the use of medical services, in contrast to the "hands off" style of the traditional fee-for-service health insurance that had previously governed American medicine. These prepaid programs have their enrollees receive their medical services in a way designed to coordinate services and eliminate unnecessary ones. Usually enrollees must have a "gatekeeper's" (a primary care physician or a utilization review person) approval before receiving care from a specialist and before being hospitalized on a non-emergency basis. All managed care plans have a common goal—to reduce health care expenditures while maintaining the quality of care. Managed care organizations tightened budgets by reducing the number of hospitalizations and the use of specialists. Many of these organizations were known as health maintenance organizations (HMOs), and as health care costs and insurance premiums soared, they grew rapidly until by 1995, over 50 million Americans received their health care in HMOs, compared with less than nine million in 1980. Tens of millions more people were in "looser" forms of managed care.

Physicians throughout the century were trained to rely heavily on technology. When it came to tests, technology, and interventions, more was better. Generations of Americans were used to having whatever medical services they or their doctors demanded, but the advent of managed care brought this to a dramatic halt. Now patients and physicians alike had to bring their case to a "gatekeeper" in the managed care business in order to have the medical procedure costs covered by the insurance provider. In the 1990s, a huge public controversy erupted over whether managed care organizations were denying needed care, whether the companies were placing profits before patients, and whether the quality of care had suffered.

Compared to other industrial nations, the United States does not emphasize primary care. Primary care is the first level of treatment after a disease or injury has occurred, and should prevent minor medical events from becoming serious and expensive problems. An inadequate primary care system may frustrate attempts to improve health and contain expenditures. The inadequacy of the U.S. primary care system may be due, in part, to misplaced incentives. In the United States, greater prestige, awards, and larger income go to specialists instead of primary care physicians. In the 1990s the HMOs brought about a shift from specialized to general medical care in the United States, hiring far fewer specialists compared than did the fee-for-service system.

By the close of the century, health care was a major political and campaign issue with most reforms languishing in Congress as Republicans and Democrats debated the issues. By the end of the 1990s, the system of private insurance and market-driven health care remained unchanged while providers and consumers alike continued to voice their frustrations with the American system of medical care.

1990S • PHYSICIANS FEES ~ Historically doctors who perform tangible procedures, such as surgery, endoscopies, or diagnostic imaging get the highest fees. Evaluation and management services where doctors examine and question the patient and prescribe a treatment, but don't actually do a particular procedure do not pay as well. Primary-care physicians, such as general internists, family practitioners, and pediatricians spend their days in office visits. In 1990 for example, internists charged a median of $110 for a comprehensive office visit for a new patient. A family practitioner might spend 45 minutes taking a medical history, doing a physical examination, and talking with the patient. By contrast, a specialist charged a median fee of $126 for spending 10 minutes to examine the bowel with a flexible fiber optic device called a sigmoidoscope.

Average salaries of medical residents ranged from about $34,100 in 1998-99 for those in their first year of residency to about $42,100 for those in their sixth year, according to the Association of American Medical Colleges.

Median net income of MDs after expenses, 1997

All physicians	$164,000
Radiology	260,000
Anesthesiology	220,000
Surgery	217,000
Obstetrics/gynecology	200,000
Emergency medicine	195,000
Pathology	175,000
General internal medicine	147,000
General/Family practice	132,000
Psychiatry	130,000
Pediatrics	120,000

SOURCE: American Medical Association

LATE 1990S • MEDICAL TRAINING
As the century drew to a close, the demographic make-up of medical schools significantly changed, with women comprising more than half of the entering students in many medical schools. The focus of the American medical school firmly shifted away from a primary function of education and research to one of patient care, largely in response to the new managed care systems. These institutions responded by expanding clinical care to make up in volume what they lost in price, treating more patients more quickly. Medical school and teaching hospital officials increasingly focused on profitability and market share, and overlooked what was happening to education and research. Ironically, at the end of the century, American medical education began to look more like it had at the beginning of the century with faculty incomes, as at the proprietary schools of the nineteenth century, depending mainly on the private practice of medicine rather than on teaching and research. Some students of American medical education expressed fears that the quality of care might not remain high in the United States if the quality of medical education and research tapered off.

At the end of the century medical education faced serious problems. With cutbacks in funding for academic medical centers, the new demands on clinical faculty members to bring in more dollars from practice (and thus the reduced time for teaching), the shortened hospital stays of patients, and the preponderance of very sick patients in hospital beds, some critics suggested it was not surprising that many students now seemed lacking in the basic clinical skills of history taking and physical examination. Also, students who began medical school as idealists became cynical as they witnessed interns and residents who treated patients indifferently and saw physicians and professional organizations adopt a permissive approach toward financial conflicts of interest, product endorsements, and collective bargaining. At the same time, imminent technical revolutions, such as the decoding of the human genome and changes in the way researchers obtain and use information, could be predicted to have major effects in the twenty-first century medical schools.

Newly trained specialists began to have problems finding practice opportunities as HMOs shifted to general medical care. The percentage of medical students seeking residency in a primary care field nearly doubled, increasing to 27.7 percent in 1995 from its lowest point of 14.6 percent in 1992 because these young doctors could not find attractive opportunities in private practice. The rise of HMOs also led to questions of a doctor surplus in the country. In the mid-1990s, there were about 240 doctors per 100,000

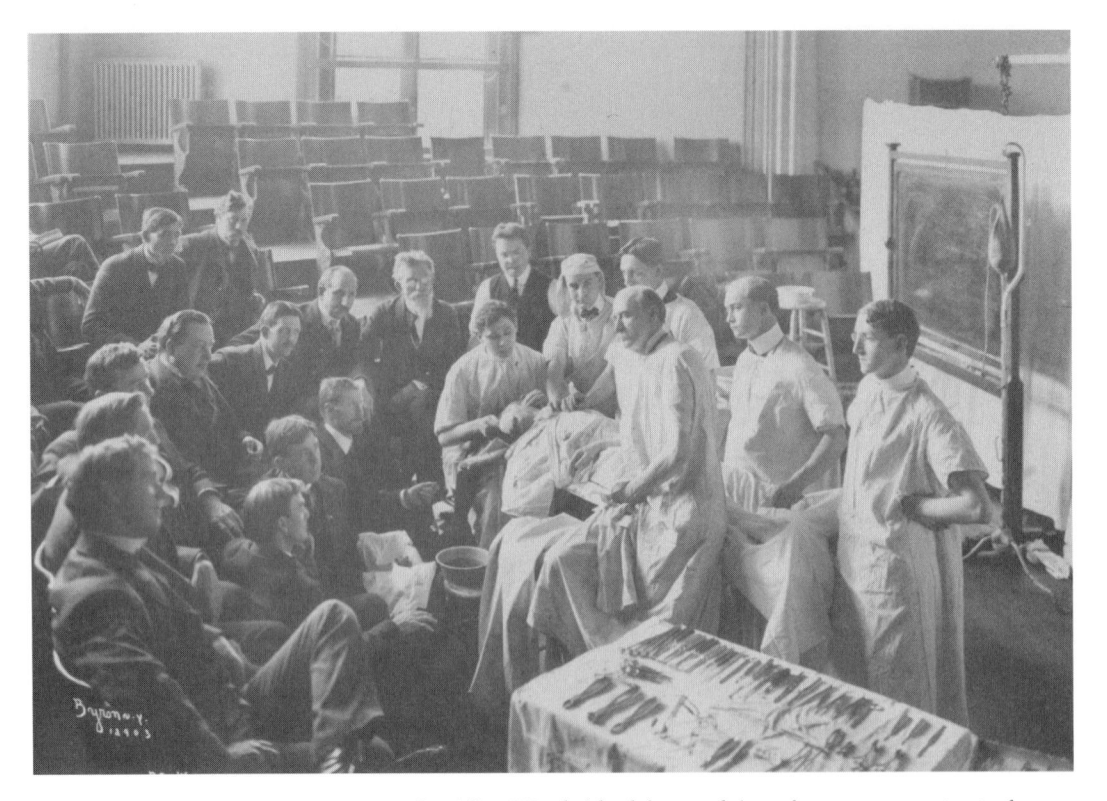

(1902) Surgery Demonstration. Dr. John Allen Wyeth (third from right) performs an operation in front of a classroom of students at New York Polyclinic Medical School and Hospital.

people in the United States, while HMOs typically used no more than 100 to 140 doctors per 100,000 enrollees. For the first time since the Great Depression, American physicians experienced job insecurity. Nurse practitioners and physician assistants might replace even primary care physicians. Consequently questions arose about reducing the number of medical students and 121 medical schools, as well as decreasing the large number of international medical graduates who did residency training in the United States and remained in the country afterwards in large numbers as practicing physicians.

Alternative Health Services Expenditures in the U.S. — 1999

Health Care Practice	Total Revenues in Millions of Dollars
Acupuncture	$790
Chiropractic	16,220
Homeopathy	610
Massage therapy	7,530
Naturopathy	530
Traditional Oriental medicine	3,360
TOTAL	$29,040

SOURCE: *World Almanac and Book of Facts, 2001.*

Dot.com Doctors

Cyberspace and its new information technologies beckoned to patients in 1999. People could spend hours browsing the Web's health sites for medical information and even chatting with a doctor on-line. In 1998 almost 25 million patients reported going online for healthcare information. Some sites were free; but some charged as much as $195 for offering diagnoses, treatment recommendations, and even prescriptions for common medical problems such as allergies and high blood pressure.

This new way of practicing medicine was controversial. Some physicians argued that certain medical practices could indeed be more efficient online rather than in person; while others raised questions about the importance of personal contact. Putting personal information online introduced security concerns and fears of hackers. Not all online pharmacies screened their patients or consulted with doctors. One woman filed a complaint with the Federal Trade Commission, revealing that not only had her young teenager purchased Viagra online, but that he was able to do it when he suffered from a bipolar disorder and was taking blood pressure medication as well.

State and federal regulators began crackdowns; Congress considered legislation to regulate the practice; and other agencies began to institute their own controls. The final word about medicine online would apply to other internet services as well—"as with most things in cyberspace, what you see is not always what you get."

SOURCE: Claudia Kalb and Deborah Branscum. "Doctors Go Dot.Com." *Newsweek*. Vol. 134: 65-66. Aug. 16, 1999.

1990s • ALTERNATIVE HEALERS IN MODERN SOCIETY ~ Alternative forms of medicine, or medical practices outside the realm of formal medicine, have always been a part of American life, perhaps in response to mainstream American medicine, which favors aggressive therapy and mistrusts other forms of treatment. In the 1980s, caesarean section for childbirth was the most commonly performed operation in the United States, and hysterectomy the second most common. In the 1990s, discussions of HRT, or hormone replacement therapy, for menopausal women recommended almost universal application of these estrogens, even though there was no clear, undisputed scientific evidence of benefits or long-term effects. New studies found familiar medications dangerous and medications came and went from the market.

The medical profession also traditionally emphasized the diagnosis, treatment, and cure of acute organic diseases, but by the latter part of the century, the great majority of patients instead suffered from chronic diseases or stress-related complaints. As many as one out of three Americans claimed to use the increasingly popular alternative medical techniques that focused on the total person or so-called "natural" approaches. Acupuncture became popular in the 1970s, and the 1980s and 1990s saw a boom in the use of herbal remedies. These medicines and remedies received

1980s-1990s

Top-Selling Medicinal Herbs in the United States—1999

Herb	Sales (in millions in 1999)	% Change 1991-1999
Echinacea	$280	65
Garlic for medicinal use	190	27
Ginkgo biloba	300	76
Ginseng	210	11
St. John's Wort	280	2,700
Saw palmetto	110	175
Combinations	1680	87
All other	1060	26
TOTAL	$4,110	66

SOURCE: *World Almanac Book of Facts*, 2001.

(1899) Two nurses walk down a spiral staircase with elaborate metal work, in the Vanderbilt Pavilion of St. Luke's hospital, located on West 114th Street, New York City.

no approval from the FDA, which classified them as food supplements, even though Americans spend as much as $27 billion a year on herbal remedies. Drug companies have not invested in herbal remedies, so there is no research data on their safety or effectiveness. Many Americans supported these alternative medical views and services, both on their own merits and as symbols of resistance to modern medical authority.

1980s-1990s • NURSING ~ Throughout much of the latter part of the twentieth century, nursing seemed to be a profession in search of an identity. Part of this came from the debates over the relative merits of diploma or associate, versus baccalaureate training programs, but it also came from the conflict nursing has always had with the medical profession. Nurses by the late century wanted a role that gave them more independence and put them on a par with physicians and not subservient to them. Part of the search for professional identity led to a change in many of the traditional functions of nursing, including bedside nursing. Many of these functions were taken over by the licensed practical nurse (LPN) and the nurse's aide.

The strains between physicians and nurses became apparent when in 1983 the AMA House of Delegates adopted a statement stating that nurses should not be expected to obediently follow all medical orders and that a nurse may take action contrary to a physician's orders to protect a patient in an emergency if a physician was not available. This resolution sent the message to the medical profession that the nurse was capable of using judgment, too.

The crucial issue at the century's end was concern about a national nursing shortage, especially in hospitals. More nurses were needed in hospitals as the century progressed because of the demands of new technology, increased paperwork, and sicker patients. Poor wages and working conditions also contributed to the shortage. Most nurses continue to be women. Nurses' wages do not compare to female professional and technical workers in other fields; nor did the same pay raises and career advancement exist in nursing compared to many other professions women entered. Hospitals took several measures to improve the recruitment and retention of RNs, addressing issues of difficult hours and low salaries. However, by century's end the supply of nurses was still inadequate to meet the demand.

1990s • HOSPITALS ～ In 1990 there were 6,650 hospitals in the United States with about 1,200,000 beds. Americans were most familiar with the community, or general, hospital, which was traditionally a nonprofit institution. Physicians admitted their patients for short periods for acute illnesses. After World War II hospitals expanded with little regard for cost; but by the end of the century, cost containment had become such a major issue that numbers of smaller community hospitals were forced to close their doors, and others began to return to a proprietary base, or become regionalized, affiliating with larger, more urban hospitals. These changes came about both because of the decreased need for acute hospital care as acute diseases declined, and because of the efforts of government and other large health care purchasers to slow the dramatic increases in health care spending. As inpatient care became less profitable, and chronic disease increased in the population, hospitals increased and expanded their outpatient services.

1970-PRESENT • COMPUTER IMAGERY, MICROSURGERY, ARTIFICIAL HEARTS, GENOME RESEARCH, FERTILITY ～ Some of the greatest advances in medicine during the century were made in body imaging. These non-invasive techniques meant that patients no longer needed to "go under the knife"—to have surgery performed for diagnosis and treatment of many diseases. At the beginning of the century, patients had X-rays available to them, and by the 1970s sonar technology borrowed from the military and used in the form of ultrasound identified body organs and medical problems without the need for surgery. Computerized axial tomography or CAT (1972) scans provided cross-sectional pictures—tomograms—of a patient's body. Computers were able to put together the information to form a picture on a computer screen to provide clear pictures inside the body. Nuclear medicine in the form of magnetic resonance imagery (MRI) (1977) had the ability to detect cancerous tissues and

1970-PRESENT

(1946) Seen here, the distilling and extraction apparatus at an insulin factory during the 1940s.

treat cancer. These advances in imaging permitted the development of new treatments for cancer, vascular and cardiac diseases, as well as a more accurate determination of the stages of a variety of disease processes. Images available on computers could be sent all over the world for long-distance diagnosis.

Microsurgery used endoscopes and fiber optics in the form of high-powered microscopes, miniature surgical tools, lasers, and tiny television cameras to perform minimally invasive surgeries that had many patients up and about almost as soon as they regained consciousness. With smaller incisions, patients had less pain and quicker recovery times. These new surgical techniques meant that patients often left the hospital on the same day they had surgeries such as appendectomies, knee surgery and gall bladder removal, rather than being hospitalized for the long periods of the past.

Artificial hearts made news during the decade of the 1980s, with high expectations that "bionic" patients might live out the rest of their life span attached to these machines. But highly publicized failures led to the Federal Drug Association cancellation of the artificial heart program. By the century's end, organ transplants, including heart transplants had become common enough to no longer make headlines.

Genetically engineered insulin was first marketed in 1982, and a license to sell genetically modified living organisms for the purpose of manufacturing recombinant proteins was granted in 1986. In that same year the Food and Drug Administration approved a genetically engineered vaccine for hepatitis B. Hopes were high that the quality of life could be improved by manipulating human genes once the complete sequencing of the human genome was accomplished.

Fertility treatments and new reproductive technologies such as in-vitro fertilization provided previously infertile couples with families. By the end of the century, it was theoretically possible for an infant to have as many as five different parents rather than the traditional two. Two individuals might contribute sperm and an ovum for in-vitro fertilization in the womb of another woman who would become pregnant and give birth as a surrogate mother for a different set of two parents who would raise the child.

As the population grew older, there were new demands for new therapies to combat problems associated with aging. In March 1997, the FDA granted approval for VIAGRA, a drug intended to address erectile dysfunction in men, and Americans watched a former presidential candidate, Robert Dole, discuss his sexual dysfunction on television in a VIAGRA advertisement. Alzheimer's disease, a neurological condition that diminishes the brain's functioning affected four million people, including one in ten individuals older than 65, and half of all those older than 85, including former President Reagan. A vaccine to prevent or treat it did not exist, and there were few other medical treatments available for this disease known as the "long goodbye."

CONCLUSION

The twentieth century was a "Health Century," marked by dramatic discoveries in technology and medical therapy. The 1950s in particular claimed a "Golden Age of Medicine," and it seemed that medical science had an unlimited potential to cure disease. The advent of the "germ theory" of disease in the nineteenth century led American medicine to focus on the diagnosis and aggressive treatment of acute forms of disease, with the consequence that, in the opinion of many, American medicine is not very good at treating the chronic diseases that marked the population by the end of the century. Americans regard themselves as naturally healthy. If they become ill, there must be a cause for the illness, preferably one that can be quickly dealt with. The American approach has cut the U.S. rate of heart attack and stroke, as well as virtually eliminating certain infectious diseases, but some diseases have not proven so open to the aggressive approach. In spite of a long search and predictions that a cure for cancer is possible, death rates from cancer have been rising. Yet American medicine and American culture still insists that the solution is in the cure, rather than the prevention of cancer.

Soaring health care costs and the advent of managed care in tandem with traditional medical attitudes made American medicine continue to advocate doing "what works," and doing it as quickly and inexpensively as possible. For example, the treatment of such chronic diseases as mental illnesses became even more controversial by 1999. Many new drugs were available for treating mental illnesses that had not been available earlier in the century, and a number of these allowed the patient to once again become a functioning member of his or her community rather than languishing in asylums. However, managed care, concluding that drugs were more effective for mental illnesses, refused to pay for long-term treatments and hospitalizations, or even many visits with a therapist. Drugs appeared to be more effective for treating many mental illnesses, but this may be simply because they work faster. While many psychiatrists recommended a course of drug therapy jointly with psychotherapy, managed care preferred the quicker and less expensive route of drug therapy.

While the twentieth century saw great medical advances, American medicine failed to foresee that the focus of care would switch from acute to chronic disease, that preventive medicine would become important, that the system of care was inadequate for the entire population, or that the cost of care would reach a crisis point. The American health care system is at once the most expensive and the most inadequate system in the developed world, and it is uniquely complicated. In 1997 the country spent about $4,000 per person on health care, as compared with the next most expensive country, Switzerland, which spent some $2,500. Yet 16 percent of the U.S. population has no health insurance at all, and many of the rest have only very limited coverage.

The hallmark of the system is its reliance on the private market to deliver and, to a lesser extent, to fund health care. Accordingly, health care is treated as a commodity provided by a huge number of competing organizations. The surest way for these organizations to thrive is to shift costs to one another by devising plans to avoid the most expensive patients—either those who are chronically ill, if payment is capped, or those who are not insured for the services they need, if payment is on a fee-for-service basis. Other developed countries provide universal health care, considering it a social service, not a commodity. By default, the market took over the American health-care system during the twentieth century, and by the century's end, the system was even more fragmented and profit-driven. Even as the role of employer-based insurance has declined, payment by government has increased, and the number of the uninsured has grown.

Doctors are more disease-oriented and less patient-oriented as the doctor's role has become more scientific. Even in the face of an AMA study that claimed that a patient's time with the doctor had gotten slightly longer during the 1990s—an

THE DAWN OF HOPE.

NATIONAL INSURANCE AGAINST SICKNESS AND DISABLEMENT

Mr. LLOYD GEORGE'S National Health Insurance Bill provides for the insurance of the Worker in case of Sickness.

Support the Liberal Government in their policy of SOCIAL REFORM.

(1911) Health insurance was an important issue in both the U.S. and Britain even as early as the turn of the century before today's astronomical medical care fees. Here, a British cartoon advocates establishing a government sponsored national health insurance program.

average increase from 20.4 minutes in 1989 to all of 21.5 minutes in 1998—patients are left feeling neglected in rushed and impersonal consultations.

When Americans looked at their health system at the close of the century, they could see enormous changes for the better. Epidemics that raged at the beginning of the century were firmly under control, and new equipment, based on atomic and computer technology, was in place, bringing better qualities of life and longer lives to many of the country's citizens. But shortcomings in the American health system still existed. While many late-twentieth-century Americans were impressed that their nation spent a larger proportion of its gross national product on health than any other developed country, they were unaware that other countries spent far less and had more to show for it than did the United States. The general rate of infant mortality in the United States remained higher than that of all but a few other developed nations and it was twice as high for black infants as for white infants. An issue in the 2000 presidential campaign was how to provide health insurance for all American children. At the century's end, American medicine was still characterized by its many-sided and constantly shifting character.

BIBLIOGRAPHY

Abenheim, Lucien, et al. "Appetite Suppressants and the Risk of Pulmonary Hypertension." *New England Journal of Medicine*. Vol. 335(9): 609-616 (August 29, 1996).

Abram, Ruth J., ed. *Send Us a Lady Physician: Women Doctors in America, 1835-1920*. New York: Norton. 1985.

Apple, Rima D., ed. *Women, Health, and Medicine in America. A Historical Handbook*. New Brunswick: Rutgers University Press, 1990.

Allison, D. B., K. R. Fontaine, et al. "Annual deaths attributable to obesity in the United States." *Journal of the American Medical Association*. Vol. 282(16): 1530-1538. 1999.

Amersbach, Gabriele. "Beyond the Myths of Aging." *Harvard Public Health Review*. Fall 2000.

"Annual Summary of Vital Statistics: Trends in the Health of Americans During the 20th Century." *Pediatrics*. Vol. 2000(106): 1307-1317, December 2000.

Berger, Melvin. *Disease Detectives*. New York: Crowell, 1978.

Cassedy, James H. *Medicine in America. A Short History*. Baltimore: The Johns Hopkins University Press, 1991.

Flegal, K. M., M.D. Carroll, R. J. Kuczmarski, C. L. Johnson, "Overweight and obesity in the United States: prevalence and trends, 1960-1994." *International Journal of Obesity*. Vol. 22: 39-47, 1998.

Guyer, Bernard, Mary Anne Freedman, Donna M. Strobino, and Edward J. Sondik. "Annual Summary of Vital Statistics: Trends in the Health of Americans During the 20th Century." *Pediatrics*. Vol. 2000(106): 1307-1317, (December 2000).

Historical Statistics of the United States: Colonial Times to 1970. U.S. Department of Commerce, Bureau of the Census, 1975.

"Looking Back on the Millennium in Medicine." *New England Journal of Medicine*. Vol. 342(1): 42-49, January 6, 2000.

Ludmerer, Kenneth M. *Time to Heal. American Medical Education from the Turn of the century to the Era of Managed Care.* New York: Oxford University Press. 1999.

Mechanic, David, Donna D. McAlpine, and Marsha Rosenthal. "Are Patients' Visits with Physicians Getting Shorter?" *New England Journal of Medicine.* Vol. 344(3): 198-204, January 18, 2001.

Payer, Lynn. *Medicine & Culture. Varieties of Treatment in the United States, England, West Germany, and France.* New York: Henry Holt, 1988.

Raffel, Marshall W. and Norma K. Raffel. *The U.S. Health System. Origins and Functions.* 4th Ed. Albany, NY: Delmar Publishers Inc., 1994.

Rickert, Edith. "The Meanest business in the World: How many Sick Women are Tricked," *Ladies Home Journal*, 30. September 1913.

Rothman, David J. *Strangers at the Bedside. A History of How Law and Bioethics Transformed Medical Decision Making.* New York: Basic Books, 1991.

Shorter, Edward. *Bedside Manners. The Troubled History of Doctors and Patients.* New York: Simon and Schuster, 1985.

Starr, Paul. *The Social Transformation of American Medicine. The Rise Of a Sovereign Profession and the Making Of a Vast Industry.* New York: Basic Books, 1982.

Statistical Abstracts of the United States. U.S. Bureau of the Census. Washington, D.C. (Various years)

Twaddle, Andrew C. and Richard M. Hessler. *A Sociology of Health.* New York: Macmillan, 1987.

World Almanac and Book of Facts. World Almanac Books, Inc. (Various years)

Wilmoth, John R. "The Future of Human Longevity: A Demographer's Perspective." *The American Association for the Advancement of Science.* Vol. 280: 395-397, April 17, 1998.

Young, James Harvey. *The Medical Messiahs. A Social History of Health Quackery in Twentieth-Century America.* Princeton: Princeton University Press, 1967.

INTERNET RESOURCES

ALL U.S. AND STATE GOVERNMENT INTERNET RESOURCES
Keyword search links to all government websites for that topic.
http://firstgov.gov/

U.S. NATIONAL LIBRARY OF MEDICINE
Index of resources for services, databases, publications, research activities, for the world's largest biomedical library.
http://www.nlm.nih.gov/

NATIONAL INSTITUTES OF HEALTH (NIH)
Extensive site of this organization which is the federal focal point for biomedical research in the U.S. Find news, health info, and databases,
http://www.nih.gov/

IMAGES FROM HISTORY OF MEDICINE
Nearly 60,000 images drawn from the collection of the History of Medicine Division at the US National Library of Medicine.
http://wwwihm.nlm.nih.gov/

MILESTONES IN U.S. FOOD AND DRUG LAW HISTORY
http://www.fda.gov/opacom/backgrounders/miles.html

SAFETY & HEALTH STATISTICS
U.S. Bureau of Labor and Statistics presents news releases, data, and reports on occupational injuries and illness.

Many are in text or pdf format.
http://www.bls.gov/oshhome.htm

WORLD HEALTH ORGANIZATION
Links to major programs, an archive of WHO statements, and guidelines for international health and travel.
http://www.who.org/

A Brief History of Nurse-Midwifery in the U.S. Although midwives have been attending births in America since its colonization, the profession of nurse-midwifery was established in the early 1920's as a response to the alarming rate of infant and
http://www.acnm.org/focus/HISTORY.htm

FEMALE PHYSICIANS
Women doctors: women physicians and women's medical education.
http://womenshistory.about.com/cs/physicians/index.htm

WOMEN'S HEALTH IN HISTORICAL PERSPECTIVE
Historical view of women's health and other physical, health, medical and body issues. Overviews and general information on women in medicine.
http://womenshistory.about.com/cs/health/index.htm

MEDICINE
HEALTH/DOCTORS/NURSES/MIDWIVES
Medicine and medical issues in women's history: a history of women in medicine and nursing, including pioneer women physicians and nurses, women's health issues through the ages, and discussions about how women have been viewed in medical history.
http://womenshistory.about.com/cs/medicine/index.htm

MEDICAL HISTORY AND MEDICAL INVENTIONS
The history of medicine and major medical inventions.
http://inventors.about.com/library/inventors/blmedical.htm

RAINFOREST
Check out these links for medicinal herbs and plants from world rainforests.
http://herbsforhealth.about.com/cs/rainforest/index.htm

UNIVERSITY OF PITTSBURGH HEALTH SCIENCES LIBRARY SYSTEM
Electronic medical journals, health information for the consumer, and a history of medicine are provided by this medical library resource system.
http://www.hsls.pitt.edu/

THE LESSON PLAN LIBRARY OFFERS HEALTH LESSON PLANS FOR TEACHERS
The Lesson Plan Library offers original health lesson plans written by teachers for other teachers.
http://school.discovery.com/lessonplans/health.html

HEALTH RELATED ISSUES
Internet directory lists links to health resources in categories like Patient Education, Nutrition, Mental Health and Women's Health.
http://www.useekufind.com/health.htm

AMERICAN ASSOCIATION FOR THE HISTORY OF NURSING
Founded in 1978, AAHN is a professional organization open to everyone interested in the history of nursing. The association's purpose is to foster the importance of history in understanding the present and guiding the future of nursing. These goals a

http://mentalhealth.about.com/library/h/orgs/bl3165.htm

THE U.S. ENVIRONMENTAL PROTECTION AGENCY
History Office provides information: documents, statistics, and other useful resources.
http://www.epa.gov/history/org/origins/goals.htm

CENTER FOR ENVIRONMENTAL HEALTH
Read recent news, general details about, history of, and a mission statement for the National Center for Environmental Health.
http://www.cdc.gov/nceh/default.htm

Joan D. Laxson

Housing and Architecture

(1925) A suburban house being moved in one piece across a road.

TIMELINE

1880-1900 ～ Massive Shifts in Populations

Increase in poor immigrants and migrant farmers into cities / Increase in tenement housing in cities / Great plains dugout and sod houses constructed / Prevalence of two- and three-story American Queen Anne frame houses / Construction of high-rise residential buildings / Completion of the Biltmore House (1895) / Indoor bathrooms prevalent in urban homes of wealthy

MILESTONES: Chinese Exclusion Act restricts immigrant workers (1882 and 1884) • Eight-hour work day inaugurated in Chicago (1886) • Capture of Geronimo ends formal warfare between whites and Native Americans (1886) • Coca Cola created (1886) • Financial crisis of 1893-1896 • Hawaiian Islands (1898) and Samoan Islands (1899) are annexed

1900-1919 ～ The Development of Urban Society

Spread of the railroad system across the country / Proliferation of crowded unsanitary tenements / Poor city services in tenement neighborhoods / Frank Lloyd Wright designs 'Prairie' houses / Rise in 'Bungalow' houses in California / Proliferation of mail order houses / NYC Tenement House Act requires that no new tenement could occupy more than 70 percent of its lot (1901) / Large apartment building and cooperative apartments are developed in New York City / World War I halts Housing Construction (1918)

MILESTONES: U.S. Army Yellow Fever Commission confirms mosquitoes as the disease carrier (1900) • Mexicans strike against the Pacific Electric Railway company for equal wages and parity (1903) • Supreme Court rules in favor of restricting working hours for women (1908) • Harriet Quimby becomes the first American woman to earn a pilot's license (1911) • Mass production of Model T Ford automobile opens suburbs for housing (1913) • Panama Canal completed (1914) • Race riots erupt in St. Louis, Chicago, and Washington, D.C. (1917-1919)

1920-1929 ～ Housing Boom

Half of American homes have electricity (1920) / For the first time more Americans live in urban than in rural areas (1920) / Forty-six percent of Americans own their own homes (1920) / Model Town designed in Radburn, New Jersey / Development of multi-lane highways and throughways / Standardization of building and housing codes / Construction of the first New York skyscrapers

MILESTONES: Women's right to vote enacted (19th amendment, 1919) • One out of every eight American workers is employed in automobile-related industries, including rubber, steel and petroleum (1920s) • First suburban shopping center opened in Kansas City (1924) • *The Jazz Singer*, first talking picture, is released (1927) • Stock market crash propels economy into the worst economic depression in American history (October 1929)

1930-1939 ~ Foreclosures and Homelessness

Falling property values due to oversupply and foreclosures / Federal Home Loan Bank provides a reserve system for lending institutions (1932) / Federal Housing Administration federally insures long-term mortgages to encourage lending institutions to make loans in a difficult market (1934) / Relocation of Dustbowl farmers (1935) / Introduction of modern architecture of the Bauhaus group / Frank Lloyd Wright Design of 'Fallingwater'

MILESTONES: Franklin D. Roosevelt appoints women to prominent posts within his administration (1932) • First successful lung surgery removes cancerous lung (1933) • Rural Electrification Act brings electricity to rural areas (1935) • Fair Labor Standards Act establishes minimum wages, maximum hours, and the abolition of child labor (1938) • Germany invades Poland, starting WWII (1939)

1940-1945 ~ The War Years

Lanham Act authorizes housing at defense plants and military bases (1940) / National Housing Act authorizes FHA mortgages in defense areas (1941) / National policy of rent control established (1942) / G.I. Bill of Rights guarantees loans to veterans for home purchases (1944) / Veterans Emergency Housing Program provides subsidies to create housing (1945)

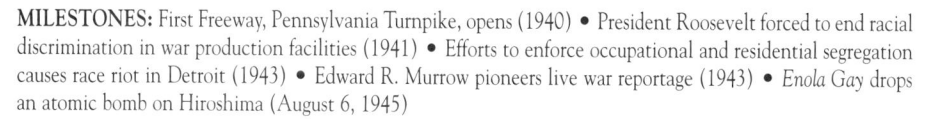

MILESTONES: First Freeway, Pennsylvania Turnpike, opens (1940) • President Roosevelt forced to end racial discrimination in war production facilities (1941) • Efforts to enforce occupational and residential segregation causes race riot in Detroit (1943) • Edward R. Murrow pioneers live war reportage (1943) • *Enola Gay* drops an atomic bomb on Hiroshima (August 6, 1945)

1946-1949 ~ Post-war Prosperity

Prefabricated housing helps fulfill housing shortage (1946-1949) / Increase in non-farm employment / Farmers Home Administration make loans available for farmers to buy or modernize their houses (1946) / Housing and Rent Act controls rents and provides subsidies for garden apartments (1947) / First Levittown suburban development constructed (1947) / Housing Act provides for slum clearance and community redevelopment (1949)

MILESTONES: Marshall Plan to restore Europe is implemented (1946) • Truman Doctrine aligns U.S. with Western Hemisphere nations (1947) • NATO established (1949) • Mao Zedong's communist party seizes power (1949)

1950-1959 ~ Flight from Cities to Suburbs

Housing starts reach 1.7 million (1950) / Federal home loan programs discriminate against minorities (1950s-1960s) / Baby Boom, low unemployment and increase in life expectancy create more housing demand / Proliferation of televisions and air conditioning in homes / Proliferation of regional shopping centers in suburbia / Interstate Highway Act passed to fund a vast network of high speed roads (1956) / Nationwide motel chains established / Proliferation of ranch-style houses / Federal urban renewal program attempt to revive inner cities / Pruitt-Igoe public housing project in St. Louis builds 2,800 apartments, which the tenants hate (1955) / Housing Act authorizes loans to private nonprofit corporations to build elderly housing projects (1959)

MILESTONES: 33,600 American combat deaths and 20,600 non-combat deaths in Korean War (1950-1953) • First McDonald's opens (1952) • Disneyland opens (1955) • Sabin live polio vaccine introduced (1955) • Montgomery Bus Boycott propels Martin Luther King, Jr. into national prominence (1955) • Alaska and Hawaii become states (1959)

1960-1969 ~ Civil Unrest and Public Assistance

Housing Act includes mortgage interest subsidies for low- and moderate-income rental housing and a subsidy for apartments for the elderly in public housing projects (1961) / Congress authorizes grants to states and cities to finance mass transportation (1961) / Housing Act extends mortgage insurance to condominiums (1961) / Expansion of mobile home and condominium apartments market / Executive order bars discrimination in the sale, lease, or occupancy of residential property owned or operated by the federal government (1964) / Housing Act authorizes a rent supplement subsidy to qualified low-income families (1965) / National Historic Preservation Act makes the protection of historic buildings a national policy (1966) / Model Cities Act authorizes construction of turnkey projects for low-rent housing (1966) / Housing Act includes provisions designed to assist low-income families in becoming homeowners (1968) / Housing Act authorizes FHA insurance for mobile home loans up to $10,000 (1969)

MILESTONES: Soviet cosmonaut Yuri Gagarin is the first man in space (1961) • Bay of Pigs invasion (1961), Cuban Missile crisis (1962) • 200,000 civil rights supporters march on Washington with Dr. Martin Luther King, Jr (1963) • Assassination of John Kennedy (1963), Martin Luther King, Jr. (1968) and Robert Kennedy (1968) • Civil Rights Act declares that American citizens cannot be segregated in public accommodations (1964) • Miranda decision forces police to read a suspect his rights (1966) • Race riots across America, destroying many inner-city areas, start with MLK's assassination (1968)

1970-1979 ~ Abandonment of Inner-city Housing

White flight to the suburbs increases urban deterioration / OPEC embargo of oil and gas from the Middle East raises energy awareness in design / Houses are viewed as hedge against inflation / Use of single, double-wide, and triple-wide mobile units as permanent homes / Dramatic rise in median prices of new conventional single-family homes / Preservation Movement provides tax incentives to save historic buildings / Creation of housing clusters: duplexes, triplexes, and fourplexes / Creation of pre-fab and modular housing

MILESTONES: United Nations sponsors first global environmental conference (1972) • Title IX requires schools to provide for girls' sports (1972) • Pruitt-Igoe public housing project in St. Louis, built in 1955, is demolished (1972) • Minimum voting age lowered to 18 (1972) • Courts uphold the right to abortion in *Roe v. Wade* (1973) • Arab Oil Embargo and ensuing gas crisis in U.S. (1973) • President Nixon resigns over Watergate scandal (1974) • U.S. troops pull out of Saigon, which falls into Viet Cong control, ending the U.S. presence in Vietnam (1975)

1980-1989 ~ City Redevelopment and Urban Sprawl

High inflation, high interest rates, high unemployment reduce housing starts / Increase in single person households creates demand for condominiums / Failure or merger of 900 federally-insured thrift institutions / Corruption in the Department of Housing and Urban Development / Development of regional architecture / Proliferation of attached two-story single-family housing in suburbia / Warehouses turned into apartments in cities / Restoration of houses in urban neighborhoods

MILESTONES: Attempted assassination of President Reagan (1981) • First baby born from a donated embryo to an infertile mother (1984) • Immigration Reform Act makes it illegal for employers to hire undocumented workers (1987) • AIDS becomes the second leading cause of death (following accidents) among American men aged 25-34 (1989)

1990-1999 ~ Luxury Housing During Prosperous Times

Thrift institutions are no longer a force in home mortgage lending / National Affordable Housing Act provides matching funds for new construction and rehabilitation of renter-occupied and owner-occupied housing, and for privatizing public housing and multi-family properties owned or financed by federal agencies (1990) / HUD authorizes demolition of some of its worst public housing projects / Surge in construction of luxury apartment buildings / Two-car garages replaced in many wealthy neighborhoods with three- and four-bay garages

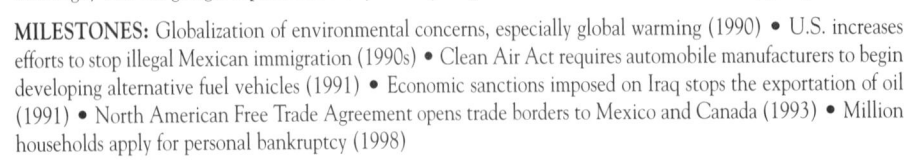

MILESTONES: Globalization of environmental concerns, especially global warming (1990) • U.S. increases efforts to stop illegal Mexican immigration (1990s) • Clean Air Act requires automobile manufacturers to begin developing alternative fuel vehicles (1991) • Economic sanctions imposed on Iraq stops the exportation of oil (1991) • North American Free Trade Agreement opens trade borders to Mexico and Canada (1993) • Million households apply for personal bankruptcy (1998)

INTRODUCTION

A house is, in its most elementary sense, shelter from nature's discomforts and dangers. It is more, however; it is a means of sequestering the basic human social and economic unit, the family. Houses are also the building blocks of neighborhoods and communities. To the concept of the house as a refuge, the nurturing place for the family and integral to communities, the twentieth century added the concept of social well-being—that good housing can promote good behavior and bad housing, bad behavior. The twentieth century also brought the realization that a house can contain toxic substances, making people physically unwell. In addition, modern concepts of housing are beginning to include the idea that housing should be resistant to the forces of nature in a much more advanced fashion than formerly has been the case — houses should withstand fires, earthquakes, floods, tornadoes and hurricanes as well as long periods of use. Thus greater and greater burdens have been placed on the architects, builders and policy makers who are responsible for the nation's housing.

Housing is an essential component of the country's economy, and a prime indicator of national economic direction. Home ownership is usually the major form of investment for individuals and households and the key to financial stability and upward social mobility. Home ownership of a certain type is the "American Dream," the goal toward which immigrants and young families strive. Housing costs are also typically the principal category of household expenditure, not only in terms of rent or purchase price, but also in terms of maintenance and operation.

Housing constitutes a major problem for any society that is urbanized. The demand for housing in urban areas raises the value of land and buildings and creates housing shortages, always more punishing to the urban poor, those who cannot afford the high cost of housing in cities. Private enterprise has not been able consistently to supply quality housing to the poor. Huge strides have been taken, however, in this regard and the overall quality of housing in the United States has improved greatly over the course of the twentieth century, mostly through the actions of the free-enterprise system. Still, there is an abundance of problems left to be solved with regard to the inadequacies of housing in the United States.

Houses can possess, or lack, functional utility, beauty, comfort, sanitation, space, structure, tranquility, security, safety, convenience, light, clean air, compatibility with surroundings, reasonable maintenance costs, the preservation of tradition or the excitement of change. They embody physical, geographic, social, economic, demographic and artistic principles. Many changes have taken place in the science, art and governance of building houses over the course of the twentieth century.

LATE 1800s • MASS IMMIGRATION AND MIGRATION ~ Industry transformed America between the Civil War and the beginning of the twentieth century from a rural, agricultural nation to one of rapidly growing cities, a continuing influx of European immigrants, thousands of machine-filled factories and mills and a vast railroad network. By the end of the century, plants and mills located along the nation's rivers were operating twenty-four hours a day and filling the air with

LATE 1800s

smoke and other pollutants. As industry expanded and farming became mechanized, workers continued to migrate to these industrial centers.

The growth in population that accompanied industrialization was comprised of mass immigration from Europe, migration from farms and small towns to larger centers of population, in addition to the normal increase from new births. Also, as cities expanded, they incorporated smaller municipalities into their city limits. The country grew from 50,200,000 people in 1880 to 76,000,000 in 1900. Of these totals, in 1880, 8,700,000, or 17 percent, lived in cities of 25,000 or more; by 1900, 19,800,000, or 26 percent, lived in such cities. Chicago tripled in size between 1880 and 1900 and New York grew from two million people to three-and-one-half million.

Over nine million immigrants arrived in the United States between 1880 and 1900. Whereas earlier immigrants had come from northern and western Europe, especially Great Britain, Germany, Ireland and, except for the Irish, were predominantly Protestant, those of the last two decades of the century came mostly from southern and eastern Europe, especially Poland, Russia and Italy, and were mainly Catholic, Jewish or Eastern Orthodox. This latter group typically remained in urban enclaves, not assimilating into the country's general population as the earlier immigrants had. These resulting concentrations of poor immigrants, migrants from farm areas and other low-wage workers within large cities presented problems, one of the most pressing of which was housing.

1890s • PROBLEMS WITH URBAN HOUSING ~ Because most nineteenth-century workers walked to work, people either had to be housed near centrally-located factories or industry had to be dispersed throughout the city so that they could live in less crowded conditions. The latter was often not practical, as factories usually had to be near water or rail transportation so that they could receive supplies and ship their products. The demand for land near the centers of employment drove its value up and builders, seeking to maximize their profits, built worker housing so densely in some center cities that the occupants were deprived of adequate ventilation and natural light. Sewers, water service lines and other infrastructure components were installed quite randomly without proper municipal planning and

(1937) A Russian Orthodox church built by a colony of 50 White Russians, formerly loyal to the Tsar, near Lakewood, New Jersey. The immigrants are aided by the New Deal's Rural Rehabilitation Project.

coordination in late nineteenth century cities and developers often did not provide adequate plumbing.

The Census of 1890 counted 12,690,152 families in the United States, which was 11 percent more than the number of dwelling units, with an even worse housing ratio in the industrialized cities of the eastern seaboard. By 1900 greater New York City had the highest population density in the world. There were 80,000 tenements housing a population of 2.3 million people, representing three-quarters of the city's total population. In 1890 Jacob Riis published *How the Other Half Lives*, a shocking description of slum life among New York City immigrants.

Tenements, buildings for the occupation of multiple tenant families, were the dominant form of housing in New York. These four- and five-story buildings, which covered 100 percent of their lots, were windowless except in the front and the rear. They were divided into railroad flats, so called because the flats were long and narrow, with one windowless room after another. In the 1880s an architectural competition to improve tenement design resulted in "dumbbell" buildings, so-called because they had recessed areas in the center portions of their perimeters that permitted windows to be opened on to air shafts. Approximately 400 of these dumbbell tenements were built in the 1880s and although an improvement they still did not solve the problems of crowding or of inadequate light and ventilation.

Tenements were also extensively built in Boston, Chicago and Philadelphia. Chicago's tenements were mostly constructed of wood and were large houselike buildings crowded together closely but with small side yards. In many cities tenements were old houses that had been awkwardly, but profitably for their owners, divided into separate living units. The tenement was not typical in the South where low-wage labor was supplied by African Americans, who lived in tiny houses on tiny lots in dilapidated neighborhoods, usually on the outskirts of town or near the railroad tracks. Shotgun houses, containing a single row of rooms and sited on narrow lots, were common in the South.

LATE 1900s • HOUSING ON THE GREAT PLAINS ~ Housing conditions in the late nineteenth century on the Great Plains were quite different from tenement house living, but perhaps equally shocking. New settlers on the treeless plains usually first constructed a dugout or a sod house. A dugout was a hole in the ground or in the side of a creek bank, built up with walls of sod, whereas a sod house was constructed entirely of blocks of sod, laid up like bricks, with a brush, grass and sod roof. "Soddies" were constructed to last for six or seven years generally, but some of the larger ones with better roofs and interior plastering lasted much longer. Sod houses were fireproof, which was important where prairie fires were rampant, and they provided excellent insulation. The misery of living in them came from the fact that they leaked badly when it rained, they allowed snakes, insects and other creatures to invade the interior, and they were very hard to keep clean. Another misery of living on the open prairie was the intense isolation and loneliness, something the city tenement dweller would not have found familiar.

Once the railroads were extended across the Great Plains, the people living on farms and in the multitude of small towns were no longer dependent on local building materials. Lumber and

1890s

other supplies could be moved efficiently over distances. Lumber yards became typical businesses in the towns along railroad routes. Soon the vernacular houses built of sod, logs, stone and heavily-hewn wood framing were replaced with lightly-framed wood structures. In fact, the railroads changed the traditional building materials and construction techniques for vernacular houses throughout the country.

1890s • Single Family Houses

In the last decades of the nineteenth century, a variety of types of two- and three-story frame houses, mostly in the very flexible American Queen Anne style with gabled roofs, projecting porches and decorated surfaces, constituted the prevalent type of house for the people of the United States who lived in single-family detached housing. Although Queen Anne architecture was not usually considered appropriate for densely-developed city housing, San Francisco developed a row version of the style that became its characteristic housing for rich and poor alike.

Masonry row dwellings based on English models were the typical form of housing in the central core of cities that had been developed before 1850, particularly those of the Northeast. Many of these row houses were substantial three- and even four-story dwellings. Well-built, adaptable to combinations of residential and commercial use or to apartments, and architecturally handsome, thousands of them have survived into the twenty-first century, even though they are atypical of American housing in general.

(1911) Portrait of a man sitting in front of a sod house next to a shovel with ears of corn hanging from its handle, Newell, South Dakota. The house has a wooden door, a window and a stovepipe protruding from the roof.

1890s • EARLY HIGH-RISES ~ By 1892 steel frame construction and electric elevators had made high-rise residential buildings feasible. In New York apartment houses had been constructed since the 1870s, the idea imported from Paris, but had been restricted to low-rise buildings. The 340-unit, seventeen-story Ansonia, built in New York in 1903, covered an entire city block at a stop on the new subway system then under construction. The building had shops in the basement, a roof garden, and two swimming pools. It had heavy fireproof partitions between apartments that also made it soundproof. Such apartments in New York were much like private houses in their roominess and amenities. In Chicago a new group of apartment buildings was constructed after the fire of 1871, to accommodate the numbers of people who wanted to live along the lakeshore.

1890s • WHERE THE RICH LIVED ~ In the last decade of the nineteenth century the United States had become the largest producer of industrial goods in the world. The wealthy entrepreneurs who had amassed huge fortunes from America's industrial revolution usually lived in showy splendor and often had two or more houses, among which they moved seasonally. Their houses were quite large and had extensive landscaping. An impressive number of summer homes for the wealthy were built in Newport, Rhode Island, among them the Breakers, a Beaux Arts landmark designed by Richard Morris Hunt, and dating from 1892.

Living in the country on estates that included sweeping views, woodlands, pastures, accessory buildings, gardens and water features, was also an ideal of the wealthy. Biltmore, completed in 1895 near Asheville, North Carolina, for George Washington Vanderbilt, is the largest private house ever built in the United States. It contains 255 rooms, has a floor area exceeding four acres and a facade that is 375 feet long. It was originally sited on 125,000 acres of woodland. Biltmore's banquet hall, planned to display five sixteenth-century tapestries, is 74 feet long, 42 feet wide, and 70 feet high. This magnificent house embodies American wealth, power, cultural aspirations and a period in history when the wealthy had many servants, entertained

(1899) Exterior of the the Elbridge T. Gerry residence, located on Fifth Avenue and East 61st Street, New York City. Gerry was a prominent lawyer and philanthropist. The house was demolished in 1927, the year of Gerry's death, and replaced by the Pierre Hotel.

1890s

lavishly and when career-less wives were at home to keep track of it all. Richard Morris Hunt designed the property and Frederick Law Olmstead the grounds. Hunt had been the first American to complete architectural studies at France's world famous Ecole des Beaux Arts and Olmstead was America's premier landscape architect. With its many spires, pinnacles, turrets, gables and chimneys set against a steeply-pitched roof, the Biltmore House is a brilliant example of the Chateauesque style.

Other mansions built at the end of the Gilded Age were designed by European-trained architects in the Italian Renaissance, Beaux Arts, Tudor and Colonial Revival styles. Academic Eclecticism in architecture stressed correct historic interpretation of European styles in terms of their logic, symmetry, and proportion.

BOOM AND BUST IN THE 1890S

In the 1880s urban houses were just beginning to be equipped with electric lights, central heating and indoor bathrooms. These technological improvements were much more prevalent in the homes of the wealthy; the majority of houses still did not have electricity, running water, central heating or indoor plumbing. Nevertheless, the basic model of the contemporary functional house had been developed by 1890.

Dispersion of the population away from the centers of cities was still very limited in the late nineteenth century, but forms of public transportation, primarily electric streetcars, were becoming more prevalent and as the routes were extended, new housing developments appeared farther and farther from the city centers. In 1890, only 51 municipalities had electric streetcar lines, but by 1895 there were over 850 systems and 10,000 miles of trolley lines operating in the country.

A nationwide speculation boom in land acquisition and subdivision of building lots was underway in the 1880s. By the end of 1892, the housing market in the United States was oversupplied. For the preceding six years housing starts had averaged 333,000 units annually, and had peaked at 381,000 in 1892, whereas the annual average rate of household formation during these years was only 220,000. The financial crisis of 1893-1896 brought business failures, tight money, unemployment of 10 percent and labor disturbances. Despite this slump, the period between 1880 and World War I was one of rapid economic and urban growth.

The role of the federal government in housing in the nineteenth century was minimal. In 1892 Congress passed a resolution to investigate the slum conditions in cities with populations of 200,000 or more; the study was to be carried out by the U.S. Department of Labor. Because only $20,000 was appropriated for the purpose, the study had to be limited to parts of Baltimore, Chicago, New York and Philadelphia instead of the sixteen cities that met the population criterion. No significant findings resulted.

1900-1920 • THE DEVELOPMENT OF URBAN SOCIETY ~ The cities of the United States continued to grow rapidly in the period between 1900 and 1920. In 1860 four times as many people lived in rural areas as in urban areas but by 1920 rural and urban populations were approaching equality. The population of the United States was becoming increasingly urban for a number of reasons, including the huge expansion of industry and trade, the spread of the railroad system across the country, the development of ports, the mechanization of farming operations that left former agricultural workers without jobs, continuing immigration from Europe primarily to cities, the growth of government and the development of specialized functions in certain areas such as hydroelectric power in Buffalo, New York, beer brewing in Milwaukee, Wisconsin and oil well drilling in Tulsa, Oklahoma.

The greatest population growth in the first two decades of the twentieth century took place primarily where the greatest cities were developing. The growth of the North Central region, which increased by 7,700,000 between 1900 and 1920, was centered in the growth of Chicago, Detroit, Minneapolis, St. Louis and Kansas City. The growth of the Middle Atlantic states, which increased by 6,800,000, was centered in New York, Baltimore, Philadelphia and Pittsburgh. The Mountain and Pacific sections grew rapidly also, but the South lagged behind, its cities not developing at the same pace during this period. The cities that had more than one million population by 1920 were Chicago, Philadelphia and New York and those that included 500,000 to one million were San Francisco, Los Angeles, St. Louis, Detroit, Buffalo, Cleveland, Pittsburgh, Baltimore and Boston.

The chart below shows the proportions of the population living in the variously-sized municipalities of the country in 1900 and in 1920.

1900 • URBAN POPULATION BY SIZE CATEGORY ∼ As the United States became primarily an urban country, its people had to adapt to new ways of life. In the first two decades of the century the population of American cities increased by twenty-four million people. The increase was comprised largely of poor people who had lived in rural areas and had come to the cities to work in industry at low-paying jobs. Many of these people, if they were immigrants, did not initially speak English. The Afro-Americans who came from the agricultural South to northern cities faced the same discrimination and segregation they had known in the South. Catholics, Jews, Irish, Italians, Slavs and Hispanics also

Percent of the Population Living in Urban and Rural Areas

Size of City	1900	percent	1920	percent
100,000+	14,208,347	18.7	27,429,326	26.0
50,000-100,000	2,709,338	3.6	5,265,408	5.0
5,000-50,000	10,343,072	13.6	17,077,334	16.1
2,500-5,000	2,899,164	3.8	4,385,905	4.1
Total Urban	30,159,921	39.7	54,157,973	51.2
Rural	45,834,654	60.3	51,552,647	48.8
Total Population	75,994,575	100.0	105,710,620	100.0

SOURCE: *Historical Statistics of the United States, Colonial Times to 1957*, Bureau of the Census, 1960, p. 14.

faced prejudicial hiring practices and segregated housing.

Segregation was not the only problem related directly or indirectly to housing. The crowded unsanitary tenements, poor systems for collecting trash and garbage, undependable infrastructure components such as water, sewer, utility and transportation systems, inadequate police and fire protection and corrupt public officials were all housing problems. That city and federal governments were not disposed to carry out the needed urban reforms until it was almost too late in the 1930s, made the cities unsafe, unhealthy and unpleasant, hard places to live for those who had very little choice but to stay there.

1900-1919 • THE PROGRESSIVE ERA

In the period before World War I a comprehensive movement of social and political reform that had begun in the late nineteenth century and was known as progressivism influenced many aspects of American life. Progressives opposed 1) the widespread corruption and ineptness of governments, particularly municipal governments; 2) the growth of monopolies and the concomitant exploitation of American workers, farmers and natural resources, 3) the ostentatious lifestyles of the wealthy and 4) the wretchedness of slum housing.

Progressivism was predominantly a middle-class reform movement. The wealthy found themselves the target of it and the poor perceived themselves as powerless to effect change. Theodore Roosevelt, who became president in 1901, supported progressive principles. He was the first president since the rise of the big corporations to insist on the principle of government supremacy over business as well as being the first president to realize the importance of conservation of the nation's natural resources.

1900-1910 • NEW DESIGN CONCEPTS

Progressivism was reflected in American house styles in the period preceding World War I. The architect Frank Lloyd Wright saw the heavily-ornamented houses of the late nineteenth century as part of the "pernicious social fabric," and set out to design the ideal suburban house for the independent American family, a free-standing house on its own plot of ground. He termed his new designs Prairie Houses. They were one-story, horizontally-aligned houses with simple but dramatic lines and a revolutionary lack of ornamentation. Wright also proposed that American housing development be spread over the entire country with each family occupying one house on one acre of land. A vast network of roads could link it all together, in a culture without cities. It was in many ways a prefiguration of the suburban culture that would emerge after World War II.

Prairie Houses had a new form of interior design that featured large fireplaces in the center of the house, an open flowing floor plan that was much less formal than that of nineteenth-century houses, built-in furniture, artfully crafted woodwork, stained glass windows, murals and sculpture. The symbolism of the houses was sanctuary for the American family, natural surroundings, escape from the crowded conditions of the city and rejection of the artificiality of overwrought design. Wright's houses were American originals, stunningly beautiful and at the same time extremely functional, a combination that earned them and their architect lasting distinction.

After 1905, the Craftsman bungalow house, another expression of progressivism, arose in California and was widely adopted by the American people, becoming in fact a national phenomenon. Bungalows quickly replaced the larger, more formal, Queen Anne Victorian houses that had set earlier standards. Bungalows were mostly one- or one-and-a-half-story houses with low-pitched, gabled, overhanging roofs, separately-roofed front porches, and prominent wood, stone or stuccoed porch columns that extended to the ground rather than to the level of the porch floor. They were built of wood, sometimes covered with shingles, sometimes with stucco. Their ornamentation was limited to simple wood bracing and the exposed rafters of the extended roofs.

Although bungalows were typically smaller than the houses that previously had been common, they were built in a wide range of sizes, from large expensive houses for the wealthy, to 600-800-square-foot versions on tiny lots in suburbs. In their varying sizes, they were built to accommodate the latest technologies such as full bathrooms, central heating, water heaters, washing machines, built-in kitchen cabinetry and refrigerators. They simplified living by having rooms serve more than one purpose. Most of the rooms were accessible through wide arched openings rather than through doors kept closed to preserve the heat from coal stoves. Kitchens and bathrooms were efficiently organized and were finished with smooth, white, easy-to-clean porcelain, enamel, tile and linoleum surfaces. The Progressive Era placed great emphasis on sanitation; some progressives even called themselves "sanitarians." It was the age in which, with the help of modern plumbing and appliances, Americans adopted "household science." It was also the age of fewer servants; whereas in 1890 two-thirds of wives of men in business had full-time servants, by 1924 only one-third did.

The Progressive house styles found a receptive audience in America at the turn of the century. They were thought to represent honesty, democracy, the family and integration with a natural setting. They were a new American type of housing that rejected the domination of the upper classes. They incorporated the first truly revolutionary changes in interior spatial arrangements in two centuries. The spaces were smaller, better connected and informal. Gone were entrance halls, formal dining rooms and parlors, replaced by breakfast nooks and casual living rooms. Bedrooms were for the first time located downstairs; Victorian propriety that had required bedrooms to be out of sight no longer prevailed. There was less clutter: the ornate Victorian furniture, heavy draperies and multitudinous knickknacks were gone. Americans had used the formal Victorian house to train themselves to live properly; having

---

Mail Order Houses

Beginning in 1900, houses were available by mail. Sears Roebuck and Montgomery Ward offered in their catalogs almost complete houses, all the components precut, notched, and numbered for assembly, for between $1,000 and $2,500. The materials included the nails, the varnish, the plans and even estimates of the cost of labor and materials to assemble and finish the house. These early prefabricated houses were shipped in railroad cars and moved by horse and wagon to their sites where the homeowner only had to supply the foundation and the chimney and have it all put together.

1900-1920

(1924) New home construction was a new industry in the 1920's for the middle class. Seen here is a moving advertisement for a builder who builds new middle income homes for people.

learned, they were ready for efficiency, cleanliness and democratic simplicity.

1900-1920 • HOME OWNERSHIP Home ownership is an ideal to which most people aspire. However, the period between 1900 and 1920 was still characterized by a large proportion of rental housing because of the prevalence of immigration and migration into cities and the low wages paid by industry. Excluding farm units, the proportion of owned dwelling units increased somewhat from 36.5 percent to almost 41 percent between 1900 and 1920 as shown in the chart below, a long-term trend that would eventually bring home ownership to nearly 67 percent over the course of the twentieth century. However, with farm dwellings included, the proportion of owned dwellings decreased slightly between 1900 and 1920, from 46.7 percent to 45.6 percent as shown in the following chart.

Although home ownership excluding farm dwellings was rising on a national average by 1920, it varied widely on a regional basis and from city to city. The cities with populations exceeding 100,000 that had the highest proportions of home ownership in 1920 were Des Moines: 51.1 percent, Grand Rapids: 50.2 percent, Toledo: 49.4 percent, Omaha: 48.4 percent, Youngstown: 47.8 percent, Kansas City: 47.6 percent, Reading: 46.6 percent, Baltimore: 46.3 percent, Seattle: 46.3 percent, and St. Paul: 46.1 percent. Affordable housing was more widely available in these cities; in New York City, home ownership was only 12.7 percent of the total. The state with the highest proportion of home ownership was North Dakota with 65.3 percent and the two states with the lowest share were New York with 30.7 and Georgia with 30.9.

Along with increasing home ownership, a growing proportion of home mortgages was also a trend in the first twenty years of the twentieth century. In 1900, 32 percent of all owned dwelling units were mortgaged; by 1920 approximately 40 percent were mortgaged.

1890-1900 • HOUSING CONDITIONS

By 1900, rapid industrialization, urbanization, immigration and internal migration had taken their toll on American housing conditions. In 1894 the New York City Board of Health reported that there were 39,000 tenement buildings in the city. The inspectors visited 8,441 dwellings that year, finding structural or sanitary deficiencies in 2,425. Only 306 out of 255,033 persons surveyed at that time had access to bathtubs and 83 percent used toilets that were located outside of their dwellings. Over sixty percent of the buildings surveyed had their water supply in the hall of the building or in the yard; the remainder had their water supply in their apartments. More than half of the buildings had inadequate or no fire escapes. The Tenement House Commission of 1900 was appointed by Governor Theodore Roosevelt to investigate housing conditions in New York City and Buffalo. The recommendations of the 1894 Tenement House Committee and the Tenement House Commission of 1900, although not acted upon immediately, led to the Tenement House Act of 1901. This Act required, among other provisions, that no new tenement could occupy more than 70 percent of its lot, and that the size of lots should be at least 50 feet in width and 100 feet deep. This legislation was effective in that new tenements had to be constructed in conformance with it and as a result living conditions were improved for some tenants. The act was also effective

Occupied Non-Farm Dwelling Units 1900-1920

Year	Total	Owner-Occupied		Renter-Occupied	
1900	9,779,979	3,566,809	36.5%	6,213,170	63.5%
1910	13,672,044	5,245,380	38.4%	8,426,664	61.6%
1920	17,229,394	7,041,283	40.9%	10,188,111	59.1%

SOURCE: *U.S. Census of Housing*, 1950, Vol. I and 1956 *National Housing Inventory* Vol. III.

All Occupied Dwelling Units 1900-1920

Year	Total	Owner-Occupied		Renter-Occupied	
1900	15,428,987	7,205,212	46.7%	8,223,775	53.3%
1910	19,781,606	9,083,711	45.9%	10,697,895	54.1%
1920	23,810,558	10,866,960	45.6%	12,943,598	54.4%

SOURCE: *U.S. Census of Housing*, 1950, Vol. I and 1956 *National Housing Inventory* Vol. III.

1890-1920

in that it set an example for other states to follow. Restrictive tenement house laws were passed in thirteen states between 1900 and the beginning of World War I. However, the Tenement House Act made tenement development generally unprofitable in New York City and many of the old tenements were continued in long-term use, their landlords resistant to their demolition or renovation and public sentiment generally against any interference by the government in private property development. Furthermore, World War I put an end to social reforms and housing legislation; the conservative political reaction that followed World War I lasted until the dark days of the 1930s.

Almost no attention was given to rural housing conditions in this period. The 1920 Census reported that seven percent of U.S. farms had gas or electric lighting and ten percent had running water in their dwellings, while at the same time reporting that 38 percent had telephones. The fact was that most farms did not have electricity until just before World War II and many houses in rural areas did not have indoor plumbing or central heating until after the war.

As Americans purchased their own homes, the quality of their housing rose because rental housing construction is generally, although not always, of a lesser quality. When new amenities were added to American housing, they were usually added from the top down. At the beginning of the century, electric lights, interior plumbing and central heating were just beginning to be installed routinely in certain kinds of housing. They first appeared in the houses built for the city-dwelling wealthy and last in the houses of the rural poor. On the continuum between these two extremes, these amenities were added to owner-occupied houses before rented houses, in new construction before old and in cities before rural areas.

1900-1920 • HOUSEHOLDS

Expenditures for public health had increased between 1900 and 1920 and infant mortality had begun to drop as a result. Whereas in 1900, 16.5 percent of all babies died before their first birthday, by 1920 this had been reduced to approximately 8.5 percent. Despite this drop in infant mortality, and despite that in 1900 half of all Americans lived in households of six or more persons with fewer than 1 percent of the population living alone, households were becoming smaller because of a decreasing birth rate.

The average number of people per occupied unit fell between 1900 and 1920 from 4.8 to 4.3. The makeup of households was otherwise fairly stable in the period between 1900 and 1920. In 1910, 80 percent of all households were headed by a married couple; this number would decrease only slightly until the 1930s when it would fall more sharply. Between 1900 and 1920 the male head of the household was typically the wage earner; very few married women worked outside of the home and once they had children, almost none did. Often elderly parents lived with one of their married children and were supported by the male wage earner of their son or daughter's family. The median age at first marriage was 26 for men in 1900 and 22 for women. By 1920 the median first marriage age had dropped to less than 25 for men and was just above 21 for women. The divorce rate was .4 percent in 1900; by 1920 it had risen to .8 percent. Eventually, most of these characteristics of the average American household would change and the forms and patterns of housing would change with them.

1900-1920 • APARTMENT LIVING ~ Many wealthy people were moving away from the old center cities at the beginning of the twentieth century. The residential heart of old Chicago, the citizens, mansions and grand avenues which had been so prominent throughout the nineteenth century, was gradually abandoned as the wealthy moved north of the city. There were notable exceptions to the trend such as Beacon Hill in Boston, Gramercy Park and Washington Square in New York, and Mainline Philadelphia. Despite the movement out of the center cities, there continued to be people who wanted to live near the cultural and commercial attractions of the downtown. The high cost of land in center cities made single-family houses impractical to build after 1900 and a new form of housing was needed. Although the concept of apartment living had been imported to the United States from Europe, it was considered somewhat amoral and dangerous. Eventually, however, city dwellers came to the realization that they could, by living in an apartment, both continue to participate in the dynamism of city life and at the same retreat when they felt like it to quiet, privacy and security away from the hubbub of the streets.

Steel frame construction and electric elevators meant that apartment buildings could be taller than ever, thus providing views and separation from the street. Restaurants and shops, and modern amenities such as air conditioning and central heating were available in newly-constructed buildings. At first, apartment buildings were developed with staffed laundry facilities in the basements, elevator operators, concierges in the lobby and a full range of building employees. Elevator apartment buildings were particularly able to take advantage of scenic areas such as Central Park in New York, Rock Creek Park in Washington, D.C. and the lakefront in Chicago. By 1900 large apartment building development was becoming common in these cities and they were soon followed by San Francisco and Boston. The development of large apartment buildings enabled housing to compete successfully with other land uses for good locations that would have been otherwise too expensive for housing.

Whereas these high-rise buildings were appropriate for expensive sites, where land was less expensive, mid-rise apartment buildings of four-to-seven stories, or walk-up buildings of three or fewer stories could be profitably developed.

Cooperative apartments—apartments in which the tenants own shares in the entire building, rather than their units— were first developed in New York to circumvent the tenement laws that would have restricted their size and height.

1914-1920 • WORLD WAR I ~ World War I broke out in 1914 and the United States became a participant in 1917. Housing construction came to a virtual halt. The government took over the management of the railroads, the merchant fleet, the production of war materiel, and built emergency housing for war workers. At the end of the war there was an acute housing shortage. Prior to the war housing production had annually averaged about 440,000 new dwellings which had kept severe shortages from developing. The cost of building a house had doubled during the war and consequently in 1919, new construction starts, instead of reducing the shortage, were at only 315,000 units and those of 1920 at only 247,000 units. The shortage in dwelling units was over one mil-

1920-1929

lion by the end of 1921. Years of progress in providing housing had been lost. With dwelling units in such a shortage, the heightened demand for rental units raised rents and lowered maintenance. Overcrowding was rife as many single-family houses were converted to apartments and families even doubled up to live two to a unit.

The era of progressivism that had been so reform-minded ended with World War I. The war brought disillusionment and stifled idealism. Warren G. Harding was elected president in 1920, as an advocate of a return to "normalcy;" however, what would follow, although it was not the reform mindset of progressivism, was anything but normal.

1920-1929 • PROSPERITY ～ The United States began to experience an unprecedented economic prosperity after 1923 as investment poured into new industries, including the automobile industry, and as people rushed to acquire the many durable goods that were just then available. One of the greatest housing booms in the history of the country began in 1923 and lasted until the middle of 1927. This housing boom resulted from a combination of factors. There was the backlog of demand for housing resulting from the low rate of production during World War I and the period immediately subsequent. Other factors included full employment, continued population growth, rising income levels, stable costs of labor and materials, and the new affordability of the automobile, which stimulated construction in the suburbs where land was cheaper.

More than seven million new dwelling units were started in the 1920s, 5,600,000 of them in urban areas of 2,500

Non-Farm Dwelling Units (DU), 1920-1930
(in thousands)

Year	Total	1-Family		2-Family		Multi-Family		Costs*	Per Unit
1920	247.0	202.0	82%	24.0	10%	21.0	8%	1,710	$6,923
1921	449.0	316.0	70%	70.0	16%	63.0	14%	1,795	$3,998
1922	716.0	437.0	61%	146.0	20%	133.0	19%	2,955	$4,127
1923	871.0	513.0	59%	175.0	20%	183.0	21%	3,960	$4,546
1924	893.0	534.0	60%	173.0	19%	186.0	21%	4,575	$5,123
1925	937.0	572.0	61%	157.0	17%	208.0	22%	4,910	$5,240
1926	849.0	491.0	58%	117.0	14%	241.0	28%	4,920	$5,795
1927	810.0	454.0	56%	99.0	12%	257.0	32%	4,540	$5,605
1928	753.0	436.0	58%	78.0	10%	239.0	32%	4,195	$5,571
1929	509.0	316.0	62%	51.0	10%	142.0	28%	3,040	$5,972
TOTAL	7034.0	4271.0	61%	1090.0	15%	1673.0	24%	36,600	$5,203

*In millions of dollars

SOURCE: *Historical Statistics of the United States, Colonial Times to 1957*, U.S. Bureau of the Census, Washington, D.C., 1960, p. 393.

or more. Housing starts rose from 247,000 in 1920 to 937,000 units in 1925, a figure that was a new high and was unsurpassed for the next twenty years. Production declined to 753,000 units in 1928, then dropped to 509,000 units in 1929. The chart shows the annual dwelling unit starts by category and average dollars expended.

1920-1929 • SURGE IN APARTMENT CONSTRUCTION ~ Over the decade, 4,271,000, or about 61 percent of the total units started, were single-family dwellings; 1,090,000, or 15 percent, were two-family dwellings, and 1,673,000, or 24 percent, were multi-family units. This was an unprecedented surge of new apartment construction. Previously apartment development was mostly tenement development in cities or conversions of row dwellings or large houses to multi-family use. Apartment construction rose in proportion to the total number of new dwelling units, reaching a peak in 1927 when they were 32 percent of total housing starts. As the boom proceeded the number of units in the individual projects grew larger. In Chicago, the majority of building permits issued for the entire decade of the twenties was for apartments. In Los Angeles, many apartments were built and in 1928, 53 percent of building permits issued were for apartments. Even row-dwelling cities such as Baltimore and Philadelphia began to develop apartments.

The highest number of multi-family units, 33 percent, were started in the 1920s in the Northeast part of the country; the Midwest was second with 27 percent; the South was third with 24 percent; and the West developed 16 percent. More housing was created in New York City in the 1920s than at any time previous or since. Two-thirds of the new dwelling units built in New York were apartments and many of them replaced dilapidated housing; between 1920 and 1929, 43,000 old tenements were torn down. The construction of large apartment buildings in the Bronx in the 1920s resulted in a mass Jewish exodus from the Lower East Side of Manhattan. The Jewish population of the Bronx rose from 382,000 in 1923 to 585,000 in 1930, while the Jewish population on the Lower East Side fell from

Garden Apartments

~

The apartment boom of the 1920s initiated the widespread development of garden apartments, expansive developments built with open green space between the buildings, more or less the opposite of city tenements in concept. Garden apartments were built on the edges of cities where land was sufficiently inexpensive to allow the purchase of several acres. In this same period in large and middle-sized cities, many three-story, walk-up apartment projects were built. These buildings typically had four to eight units in a building and were built in groups. They were plain buildings with few amenities, a far cry from the luxury elevator buildings on Central Park in New York. They were prevalent in many cities of the Northeast and Midwest. In California and other southwestern cities bungalow courts, which had several free-standing bungalows arranged around a central courtyard, began to appear in large numbers.

706,000 to 297,000 in the same period. *(See Appendix A, 1920s, for more statistics)*

Despite all this new apartment construction, home ownership rose significantly from 1921 to 1928, increasing by 2.8 million, whereas renters increased by only 1.8 million. This increase in home ownership was due to many of the same factors that had produced the housing boom: the supply of mortgage money, rising income levels and the availability of the automobile that made the suburbs attractive places to live. In addition the decrease in the number of poor immigrants entering the United States after 1924 that resulted from a more restrictive immigration policy, decreased the demand for rental units.

1920-1929 • SUBURBAN DEVELOPMENT ∼ Mass production of first the Model T Ford, then other cars, made individual transportation available to the masses. By 1928 there were twenty million cars on the streets and roads of the country. Car ownership exceeded home ownership by about fifty percent. Cars had become necessities rather than luxuries. The automobile changed American life in many ways, one of which was housing development patterns. Cars provided an easier way for people to commute between work and home. The star-shaped cities, with their public transit line spokes lined with Victorian houses, began to fill in the areas between the spokes and grow outward with the popular bungalow styles predominating. These new suburbs were primarily Anglo-Saxon Protestant enclaves; the rich cultural diversity of the central cities was not regarded as desirable by many Americans of this period. What the new suburbanites wanted was to leave the problems of

(1908) An Early Ford. American inventor and manufacturer Henry Ford (1863 - 1947) drives an early tractor, which he called an 'automobile plow,' powered by a 1904 Model-B type engine on one of his farms near Dearborn, Michigan. One could use this "car-plow" on either the farm or the roadway.

the unsafe and unclean center cities behind. Representative of this attitude was the Ku Klux Klan, which in its heyday in the 1920s crusaded against racial minorities, Catholics and Jews. The Klan became so strong that a resolution denouncing it was only narrowly defeated in the Democratic Convention of 1924. The movement gained its greatest strength in the South and the Midwest, among descendants of the first white Protestant settlers. Its power had begun to wane by 1928.

Architects Clarence Stein and Henry Wright designed the model town of Radburn, New Jersey in 1928. Projected for 25,000 people and surrounded by a green belt, it was the first of its kind. The main arterial streets were on the periphery and houses were located on *cul de sacs* to reduce traffic. Radburn included local amenities such as public schools and retail shops.

In addition to cars, the 1920s brought their adjuncts, not all of them attractive. They included multi-lane highways and throughways, gasoline service stations, traffic lights, motor courts, roadside restaurants, produce stands, billboards and used-car lots. Some business was drawn away from the central business districts of cities and some inner city residential areas began to suffer deterioration, although this was not nearly as serious as it would become after World War II.

1920s • Housing Styles ~ As America returned to laissez-faire individualism and disinterest in social reforms prevailed, the Academic Eclectics continued to design grand houses based on European traditions for wealthy Americans and a variety of revival styles including Tudor, Spanish, and Dutch Colonial. Colonial became popular for small houses. Some of these styles transformed bungalows as was the case of the Spanish bungalows of the west coast. Concrete and cinder blocks for foundations and stucco as a protective and long-lasting siding material were new in this period. Old houses were totally out of favor because they were not readily adaptable to modern conveniences and lifestyles. The garage was a new addition to the modern house. At first garages were built on alleys as far from the house as possible; by the end of the decade, however, they were being built at the front of the lot with a driveway from the street.

1917-1926 • Regulation of Real Estate ~ By 1917 approximately 500 municipalities were run by city commissions or city managers who coordinated the administrative work of the municipality. In the 1920s many cities adopted city-manager and commission forms of government. By the end of the 1920s most cities had established minimal standards for housing and for regulating land use through zoning ordinances. Zoning ordinances were upheld when challenged in 1926 by the U.S. Supreme Court. Zoning meant, among other things, that single-family residential areas could be protected from intrusive land uses. Building and housing codes and city planning also became standard. In addition to these municipal regulations, homeowners' associations and developers created exclusionary covenants that included minimum lot and house sizes and building costs to protect middle-class residential areas from incompatible types of development. Zoning, city planning and building codes eventually worked together to produce a housing uniformity, particularly in suburban areas, the desirability of which eventually became controversial.

1927-1929 • END OF THE BOOM

The boom in suburban development, which had been filling the open spaces in the outskirts of cities, began lagging somewhat after 1927, although the boom in apartment house construction and office building construction was still going full tilt in 1929. This development was not taking place where poor people lived but rather at the centers of big business and residential wealth. In New York the old Waldorf-Astoria hotel was torn down to make room for the Empire State Building, and John D. Rockefeller, Jr. had architects working on plans for a large mid-town development that would become Rockefeller Center. The Chrysler Building and other major New York skyscrapers were under construction. At the same time most of the other cities of the United States were also engaged in building ever-taller buildings to express American exuberance over the country's successful technology and financial prosperity.

The 1920s were the last period of laissez-faire housing development in the United States. By 1928, the housing market was overbuilt and vacancy and foreclosures were increasing. From 1926 to 1928 the housing stock increased by about three million units whereas the increase in the number of households in the same period was only 1.6 million. Finally in response to the housing oversupply, production dropped in 1929 to 509,000 units. While this was going on the stock market was rising to new heights.

(1929) View of the tower of the Chrysler Building under construction, New York City. Designed by William Van Alen.

The 1930s • Economic Chaos

The momentum of housing overproduction was initially difficult to slow because of the large number of units that were already underway, but by 1933, the housing industry, along with the rest of the economic and financial structure of the country, was in a stall. Approximately 14 million people, or 25 percent of the labor force were unemployed, and numbers of others had been reduced to working part time. Non-farm disposable income dropped from $77 billion in 1929 to $47 billion in 1932. From mid-1929 to mid-1932, the value of the stocks listed on the New York Stock Exchange had gone from $90 billion to about $16 billion. Ultimately the total value of all stocks dropped to less than 12 percent of their former prices. Housing production in 1932 was only 134,000 dwelling units, down to 26 percent of the 509,000 units produced in 1929. Multi-family construction starts had been 142,000 in 1929, but were down to 9,000 units in 1932.

Even though the rate of starts of new construction fell drastically, 2.5 million dwelling units were added to the supply of American housing in the four-year period, 1929-1932, due to the numbers of units brought to completion and also to subdivisions of existing apartments into smaller apartments to meet declining income levels. Because private enterprise was not providing sufficient low-cost housing, some families were doubling up while some houses were vacant. The new supply of 2.5 million dwelling units exceeded new household formation during this period by 1.5 million, driving values down and resulting in a vacancy rate of thirteen percent as compared to eight percent in 1928.

Property values fell by more than 25 percent in nonfarm areas from 1929 to 1932, wiping out homeowner equity. With income levels falling, mortgage debt increased from 36 percent in 1928 to 61 percent in 1932. At the same time that property values fell because of oversupply and diminished purchasing power, the drastic reduction in residential construction by two-thirds of what it had been caused sudden large decreases in employment, reduced sales and production of building materials, and loss of business profits. Construction workers were approximately one-third of the unemployed by the mid-1930s.

Wealth in the United States in 1929 remained concentrated at the top with 5 percent of the population earning 30 percent of personal income, even though the per-capita gross national product had increased by 65 percent since 1900. In 1929 at least 78 percent of the population had family incomes of less than $3,000 a year and 40 percent of the total population had family incomes of less than $1,500 per year. (The purchasing power of the dollar changes over time: goods and services costing $2,500 in 1929 were available in the period of 1932-1939 for $2,000, but the same goods and services, because of inflation, cost $24,000 in 1999). When the Depression struck, family incomes fell, not only to reflect the depressed dollar, but also in real terms as employment declined. The deflated value of the dollar had the effect of adding 25 percent to mortgage payments and other debt. Banks began suffering from an absence of deposits and uncollected mortgage payments and could not make new loans or extend existing ones. Over 725,000 foreclosures took place in the 1929-1932 four-year period; by mid-1933 the rate of mortgage foreclosures was approaching 1,000 per day. Beyond foreclosures, mort-

1930s

gage payments and rental payments were delinquent and people were frequently not paying their property taxes.

1930s • Homelessness ~ Homelessness was the very visible result of the increasing number of foreclosures and evictions. People were sleeping in parks, doorways and packing boxes or living in Hoovervilles, which were groupings of makeshift shacks on vacant lots, under bridges or on the edges of cities. The homeless scrounged food where they could and stood in bread lines and went to soup kitchens. Some drifted, hitchhiking, riding in railroad boxcars, going from town to town, begging for food. In 1929 there were an estimated 14,000 transient people in the United States, in 1931, about 190,000, and in 1933, one million. There were among them approximately 200,000 homeless children.

The hopelessness of the mid-1930s was reflected in the birth rate, which fell from 27.7 per 1,000 population in 1920 and 25.1 in 1925 to 21.3 in 1930 and 18.7 in 1935. It would not be that low again until the 1970s. The marriage rate also fell. The annual number of marriages per one thousand women over the age of fifteen was 52 in 1931, the lowest it had ever been previously. By 1946 the rate had risen to 118. It would not be as low again as it was in 1931 until 1995. In response to lower birth rates and decreased incomes, speculative builders built smaller housing units. One-and-one-half-story cottages and one-room efficiency or studio apartments became common.

1932-1935 • Coping with the Depression ~ With the country in economic collapse, social chaos threatened the governing structure. Capitalism

(1936) Houses in an African-American district of Atlanta, Georgia.

seemed to many to have failed and even political moderates were considering socialism as a possible alternative. Those in power were not solving the problem and had to be replaced by those who would. The prevailing idea that there should be no government interference in private enterprise and that the individual was the only one responsible for providing for himself was no longer a tenable concept. The millions who were out of work, homeless, and hungry clearly had not caused their conditions. The need for a minimum level of shelter for those who could not afford to pay for it, which previously had not been perceived as a government responsibility, was now perceived as an obvious government responsibility, at least politically. Whereas the country's long-term emphasis had been on industrial and territorial expansion and on the needs of the middle class, the primary emphasis was now on the needs of the unemployed, the poorly-housed, the homeless, and the hungry.

The Depression ended the political dominance of the Republican Party that had begun in 1890. Franklin Roosevelt was elected overwhelmingly in November of 1932 and the Democrats captured both houses of Congress by large majorities. President Hoover had been rejected by the voters for failing to take bold enough steps to deal with the country's escalating problems.

By the time of Roosevelt's inauguration in March of 1933, the banking system had collapsed. Housing starts were at 93,000 units, the lowest they had been since 1879. The new president began work immediately on a series of radical programs to address the various economic, financial, and social crises facing the country. He appeared before Congress, time after time, introducing a series of legislative acts. By the time Congress had adjourned three months later, the major legislation that had been passed included the Emergency Banking Relief Act, the Federal Emergency Relief Act, the Agricultural Adjustment Act, and the Federal Securities Act. The new agencies that had been created were the Civilian Conservation Corps, the Tennessee Valley Authority, the Home Owners' Loan Corporation, the National Recovery Administration and the Public Works Administration.

1932 • FEDERAL BACKING OF MORTGAGE BANKS ~ The Hoover Administration, in an attempt to stop property loan foreclosures, had created the Federal Home Loan Bank system in 1932, with twelve regional banks, to provide a reserve system for lending institutions. Funding for the system was to come from debt obligations such as bonds and not from the federal budget. Members of the system included savings and loans, savings banks, and insurance companies; as members they were subject to regulation by the five-member Federal Home Loan Bank Board. The system was a good one and would be kept, but in the face of the overwhelming and ever-climbing number of loan foreclosures, the Federal Home Loan Bank system by itself could not overcome the problem.

Roosevelt took stronger action. The construction industry, particularly the residential component, was a major focus of the new administration's effort to revive the economy. With so many construction workers in the ranks of the unemployed and with the boost to manufacturing that would be entailed, an increase in new housing starts would not only better house people, it would benefit the economy generally. In addition, reform of the mortgage lending structure, slum removal, and community planning could be incorporated in the housing programs. *(See Appendix A, 1930s, for more statistics)*

1932-1938 • RELOCATING DUST BOWL FARMERS ~ In the early 1930s, the dust storms hit the Great Plains. First there was a drought with high temperatures, and then the wind began to blow. All of the ploughed-up acreage that had been committed to crops to meet the demands of the market during World War I, no longer held in place by the extensive root systems of the prairie grasses, rose in walls of dirt over the whole of the plains. In some states rain was absent for months at a time and temperatures remained over 100 degrees for week after week in the summer months. Farms became great dunes of shifting dirt and sand.

Farmers had suffered from low crop prices since the boom times of World War I, which had lured them into heavily investing in machinery as well as plowing up more of their land. The drop in demand for wheat and corn after the war left them in poor financial condition. During the first years of the Depression many Midwestern farmers lost their farms to tax sale or foreclosure. When the dust storms came, more and more families abandoned their farms and migrated elsewhere, mostly westward. In 1936, in southeastern Colorado, a survey showed that approximately one-half of the existing farmhouses had been abandoned. The Roosevelt administration created the Resettlement Administration to remove farm families that were victims of the Dust Bowl in the Midwest to farms developed out of federal lands. The Resettlement Administration projects also included the three greenbelt towns that were built: Greenbelt, Maryland; Green Hills, Ohio; and Greendale, Wisconsin. These new-town projects were comprised of about 15,000 dwelling units.

1934 • CREATING THE FEDERAL HOUSING ADMINISTRATION (FHA) ~ The National Housing Act of 1934 created the Federal Housing Administration (FHA), which undertook an entirely new program of federally insuring long-term amortized mortgages to encourage lending institutions to make loans in a difficult market. The activities of FHA were to be financed by insurance premiums, fees, and the interest on invested reserves. Title I of the Act authorized insurance of loans up to $2,000 for repairs and improvements to nonfarm residential properties. Title II authorized insurance on unpaid balances of mortgages on small houses and rental projects. Title III authorized nationally chartered mortgage associations to purchase FHA-insured mortgages in the secondary market. These associations could raise funds by issuing debt instruments such as bonds and notes. The Act also created the Federal Savings and Loan Insurance Corporation to insure the accounts of savings institutions, in a manner similar to that of the Federal Deposit Insurance Corporation, which had been established early in the Roosevelt years to insure bank deposits.

The loans permitted were 1) limited to 1-4-family properties, 2) the values of the properties could not exceed $20,000, 3) the amount of the mortgage was limited to 80 percent, 4) the term of the mortgage was limited to twenty years and 5) the interest rate could not exceed five percent. The high (80 percent) loan-to-value ratio eliminated the need for second and third mortgages. Financial institutions were willing to make these federally-insured loans. FHA appraisal standards were strict and the secondary market for mortgages grew because of the ability to rely on these appraisals. Another consequence of the FHA program was that builders were willing to undertake the construction of large numbers of dwellings at one time. This brought about an increased standardization of housing types on large tracts of land around the edges of cities.

The opportunity to form a national mortgage association was shunned by the wary private financial sector and consequently, in 1938, Roosevelt requested the FHA administrator to establish the Federal National Mortgage Association (FNMA) as a subsidiary of the Reconstruction Finance Corporation, which had been established in 1932 under the Hoover administration. The new secondary market mortgage association soon came to be called Fannie Mae. Before the year was over Fannie Mae had authorized and purchased 26,276 mortgages, amounting to over $100 million, at an average of just under $4,000 each. While Fannie Mae bought insured mortgages on new houses, including large-scale housing projects, its parent, the Reconstruction Finance Corporation, continued to buy insured mortgages on older houses.

The American Federation of Labor had been persuaded to support a public housing program for low-income families in 1934 during a campaign for a public housing bill. Both support and opposition for public housing emerged. The National Association of Real Estate Boards was opposed as was the National Retail Lumber Dealers Association whose members objected because the buildings were not to be wood. In January 1935 the National Public Housing Conference drafted a public housing bill that died in committee. The bill was recast with the emphasis on relief of unemployment rather than public housing and the Housing Act of 1937 was finally passed and signed into law September 1 of that year. Its stated purpose was: ...to provide financial assistance to the states and political subdivisons thereof for the elimination of unsafe and unsanitary housing conditions, for the development of decent, safe, and sanitary dwellings for families of low income, and for the reduction of unemployment and the stimulation of business activity, to create a United States Housing Authority, and for other purposes.

The United States Housing Authority was to be a permanent agency within the Department of the Interior. Several amendments were made to the bill before it was passed, including restrictions on the amounts spent for units in cities of less than 500,000 population of $4,000 per unit and $1,000 per room; in larger cities the limits were $5,000 per unit and $1,250 per room. For each unit built, one slum unit had to be eliminated or repaired, a feature that was termed "equivalent elimination." No more than ten percent of the funds were to be spent in any one state. No loans made by the Housing Authority were to be for more than 90 percent of the cost of the project. The rate of interest was to be 0.5 percent above the current federal borrowing cost, paid back in 60 years. The local housing authority paid an annual payment in lieu of local property taxes equal to 10 percent of the rent of the projects (rent without utilities). The decision to have public housing or not was left to the local housing authority.

1930s

Congress increased the appropriation for the United States Housing Authority from $500,000 to $800,000,000 early in 1938 in response to a new downturn in the economy that had started in August of 1937. The government had cut relief and recovery spending because of pressure from the business community for a balanced budget, but because private enterprise was not committing capital and increasing employment, the newly-re-elected Roosevelt administration once again had to strongly intervene. By November of 1938 commitments of $576,000,000 had been made to build public housing in fourteen cities. At the same time FHA terms were liberalized, which led to increased private construction.

During the 1930s, federal housing policy was revolutionized to include the concepts that housing is within the purview of the government, that individual homeownership is the preferred form of housing, that federally-backed financing can be used to accomplish that goal, and that slums can be cleared and public housing built cooperatively between federal and local governments. The government thus intervened in the private market to accomplish worthy social and economic goals. The intervention of the federal government stopped socialism and the drastic diminution in the value of American housing. The Federal Housing Administration's program formed the basis of a huge increase in housing construction that would take place over the remainder of the twentieth century. Large volume builders, relying on FHA-insured mortgages, began to expand their activities in the mid-1930s. In 1936 housing starts began to rise and in 1937, starts were 336,000; in 1938 they were 406,000; and in 1939, 515,000.

1930s • Housing Styles for the Working Class ~ A group of European architects fleeing the Nazis came to the United States in the 1930s, bringing with them the Bauhaus functional architecture that came to be called the International style. Although Frank Lloyd Wright had created an architecture that contrasted markedly with traditional

---

Mobile Homes

By 1936, between 160,000 and 200,000 mobile homes, then called "trailers," were in use. The first trailer was made at home in the summer of 1929 by Arthur G. Sherman, a bacteriologist who wanted to take a small house on wheels behind the family car on vacations. Wherever he and his family took the trailer it attracted so much favorable comment that he built more and exhibited one at the Detroit Automobile Show in 1930. Soon he and other manufacturers were making them on a regular basis. In addition to being an inexpensive place to sleep and eat on a vacation they were ideally suited for people who had to move from place to place looking for work. They also served as temporary housing for construction workers and permanent housing for factory employees and military personnel. By 1939 approximately 287,000 were in use. Two travel associations were formed in response to the trailer phenomenon, the Automobile Tourist Association and Tin Can Tourists.

styles, his work was a synthesis of rationalism and expressionism. Wright's work was related to Americanism, to the natural setting, to the traditions of the family and to craftmanship. The architecture of the Bauhaus group, which included Walter Gropius, Ludwig Mies van der Rohe, Marcel Breuer and Charles Edouard Jeanneret Le Corbusier, was rationalistic, international rather than nationalistic, expressive of technology rather than nature and engineered rather than crafted. It rejected anything aristocratic or bourgeois (middle class) in character and instead was associated with socialism and the worker class. Le Corbusier particularly rejected the concept of the home as a place imbued with meaning and tradition. "Styles are a lie," he said, and "the house is a habitable machine."

Pre-International style modernism in the United States, in addition to the work of Frank Lloyd Wright, took the forms of Art Deco in the 1920s and Streamline Moderne in the 1930s. Art Deco was a flamboyant style, popular for apartment buildings and theatres; its most famous building is the Chrysler Building in New York. Streamline Moderne, a less ostentatious style, replaced Art Deco in the 1930s. Houses and commercial buildings built in the Streamline Moderne style had flat roofs, horizontal lines and banding, rounded corners, glass blocks, and stucco finishes. The decorative counterpart of this architecture was called Art Moderne.

International style houses were much more austere. They were built with stark expanses of flat walls with no roofline, window, or door trim, groupings of metal casement windows, and an asymmetrical facade. Colors were very limited; white predominated. Interiors were painted white and had low ceilings. Mass-produced components were used as much as possible. Edward Durell Stone designed the first International style house on the East Coast in 1933 in Mount Kisco, New York. Richard Neutra had built one in Los Angeles in 1928. Walter Gropius' own house, built near Boston in 1937, was constructed with components ordered from American catalogs.

The schools of architecture, many architects, professional architecture magazines and journals, the Museum of Modern Art, and public housing officials favored modernism in its various forms in the 1930s, whereas the general public diverged, continuing to favor traditional styles. Home design and decorating magazines still featured colonial and other traditional styles.

The International style was adopted in the 1930s for public housing, perhaps because of its association with the working class or because the government wished to convey a modern image. Under the official policy of equivalent elimination, public housing projects were typically built where old slums had been. Large acreages were cleared in cities such as New York, Philadelphia, St. Louis and Baltimore, the residents having been evicted and moved elsewhere, and new high-rise towers constructed with broad expanses of grass between them. The buildings were starkly modern, people soon grew to hate them. Trapped in their high-rise warrens, they had lost their old neighborhoods and consequently their identities as people who lived at certain addresses, on certain streets, in certain neighborhoods. They were now imprisoned in "the projects," too-readily-identifiable enclaves of tall buildings set at angles to the normal street grids and facing inward onto courtyards rather than toward, and with a view of, a street with

1930s

its passing panorama of human activity. Crime and vandalism were soon out of control in many of these large International style projects. The intent of the Bauhaus architects, although laudable–they were trying to better the living conditions of the working classes–was lost among the hopelessness and the disadvantages suffered by the urban poor.

1930s • Precursors of the Future ~ Frank Lloyd Wright's Usonian houses, which he designed in the mid-1930s for a nation that could not afford his elegant Prairie Style houses, were small practical homes in simple, modern shapes, streamlined, but built of appealing natural materials. They were oriented to their backyards, accessed through glass sliding doors opening onto a patio, providing privacy and opening up the house to the light. Wright put these houses on concrete slabs. Inside a dining alcove was open to both the kitchen and the living room. This practical house design was one of the forerunners of the ranch house that would become so popular in the 1950s.

Some examples of houses of the future verged on fantasy. The "House of Tomorrow" featured in the 1933 Chicago World's Fair, which had as its theme "Science is the determining factor in progress" was a twelve-sided structure of glass and steel sections bolted together and supported on a cantilevered frame. It had an airplane hangar in the basement and was fully air-conditioned.

As exhibited at the 1939 New York World's Fair, the home kitchen had undergone design changes during the 1930s, even though many people could not afford the newest innovations. A streamlined kitchen, based on a scientifically organized work process, had emerged. The components of the kitchen were all standardized and interchangeable. The various machines, refrigerators, sinks, ranges, dishwashers and garbage disposers, were for the first time built into cabinetry. The kitchen was becoming the command center of the house, all buffed and presentable for viewing, a far cry from the nineteenth-century kitchen hidden away in the basement, in a sepa-

---

Restoring America's History

~

The restoration of Colonial Williamsburg began in 1927 and was completed by 1937. John D. Rockefeller was the financial force behind this project, which was first suggested by Dr. W.A.R. Goodwin, rector of the local Bruton Parish Church. Williamsburg, originally laid out in 1666 with broad, tree-lined streets and public squares, was a town significant in both history and architecture. Christopher Wren designed its College of William and Mary in the late Renaissance style. Its Governor's Palace, Old Court House, Capitol, Raleigh tavern, and many other buildings exemplified some of the best architecture of Virginia and Colonial America. Sixty-six Colonial buildings were repaired or restored, eighty-four were reproduced on their original foundations and the landscaping and street improvements were all restored to their appearance in Colonial times. This first example of "living history" greatly influenced American home design. Its architecture was the antithesis of the International style, but both would be very influential in the coming decades.

(1940) The winter home of American architect Frank Lloyd Wright, 'Taliesin West', in Scottsdale, Arizona.

rate building outside the house as in the South or at best at back of the house where it was not meant for viewing.

In 1935 Frank Lloyd Wright designed Fallingwater on Bear Run in a rugged area of the Allegheny Mountains south of Pittsburgh, a work of such genius that it remains as the outstanding house designed in the twentieth century. In this house Wright combined his distinctive organic architecture with the rational geometric forms of the International style. The house's vertical elements are of stone and the horizontal of concrete, but it hovers over the waterfall, seemingly weightless. With Fallingwater Wright turned the International style to his own ends and created a masterpiece.

1940-1945 • WAR-TIME HOUSING

(See Appendix A, 1940s, for housing statistics) Despite the growing totalitarianism in Europe and Adolph Hitler's aggressive actions, the Congress of the United States, reflecting the isolationist positions of most Americans, passed a series of Neutrality Acts in 1935-1937. However, beginning in 1940, U.S. leaders began to prepare for a possible war. The United States began supplying war materials to Great Britain in its efforts to resist the Axis powers. Production began in 1940 and in the period between 1940 and 1945, with a massive effort, U.S. factories not only equipped the United States military, but also significantly supplied Great Britain, the Soviet Union and other allies with armaments, producing in total twice the war material production of all of the Axis powers combined. In addition, U.S. farmers increased their production by one-third, enabling the United States to supply other countries with needed food.

Beginning in 1940, Congress legislated a range of public provisions for housing. In June of 1940, funds were appropriated to purchase stock in the Defense Homes Corporation, which would in time complete 8,000 housing units. Also

1940-1945

in June of 1940, the U.S. Housing Act was amended to permit defense housing to be built using public housing loan and subsidy funds. In July of 1940 an Office of Defense Housing Coordinator was created in the Council of National Defense to plan and carry out defense housing programs, in cooperation with private enterprise. In September, Congress appropriated $100 million for the construction of defense housing by the Navy and War Departments. In October, the Lanham Act authorized the Public Works Agency, and subsequently, the Federal Public Housing Authority, to use appropriated funds to build housing at defense plants and military bases. In March of 1941 the National Housing Act was amended to authorize insurance of FHA mortgages in defense areas and firm advance commitments to builders. In January of 1942 a national policy of rent control was put into place to prevent landlords from exploiting the shortage of rental facilities. In February of 1942 President Roosevelt merged the sixteen federal agencies that were handling federal defense housing into the National Housing Agency. All publicly financed housing operations were consolidated into the Federal Public Housing Authority, which encompassed the former United States Housing Authority.

The conflict between private and public housing interests resurfaced in the face of the exigencies of impending war and continued after war was declared. In 1941 the War Production Board moved to close down private defense housing and turn all construction over to public housing agencies. The Home Builders' Association, a national builder group that eventually became the National Association of Home Builders, persuaded government officials that they needed the cooperation of private enterprise to build the needed housing. Millions of defense workers who had migrated to defense plant locations were futilely looking for places to live and their housing problems were causing high labor turnover. Private enterprise builders relocated at military installation and defense plant locations and began the mass production of the needed housing. Carrying out the wartime housing programs required great ingenuity and effort. Builders had to experiment with prefabrication and assembly line production while coping with growing shortages of lumber and other building materials as well as bureaucratic red tape. All non-essential new construction, i.e., non-defense-worker housing construction, was prohibited and the costs and supplies of building materials were placed under government controls. (See Appendix A, 1940s, for more statistics).

Non-Farm Housing Starts
(in thousands)

Year	Total	Private	Public	Cost
1940	602.6	529.6	73.0	$3,825
1941	706.1	619.5	86.6	4,000
1942	356.0	301.2	54.8	3,775
1943	191.0	183.7	7.3	3,600
1944	141.8	138.7	3.1	3,500
1942-1944	688.8	623.6	65.2	
1940-1944	1,997.5	1,772.7	224.8	

SOURCE: *Historical Statistics of the United States, Colonial Times to 1970*, U.S. Bureau of the Census, Washington, CD, 1975.

1943-1944 • FHA HOME FINANCING
~ In October of 1943 Congress authorized an additional $400 million for FHA home financing. In the Spring of 1944 the Senate Committee on Postwar Economic Policy and Planning established a subcom-

(circa 1940) Strawberry Manor. World War II brought a new type of house to the market, the pre-fabricated house. Builders devised factory-built insulated wall panels; used standardized, pre-cut components of all kinds; lightweight metal framing, including girders and trusses that allowed for greater spans; and in the face of the lumber shortage, even experimented with an all-steel house. Seen here is a high-angle view of two rows of tract houses in the Strawberry Manor subdivision situated in the hills of California.

mittee on housing and urban development, chaired by Senator Robert Taft, which began a five-year legislative process that would culminate in the Housing Act of 1949. Private interest groups convened in 1944 at the National Housing Conference and reaffirmed their opposition to public housing on anti-socialism principles. In August of 1944 Congress passed the Serviceman's Readjustment Act, known has the G.I. Bill of Rights, guaranteeing loans to veterans for home purchases. In October of 1944 the War Production Board and the National Housing Authority relaxed some housing controls, but shortages of materials, especially lumber, continued to grow worse through 1945. Eventually ten million veterans returned home to the United States and the number of families needing housing rose to three million. Although price and rent controls were still in effect, civilian residential construction was once again allowed by the fall of 1945, but it was too late in the year to bring new housing starts above 326,000.

1942-1945 • CONSTRUCTION INNOVATION ~ World War II significantly changed housing production. In order to meet the demand for war worker housing, builders had created many innovative ways to build houses, particularly in the areas of prefabrication. Builders devised factory-built insulated wall panels; used standardized, pre-cut components of all kinds; lightweight metal framing, including girders and trusses that allowed for greater spans and in the face of the lumber shortage, even experimented with an all-steel house. From the aircraft industry new glues and gluing methods came into

1942-1945

1945-1950

use and from advances in electronics came automatic controls for home electrical and mechanical systems. Plastic pipe for plumbing systems was first used during the war. The poured concrete foundation became standard. Some 200,000 totally prefabricated houses were manufactured during the war, but new homes mostly were a combination of factory-built components and on-site assembly. Many technological advances were made with the help of engineers, architects, and professors at leading universities such as the Massachusetts Institute of Technology. This cooperative effort established the basis for the hugely expanded post-war construction industry. The war forever changed the small, craft-oriented builder base of the house construction industry to one more compatible with the rest of American industry in general.

1945-1950 • POST-WAR HOUSING ~ Americans came out of World War II with higher incomes to buy better housing. Personal savings rose between 1941 and 1945 by $161 billion as compared with $24 billion in the previous five years. Nonfarm disposable personal income had almost doubled, going from $68 billion in 1940 to $133 billion in 1945, an increase of 30 percent adjusted for inflation. As a result of this increase, mortgage debt as a proportion of personal income fell from 61 percent in 1932, to 28 percent in 1941, and to 18 percent in 1945. The proportion of nonfarm home ownership rose from 41.1 percent in 1940 to 50.8 percent in 1945, the fastest increase of such magnitude to take place in the twentieth century. Contributing to the increase in home ownership was a decrease of nearly one million rental units sold by landlords who found them no longer profitable under rent control.

During World War II population growth in the United States shifted to the South Atlantic and the Pacific states. Not only were many of the huge military installations located in these areas, such as Seattle and San Diego on the west coast and Norfolk-Portsmouth in the South Atlantic region, but many military personnel, who had traveled from farm areas for the first time during the war, settled on one or other of the coasts when the war was over, thereby decreasing the population of rural areas in the Midwest. The total shift of population during the war was between eight and ten million people. By 1950 the Census of Housing showed a 23 percent gain over 1940 in the numbers of housing units in the South Atlantic states and a 49 percent gain in the Pacific states.

1945-1949 • BOOM IN HOUSING STARTS ~ There was a general anticipation that when the war ended there would be another depression like the one after World War I, but it never materialized. Non-farm employment increased by over 2.5 million from 1945 to 1946. Post-war prosperity ensued despite huge expenditures by the federal government to aid war-devastated Europe and maintain the U.S. military in the face of the Cold War. The Federal Reserve System supported government bonds, which yielded only a little over two percent, at par for the first six years after the war. Many factors contributed to the huge boom in post-war housing including the housing shortage that had built up, the $400 million authorized by Congress in October of 1943 for additional FHA financing, the increase in the loan-to-value ratio for FHA loans to 90 percent, the passage by Congress in 1944 of the GI Bill of Rights guaranteeing home loans to veterans, the rising marriage and birth rates, increased income and employment levels, the deductibility of property taxes and mortgage interest from growing income taxes and the fact that lending institutions wanted to liquidate their government bond portfolios and invest in mortgages and commercial loans that could provide higher yields.

After a slow beginning in 1945, housing starts exploded upward for the rest of the decade. Housing starts in 1946, the first year after the war had ended, were higher than they had been in 1925, the previous record year, and climbed to nearly 1.5 million in 1949. As the chart below shows, the average per-unit cost of housing more than doubled between 1944 and 1949. From 1940 to 1945, the increase in the cost of living for moderate income families was approximately 28 percent and in the period 1945-1949 it was about 32 percent. New starts of single-family houses predominated after the war, ranging between 80 percent and 90 percent. Rural housing, which had been neglected throughout the Depression and war years, was given a boost by the 1946 creation of the Farmers Home Administration within the Department of Agriculture, which made loans available for farmers to buy or modernize their houses.

1945-1955 • HOME LOANS TO VETERANS

The Veterans Administration loan-guarantee program was a major factor in the successful housing of America's returning veterans in the postwar period. In 1945, the maximum amount of the loan guarantee was increased from $2,000 to $4,000 and the loan term was increased from twenty to twenty-five years, but even these more favorable conditions were not sufficient to entice large numbers of lenders to make house loans to returning GIs. Two-thirds of VA loans made before 1950 were made to finance existing rather than new houses. However, in 1950 the loan guarantee was increased to $7,500 and the loan term to thirty years. The maximum interest rate for the program was 4.0 percent until 1953 when it was increased to 4.5 percent. After 1950 the number of annual housing starts financed with VA loans exceeded 100,000 and reached a peak in 1955 with 393,000 or 24 percent of all private non-farm housing starts.

The VA program, unlike others, allowed lenders to lend 100 percent of the market value of the property, with the VA insuring up to 60 percent, capped at $7,500. In addition to straight VA-insured loans, VA-FHA combination loans were available with FHA insuring the first 80 percent and the VA the remaining 20 percent.

In January of 1945 veterans were given preference in obtaining building materials. In February, President Truman announced "The Veterans Emergency

Non-Farm Housing Starts
(in thousands)

Year	Total	Private	Public	Cost
1944				3,500
1945	326.0	325.0	1.0	4,625
1946	1,023.0	1,015.0	8.0	5,625
1947	1,268.0	1,265.0	3.0	6,650
1948	1,362.0	1,344.0	18.0	7,725
1949	1,466.0	1,430.0	36.0	7,525
1945-1949	5,445.0	5,379.0	66.0	
1940-1949	7,442.5	7,151.7	290.8	

SOURCE: *Historical Statistics of the United States, Colonial Times to 1970*, U.S. Bureau of the Census, Washington, D.C., 1975.

1946-1948

Housing Program, proclaiming the need for 2.7 million new dwellings by the end of 1947. This program provided subsidies for the production of building materials, set up allocations and priorities for residential builders to purchase equipment, established veterans' preference in new sales and rental housing, and continued price controls on materials to prevent runaway inflation in the face of the strong demand for housing. President Truman appointed a Housing Expediter to handle the veterans' housing crisis. A proposal to set price ceilings on sales of houses and house sites that was part of this emergency program was defeated in Congress. The rest of the program, although it had been successful for a year, was ended in January of 1947 after Republicans gained control of Congress in late 1946.

1946-1948 • APARTMENTS AND RENTAL HOUSES ~ In May of 1946 Congress expanded FHA's mortgage insurance program by a billion dollars, part of it targeted for large-scale rental housing. The year 1947 was a banner year for apartment construction. Title VI of the Housing Act (Sections 603 and 608) as well as rent control on existing apartments and veterans' preferences, were all extended by the Housing and Rent Act of 1947. FHA Title VI Section 608, garden apartment loans, which could be 90 percent of market value, and which Congress made even more attractive in 1948 with 27-year terms and 4 percent interest rates, earned more money for FHA than any other program and made it one of the few government programs to show a profit. More than 400,000 apartment units were produced, with rents ranging from $40 to $90 per month. Also in June of 1947 a new Section 603 of FHA Title VI went into effect, making 90 percent mortgages available on one- to four-family buildings.

The Housing Act was further amended in the post-war period by Title VII, providing yield insurance on rental housing, Title VIII, providing rental housing for civilian and military personnel adjacent to military installations, Title IX, providing sale and rental housing during the Korean War for defense-industry areas, and a cooperative housing FHA mortgage insurance program, Section 213. Rent control lasted until 1953, through the fighting in Korea.

PUBLIC HOUSING

Construction of public housing units had remained at a low ebb during and after the war. An American Public Health Association report in 1948 had proposed that slum neighborhoods be treated in a comprehensive manner. Housing discrimination and racial segregation were recognized as major problems. As planning for new public housing for low-income renters got underway, the National Association of Home Builders and the National Association of Real Estate Boards announced their opposition to public housing in general and to the continuation of the National Housing Agency in the post-war period. Ranged against them in support of public housing, urban renewal, and a comprehensive approach to housing problems, was a coalition of labor organizations, the National Public Housing Conference, the National Association of Housing Officials, and the National Committee on Housing.

Senator Taft's Subcommittee report in August of 1945 was a major setback for the private housing lobby. The report supported the National Housing Agency and a comprehensive public housing program.

In July of 1947 both houses of Congress authorized a joint committee to study all phases of housing. The majority supported the recommendations of Senator's Taft's committee. The Housing Act of 1949, passed after President Truman's 1948 election victory, favored a "decent home and a suitable living environment for every American family." It provided for continuation of the NHA, slum clearance and community redevelopment, construction of low-rent public housing to the extent of 810,000 units in six years, housing research, continuation of the Housing Census, and loans for farm housing.

1950s • IMPROVEMENTS IN HOUSES ~ As the United States continued its emergence from the Depression and War years, those who could afford it — and they were a greater proportion than ever — largely fled the cities leaving behind a poor minority population, a diminished commercial core, and growing slums. At the beginning of the decade about 20 percent of the U.S. population were living in the suburbs. The upward trend in owner-occupancy had reached 55 percent as shown on the following chart.

Owner Occupancy 1930-1950

Year	1930	1940	1950
All Units	47.8%	43.6%	55.0%
Non-farm	46.0%	41.1%	53.4%
Farm	53.9%	53.2%	65.7%

By 1956 the owner-occupied portion of total nonfarm occupancy would rise to 59 percent, a huge increase over the 41 percent of 1940. (*See Appendix A, 1950s, for more statistics*)

The 1950 Census showed a slight improvement in the physical condition of the country's housing, an improvement compatible with a higher ratio of home occupancy, but also reflecting the greater prosperity that people had begun to enjoy. Houses had more bathrooms. As compared with 20 percent in 1940, only 15 percent of occupied dwelling units were overcrowded, averaging more than one person per room. In 1950, 71 percent had flush toilets as compared with 60 percent in 1940 and 69 percent had private bathtubs or showers compared with 56 percent in 1940. The average value of non-farm dwelling units was $7,400 as compared with $3,000 in 1940 and the medium rent was $42, up from $27 in 1940. By 1950 more than 85 percent of American farms had public electricity as compared with only about ten percent in 1935.

1950s • HOUSING DEMAND/HOUSING STARTS ~ The overwhelming postwar demand for new housing continued in 1950. Marriage and birth rates continued to be high; the baby boom was well underway. The country seemed intent on marrying, settling down in a nice new house in the suburbs and raising a family. Unemployment was low, wages were up, mortgages were available at reasonable rates and low down payments, new cars, and refrigerators and other modern appliances were once again available. The prospects for a longer, more healthful life, thanks to antibiotics, vitamins and better medical care, were excellent. Life expectancy had increased from 49 years in 1900 to 68 years in 1950.

Americans were also much better off financially than they had been during the first fifty years of the century. Millions had been raised above the poverty level by the World War II-engendered prosperity. Incomes were much more evenly distributed by 1950 than they had been in 1929 when 5 percent of the population garnered 30 percent of the national income; by 1950 the highest earning 5 percent were earning less than 20 percent of total income. Disposable real income had risen 74 percent between 1929 and 1950 and by the 1950s approximately 60 percent of Americans had incomes that classified them as middle-class. Americans bought eight million new cars in 1950; they also bought many refrigerators, washers, dryers, dishwashers and televisions. By 1950, Americans were paying an average 26 percent of their family income for housing, including utility costs and furnishings. This percentage had been 25 percent in 1901 and 29 percent in 1929 and would remain between 20 percent and 30 percent through 1997.

Increased earning power, increased household formation, a higher birth rate and people living longer meant a tremendous demand for housing. The construction industry responded by intensifying the trend of mass production it had begun in the last years of the 1940s. In addition, the federal government continued the upward trend of construction of public housing units begun in 1949, reaching a peak in 1951 with 71,200 units, or 4.8 percent of total units started. It reached a second peak in 1958 with 67,800 units or 4.9 percent of the total. Housing starts as a percentage of the existing housing stock reached a high for the twentieth century of 4.75 percent in 1950 when 1,951,900 housing units, more than one-third of them in the suburbs, were started. In addition, 63,100 mobile homes were sold in that year, bringing total new dwelling units to 2,015,000.

North Korea attacked South Korea in June of 1950 and President Truman declared South Korea the place to draw the line against communist aggression. U.S. troops made up the bulk of the UN

Housing Starts 1950-1959

Year	Private Units		Public Units		Total Units	
1950	1,908,100	97.8%	43,800	2.2%	1,951,900	100.0%
1951	1,419,800	95.2%	71,200	4.8%	1,491,000	100.0%
1952	1,445,400	96.1%	58,500	3.9%	1,503,900	100.0%
1953	1,402,100	97.5%	35,500	2.5%	1,437,600	100.0%
1954	1,531,800	98.8%	18,700	1.2%	1,550,500	100.0%
1955	1,626,600	98.8%	19,400	1.2%	1,646,000	100.0%
1956	1,324,900	98.2%	24,200	1.8%	1,349,100	100.0%
1957	1,174,800	96.0%	49,100	4.0%	1,223,900	100.0%
1958	1,314,200	95.1%	67,800	4.9%	1,382,000	100.0%
1959	1,494,600	97.6%	36,700	2.4%	1,531,300	100.0%
TOTAL	14,642,300	97.2%	424,900	2.8%	15,067,200	100.0%

SOURCE: *Historical Statistics of the United States, Colonial Times to 1970*, U.S. Bureau of the Census, Washington, D.C., 1975.

(1986) Rows of suburban houses set in a circular plan in Sun City, Phoenix, Arizona.

troops fighting in Korea. The stalemated war dragged on until an armistice was signed in 1953. During the war there was a new shortage of building materials. Strict controls on credit were imposed to curtail housing and inflation, and wage and price controls were re-imposed. Housing starts slowed, declining to 1,491,000 in 1951, 1,503,900 in 1952 and 1,437,600 in 1953. General Eisenhower became president in 1953, a Republican who had promised to keep tight controls on the budget, but who had also promised to support the housing program mandated by the Housing Act of 1949. The Korean War over, 1954 housing starts rose to 1,550,500 and then to 1,646,000 in 1955. Pent-up demand had been satisfied by 1956 and the housing market was more or less at equilibrium with new production equaling new demand. There was a decrease in 1956 to 1,349,100 and then to 1,223,900 in 1957 as the economy moved through a minor recession. In 1958, a rising trend began with 1,382,000 starts, and in 1959 the number of starts were 1,531,000. Alaska and Hawaii became states of the union in 1959 and added to the demand.

THE EXPANDING SUBURBS

The new American middle class wanted the suburban houses that prosperity could make available to them in the postwar period. The ideal of a single-family house for the nuclear family on a generously-sized lot away from the deteriorating inner-city was embraced by a very large component of the population. In a way it was a return to living in rural conditions as contrasted with the dangerous jumble of city life. Iconoclasts continued to favor living in elevator apartment buildings in big cities, or in rural settings, but for many who worked in cities and towns of all sizes, the suburbs were becoming the place to be. If the family owned one car, the principal wage earner could commute to work; many husbands carpooled so that wives could use the car during the day to buy groceries, drive the children to school and do all the other errands. People had been flocking to the cities from the farms and small towns for decades; now they were leaving the cities in droves for the suburbs.

The Back Yard Society: Come in the Back Door, Please

As the decade of the 1950s progressed, some real changes in socialization patterns emerged. Television and air conditioning enticed people to spend more time inside their houses. Also, whereas socialization in urban settings had been oriented toward the front door and the street, with people gathering on their front steps, their front porches or in their living rooms next to the front door, in the new suburban lifestyle of the 1950s, the focus moved toward the back, to the fenced-in back yard, the patio and the newly socially acceptable kitchen-dining area. Life was both more private and more homogeneous. Barbecuing on the rear patio became a new, less formal, way to entertain. People began to drive their cars into the driveways or their garages and enter their houses through the back or side doors. Eventually the front door was little used. The living rooms behind the front door were also abandoned in favor of the basement "rec" room where the television was. Americans were beginning to be entertained less by each other, by conversation and by participation in organized social life. Builders soon eliminated public sidewalks as social life changed from the front of the house to the back. Children who wanted to ride tricycles, bicycles or scooters, or roller skate had to take to the streets. Alleys were also eliminated as driveways and garages moved to the fronts of lots and trash pickup and other services moved to the streets.

Builders were quick to supply the houses that suited this lifestyle. They could acquire large tracts of land relatively inexpensively at the perimeters of towns and cities, secure government-insured advance financing, install streets and other infrastructure and mass produce standardized housing. In 1947, William Levitt and Sons had purchased a large tract of farmland on Long Island, New York, installed streets and other necessary infrastructure, and then built 17,000 standardized houses for a population of over 50,000. The company prefabricated building parts and had them shipped to sites where they were assembled in rows. Levitt went on to build a number of other such developments and other developers followed suit, although mostly on a smaller scale. This style of mass production typified single-family housing development, especially in the early 1950s.

As large-scale single-family housing developments proliferated, retailers began to build branches of their downtown stores in the suburbs. The first shopping centers were in-town strip centers developed before World War II. They were rows of stores set back from the street with paved parking areas in front, and they came into being when the use of the automobile became prevalent. After World War II regional centers were developed—much larger collections of suburban stores set in the centers of huge paved parking lots. Eventually downtown commerce began to feel the loss of business as suburbanites bought much of what they needed in the new shopping centers. Also, increasingly shopping centers became locations for social interaction, competing in that regard with central business districts, although throughout the 1950s, central business districts continued to draw people to shop and be entertained.

Commuter roadways had become clogged with traffic by the mid-1950s. The Interstate Highway Act (1956), a national, centrally-designed, ultimately $100 billion program that resulted in 41,000 miles of new highways and expressways, was underway as the decade ended and had begun to spur real estate development of all kinds. Land values around the 4,000 or so interchanges of these new highways soared as they became prime locations for shopping centers, motels, service stations and restaurants. Nationwide motel chains came into being and by 1958, 3,000 motels a year were being built. The highway program also encouraged people to travel more, to take vacations by car and to buy vacation homes. By 1960, approximately 100,000 vacation and resort homes had been built, double the 1950 figure.

The inner cities did not benefit as much from the Highway Act. Elevated roads, ramps, limited-access roadways and tunnels were built to provide fast access into and out of the center cities for commuters. These roads and their attendant structures severed and destroyed urban neighborhoods. The traditional urban fabric in many cities was damaged by automobile access to a much greater extent than was necessary. The old mass transit routes were interrupted, underfunded and abandoned.

During 1951-1952, self-sufficient newtowns, planned communities that included housing of various types, shopping, schools, parks, recreational facilities and places of employment were built, styled after the prototype in Radburn, New Jersey, designed in 1929. Two prominent newtowns of the early 1950s were U.S. Steel's Fairless Hills and William J. Levitt's Pennsylvania Levittown, both near Morrisville, Pennsylvania. Fairless Hills was built on an original site of 2,000 acres and Levittown began with 5,000 acres. This was affordable housing of the monotonous type, but it had a broad appeal in the early 1950s.

1950s • HOUSING DESIGN ~ One of the reasons new houses in the suburbs were standardized and simplified was that the costs of materials and labor had risen to an extent that builders could not otherwise provide a modern house complete with the amenities that the market expected. Construction costs increased 85 percent in the period 1946-1956 at the same time that the Consumer Price Index increased only 51 percent. Starter houses built in the late 1940s and early 1950s were often just four and one half rooms, consisting of two bedrooms, a kitchen, one bathroom and a living room, quite often as small as 650 square feet in area. The first suburban post-war houses were built on the edges of existing neighborhoods and were simplified versions of traditional styles. The steep roofs were lowered and most ornamentation, with perhaps the exception of decorative but non-functional, window shutters, was stripped off.

The ranch house, the most prevalent house style of the 1950s, was first devel-

1953-1956

oped in California in the 1930s. Its origins were a combination of Spanish Colonial, the Craftsman house and Frank Lloyd Wright's Prairie and Usonian ideas. Ranch houses were single-story, wide houses with horizontal lines, low roofs, and overhanging eaves, set lengthwise on their wide lots. When garages were added to the ranch house, they widened the horizontal look even more. In many parts of the eastern United States these houses at first were called "ramblers."

A split-level version of the ranch house was developed that was popular with the public but criticized because the strong horizontal exterior of the ranch style had been fractured into three levels. The theory behind the split level was that there should be three basic areas in a house, the noisy area, which was the below-grade garage and the recreation room, the relatively peaceful on-grade living-dining-kitchen area and the sleeping rooms and bathrooms, which were situated over the lowest level.

1953-1956 • CONSTRUCTION TECHNIQUES ~ In 1953 James T. Lendrum, director of the Small Homes Council of the University of Illinois, published the results of his research in a document for builders entitled "Ten Ways to Cut Costs." The ten ways were: 1) build on an interior module; 2) precut all framing material, using engineered drawings and cutting schedules; 3) use tilt-up exterior walls and build them flat on the slab for speed; 4) use a long-span roof truss; 5) apply wallboard on ceiling and side walls before partitioning; 6) lay entire finished floor before partitioning to avoid working around small, irregular spaces; 7) place windows at the top of exterior walls; 8) make all ceiling heights exactly

(1946) A Swift Solution. Tournalayer provides one answer to acute post-war housing shortage by building a low-cost concrete house in only 24 hours. The machine drops a portable mold into which it pours concrete, and allows it to set before removing the framework.

8 feet 3/8 inches; 9) use prebuilt storage walls and use them as closet and interior partitions and 10) use a double wall around plumbing to eliminate cutting and fitting. These guidelines were both influential on and reflective of, mass-builder standards in this period.

Double-pane, pre-built window units came into use in the 1950s as did aluminum-framed windows, storm windows, gutters, storm doors, siding, roofing, prefabricated panels, and even structural components. Plastics were introduced in the mid-fifties and were used for counter tops, vinyl flooring, wall tiles, paneling, shower stalls, light ceilings and skylights. Wall-to-wall carpet became standard in all areas of the low-ceilinged interiors except kitchens, bathrooms and recreation rooms. Asbestos in floor tiles, ceiling tiles and insulation were common.

As the decade progressed suburban house development diversified. Builders hired architects, built model houses, and sponsored housing shows, competing to draw the buying public and to offer the best design and construction quality for the least money. New house designs were constantly featured in popular magazines, further influencing public tastes and demands. By 1956, the housing shortage had been met and a second wave of larger suburban houses was being built for families who were ready to improve their lifestyle and sell their former homes to newly-formed families. For these more expensive houses, builders employed post and beam construction to open up more interior space, used large areas of glass and natural wood interiors, added more luxurious kitchens and baths and landscaped much more extensively.

1948-1960 • THOSE EXCLUDED

While this realization of the American dream was going on in the suburbs there were many people in the deteriorating inner cities who were not enjoying the same benefits. Generally they had little choice. In 1900 three-fourths of African-Americans lived in the rural south; by 1950 fewer than one-fifth did. In the 1940s the number of African-Americans living outside the South increased from 2,360,000 to 4,600,000. Northern employers actively recruited African Americans from the South to work in industries once the tide of European immigration had been stemmed. Eventually 6.5 million African Americans left the South. The peak of the migration coincided with the exodus of white families to the suburbs that began in the 1940s and continued throughout the 1950s and 1960s. Sixty-two percent of Washington, D.C.'s racial change in this period was attributable to white out-migration, 17 percent was African American in-migration, and 21 percent was attributable to the natural increase of the African American population.

In 1950, Washington, D.C., the nation's capital, was still racially segregated. African Americans were excluded from the restaurants, hotels, department stores and theaters patronized by whites. Public schools were segregated by law as they were in many other states. President Truman had desegregated the armed forces in 1948 and in that year the Supreme Court struck down racial and religious housing covenants on the grounds that they were judicially unenforceable, but segregation in Washington, D.C. was a long-standing cultural tradition, mandating that African Americans could not buy or rent houses in white neighborhoods. However, in 1953 the Supreme Court made a decision that opened restaurants to African Americans

1954-1959

and soon they were admitted to all department stores and theatres. In 1954, the doctrine of separate but equal was negated by the Supreme Court in *Brown vs. the Board of Education*. Federal housing officials began to realize that they should eliminate language that permitted segregation from all federal regulations.

Public housing projects built since the 1930s were often segregated, usually at the urging of the local housing authorities, but certainly with the concurrence, albeit reluctant concurrence, of federal officials. Nor had the federal government been interfering with lending policies that regarded African American and mixed-race neighborhoods as carrying a much higher risk. After 1954, the legal structure of race segregation was challenged everywhere, although it would be ten years before segregation in public housing was explicitly addressed.

1954 • THE FEDERAL ROLE ~ When Dwight D. Eisenhower began his first presidential term in 1954, it was widely expected that the role of the federal government in housing would be curtailed. Instead the federal housing policies carried out by the Eisenhower administration followed the trails blazed in the 1930s. An advisory committee recommended to the president: 1) the reorganization of the Housing and Home Finance Agency (formerly the National Housing Authority), 2) a program of special assistance for low-income families, 3) a vigorous attack on slums, 4) conservation and utilization of existing housing and 5) an increase in the volume of new housing. The president accepted these recommendations. *(See Appendix A, 1950s, for more statistics)*

1954-1959 • URBAN RENEWAL ~ The 1954 Housing Act provided for a continuance of the urban renewal program set up in the Act of 1949, to be carried out by private developers but overseen by the federal government. Communities had to develop a Workable Plan before they could receive assistance in slum clearance, urban renewal or public housing. The Workable Plan had to meet seven criteria: health and safety standards, a plan for future development, a specific identification of blighted neighborhoods, an administrative entity to coordinate and execute programs, adequate financial resources, provisions for housing the displaced and a program to fully inform the community at large of what was going to take place. By the end of 1959, 1,000 cities were developing or had developed Workable Plans. The comprehensive programs undertaken by cities to clear and redevelop their slums included planning efforts, new zoning regulations, the construction of streets and recreational areas and the provision of transportation, education and employment. Redevelopment might be entirely residential or mixed residential, commercial and institutional. Early programs in the 1950s were carried out in Washington, D.C., Philadelphia, New Haven, Pittsburgh, Boston, New York and Chicago, among others.

In Washington, D.C., to cite one example, the federal government approved a plan for redevelopment of a 550-acre triangle of land along the Washington Channel of the Potomac River that was said to be one of the worst slums in the country. A mostly poor African American population lived in brick row dwellings built in the nineteenth century. The National Capital Planning Commission began working on its redevelopment in 1951, hiring the architect, Cloethiel Smith, to do the design work. The properties were acquired by eminent domain and cleared of buildings. Mortgage lenders said that middle-income people would not be willing to live in the Southwest section of the city, despite that it was directly southwest of the United States Capitol. Although there were many difficulties in bringing what came to be called "The New Southwest" to completion, it eventually became a successfully redeveloped area of elevator apartment buildings, modern townhouses, government and private office buildings, subway stations, hotels, a popular legitimate theater (Arena Stage), stores, waterfront restaurants and marinas. By 1959 there were 500 urban renewal projects in 300 cities.

A major problem associated with urban renewal projects was relocating the displaced residents who lost their homes in the process. In 1956 Congress authorized the payment of moving expenses as part of urban renewal projects, setting a ceiling first of $100 and raising it in 1959 to $200. Not all former residents were willing to accept assistance in moving to new quarters, but 23,900 former residents of Southwest in Washington, D.C. were assisted by the National Capital Housing Authority in finding replacement housing.

1946-1956 • GOVERNMENT FAILURES ~ In 1955 the Pruitt-Igoe public housing project was opened in St. Louis. It was named after two World War II heroes, one African American and one white. The project was designed by Minoru Yamasaki in the best modernist style with 2,800 apartments in fourteen-story, steel, glass and concrete blocks separated by open space but connected on each floor with covered walkways. The design won an award from the American Institute of Architects. As costs mounted during construction, quality was reduced and the landscaping was eliminated. Services to the tenants were reduced to a minimum. The tenants, mostly migrants from the rural South, hated their environment and it became a hell on earth. It was dynamited in 1972 at the request of the tenants.

The federal government continued to support private multi-family and single-family production with mortgage insurance programs during the 1950s. FHA 608, a multi-family program, however, erupted as a major housing scandal in the mid-1950s. The program, started in 1946, had been intended to remedy the critical shortage of rental apartments and this it had done with some 7,000 developers efficiently producing hundreds of thousands of units mostly between 1946 and 1950. But because FHA reviewers had accepted the cost estimates and project specifications submitted by developers without really checking into them, developers had been given, in many cases, loans that exceeded their actual costs, thereby earning excessive profits at considerable cost to the American taxpayer. A 1954 probe found that in 1,417 cases out of 1,547 investigated, windfalls of $113 million had been gained through padded cost estimates and specifications. A number of FHA officials were fired or resigned and by the end of 1956, 750 indictments had been issued. Thereafter the multi-family FHA insurance program required certified detailed cost estimates to be submitted by developers.

1950s • GOVERNMENT HOUSING LOANS ~ During the decade, 2,293,053 Veterans Administration loans were made on new single-family houses,

1960s

at an average loan amount of $11,165, the houses selling for an average of $12,100. Loans were made on 1,313,811 existing houses at an average of $9,281 per loan, the houses selling for an average of $10,830. The Farmers Home Administration made 36,638 rural housing loans in the 1950s totaling $216,959,575, at an average of $5,922. The Community Facilities Administration granted low interest rate loans to universities and colleges for dormitories, student unions and dining halls. By 1959 a total of $1.175 billion had been spent on 890 higher-learning-institution projects.

The Housing Act of 1959 authorized the Housing and Home Finance Agency to make direct loans to private nonprofit corporations to build elderly housing projects. Mortgage insurance amounts were increased, there were additional grant authorizations for urban renewal, increases in relocation payments for families and businesses in urban renewal areas, authorization for 37,000 public housing units, provision for acquisition of land in urban renewal areas at fair market value, additional authorization for college and military housing and also for farm housing research. The total mortgage insurance amount for the Public Housing Administration was increased from the $3 billion authorized in the 1956 Act to $8 billion.

1960s • Building Neighborhoods, Not Just Houses ~

The 1960s were the years in which the public realized that simply tearing down the slums and building new housing structures would not fix the problems of America's cities and its poor. The "suitable living environment" of the stated goal of the Housing Act of 1949 came to the fore after a decade of failure to produce "decent homes." As the middle class continued to depart from the center cities for the suburbs and as public housing continued to turn into institutionalized new slums, the real nature of what makes a home had to be re-examined. President Lyndon Johnson in his March 1965 speech "The Problems of the Central City and Its Suburbs" said "We want to build not just housing units, but neighborhoods; not just to construct schools, but to educate children; not just to raise income, but to create beauty and end the poisoning of our environment."

Although the urban renewal programs of the 1950s and early 1960s were controversial, they did achieve certain goals, including new infrastructure and modern replacement buildings that were to an extent successful in retaining or reclaiming middle-class residents and businesses within cities. City and federal governments had seen the concept of luring back and retaining the middle class as crucial to the problem. Critics, however, saw whatever gains there were at the cost of the destruction of the traditional urban architecture and neighborhood structure.

1960s • Urban Preservation ~

There began in the early 1960s a countermovement of people who saw the value of preserving and refurbishing older urban buildings, moving into inner-city neighborhoods, and individually reclaiming with hard work the buildings built before the advent of modern architecture. In the 1960s, a national preservation movement emerged in direct reaction to urban renewal programs that removed whole neighborhoods, the interstate highway program that slashed through the traditional urban fabric, and the ongoing federal program that replaced nineteenth-century government office buildings with bleak modern structures. Two books that strongly influenced the preservation movement were Jane Jacobs' *Death and Life of Great American Cities* (1961) and Martin Anderson's *The Federal Bulldozer* (1967). An earlier book, John Kent's *The Crack in the Picture Window* (1956) discussed suburban disadvantages, and remained popular into the 1960s.

A National Historic Preservation Act was passed by Congress in 1966 that made the protection of historic buildings a national policy. Worthy properties began to be identified, documented and listed on local landmark registries or on the National Register of Historic Places. From the mid-1960s on, historic houses particularly, but also all kinds of elegant older buildings, slowly began to be rehabilitated to their original splendor.

1960s • Urban Conflict ~ The 1960s were a decade of confrontations, confrontations over the war in Vietnam, confrontations between preservationists and bulldozers and worst of all, the racial confrontations in the cities. Despite the ongoing efforts of governments at the federal, state, and local levels, by the mid-1960s, as a result of the social and physical transformation of the cities that resulted from white flight to the suburbs, the cities were in crisis. The civil disturbances that began in 1965 and which resulted in the widespread burning and looting of property as well as the injury and death of people led to further flight to the suburbs. Confrontations over the lack of housing, jobs, schools, adequate transportation, political representation and public services in cities that had largely been abandoned to the poor were ongoing. The assassination of three major political figures, one of them an American president, during this decade,

(1963) Protesters marching with placards outside Penn Station to save the building from demolition, New York City.

added to the shame many Americans already felt about the country's social and political policies. During the 1960s, and particularly the latter part of the decade, the United States was a disturbed and deeply divided society.

1965-1969 • Housing Starts and Interest Rates ~ Business was in an expansion mode and the securities market was booming in 1965 when the Federal Reserve System, in order to restrain rising inflation, precipitated a

1960s

tight money crisis that brought housing production to its lowest level since 1945. Housing starts did not regain the 1965 level until 1968. Conventional housing starts then remained at the 1968 level through 1970. Despite the Federal Reserve System's 1965 intervention, inflation continued to advance under the federal policy of "guns and butter," that is, financing the "Great Society" and the war in Vietnam simultaneously without price controls. In 1969 the Federal Reserve again tightened the money supply, but this time the impact on the mortgage market was minimized through the intervention of Fannie Mae and the Federal Home Loan Banks. During 1969 and 1970 the outstanding mortgage debt held by Fannie Mae rose from $11.4 billion to $20.7 billion and the outstanding advances of the Federal Home Loan Banks increased by $5.3 billion. During this period average mortgage interest rates for conventional loans rose from 6.57 percent in April of 1968 to 7.47 percent in April of 1969, then to 8.23 percent in April of 1970. The restrictive monetary policies of the latter years of the 1960s were reversed early in 1970 and housing production began to rise. Housing starts, excluding shipment of mobile homes, as shown on the chart, average 1,419,000 total units per year, in these ten years. (*See Appendix A, 1960s, for more statistics*)

1960s • MOBILE HOMES ~ The private market came up with a very successful form of low-cost, prefabricated housing in the 1960s. Mobile homes had been around since the 1930s, but between 1960 and 1970 when assembly line techniques were greatly improved, the mobile home market began to expand rapidly. Mobile homes were much cheaper than conventional homes of the same size; they required no permanent foundation, and were delivered fully furnished. Because they were personal property, not real estate, they were not subject to building codes or property taxes. One negative aspect of these low-cost houses was their relatively short economic life compared to conventional houses. The majority of mobile home owners, who did not own their sites, usually paid rent to park them, which was high relative to their value. In addition, mobile homes were more vulnerable to damage from windstorms and tornadoes and were often located on flood plains.

Total housing starts, including shipments of mobile homes grew from 1,399,700 in 1960 to 1,912,690 by 1969; this growth was due primarily to the increase in the number of mobile homes being added to the housing stock as conventional dwelling unit production was fairly level during the decade.

The Housing Act of 1969 authorized FHA insurance for mobile home loans up

Total Housing Starts
(Excluding Mobile Homes)
(in thousands)

Year	Total	Private	Single-Family		Public
1960	1,296	1,252	995	79%	44
1961	1,365	1,313	974	74%	52
1962	1,492	1,463	991	68%	30
1963	1,635	1,603	1,012	63%	32
1964	1,562	1,530	972	64%	32
1965	1,510	1,473	964	65%	37
1966	1,196	1,165	779	67%	31
1967	1,322	1,292	844	65%	30
1968	1,545	1,507	900	60%	38
1969	1,500	1,467	811	55%	33

SOURCE: *Statistical Abstract of the United States*, 1970. U.S. Bureau of the Census.

Number of Mobile Homes Shipped

Year	Number
1960	103,700
1961	90,200
1962	118,000
1963	150,840
1964	191,320
1965	216,470
1966	217,300
1967	240,360
1968	317,950
1969	412,690
Annual Average	205,883

SOURCE: *Current Construction Reports, Housing Starts.* C-20 series.

to $10,000. By 1970, the Federal Home Loan Bank Board had authorized savings and loan associations to finance mobile home sales.

1960s • FEDERAL HOUSING PROGRAMS

Two major commission reports, that of the United States Commission on Civil Rights and that of the Commission on Race and Housing, by the end of the 1950s, had recommended that the President of the United States take direct action to effect equal opportunity in housing. These commissions reported the existence of widespread discrimination in housing, including federally-assisted housing. In November of 1962, President Kennedy issued an Executive Order barring discrimination in the sale, lease or occupancy of residential property owned or operated by the federal government.

Federal legislation in the 1960s included assistance to particular groups such as the elderly and the handicapped living in government-assisted housing. Programs were devised for moderate-income households as well as those in the low-income category. And there was a succession of programs providing public subsidies to private developers as well as increasing privatization of public housing through turnkey programs.

The 1961 Housing Act repealed the requirement that cities must have a Workable Plan, as required by the 1954 Housing Act, before they could participate in programs that provided assistance for those displaced by slum clearance and urban renewal. The Act included mortgage interest subsidies for low- and moderate-income rental housing. The beneficiaries of these direct loans were tenants ineligible for public housing but too poor to afford open market rental housing. The act also provided a subsidy for apartments for the elderly in public housing projects that were experiencing operating deficits. This was the first federal public housing subsidy to cover operating expenses.

In May of 1964 President Johnson described the urban crisis facing the United States. He outlined his plan for the "Great Society" and declared a "War on Poverty," in which better housing was to play a major role. Johnson then pushed for urban mass transportation legislation that was passed by Congress, authorizing grants to the Housing and Home Finance Agency to help states and city agencies in financing mass transportation. Johnson's 1964 Task Force on Metropolitan and Urban Problems tackled the problems of the cities.

The 1965 Housing Act authorized a rent supplement subsidy allowing federal payments to offset a portion of the market rent of qualified low-income families. There was also a subsidy program that authorized local public housing authorities to lease privately-owned rental units and make them available to low-income families. Both of these provisions were designed to allow people to escape the stigma of living in public housing projects.

1966-1972 • MODEL CITIES AND LOW-INCOME FAMILIES ～ In November of 1966, the Demonstration Cities and Metropolitan Development Act was passed, out of which came the Model Cities Program. It authorized grants and technical assistance to help communities establish programs to rebuild or restore blighted neighborhoods through federal aid in combination with local resources. More than one thousand cities applied; Detroit, Philadelphia and St. Louis were among the first chosen. When a city was designated a Model City project, it received a one-year planning grant for developing a comprehensive plan detailing the improvements that would be made. By 1967 Model Cities programs had been established in sixty-three communities. The 1966 Act also authorized construction of turnkey projects of low-rent housing. Under this program, private developers proposed to build projects and local housing authorities contracted to buy the finished products using federal funds. Builders could readily obtain private market financing. The turnkey program resulted in more than 200,000 units under contract by 1972.

The Housing Act of 1968 included provisions that were designed to assist low-income families in becoming homeowners. Lenders received subsidies that allowed buyers to pay only a one percent interest rate. Mortgages were to be insured by FHA. Properties in older urban areas became eligible for mortgage insurance. Low- and moderate-income families with poor credit histories were eligible for mortgage insurance. Another section covered rental housing for low- and moderate-income families were eligible for rental housing. Subsidies reduced the interest rate the developer paid to one percent. FHA insured the loans. The mortgage interest subsidy was very attractive to developers even though rents were limited to 25 percent of the tenant's income. The 1968 Act also included 1) authorization of the sale of public housing units to tenants; 2) restriction of new construction of high-rise public housing to the elderly and families without children; 3) a Special Risk Insurance Fund for some of FHA's programs; 4) the founding of the National Corporation for Housing Partnerships; 5) authorization for HUD to guarantee debt obligations of private new communities; 6) a federal program of reinsurance against riots and other civil disturbances; 7) creation of a national flood insurance program; 8) federal regulation of interstate land sales; 9) partition of the Federal National Mortgage Association into two entities: a private Fannie Mae corporation and the Government National Mortgage Association (Ginnie Mae), to operate the special assistance, management, and liquidating functions of the former Fannie Mae and 10) authorization for Fannie Mae to securitize FHA and VA mortgages.

1965-1969 • CIVIL RIGHTS AND RIOTS ～ The Civil Rights Act of 1964 was a major legislative achievement. Title VI barred racial discrimination in any housing requiring federal funding assistance, not merely federally-owned housing. However, FHA and VA mortgage programs were not included. At the same time that so much progress was being made in outlawing racial discrimination in all areas of American life, riots began taking place in a number of cities. Five days after the Voting Rights Act of 1965 was signed, a riot broke out in the Watts neighborhood of Los Angeles that killed 34 people, injured more than 1,000, destroyed 200 buildings by arson and damaged 400 more with total property losses amounting to $40,000,000. Some 4,000 people were arrested. Riots continued to take place every summer from 1965 through 1968. In Detroit in 1967, 43 people were killed and more than 1,000 injured. More than 2,700 businesses were looted. Whole sections of the city, including many houses, were burned, a total area of fourteen square miles. After the murder of Dr. Martin Luther King in April of 1968, organized violence destroyed several commercial areas of Washington, D.C., including the Seventh Street, N.W., the 14th Street, N.W. and the H Street, N.E. shopping corridors.

The Civil Rights Act of 1968, enacted soon after the murder of Dr. King, established equal opportunity in housing as the official policy of the United States. It extended this policy to cover all federally owned or assisted housing beginning immediately, conventionally financed apartment units in 1969, and the sales of most single-family houses in 1970. The law forbade discrimination in housing on the basis of race, color, creed or national origin. By 1968 twenty-three states and 155 municipalities had passed laws banning discrimination in the private housing market.

1965 • THE NEW DEPARTMENT OF HOUSING AND URBAN DEVELOPMENT

∼ The creation of the cabinet-level Department of Housing and Urban Development (HUD) had first been proposed by President Kennedy, however, it was not until 1965 that the legislation was enacted. All of the duties and functions of the Housing and Home Finance Agency, the Federal Housing Administration, and the Federal National Mortgage Association were transferred to the new department. President Johnson appointed Robert Weaver to be Secretary; the former Administrator of HHFA was the first African American cabinet member in the country's history. The Veterans Administration loan guaranty program, the Federal Home Loan Bank Board, and the Farmers Home Administration remained outside of the new department. The Housing and Community Development Act of 1968 gave the newly-created department the responsibility for 26 million housing units over the next ten years, with an emphasis on low and moderate income housing.

In 1969 Richard Nixon became President and he appointed George Romney, a former governor of Michigan, as Secretary of HUD. Additional legislation in 1969 and 1970 supplemented the Housing Act of 1968 by 1) limiting rent in public housing to 25 percent of family income; 2) creating the Federal Home Loan Mortgage Corporation (Freddie Mac) to purchase conventional mortgages and convert them to mortgage-backed securities; 3) providing income tax relief for new rental housing through the 1969 Tax Reform Act; 4) authorizing HUD to conduct an experimental housing allowance program to see whether this might be an alternative to other forms of housing subsidy; 5) authorizing FHA insurance of mobile home loans up to $10,000 and 6) requiring an environmental impact statement in connection with federal actions affecting the quality of the environment, including housing developed with federal assistance.

1960s

1960s • MERGERS AND ACQUISITIONS ~ During the 1960s the private segment of the housing industry became more national in its scope. Large corporations, such as ITT, General Electric, Westinghouse and Boise Cascade, which formerly had nothing to do with building houses, began to acquire builder companies and to develop and market private dwellings. Independent builders, always vulnerable to cyclical economic changes and the chronic undercapitalization that made their business so risky, were at first pleased to be undergirded by these giant corporations. However, the strong individualism and self-direction of housing entrepreneurs was lost in the multiple layers of decision making in these large corporations and in many cases the new associations were far from successful.

1960s • APARTMENTS ~ In 1960, except for several of the largest cities in the country, the housing in most municipalities consisted of single-family houses and small apartment buildings. The New York Standard Metropolitan Area had as many apartment units in buildings of ten or more units as the next twenty-three metropolitan areas combined, and Manhattan by itself had more apartment units than the Los Angeles and Chicago metropolitan areas together. On an average, only about five percent of housing units in most metropolitan areas, exclusive of New York, Chicago, Los Angeles, Miami and Washington, D.C., were in apartment buildings of ten or more units. Exclusionary zoning had kept apartment buildings out of separately incorporated suburbs. In 1960, 80-90 percent of apartment buildings with more than ten units were located in the central cores of large metropolitan areas.

Apartment construction began to shift to suburban locations in the 1960s. Middle-class garden apartments were built at highway nodes and near centers of employment. Apartment construction, to some extent, is a function of the zoning and cost of land although it also requires a population base. In the immediate post-World War II period land was relatively inexpensive and large tracts could be acquired and improved with single-family houses in great numbers. With households growing smaller by the middle of the 1960s as the baby boom ended, and with higher per-household incomes than ever before, a new demand for apartments arose that was not based entirely on newly-weds or retirees. Apartment construction began the decade with 18.3 percent of total housing starts, rose to 32.2 percent in 1965 and to 42.7 percent in 1969.

Luxury apartment buildings with large units returned to the American building scene in the mid-60s. These buildings were well-built, attractive structures with amenities such as balconies, swimming pools, big lobbies and tenant services such as guest screening, message and package reception and security features. Tenants did not have to worry about cutting the grass, taking the trash out to the curb, relighting the pilot light on the water heater or changing filters in the air conditioning units; these chores and others were taken care of by the building staff.

Condominium apartments, apartments that one could buy rather than rent, appeared in mainland United States as legal entities in the 1960s. Just as owning one's own house allows pride of ownership, deduction of mortgage interest and property taxes from income taxes, and the accrual of wealth through the investment of a small amount of equity, so does owning a condominium provide the opportunity for these benefits. The Housing Act of 1961 extended mortgage insurance to what soon became known as "condos."

An ostensibly similar apartment ownership method, called cooperatives or "co-ops" had been popular in large cities for many decades. Co-ops were successful in upper-income buildings only. A co-op building is a single property; an apartment occupant owns a proportionate share of the corporation that owns the property.

1960-1969 • PUBLIC HOUSING ～ The number of low-rent public housing units also increased more rapidly than had been the case prior to the late 1960s. According to Census data, there were 593,000 such units in the United States in 1960 and by 1969 the number had increased to 1,035,000 units. Approximately half of this increase was attributable to turnkey housing built by private developers for public housing authorities or to the public lease or purchase of existing private housing. A substantial portion of the added units had been designed for the elderly and occupancy of public housing units by the elderly had risen to 20 percent by the end of the decade. The median income of the occupants of public housing had dropped by 1969 to 30 percent of the median family income in the United States, as compared to 45 percent in 1957 and 63 percent in 1948, partially because of the increase in the numbers of the elderly. Public housing projects, experiencing reduced income and rapidly rising operating expenses due to inflation, began to suffer net losses. Various legislative amendments enacted between 1968 and 1971 further reduced rental income. The physical conditions of public housing projects began to show deterioration as these stresses increased at the end of the decade.

1970-1972 • SOCIAL DISRUPTION ～ Many of the social disruptions of the 1960s continued in the 1970s: the Vietnam War and the demonstrations against it, racial hostilities, the abandonment of inner-city housing and the resistance of suburban neighborhoods to incursions of subsidized housing. In the middle of the decade things got worse as OPEC embargoed oil and gas from the Middle East, inflation and recession hit simultaneously, President Nixon self-destructed over Watergate and the housing programs of the federal government were revealed to be plagued with fraud and plunder. As a result of the energy crisis, solar collectors sprouted on the roofs of houses and other buildings, joining the television antennae of the fifties and sixties. The failure of modernism as the architectural concept needed to save the working class poor was dramatically demonstrated when the seventeen-year-old Pruitt-Igoe public housing project in St. Louis was dynamited in 1972. In the second half of the seventies Americans sought a return to tradition in their architecture and, the war in Vietnam over, turned away from political involvement. Houses became larger as they were recognized as the best hedge against inflation and the most important sources of wealth creation for families. The seventies were the decade when women went to work outside the home in large numbers and non-traditional households, such as those of unmarried couples, created an additional demand for housing.

1970-1974 • HOUSING STARTS ～ New total housing unit starts for the decade were at a record high, largely because of increases in apartment construction and the manufacture of new mobile homes. When mobile homes

1972-1980

shipped by manufacturers to dealers are added to starts of conventional units, the total for new housing units in the decade were an astonishing 21,482,000. This production level was at a rate of approximately one new dwelling unit for every ten people in the country. The higher level of demand for apartments in this period was caused by lower real income levels relative to the prices of single family houses at the end of the 1960s and the beginning of the 1970s. Starts of multi-family housing were between 44 percent and 45 percent of conventional dwelling unit starts in each year beginning in 1970 and ending with 1974 and between 35 percent and 36 percent of total units including mobile homes. Multi-unit starts decreased after 1974, both in actual numbers and as a proportion of total units, ranging between 25 percent and 34 percent of conventional starts. *(See Appendix A, 1970s, for more statistics)*

1972-1980 • More and More Mobile Homes

By 1972 mobile home sales were eighty percent of all single-family houses sold at prices under $20,000. By the mid-1970s more than eight million people lived in 3.4 million mobile homes in the United States. It was during this decade that single, double-wide, and triple-wide mobile units began to be widely used as permanent homes. Increasingly, slab and raised foundations were constructed under mobile homes. Also they were being more attractively sited in many places with landscaping and proper spacing. Mobile home shipments began to fall in 1974 and remained at a diminished level for the rest of the decade indicating that the backlog of demand had been met. In the period 1974 to 1980 during which mobile home sales totaled 1,900,000 units, the stock of mobile homes increased by only about 500,000 units, affirming the relatively short economic life of this type of housing.

(1940) A Trailer Home. Early Trailer Homes were very poorly built and often were only used by the very poor. Seen here a migrant family from Amarillo, Texas, outside their trailer home.

Conventional Housing Starts 1970-1979
(in thousands)

1970-1979

Year	Total	In SMSAs	Private	Pub	S-Fam	2-4 DUs	5+DUs
1970	1,469	1,034	1,434	35	815	96	558
1971	2,085	1,519	2,052	32	1,153	133	799
1972	2,379	1,733	2,357	22	1,311	151	917
1973	2,057	1,502	2,045	12	1,133	124	800
1974	1,352	932	1,338	15	889	77	387
1975	1,171	767	1,160	11	896	68	208
1976	1,548	1,048	1,538	10	1,166	89	292
1977	1,990	1,378	1,987	3	1,452	122	415
1978	2,023	1,433	2,020	3	1,436	125	463
1979	1,749	1,242	1,745	4	1,196	123	430
Total	17,823	12,588	17,676	147	11,447	1,108	5,269

SOURCE: *Statistical Abstract of the United States*, 1980, U.S. Bureau of the Census

1970-1979 • INFLATION AND REAL ESTATE PRICES ~ During the 1970s inflation combined with an economic slowdown to produce what was termed "stagflation" measured by "the misery index," which was a nickname for the sum of the inflation rate and the unemployment rate. The inflationary trend had begun in the late 1960s when the federal government chose not to impose price controls and paid for the war in Vietnam by just creating more money. The Consumer Price Index rose from 119.1 in 1970 to 230.0 in 1979, an increase of 93 percent. The government's decision not to control inflation negatively affected the housing industry in 1974-1975. Beginning in 1973, oil and gas prices rose precipitously because of the OPEC oil embargo, which exacerbated inflation. As consumer prices and unemployment went up, housing starts dropped by nearly one million units from 1973 to 1974.

Total Dwelling Unit Starts

Year	MobHms	Conventional	Total	% MHs
1970	401,000	1,469,000	1,870,000	21.4
1971	497,000	2,085,000	2,582,000	19.2
1972	576,000	2,379,000	2,955,000	19.5
1973	567,000	2,057,000	2,624,000	21.6
1974	329,000	1,352,000	1,681,000	19.6
1975	213,000	1,171,000	1,384,000	15.4
1976	246,000	1,548,000	1,794,000	13.7
1977	277,000	1,990,000	2,267,000	12.2
1978	276,000	2,023,000	2,299,000	12.0
1979	277,000	1,749,000	2,026,000	13.7
Totals	3,659,000	17,823,000	21,482,000	17.0

SOURCE: *Statistical Abstract of the United States*, 1980, U. S. Bureau of the Census

1970s

The median prices of new conventional single-family dwellings rose dramatically in the 1970s. The increase in the median prices of all new houses was 169 percent from 1970 through 1979. Houses in the Northeast, where early in the decade unemployment was the most severe, increased 116 percent; in the North Central section, 162 percent; in the South, 182 percent; and in the West, 190 percent. During this period the National Consumer Price Index increased by 93 percent, indicating that the prices of houses were increasing at a faster rate than inflation. Homeowners' equity, that portion of the value of their dwelling units over and above the mortgage debt balance remaining on them, grew rapidly in the 1970s, allowing employed homeowners to trade up; that is, sell their houses, pay off the mortgages, take the equity and purchase better, more expensive houses, thereby easily moving up the wealth ladder. The average price of mobile homes also rose dramatically in the latter part of the decade, going from $9,300 in 1974 to $17,600 in 1980, or 89 percent increase over the six-year period.

Economist Alan Greenspan estimated that in 1977 the market value of the nation's entire stock of single-family, owner-occupied houses was increasing at an annual rate of $62.2 billion. He also estimated that new mortgages were growing at a $60.2 billion annual rate so that almost all of the increase in housing value was being "monetized;" or cashed in, as new and extended mortgage debt. This money was then circulating in the economy, bringing the United States out of the mid-1970s recession and spurring more housing production. Houses were regarded as a top form of investment for families and particularly as a safe hedge against inflation. Studies in 1977 showed that capital gains from housing were at the time triple the gains taken by private investors in the stock market.

1970s • HOUSEHOLD DEMOGRAPHICS

∼ Whereas the slowing of population growth that had begun with the drop in the birth rate in 1964 continued during the 1970s, the growth rate of households was accelerating. The population group from age twenty to thirty-four, the prime household-formation group, increased by nearly 25 percent in the 1970s. Also the divorce rate, the number of unmarried couples living together and the incidence of people living alone contributed to the increasing numbers of households. The proportion of single-person households went from 17 percent in 1970 of the total population to 22.2 percent in 1979. The proportion of the total population that was single increased from 16.2 percent in 1970 to 20 percent in 1979 and the proportion that was married decreased from

Median Sale Prices of Conventional
Single-Family Houses

Year	U.S.	Northeast	North Cntrl	South	West
1970	$23,400	$30,300	$24,400	$20,300	$24,000
1971	25,200	30,600	27,200	22,500	25,500
1972	27,600	31,400	29,300	25,800	27,500
1973	32,500	37,100	32,900	30,900	32,400
1974	35,900	40,100	36,100	34,500	35,800
1975	39,300	44,000	39,600	37,300	40,600
1976	44,200	47,300	44,800	40,500	47,200
1977	48,800	51,600	51,500	44,100	53,500
1978	55,700	58,100	59,200	50,300	61,300
1979	62,900	65,500	63,900	57,300	69,600

SOURCE: *Statistical Abstract of the United States*, 1980, U.S. Bureau of the Census.

71.7 percent to 66.2 percent. (The remainder were widowed or divorced.) The average household size fell from 3.14 in 1970 to 2.94 in 1975, 2.81 in 1978 and 2.78 in 1979. The 1970 Census of Housing showed that fewer than ten percent of the households in the country were living in substandard housing as compared with nineteen percent in 1960.

The 1970s were the years in which women moved out of homemaker roles and into outside employment, and lenders began to accept female wages as credit-worthy on a long-term basis. Two salaries could buy better houses. Single women also bought condominiums and rented apartments. During the 1970s there was a 50 percent increase in the number of women heading households and a 100 percent increase in unmarried couples sharing a household.

In 1900, 62 percent of the total population of the United States lived in the colder parts of the country, the Northeast and the Midwest; by 1975 approximately 51 percent of the population lived in the warmer areas, the West and the South, and 49 percent lived in the Northeast and the Midwest.

1970-1973 • FAILURE OF FEDERAL PROGRAMS ~ The Housing and Urban Development Act of 1970 continued the programs of President Johnson's Great Society. It provided for increased spending for many of the programs of the 1968 Act. A revenue-sharing program enacted in 1972 gave more flexibility to state and local governments in the utilization of tax dollars, allocating funds one-third to the state and two-thirds to the local government.

In January of 1973, just after the 1972 re-election, President Nixon's Secretary of Housing and Urban Development,

(1906) San Francisco. The "great earthquake" of 1906 in San Francisco was one of the first natural disasters in which the federal government assisted the local population in clean up efforts. Seen here, pedestrians examining frame houses, which lean to one side on the verge of collapse after the earthquake.

George Romney, suspended the housing subsidy programs that had been enacted in 1968, 1969 and 1970, and resigned. The Section 235 and 236 programs were the subject of widespread scandals involving developers, real estate agents, appraisers, FHA officials and lenders. The subsidies for sale housing attracted charlatans who made cosmetic repairs to shoddy dwelling units and sold them to the poor at excessive prices. The 236 apartment program's features attracted developers in large numbers because of the subsidized mortgage interest rates and because the program encouraged more expensive housing in better locations than normally was the case for subsidized housing. The better quality of construction resulted in less resistance to the projects by residents of the neighborhoods in which they were to be built and the higher costs resulted in higher depreciation tax write-offs for the developers. The rent projections had been at too high a level and the expenses at too low a level, resulting in unrealistic net income estimates and consequently, unrealistic market values.

Unfortunately, even at one percent mortgage interest rates, low-income people could not afford to buy the new houses and poor renters could not afford to rent in the new apartments at the rents that were needed to sustain the projects. In the years of 1970-1972, the Section 235 and 236 programs had insured 400,000 houses under Section 235 and 335,00 apartments under Section 236, the largest number of subsidized housing units ever insured in such a short time period, but the abuse was rampant and FHA had failed to control it. Tens of thousands of dwelling units were eventually abandoned, making the federal government one of the largest slum owners in history. Because the programs had been underway for only three years and had obviously been abused by sloppy administration, some critics contended that their problems could have been corrected over time and the costs could have been justified in a country that provides huge subsidies to higher income families in the deductibility of mortgage interest and property taxes. The Nixon administration maintained, however, that it was preferable to utilize less expensive existing housing and provide housing subsidies directly to the needy rather than subsidies to builders and lenders.

Other housing programs included in the 1968 Housing Acts were also suspended in the 1973 moratorium, but were later reinstated. However, Section 223(e) covering housing in inner city areas and Section 237 covering potential buyers who were marginally credit risks produced very little housing for low-income people. The one successful program that had been kept was the 1965 Section 23 program that authorized subsidized rentals in private buildings.

Another failure was Operation Breakthrough. Secretary Romney, mindful that the Russians were building two million manufactured housing units each year, had announced Operation Breakthrough, with great fanfare in May of 1969. It was to be an experimental program for reducing housing costs through the improvement of technology, carried out in cooperation with private industry. Twenty-two firms were picked to build 2,000 prototype houses in ten states. The houses were modulized, panelized and otherwise industrialized, but the overhead costs were so high they were impractical for a housing industry always subject to the uncertainties of economic cycles. The program ended in ambiguity and confusion. Operation Breakthrough did, however, result in building code reform and some new agreements with organized labor.

The New Communities program authorized by the Housing Act of 1968 had resulted in guarantee commitments for thirteen new communities. Partially as a result of the 1974-1975 recession, which combined decreased demand and inflation, the program began encountering serious financial difficulties and was brought to a halt by legislation in 1979.

The provisions of the housing legislation of 1968-1970 that remained in place included the flood insurance, civil disturbance insurance, interstate land sales registration and the housing partnership program as well as Fannie Mae, Ginnie Mae and Freddie Mac, all three of which were effective in supporting mortgage lending. The experimental housing allowance study program, authorized by Section 504 of the Housing and Urban Development Act of 1970, was underway by 1973.

1974-1978 • REHABILITATING HUD ~ James T. Lynn was appointed as the new Secretary of Housing and Urban Development after George Romney's departure. Congress, threatened by a Nixon veto, abandoned the former housing subsidy programs, except for honoring previous commitments and the Section 202 program for the elderly and handicapped in a modified form. The Housing and Community Development Act of 1974 substituted for all of the former rental subsidy programs a new one called Section 8, which provided federal subsidies for low-income tenants in new construction and rehabilitated buildings, as well as in existing private properties. A moderate rehabilitation program was added in 1978. The subsidy contracts were to be for fifteen years for existing housing and twenty years for new construction and substantial rehabilitation. Eligibility was mostly limited to tenants with incomes below 80 percent of the local median income, but 30 percent had to have incomes below 50 percent of the median income. Both new construction and substantial rehabilitation projects were eligible for FHA-insured financing. Section 8 also placed more of the control of low and moderate income subsidized housing with local housing authorities rather than with the federal government.

The 1974 Housing Act also authorized the spending of $7.9 billion in block grants for community development. Local officials were required to survey low- and moderate-income housing needs and to establish a Housing Assistance Plan for meeting those needs. This plan was a prerequisite for receiving community development funds and was designed to work with the Section 8 program.

The Section 8 housing program set a new record for costs. With a partial return to new construction under Presidents Ford and Carter, from 1974 to 1980, 1,028,000 Section 8 units were committed to funding and the total annual commitment under Section 8 housing was $2.1 billion per year, nearly equal to the $2.2 billion annually being paid for all government-owned public housing units under a program that had started in 1933. Of the 1,028,000 units committed between 1974 and 1980, 321,000 were in new construction and 707,000 were in existing construction.

The Home Mortgage Disclosure Act of 1975 required lending institutions located in standard metropolitan areas to report by Census tract or zip code the number and dollar amounts of mortgage loans and home improvements loans made. The Equal Credit Opportunity Act of 1976 addressed discrimination on the basis of gender or marital status and then was extended to cover age, race, color, religion, and national origin. The Community Reinvestment Act of 1977 encouraged financial institutions to extend credit within their financial communities, including low- and moderate-income neighborhoods.

1972-1980 • TENANT PREFERENCES IN SUBSIDIZED HOUSING ~ The Experimental Housing Allowance Program, authorized by 1970 legislation and begun in 1972, was completed in 1980. The program included three experiments: 1) a demand experiment, to determine the behavior of renters receiving direct dollar housing allowances, 2) a

1960s-1970s

supply experiment, studying the impact of housing allowances on housing markets and 3) an administrative agency experiment, examining the problems and costs of delivering housing allowances. Some 30,000 households in twelve different locations participated. The experiment cost $160 million, half of which was paid to the participating renter households. At the end, not much had been determined except that perhaps federal housing standards were out of touch with the preferences of poor families. In order to qualify for an allowance, a family had to live in a standard unit, in line with housing codes developed by building code or public health officials, and when given the choice of moving out of a substandard unit in order to be eligible for the housing allowance, many of them chose to stay in the substandard unit.

The U.S. Supreme Court in *Gautreaux v. Chicago Housing Authority* found that Chicago's public housing program was racially discriminatory. As a means of redress, residents of Gautreaux received Section 8 rental housing certificates to move to private apartments elsewhere in Chicago or in the suburbs. Some 4,000 people participated in the program, beginning in 1976, including many who relocated to predominantly white suburbs.

A new movement of consumerism in the 1970s led to some real changes in the housing industry. Ralph Nader led a movement against the shoddy construction of mobile homes that brought about better standards of design and building materials. Another result of the consumer movement was the Home Owners Warranty Program of the National Association of Home Builders that began in 1974, whereby member builder firms joined a voluntary program to provide a one-year warranty for all new houses that they built.

An environmentalist movement began in the 1970s with the celebration of Earth Day on April 21, 1970. Many new laws and regulations governing real estate development came out of this new movement. The no-growth movement emerged as the key issue in land use planning during the 1970s. Local jurisdictions began to plan for more orderly growth rather than encouraging all who wanted to develop.

1960s-1970s • GENTRIFICATION

The preservation movement and the desire among young people to break out of the suburban mode led to a return to urban living. Nineteenth-century row house neighborhoods in cities such as Baltimore, Washington, D.C., Boston, Philadelphia, San Francisco and some smaller old cities as well, were being acquired and restored by urban pioneers in the 1960s, and in the 1970s this trend was in full swing. The houses were inexpensive, having long been in disfavor; they were outdated in terms of their plumbing and mechanical systems and they had everything suburban houses did not, namely, high ceilings, great tall windows, beautiful old woodwork, fireplaces, chandeliers and style. They also were in real neighborhoods with sidewalks, small city parks, old trees and proximity to stores and downtowns. They lacked the extensive but little used front lawns of the suburbs and instead had front yards enclosed with low wrought iron fencing that kept a feeling of openness while still delineating the space. Residents could walk to the corner stores that had not been zoned out of existence. Historic districts were created in many cities that placed legislative controls on demolition, new construction and exterior remodeling. In towns such as Charleston, South

Carolina and Savannah, Georgia, whole downtowns and the surrounding residential areas were undergoing restoration and attracting visitors and new residents. By the late 1970s prices in historic areas of cities had increased greatly.

1960s • NEW HOUSING DESIGN ~ In the 1960s modernism dominated architecture as never before and as never again. In 1966 the architect Robert Venturi wrote a book *Complexity and Contradiction in Architecture* in which he advocated a change in modernism that would introduce a new vitality to what had become a dead form. His designs reintroduced elements of traditional design but used them in different ways, ways that were the beginning of a new architecture that came to be called Postmodernism. This architecture is related to its context, picking up elements of the buildings around it, but rearranging them in original ways. Rounded and molded facades replaced the harsh rectangles of modernism; columns were reintroduced and facades took on color and new forms of ornamentation, with designs complementing the existing surroundings, but introducing new and more lively forms.

Developers of single-family houses also began to introduce new versions of classical styles in the 1970s although with much less originality than the Post-modern architects. Mansard roofs appeared on houses, shopping centers and small commercial buildings in the 1970s. The Neo-French style for more expensive houses appeared in the early 1970s. This popular house style has high-hipped roofs and rounded-top dormers that pierce the cornice line. A Neo-Tudor house style also became popular around 1970, a less authentic version of the early Tudor houses. This version generally has sharply pitched front gables with half-timbering on the upper part of the house. Colonial styles had never completely disappeared from the single-family housing market, but a more varied range of these appeared in the 1970s. These styles have remained popular with builders and the house-buying public through the remainder of the twentieth century.

Single-family houses had begun to get larger in the mid-1960s and some of the rooms that had been eliminated in the post-World War II period were added back, such as dining rooms and entry halls. Three bedrooms and two bathrooms became standard in the 1970s. Urban land costs rose sharply in the 1970s with inflation, the costs to implement the many new regulations governing subdivision and development, and with the real shortages of land in the most popular areas. As a result developers began to build two-story houses again to more efficiently utilize land while providing the same amount of living space.

In the late 1970s builders began to create new types of housing clusters including duplexes, triplexes, and fourplexes. Large landscaped developments often included a mix of detached houses, apartment buildings, and townhouses on narrow lots. The larger of these developments were set in park-like surroundings with trees, open space, water features and sometimes golf courses as well as swimming, tennis and other community and recreational facilities, and often a small shopping center, an elementary school, and church sites.

1970s • ENERGY CONSERVATION ~ In response to the energy crisis in the 1970s builders began to introduce energy-conserving features. Solar collectors that converted the sun's heat to stored energy became common sights in the 1970s but they were never very popular and when the energy crisis was over they were abandoned. Utilizing passive solar energy entails modifying design and construction to make a structure more receptive to the sun's heat and then conserving that heat. During the decade earth-bermed houses, which were built into real or artificially-created hillsides, were a new way of approaching energy efficiency. They were also a way of protecting a house from the devastating effects of tornadoes. Massive walls of masonry, such as those traditionally used in the Southwest, were sometimes used to decrease energy consumption. Wood-burning iron stoves and fireplaces had a resurgence.

The National Association of Home Builders built a 1,200-square-foot energy-efficient demonstration house in 1977 using products and technology that its members could readily obtain. Some of the ideas that were incorporated into its design were siting concepts that had commonly been used prior to the availability of central heating and air conditioning. For instance, traditionally houses were sited where they could catch the breezes; in the South, the front and rear doors were usually connected by a long hall to allow the breeze to blow through. Many houses were built only one room wide with windows on both sides to achieve this effect. Houses in New England were built with no windows or very small windows on the north side. Windows on the south were maximized to capture the sun's warmth in the winter, but trees were planted to shade them in the summer. Overhanging eaves have always been a feature of houses to provide protection from the sun. Many of these features had been given up in the decades of mass-producing houses after World War II when energy sources were thought to be inexpensive and inexhaustible.

1970s • HEALTH HAZARDS ~ One of the major energy-conserving features that first appeared in the 1970s was the extensive use of insulation, in walls, in double-pane glass windows, in attics and wrapped around water heaters and plumbing pipes. In some cases too much insulation was used and houses could no longer "breathe," keeping in toxic gases and rotting wood with trapped moisture. A type of sprayed-in foam insulation that expanded to fill the spaces between exterior and interior walls was installed in many houses in the 1970s. In 1982, the Consumer Product Safety Commission banned urea-formaldehyde foam insulation in residences and schools because it could release formaldehyde gas at high levels, especially immediately after installation. It was estimated that some 500,000 residences had this type of insulation. The 1970s were also the period during which the dangers of lead paint, radon gases, asbestos and fiberglass were beginning to be realized. Asbestos is a nonflammable, natural mineral fiber that was widely used in structures of all kinds built between 1945 and 1970. Asbestos fiber poses a threat to human health when "friable" or loose in the air so that it can be breathed into the lungs where it lodges in tissues and causes asbestosis. The range of dangers covered by the "sick building" concept was eventually expanded to include molds that accumulate behind drywall, bacteria in air conditioning systems that cause respiratory illnesses and toxic fumes from chemically-treated carpeting and furnishings.

1970s • PRE-FAB HOUSES ~ For many decades there was a movement to achieve some technological innovation that would greatly reduce the cost of housing construction and maintenance. Manufactured houses took three forms in the 1970s, the precut house for which the lumber is precut, assembled and numbered in a factory for shipment as a package. Approximately 26,000 precut houses were manufactured and shipped to buyers in 1979. The second type, the panelized house, is the most popular form of manufactured housing. These are delivered to building sites as wall panels, eight feet high, in varying lengths, but usually twenty to thirty feet long. Exterior wall panels are insulated and have siding on one side with the windows and doors pre-installed. Interior wall panels are framed and covered with wallboard and have the electrical and plumbing components in the walls. The exterior of these houses can be of wood, metal or vinyl. Approximately 314,000 of these were built in 1979. The third type is the modular house, which is shipped in three-dimensional sections forming the front and back halves of the house. The two halves are set on a foundation with a crane then joined at the ridge of the roof. They come to the site complete with painted walls, installed kitchens and baths and carpeting on the floors. Only a week's work is required to install and finish the house. More than 43,000 modular houses were produced in 1979.

Despite the many efforts that have been made to create the American dream single-family detached house by assembly-line industrialization, the prefabricated housing industry has never been able to dominate the housing industry, which is still the purview of the on-site builders. They have made vast improvements in their techniques since the days of the craftsman builders. Subcontracting of various facets of the work as well as increased use of manufactured standardized components and easier assembly methods using power tools of all kinds have drastically cut costs and hastened the process, while still allowing the general contractor to control the schedule and the process and not be dependent on a manufacturer's shipments.

The housing industry creates much more employment than is involved on the immediate site, from the lumber industry to the manufacture of the electrical, plumbing, heating, ventilating, hardware, lighting, various floorings and appliance components.

1980s • HOUSING STARTS ~ In January of 1981 Ronald Reagan took office as President of the United States. The decade began with high inflation, high interest rates, and high unemployment. Conventional mortgage rates reached a high of seventeen percent in 1981. Unemployment was nearly eleven percent in late 1982. In response to high costs and low demand, starts of new housing units, including placements of mobile homes, fell to approximately 1.3 million units in 1981 and 1982.

The Federal Reserve, which sets the cost of money in response to inflation, commenced lowering rates in 1982 as the economic recovery began. By 1983, housing starts had risen to almost the annual two million level that had been achieved throughout the 1970s. By 1986 unemployment had fallen to 7 percent. Mortgage lending rates decreased to 9 percent in December of that year. The rate of inflation fell from 13.5 percent in 1980 to 3.2 percent in 1983, where it remained until 1987 when it began rising slowly, reaching 5 percent in 1990. (See *Appendix A, 1980s, for more statistics*)

Private Housing Starts 1980-1989
Excluding Mobile Homes
(in thousands)

Year	Total	1-Family		2-4 Units		5+ Units		Condos	
1980	1,292	852	66%	110	9%	331	26%	186	14%
1981	1,084	705	65%	91	8%	288	27%	181	17%
1982	1,062	663	62%	80	8%	320	30%	170	16%
1983	1,703	1,068	63%	113	7%	522	30%	276	16%
1984	1,750	1,084	62%	121	7%	544	31%	291	17%
1985	1,742	1,072	62%	93	5%	576	33%	225	13%
1986	1,805	1,179	65%	84	5%	542	30%	214	12%
1987	1,621	1,146	71%	65	4%	409	25%	196	12%
1988	1,488	1,081	73%	59	4%	348	23%	148	10%
1989	1,376	1,003	73%	55	4%	318	23%	118	9%
Totals	14,923	9,853	66%	871	6%	4,198	28%	2,005	13%

SOURCE: U.S. Bureau of the Census: *Statistical Abstract of the United States, 1992*

Dwelling Unit Starts
1980-1989 With Mobile Homes

Year	Conventional	MobHms	Total	% MH
1980	1,292,000	233,700	1,525,700	15.3%
1981	1,084,000	229,200	1,313,200	17.4%
1982	1,062,000	234,100	1,296,100	18.1%
1983	1,703,000	278,100	1,981,100	14.0%
1984	1,750,000	287,900	2,037,900	14.1%
1985	1,742,000	283,400	2,025,400	14.0%
1986	1,805,000	256,100	2,061,100	12.4%
1987	1,621,000	239,200	1,860,200	13.0%
1988	1,488,000	224,300	1,712,300	13.1%
1989	1,376,000	202,800	1,578,800	12.8%
Totals	14,923,000	2,468,800	17,391,800	14.2%

SOURCE: U.S. Bureau of the Census: *Statistical Abstract of the United States, 1992*

Of the total mobile homes placed for residential use in the period 1980-1989, 64 percent were placed in the South, 15 percent in the West, 14 percent in the Midwest, and 7 percent in the Northeast. The average sale prices of these units rose steadily from $19,800 in 1980 to $27,200 in 1989. The averages were highest in the West and lowest in the South. Mobile homes as a percentage of total dwelling unit starts had reached over 21 percent in some years of the 1970s, but fell in the 1980s. New mobile homes placed as residences had fallen to 12.8 percent of total units by the end of the 1980s.

During the 1980s, the rate of population growth continued its long-term decline to 1.1 percent per year. The migration from farm areas was minimal and legal immigration had increased slightly to about 600,000 annually. The trend to smaller and smaller household size slowed with the average dropping from 2.78 at the beginning of the decade to 2.66 at the end. New annual household formation declined over the decade from 1.8 million to 1.3 million. The number of households headed by females rose by 12 percent over the decade and the number of unmarried couples increased from 1,589,000 to 2,856,000. Single-person households increased, from 18,296,000 in 1980 to 22,999,000 in 1990. Single-persons were 35 percent, and female-headed households, 23 percent, of total renter households so that 58 percent of all households were not the traditional nuclear family.

In 1980, 545,000 single-family privately owned houses were sold; sales fell to 436,000 in 1981 and to 412,000 in 1982. In 1983 sales increased to 623,000 and then 750,000 in 1986, the highest number of annual sales of single-family houses in the decade. The total sales of single-family houses for the years 1980-1989 were 6,090,000, at an average of 609,000 per year. Median prices for single-family houses began to rise significantly in 1983 and by the end of the decade had almost doubled, unadjusted for inflation. (*See Appendix A, 1980s, for more statistics*)

1982-1989 • THE SAVINGS AND LOAN CRISIS

The highly-regulated thrift institutions (savings and loans and mutual savings banks) became popular in the Depression, when as a result of federal mortgage insurance, they became intrinsically associated with financing housing with fully-amortized, fixed-rate, long-term, level-payment single-family-house mortgages. After World War II a high rate of savings, economic expansion and an increasing demand for housing brought great prosperity to the thrift institutions, because of the spread between the interest rates they paid to their depositors and the higher rates they charged for mortgages. In the 1960s however, commercial banks began competing for deposits and when they were allowed to raise their rates in 1966, the thrifts had their first experience with disintermediation — the withdrawal of funds from one institution to be placed in another. Regulation Q, passed by Congress in 1966, saved the thrifts temporarily by allowing them to pay depositors one-half of a percent more for funds than commercial banks, but inflation in subsequent years drew investors away from banking and savings institutions in general into other debt and equity investments.

In the late 1960s the secondary mortgage market institutions of Ginnie Mae, Fannie Mae and Freddie Mac developed security instruments based on pools of mortgage loans which then were actively bought and sold by investors, creating a dependable source of mortgage funds.

Median Sale Prices of New Conventional Single-Family Houses

Year	U.S.	Northeast	Midwest	South	West
1980	$64,600	$69,500	$63,400	$59,600	$72,300
1981	68,900	76,000	65,900	64,400	77,800
1982	69,300	78,200	68,900	66,100	75,000
1983	75,300	82,200	79,500	70,900	80,100
1984	79,900	88,600	85,400	72,000	87,300
1985	84,300	103,300	80,300	75,000	92,600
1986	92,000	125,000	88,300	80,200	95,700
1987	104,500	140,000	95,000	88,000	111,000
1988	112,500	149,000	101,600	92,000	126,500
1989	120,000	159,600	108,800	96,400	139,000

SOURCE: U.S. Bureau of the Census: *Statistical Abstract of the United States*, 1992

1982-1989

These mortgage pools grew through the 1970s to $130 billion or twelve percent of outstanding mortgage debt in 1980. At the beginning of the 1980s, the thrift institutions still dominated housing finance, issuing approximately one-half of all mortgages at fixed interest rates. Recession and inflation reduced the annual growth rate of outstanding mortgage debt from 16 percent in the late 1970s to 7 percent in 1981 and 3 percent in 1982. However, this was only the beginning of what would happen to the thrifts as the result of deregulation during the 1980s.

The Depository Institutions Deregulation and Monetary Control Act of 1980 authorized a phased-in removal of the Federal Reserve System's Regulation Q ceiling on interest rates that could be paid to depositors by thrift institutions and authorized them to invest up to twenty percent of their assets in real estate and consumer loans, commercial paper and corporate debt securities. In addition this legislation raised the ceiling on individual insured accounts from $40,000 to $100,000.

Disintermediation away from thrift institutions to money market mutual funds in 1981 and 1982 brought about the failure or merger of nearly nine hundred federally-insured thrift institutions. In reaction Congress passed the Depository Institutions Act of 1982, allowing thrifts to offer federally-insured money market accounts at market interest rates, to invest in residential and commercial real estate loans on a broadened basis, and to invest in government and corporate securities, consumer loans, and equipment leasing. The thrifts soon attracted large amounts of deposits into their new money market checking accounts and growing number of insured savings accounts, together to the extent of over $63 billion net new deposits in 1983 and $57 billion in 1984. But the rates the thrifts were paying on these accounts were higher than the rates they were collecting on their long-term mortgage commitments. As a result they began to issue adjustable rate mortgages, with interest rates rising and falling with the costs of funds to the thrifts and graduated-payment mortgages on which the monthly payment increased according to a fixed schedule.

The amount of outstanding mortgage debt increased by 11 percent in 1983 and 14 percent in 1984. Loans were also made with the builder "buying down" loans by paying a portion of the interest rate during the early years of the loan. Often when borrowers faced their first increased loan payment, they walked away from the loan, especially if the loan principal was greater than the value of the property. Thrifts were also granting permanent and construction loans on overvalued real estate projects. Mortgage debt as a percentage of disposable personal income had risen to 71 percent by the end of the decade, the highest debt burden in history.

After 1984 new deposits in thrift institutions declined sharply and net earnings were greatly reduced by the refinancings of 1986 when mortgage interest rates fell. Finally, the Federal Savings and Loan Insurance Fund was bankrupted and the thrift industry moved toward a state of collapse. Major thrift failures initially occurred in Ohio and Maryland but the losses were primarily in the Southwest and California where economic recovery had been slow. The rampant greed and mismanagement that had ensued after deregulation as well as much outright fraud resulted in one of the worst financial disasters ever to have taken place in the United States.

In 1989, Congress enacted FIRREA (the Financial Institutions Reform, Recovery, and Enforcement Act) in order to reorganize the many insolvent thrift institutions and to establish better standards for those institutions that would remain open. The Federal Home Loan Bank Board was replaced by the Office of Thrift Supervision and given the power to charter federal savings and loan institutions and savings banks and to set capital standards for both federal and state-chartered institutions. An independent Federal Housing Finance Board was established to oversee the operations of the twelve Federal Home Loan Banks. The Resolution Trust Corporation was established to manage the assets and liabilities of insolvent institutions. New capital requirements were imposed on thrifts that were similar to those for national banks. They included limitations on investments other than home mortgages and excluded investments in junk bonds, required the development of uniform accounting standards for thrifts and banks, increased penalties for fraud, and required bank and thrift regulatory agencies to adhere to minimum appraisal standards, which were established by the FIRREA-recognized Appraisal Foundation.

The thrift institution mortgage debt share decreased from 50 percent in 1980 to 27 percent in 1990, displaced in the housing mortgage market by the securities based on the Ginnie Mae, Fannie Mae and Freddie Mac mortgage pools. By 1990 secondary market mortgage pools were $1.1 trillion or 37 percent of the outstanding residential mortgage debt of $3.0 trillion.

1980s • Federal Programs ~ In the period between 1974 and 1980, construction of 867,000 new subsidized housing units was completed: 158,000 public housing units, 321,000 Section 8 units, 82,000 Section 235 units, 216,000 Section 236 units, 28,000 Section 202/8 units for the elderly and 62,000 units under the 1965 rent supplement program. In addition, 752,000 existing units were placed in service: 45,000 public housing units and 707,000 Section 8 units.

More emphasis was placed on the use of existing buildings during the Reagan and Bush administrations with 804,000 new subsidized units completed and 973,000 existing units placed in service. A portion of the units completed after 1980 had been committed by the Carter administration. The Housing and Urban-Rural Recovery Act of 1983 repealed the authority for new construction and substantial rehabilitation under Section 8, except for Section 202 which provided units for the elderly and handicapped. This 1983 legislation also provided grants for emergency shelters for the homeless.

The Housing and Community Act of 1987 established the housing voucher program, a tenant-based program that issued vouchers to eligible tenants for five-year periods, allowing them to choose among available qualifying housing units. Because the housing had to meet certain standards, tenants with vouchers were not always able to find housing that was acceptable.

By 1990 there 1,405,000 public housing units in the United States and 2,981,000 units being used for other subsidized programs, (most of them, 2,500,000, in Section 8 programs) bringing the total number of subsidized units to 4,386,000. Of these total units approximately 40 percent were for the elderly. Most subsidized tenants were paying 30 percent of their income, rather than the earlier-required 25 percent. Eligibility for

1980s

Section 8 occupancy had been reduced from 80 percent of the local median income to 50 percent. Expenditures for subsidized housing programs rose from $8.6 billion in Fiscal Year 1980 to $15.6 billion in Fiscal Year 1990 in 1990 dollars.

In 1989 a series of major scandals in the Department of Housing and Urban Development (HUD) involving Section 8 moderate rehabilitation confronted the Bush administration. The scandals, which involved political influence in the awarding of funds, reached the highest levels of the department, including the Secretary, who in Congressional hearings, invoked the Fifth Amendment and refused to testify on the grounds of possible self-incrimination. The Department of Justice conducted criminal investigations of HUD operations that resulted in prosecutions and convictions. The new Secretary of HUD, Jack F. Kemp, suspended the moderate rehabilitation program and announced proposals to prevent a recurrence of the abuse that had occurred in the program.

The Department of Housing and Urban Development Reform Act of 1989 removed some of the department's flexibility and discretion in awarding funding, required the registration of consultants and lobbyists, appointed a chief financial officer for HUD, a comptroller and an audit for the FHA, eliminated mortgage insurance for investor-owned single-family houses and for land development, required reviews of the financial status of coinsurance lenders twice a year and authorized a study of private agency review of FHA applications. The 1989 act also established a National Commission on Severely Distressed Public Housing and implemented a 1988 demonstration program permitting state agencies to take over the management of foreclosed HUD properties.

1980s • HOMEOWNERSHIP AND HOMELESSNESS ~ Although the national homeownership rate declined slightly in the 1980s, from 64.4 percent to 64.2 percent, the homeownership rates for both married couples and single-person households rose over the decade. Home-ownership rose from approximately 75 percent to approximately 79 percent for married couples and from approximately 45 percent to approximately 47 percent for single-person households. The national homeownership rate was negatively affected, although only very slightly, by the increase in the number of single-person households. The highest homeownership ratio was among those in the age 55-65 group, 80 percent of whom owned their own homes, most of them mortgage free.

At the other end of the scale were the homeless, visible in every large city in the 1980s, sleeping in parks, over steam vents, under overpasses, their belongings piled in shopping carts. Their numbers reached an estimated 500,000 to 750,000 during the decade. A considerable proportion of the homeless have severe mental or addiction problems and in another age would have been institutionalized. Most cities converted buildings to shelters where the homeless could sleep at night, but these quickly became quite dangerous. Federal legislation in 1983, 1986 and 1987 authorized funds in support of local and private efforts to help the homeless.

1980s • HOUSING DESIGN AND NEW LOCATIONS ~ There was a revival of interest in regional architecture in the 1980s. This movement was in conflict with the universalist character of Modernism, classicism, Postmodernism and Deconstructivism, but in harmony with Frank Lloyd Wright's tenets at the beginning of the century. The world mood

(1940) Adobe housing is now a very sought after style in the southwest for its character and appearance blend seamlessly with the house's surroundings.

was one of regional autonomy and ethnicity. Spanish Colonial styles, Southwest adobe styles, New England Colonial styles and others became popular in housing design. There was a thoroughgoing rejection of the 1950s type of banal suburban house and a new interest in houses with picturesque qualities, with asymmetrical massing, with distinct character.

Apartments began to be installed in restored downtown commercial areas, in old warehouses on waterfronts, as well as newly constructed in urban and suburban locations. Apartment locations became more romantic and apartments more widely accepted as a way to live. Many of them were located near some type of amenity, a view, a lake, near shopping or a rapid transit station, or in an area with recreational facilities.

Houses became larger in the 1980s. In 1980, 21 percent of new single-family, privately-built houses contained less than 1,200 square feet of area, whereas in 1990 only 11 percent were that small. In 1980 13 percent contained 2,000 to 2,400 square feet; by 1990, 17 percent were in this category. Whereas in 1980, only 15 percent of new houses were 2,400 square feet or larger, by 1990, 29 percent were. The median size was 1,595 square feet in 1980 and 1,905 square feet in 1990 and the mean size was 1,740 square feet in 1980 and 2,080 square feet in 1990. The incidence of new two-story houses increased over the decade from 31 percent in 1980 to 49 percent in 1990. Houses with four or more bedrooms increased from 20 percent in 1980 to 29 percent in 1990 and houses with 2.5 or more bathrooms rose from 25 percent in 1980 to 45 percent in 1990. New houses with one or more fireplaces rose from 56 percent to 66 percent and new houses

1980s

with air conditioning rose from 63 percent to 76 percent.

The role of houses in the United States had changed by the 1980s. Families were no longer the traditional father, mother and children using the house intensely. A busy new lifestyle characterized the American way of life. During the day no one was at home and more often than not members of the family only rushed in to change clothes, pick up sports equipment and be off again. The house was a place to sleep and keep one's belongings. Restaurants of all types were serving more meals than ever. Rooms for formal entertaining were scarcely used at all. But still houses grew larger and larger as their investment value increased although households were smaller and smaller.

1980s • Townhouses ~ Developers began building inexpensive attached two-story single-family housing in suburban developments in the 1980s. Called townhouses, they were a modern version of the venerable urban brick row houses of the nineteenth century. Built for some of the same reasons—they were less expensive and took up much less land, they were often held to be inappropriate for the wide open spaces of the outer suburbs. They were an alternative to condo apartment ownership. In the West, a one-story patio house variation was developed.

Mid-1980s • Refiguring Old Neighborhoods ~ By the mid-1980s a totally new phenomenon was taking place in established urban residential neighborhoods where large houses were

(1925) Sometimes people did not have to tear down their old housing to create new larger homes – nature would do this for them. Seen here a toppled house which was carried more than 50 feet in the great U.S. cyclone disaster.

814 ~ Housing and Architecture

being built on small, but very well-located lots. Termed "bulkification," this development was supplying quite grand new houses in old neighborhoods, but often in a very incongruous way. Smaller older houses were being torn down and replaced or lots were being subdivided with new houses built on the newly-created lots in close proximity to the original house. Where zoning permitted this to happen, a clamor sometimes arose to change the minimum permitted lot size, or to control demolition of existing houses. Formerly quiet, uncrowded neighborhoods with large yards and old trees became densely, and many would say, inappropriately developed.

Conflict between social classes also occurred in old urban neighborhoods where younger, more affluent, "yuppies" have purchased old houses on a wide scale and "restored" them. Often the former ethnic inhabitants have felt displaced by restoration, which in a purer form would be a way of renewing good housing stock without displacing the inhabitants. No city better demonstrates this trend than Chicago, with its many urban neighborhoods, well-served by urban mass transit. Young people in great numbers began moving back to urban Chicago neighborhoods where they have every convenience, including proximity to their work, but where they have displaced the traditional populations of these neighborhoods as prices and property taxes are driven up by market demand. In many of these neighborhoods single-family dwellings have been rapidly converted to multiple units and new construction, often condominiums, but also large single-family dwellings, interspersed wherever lots are available. Existing buildings have been enlarged to the maximum lot coverage and height permitted. Chicago is one of the cities in the United States where prices soared in urban areas following the substantial and general rise in housing prices all over the country during the 1970s.

1990S • THE BEGINNING OF THE DECADE ~ The 1990s began with economic recession and high short-term interest rates. Inflation, as measured by the increase in the Consumer Price Index was 6.1 percent at the end of 1990 as compared with the end of 1989, but by December 31 of 1991 the CPI had increased by only 2.8 percent over December of 1990. Housing starts, including manufactured homes, were relatively low in 1990 and 1991, totaling 1,388,400 and 1,188,300 units, respectively, in those two years. By 1990, the role of the FHA and VA in financing new housing had declined to approximately 17 percent of new housing starts. Mortgage bankers, and in small communities, commercial banks, had become the principal sources of home mortgage lending, backed by the huge secondary mortgage market, consisting of agencies such as Fannie Mae, Freddie Mac and Ginnie Mae buying packages of mortgages from the primary lenders.

By 1990 population growth in the outer ring of suburbs of urbanized areas was over half of the total population of all urbanized areas. These suburban areas were no longer just residential — many of them were "edge cities," that offered more jobs than bedrooms and some experts were predicting that the United States would never again have the strong, culturally-diverse, centralized cities of former days, that the edge cities would predominate in the future.

1988-1992 • HANDICAPPED ACCESS LEGISLATION ~ The Fair Housing Amendments Act of 1988 extended non-

1988-1992

discriminatory treatment with regard to housing, to individuals with disabilities. This legislation provided that, in buildings ready for first occupancy after March 13, 1991 with an elevator and four or more units: 1) public and common areas must be accessible to persons with disabilities, 2) doors and hallways must be wide enough for wheelchairs and 3) all units must have an accessible route into and through the unit, must have accessible light switches, electrical outlets, thermostats and other environmental controls, reinforced bathroom walls to allow installation of grab bars and kitchens and bathrooms fully usable by people in wheelchairs. In buildings of four or more units but no elevator, these standards apply to ground floor units.

The Americans with Disabilities Act of 1991, which took effect in January of 1992, required that all commercial and public accommodations, including all public meeting places and public transportation facilities, be readily accessible and safely usable by persons with disabilities. This landmark civil rights legislation immediately began to influence the design of commercial buildings, particularly with regard to entrances, sidewalks, parking, restrooms and hallways. To be accessible, a building must have no barriers to persons with disabilities. The law is applicable to both new and existing construction although certain exceptions for small and owner-occupied buildings were made. ADA was intended to be implemented through court decisions that established consensus and precedent. Businesses, organizations and local governments that chose initially to ignore ADA often found themselves facing fines and remedial actions mandated by courts to make their facilities accessible to people with disabilities.

1990 • SUBSIDIZED HOUSING LEGISLATION ~ The first comprehensive housing legislation since 1974 was the National Affordable Housing Act of 1990, which reflected the diminished role of the federal government in subsidized housing and the increased part to be played by state and local housing authorities. Existing housing was retained as the principal form of subsidized housing although a limited amount of new construction was authorized.

The two principal new programs of the 1990 act were the HOME Investment Partnership program and the Homeownership and Opportunity Through HOPE program. HOME was designed as a block grant program requiring local matching funds and was to be used for new construction and rehabilitation of renter-occupied and owner-occupied housing and also for tenant-based rental assistance. HOPE also required matching funds. It was aimed at privatizing public housing and multi-family properties owned or financed by HUD, the VA, the Farmers Home Administration, the Resolution Trust Corporation and state and local governments.

The 1990 act also provided assistance for the homeless; further stiffened FHA mortgage insurance requirements; added enhancements to subsidies for low-rent multi-family properties such as a guaranteed eight percent return on equity and aid in financing capital improvements; extended funding for the operating and modernization costs of public housing; authorized funds to replace expiring Section 8 contracts and authorized funds for converting the Section 202 program for the elderly and handicapped from a loan program to a capital grant and rental assistance program. Housing assistance programs were to be coordinated with education, job training and supportive services to encourage family self-sufficiency. The goal was to move people away from dependency on the government, a goal that was in line with the common public perception that welfare perpetuated a cycle of family dependency.

As of 1990, it was becoming evident that the significantly reduced growth rate of subsidized housing (with new construction virtually eliminated) and the enhanced role of state and local authorities was probably the long-term trend. Nevertheless, costs did not decrease, as the nation's stock of subsidized housing aged and deteriorated and the cost of maintaining it grew. In January of 1993 William Clinton became President and a Democratic Congress was installed. After the Congressional elections of 1994, however, a Republican-majority Congress was in place, ready to move the country to a more conservative position, including a more conservative approach to funding subsidized housing.

Between 1990 and 1994, the number of assisted housing units eligible for payment increased from 4.4 million to 4.7 million. The increase included 48,000 new dwelling units resulting from the HOME program of the Housing Act of 1990. However, in 1993, the Budget Reconciliation Act froze discretionary federal spending through 1999. HUD's budget, which was almost entirely discretionary spending, was 90 percent committed in advance, so the possibilities for new programs were extremely limited. The regional offices were eliminated under Secretary Henry Cisneros. More services were provided for the homeless and lending laws were to be more strictly enforced. HUD authorized the demolition of some of its worst public housing projects and worked to dispose of its large inventory of multi-family properties and mortgages. By 1996 the federally-assisted housing programs remained at approximately 4.7 million units, the level that had been attained in 1994.

1990-1999 • NEW HOUSING CONSTRUCTION AND PRICES ∼ The total monies spent in the ten-year period 1990-1999 on private residential construction put in place in the United States was $2.025 trillion, significantly more than the total $1.232 trillion spent on private non-residential buildings in the same period.

New housing starts began to recover in 1992 and increased every year of the decade thereafter. Manufactured (mobile) homes were a significant portion of new housing starts, reaching a high of 18.7 percent of total starts in 1995. Still criticized as being too vulnerable to windstorms and flooding, manufactured housing was nevertheless during the 1990s a significantly-growing sector of housing, particularly with the elderly. People under age 34 also occupy a disproportionate share of manufactured housing. By the end of the century approximately 19 million people were living full time in more than eight million manufactured homes.

In the final year of the decade, 1999, housing starts totaled 1,989,600, which included 348,700 new manufactured homes. In the overall decade the largest number of new housing starts, nearly 44 percent of the total, took place in the South. The West was second with 24.5 percent; the Midwest third with 22 percent and the Northeast fourth with 9.5 percent.

The median sale prices for new privately owned housing units increased by 30 percent in the 1990s. The Northeast had the highest median sale prices

Housing Starts 1990-1999
(In Thousands)

Year	Single-Family	Multi-Family	Manuf.Homes	Total
1990	894.8 64.4%	298.0 21.5%	195.4 14.1%	1,388.2
1991	840.4 70.7%	173.5 14.6%	174.3 14.7%	1,188.2
1992	1,029.9 73.0%	169.9 12.0%	212.0 15.0%	1,411.8
1993	1,125.7 73.6%	162.0 10.6%	242.5 15.8%	1,530.2
1994	1,198.4 68.8%	258.7 14.8%	286.1 16.4%	1,743.2
1995	1,076.2 64.6%	277.9 16.7%	310.7 18.7%	1,664.8
1996	1,160.9 64.6%	316.1 17.6%	319.7 17.8%	1,796.7
1997	1,133.7 64.0%	340.3 19.2%	296.5 16.7%	1,770.5
1998	1,271.4 65.3%	345.5 17.7%	331.0 17.0%	1,947.9
1999	1,302.4 65.5%	338.5 17.0%	348.7 17.5%	1,989.6
Totals	11,033.8 67.2%	2,680.4 16.3%	2,716.9 16.5%	16,431.1

SOURCE: U.S. Bureau of the Census: *Current Construction Reports*, series C20

Median Sale Prices of New Conventional
Single-Family Houses

Year	U.S.	Northeast	Midwest	South	West
1990	$122,900	$159,000	$107,900	$ 99,000	$147,500
1991	120,000	155,900	110,000	100,000	141,100
1992	121,500	169,000	115,600	105,500	130,400
1993	126,500	162,600	125,000	115,000	135,000
1994	130,000	169,000	132,900	116,900	140,400
1995	133,900	180,000	134,000	124,500	141,400
1996	140,000	186,000	138,000	126,200	153,900
1997	146,000	190,000	149,900	129,600	160,000
1998	152,500	200,000	157,500	135,800	163,500
1999	160,000	N/A	N/A	N/A	N/A

SOURCE: U.S. Bureau of the Census: *Statistical Abstract of the United States*, 1999

throughout the decade; the 1998 median price was 26 percent higher than that of 1990. Prices in the West were the second highest but the rate of increase by 1998 was only 11 percent. The Midwest had the highest rate of median sale price increase at 46 percent, but the price levels remained below those of the Northeast and the West. The South, which had the lowest price levels, showed the second highest rate of increase at 37 percent.

The average sale price of a manufactured home in 1999 was $43,600 as compared with $27,800 in 1990. In 2000, 250,550 manufactured homes were shipped by 280 manufacturers.

1995-2000 • PROSPERITY AND HOUSING ~ In the second half of the 1990s, the majority of the citizens of the United States were experiencing tremendous improvements in material benefits as the economy, particularly the technology sector, grew rapidly and the stock market soared to unprecedented heights and remained high through the end of 1999. Unemployment remained low through the end of the decade. Inflation, as measured by the rise in the Consumer Price Index, was down to 2.9 percent by the end of 1992, 2.7 percent by the end of 1993 and 1994, and 2.5 percent in 1995. Inflation rose to 3.3 percent at the end of 1996, then decreased to 1.7 percent in 1997 and 1.6 percent in 1998. It began to rise again in 1999, reaching 2.7 percent by the end of the year and by the end of 2000, had risen 3.4 percent.

In 1999, poverty as measured by the federal government's poverty threshold, which is based on the cost of groceries for a family of four multiplied by a factor of three, decreased to its lowest level in twenty years. Only 12 percent of the total population were below this level. The incidence of poverty was 10 percent for Whites, 24 percent for African Americans, and 23 percent for Hispanics. The poverty levels in 1959, when the federal government began its official measurements, were 18 percent for Whites and 55 percent for African Americans. Hispanic poverty was not measured until 1972, at which time it was 23 percent; it subsequently rose to above 30 percent and then fell to the 23 percent level of 1999.

Houses grew larger and larger in the 1990s. By 1999, the average new house had two or more stories, three bedrooms, 2.5 bathrooms, central heating and air conditioning, a working fireplace and a two-car garage. Its average size was 2,250 square feet, 50 percent larger than the average new house in 1970. By 1997, 99 percent of American dwelling units had electricity as compared with 2 percent in 1900; 98 percent had flush toilets as compared with 10 percent in 1900; 93 percent had central heating whereas only 8 percent did in 1900; 99 percent had a refrigerator, 76 percent a clothes washer, and 78 percent air conditioning whereas no households had these in 1900.

The average new apartment in 1999 had two bedrooms, two bathrooms, and was centrally air conditioned. The average size of new apartments increased from 1,005 square feet in 1990 to 1,105 square feet in 1999. A surge of construction of luxury apartment buildings took place in the late 1990s in the downtown areas of large cities. Many people, in cities such as San Francisco, Chicago and Boston, decided they preferred to live downtown as opposed to the suburbs, and brought to these center cities a renewed vitality and significant upgrades of the housing stock.

As new houses became larger and more luxurious, the standard two-car garage was replaced in many wealthy neighborhoods with three- and even-four bay garages, including one large space for the family's boat. The quality of housing construction, fixtures, and equipment increased. Homogeneous subdivisions

1980s-1990s gave way to a new diversity of house design types and price levels, within any one development, and at the upper end of the housing scale custom-built houses incorporated even greater craftsmanship and originality.

No clearly identifiable architectural trends emerged as the vast majority of housing styles were re-workings of traditional designs. Post-modernism continued to be expressed in architect-designed single-family houses. Mobile homes, the industrial solution to the need for modest-income housing, continued to be an important component of new housing, with ever-more luxury incorporated into interior finishes. Recreational vehicles, a drive-it-yourself travel house with air conditioning, plumbing and kitchens, had become popular in the 1970s and 1980s. In the second half of the 1990s, recreational vehicles grew into the motor home coach, the latest innovation in a nation experiencing great prosperity. These motor home coaches, equivalent in size to large buses, are luxuriously finished and equipped, and sell, in some cases, for in excess of $1 million.

1980s-1990s • GATED COMMUNITIES

~ By 2000 there were approximately 20,000 gated communities in the United States with some eight million residents. Access to these collections of houses is generally restricted to residents and their guests with special arrangements made for trash pickup and services of other kinds. The concept was not new: Hollywood stars lived in enclosed compounds in the 1920s and 1930s. In the 1950s and the 1960s, retirement communities, some of them centered around golf courses, often had limited access. However, the real growth in this type of community began in the 1980s and has continued to the end of the century.

Gated communities are a form of social segregation. They provide a feeling of security and exclusivity to their inhabitants, but may convey the message that the greater area around them is dangerous. They are an extended form of the elevator apartment buildings that have locked doors, through which residents and guests are admitted via security codes or a guard stationed in the lobby. Gated communities are not necessarily located in areas in which there are problems with crime; in many cases they may be functioning to reduce vehicular traffic and to provide a more exclusive social environment for their residents.

Completed in 1911 for the Deputy Postmaster General of the United States, Perry Heath, who created the rural route system, this mansion in Washington, D.C., designed by architect James Hill, is one of the best examples of beaux arts style. Fallen into severe disrepair, it was fully restored in 1987 by Walton and Deborah Beacham.

1966-1999 • HISTORIC PRESERVATION

~ The public interest in historic preservation that has emerged and grown so tremendously in the United States over the last thirty years of the twentieth century has constituted a major social, as well as economic, change. Preservation of historic sites, buildings and cultural artifacts was rare when the National Historic Preservation Act of 1966 was passed. At the end of the century the preservation movement is concerned with the whole built and natural environment and has for the most part, been accepted as culturally appropriate. Preserved and/or restored buildings, historic districts and scenic areas are strongly linked with tourism, with successful commercial ventures of all types, and with housing. Touring historic houses has become a popular entertainment. No longer are old buildings regarded as obstacles to progress, rather their restoration and use often is the key to progress.

The Tax Reform Act of 1976 initiated beneficial depreciation schedules for owners who rehabilitated income-producing older structures and at the same time demolition costs and accelerated depreciation schedules were denied to owners who demolished historic buildings. The Secretary of the Interior's Standards for Rehabilitation and Guidelines for Rehabilitating Historic Buildings, which had to be met to obtain the offered tax benefits, were developed as a result of the 1976 act and these standards have remained in effect. The Revenue Act of 1978, permitted a ten percent investment tax credit for the rehabilitation of older income-producing properties that encouraged many building owners to improve their properties following the new standards.

The Economic Recovery Tax Act of 1981 provided an even more beneficial set of economic incentives for the preservation and rehabilitation of historic structures that included a fifteen-year depreciation schedule and a 25 percent investment tax credit for income-producing certified historic structures. The entire shell and rehabilitation cost of certified historic investment properties, renovated according to the secretary of the interior's guidelines, could be written off using the straight-line method over fifteen years, thus allowing depreciation of 100 percent of rehabilitation expenditures. In 1982 this provision was modified; the taxpayer had to reduce the property's depreciable basis by one-half of the 25 percent rehabilitation tax credit. The Economic Recovery Tax Act of 1981 attracted large-scale developers to historic preservation and helped to create many urban revitalization projects. Nearly 17,000 projects involving certified properties worth approximately $11 billion were developed between 1976 and 1986 in direct response to the preservation tax incentive program.

Unfortunately for the preservation movement, some of the most favorable provisions of the 1981 Tax Act failed to survive the 1986 overhaul of the Internal Revenue Code. The 25 percent investment tax credit was reduced to 20 percent and the amount of the tax credit that any one taxpayer could use in any year was capped at $7,000. In addition, one of the most attractive features, the ability to apply the tax credit to the income earned from other projects, was dropped.

In 1995 the Historic Homeownership Assistance Act was introduced in the U.S. Congress, proposing a new 20 percent investment tax credit for certified rehabilitation of historic residential property. The credit, proposed to be capped at $50,000, would apply to condominiums, cooperatives and single-family and multi-family houses registered individually or as part of a historic district at the local, state or national level. The tax credit could be transferred to the buyer of a rehabilitated property and a homeowner could transfer unused portions of the credit to a mortgage lender who would then reduce the interest on the homeowner's mortgage. This type of tax credit, already available in some states, was still pending in the U.S. Congress in 2000.

2000 • AT THE CLOSE OF THE CENTURY ~ The number of households in the United States reached 105,480,101 by 2000. Of these, 71,787,347, or 68 percent were family households and 54,493,232 or 51.7 percent were married couple family households. Family households headed by females with no spouse present rose 18.5 percent to 12,900,103. As the population aged, married couple family households with children increased only 3.9 percent over 1990 to 24,835,505 or 23.5 percent of total households and 45 percent of married couple family households. The average family size declined from 3.17 in 1990 to 3.14 in 2000 and the average household size declined just slightly from 2.6 in 1990 to 2.59 in 2000.

Non-family households increased 23.6 percent between 1990 and 2000 to 33,692,754 and individuals living alone grew 18.4 percent to 27,230,075, or 25.8 percent of all households. The number of households with individuals 65 years and older were 24,672,708 or 23.4 percent. There were 5.5 million unmarried couple households in 2000 as compared to 2,856,000 in 1990. The number of single mother households grew to 7.5 million and the number of single father households to 2.2 million. Approximately 48 percent of all householders were unmarried. The number of households including individuals under 18 years of age were 38,022,115, or 36 percent of total households. Married-couple families with children (24,835,505) were 65 percent of these households.

The number of housing units in the United State increased to 115,904,641 in 2000 with 105,480,101 or 91 percent occupied. Of the vacant housing units 3,578,718, or approximately one-third were seasonal, recreational, or occasionally-used units. Of the fully-occupied units, 66.2 percent or 69,815,753 were owner-occupied and 33.8 percent or 35,664,348 were renter-occupied units. The average household size of the owner-occupied units was 2.69 and of the renter-occupied units, 2.4.

CONCLUSION

The democratic process in the United States presents its citizens with many choices and the houses in which people choose to live are among the major choices they will make in their lifetimes. Although for most people, the choice of housing is limited by income, by technology, and by the imagination, for Bill Gates, owner of one of the most luxurious new houses built at the end of the twentieth century, the choices were much wider than they were for George Washington Vanderbilt in 1895, although they both are exemplars of great wealth in their respective times. Mr. Gates could have as large a house as he wishes, but he has chosen to build one that is only one quarter the size of Mr. Vanderbilt's *first floor*. On the other hand, Mr. Vanderbilt would undoubtedly be quite bewildered by the technology and the imagination that pervades Mr. Gates' new house.

APPENDIX A

Some Additional Housing Statistics

1920s • Because Americans were earning more money and putting more of it into financial institutions, abundant mortgage funds were available at reasonable interest rates to make the housing boom of the 1920s possible. Total non-farm residential mortgage debt increased from $9.4 billion in 1920 to $27.2 billion in 1928 and mortgage debt as a portion of disposable personal income increased from 14 percent in 1920 to 36 percent in 1928. The multi-family portion of the outstanding debt rose from 20 percent in 1920 to 32 percent in 1928. Mortgages, as they had been for many years, were short-term, usually renewable every year or every three years and the amounts of the mortgages were a low percentage of the total value of the property so that junior mortgages usually had to be taken out at higher interest rates. Mortgage funds were loaned by individuals, by savings and loans, mutual savings banks, commercial banks, and life insurance companies.

1930s • President Roosevelt appointed John H. Fahey, a New England investment banker, as chairman of the Federal Home Loan Bank Board and it was given expanded powers. The Home Owners' Loan Corporation (HOLC) was established under the FHLBB to refinance the mortgages of homeowners threatened with foreclosure and to lend money to make needed repairs and to pay property taxes. HOLC had authority to issue low-interest bonds up to $2 billion. Eligibility for loans was limited to nonfarm properties appraised at $20,000 or less and loan amounts were limited to 80 percent of appraisals or to $14,000, whichever was lower. Loans were to be amortized at 5 percent over terms of fifteen years. This was a totally new form of property loan; the common practice was a 3-5-year, low loan-to-value-ratio non-amortized loan with the principal not due until the term ended. During the period between June 1933 and June of 1935, HOLC received 1,886,491 applications for loans, on about one-fifth of the country's nonfarm, owner-occupied dwellings. Approximately 50 percent of the applications were rejected or withdrawn, but one million refinancing loans totaling $3.1 billion were made from these applications. HOLC stopped accepting loan applications in 1935. Although 20 percent of HOLC borrowers defaulted, when HOLC was liquidated in 1951 it had made a slight profit. It has been credited with saving the homes of at least 750,000 families, keeping lending institutions in business, and keeping property taxes paid, all at no drain on the federal budget. Total mortgage debt on nonfarm properties reached a low in 1937 of $23.3 billion.

The National Industrial Recovery Act, passed in 1933, authorized funds for slum clearance and low-income housing. The Housing Division of the Public Works Administration built 22,000 low-rent housing units by direct federal construction programs in 37 cities between 1934 and 1937. The land for these projects was taken through federal eminent domain and this practice was challenged by a lawsuit, which was upheld in the Sixth Circuit Court of Appeals in July of 1935, bringing a halt to the program.

1940 • The 1940 Census for the first time included a complete count of housing units. The information collected also included sizes, types, price ranges, conditions, tenure, facilities, equipment and vacancy. A total of 37,325,470 dwelling

1940s

units were counted, of which 34,854,532 or 93.4 percent were occupied and 2,470,938 or 6.6 percent were vacant. Of those occupied, 15,195,763 or 43.6 percent were owner-occupied and 19,658,769 or 56.4 percent were renter-occupied. The proportion of owner-occupancy was down from the 47.8 percent of 1930; the Depression had set back the American ideal of home ownership.

The average family or household size in 1940 was 3.8, a continuation of the declining trend; the comparable numbers had been 4.3 in 1920 and 4.1 in 1930. The average household sizes for nonfarm areas were even lower: 4.2 in 1920, 4.0 in 1930, and 3.7 in 1940. The population of the United States had increased by more than seven percent between 1930 and 1940, but new construction lagged considerably behind new household formation in a reversal of the situation in 1930.

Single-family dwellings reported in the 1940 Census comprised 73.7 percent of the total; 15.8 percent were in two-to-four-unit buildings, and 10.5 percent were in buildings of five or more units. Of the total of all units, 21,616,352 or 57.9 percent were located in urban areas. The median value of all units was $3,000; the median monthly rent was $27. The median housing unit was twenty-five years old; forty percent of the units were more than thirty years old. One in every five families or 20 percent lived in crowded conditions, in other words, occupied housing that provided them with less than one room per person. Twenty-four percent or 8.2 million of the occupied units had no gas or electricity, 4.3 million or twelve percent had no central heating or stoves, and 10.9 million or thirty-one percent had no refrigerators. More than eighteen million units or almost half of the total units needed major repairs or had no private bathrooms. The physical conditions of rural dwellings was considerably more deteriorated than those of urban units.

The New Deal had affected only partial economic recovery. Wealth was more equally distributed than it had been in 1929, but real wages were still below the level of that year. Unemployment remained unacceptably high. The national budget deficit had risen over the 1930s from $7 billion to $20 billion. It would take the outbreak of World War II to bring about full economic recovery and full employment.

The 602,600 housing starts in 1940 and the 706,100 in 1941 include both civilian non-defense-related and defense-related housing starts. The 356,000 housing starts in 1942 reflect the fact that civilian housing was no longer allowed; most of these housing starts were defense related. During 1943 unmet defense housing needs began to decline and consequently housing starts dropped to 191,000 and then to 141,800 in 1944. Public housing starts totaled only 224,800 in the five-year period 1940-1944 and occurred mostly in the pre-war years as shown on the chart below. Not included in the figures in the chart are the 583,000 units of temporary housing — totally prefabricated buildings, dormitories, and trailers. Cost controls kept the average per-dwelling-unit price level during the war. Private-enterprise construction starts were 88.8 percent of the total during the five-year period and 90.5 percent of the total during the war years of 1942-1944.

1950s • The Census of 1950 reported that there were 45,983,398 dwelling units, of which 42,826,281 or 93.1 percent were occupied, 55 percent of them owner-occupied. Of the total units, 29,569,073, or 64 percent, were in urban areas and 25,626,381 or 55.7 percent, were in metropolitan areas. In 1950 the ten largest cities in the United States had a population of about 22 million or approximately fifteen percent of the total population.

Although the Housing Act of 1949 had authorized construction of 810,000 units of public housing or 135,000 units per year, no attempt was made to build that many units. The administration had to work hard to convince the Bureau of the Budget and Congress that 35,000 units should be the goal for 1954. During the remaining six years of the decade starts were made on 215,900 public housing units, at an average of 36,000 per year. At the end of 1959 there were 585,000 dwelling units owned or supervised by the Public Housing Administration. The total public housing starts in the decade were 424,900.

The Housing Act of 1954 was passed in August of that year. As authorized by that act, the Housing and Home Finance Agency was reorganized to include the Federal Home Loan Bank Board, FNMA (Fannie Mae), the Public Housing Administration, the Urban Renewal Administration, and the Community Facilities Administration. The latter two were new entities. There was some expert opinion expressed at the time that federal housing functions having to do with market demand should be separated from the functions having to do with social need, but this advice was not followed. The 1954 Act rechartered FNMA (Fannie Mae) to be funded by private rather than federal capital with the intent that it would become a private corporation in time. A new program of FHA mortgage insurance was authorized for rehabilitation of existing urban dwellings in slum clearance and urban renewal areas (Section 220) and for rehabilitation of dwellings for families displaced by urban renewal projects (Section 221). Because appraisals made for FHA multi-family projects were often so low that developers could not borrow enough money to build the projects, in 1959, Section 221 was amended to permit estimated construction costs to be substituted for the comparison approach to market value in establishing the basis for loans, thereby mixing the federal government's credit and welfare functions.

1960s • From 1950 to 1960 the baby boom had helped push the population up by 28.5 million from 150,845,000 to 179,326,000. In the decade of the 1960s, the population grew by another 24,900,000 to 203,210,000. In 1960, there were 53 million households in the United States; by 1970 the number of households had grown to 63 million. The baby boom ended in 1964 when the birth rate began to drop, decreasing from the 23.3 per 1,000 population it had been in 1960 to 18.4 by 1970. With the decrease in the birth rate the average household size dropped from 3.4 persons in 1960 to 3.1 in 1970. However, the number of households increased as both the marriage rate and the divorce rate increased. The marriage rate was 8.5 per 1,000 in 1960 and 10.6 per 1,000 in 1970. Divorces were 2.2 per 1,000 in 1960 and a much higher 3.5 in 1970 after no-fault divorce laws, allowing divorce by mutual consent, were adopted throughout the United States beginning in 1967. The population after 1964, despite the drop in the birth rate, was sustained by new immigration from Mexico, the Caribbean, Asia, and sub-Saharan Africa that was the result of the Immigration Act of 1965 and that increased population by about 1

1960s-1970s

percent per year. By the early 1960s, African American migration from the South had dropped significantly, but the out-movement of whites from the central cities had increased. By 1966, nonwhites were 23 percent of the population of all cities over 250,000, nearly double the proportion in 1950. The percentage of the population 65 years and older increased over the decade, going from 9.2 in 1960 to 9.6 in 1969.

The Census of 1960 reported 58,326,357 housing units, of which 91 percent or 53,023,875 were occupied. Of those occupied, 32,796,720, or 62 percent were owner-occupied and 20,227,155, or 38 percent were renter-occupied. Of the total units 40,763,865 or 70 percent were located in urban areas and 36,386,215 or 62 percent were located in metropolitan areas. Of the occupied units, 49,458,000 or 93.3 percent were nonfarm units and 3,566,000 or 6.7 percent were farm dwelling units. Of the total units, 10,591,000 or 18.2 percent were reported to be substandard, i.e., dilapidated or to have plumbing deficiencies such as no hot and cold running water, private flush toilet, or private bathtub or shower.

As of 1960, the median value of all owner-occupied units was $11,900; by 1968 it was $15,400, and by 1969, $16,200. The median monthly rent for all renter-occupied units was $58 in 1960, $78 in 1968, and $84 in 1969.

The number of mortgaged nonfarm, owner-occupied dwelling units in 1960 were 15,816,000 or 56.8 percent of the 27,862,000 nonfarm, owner-occupied total units. By 1965 savings and loan institutions held 41 percent of the outstanding nonfarm residential mortgage debt, up from the 31 percent of 1956. Insurance companies were making fewer residential loans, preferring instead the more lucrative commercial development market. Commercial banks and mutual savings banks each held about fifteen percent of nonfarm residential mortgage debt. Private mortgage insurance companies grew rapidly during the 1960s. They insured the top 20-25 percent of mortgage loans on one-to-four-family properties at one-half the cost of the FHA premium for this coverage. The first of these companies was The Mortgage Guaranty Insurance Company (MGIC) organized in 1957. The number of VA loans being made were decreasing as the number of veterans entering the home purchase market declined, but FHA-insured loans remained stable.

1970s • The total number of housing units in the United States in 1970 was 68,679,030, of which 63,449,747 or 92.4 percent were occupied units. Of these, 39,885,180 or 62.9 percent were owner-occupied and 23,564,567 or 37.1 percent were renter-occupied. Over the decade the total number of housing units increased 28.7 percent to 88,411,263. Occupied units increased 26.7 percent to 80,389,673 and the owner-occupancy level increased to 64.4 percent. Over the decade the population of the United States increased only 11.4 percent, from 203,849,000 in 1970 to 227,061,000 in 1980. The increase in the number of occupied housing units of 16,939,926 was 73 percent of the increase in population of 23,212,000, reflecting the increasing number of single- and two-person households.

1980s • Whereas single-family houses had been 68 to 76 percent of new starts in the second half of the 1970s, in the 1980s, single-family houses fell to 62 to 63 percent in 1982-1985, after which they rose to 71 to 73 percent in 1987 through 1989. Multi-family production increased during the mid-1980s as a result of builders taking advantage of changes in the federal tax code that 1) shortened the period over which investment buildings could be depreciated and 2) permitted advantageous treatment of passive losses. From 1983 through 1986, multi-family unit starts were 635,000, 665,000, 669,000 and 626,000 units respectively. Over the decade, new starts of condominium units averaged 13 percent of total starts, but condominiums, which reached a peak of 291,000 units in the mid-1980s had retreated to 118,000 new starts in 1989. The Tax Reform Act of 1986 rescinded the favorable treatment of depreciation and passive losses for apartments that had been included in the 1981 Tax Act.

In 1980 there were 88,411,263 total housing units in the United States, of these 80,389,673, or 90.9 percent were occupied. Of these latter, 51,794,545 or 64.4 percent were owner-occupied and 28,595,128 or 35.6 percent were renter-occupied. Housing units located in metropolitan areas were 65,116,035 or 73.6 percent of all units with 23,295,228 or 26.3 percent in non-metropolitan areas. In 1980 approximately 85 percent of owner-occupied dwelling units were single-family detached dwelling houses and less than 4 percent were attached (semi-detached or row) houses. Approximately 4.5 percent were in buildings containing 2 to 4 units and less than 2 percent of owner-occupied dwelling units were in structures containing five or more units. Approximately 6 percent of owner-occupied dwellings were mobile homes.

Some 27 percent of renter-occupied units were in single-family detached houses; about 4.5 percent were attached. Just over 27 percent were in structures containing 2-4 units; just over 12 percent were in 5-9-unit structures; about 10.5 percent were in structures with 10-19 units; and 7.5 percent were in 20-49-unit structures; and slightly over 9 percent were in structures with more than 50 units. Mobile homes comprised 2.6 percent of the total rental units. These percentages were very little changed by the end of the decade.

1990s • The U.S. Census of 1990 showed 93,347,000 households, a 15.5 percent increase over the 80,776,000 of 1980, but a slowing of the rate of growth in the number of households, which had increased 27 percent in the 1980s. The number of family households, 66,090,000, were 71 percent of total households. The number of married-couple family households, at 52,317,000, were 56 percent of the total number of households and 79 percent of the family households. The number of married-couple households with children living at home was 25.6 percent of the total number of households as compared with 30.8 percent in 1980, 38.8 percent in 1970, and 45 percent in 1960. Family households headed by females with no spouse present, at 10,890,000, were 11.6 percent of total households and 16.5 percent of family households. Family households headed by males with no spouse present, at 2,884,000, were three percent of the total households and 4.4 percent of family households.

The average family size decreased from 3.29 people in 1980 to 3.17 people in 1990 and the average household size decreased from 2.8 in 1980 to 2.6 in 1990. Of the 27,257,000 non-family households, 22,999,000 or 84 percent (24.5 percent of total households) were people living alone. The number of people living alone increased 26 percent between 1980 and 1990, but had increased by 69 percent between 1970 and 1980. There were approximately 2,800,000 unmarried couple households in 1990. The proportion of householders sixty-five years of age and older rose to 20.1 percent in 1990. All of these factors influence housing choices.

The total number of housing units in the country in 1990 was 106,283,000, of which 94,224,000, or 88.6 percent were occupied units. Of the occupied units, 60,248,000 or 63.9 percent were owner-occupied and 33,976,000 or 36.1 percent were renter-occupied.

The single-family detached house has long been identified as the American ideal housing unit. However, the proportion of total single-family detached houses in the United States declined, going from 68.8 percent at the peak of dominance in 1960, to 66.2 percent in 1970, then to 61.8 percent in 1980, and 59.0 percent in 1990. Single-family attached houses (rowhouses, townhouses and duplexes) increased somewhat as a proportion of the total housing inventory between 1980 and 1990, from 4.1 percent to 5.3 percent. Housing in buildings of two to four units declined from 11.2 percent of the total in 1980 to 9.7 percent in 1990. Multi-family units in buildings of five or more units remained proportionately level, from 15,478,306 (17.8 percent) in 1980 to 18,104,610 (17.7 percent) in 1990. Mobile or manufactured (mobile) homes increased 68 percent, from 4,401,056 and 5.1 percent of the total in 1980 to 7,399,855 and 7.2 percent of the total in 1990.

The highest proportions of single-family detached houses in 1990 were in the Midwest states of Iowa (74.6 percent), Nebraska (72.5 percent), Kansas (71.6 percent), Oklahoma (71.5 percent), Arkansas (70.8 percent), Missouri (70.3 percent), and Indiana (70.1 percent). Nevada and Florida, which once had predominately single-family detached houses (80.7 percent and 74.0 percent, respectively, in 1940), in 1990 had 45.5 percent and 49.7 percent. The states with the highest proportions of apartments in buildings with five or more units were New York (32.8 percent), Hawaii (31.4 percent), and Nevada (25.2 percent). The states with the greatest proportion of mobile homes were South Carolina (16.9 percent), Wyoming (16.5 percent), New Mexico (16.3 percent), North Carolina (15.3 percent), West Virginia (15.2 percent), Arizona (15.1 percent), and Montana (15.0 percent).

BIBLIOGRAPHY

Abstract of the 12th Census 1900. U.S. Census Office, 1902.

Abstract of the 15th Census of the United States, 1930. Bureau of the Census, 1930.

Alexander, Theron. *Human Development in an Urban Age.* New York: Prentice-Hall, Inc., 1973.

Caplow, Theodore, Louis Hicks, and Ben J. Wattenberg. *The First Measured Century, An Illustrated Guide to Trends in America, 1900-2000.* The American Enterprise Institute Press, 2001.

Doan, Mason C. *American Housing Production, A Concise History, 1880-2000.* Lanham, MD: University Press of America, Inc., 1997.

Fish, Gertrude Sipperly, ed. *The Story of Housing.* New York: MacMillan Publishing Company, 1979.

Ford, Larry R. *Cities and Buildings, Skyscrapers, Skid Rows, and Suburbs.* Baltimore: The Johns Hopkins University Press, 1994.

Gelernter, Mark. *A History of American Architecture, Buildings in Their Cultural and Technological Context.* Hanover, NH: University Press of New England, 1999.

Hildebrand, Grant. *Origins of Architectural Pleasure.* Los Angeles: University of California Press, 1999.

Historical Statistics of the United States, Colonial Times to 1957. Bureau of the Census, 1960.

Kostof, Spiro. *American by Design.* New York: Oxford University Press, 1987.

Mason, Joseph B. *History of Housing in the U.S. 1930-1980.* Houston: Gulf Publishing Company, 1982.

McAlester, Virginia and Lee. *A Field Guide to American Houses.* New York: Alfred A. Knopf, 1996.

Statistical Abstracts of the United States. 1940, 1960, 1970, 1980, 1992, 1997 and 1999. United States Department of Commerce, Bureau of the Census.

U.S. Census of Housing, 1950, Vol. I and *1956 National Housing Inventory, Vol. III.* Bureau of the Census.

Welfeld, Irving. *Where We Live, A Social History of American Housing.* New York: Simon and Schuster, 1988.

Wolfe, Tom. *From Bauhaus to Our House.* New York: Farrar Straus Giroux, 1981.

Wright, Gwendolyn. *Building the Dream: A Social History of Housing in America.* Cambridge: MIT Press, 1992.

INTERNET RESOURCES

National Association of Home Builders.
www.nahb.org

Bureau of the Census Types of Housing
http://www.census.gov/hhes/www/housing/census/historic/units.html

Government Publications on Construction and Housing from Masonry to Rent Subsidies
http://www.census.gov/prod/www/abs/cons-hou.html

Americans with Disabilities Act
http://www.usdoj.gov/crt/ada/publicat.htm
http://www.usdoj.gov/crt/ada/pubs/10thrpt.htm

The Fair Housing Act
http://www.hud.gov/fhe/fhehous.html

The Biltmore Estate
http://www.westernncattractions.com/biltmore.htm

FAIR HOUSING - HOUSING DISCRIMINATION
Fair housing law and housing discrimination for the apartment dweller. Know when discrimination happens and how to pursue a complaint.
http://apartments.about.com/cs/fair/index.htm

HOUSING AND HOMELESSNESS
Resources related to housing and homelessness in the United States
http://usgovinfo.about.com/cs/housing/index.htm

ARCHITECTURE SITE
Links to various aspects of architecture
http://architecture.about.com/index.htm

ARCHITECTURE AND SOCIAL STUDIES
Use this directory to find ideas and general resources for combining social studies, geography and history lessons with

discussion of architecture and building design. Teaching aids for all ages.
http://architecture.about.com/cs/socialstudies/index.htm

ARCHITECTURE HISTORY TIME LINE - HISTORIC PERIODS AND STYLES
History of architecture, with photos and resources for exploring architectural periods and styles, from prehistoric to modern times
http://architecture.about.com/cs/timeline/index.htm

Judith Reynolds

IMMIGRATION

~

(1907) A Polish emigrant boarding the 'General Grant'.

TIMELINE

1820-1899 ~ Coming to America

Factories employ entire families of immigrants (1820s-1830s) / Old Immigration from England, Ireland, Scandinavia, and Germany (1830-1870) / Fourteenth Amendment declares that all persons born or naturalized in the U.S. are citizens (1866) / New Wave immigration, mainly from Southern and Eastern Europe (1880-1920) / Supreme Court rules in *Plessy v. Ferguson* that a person with mixed blood should be considered black (1896) / Chinese Exclusion Act restricts immigrant workers (1882 and 1884)

MILESTONES: Fugitive Slave Law requires the return of runaway slaves to their owners (1850) • Land Act gives whites in California legal control over Mexican property and voting rights (1851) • Homestead Act promises land to pioneer settlers in the west (1862) • Fifteenth Amendment declares all men eligible to vote without regard to race (1870) • Open door trade policy with China initiated (1899) • Philippine uprising after Spanish American War (1899-1902)

1900-1919 ~ Mass Migration

Chinese immigration banned except for diplomats, students, and merchants (1900) / Mexicans strike against the Pacific Electric Railway company for equal wages and parity (1903) / The only foreign born residents of the U.S. ineligible for citizenship are Asians (1913) / Seven thousand Japanese plantation workers in Hawaii stage a four month long strike (1909)

MILESTONES: Mass migration of workers across the nation (1915-1919) • Child labor abuse made a federal crime (1916) • War Labor Board created to protect labor (1917) • Unions fall into government and public disfavor (1919-1920)

1920-1929 ~ Restricting Immigration

Restricted Filipino immigration; unlimited Western Hemisphere immigration (1920s) / Permanent immigration quotas imposed (1921 and 1924) / Japanese and Filipino farm workers strike against Hawaiian plantation owners (1920 and 1924) / Cable Act declares that an American woman married to an alien loses her citizenship (1922)

MILESTONES: Formation of the Negro National League in baseball (1920) • Bessie Coleman becomes first African-American female pilot, earning her license in France because of segregation in the U.S. (1921) • The Olympic Winter Games are separated from the Games of the Olympiad, the official title of the Summer Games (1924)

1930-1949 ~ Resentment and Fear of Immigrants

Filipino immigration is restricted to 50 people a year (1934) / Executive Order 9066 requires internment of Japanese Americans living on the West Coast (1942) / "War brides" immigration permitted (1943-1946) / Women, blacks and immigrants increase the work force from 46 million in 1940 to 60 million in 1945

MILESTONES: Holocaust results in the massacre of millions of Jews and disenfranchised people in Germany and Eastern Europe (1939-1945) • U.S. freezes Japanese assets (1940) • First atomic explosion, developed by German and American scientists, occurs in Los Alamos, New Mexico (1943) • Establishment of the All-American Girls Professional Baseball League (AAGPBL) (1943) • Ukrainian immigrant Igor Sikorsky builds the first successful helicopter (1939) • Housing Act provides for slum clearance and community redevelopment (1949)

1950-1979 ~ Refugee Immigration

Asian intellectuals immigration permitted (1950-1980) / McCarran-Walter Act permits Japanese to apply for citizenship (1952) / Immigration and Nationality Act removes Japanese quota restriction (1965) / Vietnam refugee immigration permitted (1970-1975) / Cuban refugees immigration permitted (1975-1990)

MILESTONES: Federal troops intervene to enforce Little Rock integration orders (1956) • Supreme Court applies the Bill of Rights to state court proceedings (1960s) • Evidence seized in illegal searches cannot be used in state court trials (1961) • Civil Rights Act prohibits discrimination in employment (1964) • *Hernandez v. Texas* rules that Mexican Americans are white (1954)

1980-2001 ~ Hispanic Immigration

Soviet refugee immigration permitted (1980-1995) / Amnesty granted for illegal immigrants in the U.S. (1986) / Supreme Court rules that a child of an American mother, regardless of where it was born, automatically becomes a U.S. citizen while the child of a foreign mother by an American father must apply for citizenship (2001)

MILESTONES: President Jimmy Carter imposes a U.S. boycott of Moscow Summer Olympics due to Soviet invasion of Afghanistan (1980) • U.S. attempts to stabilize Central American countries (1980s) • Russell Higuchi becomes the first scientist to clone an extinct animal's DNA segment (1983) • Fall of the Berlin Wall begins breakup of the Soviet Union (1989) • North American Free Trade Agreement opens trade borders to Mexico and Canada (1993)

Introduction

America has always viewed itself, whether correctly or not, as the melting pot of the world, blending immigrants of many cultures into one. Regardless of whether a person was a Spanish explorer, one of the Pilgrims of the Plymouth Colony, or the country's first president, he or she was an immigrant to what would become the United States. Arguably, Native Americans were the first immigrants, arriving in North America from Asia or another continent thousands of years before the Europeans. Accordingly, from its original roots, the United States was and is a country made of diverse peoples from many countries.

It seems as though the very first European settlers of the United States did not really want to come here at all. They were either escaping some sort of persecution at home, retreating from their homelands in order to find more food and land, or were convicts sent by the British to serve out their terms in the colonies. This mosaic of diverse peoples endured social and religious conflict until the colonies won their independence from England. With the rise of the new nation came the rise of a new nationalism and the population of the United States was transformed from a diverse group of immigrants trying to tame a wilderness to a fairly homogenous, Anglo-dominated population and a desirable place to live for the white, western European. New immigrants even sold themselves into servitude in order to afford the expensive, long, dangerous, trip to the colonies.

After the settlement of the first colonies, the first large "wave" of immigrants, albeit unwilling immigrants, were slaves. From the early 1700s to 1807 when Congress prohibited importing slaves, over 500,000 African people were taken from their villages, sold into slavery and brought to the United States to serve mostly as field hands. Forced to change their names, speak a new language, work without pay and under brutal working conditions, their process of assimilation into American society was inaugurated. Little did this pattern change for other immigrants who followed. Although they were not slaves, they were expected to assimilate into American society.

The first "official" large wave of immigrants came from western European countries. The young United States government sought to increase its population and accordingly supported an unrestricted 'come one, come all' immigration policy. It was not inexpensive to travel to the United States so to attract new populations the government offered cheap or free land grants. Agriculture was the main industry. Coming mainly from England, Ireland and Scandinavia, these wealthy or upper middle class white Europeans tended to assimilate into American culture quite easily and quickly established themselves economically. It was quite a different story for the second "official" large wave of immigration.

The second wave of immigrants, in contrast to the first, came largely from eastern and southern Europe. This second wave

> *Give me your tired, your poor, your huddled masses yearning to breathe free, the wretched refuse of your teeming shore. Send these, the homeless, tempest-tossed to me, I lift my lamp beside the golden door.*
>
> From a poem by Emma Lazarus, engraved on the Statue of Liberty

were poor; they came looking for work that was unavailable in an overcrowded Europe. There were so many of these immigrants—about 25 million between the late 1880s and the 1920s and as many as 5,000 a day—that the United States government needed an organized and efficient method of admitting them to the country. Erected in 1886, the main entry point for European immigrants to the United States was Ellis Island located outside New York City, in New York Harbor. Immigrants who had crossed the Atlantic by ship in third class, or steerage, were herded through this "gateway" into America in what proved to be a humiliating experience for many of them. Here the beginning of the assimilation process took place; often, the immigration officer would change or Americanize the immigrant's name in a process through which immigrants were encouraged to abandon their native customs and cultures. It cannot be emphasized enough that only the poor went through this process. The wealthy, though arriving in much smaller numbers during this time, usually were admitted while still on board their ships and were let off in New York City itself; they were not required to make the ferry trip to Ellis Island to undergo further medical and legal inspections. Therefore, the wealthy tended to keep their original names, while the poor did not. This beginning of the assimilation process is where we also begin the story of twentieth century immigration.

In 1910, 1.04 million people arrived in the United States; among a population of 92.4 million of which 13.5 million (12.5 percent) had been born in another country. By 1990, only 700,000 people immigrated (in addition to the legalization of half a million formerly illegal immigrants) into an official population of 248 million (thus a 2.8 percent immigration rate in 1990). This radical drop in immigration is the result of shifting attitudes and policies that Americans and their government adopted toward foreign-born people.

1830-1930 • TWO MAIN WAVES OF EUROPEAN IMMIGRATION

From 1830 to 1920 the United States experienced two large waves of immigration. The first, 1830 to 1882, were mainly Western Europeans. In this period more than ten million people arrived from England, Ireland, Germany and the Scandinavian countries. During the second wave, 1882 through 1920, the 22 million immigrants included a huge influx of Southern and Eastern Europeans as well. After stringent quotas were inacted in 1921 and 1924, most immigrants in the 1920s were from the Western Hemisphere, especially Canada and Mexico. Their ethnic origins and the economic structures of their new communities in America shaped the lives of immigrant families wherever they settled. The first wave of immigrants had already established their identity by the time the second wave of immigrants arrived in the United States. Because the ethnic origins of each wave of immigrants were so different and because the second wave was so large, the two waves clashed for a long period. Table 1 shows the relationship between the two immigration movements during the period between 1900 and 1930. In 1930, of the 26 million "foreigners" in the United States, 14.2 million were from the "new" wave of immigration. To have been a member of either community at this time must have been overwhelming, for the big industrial cities were overcrowded with immigrant populations that had to find their own way into American culture and life.

Table 1

	Total Population	Native Population Total	Native Parents	Foreign Parents	Foreign Born	Native
1930	122,775,046	108,570,897	82,488,768	26,082,075	14,204,149	88.4%
1920	105,710,620	91,789,928	68,994,682	22,795,246	13,920,692	86.8%
1910	91,972,266	78,456,380	59,491,427	18,964,903	13,525,886	85.3%
1900	75,994,575	65,653,299	49,456,178	15,697,121	10,341,276	86.4%

SOURCE: Compilation from *The World Almanac and Book of Facts*, 1915 to 1970

THE "NEW IMMIGRATION" INTO INDUSTRIAL AMERICA 1865-1920

1850-1890 • OLD IMMIGRANTS— WHERE THEY LIKED TO SETTLE ~ The high proportion of Norwegian, Swedish, Dutch, Swiss, and British immigrants (the "old" immigration) settled in rural communities because they arrived in the United States at a time when abundant quantities of cheap or free land were available. These were the groups on whom the land-grant railroads and the immigration bureaus of the northwestern states had concentrated their advertising campaigns. Important, too, was the fact that these were relatively prosperous groups, many of whose members possessed the capital necessary to embark on American farming.

In 1920, for the first time in American history, a decline in rural population was recorded, to less than 50 percent of the total population. A 1921 Census report on urbanization showed that 51 percent of Americans lived in cities and that the number of farm residences had dwindled by 30 percent. Table 2 shows the steady decline from 1900 to 1930.

1890-1930 • NEW IMMIGRANTS— WHERE THEY LIKED TO SETTLE ~ According to the Dillingham Commission, immigrants from southern and eastern Europe (the "new" immigration) were more prone to congregate in cities than those from northern and western Europe

Table 2

	1900	1920	1930
Urban Population	30,160,000	54,158,000	68,955,000
Rural Population	45,835,000	51,553,000	53,020,000

SOURCE: Compilation from *The World Almanac and Book of Facts*, 1915 to 1970

(circa 1912) Street scene of Orchard Street, on the Lower East Side of New York City, home to many of the city's Jewish inhabitants. Children roam the street, as men and women walk under the awnings of grocers and businesses, some with signs in Hebrew. Several horse-drawn carriages are parked along the garbage-strewn curb, and tenement buildings line the block.

(the "old" immigration). At the top of the list for city dwellers were natives of Ireland and Russia, of whom more than 80 percent lived in urban communities, while 75 percent of Italian and Hungarian immigrants settled in cities. Less than half the American-born population was urban, however, and the only immigrant groups with a lower percentage of urban dwellers than the natives were the Norwegians and the Montenegrins. Table 3 shows the largest American Cities of the time with the growth rate largely coming from immigrants.

1880-1910 • IMMIGRANT FARMERS
~ Even though the vast majority of "new" immigrants settled in urban areas, some others, especially the Czechs and the Germans, chose farm life. By 1910, almost one-third of all Czech immigrants, and an even higher proportion of the second generation, were engaged in agriculture, mostly in the prairie states of the Mississippi Valley, Nebraska and Texas.

Table 3: Ten Largest Cities

1890	1900	1930
New York City	New York City	New York City
Chicago	Chicago	Chicago
Philadelphia	Philadelphia	Philadelphia
Saint Louis	Saint Louis	Detroit
Boston	Boston	Los Angeles
Baltimore	Cleveland	Cleveland
San Francisco	Baltimore	Saint Louis
Cincinnati	Detroit	Baltimore
New Orleans	Cincinnati	Boston
Pittsburgh	Los Angeles	San Francisco

The Dillingham Commission

In 1906 Senator William Dillingham introduced a bill to Congress whose intent was to restrict immigration and to control the number of immigrants settling in cities. It required a raise in the head tax on immigrants; it excluded people of poor health and physique from entering the United States, and it established a Division of Information in the Immigration Service to help new immigrants locate jobs in less densely settled areas of the country. Included in this bill were allocations for a commission to be set up to study the impact of immigration on the United States: hence the Dillingham Commission. The bill passed in 1907.

1890-1900

The Russo-Germans, finding the soil and climate of the plains not to be dissimilar to those of their homeland, were clustered together in hundreds of small communities in Kansas, Nebraska, Iowa, Minnesota, and Dakotas.

The Slavic, Italian, and other "new" immigrants did not take up farming for several reasons. Not only were these people reluctant to become separated from their own groups, which had congregated in cities, but also a large portion of these immigrants did not initially intend to remain permanently in the United States. Most of the late nineteenth-century immigrants were almost completely without capital and could not afford to establish farms even if the land was given to them. Typically, (apart from Czechs and the Russo-Germans) Southern and Eastern European immigrants shunned the Great Plains. Not only were the limitless expanses forbidding, but also plains farming required reapers, binders, and wire fences that were all very expensive.

1890-1900 • Employment Opportunities for Urban Immigrants

By the time the new wave of immigrants had reached America, industrialization had eliminated much of the need for skilled labor. In the bituminous coal fields, for example, the skill and experience which had been necessary for pick or hand mining became unnecessary once mechanical cutters began to be used on the coal face. In cotton manufacturing, unskilled and inexperienced immigrants could, after brief training, operate automatic looms which took over work

Table 4: Immigrant Enclaves

Population	Before 1890	After 1900
Pennsylvania	English Irish Scottish Welsh American Born	Slovak Polish Italian
New England	British Irish French Canadian	Polish Portuguese Greek Syrian
New York Chicago	German Bohemian	Russian Jews Italian

SOURCE: Compilation from *The World Almanac and Book of Facts*, 1915 to 1970

(circa 1900) An immigrant family in a New York slum.

formerly performed by highly trained weavers. Because many manufacturing plants that required unskilled laborers were located in urban areas, poor immigrants who were unskilled or could not speak English provided a good labor pool.

As Table 4 shows, the "new" immigrants picked up employment that the "old" immigrants had previously filled. Before 1890, most of the miners in Pennsylvania had been American-born or English, Scottish, Welsh, Irish, or German immigrants. After 1900, the miners were largely Slovak, Magyar, Polish and Italian. In the same period, in the New England textile industry, what had been a wholly British, Irish and French-Canadian work force, saw a significant influx of Poles, Portuguese, Greeks and Syrians. In the garment trades of New York and Chicago, the majority of employees that originally had been German, Bohemian, or Irish, were replaced by Russian Jews and Italians. In 1910, 57.9 percent of all industrial employees were foreign born, and nearly two-thirds of those were from Eastern or Southern Europe.

1890-1910 • HOW NEW IMMIGRANTS SETTLED IN CITIES ~ Immigrant life was organized almost wholly along the lines of nationality. Each group exhibited strong tendencies to live in separate areas and to move elsewhere whenever newcomers appeared. In the generation after the Civil War, New York's Lower East Side experienced almost a complete change in population. Formerly the stronghold of the Irish and the Germans, its character changed as these groups retreated to Brooklyn in the face of Russian Jewish and Italian immigration; while the Italians took over the old Irish neighborhoods, Russian and Polish Jews pressed into the German districts. In Chicago, Bohemians and Poles took over areas, that had been Irish, German or Scandinavian in character.

Table 5

Legislation Time-Line

1830 1840 1850 1860 1870 1880 1890	1900 1910 1920 1930 1940 1950	1960 1970 1980 1990
Open Unrestricted Immigration Policy	50 cent tax per person Quota System Literacy Test	Refugee, Skills, & Family Preference

1882-1924

Yet to refer to these ethnic areas as "Little Italy" or "Little Poland" only told half the story, for immigrant clannishness was based on provincial rather than national loyalties. For example, New York's Italians, Neapolitans and Calabrians clustered together in the Mulberry district; a colony of Genoese occupied Baxter Street and Sicilians lived on Elizabeth Street; west of Broadway up to the Eighth and Fifteenth wards North Italians predominated; and finally a small group of Austrian Italians was to be found on Sixty-ninth Street, near the Hudson.

The congested, decayed districts into which the "new" immigrants swarmed exemplified the worst evils of city life. New York provided the most conspicuous example of poverty and overcrowding. The new type of slum—the "dumb-bell" tenement—forced immigrants into new levels of compression and degradation. Five stories high, honeycombed with tiny rooms lacking in both light and proper sanitation, the grim structures became the haven of disease, crime, and immorality. In New York's Italian Mulberry bend, unsanitary and overcrowded conditions resulted in the heaviest infant mortality rate in the city as well as the highest incidence of tuberculosis.

But New York was far from being the only place scarred by immigrant slums. Boston, Pittsburgh, Kansas City, Buffalo, and Jersey City all had notorious tenement districts. So, too, had smaller places like Lowell, Massachusetts, where the area known as "Little Canada" was said to have a population density greater than anywhere else in the United States outside the Fourth ward of New York City. The Dillingham Commission, anxious in 1910 to compare immigrant and native tenement conditions, was unable to locate a single tenement occupied by a native-born American.

Table 6

	Chinese Population		Japanese Population	
	1930	1920	1930	1920
Total United States	74,954	61,639	138,834	111,010
California	37,361	28,812	97,456	71,952
Washington State	2,195	1,263	17,837	17,387
New York	9,665	5,793	2,930	2,628

SOURCE: Compilation from *The World Almanac and Book of Facts*, 1915 to 1970

1882-1924 • THE MOOD OF AMERICA ABOUT IMMIGRANTS: DEMAND FOR RESTRICTION ~ Through common misconceptions about immigrants and crime that the "new" immigrant slums fostered, restrictions on immigration policy were demanded by the American public. The dedication ceremonies for the Statue of Liberty in October 1886 took place, ironically enough, at precisely the same time Americans were beginning to seri-

(circa 1900) A market in San Francisco's Chinatown.

ously doubt the wisdom of unrestricted immigration. Already the first barriers had been erected against the entry of "undesirables". In response to public pressure, Congress had already suspended Chinese immigration and had taken its first steps to regulate the European influx. This period marked the opening of a prolonged debate which was not to culminate until the 1920s when the enactment of restrictive codes in 1921 and 1924 brought the era of mass immigration to a close.

1885-1925 • IMMIGRATION RESTRICTION AGAINST ASIANS ~ In California, nativism took the form of a virulent anti-Chinese movement. As one can see from Table 6, the American West had the largest proportion of Asians in the country. The indiscriminate anti-foreignism that had characterized California's gold-rush days soon gave way to a concentrated hostility toward the Chinese, who had become the largest and most conspicuous non-European element in the state. Antipathy stemmed largely from the mistaken belief that the Chinese were "coolies" and as such constituted a servile class whose existence degraded and threatened free labor. It was also widely believed that the Chinese were an unassimilable, even subversive group, and that their customs and social habits were a social menace. Accordingly, in May 1882 the Chinese Exclusion Act suspended Chinese immigration for a period of ten years, forbade naturalization of Chinese, and imposed other restrictions on them.

First coming to the United States between 1885 and 1924, Asian immigrants were predominately male; only wealthy Asian men were able to bring brides to the United States. As of 1910 there were 1,413 Chinese men to every

100 Chinese women. The sex ratio was still skewed in 1940 when there were 258 men to every 100 women. In contrast to the extended family networks in traditional Chinese culture, until recent decades many Chinese-American households consisted of single men living alone.

European immigration restriction involved different considerations than Asian immigration restriction. This suspension was not intended as a repudiation of the traditional immigration attitudes. Chinese immigration, it was argued, was a separate issue involving wholly different considerations from those applying to the European movement.

While those who wished to restrict European immigration were failing to secure anything but a succession of mildly exclusive and largely ineffective statutes, the opponents of Asian immigration were winning with striking success. The two issues continued to be separate; the agitation for Asian exclusion remained almost wholly a concern of the far West, while support for the restriction of the European movement still came largely from the East coast. Yet, in an age of growing race-consciousness, the attitudes evoked by these issues were reflected in the clash between the "strange" cultures of the Asians and the more recognizable cultures of the Europeans.

1905 • BIG BUSINESS OPPOSES RESTRICTIONS — During the years following the initial Asian Immigration restrictions, steamship companies and industrial interests fought legislation that might restrict the immigrant flow. It helped these interests that representatives of western states argued that since New York and Boston derived great benefits from immigrant traffic, they should be prepared to take the bad along with the good. What finally brought matters to a head between big business and public discrimination was New York's threat to close down the immigrant depot at Castle Garden (the main entry point for this immigration) unless federal aid was forthcoming. To close down this entry point would cause havoc to immigration all over the United States. A general realization of the abuses between states that were immigration entry points and the federal government that would follow resulted in the first congressional immigration law in August 1882, which imposed a 50 cent tax upon every Italian passenger. Moreover, it excluded convicts, lunatics, idiots, and those libel to become a public charge from entering the country. The prohibition was not to apply to skilled labor needed for new industries, nor to artists, actors, lecturers, singers,

(1921) Uncle Sam putting the Quota Act in place. The act limits immigration to 3% of the number of foreign born nationals in the census of 1910.

> ## Angel Island
>
> Between 1910 and 1940, Asian immigrants were processed through Angel Island located in San Francisco Bay. Some of the 175,000 Chinese immigrants passed through Angel Island in a few days, but the average detention time for Chinese workers was two to three weeks and often several months. A few were forced to remain on the island for nearly two years.

and domestic servants; and individuals in the United States were not to be prevented from assisting the immigration of their relatives and personal friends.

1905 • ORGANIZED LABOR SUPPORTS RESTRICTIONS ~ While big business interests were chief defenders of an open gate policy, organized labor opposed it. Around 1905 employers began to make great efforts to check union growth, partly through the practicing of "balancing nationalities." Big business thought that by "balancing nationalities" there would not be enough of one particular group or nationality to unite and form unions. Up until that point there had been no clear-cut division between the big business that supported free immigration and the labor that worked for them.

1890S • RACIST INTELLIGENTSIA SUPPORT RESTRICTIONS ~ In 1894, the New England intelligentsia, worried about the future of their "race" and class, formed the Immigration Restriction League. Unprepared to commit itself to the exclusion of immigrants upon a frankly "racial" basis, the League hit upon the device of a literacy test as a more devious but equally effective method of excluding "undesirable classes" from southern and eastern Europe. Both Houses in Congress passed the bill but in his last days in office President Cleveland vetoed the measure as an unworthy repudiation of America's historic role as an asylum for the oppressed. Twenty years were to elapse before the campaign for a literacy test was carried to a successful conclusion.

1900-1930 • IMMIGRANT INFLUENCE ON LITERACY TEST RESTRICTIONS ~ With a relatively small percentage of voting immigrants from Eastern and Southern Europe one may ask, "Why did it take so long to finally pass the literacy test as law?" The force behind the opposition to the literacy test was the growing importance of foreign-born voters and the emergence of the "new" immigrants as an influential pressure group. As Table 7 shows, by 1930 there were significant numbers among the immigrant population that were of voting age. Until about 1900 the immigrant population, especially the Irish, associated with the Democratic Party in large enough numbers that it forced advocates of immigration restriction legislation to appeal to the Republican Party. But as an increasing number of Italian, Slavic, and Jewish voters became attracted to the Republican Party, the GOP was forced to take their wishes into account as well. This explains the strenuous efforts of Republican speaker Joe Cannon to defeat an attempt in 1906 to attach a literacy test

Table 7: Foreign Born Population By Country of Birth and Age 1930

	Population	Under 10	Under Age 10 Percent of Pop	Age 10 – 24 Percent of Pop	Age 24 – 25 Percent of Pop	Age 45 – 64 Percent of Pop	Age 65 & Older Percent of Pop
All Countries	13,366,407	149,479	1.1%	8.5%	41.8%	36.1%	12.4%
Italy	1,790,424	20,719	1.2%	9.1%	52.3%	31.7%	5.7%
Poland	1,268,583	5,691	0.4%	7.1%	53.6%	33.1%	5.8%
Germany	1,608,814	19,565	1.2%	6.4%	25.9%	40.5%	25.9%
Russia	1,153,624	3,183	0.3%	5.9%	50.8%	33.9%	6.1%
Canada	907,569	34,582	3.8%	16.9%	31.9%	33.1%	14.6%
England	808,672	8,015	1.0%	78.0%	33.9%	40.5%	17.3%

SOURCE: Compilation from *The World Almanac and Book of Facts*, 1915 to 1970

1900-1920

to an immigration bill. Equally significant was the omission of immigration restriction from the Republican platform between 1904 and 1912, which the party had regularly included for more than a decade before.

1900-1920s • NATIVISM RECEIVES A BIG PUSH WITH WORLD WAR I

What ultimately influenced the passage of the literacy act was derived from the anxieties provoked by the European War. World War I was a major turning point in the history of American protectionism – in the sense that Americans were very protective of their own, very new, nationality. The war made Americans aware, as never before, of the persistence of Old World ties, and thus, of their own disunity. The conflict between defending one's new country and staying loyal to one's heritage bred a strident demand for a new type of American attitude: a loyalty involving conformity to the generally accepted American concept of devotion to country, the English language, and traditions. This promotion of a nationalistic spirit, generally espousing being "100 percent American," proved to be more than just a war-time phenomenon. Persisting into the 1920s, it became an essential doctrine of the movement that carried the restrictionists to victory.

1916-1920 • BIAS AGAINST GERMANS

Germans became the victims of a fresh wave of xenophobia (fear and hatred of strangers and foreigners) that came in the wake of America's entry into war. The belligerent nationalism, which had earlier characterized the country's preparedness to go into war, now erupted into hysterical anti-Germanism. Despite the fact that the mass of German-Americans supported the declaration of war on Germany, wild rumors circulated of spying and sabotage. Zealous patriots, now thoroughly infected by the intolerant, coercive spirit of 100 percent Americanism, proclaimed that loyalty demanded the complete eradication of German culture. Accordingly, teaching German was in many places prohibited, German opera and music were shunned, and buildings with German names were re-christened; even sauerkraut became "liberty cabbage," while hamburgers turned into "Salisbury Steaks."

1910s • Immigrant Assimilation into Mainstream America ~ With the rise of wartime nationalism the Americanization movement underwent rapid metamorphosis. From 1915 onward, the Americanization of the immigrant became a patriot's duty, absorbing the energies of thousands of schools, churches, fraternal orders, patriotic societies, and civic and business organizations. In their eagerness to promote national unity, zealous patriots subjected immigrant groups to high-pressure sales campaigns designed to promote naturalization, the learning of English, and respect for American institutions and ideals. These had been the aims of the prewar Americanizers, too, but not until American nationalists began to demand a completely conformist loyalty was the effort to teach immigrants things such as personal hygiene and industrial safety jettisoned in favor of persuading them to forget their Old World heritage.

Many immigrants reacted bitterly. They felt humiliated at the suggestion that their cherished ways of life were proof of their inferiority. Having evolved from an instrument of social welfare into one of social solidarity, the Americanization movement survived briefly into the postwar era to play its part in the crusade against Bolshevism. With the arrival of Russians fleeing the Bolsheviks, an America convinced that a communist threat was brewing, fell completely under the domination of the super patriots.

(1940) Immigrants crowd a Brooklyn post office at the start of the four months they are allowed to register. They are asked to fill in forms and have their fingerprints taken in a U.S. effort to keep out fifth columnists, such as communist sympathizers.

1920s

The continuing concern for national homogeneity also explained the post war xenophobia. New nationalism turned its attention from resident aliens (foreign-born citizens) to the question of immigration restriction. Since the literacy test had been enacted in 1917, questions of immigration policy had remained largely in suspension. But resumption of large scale European immigration, coinciding as it did with sharp economic declines in 1920 and 1921 in Europe, stimulated fresh agitation for restrictions that ultimately reduced immigration to a trickle.

1920s • Anti-Semitism and Racism

During the early 1920s, anti-Semitism increased markedly, especially in the rural regions. Social discrimination against Jews increased, and an anti-Semitic ideology took form, focusing upon an alleged conspiracy by Jews and disseminated through such publications as Henry Ford's notorious *Dearborn Independent*. Anti-Semitism was partly responsible for the resurrection and astonishing growth of the Ku Klux Klan, which after 1920 spread like wildfire in the South and Middle West and which reached a membership peak of two and a half million by 1923. The heart of the Klan's nativism was virulent anti-Catholicism and anti-Semitism, although Klansmen perpetrated their terror on all racial, ethnic, and religious minorities.

This period also saw a rise in racist literature. Madison Grant's *Passing of the Great Race*, though originally published in 1916, found its largest audience at the end of World War I. The book pointed to the dangers that the Italians and other immigrants posed by what they called "mongrelizing" the American race. Thanks to the writings of a group of popular authors who had absorbed Grant's teachings, the racist philosophy of the intellectuals filtered down throughout all of America at the time. Especially influential in popularizing the doctrine of Nordic Superiority was a series of articles in 1922 in the *Saturday Evening Post* by Kenneth Roberts, who warned that a mixture of Nordic with Alpine and Mediterranean stock would produce only a worthless race of hybrids. About the same time, publication of the results of the United States Army's wartime psy-

Table 8: Jewish Immigration 1908 - 1943

	Total Immigration	Jewish	Percent Jewish
1908 - 1914	6,709,357	656,397	9.78%
1915 - 1920	1,602,680	79,921	4.99%
1921	805,558	119,036	14.70%
1922	309,556	53,524	17.30%
1923	522,919	49,719	4.50%
1924	706,896	49,489	7.07%
1925	294,314	10,267	3.30%
1926	335,175	11,483	3.40%
1927	307,225	11,639	3.80%
1928	279,678	12,479	4.46%
1929	241,700	11,526	4.77%
1930	97,239	5,692	5.86%
1931	35,576	2,755	7.74%
1932	23,068	2,372	10.28%
1933	29,470	4,134	14.03%
1934	34,456	4,837	13.84%
1935	36,329	6,252	17.21%
1936	50,244	11,352	22.59%
1937	67,895	19,736	29.07%
1938	82,998	43,450	52.35%
1939	70,756	36,945	52.21%
1940	51,776	23,737	45.85%
1942	28,781	10,608	36.86%
1943	23,725	4,705	19.83%

SOURCE: Compilation from *The World Almanac and Book of Facts*, 1915 to 1970

chological tests on soldiers helped further condition the public to racist thinking. The fact that soldiers from Southern and Eastern Europe had markedly lower IQ scores than those from Northern and Western Europe and the United States was thought to be conclusive proof of Nordic intellectual superiority.

1920-1930s • THE CONSEQUENCES OF RESTRICTION

It was American immigration policy that brought an end to the century long mass movement of peoples from Europe. The adoption of a quota system, heavily weighted in favor of natives of Northern and Western Europe, all but slammed the door on the Southern and Eastern Europeans who had formed the bulk of arrivals in the prewar and immediate post World War I periods. The result was that European immigration slumped from over 800,000 in 1921 to less than 150,000 by the end of the decade. From 1924, the national origins system doubled the British quota while drastically reducing those of Germany, Scandinavia, and the Irish Free State. Thus, despite the fact that German, Scandinavian, and Irish immigration had, during the twenties, outnumbered the British by almost three to one, Great Britain was now given a quota larger than the totals of all other countries in northwest Europe combined.

In the fall of 1930, in response to demands that immigration be further reduced during the economic crisis of the Great Depression, the Hoover administration ordered a more rigorous enforcement of the 1917 clause in the immigration act "prohibiting the admission of any persons likely to become a public charge." This strict reinforcement was not abandoned until 1937 and insured the exclusion of all but the most prosperous European immigrants. During the decade in which quotas were mostly unfilled, fewer than 350,000 Europeans entered the United States. And, in some years, more people left the country than entered it. The net gain of population from immigrants between 1931 and 1940 was negligible.

1930s • FLEEING NAZI GERMANY

During the 1920s, those who arrived from Europe were almost entirely relatives of those who had entered the United States earlier. But from 1933 onward immigration included a considerable proportion of refugees from Nazi Germany. As one can see from Table 8, this was particularly so after 1938, when the percent of Jewish immigrants rose from roughly 30 percent to over 50 percent of total immigration. This can be partly explained by the 1938 *Anschluss* (non-aggression pact) with Austria and the intensification of Hitler's anti-Semitic campaign. Since Congress refused to consider liberalizing the immigration laws during the Depression, only a fraction of the refugees were able to reach the United States. It is true that as early as 1934, President Roosevelt demonstrated some sympathy with the refugees by instructing American consuls to treat their applications for admission with all the humanity and consideration possible under the law. Moreover, in 1940 the situation was further eased when the State Department rescinded German quotas by permitting consuls outside Germany to issue visas to German refugees. Yet, as long as the Depression lasted, there was little inclination in America to lower the barriers imposed by the quota system, and the 250,000 refugees admitted to the United States in the period 1934-1941 came within the limits of the existing laws.

1933-1950

1933-1940 • European Brain Drain

In addition to being on a much smaller scale, the refugee influx differed in other ways from the mass movements of the nineteenth and early twentieth centuries. For one thing it was not the free flow of individuals, but a highly organized and regulated movement. For another, the refugees came from an entirely different background than the bulk of earlier immigrant populations. Largely, though not exclusively Jewish, they were predominantly middle class. These immigrants were of urban origin, mostly white-collar workers, professional and business people, and manufacturers. Many had achieved eminence in the arts, science, and scholarship; some of the best known were Albert Einstein, Thomas Mann, Walter Gropius, Bruno Walker, and Paul Tillich. No fewer than twelve of the refugees were Nobel Prize winners while hundreds of others were men and women of almost equal distinction.

The mere presence of this new type of refugee greatly enriched American life. Those immigrants with capital, for instance, introduced a variety of new industries to the United States and were responsible for making New York the world-trading center of the diamond and jewelry trades. Refugee scientists figured prominently in the development of the atomic bomb. Widely dispersed throughout the country, partly as a result of their occupations and partly because of the reluctance of Jews to incur nativist criticism by massing themselves together, this uniquely gifted and cultivated group did much to increase American appreciation of the best in European culture.

The immediate post World War II period demanded that most of the available ships be used to bring the soldiers home from Europe, and emigrant transportation facilities remained extremely limited. But as conditions improved, the continuing prosperity of the United States attracted appreciable numbers of immigrants from the countries favored by the quota system. From Britain and Germany especially came the skilled artisans, people from small business, and clerical workers who had bleak futures at home. In addition to independent immigrants came the European wives, fiancées, and children of American service personnel. Quota requirements were relaxed for their benefit, and some 150,000 wives and fiancées, 25,000 children, and a few hundred husbands entered the United States from Europe in the five years after the war. Further amendment to the law in 1947 in favor of Asians permitted the entry of nearly 5,000 Chinese and about 800 Japanese wives.

1946-1950 • Post World War II Immigrants

Prior to a presidential directive of December 1945, refugees had been given only priority within the existing quotas. But since most displaced persons were from countries with low quotas, only 41,000 were able to enter the United States between 1945-1948. Finally, the Displaced Persons Act of 1948, as amended in 1950, provided for the admission of some 400,000 people during a four-year period. As Table 9 shows,

Table 9

1948	All Countries	Europe	Asia
Emigration from U.S.	20,875	10,258	3,220
Immigration into U.S.	170,570	103,544	10,739

SOURCE: Compilation from *The World Almanac and Book of Facts*, 1915 to 1970

European Immigration during 1948 was extensive. By the end of this four-year period, the great majority of those uprooted by World War II had been resettled.

1920s • FILIPINO IMMIGRATION ~ The decline of European immigration in the late 1920s led to increased arrivals from those areas exempted from the quota system. One such area was the Philippine Islands, which for a decade after 1924, enjoyed the distinction of being the only Asian country whose inhabitants the United States had not excluded, mainly because the Hawaiian Islands needed farm labor. In late 1920 there were only about 5,000 Filipinos in the continental United States. A decade later, the number was more than 50,000. Almost wholly male, the Filipino immigrants were heavily concentrated in the Pacific Coast States, where they were chiefly employed as seasonal agricultural workers.

Though the number of arrivals had been relatively small, a demand for Filipino exclusion by the American public grew steadily after 1928. In the forefront of this agitation were the west coast labor unions, though a strong resistance came from patriotic societies anxious to support Asian exclusion. During 1929 and 1930 came a rash of anti-Filipino demonstrations in California and Washington. The chief complaint in the clashes between Filipino and whites was the alleged immorality, criminality, and the inability of Filipinos to assimilate into American culture. Ultimately, the dispute was ended by the Depression when most of the Filipino laborers in the United States became destitute as agricultural production plummeted in the Dust Bowl and they had to have assistance to return home. This fact, combined with the 1934 Philippine Independence Act, resulted in making Filipino population in the United States negligible.

(1950) A woman boards a bus to Chicago with her children. They have just arrived in New York on the last boatload of displaced persons from Europe.

1924 • WESTERN HEMISPHERE IMMIGRATION ~ The 1924 decision to exempt the Western Hemisphere from the quota system was in part a concession to the southwest ranchers and farmers who had grown to rely heavily upon Mexican labor. But another influence was the strength of Pan-Americanism. The restrictive immigration laws were essentially an expression of American antipathy to Old World traditions; as a consequence of its isolationism, the United States tended to establish closer relationships to other American countries so it was natural to put immigration from them on a special footing. For more than a decade after 1924, restrictionists pressed for the abolition of the Western Hemisphere exemption. But, although Mexican immigration was checked by administrative action during the Depression, every demand that immigration from the Americas should be placed on a quota basis was rejected in the interests of what eventually became known as the "Good Neighbor" policy.

1920s • Canadian Immigration ~ For a time, the most active immigration was from Canada. Since the American Revolution, Canada and the United States had been regularly exchanging populations, the tide at one time setting in a southerly direction, at another to the north. And while the balance had swung in Canada's favor during the settlement of her prairie provinces just before World War I, the 1920s saw a wave of Canadian immigration into the United States. By 1930, however, the immigration from Canada had largely run its course. As a result only about 100,000 Canadians entered the United States during the 1930s; after World War II the rapid industrialization in Canada created no incentive for its inhabitants to move to the United States.

1900-1920s • Mexican Immigration ~ More persistent, and more conspicuous, was the immigrant influx from the southwest border. Immigration from Mexico began on a large scale about 1900, when railroad-building and phenomenally rapid agricultural expansion in the Southwest created a demand for cheap, unskilled, migratory labor. During the next thirty years, as the citrus fruit and vegetable industries boomed and the center of cotton cultivation marched steadily westward, Mexican immigration increased proportionally. The number of Mexicans who officially entered the United States rose from 49,000 in 1901–1910 to 219,000 in 1911–1920 and then to 459,000 in 1921–1930. But actual arrivals, especially in the 1920s, were well in excess of these figures because many Mexicans entered illegally due to their inability to fulfill the literacy test requirements, and because of the expense and delay involved in obtaining American visas. From 1930 to 1945 American labor contractors were smuggling large numbers of so-called "wetbacks" (they were referred to as 'wet backs' because their backs were wet after swimming across the Rio Grande into the United States.

By 1930 there was a considerable concentration of Mexicans in Colorado and Kansas. By 1934, the majority were to be found in Texas, Arizona, and California. Mexican laborers were employed chiefly in the cultivation and harvesting of fruits, vegetables, cotton, and sugar cane. In the production of all of these commodities these immigrants formed the backbone of the Southwest's labor force. In 1940, an acute shortage of labor in the Southwest caused the United States to reach an agreement with Mexico. From 1942 onward, the U.S. government undertook the organized recruitment of Mexicans for seasonal agricultural work and railroad maintenance. By 1945 the number of Mexicans born in the United States exceeded two and a half million, and both legal and illegal immigration swelled the total even further. The increasing mechanization of the farm industry narrowed the employment opportunities in the Southwest and caused the population to fan out in the 1950s, first to the Rocky Mountain states and then to the Middle West. There were also increasing numbers entering industial jobs, especially in Chicago, Toledo, and Detroit.

1920-1930 • Feeling at Home in America ~ By drastically limiting the volume of European immigration, the restrictive policy adopted in the 1920s accelerated the Americanization of those groups that had come earlier. With reinforcements no longer arriving from across the ocean, ties with Europe were gradually weakened. The gradual disintegration of the ethnic ghettos helped produce a similar result. As immigrants grew more familiar with conditions in the United States, they burst from their occupational and residential confines and moved nearer to the mainstream of American life. Table 10 shows the migration from New York City proper to the suburbs from 1920 to 1930.

During the prosperous decade of the 1920s, more than 90,000 of New York's Italians moved out of the city into suburbs. The population of the congested districts of East Harlem and the Lower East Side moved to Westchester and Long Island. Similar movements were discernible among the Italians of Chicago, Boston and Philadelphia. The depression slowed down the exodus, but by 1940 less than half of New York's Italian-born immigrants lived in the so-called Italian areas. The same tendency toward dispersion was to be found among the Poles of Buffalo, the Czechs of Chicago, and the Boston Irish. Although each group tended to re-congregate in the suburbs, they were no longer restricted to their urban contacts. For the immigrant, escape from the ghetto was the first great stride toward the anonymity of American middle-class life.

To the second generation, which had never known the old country, the ethnic tie became increasingly meaningless. Culturally estranged from their parents by American education, and wanting nothing more than to become and to be accepted as Americans, many second-generation immigrants made deliberate efforts to rid themselves of their heritage. The adoption of American clothes, speech, and interests, often accompanied by the shedding of an exotic surname, were all part of the process whereby cultural customs were repudiated as a means of improving status.

1942-1945 • ASIAN AMERICANS DURING WORLD WAR II ~ For Asian Americans it was a different story. Despite the fact that this was the second time within twenty-five years that the United States had been at war with Germany, and most Americans regarded Germany as the

Table 10: Foreign Born Population in New York City 1920 - 1930

	Manhattan	Brooklyn	Bronx	Queens	Staten Island	Total 1930	Total 1920
All Countries	641,618	868,770	477,342	266,150	39,500	2,293,400	1,991,547
Italy	117,740	193,435	67,732	50,307	11,036	440,250	390,832
Russia	69,685	219,483	135,210	16,571	1,482	442,431	479,797
Irish	96,861	53,571	38,816	27,139	4,244	220,631	203,450
Germany	69,111	56,134	43,349	64,007	4,987	237,588	194,154
Poland	59,120	106,714	55,969	14,344	2,192	238,339	145,679

SOURCE: Compilation from *The World Almanac and Book of Facts*, 1915 to 1970

major enemy, most Americans did not question the loyalty of Americans of German origin. Less fortunate were the Japanese aliens and the Americans of Japanese ancestry. For half a century or more, the people of the nation at large, especially those on the West Coast, had built up a stereotyped image of the Asian immigrant as a sly, unscrupulous, and subversive element. Japan's secret attack on Pearl Harbor supported this stereotype. Thus in the early months of 1942, with a series of Japanese victories, few voices were raised in opposition of a great wrong; more than 110,000 people of Japanese ancestry, two thirds of whom were American citizens, were transferred by the U.S. Army to ten relocation centers in the isolated parts of the western, mountain, and plains states. There, behind barbed wire and under armed guard, the majority of evacuees sat out the war, cut off from their homes, deprived of their occupations and much of their property, and denied constitutional and legal rights.

Not surprisingly, the evacuees were severely shaken, sometimes demoralized, by the treatment they received. More than 5,000 Japanese Americans renounced their American citizenship during the course of the war, though a number of them subsequently reclaimed it, and a slightly larger number returned to Japan at the first opportunity. Yet the majority remained staunchly loyal to the United States, and more than 12,000 people born of Japanese parentage served with honor in American combat units during World War II.

Having proved their loyalty, most Japanese Americans in the postwar era were able to readjust and even realize greater success than before the war. Though the majority returned to the Pacific coast, others spread throughout the nation and developed flourishing communities in cities like Chicago, Minneapolis, Denver, Philadelphia, and Cleveland. At the same time, a broader range of jobs became available to them. Before 1941 most Japanese Americans had been farmers, gardeners, fisherman, and domestic servants. Because of the wartime shortage of workers, however, considerable numbers were allowed to leave relocation camps to take up industrial and other employment in the Middle West and the East. After 1945, with discrimination against them on the wane, even in the far West, Japanese Americans became

(1942) Civilian Exclusion Order issued in San Francisco forbidding all persons of Japanese origin, both alien and non-alien, to enter certain military areas.

(circa 1955) Interior view of a hallway inside a building on Ellis Island, with desks, chairs and bedding stacked in the hall and paint flaking from the walls and ceiling, New York City. The Ellis Island station was permanently closed in 1955.

1960-1990 • REFUGEES, FAMILY REUNIFICATION, AND SPECIAL SKILLS

~ In 1960, Ellis Island was a crumbling ruin. Abandoned as an immigrant landing depot six years earlier, it seemed to conform to the belief of many Americans that mass immigration was a closed chapter in American history. Immigration was negligible during the Depression and World War II era, and had decreased during the 1950s to a mere 250,000 people a year, barely a quarter of the record levels of 1901–1910. Nor did any appreciable increase seem likely, for the restrictionist national-origins system still remained in place. Under that system the favored countries of Northern and Western Europe received no less than 85 percent of the total quota, which they never used, while countries in Southern and Eastern Europe were limited to quotas of a few thousand per year and Japan, China, and other Asian countries were each allowed only 100 immigrants. Western Hemisphere countries were exempt from the quota system but the flow from them had been severely checked. Immigration appeared to be subsiding and even the refugee problem seemed manageable since nearly all of the 30 million uprooted World War II Europeans had been resettled.

However, far from being over, mass immigration was about to resurge. Immigration and Naturalization Service officials counted 3.3 million immigrants in the 1960s, 4.4 million in the 1970s, and 7.3 million in the 1980s. Yet these totals

1960-1990

took no account of an illegal influx whose dimensions can only be guessed at but certainly ran into the several millions. More striking even than the scale of movement was its change in composition. Of the 41 million immigrants who had arrived in the United States between 1820 and 1960, no less than 85 percent had come from Europe, only 13 percent from western hemisphere countries, and a mere two percent from Asia. Even as late as the 1950s Europeans made up over one-half of all the newcomers. Starting in the 1960s, however, a dramatic progressive shift occurred toward Third World countries. By the 1980s, Europe was contributing barely ten percent of the total, whereas the Western Hemisphere countries were sending 45 percent and Asia was contributing an additional 41 percent. A further related departure from past patterns was a different demographic profile of immigrants. During the nineteenth and early twentieth centuries a substantial majority of the immigrants had been male, mostly young and usually unmarried. After 1960 females outnumbered males; there were more married immigrants than single ones, and while people of prime working age continued to predominate, their total share dropped. There was also a major switch, among legal immigrants at least, from mainly unskilled labor to a highly educated labor force. Whereas in the 1900s, 70 percent of the arrivals had been either laborers or domestic servants, the proportion in the 1970s had dropped to less than 20 percent, and the proportion of professional, technical, and managerial workers had risen from one percent to nearly 25 percent.

1965-1976 • NEW IMMIGRATION RESTRICTIONS ~ The Immigration

(1957) Hungarian refugee Bela Feher with his wife Lucy and their three children Vera, Cseve and Michael, walking along Main Street in Patchogue, Long Island, their new home.

and Nationality Act of October 1, 1965, which became effective on July 1, 1968, swept away the national origins system. Instead, this new act applied to all countries in the Eastern Hemisphere a complex system of preferences and priorities based either on family unification, the possession of needed skills, or refugee status. The act imposed a 20,000 person maximum for any one country in the Eastern Hemisphere. The available visas were granted as follows: 74 percent to non-immediate relatives of people already in the United States, 20 percent to persons with special skills, and the remaining six percent to refugees. Far from being a nation with "open borders" this new policy was designed to maintain immigration at existing levels. The Eastern Hemisphere total limit of 170,000 per year was scarcely more generous than the 155,000 previously allowed under the old system. What is more, Western Hemisphere countries, who were never before subject to numerical limitations, were given a total of 120,000 spots—on a first come, first served basis. Thus, for a time the United States had two immigration systems, one for each hemisphere. This lasted until 1976, when the 20,000 per-country limit and the preference categories were extended to the Western Hemisphere.

1960s • IMMIGRATION BOOM ~ The result of this new act would create a massive brain-drain from developing countries and increase Asian immigration by 500 percent, a totally unexpected outcome. Nor was it foreseen that it would stimulate illegal immigration. Further, the Act's framers would have been surprised to learn that close relatives and refugees would have been admitted in such numbers that, in practice, admission would greatly exceed the annual legal ceiling of 290,000.

Table 11: U.S. Immigration
(In thousands)

	1951 - 1960	1961 – 1970
From All Countries	2,515.5	3,322
Asia Immigration	153.3	427.8
China	25.2	109.8
India	3.4	10.3
Japan	46.3	40.0
Jordan	5.8	11.7
Korea	6.2	34.5
Lebanon	4.5	15.2
Philippines	19.3	98.4
Turkey	3.5	10.1
Vietnam	2.7	4.2
America Immigration	996.9	1,716.4
Argentina	19.5	49.7
Brazil	13.8	29.3
Canada	378.0	413.0
Columbia	18.6	72.0
Cuba	78.9	208.5
Dominican Republic	9.9	93.3
Ecuador	9.8	36.8
El Salvador	5.9	15.0
Haiti	4.4	34.5
Honduras	6.0	15.7
Mexico	299.8	453.9
West Indies	29.8	133.9

SOURCE: Compilation from *The World Almanac and Book of Facts*, 1915 to 1970

Congressional expectations were that immigration from Southern and Eastern Europe would grow as a result of the 1965 reforms. This proved to be true during the succeeding decade, when there was a substantial influx from Italy, Greece, Portugal, and Yugoslavia. But as Table 11 shows, this is clearly not what happened. Once the backlog of relatives waiting to emigrate under the quota system had been admitted, immigration from Italy, Greece, Portugal,

1980-1990

and Yugoslavia fell. Meanwhile Asia, the Caribbean, and Latin America were steadily gathering strength. In 1965, Canada, Mexico, the United Kingdom, and Germany headed the list of countries sending immigrants to the United States; by 1973, the largest immigrant populations were from Mexico, the Philippines, Cuba, and Korea. Table 12 shows not only how great the number of Mexican immigrants had become by 1976 but also that China (including Hong Kong and Taiwan), India, and the Dominican Republic had ousted Canada and the United Kingdom from the top ten countries providing the most immigrants. Thereafter, Third World countries predominantly filled the numerical quotas and countries like Vietnam, Iran, Lebanon, Ethiopia, El Salvador, and Haiti became major contributors to the U.S. immigrant population. Just as the sailing ship and then the steam ship had bridged the Atlantic for nineteenth-century Europeans, so too did cheap airplane travel bring the United States within reach for Asians and Latin Americans, or at least for those with enough money to pay for an airplane ticket and sometimes for a bribe to secure an exit permit.

Table 12

Immigrants 1976 -1986

Mexico	720,000
Vietnam	425,000
Philippines	379,000
Korea	363,000
China	331,000
Cuba	258,000
Dominican Republic	211,000
Jamaica	200,000
United Kingdom	150,000
Canada	129,000

SOURCE: Compilation from *The World Almanac and Book of Facts*, 19

1980-1990 • POPULATION CENTERS OF THE NEW IMMIGRANTS

Despite the large influx of Third World immigrants, the fears of some Americans that the nation was being swamped were off the mark. Although the foreign-born population rose from 5.2 percent in 1960 to an estimated 7.8 percent in 1990, it remained low in comparison to the peak of 14.7 percent in 1910. Yet in some states immigration had more of an impact than on the rest of the country. Almost 70 percent of the newcomers settled in six states—California, New York, Florida, Texas, Illinois, and New Jersey—with 40 percent of those settling in New York and California alone.

Table 13 shows the 1980 population distribution of the largest immigrant populations. In 1985, three cities—Los Angeles, Miami, and New York—had populations of more than 25 percent foreign-born. Each of these three cities had its own distinctive ethnic patchwork. Miami's immigrants were overwhelmingly Hispanic, mostly Cuban. Los Angeles was more cosmopolitan with large resident populations of Iranians, Salvadorians, Armenians, Chinese, Koreans, Vietnamese, Filipinos, and Arabs—more than two-thirds of the population was already Hispanic, with Mexicans easily the largest group. In New York City, the mix of immigrants was bewilderingly broad. In 1985, more Dominicans lived in New York than in any city but Santo Domingo; more Haitians than anywhere but Port-au-Prince; more Greeks than anywhere but Athens; the city also had more Jamaican, Russian, and Chinese residents than anywhere outside Jamaica, the U.S.S.R., and mainland China. In addition, there were thousands of people from Ireland, Korea, India, and Ecuador. Moreover, there were sizable Ethiopian, Argentinean, Afghan, and Senegalese communities.

1965 • SKILLED LABOR ~ The preference given to skilled workers by the 1965 immigration law opened the door widest to Asians. While in 1973 fewer than 73 percent of immigrants possessed technical or professional skills, 54 percent of those were Asians and within this group, 83 percent were Indians. Most of the educated immigrants were scientists, engineers, managers, computer analysts, and doctors. These professionals were not only attracted to the United States by high salaries but also by working conditions and resources not available at home. In the 1950s the chronic shortage of physicians in American hospitals had been met largely by Europeans and Canadians, but after 1965 the new influx of doctors came from the Philippines, Korea, Iran, India, and Thailand. By 1974, foreign-born physicians made up one-fifth of the American total. There were more Iranian doctors practicing in New York City in 1974 than in the whole of Iran.

1965 • FAMILY REUNIFICATION ~ The arrival of Asian professionals represented only the first wave of an escalating immigrant movement. The family unification provision of the 1965 law allowed a perfectly legal but wholly unanticipated pattern of immigration known as "pyramiding" to develop. The case of a Filipino nurse, cited in *Time* magazine in 1982, exemplified this process. Having entered the country on a temporary work permit ten years earlier, she obtained resident status, which enabled her to have her parents admitted. A few years later, having become a citizen, she sponsored her nine brothers and sisters. The brothers and sisters, in turn, secured entry visas for their children and spouses. A total of forty-five people were admitted into the United States thanks to the one nurse who originally immigrated. The children and spouses of the brothers and sisters then started their own "pyramids."

1960-1990s • MEXICAN IMMIGRANTS ~ Mexico contributed more immigrants to the United States between 1960 and 1990 than any other country—about 18 percent of the total admitted. The official statistics reveal a steadily rising tide; 450,000 in the 1960s; 640,000 in the 1970s; 1,600,000 in the 1980s. If undocumented aliens could be included, the total for the years 1960–1990 would be substantially higher—perhaps as many as five million. Along with heavy immigration, an exceptionally high birth rate contributed to the phenomenal growth of

Table 13: 1980 Population

	Total	White	Black	American Indian	Asian	Other	Spanish Origin
Los Angeles	2,966,763	1,816,683	505,208	16,595	196,824	432,253	815,989
Miami	346,931	231,069	87,110	329	1,861	26,562	19,087
New York City	7,071,030	4,293,695	1,784,124	11,824	231,505	794,882	1,405,957

SOURCE: Compilation from *The World Almanac and Book of Facts*, 1980

the Mexican population. The population has increased by 30 percent each decade since 1960, reaching an estimated ten-and-a-half million by 1985. The Chicano population remained heavily concentrated in the Southwest; in 1980 nearly half were in California, another third in Texas, and large numbers in Arizona and New Mexico. Mainly poor and unskilled, Chicanos lagged behind other groups socially and economically. Unemployment rates for them as a group were well above the national average. They worked largely in low-paying, dead end jobs as unskilled laborers. Educational levels were likewise depressed; the Chicano drop-out rate in Los Angeles high schools was between 35 and 50 percent. Social scientists seeking reasons why the nation's second largest minority group failed to experience higher achievement pointed to a reluctance to learn English or to put down roots because of the proximity of the Mexican border. They chose to live in cultural isolation within self-contained communities, maintaining strong linguistic, psychological and family ties with Mexico. Through frequent return visits, Chicanos viewed themselves as sojourners rather than permanent residents. One indication of this tendency was demonstrated in the much lower naturalization rates among Mexicans.

1963 • CARIBBEAN IMMIGRATION ~ Rivaling Mexico as a source of immigration were the densely populated and impoverished subtropical islands of the Caribbean, formerly Spanish, Dutch, British or French colonies. Apart from Cubans, the largest group of Caribbean immigrants were Dominicans, Haitians, and Jamaicans. In the 1960s a sizable proportion of blacks from the Dominican Republic and Haiti were professional, middle class people but later the great majority consisted of illiterate peasants fleeing extreme rural poverty and political instability. The immigrant Dominicans and Haitians clustered mainly in and around New York City. There, like the Puerto Ricans immigrants, they were restricted by their lack of education and skills to poorly paid factory and service jobs. In addition, they were cut off culturally from native American blacks.

West Indian immigration began when Great Britain adopted a restrictive policy in 1962. By the 1970s, immigration from the newly independent countries of Jamaica, Trinidad and Tobago, Guyana, Barbados, and Bahamas had grown to 25,000 a year and thousands came illegally. As in the past, a high proportion were professional, white collar workers, but there were also growing numbers of female domestic servants. Although dispersed in places as far as Miami and Los Angeles, the great majority flocked to New York City. Their passion for education gave the West Indians a head start over other immigrants, and by every measure of achievement they were highly successful. By the early 1970s their median family income was 40 percent higher than that of American blacks and they owned half the black businesses in New York City. Social contacts with other American blacks remained limited, and intermarriage was rare.

1945-1990 • REFUGEES ~ Between 1945 and 1990 an estimated three million aliens, or foreign-born residents, were admitted into the United States as refugees—about one quarter of the total immigrant population. Once admitted, they were treated with unprecedented liberality by the federal government. Whereas regular immigrants were left to fend for themselves, successive administrations housed refugees, and paid for resettlement, health care, education and general assistance. As American generosity to refugees was at times greater than the generosity shown by other countries, it was also selective and aimed at supporting anti-communist foreign policy. The Refugee Escape acts of 1957 and 1965 defined refugees as people fleeing communism or communist-dominated lands. This rather loose definition served as a measuring stick for admission to the United States that allowed over 90 percent of the refugees admitted after 1945 to come from countries with Marxist governments. They included 875,000 Cubans, 750,000 Indochinese, and at least 600,000 Eastern Europeans from behind the Iron Curtain. By contrast, there was an unsympathetic reception from those fleeing right wing dictatorships friendly to and sometimes supported by the United States. The refugee act of 1980 provided that refugees thenceforth be admitted in limited numbers—50,000 per year. It also redefined refugee to mean "persons fleeing persecution or fear of persecution." The extended refugee quota soon proved to be too low and had to be increased more than once. The Executive (presidential) Branch had the sole discretion to determine who qualified as a refugee, and it freely admitted applicants from communist countries while making only token efforts to assist refugees from other countries.

1960-1980 • CUBAN REFUGEES

In the thirty years after Fidel Castro came to power in Cuba, nearly 10 percent of its population emigrated to the United States. They came in three main waves. The first, numbering about 155,000, began with the Cuban revolution in 1959 and accelerated until the Cuban Missile Crisis of 1962, which led to suspension of direct flights from the United States to Cuba. After three years, a second wave arrived, bolstered by Castro's announcement that anyone who wished to leave Cuba could do so, and when President Johnson proclaimed an open door for Cubans. The two governments established a daily airlift; by the time it ended in 1973, over 380,000 Cubans had emigrated. A third wave came in the spring of 1980, when Castro suddenly announced that any Cuban could leave if his or her American relatives came to the port of Mariel to claim them. The offer triggered a remarkable sea-lift. Cubans from all over the United States converged at Key West, hiring vessels to conduct an emergency rescue operation. Angered and embarrassed by Castro's radical policy shift, the Carter administration vacillated in its commitment to accept these Cubans. Having originally attempted to stop the chaotic flow of immigrants to Florida, Carter offered the refugees "an

(1960) A billboard on the Miami waterfront after Fidel Castro came to power, proclaiming Cuba's liberation from a dictatorship and inviting American support.

1960-1980

open heart with open arms", only to put a dramatic halt to it all after 130,000 Cubans arrived in less than five months.

The Cuban immigrants of 1959-1962 were more truly refugees than their successors in that they were strongly anti-Castro and were possibly in political danger. They were extremely well educated, brought money with them, along with considerable skill. At first many regarded themselves as temporary exiles. But after the Bay of Pigs disaster, in which private Cuban American citizens attempted to invade Cuba with the clandestine assistance of the U.S. government, they gradually became reconciled to the fact that they were in the United States to stay. Those who followed between 1965 and 1973 differed from the first in two ways: they came for economic rather than political reasons and they were mostly blue-collar workers. The 1980 wave represented a further downward shift in socioeconomic status: the new Cuban immigrants were generally poor and unskilled and a large portion were single men. As it was later revealed, the 1980 wave was Castro's attempt to rid Cuba of its undesirables and criminals. The climate and proximity to Cuba explains why the first wave settled mainly in Miami. Despite the efforts of the United States government to disperse the subsequent arrivals, Miami's appeal persisted. In 1975, more than 40 percent of the Cubans living in the United States resided in Miami.

Table 14: 1980 Population

	Black	Hispanic
Florida	1,342,478	857,898
Miami	87,110	19,087

SOURCE: Compilation from *The World Almanac and Book of Facts*, 1980

The relative affluence and anti-Communist fervor of the first wave of immigrants earned the Cubans a warm welcome, but later comers, especially in the 1980 wave, received an unfriendly reception, especially because of the criminal element of some of the Cuban immigrants. The sudden growth of the Cuban population overwhelmed the communities of southern Florida, besides touching off an alarming crime wave. The simultaneous arrival of 30,000 Haitians added further to the region's problems. Some establishments moved out, while poor Miami blacks, fearful of being crowded out of jobs, vented their resentment in riots.

Because of the affluence and education of the first Cuban immigrants, and because of the significant voting power they possessed, the Cubans in Miami became increasingly influential, both locally and in national political campaigns, fiercely objecting to any U.S. policy that would strengthen Castro's stronghold on the country, from banning sugar cane imports to opposing returning Elian Gonzales—the Cuban boy who was rescued at sea when his ship full of refugees sank—to his father.

1975 • VIETNAMESE REFUGEES

Before the fall of Saigon, in April 1975, there had been little immigration from Indochina, except for a few thousand Vietnamese wives of American servicemen. But the sudden communist victory in the Vietnam War precipitated the panic-stricken flight of thousands of refugees. Vietnamese who had served the American-supported Thieu regime feared Vietcong reprisals and hastened to escape by any means. They were joined by those who simply found the prospect of communist rule intolerable. By the end of 1975, 130,000 Vietnamese had found refuge in the United States. Their arrival was both resented by those fearing job competition and by others who disapproved of America's involvement in Vietnam. In an effort to ally the public, the government attempted to disperse the Vietnamese throughout the country, but within months they had congregated through secondary migrations in states like California and Texas which had long-established Asian communities.

1980s • Russian Refugees ~ The changing face of Soviet Communism in the late 1980s created a refugee emergency which posed considerable problems for the United States. In the wake of President Gorbachev's sweeping reform program in 1987, separatist movements manifested themselves. Together with the Armenian earthquake in December 1988, these events exacerbated the American refugee problem. Even without these two events the refugee problem had reached huge dimensions with the liberalization of the Soviet immigration policy. For years the United States had pressured the U.S.S.R. to allow its people, especially its Jews, to emigrate freely. When Gorbachev relaxed restrictions in 1987, the United States proved unable or unwilling to accommodate more than a portion of the rapidly escalating number of refugees clamoring for admission.

Perhaps 80 percent of those who wanted to leave the Soviet Union were Jews. They were alarmed at the rise in ethnic nationalism that had renewed anti-Semitic feeling. The overwhelming majority of Jewish refugees wanted to go to the United States, and growing numbers were able to do so. Notwithstanding the bureaucratic delays in obtaining an exit visa, the limited number of direct flights to the United States, and the requirement that immigrants could not take more than $140 with them, the number of Soviet refugees entering the United States soared from a handful in the early 1980s to 8,000 in 1987, 19,000 in 1988, and 43,000 in 1989. If the initial American response was generous, it gradually became less so. The growing scale of the movement alarmed officials as early as the summer of 1988. The American Embassy in Moscow, inundated by applications from Jews eager to leave, was forced to suspend the requirements of refugee visas. The rising costs at home to relocate and resettle these refugees was estimated in the tens of billions of dollars.

Many of the newly arrived Soviet Americans settled in Los Angeles, which had a long-established Russian community. Other Soviet Jews gravitated to the east coast, half to New York, especially Brighton Beach at the southern tip of Brooklyn whose Jewish character dates back to the 1930s. Few of the new arrivals were religious; many had never been to a synagogue and some were of mixed marriages. A large portion were professionals and skilled technicians—engineers, computer programmers, scientist and teachers—for whom jobs were hard to find because their qualifications were not recognized and they lacked proficiency in English. Many were forced into low level employment, others faced the prospect of unemployment for the first time in their lives. Since culture shock was acute, there was not a little disillusionment. Soviet Jewish women, however, entered the work force more freely than the men.

1990s • Illegal Aliens ~ The most recent concern of United States immigration authorities has been people entering the country illegally. By far one

(1948) Members of the Texas Border Patrol guarding illegal Mexican immigrants captured close to the Mexican border. They will be questioned in the hope they have information leading to the capture of the gangs of murderers who prey on the captured immigrants returning to Mexico.

Table 15: 1996 Estimate of the Numbers of Illegal Aliens and the Source Countries

Country	1996
Mexico	2,700,000
El Salvador	335,000
Guatemala	165,000
Canada	120,000
Haiti	105,000
Philippines	95,000
Honduras	90,000
Poland	70,000
Nicaragua	70,000
Bahamas	70,000
Colombia	65,000
Ecuador	55,000
Dominican Republic	50,000
Trinidad & Tobago	50,000
Jamaica	50,000
Pakistan	41,000
India	33,000
Dominica	32,000
Peru	30,000
Korea	30,000
Other	744,000
Total	5,000,000

SOURCE: The Immigration and Naturalization Service, 1996

1990s of the largest voting concerns of the very late twentieth century in California, Texas, New York, and Florida is the issue of illegal aliens. It has prompted so much controversy that the issue alone tends to divide these states, and even parts of the country, along ethnic roots.

The Immigration and Naturalization Service estimated there were five million illegal aliens living in the United States in 1996; 275,000 are added to their number every year. It is also estimated that over one million transient illegal aliens are in the United States at any given time. These estimates would be much higher if the U.S. had not given amnesty to nearly three million illegal aliens in 1986, allowing them to become legal aliens.

ARGUMENTS SUPPORTING THE RESTRICTION OF ALIENS

ILLEGAL ALIENS UNDERMINE LEGAL IMMIGRATION • One of the biggest arguments against illegal immigration is that the presence of illegal immigrants undermines the ability of people waiting to get into the United States legally. Over three-and-a-half million eligible people are waiting to be admitted as immigrants to the U.S.; some of them have been on that list for eighteen years. Illegal aliens are accused of not only 'jumping the line' in front of those waiting legally but also of disrespecting the United States itself by ignoring its laws. About half of all illegal aliens enter the United States legally (on tourists or student visas, for example) and then stay on illegally. The other half enter completely illegally by hiding in cargo storage areas, or crossing the large, unguarded United States border.

THE COST OF ILLEGAL IMMIGRATION • One of the oldest arguments against free unrestricted immigration is that it hurts employment in the United States. It is estimated that illegal aliens displace 650,000 American workers every year, at a cost of $3.5 billion a year. In addition it is argued that the cheap labor that illegal immigration provides depresses the wages and working conditions of the working poor.

The U.S. welfare system comes under attack from many different directions but illegal aliens pose a serious problem for the system. What is the U.S. government to do with the very poor and the very sick? On the one hand, should these immigrants be entitled to the same privileges of legal residents because they have not paid for these services through taxes? On the other hand, should the U.S. government let someone suffer, die, or infect the rest of the population? This raises the following dilemma. Currently, many illegal aliens are allowed to receive welfare without fear of deportation. But some abuse this law by document fraud. In many U.S. cities, false documents can be bought on the street for as little as $40. With false documents, an illegal alien's "right" to work or to receive welfare goes unquestioned.

Document fraud and the debate over welfare adds additional cost to the United States government. With the cost of displacing American workers, the cost of giving welfare to needy illegal aliens, and the cost of providing them general services, it is estimated that the annual cost of illegal immigrants is $19 billion (even after giving credit for their tax contributions).

PREFERENTIAL TREATMENT • In order to understand twentieth century America one must be able to understand its inhabitants. Because the United States was and continues to be founded by immigrants, immigration may be one of the keys to that understanding. U.S. immigration and immigration policy has frequently changed and evolved during the twentieth century. From the predominant populations of eastern and southern Europeans at the beginning of the century to the melange of different countries by the end of the century, the influence of immigrants is difficult to assess. However, United States immigration policy is a little easier to pinpoint.

United States immigration policy was unrestricted until the twentieth century. Cultural typecasting of certain people from certain countries caused the original policy change. These misconceptions changed citizens' sympathy for immigration. Examples of these American cultural perceptions can be seen in the early restriction policies toward Asians and the country quotas against Southern and Eastern Europeans. These quotas were so severe that finally a point was reached where very few people were allowed to immigrate at all during the 1920s to 1940s.

RELIGIOUS AND POLITICAL FAVORITISM • Religious preference or bias also played an important role in immigration policy. Typecasting of Jews initially caused restrictive policies towards them. However, once World War II pointed out the dangers of stereotyping people, policies towards Jews reversed. Jewish people then became the favored of the religious immigrant groups to such an extent that in 1980, the United States admitted even non-practicing Jews from Russia seemingly without question. Certainly, the United States, political relationship with a certain country forged its immigration policy. For example, Cubans before Castro's takeover were not given the preferential treatment they were later given in the 1970s and 1980s.

PREFERENCE TO FAMILY MEMBERS • The one policy that has remained steadfast throughout the twentieth century is the partiality given to family members of current U.S. citizens or residents. Family unity has been the cornerstone of American immigration policy since it began. Even the extremes such as the pyramiding effect of the late twentieth century were not rescinded in the name of family ties.

GROWING OPPOSITION TO IMMIGRANTS • In 1994, the debate over immigration had become heated once more. In polls broken down by ethnicity, white Americans appear to be more inclined to favor decreased immigration or believe that immigrants are more of a burden on American society than other groups. The belief that immigrants, especially illegal ones, are a drain on the taxpayer was the driving force behind a California, grass roots movement to deny illegal immigrants free state services under Proposition 187.

Ironically, Proposition 187 was not merely a white supported issue. Asian Americans and other smaller California ethnic groups were largely in favor of the bill. The only group that did not support the Proposition were Latino voters, who were largely offended by the rhetoric and provisions that the bill offered. As they perceived it, the bill was aimed not just at undocumented aliens but also the Latino community. Although California Latinos opposed Proposition 187, Latinos in other parts of the United States supported reducing the number of immigrants. For example, a poll taken by *The Washington Times* just a year later showed that more than 65 percent of Latinos in the United States either 'agreed' or 'strongly agreed' that the nation was accepting too many immigrants. Clearly California was reflecting a new nation-wide attitude.

CENSUS 2000 • The changing face of American immigration came full circle in the year 2000. The 2000 Census was the most comprehensive census to date—not only extensive in its thoroughness to find every American but also extensive in its questioning. For the first time, Americans had the opportunity to describe themselves as more than one ethnic group on the questionnaire. Close to seven million people identified themselves as coming from more than one culture. This significant number, 2.4 percent of the nation, reflects America as a melting pot like never before. However, it may be misleading to call America a melting pot in the year 2000; it is more like a tossed salad. The people who identified themselves as multi-racial lived in states that have long been inter-racial, like Alaska and Hawaii. Although in some Southern states people identified their race along traditional lines, it is not merely the lingering attitudes of segregation that accounts for America's tossed salad description.

In general the changing face of America is becoming a darker shade, though still segregated. Whites, blacks and Asians largely live among themselves. The average white person lives in a neighborhood that is roughly 80 percent white and seven percent black. In contrast, the average black person lives in a neighborhood that is 33 percent white and 51 percent black. In cosmopolitan Southern cities blacks and whites are the most synthesized, due to young and professional blacks moving to Southern urban areas. However, the largest city in the United States, New York City, ranks in the top ten of being the most segregated, superceded only by Newark, New Jersey, and Nassau and Suffolk Counties on Long Island.

All of these figures are a reflection of the early years of immigration. Yet, the story of recent immigration is an interesting one. According to the 2000 Census, the Hispanic population expanded by 58 percent to 35.3 million people since 1990. This makes the Hispanic population on par with or outnumbering the African American population. In Florida Hispanics now eclipse African Americans in population and in California they not only outnumber African Americans but make up one-third of the population. The fastest growing county in the nation, Clark County, Nevada, owes its new accolade to the rise in Hispanic immigration. Clark County has doubled in size since 1990 to 1.4 million people. The non-Hispanic white population that used to be the largest majority of the United States is now becoming the minority in some states. For example, whites are almost the minority in Texas.

2000
FUTURE IMMIGRATION LAWS

Future immigration policy in general is a greatly debated topic. Here are some of the most influential arguments for and against immigration policy in the future.

POPULATION CONTROL • The formation of the Federation for American Immigration Reform (FAIR) by the environmentalists in 1979 marks the entrance of environmentalism in the immigration debate. Early restrictionists' movements did not address the connections between the environment, population, and immigration. Essentially, proponents of this view think that immigrants and refugees should be admitted into the United States without regard to race, national origin, color, religion, gender or sexual preference. That being said, the nation cannot solve its environmental problems without facing the population issue. The largest portion of American population increase is attributable to immigration; therefore, immigration to the United States must be curtailed.

IMMIGRATION THROUGH THE BACK DOOR • The problem started in 1965 with the imposed restriction of Western Hemisphere immigration. Mexicans soon discovered that it was very difficult to enter the United States legally, and so they came without proper documentation. Later, Central Americans discovered how hard it was to immigrate to the United States and they too came without proper documentation. Thus, closing the 'front door' on immigration in the 1965 act fostered 'back door' illegal immigration. The only way to close the back door was to develop an effective way to patrol the nation's borders and catch those who overstayed their visas.

A potential solution came in 1986, when the Immigration Reform and Control Act increased border patrols and created sanctions on American employers who employed illegal aliens. In turn it granted illegal aliens already residing in the United States amnesty—admitting nearly three million persons.

It quickly became apparent that the IRCA was not a success. Apprehension of illegal aliens was averaging over one million a month before the IRCA; ten years after, the inflow of illegal aliens had increased by 20 percent. Employers were the main culprits. Beefing up the borders at El Paso and San Diego in 1994 (Operation Gatekeeper) proved futile. It just forced illegal border crossers to try somewhere else. Even if the borders were secure, by the mid-1990s more than half of the undocumented aliens were estimated to enter with some type of temporary visa, then remained in the United States illegally. Center for Immigration Studies head David Simcox lamented that there was practically no deterrence to stop people from coming and overstaying; as late as 1995 the INS had no effective program to seek out such immigrants. Even if they came with fake documents, the INS lacked personnel to conduct thorough checks.

Refugees also became a problem. Presidential parole was first granted to Cubans, then to Indochinese, and finally blanket paroles were letting in legal aliens at a much higher rate than the country could handle. The blanket paroles loosened the definition of asylum seekers as well. In the 1980s tens of thousands of persons reaching the United States without proper immigration documents requested asylum. Because the backlog grew to over 400,000 by 1994, the INS could not dispose of their cases quickly. The agency gave them working papers and scheduled a hearing later. Often they did not show up for their hearing; even if they did and were rejected, they were ordered to depart voluntarily. Soon many immigrants knew that if they could reach the United States, they could stay just by claiming political asylum.

The problem was that the definition of asylum no longer applied to people fleeing a country at war. Should women who are treated as second-class citizens be granted asylum? An African woman, fleeing genital mutilation, did win asylum in 1996. What about Chinese who disagreed with China's policy of one child per family? Had this policy not led to forced sterilization and abortions? Should gays be allowed to enter on grounds of asylum? In 1994, Attorney General Janet Reno issued a directive allowing political asylum for foreign nationals on the grounds that they were homosexuals. Moreover, individuals with AIDS or HIV had been barred from entering the country but in 1995 the President's Advisory Council hinted that such persons might be granted waivers and even asylum.

TERRORIST IMMIGRANTS • Worse yet were terrorists immigrating to the United States and asking for asylum. Mir Aimal Kansi of Pakistan, whose legal visa had expired, applied for asylum. While waiting for a decision, he purchased an AK-47 weapon and killed two Americans outside CIA headquarters in Virginia, then promptly fled back to Pakistan. Sheik Omar Abdel Rahmen, who was charged and convicted of plotting to blow up New York City's World Trade Center and who was wanted in Egypt for involvement in the assassination of Anwar Sadat, should not have been admitted into the United States at all. Once in the United States, he moved his residence, changed his name, and received a green card from the INS. The authorities caught up with him and revoked his status, but then the Sheik applied for political asylum. The case was pending when the World Trade Center exploded in 1993.

THE ECONOMIC DEBATE • Defenders of the economic debate claim that the United States needs large numbers of unskilled laborers and immigrants to supplement the labor pool. However, the rapid growth in technology, especially computer technology, has created a demand for professional immigrants who are abundant in the Pacific Rim countries, China, India and Pakistan. Restrictionists who oppose opening the doors for highly skilled technicians charge big business with not bringing the best and brightest but rather the cheapest, which drives down the wages of American professionals as well. Since 1990, at least six million foreign workers, both skilled and unskilled, have been thrown into competition for American jobs.

CONCLUSION

Defenses and attacks of the American immigration system will no doubt continue in the future. Second and third generation immigrants made up slightly less than ten percent of the American population in 1997 compared to a high of 15 percent in the early twentieth century. Yet, the foreign-born population residing in the United States has nearly doubled since 1970 and immigration is running at record highs. Moreover, immigration is no longer predominately European. If the economy experiences another recession or sluggish growth, then anti-immigration sentiment could gain momentum. If the economy is doing well, then a 'business as usual' attitude may accelerate. However, even among the immigrant population, the American public is becoming more and more restrictionist no matter what the economy produces.

BIBLIOGRAPHY

Bernard, William S., Carolyn Zelony, and Henry Miller, eds. *American Immigration Policy – A Reappraisal.* New York: Harper Brothers, 1950.

Carpenter, Niles. *Immigrants and Their Children 1920.* Washington, DC: U.S. Government Printing Office, 1927.

Chiswick, Barry R. ed. *The Gateway : U.S. Immigration Issues and Policies.* Washington, DC: American Enterprise Institution For Public Policy Research, 1982.

Hing, Bill Ong. *Making and Remaking Asian America Through Immigration Policy 1850-1990.* Stanford: Stanford University Press, 1993.

Hirchman, Charles, Phillip Kasinitz and John Dewind, eds. *The Handbook of International Migration,* 1999.

Jones, Maldryn Allen. *American Immigration.* Chicago: University of Chicago Press, 1960.

King, Desmond. *Making Americans.* Cambridge: Harvard University Press, 2000.

Koehn, Peter H. *Refugees From Revolution: U.S. Policy and Third World Migration.* Boulder: Westview Press, 1991.

Loesher, Gil and John A. Scanlan. *Calculated Kindness: Refugees and America's Half Opened Door 1945 – Present.* New York: Free Press/ McMillian, 1986.

Lyman, Robert ed. *The World Almanac and Book of Facts for 1931.* New York: The New York World Press, 1931.

Maharidge, Dale. *Becoming White Minority.* New York: Random House, 1996.

Portes, Alejandro and Ruben G. Rumbaut. *Immigrant America.* Berkeley: University of California,1996.

Readers Digest Almanac and Yearbook 1980. New York: W.W. Norton, 1980.

Williamson, Clinton, Jr. *The Immigration Mystique*. New York: Basic Books, 1996.

INTERNET RESOURCES

American Family Immigration History Center. This is the entry to the official Ellis Island website where passenger arrivals to New York can now be searched online. Since handwritten records have been transcribed and entered into this searchable database, they may contain typos due to unclear handwriting.
http://www.ellisisland.org

ACLU: Immigrant Rights - American Civil Liberties Union information resources, position statements, and activities related to the rights of immigrants in the United States.
http://www.aclu.org/issues/immigrant/hmir.html

U.S. IMMIGRATION HISTORY
Historical Trend in Immigrant Arrivals 1821 to 1995. Data on immigration by decade and by geographic region taken from the Statistical Yearbook of the Immigration and Naturalization Service.
http://www.fairus.org/html/03002606.htm

American Women's History: Immigrant Women
http://www.mtsu.edu/~kmiddlet/history/women/wh-immig.html

Immigrant Arrivals: A Guide To Published Sources - Research guide and bibliography presented by the Library of Congress.
http://www.loc.gov/rr/genealogy/

NARA Immigrant and Passenger Arrivals on Microfilm - An index to genealogical microfilm rolls published by the National Archives and Records Administration.
http://www.nara.gov/publications/microfilm/immigrant/immpass.html

Immigration and Border Control Suggestions for addressing underlying economic causes of illegal immigration, rather than merely responding to symptoms.
http:/www.wordwiz72.com/migra.html

Census of Population and Housing, 1990-U.S. Census of population and housing.
http:/www.census.gov

Veryan B. Khan

Individual Prosperity and the American Dream

~

(1885) Illustrated view of the Chinese Quarter in San Francisco, California, late 19th century. People walk in the streets, carrying buckets and talking with vendors. A small dog barks in the street.

TIMELINE

1890-1919 ~ Striking it Rich

Indians massacred at Wounded Knee (1890) / Alaskan gold rush begins in 1897 a year after the discovery of gold in the Klondike; peaks the following year / Sixty percent of the country's population lives in rural areas; ten percent of students graduate from high school (1900) / Spindletop oil plume gushes, and the Texas black gold rush begins (1901) / Henry Ford institutes the five-dollar day for his factory workers (1914)

Milestones: *Plessy v. Ferguson* declares it illegal for blacks to ride in the same railroad car as whites (1896) • Spanish American War (1898) • Chinese immigration banned except for diplomats, students, and merchants (1900) • Andrew Carnegie gives $350 million for social causes (1900-1919) • Lee De Forest invents the vacuum tube, essential to the development of electronics (1906)

1920-1929 ~ Good Times

For the first time, more Americans live in urban areas than in rural ones; forty-six percent of Americans own their own homes (1920) / Ford Model T costs $290 (down from $950 in 1908), and is now accessible to many working Americans, including those who work in Ford factories (1924) / Sixty-three percent of Americans live in homes with electric lights (up from 16 percent only 15 years before) (1927) / Mail order catalogues and magazines bring fashion awareness to every household (1925-1929) / Workers laid off and production cut back due to over-production and large stocks of unsold inventory (1929)

Milestones: Nineteenth Amendment passed, giving women the right to vote (1919) • Invention of Freon makes widespread home refrigeration feasible (1920s) • Permanent immigration quotas imposed (1924) • First national radio networks begin, NBC (1926), CBS (1927) • Penicillin is discovered (1928)

1930-1945 ~ A Troubled Economy

Thirty percent of students graduate from high school (1930) / Fifteen million Americans are out of work, nearly 25 percent of the population (1933) / The Federal Housing Administration provides government-insured mortgages, bringing home ownership within the reach of more Americans than ever before (1934) / 50,000 coal miners strike in Birmingham, Alabama against exploitation (1934) / Fair Labor Standards Act establishes minimum wages, maximum hours, and the abolition of child labor (1938) / The G.I. Bill extends government assistance for home ownership even further (1944)

Milestones: Women dominate the professions of teaching, nursing, and social work (1930) • Working wives are publicly criticized as selfish and "a menace to society" (1930) • Amelia Earhart is the first woman to complete a solo transatlantic flight (1932) • Adolph Hitler rises to power in Germany (1933) • American corporations spend $80 million a year spying on their employees (1935) • Ukrainian immigrant Igor Sikorsky builds the first successful helicopter (1939) • *Enola Gay* drops an atomic bomb on Hiroshima (August 6, 1945)

1946-1959 ~ Post-war Boom Times

Mendez v. Westminister desegregates Mexican American education rights (1946) / The first Levittown is completed in Hempstead, New York, marking the start of the postwar suburban boom (1947) / Diner's Club introduces the first general-purpose credit card (1950) / 154 millionaires in the U.S. (1954) / White-collar jobs outnumber blue-collar positions for the first time in American history (1955) / The Interstate Highway Act provides for the construction of more than 40,000 miles of roads, facilitating suburbanization (1956)

Milestones: House Committee on Un-American Activities begins communist "witch hunt" (1947) • Jackie Robinson integrates professional baseball (1947) • U.S. recognizes Israel as a sovereign state (1948) • *Brown v. Board of Education* rules that school segregation is unconstitutional (1954) • Disneyland opens (1955) • First fully enclosed shopping center built in Minnesota (1956)

1960-1979 ~ Civil Rights

Seventy-five percent of students graduate from high school, a rate that remains constant throughout the rest of the century (1960) / Civil Rights Act declares that American citizens cannot be segregated in public accommodations (1964) / New Hampshire is the first state to reinstate lotteries (1964) / Apple II computer appears on the market (1977)

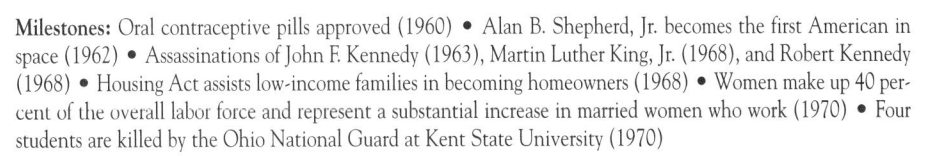

Milestones: Oral contraceptive pills approved (1960) • Alan B. Shepherd, Jr. becomes the first American in space (1962) • Assassinations of John F. Kennedy (1963), Martin Luther King, Jr. (1968), and Robert Kennedy (1968) • Housing Act assists low-income families in becoming homeowners (1968) • Women make up 40 percent of the overall labor force and represent a substantial increase in married women who work (1970) • Four students are killed by the Ohio National Guard at Kent State University (1970)

1980-2000 ~ The New Prosperity

The average house price is $70,000 (up from $37,800 only six years before) (1980) / The World Wide Web is created, opening new possibilities for communication and globalization, and changing the face of American work and leisure (1990) / Home shopping network and ATM machines encourage spontaneous buying (1990s) / 65 percent of Americans own their homes (1995) / Four percent of American families—roughly 7.1 million households—have a net worth of $1 million or more (2000)

Milestones: Hate crime legislation passed in every state (1980-1997) • 400,000 Americans die of AIDS (1987-1999) • Restaurant chain Denny's pays $50 million to settle discrimination charges (1991-1997) • A million households apply for personal bankruptcy (1998) • Hispanic population equals African American population for the first time (2000)

INTRODUCTION: RAGS TO RICHES

Harvard-educated Horatio Alger was one of the country's best-known authors at the dawn of the twentieth century, though he had not lived to see it. With at least 17 million copies of his many books in print (at a time when the country's population was only 76 million), Alger was a household name and his ideas common currency. Publishing at the rate of 3-5 books a year for much of his adult life, Alger published 120 novels in all, most of which echoed the themes of industry and frugality popularized by Benjamin Franklin more than a century before. Emphasizing merit over social status as the chief determinant of success, Alger's books offered hope to generations of Americans anxious to rise above poverty and achieve economic security, if not abundance. Their plots were simplistic and often repetitive—young man works hard and, with perseverance and a little bit of luck, ultimately succeeds—but their message of democratic equalitarianism found favor with audiences nonetheless because it articulated the crux of the American dream.

Always difficult to define, the American dream seems to center around one idea—dynamism. Progress rather than stasis can operate on both an individual level, improving one's own lot in life, and on a familial one, ensuring a better future for one's children. The exact goal may change, but the basic concept—improvement—remains the same.

Within the general theory of the American dream, there appear to be two distinct strains. The first and oldest of these is the quest for respectability. Here the goal is a middle-class standard of living to be achieved through hard work and conservative lifestyle choices. Other Americans have sought to move beyond self-sustenance, embracing the dream of financial prosperity.

1900-1970 • A PEOPLE ON THE MOVE

Those already in the United States have moved with greater frequency over larger distances than their predecessors, heading primarily to urban areas. Mobility has been a key factor in shaping the twentieth century, especially this growth of cities at the expense of the countryside. The twentieth century has been marked by urbanization, as Americans have followed the employment opportunities—industrial, corporate, and, increasingly, service-oriented—to the cities. In 1880, only twenty cities reported a population of 100,000 or more; by 1920, there were 39 such cities. (In 1990, 195 U.S. cities had more than 100,000 residents.) In 1920, urbanites comprised a majority of the population (51.2 percent) for the first time; by 1990, 78 percent of the population lived in metropolitan areas. Much of the ascendancy of urban areas was the result of a slow, but steady trickle from outlying areas, but there have been a few distinct population movements, most notably the departure of more than one million African-Americans from the rural South to the urban North after World War I, and the exodus of 800,000 agricultural laborers from the Dust Bowl of Arkansas, Texas, Missouri, and Oklahoma in the 1930s and 1940s.

These migrations did not end with the return of prosperity after World War II: more than 20 million Americans left rural areas for the cities between 1945-1970. In the 1950s, as much as 20 per-

(circa 1905) Ellis Exchange. A money exchange on Ellis Island, New York. Immigrants poured into the country from all around the world, drawn by the promise of prosperity. Although restrictive legislation drastically reduced the number of immigrants arriving between 1924-1965, immigration remained a significant factor in the century as a whole. Nearly nine million immigrants arrived between 1900-1910, another 8.7 million between 1983-1993.

Table 1: Proportion of the Population Still Residing in the State of Their Birth in 1960

Nevada	28%
Alaska	32%
Arizona	38%
Florida	38%
California	44%
Wyoming	44%
Oregon	48%
Washington	51%
New Mexico	53%
Idaho	54%

SOURCE: Historical Census Data Browser website at www.fisher.lib.virginia.edu/census

Table 2: Percentage of the Population Who Moved between 1958 and 1960

Alaska	49%
Nevada	41%
Arizona	39%
Florida	35%
New Mexico	35%
California	34%
Wyoming	34%
Colorado	33%
Hawaii	32%
Montana	32%
Texas	32%

SOURCE: Historical Census Data Browser website at www.fisher.lib.virginia.edu/census

cent of the population moved each year. In ever-larger numbers, these migrants flocked to emerging commercial centers in the South and West. The growth of the so-called "Sunbelt" and of the former frontier was evident as early as 1960, when census figures indicated the percentage of the population residing in the state of their birth. States in the South and West reported the smallest proportions of native-born residents. As Table 1 shows, in many states more than half the population had moved to another state, while Table 2 suggests significant migration in the two years between 1958 and 1960. The population boom was rapid—throughout much of the region, 30 percent or more of the residents had moved into their current home in the previous two years.

1945-1970 • RENEWED PROSPERITY

For Americans, new and old, the twentieth century began on a hopeful note. After the economic recessions that had dominated much of the 1890s, America seemed poised for recovery and indeed prosperity. Economic growth characterized the first three decades of the century. The gross national product (GNP) rose by 40 percent in the 1920s alone and mounted steadily throughout the century, peaking during the Cold War period, with a 250 percent expansion between 1945-1960. This prosperity was largely an urban phenomenon, as the rise of major corporations and their growing bureaucracies of salaried managers resulted in an unprecedented expansion of the middle class, formerly the province of select professionals. In 1955, white-collar jobs outnumbered blue-collar positions for the first time. In that year, more than 60 percent of the population could identify themselves as middle-class, earning an income of $3,000-$10,000; in 1929 only 31 percent of Americans were similarly situated. (Those earning the federally-mandated minimum wage of $1/hour in 1955 remained outside this group.) Real wages rose for the working class, as well, allowing even some factory laborers to conceive of such previously unheard of possibilities as home and car ownership. Henry Ford's implementation of the $5 day in his Highland Park, Michigan factories in 1914, a wage more than twice the average for industrial workers, marked the entrée of blue-collar workers to a middle-class standard of living. The trend continued: workers' wages tripled between 1945-1970. "Middle class" became a designation of economic means rather than occupational status in the twentieth century, and it became a realistic goal for significant numbers of Americans.

At the same time, technological innovation meant that more products were available more cheaply than ever. Wages rose and working hours fell, leaving a larger number of people than ever before with both disposable income and leisure time. Combined with more widespread availability of consumer products—made possible by a convergence of increased manufacturing and better distribution and sales tactics—this rise in real wages set into motion a consumer revolution that would dominate much of the twentieth century. Though the markedly uneven distribution of wealth and power went largely unchallenged—twenty percent of Americans remained at or below poverty level throughout the century—a certain democracy of goods was evident. The trappings of middle-class prosperity were within the reach of an ever-increasing number of Americans.

1890-1925 • IMPROVING THE QUALITY OF LIFE

Some of these trappings had a fundamental impact on quality of life. In 1900, less than one in twelve homes had electricity. Thirty years later, nearly two-thirds of American households were fully wired; by 1960, electricity was universal. Electrification had profound consequences. Homes were more safely and effectively illuminated. Residents could utilize more of their homes than they could when they relied on costly candles. They could read more: in Muncie, Indiana, library borrowing increased eight-fold between 1890-1925 as electricity became standard. And they could purchase and use new labor-saving appliances. Electrical refrigerators, for instance, not only saved time previously spent shopping for perishable items each day, but they also greatly improved food safety in the home. Commercial applications of electricity were also significant. Urban electrification allowed for improved public transportation with electric streetcars. New manufacturing processes emerged, powered by electricity. Existing businesses capitalized on the technology with longer store hours, new window displays, and eye-catching signage. New businesses like amusement parks were created. Work, home, and entertainment operated in new ways for most Americans.

Automobiles further altered daily life. Introduced in the 1890s as a luxury item, cars became almost standard in the first decades of the twentieth century, especially after the 1913 development of the moving assembly line, which drastically reduced prices. There were only 8,000 cars registered in 1900, a figure that climbed to 2.5 million in 1915 and jumped to 26.5 million in 1930. Henry Ford's car for the masses, the Model T, costing only $290 in 1924 (down from $950 in 1908) was well within reach of many working Americans. General Motors followed suit, promising a car for every budget and taste. With the simultaneous construction of new and better roads, the automobile forever changed Americans' conception of distance, allowing a new kind of mobility, even for working-class citizens.

The widespread availability of the automobile further quickened the pace of suburbanization that had begun around the turn of the century. Suburban living, previously the exclusive domain of those wealthy enough to afford personal transportation to and from the city, opened to more people of more varied backgrounds with the advent of electric trolleys, in place in more than 200 cities by 1889. By 1900, America boasted 20,000 miles of streetcar track. Boston went from city to metropolis, encompassing 31 towns by the turn of the century. These streetcar suburbs offered enormous advantages over city living, not just increased privacy and the pride of home-ownership, but healthier, less crowded environments. Americans with sufficient means fled the squalor of the city, places like Manhattan's Lower East Side tenement district, which had an average of 986.4 residents per acre, the highest population density in the world. The automobile facilitated the development of ever more distant and affluent suburbs, garden cities beyond the inner ring of compact towns accessible by streetcars.

Residents of these suburban homes also enjoyed increased availability of other consumer products. The telephone, still a novelty present in only eight percent of homes in 1900, almost 25 years after its invention, was in 40 percent of homes by 1940 and well over 90 percent by 2000. Television spread even more rapidly: the first commercial stations began broadcasting just after World War II, and by 1956, 80 percent of American homes had at least one television. That number reached 87 percent by 1960. Personal computers followed a similar path to popularity in the last two decades of the century.

The rapid proliferation of these and other expensive durable goods—vacuum cleaners, refrigerators, and the like—was due in part to another twentieth-century innovation, the installment plan. Widely

(1910) This photo of a horse-drawn suffrage wagon shows an older means of transportation crossing paths with a new mode, the electric streetcar. Note the tracks in the foreground.

used beginning in the 1910s, installment buying allowed working Americans to turn their sometimes meager earnings into real buying power. Purchasing power increased further with the introduction of the first general purpose credit card—Diner's Club—in 1950. Like many other items, the credit card was initially seen as exclusive to the rich, but it gradually trickled down to the population at large.

1998 General Purpose Credit Card Ownership by income

less than $10,000	26.3%
$10,000-$24,999	53.3%
$25,000-$49,999	75.0%
$50,000-$99,999	93.1%
$100,000+	97.1%

SOURCE: *Events That Shaped the Century.* Richard B. Stolley, editor.

1950s • Home Sweet Home
Other trappings of success and security were less material, but just as fundamental to quality of life. Over the course of the twentieth century, for instance, life expectancy increased dramatically—from 47 to 76 years—and infant mortality rates improved. The development of vaccines and antibiotics obliterated some diseases, while transforming others from life-threatening illnesses to passing nuisances. Home ownership rates approached 70 percent at the end of the century—over 90 percent in the northeast—an enormous leap since 1900. Much of the increase came in the years just before and after World War II.

The Federal Housing Administration, formed under the New Deal began insuring loans during the Great Depression. Insured loans could carry a down payment as low as ten percent, a much more manageable figure than the 50 percent down that had been customary. The FHA's credit policies became even more generous after the war, especially for veterans who qualified for the G.I. Bill: servicemen could frequently buy houses with no money down and reduced interest rates. The proliferation of federal and local tax incentives for homeowners, along with the development of prefabricated building techniques, made home ownership much more affordable at the same time as a burgeoning population generated an increased demand for housing. The population increased by more than 30 percent between 1945-1960 as a result of the baby boom—couples marrying younger and having more children more rapidly than their predecessors. In 1960, 32.24 percent of families around the country had children under the age of six

Housing shortages that had plagued urban residents during the Depression and the War—conditions that frequently forced young couples to live with their parents and put off establishing their own households—found their outlet in the suburban building boom that began as soon as the War (and its restrictions on civilian construction) ended. The first Levittown, in Hempstead, New York, was completed in 1947, consisting of 17,447 nearly identical two-bedroom Cape Cod-style homes, along with seven shopping centers, fourteen playgrounds, nine swimming pools, two bowling alleys, and a town hall. Under the G.I. Bill, veterans could purchase a Levittown house (priced at just under $8,000) for $56 a month with no down payment, less than the rent initially charged by the neighborhood's developers. The program pumped more than $20 million into the housing industry by 1950, assisting the quarter of World War II veterans who purchased about 4.3 million new homes—one-third of the new construction.

The construction boom was unprecedented. The Levitt brothers were throwing up about 2,000 homes each year—800 square foot Capes and ranches built in 27 steps; their construction crews completed a house every fifteen minutes. The 1950s saw 3,000 acres of grasslands and forests cleared each day for suburban development, and by 1970 suburban residents outnumbered their urban counterparts, 76 million to 64 million, with home ownership rates 50 percent higher than a generation earlier. Suburban development depended heavily on increased car ownership (from 26 million in 1945 to 52 million only ten years later) and the construction of road networks. The Interstate Highway Act of 1956 paved the way for more than 40,000 miles of federally financed road construction; states completed additional roads. In all, 79,000 miles of highways were built in the 1950s. Americans were truly dynamic—always on the move.

1945-1956 • GOVERNMENT-SUBSIDIZED PROSPERITY ~ The Servicemen's Readjustment Act of 1944 (better known as the G.I. Bill) that fueled so much of the postwar building boom also provided for educational stipends to be used by veterans at colleges and vocational schools, along with monthly allowances to cover living expenses. The $500 per year was enough to cover the tuition at any public and most private schools. More than half of the returning servicemen (7.8 of the 15.4 million who had served in the war) took advantage of its provisions by 1956. College enrollment reached an all-time high, and the large number of students from working- and middle-class backgrounds (financed by the G.I. Bill) served to democratize higher education, long seen as a gentlemen's pursuit. In 1947, the peak year of the education bill, veterans comprised more than 49 percent of college students. The number of Americans graduating from college each year tripled between the late 1930s and 1950, from 160,000 to 500,000. The postwar years also saw a proliferation of graduate and professional degree programs as veterans sought to continue their education. Particularly prominent were business schools that offered advanced degrees: MBA programs were founded at MIT, Carnegie Mellon, Florida State, and Georgia Tech in the years immediately following the war. Universities also initiated and expanded Ph.D. programs, changing the face of higher education as veterans entered, and eventually dominated, academe. Veterans diverged sharply from the blue-collar careers of their fathers and grandfathers, carving out a place for themselves in the respectable middle class.

1956 Careers of Veterans who Earned College Degrees under the G.I. Bill

450,000	engineers
238,000	teachers
91,000	scientists
67,000	doctors
22,000	dentists

SOURCE: www.vfw.org/magazine/oct97/32

The educational provisions of the G.I. Bill had far-reaching consequences. In a single generation, educational expectations improved dramatically. Twenty-eight percent of soldiers in World War II had dropped out of high school. Thirty-three percent had stopped after elementary school, and only 14 percent had attended college (only three percent held four-year degrees). Within ten years of the war's end, however, nearly 50 percent had enrolled in colleges or vocational schools. Their massive numbers had a profound effect on college campuses around the country. New York's situation is suggestive of the national response. To meet the heightened demand, the state university system was incorporated in 1948. New institutions appeared almost overnight—seven private colleges opened on Long Island alone during the 1950s. Existing schools, public and private, also contributed to the effort. Elmira College, a small female liberal arts college in New York's Southern Tier, temporarily opened its doors to men after the war. Veterans attended classes alongside young women for a few years, during which time there was a noticeable increase in the number of women leaving school to marry. (The college did not become coeducational until 1969.)

At Syracuse University, the single largest destination of G.I. Bill students in New York State (17th largest in the nation), the arrival of veterans altered the physical landscape of the campus. The so-called "G.I. Bulge" stretched facilities to the limit, and the university had to bring in prefabricated metal buildings from demobilized military bases to serve as classrooms for the newly swollen student body. Erected in the middle of quads, or wherever there was room on the fringe, the Quonset huts remained a fixture of the campus for several years (the "Quonseteria" dining hall stood into the 1980s). Housing the veterans presented another problem. Until living quarters could be constructed, students were bused in from temporary shelters at the nearby New York State Fairgrounds, the local Ordinance Works, and an Army Air Base. For most single students, on-campus housing took the form of hastily constructed barracks and Quonset huts at the University Farm. One hundred and seventy-five married veterans lived out their college years in trailers in a nearby apple orchard.

The impact of the G.I. Bill continued long past the expiration of its educational benefits in 1956, as veterans entered the workforce armed with advanced degrees. A 1986 government survey estimates that for every one dollar the federal government invested in the G.I. Bill ($14.5 billion all together), the country saw a return of between five and twelve dollars in increased tax revenues, thanks to the higher incomes the veterans' education netted. Since the G.I. Bill also furnished low interest business loans, guaranteeing half of a $2,000 loan with interest of 4 percent or less, many of these veterans were able to start their own businesses—300,000 did so in the 1950s. One was John Finnegan. Upon returning from the war, Finnegan took advantage of all the G.I. Bill had to offer, utilizing the tuition money to earn his engineering degree at Manhattan College and the living stipend to support his new wife. After graduating, the G.I. Bill guaranteed the mortgage on his house in suburban New Jersey, and the business loan allowed him to found J. Finnegan, Inc., the second largest sheet metal manufacturer in the New York metropolitan area through the 1990s.

1945-1965 • EDUCATION IS NOT JUST FOR VETERANS ~ The entry of the federal government into education under the G.I. Bill capped nearly five decades of dramatic improvement in American education. In 1890, a mere four percent of children aged 14-17 were enrolled in school; that figure climbed to 32 percent by 1920, 47 percent by 1930, and about 90 percent by 1960 (that proportion remained constant through 2000). The high school graduation rate also improved significantly, from roughly ten percent in 1900 to 30 percent in 1930, and about 75 percent in 1960 (in 2000, the graduation rate hovered around 72 percent, a figure that was stable throughout the last three decades of the century). College enrollment also increased throughout the century, with early growth limited mainly to wealthy citizens pursuing a classical education, and later growth dominated by veterans studying under the G.I. Bill. The

College Opportunities at the Turn of the Century

Year	Number of students	Number of colleges	Number of faculty
1870	52,000	563	5,553
1890	157,000	998	15,809
1920	600,000	1,041	48,615

SOURCE: *Events That Shaped the Century.* Richard B. Stolley, editor.

1945-1965

(1963) Black American civil rights leader Martin Luther King, Jr. (1929 - 1968) addressing crowds during the March on Washington at the Lincoln Memorial, Washington DC, where he gave his 'I Have A Dream' speech.

children of veterans made their mark, too. In 1964, when the first baby boomers reached college age, first-time enrollment at colleges ballooned to 1,037,000 from 784,000 only a year before. Overall enrollment in institutes of higher learning increased from 2.6 million students in 1950 to 7.5 million in 1970.

1950S-1960S • LIMITS ON THE PURSUIT OF HAPPINESS ~ Amid this general prosperity, however, enormous gaps were evident. Poverty continued, despite the introduction of Social Security and unemployment insurance in the 1930s and the expansion of welfare in the 1960s. African-Americans and other racial minorities often struggled to attain the same standard of living that whites enjoyed, trapped by prejudice in low-paying, sometimes dangerous jobs, and decrepit neighborhoods. Many of the middle-class accouterments that had become standard for white Americans, even those with blue-collar jobs, eluded minorities. Educational disparities contributed to this inequity.

Even after the 1954 Supreme Court *Brown vs. Board of Education of Topeka, Kansas* decision outlawing segregation in public schools, African-Americans continued to attend vastly inferior, underfunded, and understaffed schools. Two years after the Court's decision, desegregation remained a myth throughout the South—in six states, not a single black child attended a school with white peers. Ninety percent of Chicago's black children attended all-black schools as late as 1964. Despite ill-received attempts at busing in the early 1970s, de facto segregation continued throughout the nation.

To be sure, blacks did benefit somewhat from the economic boom of the early Cold War period—their median income doubled between 1940-1961, thanks in large part to a 100 percent increase in the employment of skilled black workers during the war—but it remained at about 55 percent of the median income level for white Americans, while unemployment was twice as high among the African-American community. Nearly half of all black families lived below the poverty line in 1960 (as compared to 20 percent of whites). The disparity in income translated into tangible differences in lifestyle, with African-Americans comprising only six percent of suburbanites in 1980.

Title VII of the 1964 Civil Rights Act helped to achieve some degree of equality for minorities and for women in certain educational and occupational settings, but both groups faced ongoing obstacles. Women found it difficult to advance in the professional world, though they constituted nearly half of the workforce as early as 1940. Building on their employment experiences during World War II, women joined the workforce in increasing numbers during the Cold War period; by 1980, 58 percent of adult women were employed outside the home. Despite gains in numbers, critics continued to speak of a "glass ceiling" that prohibited women from reaching upper management and executive positions. In 1990, women comprised 42 percent of the management workforce—a dramatic increase from their 17 percent in 1970—but for the most part, they remained in lower- to middle-management jobs; executive leadership continued to be a male dominated field. Long under-represented in institutes of higher learning, especially in graduate programs (even in 2000, MBA programs were 70 percent male, on average), women did not achieve parity in college enrollment until 1974 and had still not achieved equal pay by the end of the century.

Working Women

Year	Number of adult women employed outside the home
1880	2.6 million
1890	4.0 million
1900	5.1 million
1910	7.8 million
1920	8.2 million
1930	10.4 million
1940	13.0 million

SOURCE: *Events That Shaped the Century*. Richard B. Stolley, editor.

African-Americans and women are not the only Americans who have struggled to achieve equality of opportunity. Homosexuals, the disabled, and new immigrants have also frequently faced brutal discrimination in the workplace and in society at large. Beginning with the civil rights movement in the 1950s, members of these groups organized to demand access to the jobs and, indeed, the basic human rights, that would allow them to share in the American dream. As the rate of population growth among racial and ethnic minorities surpasses that of Caucasians, and as less traditional living arrangements—female-headed households, same-sex partnerships, blended families, single adults—grow in number, the dreamscape will be altered considerably. Americans may continue to hold to a similar ideal, but the paths to that goal will multiply even more.

BIGGER DREAMS

At the same time as millions of Americans worked feverishly to achieve middle-class security, another strain of the American dream became evident—the quest for affluence. While significant wealth had been widely regarded as suspect and the leisured class as effete and immoral throughout much of the nation's history, the twentieth century saw an emerging respect for and interest in personal fortune. To be sure, there had always been fabulously wealthy Americans—large landholders and plantation owners, railroad and shipping magnates, major investors and financiers—but many of these men were despised as robber barons, people who made their millions from other people's misfortunes, who built their empires on the labor of others. These imposing business figures multiplied in the twentieth century, but so did opportunities for individuals to achieve massive fortunes in other ways. By century's end, the number of affluent Americans had skyrocketed, and with their increased numbers came increased respect.

1850-1950 • GO WEST, YOUNG MAN ~ Colonized by Europeans beginning in the seventeenth century, America has long been a nation of adventurers. From the earliest explorers who left their mark along the Atlantic coast to the first English subjects who carved out settlements in Massachusetts and Virginia, people have been on the move, creeping westward at a steady pace, populating areas east of the Appalachians by the end of the eighteenth century, filling in much of the Midwest by 1850, and swarming into areas west of the Rockies in the subsequent fifty years. Government programs such as the Homestead Act of 1862, which offered 160 acres of land free to any person who occupied it for five continuous years, encouraged settlement of the plains. The 1877 Desert Land Act

1897

did much the same for points further west. Despite Frederick Jackson Turner's pronouncement that the West was closed, Americans continued to move in that direction, pulled by the promise of economic prosperity and social independence. At the same time, urban overcrowding, massive immigration, rapid industrialization, and economic recession in the East made the wide-open spaces of the western United States even more appealing.

Population statistics illustrate this continuing pattern of westward migration. The 1890s had been relatively stagnant in the West, as elsewhere, but the dawning of the twentieth century brought a massive influx of new residents. Between 1900 and 1950, the population of every western state had more than doubled. Some states experienced an even more dramatic population explosion: California, for instance, saw a sevenfold increase in population. Altogether the population of the Rocky Mountain and Pacific states quintupled in the first fifty years of the twentieth century. It tripled again in the last half of the century, with every state growing by more than 100 percent, some, like Arizona and Texas, by more than 600 percent. Even in the last decade of the century, the growth was staggering. The states with the highest growth rates between the 1990 and 2000 census were all in the West—Nevada (50 percent), Utah (23.6 percent), Colorado (23.1 percent), Washington (18.3 percent), and Oregon (16.7 percent).

1897 • KLONDIKE GOLD RUSH

Westward migration was not entirely spurred by longings for freedom. The prospect of sudden, astronomical wealth proved to be a major draw at several points throughout the twentieth century. Indeed, the century opened with a full-fledged gold rush in Alaska. News of the August 1896 discovery of gold in Rabbit (later Bonanza) Creek spread rapidly, and as soon as the routes opened the following spring, thousands of prospectors poured in, 30,000 in 1898 alone. The massive influx of people made Dawson City, a newly founded boomtown, the largest city north of San Francisco. In total, more than 100,000 people made the journey to the Klondike between 1897 and 1900. When Klondike gold dissipated, prospectors headed west to Anvil City (later Nome) where gold had been discovered in September 1898. In the 1900 census, one-third of all Caucasians in Alaska were living in Nome.

For the lucky few, panning for gold proved profitable. Individual prospectors like J.J. Clements from New York City and Clarence Berry from San Diego made more than a million dollars; others struggled to break even, after spending hundreds or even thousands of dollars travel-

Growth of Western States
(according to U.S. Census figures)

	1900	1950	2000
Arizona	(not recorded)	749,587	4,778,332
California	1,485,053	10,586,223	33,145,121
Colorado	539,700	1,325,089	4,056,133
Idaho	161,772	588,637	1,251,700
Montana	243,329	591,024	882,779
Nevada	42,335	160,083	1,809,253
New Mexico	(not recorded)	681,187	1,739,844
Oregon	413,536	1,521,341	3,358,044
Utah	276,749	688,862	2,129,836
Washington	518,103	2,378,963	5,756,361
Wyoming	92,531	290,529	479,602
TOTALS	3,773,108	19,561,525	59,387,005

SOURCE: *Events That Shaped the Century*. Richard B. Stolley, editor.

Klondike Miners - circa 1897. The Alaskan gold rushes combined to yield about a quarter of a billion dollars, but the economic benefit extended far beyond the prospectors themselves Shown here are gold miners working on W.M. Cowley's claim 22 near Bonanza in Klondike, Alaska.

ing to the Klondike and securing a claim. Vast amounts of money changed hands, not only in the buying and selling of claims, but in poker games as well. According to local legend, "Silent Sam" Bonnefield from Charleston, West Virginia, won the Klondike's biggest game ever, with a pot of $150,000. Less lucky Harry Woolrich from Billings, Montana, won $60,000 in a single night of gambling, only to lose it the next day.

The Alaskan gold rushes combined to yield about a quarter of a billion dollars, but the economic benefit extended far beyond the prospectors themselves. A journey into the Klondike required nearly

Mining Provisions

Food: Bacon, 100-200 lbs; flour, 400 lbs; dried fruit, 75-100 lbs; corn meal, 50 lbs; rice, 20-40 lbs; coffee, 10-25 lbs; tea, 5-10 lbs; beans, 100 lbs; condensed milk, one case; salt, 10-15 lbs; pepper, 1 lb; rolled oats, 25-50 lbs; potatoes, 25-100 lbs; butter, 25 cans; assorted evaporated meats and vegetables

Equipment: stove; gold pan; granite buckets; tin cups and plates; knives, forks, and spoons; coffee/tea pot; picks and handles; saws and chisels; hammer and nails; hatchet; shovels; drawknife; compass; frying pan; matches; small assortment of medicines

Clothing: 1 heavy mackinaw coat; 3 suits heavy underwear; 2 pairs heavy mackinaw trousers; 1 dozen heavy wool socks; 6 heavy wool mittens; 2 heavy overshirts; 2 pairs rubber boots; 2 pairs heavy shoes; 3 heavy blankets; 2 rubber blankets; 2 pairs overalls; 1 suit oil clothing; assorted summer clothing

one ton of supplies, food and clothing to last for a full year. People were frequently not permitted into the Alaskan interior without this outfit because of the danger of starvation and exposure. Seattle, Washington experienced a tremendous boom as a gateway city where people could purchase their supplies. For instance, in the two weeks following the arrival in that city of the *Portland*, which brought the first word of the Bonanza Creek discovery, Seattle merchants sold $325,000 worth of goods. As the number of prospectors requiring supplies—which could cost anywhere between $300 and $2,000—swelled, local merchants kept pace, selling $25 million of provisions by the spring of 1898.

1894-1903 • TEXAS OIL BOOM ~ "Black gold" also proved a major draw for Americans looking for a quick fortune. The dawn of the twentieth century saw a series of oil rushes, particularly in Texas. The first economically significant oil discovery in that state came in 1894 in Navarro County; the following three decades saw dozens of discoveries and as many boomtowns. Texas history is filled with legends of "gushers." Perhaps the most famous, and certainly the earliest, is the Spindletop gusher near Beaumont. Beginning on 10 January 1901, a 150-foot plume of oil flowed untamed for nine days. Five other gushers on the same hill appeared by April of that year, and the population of Beaumont nearly tripled in the subsequent year. In 1902 alone, there was more than $3 million of new construction, mainly residential, and more than 500 oil companies formed. This boomtown scenario was repeated all across this oil-rich state in the first three decades of the twentieth century; geologists estimate that two-thirds of Texas is potentially productive for oil, natural gas, or both. Existing towns like Wichita Falls nearly quintupled in size (from 8,200 to 40,079) in ten years, while other settlements like Tuckertown suddenly appeared on the landscape, enjoyed a few years of impressive growth and prosperity, and then disappeared when the oil stopped flowing.

Oil also proved a major economic boom in California and Alaska. Bakersfield, California grew rapidly after the discovery of oil in 1899. By 1903, the Kern River oil field in Bakersfield was turning out 17 million barrels a year, making California the top oil producer in the country for a time. Major commercial oil development began in Alaska in the 1950s. The discovery of the continent's largest oil field at Prudhoe Bay in 1968 and the completion of the Trans-Alaska Pipeline System in 1977 have brought thousands of people and millions of dollars to the state.

1920s • REAL ESTATE SPECULATION ~ The discovery of oil and other natural resources in places like Texas and

---

Kilgore, Texas, one of these boomtowns, managed to hold onto its wealth a little longer than most, boasting at one point the richest acre in the country, a block that contained 200 oil wells that together produced more than 2.5 million barrels of oil. Local legend portrays Kilgore's oil as manna from heaven. As the story goes, the town's 700 residents gathered one hot Sunday during the drought-ridden summer of 1930 to pray for relief. Later that day, a gusher appeared in the town, and by Monday the population had swollen to nearly 25,000, ushering in more than 30 years of oil-based prosperity. Kilgore's fantastic tale is preserved to this day in the town's East Texas Oil Museum.

California drove land prices wildly upward. The nascent village of Tuckertown saw prices per acre rise from as little as $10 before the gusher to $500 after the boom. The fury was short-lived, however. Only a few years after oil production peaked in 1925, the land stopped producing; Tuckertown subsequently suffered a series of fires and was never rebuilt.

This pattern of boom and bust was certainly not unique to oil regions. Real estate speculators in places like south Florida also accumulated vast amounts of wealth very quickly, only to lose it all in a matter of years. Miami, a virtually uninhabited (and uninhabitable) swamp at the turn of the century, rapidly became a popular vacation destination by the mid-1920s. Newly accessible by Henry Flagler's coastal railroad and a series of new highways, Miami grew from only a few dozen year-round residents in 1896 to a town of 30,000 in 1920, and to 71,000 by 1925.

Pitched to upper- and middle-class Americans alike as "America's only tropics," south Florida proved very attractive to both residents and developers. With the threat of malaria and yellow fever eradicated by more effective mosquito control, and the distance no longer so daunting thanks to the proliferation of the automobile and better infrastructure, Americans flocked to Florida by the thousands. The absence of state income and inheritance taxes, and the lack of enforcement of Prohibition further sweetened the deal. Between 1922 and mid-1925, it was practically impossible to lose money on Florida real estate. Land was plentiful and relatively inexpensive—available in tiny 50' by 120' lots for the middle class, and created daily by developers dredging the bays to fill in the shallows—and the market of prospective buyers seemed endless. Hundreds of real estate companies established offices in northern cities, selling land, and later options to buy. Driven by the same attitude that had fueled speculation in the West—get in, get rich, get out—even more developers operated on a small scale, dabbling in local projects and generally turning substantial profits. The boom rapidly came to an end, however, with a devastating hurricane in September 1926, a second one only two years later, and the stock market crash of 1929. By some estimates, 90 percent of those who invested in Florida's real estate market in the 1920s lost money.

1920s • STOCK MARKET ~ Despite the inherent risk, speculation has remained a critical path to prosperity for many Americans, particularly in the form of the stock market. Developed in the late nineteenth century to finance the new, larger, corporations, public stock exchanges offered one route to wealth by allowing Americans to own tiny portions of major companies, sharing in the corporate profits. Sometimes, the invest-

Top Years for the Stock Market
(based on total returns)

1908	45.78%
1915	50.54%
1927	37.48%
1928	43.61%
1933	53.97%
1935	47.66%
1954	52.62%
1958	43.37%
1975	37.21%
1995	36.89%

SOURCE: *It Was a Very Good Year: Extraordinary Moments in Stock Market History*, by Martin S. Fridson.

1920s

ment returns were staggering. The 1920s saw tremendous growth of the stock market, with investment returns averaging between 35-45 percent. In Wall Street's biggest year, 1933, stockholders reaped a massive 53.97 percent profit. Two years later, stocks were still showing returns of nearly 48 percent. But, of course, these enormous profits went only to the lucky few who had managed to evade the devastation of the 1929 stock market crash, in which one million investors lost more than $30 billion.

Throughout the first half of the twentieth-century, particularly after the harrowing losses of 1929, stocks remained the purview of the wealthy. Amid the prosperity that followed World War II, however, a growing number of Americans had the disposable income to dabble in the stock market, and the proportion of Americans with money invested in—and turning a profit from—stocks grew steadily. By century's end, 48.8 percent of American families owned stock.

1998 Stock Ownership by Family Income

less than $10,000	7.7%
$10,001-$24,999	24.7%
$25,000-$49,999	52.7%
$50,000-$99,999	74.3%
$100,000+	91.0%

SOURCE: *Events That Shaped the Century.* Richard B. Stolley, editor.

(1892) Kings Of Wall Street. New York's most powerful businessmen of the 1860s and the 1870s, Jay Gould (1836 - 1892) and Commodore William Vanderbilt (1821- 1885) sit opposite each other at the center table. Only the very wealthy had stock ownership during the turn of the century.

1990s • BOOM OR BUST IN THE STOCK MARKET ~ Among these individuals, success stories are common lore. Tales circulate about the 25-year old man from Queens, New York who turned his $1,100 investment into $100,000 in two short months and the Houston secretary who left her job to trade full-time and now makes $60,000 a month from her investments. Dozens of books and programs promise to teach average investors the secrets to making money on the stock market, asserting that "The stock market is one of the biggest creators of true and lasting wealth in the world today. It's one of the only ways that a little guy can start with almost nothing and grow to make THOUSANDS or even MILLIONS of dollars! The stock market has made thousands of investors rich beyond their wildest dreams in the past few years." At certain points, of course, this has been true. Those with the money to invest have reaped enormous profits during major booms, such as the dotcom explosion of the 1990s. (Incidentally, many of those offering advice on how to become a millionaire have become millionaires themselves thanks to profits from the sale of their products.)

Select Internet Stocks— October 1998-January 1999

Amazon.com	up 542.6%
Shopping.com	up 860%
EBay.com	up 905.2%
SkyMall.com	up1181.3%

SOURCE: www.zdnet.com/pcmag/news/trends

1990s • WHO WANTS TO BE A MILLIONAIRE (AND THEN SOME)? ~ Whatever their path to success, millionaires have become increasingly common in twentieth-century America. Early in the century, only a handful of men, mainly manufacturing and shipping magnates from families of long-standing wealth, could claim the title of millionaire. By mid-century, there were 154 millionaires living in the United States, a number that multiplied exponentially in the subsequent decades. In 2000, more than four percent of American households—more than 7.1 million families—had a total net worth of $1 million or more (not including their primary home). Many of those achieved that wealth during the prosperous 1990s: the number of millionaire households more than doubled between 1994 and 1999 alone. As the population grows at a rate of about one percent annually, the number of millionaire Americans grows at 17 percent.

Unlike millionaires of the early twentieth century, these modern millionaires are rarely famous heads of massive companies. Eighty percent of them work; nearly two-thirds are self-employed, many in distinctly unglamorous retail or even salvage operations. Of the more than seven million millionaires, less than 200,000 make $1 million a year or more. The millionaires' median annual income is only $131,000; their median $3.7 million wealth derives from the 20 percent of their income they invest each year.

Even more staggering than the multiplication of millionaires has been the expansion of the billionaire class. With a scant few members throughout much of the twentieth century, the group of Americans boasting a net worth of $1 billion or more has skyrocketed in the last two decades of the century—from 13 in 1982 to 170 by 1997. The magnificent wealth of two of these billionaires—Sam Walton and Bill Gates—places them among the richest Americans of all time.

Richest Americans and their businesses
(wealth converted to modern value)

1.	J.D. Rockefeller	oil	$189.6 billion
2.	Andrew Carnegie	steel	$100.5 billion
3.	Cornelius Vanderbilt	shipping, railroads	$ 95.9 billion
4.	John Jacob Astor	real estate, fur	$ 78.0 billion
5.	Bill Gates	computer software	$ 61.7 billion
6.	Stephen Girard	shipping, real estate	$ 55.6 billion
7.	A.T. Stewart	retail, real estate	$ 46.9 billion
8.	Frederick Weyerhaeuser	lumber	$ 43.2 billion
9.	Jay Gould	railroads	$ 42.1 billion
10.	Marshall Field	retail	$ 40.7 billion
11.	Sam Walton	discount retail	$ 37.4 billion
12.	Henry Ford	automobiles	$ 36.1 billion

SOURCE: "Time 100: People of the Century" www.time.com/time/time100

1962-2000

1962-2000 • WALMART AND MICROSOFT ~ Both self-made moguls, Walton and Gates, represent one path to this iteration of the American dream of prosperity. Born in 1918, Walton started his retailing career as manager of a Ben Franklin franchise in 1945 and founded his own chain, WalMart, in 1962. Four years later, he had twenty stores, and his empire grew steadily, surpassing Sears as America's largest retailer in 1991, and operating more than 3,000 stores by century's end. In 1985, this hands-on businessman was America's wealthiest citizen. The following year, he was surpassed by Bill Gates, founder of Microsoft, who became a billionaire at age 31 with the 1986 initial public offering (IPO) of his company. Like Walton, who thrived on management, Gates maintained complete control of his company for as long as possible. Neither man was particularly innovative in creating his product—discount merchandising or software—rather, they both borrowed ideas and built upon them, demonstrating their real genius in marketing. In doing so, both have become icons, paving the way for others. WalMart made possible a whole new breed of "category killers"—retailers able to corner the market for a particular product or service and drive competitors out of business; Microsoft has legions of imitators, software companies seeking some fraction of the success of this leader. And Walton and Gates themselves have followers, hoping to follow their example to fortune and fame.

Twentieth-century America offers a number of routes to wealth. The proliferation of Internet start-ups and other technology companies at the end of the century has made working for a living somewhat more profitable, with stock options considered almost standard in this sector of the economy, even for those in relatively low-status positions. Microsoft forged the way for this phenomenon, enticing employees with potentially lucrative stock portfolios. "If postwar America of the 1950s and 60s democratized middle-classness, Gates has democratized filthy-richness—or has at least started to. Get the right job offer from Microsoft, work hard, get rich; no miracle required….The Gates Road to Wealth is still a one-laner, and traffic is limited. But the idea that a successful corporation should enrich not merely its executives and big stockholders but also a fair number of ordinary line employees is (although not unique to Microsoft) potentially revolutionary. Wealth is good." The shift in attitude has been remarkable. (David Gelernter, "Software Strongman: Bill Gates" on www.time.com/time/time100/builder/profile/gates.html).

1990S • MODERN FAIRY TALES OF MARRIAGE AND MONEY ~ For others, the road to wealth has less to do with hard work than with good luck. Marriage into a wealthy family, while highly unlikely for most Americans, remains a dream for some. Etiquette books in the early twentieth century counseled young women to marry above their station when possible, selecting men with fine economic prospects, husbands with whom they would find security.

Americans watched in awe in 1956 as actress Grace Kelly married Prince Rainier III of Monaco in a modern-day fairy tale wedding. Though by all accounts unhappy with her marriage, Princess Grace remained a powerful example that this dream could come true. Enthralled by royalty, Americans followed every moment of genuine royals, particularly the English royal family (the 1981 wedding of Prince Charles and Lady Diana drew a global radio and television audience of 1 billion), and the decidedly American equivalent, the Kennedy clan. To be sure, the women who married into these dynasties were anything but Cinderella-types: all of them came from moneyed backgrounds. Even Grace Kelly, often touted as the daughter of an Irish-American bricklayer, had been raised a debutante; her father was no average mason, but rather a millionaire contractor.

The proliferation of wealth in the late twentieth-century has seen a new brand of marrying money. Until he married Melinda French in 1994 at the age of 38, software tycoon Bill Gates was steadfastly entrenched at the top of the eligible bachelor list. Though the two richest men in America (Gates and investor Warren Buffett, also married) may be unavailable, the list of single millionaires seems to mount daily, and there is no shortage of advice for catching one's very own millionaire spouse. Indeed, there are more than a dozen books in print that offer suggestions on how to marry money: as Susan Wright proclaims in the title of her 1995 book, "The rich have to marry someone—why not you?" The books' recommendations range from the practical—live and work near the wealthy so you can mingle among them and get noticed—to the philosophical—downplay the importance of money so the millionaire-in-question believes you appreciate the person, not the wealth. Acknowledging that women are far more likely than men to find a rich spouse, the books address women as their primary audience and promise them success.

Some Representative Titles

How to Snare a Millionaire by Lisa Johnson
How to Marry the Rich by Ginie Polo Sayles
How to Marry Money: The Rich Have to Marry Someone—Why Not You? by Susan Wright
How to Meet the Rich: For business, Friendship, or Romance by Ginie Polo Sayles
Gold Diggers Guide: How to Marry Rich by Thomas Schnurmacher
How to Marry Super Rich: Or Love, Money, and the Morning After by Sheilah Graham
Desirable Men: How to Find Them by Nancy Fagan

Building on this theme, newspapers and magazines around the country have furnished lists of eligible and interested wealthy bachelors, particularly around Valentine's Day. Many of these features urge women to travel to male-dominated areas like Silicon Valley near San Francisco where they will have any number of prospective suitors, men who may lack the time or social acumen for dating, but who are interested in finding a mate.

(1965) The new Mercedes Benz 600, which holds nine passengers and is so long that it occupies two parking spaces. Two women feed money into two parking meters, to accommodate the vehicle.

2000

There are even dating services in some metropolitan areas that cater to the needs of wealthy professionals. In a new twist on the mail-order bride concept, millionaires can select their women by video.

2000 • Who Wants to Marry a Multi-Millionaire?

~ In what was undoubtedly the strangest iteration of this phenomenon, 23 million Americans tuned in to watch the 16 February 2000 special "Who Wants to Marry a Multi-Millionaire?" on the FOX television network. An anonymous and unseen multi-millionaire watched as 50 women competed in a Miss America-style contest, complete with bathing suit parade and wedding gown competition, for the honor of becoming his wife. Each contestant received a free week-long vacation in Las Vegas; the top five finishers each enjoyed a $2,500 shopping spree; the winner, Darva Conger, was awarded a new car, a $35,000 diamond ring, a two-week tropical honeymoon, and, of course, the opportunity to marry the multi-millionaire whom she had never seen. She accepted his proposal and married him before an enormous television audience. Scandal erupted in the following days as millionaire Rick Rockwell's financial holdings and past criminal record came under scrutiny, and the couple's marriage was eventually annulled, but the precedent was set. A whole new kind of marriage for money had appeared.

1950-2000 • Wealth by Winning

~ The "Who Wants to Marry a Multi-Millionaire?" fiasco was certainly not the first time a television event offered the promise of wealth. The advent of television more than fifty years earlier had ushered in a new path to wealth with the game show. A popular format on radio since the 1920s, the game show became a staple of television programming. The Game Show Network, a cable channel devoted exclusively to these programs, old and new, debuted in the 1990s and has 30 million subscribers.

Some of the earliest TV game shows like "Queen for a Day" had started on radio and moved to the new medium. In this popular show, audience members competed for prizes by telling their saddest life story; the winner's wish was granted—she received gifts and services to ameliorate her desperate situation. "Beat the Clock" and "Truth or Consequences" also moved from radio to television during this period. Other 1950s game shows awarded prizes to contestants who performed silly tasks or answered ludicrous questions, often with help from celebrity guests. At their peak in the 1950s, there were 22 game shows on the air. But by far the most successful ones, in the 1950s and since, were those that offered increasingly larger cash prizes—the quiz shows.

In 1957, five of the top ten television programs were quiz shows. Two of them, "The $64,000 Question" and "Twenty-One" had consistently commanded high ratings. Debuting in 1955, "The $64,000 Question" had reached 47.5 million viewers on 32 million television sets in August 1955: that number represented nearly one-third of the American population. Drawn in by the drama of the show—in its final stages, contestants were asked only one question each week in their expert field—and by the vicarious thrill of a large cash prize, viewers tuned in faithfully until the quiz show scandal of 1958, when it was revealed that contestants were receiving the answers ahead of time. The scandal also tainted the other major quiz show, "Twenty-One," which had offered even more impressive prizes. Contestants worked their way up to the titular twenty-one points with almost limitless earning potential. Final contestant Charles Van Doren won $129,000.

Though tainted by the scandal, quiz shows returned a short time later with the premier of "Jeopardy!" in 1964. The prizes were smaller—the largest single-game winnings totaled only $34,000—but the drama was heightened by the pace of the contest and by its daily, rather than weekly, episodes. In syndication since 1983, "Jeopardy!" continues to reach 32 million viewers a week and remains the second most popular syndicated television program.

Like its 1950s predecessors, however, "Jeopardy!"'s difficult questions demand a certain degree of academic expertise: for that reason, quiz shows are inherently less democratic than other types of game shows that required less skill (and offered less valuable prizes). Networks in the late 1990s reduced that gap with the introduction of a new breed of quiz shows—spearheaded by ABC's hugely successful "Who Wants to Be a Millionaire?"—anchored more in popular culture and general knowledge than academe. NBC revived its 1950s icon "Twenty-One," while rising network FOX introduced a new spin with "Greed," a team-based show. All three appeared in the 1999-2000 season, commanding record audiences and top ratings.

The first and the longest running, "Who Wants to Be a Millionaire?" really set the tone for these new quiz shows. Contestants work their way towards the top prize of $1 million by correctly answering multiple-choice questions of increasing difficulty, calling upon three lifelines as needed—phoning a friend for assis-

1920s-1990s

tance, asking the audience for their opinion, and removing two of the incorrect answers from consideration. The application process for contestants requires the skill of correctly answering a few test questions and the luck of surviving two rounds of random computerized selection; the odds of reaching the "hot seat" are long, to be sure, but democratic enough to inspire hope among the 29 million viewers who tune in on each of the four nights "Millionaire" airs, and the thousands who clog the phone lines each time the show searches for more contestants.

Despite its top ratings, "Who Wants to Be a Millionaire?" is actually not responsible for the largest prize ever awarded on a television game show. That honor belongs to its short-lived competitor "Twenty-One," which continued to offer limitless earning potential in its second incarnation. In February of 2000, David Legler, a lieutenant in the Navy and part-time graduate student won $1,765,000 on that show before walking away.

1920s-1990s • KNOW WHEN TO HOLD THEM

Built into the format of both "Millionaire" and "Twenty-One" are provisions that allow contestants to leave at certain times with their winnings to that point, in other words, to decide how much they are willing to risk for the chance to win even more. Though it has had a somewhat checkered past in America, gambling continues to hold out the possibility of increasing one's money through any number of avenues, legal and otherwise, skilled and not.

Gambling options have always been plentiful, even in the early republic, with local dice and card games practically omnipresent. Horse racing appeared early, with the first track built on Long Island in 1665; the first organized casinos appeared in the south in the early nineteenth century. Although gambling came under fire in the reformist climate of the mid-1800s as an immoral activity that unfairly targeted the poor and was rife with corruption, illegal gaming contin-

(1955) A smiling couple celebrate with excitement after hitting the jackpot on the slot machine. A pile of coins spill out of the machine.

ued uninterrupted into the twentieth century. Often operated by organized crime syndicates, especially during 1920s Prohibition, gambling became a major industry. During the Depression of the 1930s, many forms of gambling were legalized in an attempt to stimulate the economy; the simultaneous crackdown on organized crime was intended to channel the profits gambling yielded into government coffers instead. Illegal gambling continued, however. End-of-the-century estimates place yearly expenditures on illegal forms of gaming at more than $32 billion.

In 1931, Nevada legalized almost all forms of gambling, transforming gaming from illicit activity to leisure pursuit with the opening of dozens of resort casinos in and around Las Vegas. The following decades saw legalization campaigns elsewhere as states sought to procure some of the proceeds for themselves. Frequently limited to particular forms such as horse or dog racing or to particular locations like riverboats, these newly legal gambling outlets helped make legal gaming a $40 billion industry by 1995. Only Utah and Hawaii have no legal gambling; twenty-seven states have organized casinos (mainly on Native American reservations), mostly built in the 1990s. Their success has been staggering. In 1993, 70 million people attended a Major League Baseball game, while 92 million went to casinos.

LOTTERIES

Although casinos account for 88 percent of gambling expenditures, lotteries are actually the most popular form of legal gambling, accessible to 80 percent of the population (the 210 million Americans who live in the District of Columbia and the 38 states with lotteries) and played by as many as 70 percent of the adults in those regions in any given year. The hope of winning the big jackpot leads Americans to spend nearly $319 on lottery tickets every second.

Popular in early America and frequently used as a fundraising tool for both public works and private projects, lotteries fell out of favor in the 1840s thanks to numerous scandals. They continued to flourish in the frontier West and parts of the Deep South—where they were used to help recoup losses after the Civil War—until finally outlawed everywhere in 1894. Thereafter, playing the numbers was an illegal, though wide-

Establishment of State Lotteries

1964	New Hampshire
1967	New York
1970	New Jersey
1972	Pennsylvania, Connecticut, Massachusetts, Michigan
1973	Maryland
1974	Ohio, Rhode Island, Illinois, Maine
1975	Delaware
1978	Vermont
1981	Arizona
1982	Washington, Washington, DC
1983	Colorado
1985	Oregon, California, Iowa
1986	West Virginia, Missouri
1987	South Dakota, Kansas, Montana
1988	Virginia, Wisconsin, Florida
1989	Idaho, Indiana, Kentucky
1990	Minnesota
1991	Louisiana
1992	Texas, Nebraska
1993	Georgia
1994	New Mexico
2000	South Carolina

Source: www.lotteryinsider.com

1920s-1990s

States with Highest Annual Per Capita Lottery Expenditures

South Dakota	$750
Rhode Island	$741
Delaware	$703
Massachusetts	$552
Washington, DC	$394
Georgia	$290
Connecticut	$272
West Virginia	$248
New Jersey	$227
Maryland	$231

* State with lowest lottery spending is Montana, with $33 per person

** Statistics are not yet available from South Carolina, which voted to establish a lottery in November 2000.

Source: www.lotteryinsider.com

(1936) Looking For Work. An emigrant family from Missouri looking for work in the pea fields of California. Severe hardship makes 'get rich quick" schemes very appealing

spread practice, until New Hampshire created the first modern lottery in 1964, quickly followed by other states such as New York and New Jersey. Amid the economic upheaval of the 1970s, many states turned to lotteries as sources for new revenue; twelve states founded lottery programs during that decade.

Since the legalization of lotteries in 1964, Americans have spent approximately $352 billion, despite the fact that lotteries offer the worst odds of winning of any form of gambling. Nevertheless, with jackpots that have surpassed $100 million, for many the temptation is often too hard to resist. Twenty-eight percent of those who play the lottery do so on a weekly basis, 14 percent more than once a week; thus about ten percent of the customers account for two-thirds of ticket sales (a statistic critics point to as evidence that playing the lottery can become addictive behavior). As the prize increases, so does the number of players. According to estimates from GTech, the leading supplier of lottery systems in the nation, 162 million people purchase tickets from their equipment in an average week; that number swells to 400-500 million in states with especially large jackpots that week. The largest jackpot ever in a state lottery was $118.8 million (in California). The coalition of twenty states and the District of Columbia that operates a joint lottery—Powerball—offers even larger prizes, the largest being $295.7 million in July 1998.

1970-2000 • MODERN LOTTERIES

Technological innovations promise to increase the availability of lotteries. Instant-win tickets, introduced in the 1970s, account for about 25 percent of lottery expenditures, mostly new spending, and the continual influx of new scratch games keeps customers engaged.

Internet gaming is also on the rise, with dozens of sites that offer lottery games and state lottery sales, and hundreds more that provide lottery tips and information.

YOU MAY ALREADY BE A WINNER

The Internet has also breathed new life into another strike-it-rich scheme—the sweepstakes. Thousands of websites offer games, most of them free of charge, sponsored by companies who use them as a form of advertising and market research. The prizes are generally of little value—products or small amounts of cash—but some can reach as high as $5,000 or $10,000. In exchange for personal information to be used for marketing purposes, companies offer chances to win. (One such site is, interestingly enough, www.ragstoriches.com, which offers links to dozens of games, as well as advice on increasing the chances of winning.)

While the Internet offers new possibilities, older forms of sweepstakes continue unabated—supermarket giveaways, mail-order offers, and, most notably, the major magazine sweepstakes initiated by Publishers Clearing House in 1967. PCH has awarded $160 million in cash and prizes since its founding. Its primary competitor, American Family Publishers has given out $106 million to 345,000 winners since 1978. Though the odds of winning the top prize (now $10 million in each case) are less than one in 60 million, Americans continue to return their entries in record numbers. As those who read the fine print know, purchases do not increase the odds of winning, so it is that sweepstakes are truly the only way of getting something for nothing (or at the most, for the price of a single stamp).

CONCLUSION

This logical, if absurd, terminus of the American dream of fabulous wealth stands at the opposite end of the spectrum from the middle-class dream of hard-fought and well-deserved financial security, but that may just be the point—individual (and individualized) prosperity, one America, many dreams. Implicit in them all is a sense of moving forward, of exceeding limitations and transcending current realities. The dream posits America as a promised land in which progress is possible, even probable. The barriers that stand between reality and success are all too clear for many groups—racial and ethnic minorities, the poor, women, homosexuals—but over the course of the twentieth century, they have laid claim to the dream nevertheless, asserting their right to define it, pursue it, and ultimately achieve it.

BIBLIOGRAPHY AND INTERNET RESOURCES

"Billionaires' Club: the road to success is through the high-tech industry" *PC Magazine Online* (6 October 1997) www.zdnet.com/pcmag/

Bryant, Adam. "A Millionaire Moment." *Newsweek* (13 March 2000) www.newsweek.com

Cringely, Robert X. *Accidental Empires: How the Boys of Silicon Valley Make Their Millions, Battle Foreign Competition, and Still Can't Get a Date.* New York: HarperBusiness, 1993.

Dunstam, Roger. "Gambling in California." www.library.ca.gov/CRB/

Fink, Rychard. "Horatio Alger as a Social Philosopher" in *Ragged Dick and Mark, the Match Boy.* New York: Crowell-Collier Publishing, 1962.

Fridson, Martin S. *It Was a Very Good Year: Extraordinary Moments in Stock Market History*. New York: John Wiley and Sons, Inc., 1998.

"The G.I. Bulge" on-line exhibit at www.sumweb.syr.edu/archives/ Click on "exhibits."

Hill, John R. and Gary Palmer. "Going for Broke: the economic and social impact of a South Carolina lottery." www.scpolicycouncil.com

"How to Make Thousands of Dollars by Winning at Contests: the sweepstakes game" www.gowingo.com

"Levittown at Fifty" www.lihistory.com/ Then use search for "Levittown"

"Lottery Guides" www.lotteryinsider.com

Nye, David E. *Electrifying America: Social Meanings of a New Technology*. Cambridge, Massachusetts: The MIT Press, 1990.

Smith, Anne Kates. "$9 Million Worth of Secrets: Interview with Thomas Stanley" *U.S. News and World Report* (9 June 1997)

Stanley, Thomas and William Danko. *The Millionaire Next Door*. Marietta, GA: Longstreet Press, 1997.

———, *The Millionaire Mind*. Kansas City, MO: Andrews McMeel Publishing, 2000.

Stewart, Doug. "The Madness that Swept Miami." *Smithsonian* 31:10 (January 2001): 58-67.

Stolley, Richard B., ed. *Events that Shaped the Century*. Alexandria, VA: Time-Life Books, 1998.

———, *The American Dream: The '50s*. Alexandria, VA: Time-Life Books, 1998.

———, *Turbulent Years: The '60s*. Alexandria, VA: Time-Life Books, 1998.

"Time 100: People of the Century" www.time.com/time/time100

"United States Resident Population by State" www.census.gov

"U.S. Millionaires Double in Five Years" (19 September 2000), Associated Press.

"World War II's 'Silent Army' Produced 'Silent Revolution'" www.vfw.org/magazine/
See Oct 97 issue, p. 32.

Karen S. Oakes

INVENTIONS

(1954) Dr. Vladimir Kosma Zworykin (1889 - 1982) Russian born American physicist who pioneered the development of the electron microscope and television camera examines the 'engine' of a electronic model car which can steer, stop and turn when obstructed.

TIMELINE

1500-1799 ~ The Roots of Modern Science

Nicolaus Copernicus, a Polish mathematician, develops new theories of a sun-centered universe (c. 1500) / Johannes Kepler (1571-1630) and Galileo Galilei (1564-1642) develop theories in relation to the existence of other planets and their motion / Isaac Newton (1642-1707) makes significant contributions to mathematics, physics, astronomy, and optics / Francis Bacon (1561-1626) envisions the power of science as the savior of the human race / Model steam carriage made in China (1678) / Richard Arkwright invents the spinning jenny and the power-driven spinner (1700s) / Three-wheel, steam-powered carriage developed in Britain (1786)

MILESTONES: First American city, St. Augustine, Florida settled by the Spanish (1565) • William Harvey describes the circulation of blood in England (1628) • American Revolution (1776) • Edward Jenner develops smallpox vaccination in England (1796)

1800-1899 ~ The Industrial Revolution

Eli Whitney invents interchangeable parts, making mass production possible (early 1800s) / George Goodyear invents rubber tires (1840s) / Bessemer steel process invented (1850s) / Carl Benz and Gottlieb Daimler create the essential elements of the gasoline automobile, including the spark plug (1870s-1880s) / Alexander Graham Bell with George Watson invent the telephone (1876) / Using alternating current, Nikola Tesla develops dynamos, motors, and transformers (1880s) / Thomas Edison invents the light bulb (1879) and one-horsepower generator (1881) / George Eastman invents celluloid rolls of film for use in Kodak cameras (1888) / Thomas Edison invents the phonograph (1876) and motion picture (1888) / W.K. Roentgen discovers X-rays (1895) / Guglielmo Marconi sends the first wireless message by radio waves (1897)

MILESTONES: George Stephenson builds the first public railroad, the Baltimore and Ohio (B & O) (1825) • First railroad sleeping cars introduced (1829) • Steam-powered buses in use in London (1832) • Texas Revolution against Mexico (1835) • First use of anesthetic (ether) on humans, U.S. (1842) • Transatlantic cable laid from U.S. to Europe (1857-1866) • First petroleum well discovered in Pennsylvania (1859) • Joseph Lister uses antiseptics in surgery in England (1867)

1900-1919 ~ The Beginnings of Mass Production

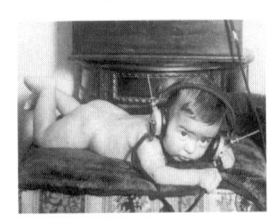

August Otto, in Germany, invents the internal combustion engine (c. 1900) / Electrolux and Hoover introduce the first vacuum cleaners (1901) / Director D.W. Griffith produces the first feature length film, *The Great Train Robbery*, which lasted eleven minutes (1903) / Lee De Forest invents the vacuum tube, essential to the development of electronics (1906) / Garrett Morgan invents the gas mask to keep firefighters from being overcome by smoke (1912) / First transcontinental phone line is established between New York City and San Francisco (1915)

MILESTONES: Color photo reproduction provides cheap, eye-catching images for advertisements (1900) • Wright Brothers fly a plane at Kitty Hawk (1903) • Scotland Yard demonstrates fingerprinting at World's Fair in St. Louis (1904) • Airmail service inaugurated (1910) • Vitamin A discovered (1912) • Pasteurization of milk begins in large cities (1914)

1920-1929 ~ The Consumer Society

Invention of Freon makes widespread home refrigeration feasible (1920s) / KDKA in Pittsburgh, the first public radio station in the U.S., begins broadcasting on November 2, 1921 / Invention of the electrocardiograph (1923) / Charles Birdseye develops a quick-freeze technique, making frozen foods possible (1924) / First miniature camera, the Leica, is produced in Germany (1925) / Introduction of the pop-up toaster (1926) / Philip Farnsworth invents the television picture tube (1927) / *The Jazz Singer*, first talking picture, is released (1927) / George Eastman invents the Kodak color film process (1928) / Walt Disney creates the first animated motion picture, *Steamboat Willie* (1929) / Vladimir Zworykin, a Russian, develops the first practical television system (1929)

MILESTONES: First commercial aircraft flights for passengers and cargo begin (1920) • First diesel engine railroad put into service (1920) • Traffic signal technology developed by African American Garrett Morgan (1920s) • First modern lie detector invented (1921) • Inkblot test introduced by Hermann Rorschach (1921) • Charles Lindbergh's solo flight from New York to Paris (1927) • Stock market crash propels economy into the worst economic depression in American history (October 1929)

1930-1945 ~ Practical Inventions

Guglielmo Marconi develops radar and microwave ovens (1930s) / First wearable hearing aid is produced (1935) / Al Gross develops the two-way radio, or walkie-talkie, used extensively during WWII (1938) / Wallace H. Carothers at the E.I. Dupont chemical company develops the synthetic fiber, nylon (1938) / Earl Tupper manufacturer of plastic war materials (1938) and later invents Tupperware (1938) / Ukrainian immigrant Igor Sikorsky builds the first successful helicopter (1939) / First atomic bomb tested in Los Alamos, New Mexico (1943)

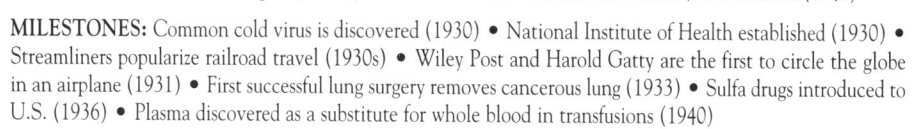

MILESTONES: Common cold virus is discovered (1930) • National Institute of Health established (1930) • Streamliners popularize railroad travel (1930s) • Wiley Post and Harold Gatty are the first to circle the globe in an airplane (1931) • First successful lung surgery removes cancerous lung (1933) • Sulfa drugs introduced to U.S. (1936) • Plasma discovered as a substitute for whole blood in transfusions (1940)

1946-1955 ~ Beginning the Electronic Age

First electronic computer, ENIAC, is developed (1946) / Transistors invented (1947) / First coast-to-coast television broadcast (1951) / Artificial pacemaker regulates heart rhythm (1952) / First color television broadcast (1953)

MILESTONES: NBC, CBS, and ABC television broadcast the House Un-American Activities hearings (1947) • Chuck Yeager breaks the sound barrier (1947) • 10 billion cans of foods are produced each year in the U.S. (1950) • Swanson introduces the TV dinner (1954) • Sabin live polio vaccine introduced (1955)

1956-1969 ~ Entering the Space Age

Kidney dialysis machine invented (1956) / *Sputnik* satellite launched by the Soviet Union (1957) / Invention of the microchip launches the technological revolution (1958) / U.S. Postal Service uses the first fax machines (1959) / Laser is invented (1960) / *Telstar* satellite makes worldwide transmission of television programs possible (1962) / *Early Bird*, first commercial communications satellite, relays television programs between the U.S. and Europe (1965)

MILESTONES: First nuclear submarine, *Nautilus*, passes underneath the North Pole (1958) • Oral contraceptive pills approved (1960) • Soviet cosmonaut Yuri Gagarin is the first human in space (1961) • First kidney transplant (1962) • Americans land on the moon (1969)

1970-1979 ~ On the Brink of Breakthrough

Electrically powered light rail systems put into service (1970) / Computerized Axial Tomography (CAT) developed in England to provide cross sectional X-rays (1972) / VCRs introduced: Betamax (1975), VHS (1976) / Steven Jobs and Stephen Wozniak create the first computers for home use, starting the computer age (1977) / Magnetic resonance imaging (MRI) scanners invented (1977) / Balloon angioplasty technique developed to reopen diseased arteries (1977)

MILESTONES: Environmental Protection Agency created (1970) • Supersonic *Concorde* put into service for passenger flight (1972) • Cable use of satellites begins (1973) • Three Mile Island meltdown causes backlash against nuclear reactors (1979) • First test-tube baby born in England (1978)

1980-1999 ~ Into the World Beyond

First space shuttle, *Columbia*, is launched (1981) / First permanent artificial heart used in a human (1982) / Compact discs invented (1983) / First commercial cellular telephones are marketed (1985) / High definition television invented (1986) / Mosaic, first Internet browser, is produced (1993)

MILESTONES: *Challenger* space shuttle explodes killing six astronauts and the first private citizen in space, Christa McAuliffe (1986) • Fall of the Berlin Wall begins breakup of the Soviet Union (1989) • World Wide Web is created (1990) • First gene therapy performed on a human to treat an immune deficiency (1990) • U.S. scientists clone a male calf (1997) • First mapping of an entire human genome (2000)

INTRODUCTION

Despite his words, Leonardo da Vinci was one of the most prolific and eclectic inventors ever. In fact, few people seem to have heeded those words, especially in the twentieth century. Throughout the five centuries prior to the twentieth century, the scientific world was in ferment—from the scientific revolution of the sixteenth and seventeenth centuries—to the Industrial Revolution and the plethora of nineteenth century inventions. The Renaissance brought an opening up to the field of philosophy and humanistic thought in Europe. Leonardo and others experimented in the field of art and literature, as well as in science.

1600s-1700s • SCIENTIFIC REVOLUTION ~ The scientific revolution of the sixteenth and seventeenth centuries in Europe created the basis for the technological innovations of later centuries. One of the first scientific fields to develop was astronomy, using mathematical calculations. Nicolaus Copernicus (1473-1543), a Polish mathematician, developed new theories of a sun-centered universe. The Danish astronomer Tycho Brahe (1546-1601) used Copernicus's theories to develop observations of the paths of the moon and the planets. Then Johannes Kepler (1571-1630) and Galileo Galilei (1564-1642) developed further theories on the existence of other planets and their motion. Both Kepler and Galilei stressed the importance of observation in scientific inquiry. The culmination of the scientific revolution was the work of Isaac Newton (1642-1707), who made significant contributions to mathematics, physics, astronomy, and even optics, and who brought to a climax the changes that had begun with Copernicus. He explained the theories of motion and gravity and the elliptical

Inventions

~

Although human subtlety makes a variety of inventions by different means to the same end, it will never devise an invention more beautiful, more simple or more direct than does nature, because in her inventions nothing is lacking, and nothing is superfluous
LEONARDO DA VINCI

*If a man builds a better mousetrap,
the world will flock to his door.*
RALPH WALDO EMERSON

I never did anything worth doing by accident, nor did any of my inventions come by accident; they came by hard work.
THOMAS EDISON

1700-1800s

orbits of planets. He developed the mathematical field of calculus and established many of the basic laws of modern physics. Important to all of these scientists was the publicity given their work and its acceptance by leaders. Rene Descartes (1596-1650) published works on the importance of the power of the mind and the use of reason—the basis for scientific thought. Francis Bacon (1561-1626) was a great scientific propagandist who envisioned the power of science as the savior of the human race. This great advancement in scientific thought and establishment of science and the scientific method as acceptable to society laid the groundwork for the great advances in technology during the Industrial Revolution of the late eighteenth and nineteenth centuries.

1800s • Early American Inventors ~ Two American inventors of the late eighteenth and early nineteenth centuries deserve mention, in part because they usually are remembered for their work in politics rather than in science. Thomas Jefferson, the third president of the United States, was a multi-talented man. Besides being a great statesman and leader, he was also a planter and architect. Three of his inventions illustrate his versatility. After spending time in Europe and observing farming techniques, he invented a new type of plow that was much more efficient and could plow more land at one time. As President, he invented a code ring (cylinder) for sending messages. The letters were scrambled on the rings of the cylinder and only a person with a matching cylinder could decode the message. Such a device was used in World War I to send messages. While in the White House, he invented a way to serve dinner and remove the dishes without opening a door. The servants could place the dishes on circular shelves that revolved by touching a spring. His house in Charlottesville, Virginia, contains many of his inventions or improvements on devices, including a dumbwaiter and grandfather's clock.

Benjamin Franklin was an even more talented inventor with wide-ranging interests. His most famous discovery was the conductivity of lightning and the invention of the lightning rod. He also invented bifocal glasses by cutting two different types of glasses in half and joining them together as one lens. Also memorable was his invention of the Franklin stove, made of steel, which heated a room much more efficiently and thus used less wood. Other inventions included the harmonica, street lamp, and white duck clothing for wear in the tropics. He also created the first volunteer fire department and was the first to describe the Gulf Stream.

1700-1800s • Industrial Revolution ~ The Industrial Revolution, which began in England in the late 1700s, focused on the transformation of manufacturing through the introduction of a new social institution: the factory. The factory brought increased productivity through the development of more efficient tools and machines and the exploitation of labor. The textile industry in England was the first to be transformed. There were all sorts of new inventions, especially the spinning jenny, the power-driven spinner of Richard Arkwright (1732-1792), and the steam engine of James Watt (1736-1819), which were housed together in a factory. Agriculture saw many changes in production also, including the enclosure of land to intensify production. The Industrial Revolution of the eighteenth century focused primarily on England.

Some Inventions Milestones

Telephone • 1876
Phonograph • 1877
Incandescent light • 1879
Generator • 1881
Skyscraper • 1885
Kodak film • 1888
Modern electric motor • 1888
Motion picture • 1889
Embalming • 1890
Electric car (first in the U.S.) • 1891
Diesel engine • 1892
Gasoline auto (first in the U.S.) • 1893
Zipper • 1893
Radio • 1895
X-ray machine • 1895
Ship-to-ship radio • 1895
Condensed soup • 1897
Color photo reproduction • 1900
Wireless messages • 1901
Safety razor • 1901
Air conditioning • 1902
Airplane • 1903
Vacuum tube • 1906
Air conditioning • 1906
Interferometer (to measure stellar space) • 1907
Synthetic plastic • 1907
Battle tank • 1916
Diesel railroad engine • 1920
Frozen foods • 1920s
Television • 1920s
Lie detector • 1921
Electrocardiograph • 1923
Liquid-fuel rocket • 1926
Iron lung • 1927
Television • 1929
Cyclotron • 1930
Microwave oven • 1930s
Modern plastics • 1930s
Electron microscope • 1931
Hearing aid • 1935

Radar • 1935
Fluorescent light • 1935
Nylon • 1938
Walkie-talkie (two-way radio) • 1938
Xerography • 1938
Helicopter • 1939
Jet engine aircraft • 1939
Tape recorder • 1940s
Nuclear reactor • 1942
Combine farm machine • 1944
Atomic bomb • 1945
Digital computer • 1946
Polaroid land camera • 1947
Transistor • 1947
Polio vaccine • 1952-55
Kidney dialysis • 1956
Remote control television • 1956
Artificial satellite • 1957
Laser • 1960
Integrated circuits • 1961
Compact disc • 1965
Fiber-optic cable • 1970
Genetic engineering • 1970s
Microprocessor • 1971
Cat scanner • 1972
DNA cloning • 1973
Pager • 1974
VCR • 1975
Ultrasound • 1975
Personal computer • 1977
MRI scanner • 1977
Cell phone • 1977
Scanning tunneling microscope • 1981
Space shuttle • 1981
Artificial heart • 1982
Compact disc • 1983
High definition television • 1986
Superconductor • 1986
Hubble space telescope • 1990
Internet • 1991

1700s-1900s

The second industrial revolution of the second half of the nineteenth century involved several countries of Europe and the United States. It is the inventions and innovations of this period that effected the tremendous changes throughout the early twentieth century.

There have been greater changes in technology in the last hundred years than in all of human history. The list of inventions on the previous page highlights a few of the inventions that have had a great impact on American society and the world in the twentieth century. Until 1900, Germany and Great Britain were the industrial and innovative leaders. However, the twentieth century belongs to the United States. As Trevor Williams stated in *A Short History of Twentieth Century Technology*, the United States had a genius for taking an invention, modifying it, and using economies of scale, making it a common item in society. Often the invention then returned to Europe for added popularity. The United States had the ability to take an invention and to create a large industry, which, in turn, brought greater production efficiency and lower costs. It then added advertising and marketing strategies, and created a household necessity. What often began as an individual or small project in Europe, became a large industry aimed at benefiting the masses, or significant groups within the masses.

Some inventions have begun as instruments of war but have become instruments for the benefit of mankind. Atomic energy is a powerful example of this. Its original use was for the atomic bomb, which helped to end World War II, but it has since been proven a useful source for electrical energy. Occasionally, something invented to solve a social problem has become invaluable during a war. The gas mask is one example. Garrett Morgan (1877-1963) in Cleveland, Ohio, invented it in 1912 to keep firefighters from being overcome by smoke. It was proven valuable when his gas masks were used to rescue men trapped in a tunnel explosion under Lake Erie. Later gas masks became essential during World War I to protect soldiers from poison gas attacks.

1900s • SEEING THE POTENTIAL IN IDEAS ~ There are several important factors to keep in mind in any discussion of inventions. One factor is that sometimes what is invented in one decade does not become known to the general public or consumers until years later. For example, the Wright brothers flew their plane at Kitty Hawk, North Carolina, in

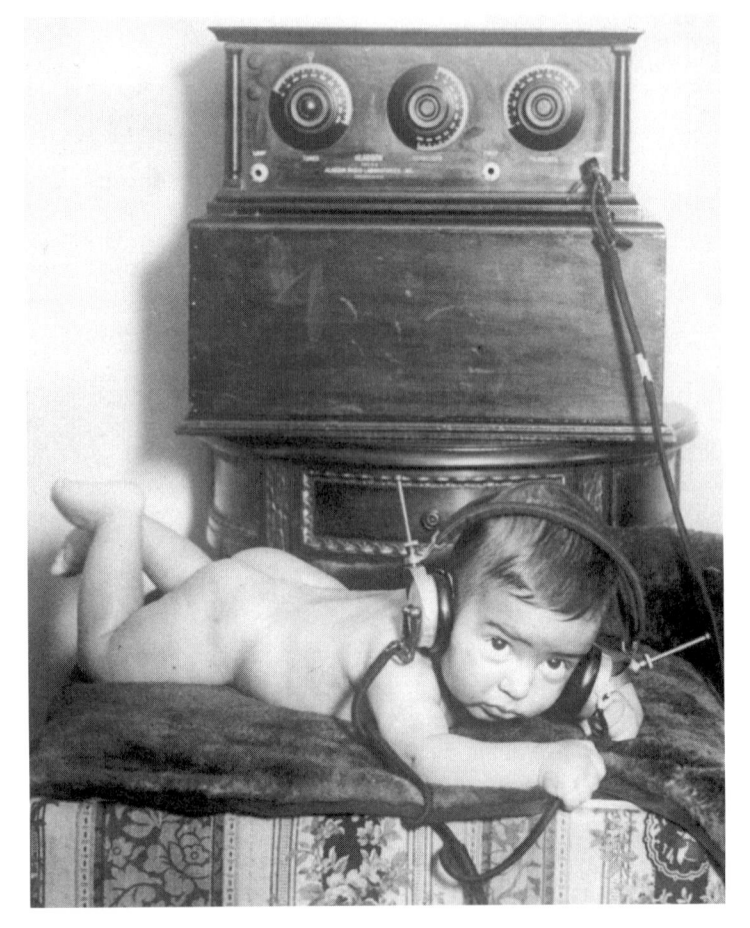

(1925) Bill Dubilier listens to the radio. Bill is the infant son of William Dubilier, whose radio mica condenser made the radio an everyday household item.

1903. For five years almost no one knew of their work. Finally, *Scientific American* published an article about it, but even then, there was little appeal. It was not until World War I (1914-1918) when airplanes were used in combat and, as a result, became significant for society as well. In the 1920s planes were used principally as mail carriers, by stuntmen, and by a few wealthy travelers. Charles Lindbergh's heroic solo flight from New York to Paris in May 1927 changed the impact of the airplane. In World War II, airplanes were a critical element, and finally in the 1950s commercial flight became common. By 1959, 45 air carriers transported some 114 million passengers.

Even television took a long time to become established. Philip Farnsworth (1906-1971) is often credited with inventing the picture tube in 1927. Vladimir Zworykin demonstrated the first completely electronic practical television system in 1929. The British and the Americans had the first public television broadcasts in the 1930s. However, it was not until the 1950s that television sets became common household items in the United States and England. Today, over 98 percent of American homes have TV sets.

Another very important factor which also must be remembered is that once an invention is accepted, it always leads to variations and improvements, often in seemingly very different directions. W.K. Roentgen (1845-1923) discovered X-rays in 1895 in Germany. In the twentieth century, this technology led not only to X-ray machines and important strides in medicine, but also to photographic film and atomic energy discoveries in the 1920s and 1930s.

Another example is Guglielmo Marconi's (1874-1937) work with extending wavelengths. The existence of electromagnetic waves had been established by 1887. Heinrich Hertz in Germany invented the first wireless telegraph in the 1880s. In 1897 Marconi first used a wireless technology to send messages. He sent the first transatlantic message in 1901. The use of extended wavelength wireless telegraphy became significant for many rescues at sea. Marconi and Ferdinand Braun shared the Nobel Prize in 1909 when Marconi was only 35. Braun was a German physicist who modified Marconi's transmitting system.

World War I gave great impetus to the use of wireless technology to send messages. In the 1920s Marconi moved from use of long waves to short waves, which could be used both day and night, and which cost less to build than long wave stations. Short waves became very important for distance radio communication. In 1922 Marconi used the reflection of wireless telegraph waves, which led to the creation of radar in the 1930s. Marconi also developed the use of microwaves, which were initially used commercially for heating ballpark hotdogs in the 1930s, but did not become popular in homes until the 1970s.

1927	1935	1947	1952	1960	2000
invention of picture tube	TV broadcasts in England/US	7000 homes with TV	6 million homes	45.5 million homes	98% of homes with TV

1876-1880

After World War II Marconi's technology and the nineteenth century theories of Christian Doppler were combined to develop the use of Doppler radar, which uses no ground stations for signals. Adapted to help navigate airplanes, the Doppler radar sends out a high pitch. When the sound waves pass through a solid, such as another plane, the waves correct the plane's course to avoid a collision. Wireless transmission also led to the development of FM radio, television, and magnetic tape recording.

Few inventions of the twentieth century originated then. Most inventions came from earlier discoveries or were improvements on earlier discoveries. By the end of the nineteenth century, many items associated with the twentieth century were already invented, including the reaper, sewing machine, telegraph, commercial rubber, commercial paper, and the linotype machine. Three of the most significant innovations of the twentieth century that began in the nineteenth century are the telephone, electricity, and the automobile.

1876 • TELEPHONE ~ The invention of the telephone eventually led to the present communications revolution. Alexander Graham Bell (1847-1922) with George Watson invented the telephone in 1876. Basically, a diaphragm vibrates in response to sound waves. The emperor of Brazil, Dom Pedro I, an admirer of Bell since a meeting at Boston University, became one of the first to use a telephone regularly. In 1878 Thomas Edison improved the Bell transmitter and his improvement was still in use in the 1950s. Edison invented a way for the voice to modulate the current supplied to the microphone instead of just causing electrical variations, which made the transmission much clearer. By 1915 the first transcontinental line was established between New York City and San Francisco. By 1919 dial phones were invented and telephone service expanded rapidly. There were 17 million phones in the United States in 1934, half of the phones in the world. By 1947, the U.S. had 32 million phones. It was not until the 1950s that long distance calls could be direct dialed. Satellite technology aided communication by telephone; one central satellite exchange could send signals to several smaller exchanges. In 1985 the first commercial cellular phones were marketed.

1880s • ELECTRICITY ~ Until the nineteenth century, mechanical engineering dominated the scientific world, but in the 1880s, electricity changed that forever. Electricity is the force that distributes energy; its existence had been known long before the twentieth century, but its power was harnessed and used for seemingly endless possibilities only in the last 100 years or so. The Greek philosopher and scientist Thales of Miletus had named electricity in 600 B.C. It is well known that Benjamin Franklin experimented with electricity produced during thunder and lightning storms. In the 1820s Michael Faraday developed electromagnets. The use of electricity was developed in England, Germany, and the United States about the same time, 1877-1880. But Thomas Edison (1847-1931), in the United States, developed the use of electricity for the common man and thus enabled electric energy to have a tremendous impact on society and twentieth century change.

Edison was a prolific inventor who once said, "I never did anything worth doing by accident, nor did any of my inventions come by accident; they came by hard work." In 1879 he invented the electric light bulb and in 1881 he created a one-horsepower generator. By 1882 he had developed a 900 hp steam-powered electric generator that lit up Pearl Street (near Wall Street) in New York City. From there uses of electricity expanded almost exponentially.

Eventually, Edison teamed up with Nikola Tesla from Croatia to develop alternating currents (AC), critical in the development of motors. Tesla championed AC when he worked for Edison and this dispute over which power was better ultimately led to Telsa quitting working for Edison, who was committed to direct current (DC). Telsa preferred alternate current because DC doesn't travel well over distance due to its inherent inefficiency and one would have to have a power plant every mile due to this fact. Edison was so convinced that AC was dangerous that he would arrange public demonstrations where he would electrocute a dog with AC. Edison referred to these demonstrations as "we are going to Tesla this dog." By 1888, Tesla had patents on alternating current (a.c.) dynamos, motors, and transformers. He later sold his patents to George Westinghouse to harness Niagra Falls for hydropower.

The importance of electricity in society today was dynamically illustrated recently when California, the largest state in the U.S., nearly ran out of electric power. Computers could not function properly; hospitals could not handle patient care; businesses could not remain open; and homes could not be heated or cooled without alternative fuel. In short, the lack of electricity totally disrupted everyday life and endangered society.

1870-1930 • THE AUTOMOBILE

Perhaps the invention that most affected society, culturally, economically, and technologically in the twentieth century was the automobile, popularized by Henry Ford (1863-1947). The groundwork had been laid in the nineteenth century. The technology, which made mass production possible, was the invention of interchangeable parts by Eli Whitney in the early 1800s. George Goodyear invented rubber tires in the 1840s. Carl Benz and Gottlieb Daimler created the essential elements of the gasoline automobile, including the spark plug, in Europe in the 1870s and 1880s. Around 1900 August Otto, in Germany, invented the internal combustion engine. In the United States George Seldon was also working on gasoline-driven automobiles. Nevertheless, by 1900 steam and electric cars still dominated the industry.

Then came Henry Ford. He was supposed to become a farmer, but he was more interested in automobiles and possibilities for mass production. He adapted Eli Whitney's invention of machine-making machines (using interchangeable parts) to create the assembly line method of automobile production. Ford used the philosophy of mass production both economically and technologically. He designed a 300-foot moving assembly line, which used teams of workers, each with a specific task to repeat for each car. The assembly line was never lower than waist-high, which aided in reducing fatigue. Ford turned out the first Model T in 1909, which he produced for the next 18 years. By reducing the cost of production through mass production on an assembly line, Ford made his Model T affordable for the common man. In 1909, the Model T cost $950; by 1926, the cost had been reduced to $290. In 1913 Ford produced 1,000 cars a day; by 1927, its last year, 15 million Model Ts had been produced. Neither the model nor the color changed from 1909 to 1927. Ford is quoted to have said, "Customers can have any color they want as long as it is black."

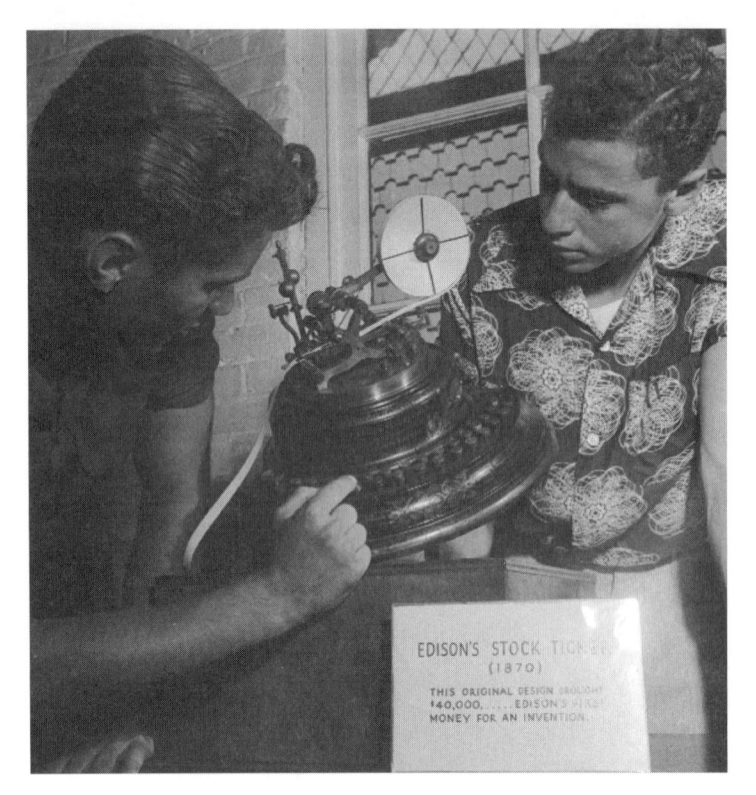

(1950) Ticker Machine. Thomas Edison (1847-1931) developed uses for electricity for the common man and thus enabled electric energy to have a tremendous impact on society and twentieth century change. In 1879 he invented the electric light bulb and in 1881 he created a one-horsepower generator. By 1882 he had developed a 900 hp steam-powered electric generator that lit up Pearl Street (near Wall Street) in New York City. From there uses of electricity expanded almost exponentially. Here, the Stock Ticker, one of Edison's early inventions, is on display in the Edison Museum, West Orange, New Jersey. He used the $40,000 raised from its sale to establish his first laboratory in Newark, New Jersey.

1860-1920

One of the major reasons for the demise of the Model T was the result of the revolution Ford created. As cars became more popular, people wanted different models and colors. The 1920s were a prosperous time and many people wanted more luxurious cars as well. Instead of one "no-frills" model, General Motors, led by Chevrolet, introduced a variety of models annually, which made earlier ones obsolete and increased sales. Many other automobile companies worked to meet the demand of the public. Eventually, Ford, too, brought out different models, replacing the Model T with the Model A in 1928.

Henry Ford not only created a technological revolution, but he also changed society and economies. Many other industries were created to support the automotive economy; transportation networks had to be built; service stations and roadside restaurants had to be established to service travelers. The popular car also was at least partly responsible for the sexual revolution of the 1920s by providing young people much more freedom. The Model T, with its rumble seat, became synonymous with the flapper. By 1929, automobile-related jobs employed one out of every eight workers in the U.S. By the 1930s, governments and society spent some $2.5 billion for maintenance and construction of roads and bridges. Thirty years later this amount had more than doubled. In 1955, auto sales were $65 billion, 20 percent of the gross national product.

1860s-1920s • INSTALLMENT BUYING

∼ The invention and development of a product is only as successful as reaching out to the public through packaging and advertising. Providing the ability for many people to buy an item is also important and was an American innovation. In the nineteenth century, Cyrus McCormick (reaper) and Isaac Singer (sewing machine) introduced the practice of installment buying. For example, a Singer sewing machine cost $125, roughly a third of an annual salary then. However, because a purchaser could pay $5 down and $3-5 a month for the machine, it became affordable for the ordinary citizen. Henry Ford also implemented the installment purchase plan for his automobiles.

1900-1920 • INVENTING USES FOR ELECTRICITY

∼ The development of the automobile industry is perhaps the most significant innovation of the first two decades of the twentieth century. (See other chapters in this encyclopedia for a more in-depth look at what it meant to the advancement of the common laborer, the emancipation of women, as well as to the development of oil, transportation, and a host of other industries.) Besides the automobile, the early 1900s were primarily noted for rapid advances in uses of electricity, including street and household lighting and the motion picture industry. In 1902 there were 100 electric billboards; by 1905, there were 2,000. Developed in London by Electrolux and in the United States by Hoover, the vacuum cleaner was introduced in 1901. The first vacuum cleaners had tubes that went through an open window to discharge the material sucked up by the machine.

1876 • PHONOGRAPH ~ The early century also saw further development of the phonograph, which Edison first invented in 1876 when he discovered how to play back messages sent by telegraph and telephone. The first phonograph used cylinders. A needle was attached to a diaphragm that vibrated in response to the sound waves of a voice. The needle made impressions on tinfoil. To reproduce the sound, another needle was attached to the diaphragm and a funnel-like horn. That needle retraced the impressions. After marveling at the first demonstrations, no one knew quite what to do with the invention. Using electricity in other ways seemed more productive, so, for many years, Edison concentrated on other possibilities. By the turn of the century, however, he returned to developing the phonograph. By 1913 he was convinced to switch from cylinders to disks (records). Disks were easier to produce and store than cylinders though, originally, their sound was not as good.

Considered a novelty at first, phonograph technology has had an important impact on society through its capability to store data. Cultural history has been preserved through the phonograph, and it served the radio and motion pictures industries well during their infancy. But more importantly, the concept of storing data to a disc, from dictophones to DVDs, revolutionized the productivity of business and science.

1888-1915 • MOTION PICTURES ~ The first decade also brought development of the motion picture industry. In 1888 Thomas Edison met with Eadweard Muybridge from England. The two envisioned the motion picture industry and developed the first kinescopes. Early kinescopes were mechanical scanning systems with motors and large rotating disks. The first motion pictures were shown in the United States in 1896. In

(circa 1900) Record label logo for Victrola RCA Victor, showing the dog Nipper looking into the horn of a Victrola. The label's slogan reads, 'His Master's Voice.'

(circa 1910) American inventor Lee DeForest (1873-1961) holding his invention, the electron tube.

1906-1920s

1903, D.W. Griffith (1874-1948) produced the first feature length film, *The Great Train Robbery* (1911), which lasted eleven minutes. This film ushered in the Nickelodeon era. Movies were silent, so theaters hired a person to play music to suit the movie scene. By 1905 there were thousands of theaters in the U.S. Most charged five cents entrance fee.

By 1914 the movie industry had moved from New York City to Hollywood, California, where it was warmer the year around and there was more space. After World War I, and for the rest of the century, Hollywood dominated the movie industry. In 1915 D.W. Griffith produced the first epic, though racist, movie—*Birth of a Nation*, about the Civil War. It was so popular that people paid as much as $2.00 to see it (a great deal of money in those days). A whole new form of entertainment influenced how millions of Americans spent their leisure time.

1906 • VACUUM TUBE ~ One of the most significant inventions of the first decade of the twentieth century was the practical use of the vacuum tube, generally credited to Lee De Forest (1873-1961) in 1906. This invention, too, first came from Thomas Edison in the early 1880s, based on his concept for the light bulb, but he made no use of his discovery. By the early twentieth century, the use of electricity was well established. De Forest, and others, built the vacuum tube in which wires and plates were contained within an airless glass cylinder or tube, *i.e.*, in a vacuum. The vacuum tubes controlled electric currents; they created signals, strengthened them, then combined or separated them. All electronic equipment from the 1920s to the 1950s used vacuum tubes. One of the first significant uses of the tube was in the development of radio, which was important in World War I and which became commercially popular in the 1920s.

1900-1920s • REFRIGERATION ~ Refrigeration, using ammonia, became an established commodity. Meat refrigeration began as early as the 1850s and brought major changes to beef production. Beef could be shipped across country and across oceans. Gradually the possibility of home refrigerators grew and by the early 1920s there were 20,000 in the U.S. With the invention of Freon in the late 1920s, refrigerators were safer and gradually became common household items. The commercial use of refrigeration greatly reduced food-borne diseases and opened markets for the distribution of products that previously could not be transported long distances. The capability to ship food products across the country changed the practice of agriculture. The development of air conditioning in the

1920s impacted a large variety of industries by improving possibilities for the manufacture and preservation of medicines, celluloid film, tobacco, and cheese.

1914-1918 • WORLD WAR I ~ World War I, from 1914-1918, created innovations and inventions which after the war were developed for consumers and which ushered in one of the most consumer oriented decades in U.S. history. Airplanes proved to be valuable instruments of war and afterward became increasingly used in commercial, and eventually, passenger aviation. The development of the gas mask from peacetime to wartime use was critical for success on the battlefield. Then after the war, both civilians and the military used it. Major innovations in weaponry—tanks, machine guns, and explosives—were adapted for civilian use. Bulldozers, backhoes, and other construction machines use tank-like tracks to propel them, and dynamite became a standard element in mining and construction.

1920s • THE AUTOMOTIVE AGE ~ The postwar decade in the United States brought a gigantic leap in inventions and innovations directed at consumers. Industries refined many advances of earlier decades. Such innovations covered the gamut from the impact of animal artificial insemination to development of film and cameras to the invention of pop-up toasters. The automobile age established a new sense of freedom and individuality. By 1929, more than half of all American families had a car; by 1930, there were more cars in New York City than on the continent of Europe. A quote by George Babbitt in Sinclair Lewis's novel, *Babbitt* (1922), sums up the automobile mood: "To George F. Babbitt, as to most prosperous citizens of Zenith, his motorcar was poetry and tragedy, love and heroism. The office was his private ship but the car his perilous excursion ashore."

1920s • SYNTHETICS ~ The 1920s began the development of synthetic products. The development of synthetic rubber in the 1920s led to many improvements for the burgeoning automobile industry. Synthetic tires could stand up much better to heat, thereby lasting longer, and they could be produced from chemicals rather than rubber trees that did not grow in abundance in the U.S. Development of synthetic rubber for tires led to inventions of better rain boots, raincoats, and many other products. Other synthetic fibers, such as rayon, also became popular for fabrics. Rayon was made from wood pulp or cotton. The cellulose was extracted, made into crumbs, and dissolved. Invented in England, rayon had been used in the U.S. since 1910. In the 1920s the industry developed to compete with wool and cotton in making strong, inexpensive fabric for mass production.

Aided also by World War I, the field of medicine saw many innovations in the 1920s. Antibiotics were discovered by 1928. Penicillin was actually discovered in London in 1928, but it did not see much use until 10 years later. It became especially important during World War II. (See the chapter on Health and Medicine).

1920s • ADVERTISING ~ Although not an invention itself, advertising drove the market for new technology during the 1920s. Ads told people what new things they needed and what new habits they should undertake so they would not be out of fashion. Advertisements helped establish a new way of living, one driven by technology and dependent on credit.

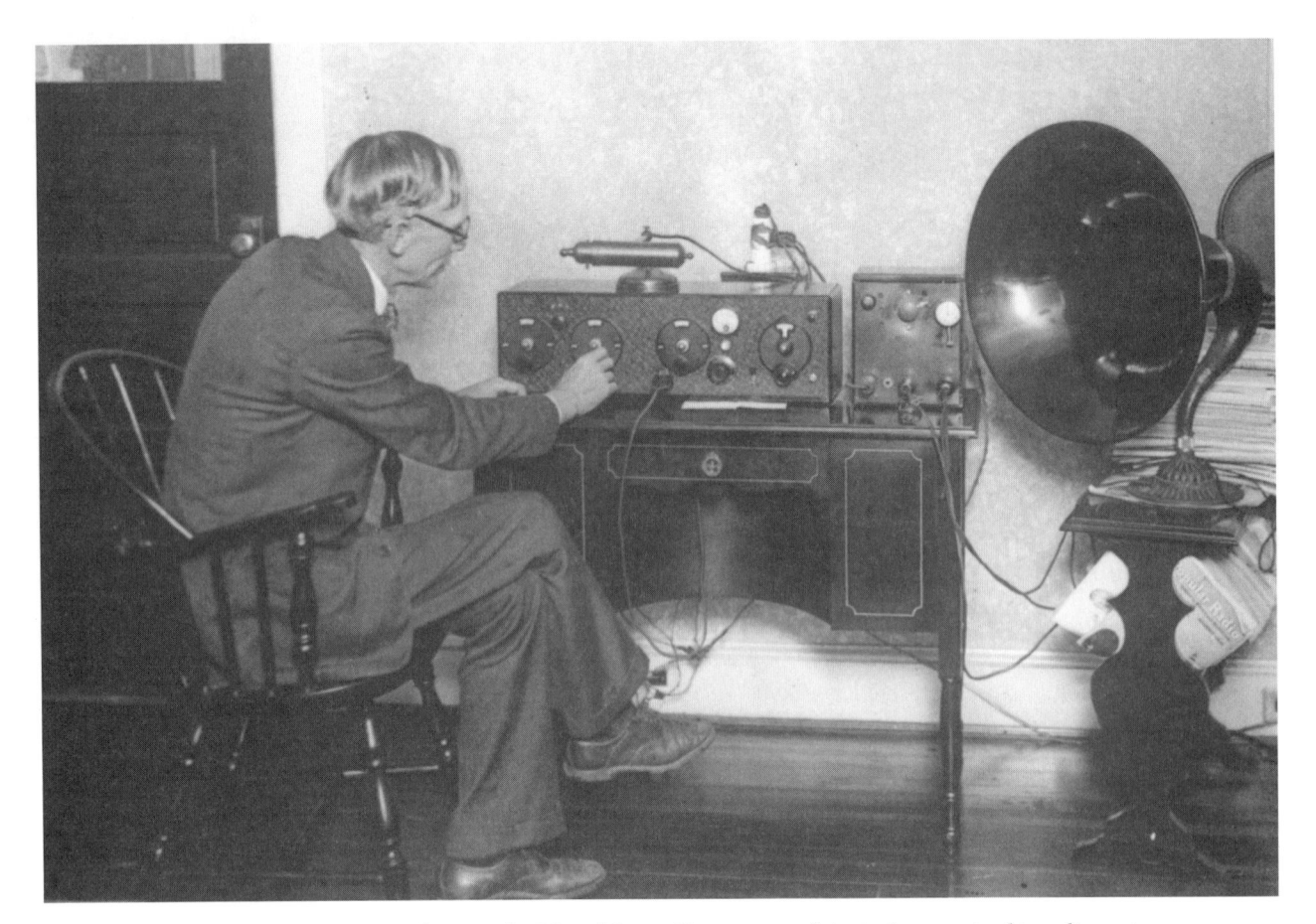

(1926) Mr. W. J. Walton, an entomologist at the United States Department of Agriculture, using his radio equipment.

1920s

They helped establish a sense of fashion and self-importance. The expansion of radio in the 1920s gave new media possibilities to advertisements, and thus, to a whole new industry that would essentially finance radio, television, and print.

1920s • RADIO ~ The wireless techniques developed by Marconi and refined during World War I were used to promote the radio industry in the 1920s. The first public radio station in the U.S. was KDKA in Pittsburgh, Pennsylvania, which began broadcasting on November 2, 1920. By 1929 there were 606 stations nationwide. Radio changed the lives of many Americans. Rural families were no longer so isolated from community or world events. Radio brought entertainment, advertising, and news to everyone. Red Barber, a sportscaster in 1924, described his amazement in listening to the radio: "A man in Pittsburgh said it was snowing there . . . somebody sang in New York . . . a banjo plunked in Chicago . . . it was sleeting in Atlanta." (from *The Century* by Peter Jennings and Todd Brewster).

Radio's popularity spread so quickly that by 1928, Republicans and Democrats spent $1.25 million of campaign money advertising on the radio. In the 1930s radio became the eyes and ears of the world as political events moved the world toward another war.

1920s • PHOTOGRAPHY ~ George Eastman (1854-1932) continued refining the film process using the X-ray technology invented in the nineteenth century and developed during World War I. Germany invented the first miniature camera, the Leica, in 1925, but Eastman, like Ford with the automobile, produced cameras and film inexpensively so that ordinary people could enjoy photography.

1920s • MOVIES ~ During the 1920s the movie industry rose to new heights of popularity. It epitomized the new sense of freedom, glamour, and experimentation in American society. European films were generally considered more artistic and psychological, but Hollywood produced popular, and profitable, movies for the masses. D.W. Griffith became the most influential movie director, developing the techniques of moving the camera around during filming and of taking shots close up and far away. He also began filming in segments instead of making the entire film in one shooting. These innovations greatly improved the quality of movies.

George Eastman had developed celluloid rolls of film in 1888 for use in Kodak cameras, but the film was flammable. In 1920 he developed the first cellulose acetate safety film for motion pictures. However, it was not until 1955 that non-flammable safety film completely replaced celluloid. Too often the heat of the film projector started fires which could send a crowded movie theater into complete panic.

In 1927 Hollywood produced the first "talking" movie, *The Jazz Singer*, starring Al Jolson. At first, sound was recorded at the same time as the film. By 1929 the technique was refined and sound was recorded on the film. Actors whose voices sounded pleasing replaced some of the great silent movie stars. Also by 1928, Eastman invented the Kodak color film process, which greatly enhanced the "talkies." Then, in 1929, Walt Disney (1901-1966) developed the first animated motion picture, *Steamboat Willie*. By the end of the decade Hollywood established the most sought-after prize in the movie industry, the Academy Awards. (See Entertainment).

1920s • LABOR SAVING DEVICES ~ The 1920s also saw the development of all sorts of useful products to ease the life of the homemaker. Thermostats and enamel coating improved the home stove and oven. Not having to worry about burning yourself and the temperature being more accurate made cooking a lot easier. Clothes washing machines became popular because one did not have to hand wash and clothes became clean much faster. Refrigerators grew in popularity, especially with the development of the safer Freon to replace ammonia. Refrigerators made the preparation of food less problematic due to food lasting longer — one did not have to worry about buying food everyday or spoiling food that was already bought. As always, one innovation led to another. For instance, the introduction of the pop-up toaster in 1926 led to new machinery for producing and packaging sliced bread. Though the zipper was invented in 1893, it was not until the B.F. Goodrich Company attached it to their rubber boots that the zipper became a staple of American life, quickly replacing buttons and snaps in popularity.

The 1920s saw many developments in food production and consumption, all of which aided the consumer. Artificial insemination of animals brought a significant change in animal husbandry and agricultural production. Animals could be fed and bred in pens. Farmers no longer had to depend on natural reproduction or on the range for feed.

1920s • FOOD PRESERVATION ~ During World War I, canned food was developed to feed soldiers far away from

1939-1945

supplies, who needed food to keep for several days or weeks. After the war, with the development of self-service grocery stores (3,000 nationwide by 1929), canned food became popular with civilians as well. By 1950 some 10 billion cans of food were produced each year in the United States.

Using principles of refrigeration developed for shipping beef, Charles Birdseye (1886-1956) developed the possibility of freezing goods for consumers. He built a frozen fish plant in New York in 1923, developed the quick-freeze technique in 1924, and by 1940 sales from frozen foods were $150 million a year.

Consumer Technology

This period saw greater development of technology than consumer goods. 1930-1940 was the decade of the Depression, not only in the U.S., but worldwide. Few people had the ability to purchase anything other than basic necessities. 1940-1945 was the period of World War II when research and development focused on innovations necessary for war use rather than consumer-related items. Nevertheless, this was a period of tremendous productivity for both the military and civilian society.

1938 • Nylon ~ In 1938 Wallace H. Carothers (1896-1937) at the E.I. Dupont de Nemours chemical company developed the synthetic fiber, nylon. It was much more versatile and easier to produce than rayon for it was created from coal, air, and water. By 1939 nylon had proved its success. It could be made into fibers, bristles, sheets, rods, and tubes. It could be used for carpets, tires, upholstery, dresses, underwear, bathing suits, lace, brushes, fishing line, or parachutes. Nylon quickly revolutionized the popular clothing industry while also assisting the war effort. In 1939, 64 million pairs of nylon stockings were produced. Nylon was so important for war materials that in 1942 the government halted the production of nylon for any civilian items.

1930s • Penicillin and DDT ~ In the areas of medicine two of the most important innovations were penicillin and DDT. Penicillin had been developed in the late 1920s but by the end of the 1930s and throughout the war, it was of critical importance as an antibiotic for the wounded. For several decades there was no antibiotic as powerful as penicillin.

DDT, a synthetic insecticide, was used first to prevent the spread of typhus and other diseases. Eventually, DDT was adopted for widespread use as a pesticide, and it eradicated many pests that attacked crops. It was very powerful, and it was not until the 1950s that people began to be aware of the harm it also did. In *Silent Spring* (1962), Rachael Carson warned of the long-term harm to the environment and people. Now DDT is banned in most countries and other pesticides have been developed with fewer side effects on birds and other elements in our environment.

1941-1945 • Military Innovations ~ Throughout the Depression of the 1930s, technological advances continued, but because of World War II, nearly all developments became connected to the war. For instance, the ballpoint pen was invented in 1938 by Ladislo Biro of Hungary, but first became important to the air force because it did not leak at high altitudes. Radar, which developed from nineteenth century theories of Doppler and Marconi, became a critical element in the war for aid in identifying enemy or ally. Its use in commercial aviation was delayed until after the war. Another development in the use of wavelengths created by the war was sonar, used especially to detect submarines. Sound waves now are used for many other purposes, especially in medicine.

1939-1945 • NUCLEAR POWER

The war also brought major advances in weaponry, including rocketry, which would become of major significance later for space exploration. Some say the world war brought one of the most significant and certainly one of the most destructive events in the history of civilization, the development of atomic power. W. K. Roentgen laid the groundwork for atomic physics in 1895 with the discovery of X-rays. Atoms contain a positive charge in the nucleus and are surrounded by a negative charge of electrons. He discovered that radioactive substances emit three kinds of radiation: alpha, beta, and gamma. The first two are particles, the third a highly penetrating radiation, akin to X-rays. Scientists later discovered that when uranium changes into radium, it emits three alpha particles and two beta particles. These are emitted at a very high speed and are quite powerful. The energy produced can be used in bombs or it can be used to heat water, producing steam, which, in turn, can drive a turbine and produce electricity.

Using these discoveries and the theory of Albert Einstein (1879-1955), that energy equals mass times the square of the velocity of light, which is a constant ($E=mc^2$), Enrico Fermi (1901-1954) discovered that if uranium, the heaviest of all the natural elements, was bombarded with neutrons, it became radioactive. Fission occurred, meaning that the uranium nucleus divided into smaller nuclei and released energy. In 1939, scientists discovered that in the uranium fission process, secondary neutrons were released, which were more numerous than those used in the original bombardment. A domino effect, or self-perpetuating chain reaction, was set up, which released a colossal amount of energy and explosion.

In 1942, during World War II, as part of the Manhattan Project that took place under the stadium at the University of Chicago, Enrico Fermi created the first chain reaction. A year later, after a series of other developments under the direction of J.R. Oppenheimer, the first atomic explosion took place in Los Alamos, New Mexico. Three years later, on August 6, 1945, the first atomic bomb was dropped on Hiroshima, followed by a second on Nagasaki on August 9. These horrific events ended the war. X-rays began as physics theory, developed into medical as well as military uses, and eventually brought about the most destructive force yet known.

Though the atomic bomb was the first use of atomic energy and the even more destructive hydrogen bomb soon followed, nuclear power has also been put to peaceful uses in providing electric energy. Many states depend heavily on nuclear power generators to provide an inexpensive source of electricity. Nevertheless, through the 1950s, the threat of nuclear holocaust remained imminent. Bomb shelters and bombing raid drills were a major public concern. It was not until perhaps the late 1970s or 1980s that the nuclear arms buildup and its worldwide threat to humanity lessened.

1940-1960 — Splitting the Atom

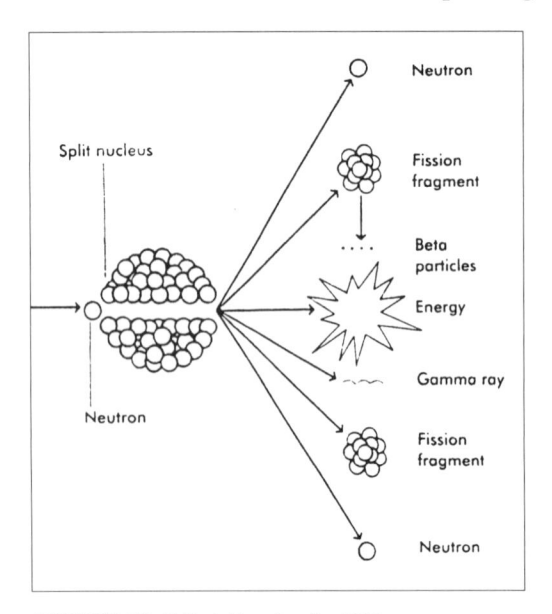

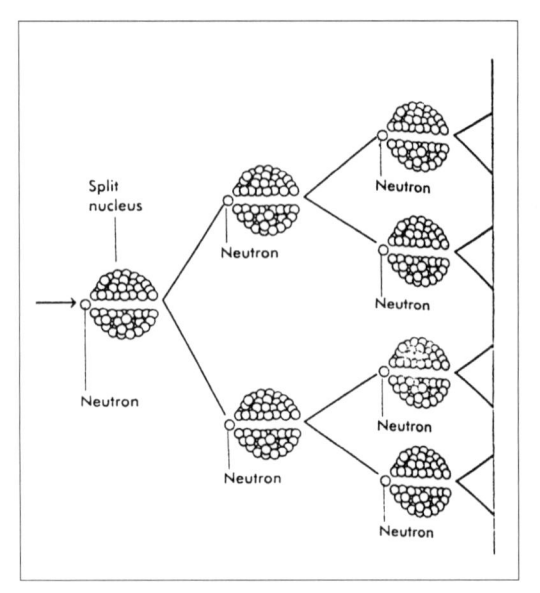

SOURCE: *World Book Encyclopedia*, 1995.

1945-1960 • POST-WAR CONSUMER PRODUCTS ~ Again, once the war was over and the focus shifted from innovation and invention for military purposes, there was a huge growth in consumer products. Just as popular culture and consumerism flourished in the 1920s, so it did in the 1950s. Because nearly all industrial production was geared to war in the early 1940s, after the war there was a huge pent-up demand for goods from synthetic clothing to appliances to housing. Material culture thrived and the U.S. entered a consumer age that has not yet ended.

One example of the military to civilian shift is the development of the two-way radio, or walkie-talkie. In 1938, Al Gross (1918-2001), also known as Phineas Thaddeus Veeblefetzer, pioneered the citizen's band radio. During the war his ground-to-air battery-operated two-way radio, using high frequencies, proved invaluable to the military in conducting surveillance behind enemy lines. Gross also developed the circuitry for personal pocket pagers, which were not consumer-cherished items until the 1980s and 1990s. Some say he provided the idea for cartoon character Dick Tracy's two-way wristwatch radio.

1940s-1950s • PRE-FABRICATION ~ The post-war building industry would benefit from another wartime industrial innovation, prefabricated units. One of the most significant was the Bailey bridge, which could be set up quickly after a bombing raid. Quonset huts, inexpensive though unattractive housing, could be moved quickly into areas with an immediate need to house soldiers. Since World War II Bailey bridges have been used after disasters such as hurricanes or floods have washed out permanent structures. Overcrowded schools often use prefabricated modular classrooms until a permanent building can be completed. The units can be moved from one part of a school district to another as needed. Immediately after the war, Quonset huts were often used to house returning military and their families until the housing shortage could be overcome.

Growth of Nuclear Energy Production

Leading Nuclear Energy Producing Countries

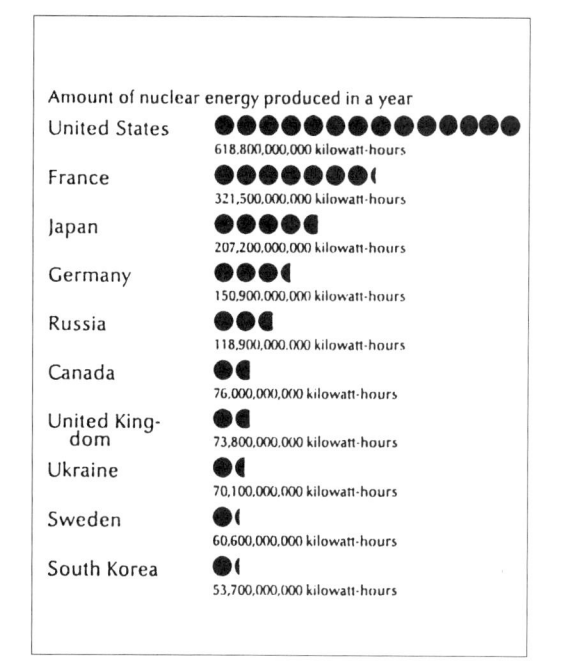

1957-1969

Amount of nuclear energy produced in a year

United States	●●●●●●●●●●●●	618,800,000,000 kilowatt-hours
France	●●●●●●(	321,500,000,000 kilowatt-hours
Japan	●●●●(	207,200,000,000 kilowatt-hours
Germany	●●●(	150,900,000,000 kilowatt-hours
Russia	●●(	118,900,000,000 kilowatt-hours
Canada	●(	76,000,000,000 kilowatt-hours
United Kingdom	●(	73,800,000,000 kilowatt-hours
Ukraine	●(	70,100,000,000 kilowatt-hours
Sweden	●(	60,600,000,000 kilowatt-hours
South Korea	●(	53,700,000,000 kilowatt-hours

Growth of Nuclear Energy Production chart: World and United States, Millions of kilowatt-hours. 1992: 2,017,000 (World); 1992: 618,800 (United States).

SOURCE: *World Book Encyclopedia*, 1995.

1957-1969 • PIONEERS IN SPACE
Another military weapon, rockets, had been developed in the Soviet Union, Germany, and the United Sates in the late 1920s and 1930s. Rockets were significant weapons during World War II, but afterward they were used nearly as much for space exploration as for mass destruction. It was the Soviet Union that first used rockets to send up the first spaceship, *Sputnik*, in 1957. The significance of a Soviet "first" profoundly affected U.S. society, both as an impetus to the space industry and as a catalyst for educational changes. Since then there has been great emphasis put on math and sciences in American schools. By the end of the 1950s, the U.S. government established the National Aeronautics and Space Administration (NASA) and named the first seven astronauts.

(circa 1915) The father of American rocket science, physicist Dr. Robert H. Goddard (1882-1945) next to a rocket apparatus.

INVENTIONS

1950s

As has been true with so many technological innovations throughout history, even in the space industry something invented for one use became popular for consumers. For space suits Velcro was much more practical than snaps, buttons, or zippers and could be used for heavy objects as well. Space-walking astronauts today use 173 Velcro strips to hold tools to their space suits. In consumer society, Velcro is used in any number of ways, including medical paraphernalia, shoes, and clothing.

1950s-PRESENT • PLASTICS ~ After the war, United States society entered the plastic age. Everything Americans used seemed to be derived from some form of plastics, from pipes to appliances to dishware. In the movie *The Graduate* (1967), Dustin Hoffman, the title character, was offered one word of advice for future success: "plastics." It would be difficult to imagine society without the use of them. By the 1970s, the U.S. produced 1.7 million tons of polystyrene, 1.5 million tons of PVC (cables and pipes), and 500,000 tons of polyurethane (foam). By the end of the century, American companies were producing 20 million tons of plastics each year. Such is the quantity of plastics used that in the next century, emphasis must be focused on creating a biodegradable plastic or a reusable plastics industry in order to protect the environment, as well as not to run out of the source of plastic, petroleum.

1945-1960 • CONSUMER ITEMS ~ Washing machines and refrigerators were introduced to homes in the 1920s, but only several thousand households had them. By 1960 there were over 47 million homes with washing machines and over 50 million with refrigerators. Home dishwashers and air conditioning even better demonstrate the rapid growth of consumer appliances in the 1950s. Neither became part of American society until after the war. By 1960, however, 3.2 million households had dishwashers and 6.5 million had air conditioning. By 2000, in some parts of the country nearly every home had air conditioning, and most middle-class homes throughout the nation have automatic dishwashers.

Bottling, packaging, fast food, and self-service all became huge industries in the 1950s. For example, in 1940, 286,000 tons of aluminum was produced a year. Some 15 years later, over 2 million tons was produced annually. The entire bottled water and soft drink industries depend on two post-war consumer-driven materials: plastic and aluminum.

1950s • TELEVISION ~ Though the picture tube was invented in the 1920s and broadcasts began in the 1930s, it was not until the 1950s that televisions became a staple of society. By 1960 there were over 45 million in American homes. Television had an even greater impact on society than radio. Television even changed eating habits of Americans through the invention of the TV dinner, to be consumed while viewing TV. In 1955 Swanson alone sold 25 million TV dinners a year.

The debate continues as to whether television has created social change or television broadcasters have picked up changes in social mores. Many argue that as children watch more and more television, they communicate less with peers and parents. Many claim that the violence and sexual behavior displayed on television have had a negative impact on adolescent behavior. Some argue that television is responsible for a degradation of moral values in American society.

Important Dates in Television

1927	Philip Farnsworth invents the picture tube
1929	Vladimir Zworykin demonstrates the first practical television system
1939	NBC made first regular telecasts in the United States
1946	Television boom begins
1951	First coast-to-coast telecast—President Truman opening the Japanese Peace Treaty Conference in San Francisco
1953	Color telecasts begin
1954	Television coverage of Army-McCarthy hearings
1960	Presidential candidates Kennedy and Nixon debate on TV
1965	*Early Bird*, first commercial communications satellite, relays TV programs between U.S. and Europe
1967	Congress establishes Corporation for Public Broadcasting to help public TV
1969	Moon landing
Late 1960s-1970s	Daily footage of Vietnam War
1973	Television coverage of Watergate hearings
1974	Nation watches President Nixon's resignation speech
1985	Worldwide audience of 1.5 billion people watches "Live Aid" benefit concert
1993	Fox network begins first new network since 1950s

SOURCE: *World Book Encyclopedia*, 1995.

The growth of the television industry is indicative of the growth of consumer-oriented innovations after World War II. In 1939, NBC began the first regular telecasts in the United States. In 1951 the first coast-to-coast broadcasts occurred with President Truman's Japanese Peace Conference in San Francisco, California. The first color broadcasts came just 2 years later. In 1962 the *Telstar* satellite made it possible to transmit and receive programs throughout the world. And by 1969 society could watch men landing on the moon.

1947 • TRANSISTORS ~ One of the major innovations that changed the electronics industry after the war was the invention of transistors. Vacuum tubes prevailed in all electronic equipment for

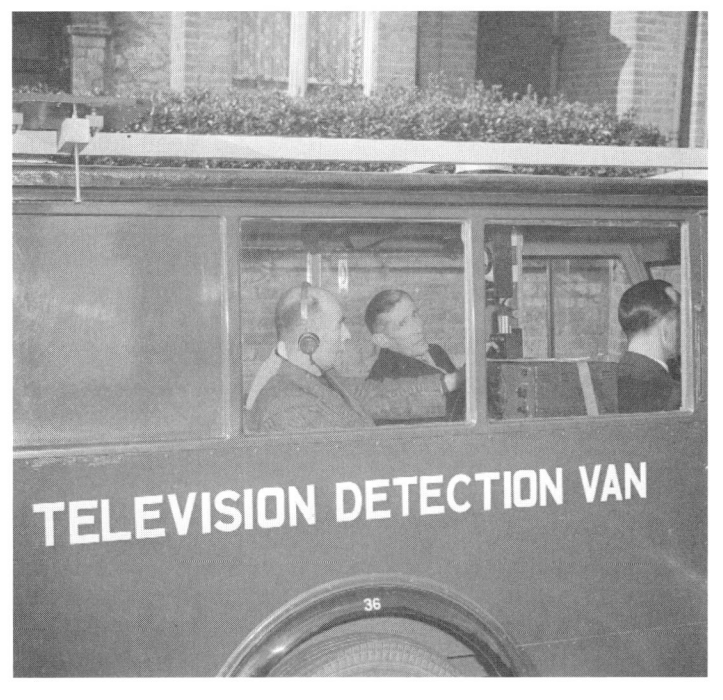

(circa 1952) Arthur Nickson, at work in a television detector van used to find and prosecute unlicensed domestic viewers.

INVENTIONS ~ 919

1958-1980s

nearly fifty years. Then in 1947 Americans John Bardeen, Walter Brattain, and William Shockley invented the transistor. Transistors follow the same principles as vacuum tubes, but they are smaller, more reliable, and need less power. The transistor transformed large, heavy appliances into small, easy to move appliances. The personal computer and other consumer electronic devices were made possible using the same principle.

1958 • MICROCHIP ~ In 1958 came the invention that launched the technological revolution, an invention that has changed the world as much as the light bulb, telephone, and automobile. By the late 1950s, circuit designs were so complex they required miles of wires, millions of soldered connections, and thousands of transistors. That year Jack Kilby began work at Texas Instruments and came up with the solution: eliminate the wires in an electronic circuit. He successfully demonstrated his wireless circuit on September 12, 1958, the date of the birth of the microchip. (Robert Noyce came to a similar solution and is named the co-inventor.) As with many inventions, development into commercial uses took 10-20 years.

THE ELECTRONIC AND SPACE AGE

The list of innovations and inventions after World War II seems almost endless. The 1960s continued the trend toward refinement of previous inventions. Probably the most important innovations came in the fields of medicine and space, rather than in consumer or popular culture aspects of society.

1950-1980 • MEDICINE ~ Not all inventions in the postwar period concerned consumer or military items. One of the great breakthroughs to preventive medicine occurred in 1953 when Jonas Salk (1914-1995) introduced a polio vaccine that included inoculation against all three polio types in one shot. The vaccine was tested on 1.8 million children in 1954 and proved effective. By 1981 Albert Sabin (1906-1993) had developed an oral polio vaccine using a weakened form of the virus. It proved easier to transport and administer than the inoculation. By the end of the century, polio had been nearly eliminated throughout the world.

In 1967 Michael DeBakey performed the first heart implant to assist a human heart. He was also instrumental in work on artificial hearts, coronary bypass surgery and aneurysm repair. In 1978 Robert Jarvik created the artificial heart; the work of these scientists has provided doctors with the tools to perform transplant and artificial organ surgery, nearly a commonplace occurrence in modern medicine.

1961-1981 • SPACE ~ As had been true before, many innovations or inventions began elsewhere, but it was in the United States that the mass production or large industry developed. In 1961 Yuri Gagarin of the Soviet Union became the first human in space. But under Presidents Kennedy and Johnson, the U.S. space industry flourished. NASA's mission was to explore space, not just orbit the earth. Throughout the 1960s the U.S. matched any Soviet advancements. In 1969, Neil Armstrong of the United States became the first human to step on the moon. Since then, the U.S. has sent space ships to the ends of the solar system and beyond. Communications satellites began in 1962 with *Telstar*. By 1971 space sta-

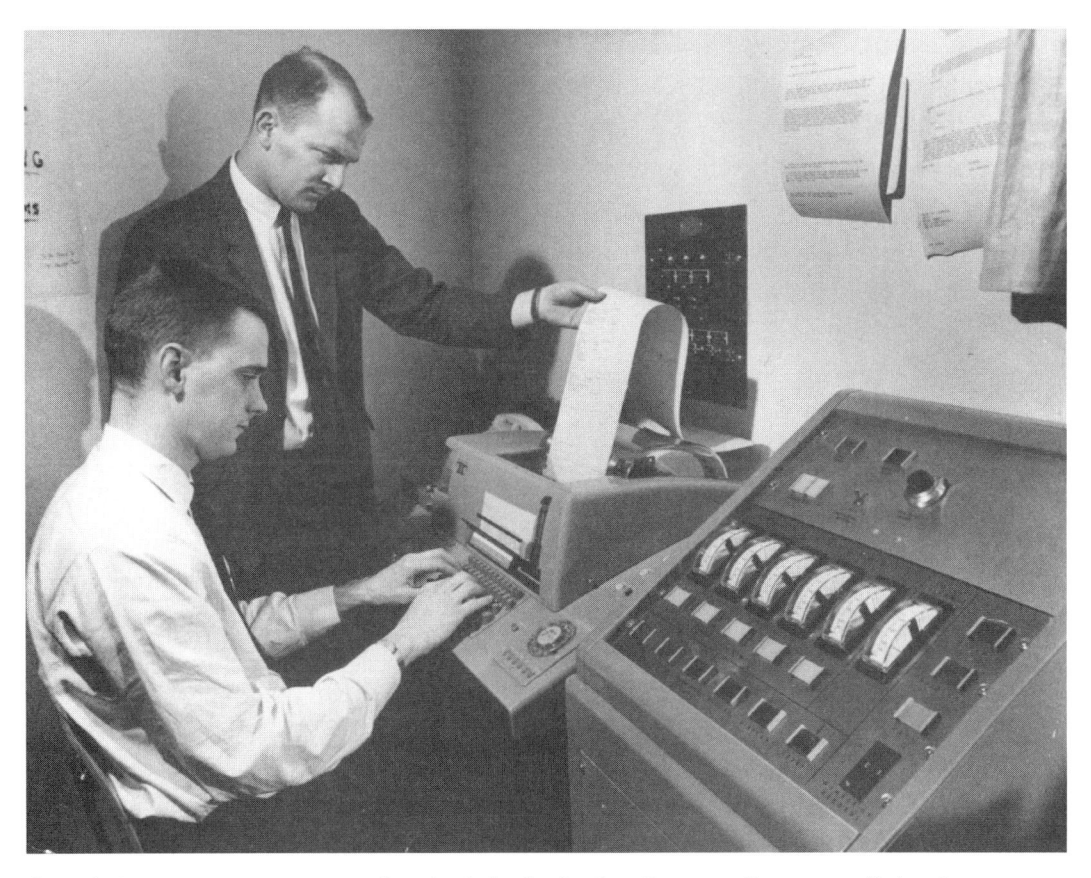

(1968) A systems engineer mans the telex link of a Student Response System installed at Syracuse University, New York by the General Electric Research and Development Center. The computer analyzes the answers given by students to multiple-choice questions and relays them back to the teacher with a rundown of percentages.

tions existed, and by 1981 the U.S. had reusable space vehicles. By 2000 the U.S. and Russia worked together on space endeavors. The proliferation of satellites has created global communication systems as well as provided a tool for the scientific exploration of the Earth, oceans, weather, and outer space. Space exploration has also produced psychological effects on society, opening our imaginations to scientific possibilities that were once only the realm of science fiction.

1970s • ELECTRONIC CONSUMER DEVICES ~ The decade of the 1970s began the Electronic Age. Magnetic tape recordings were developed in the 1930s, but the tape cassette craze did not arrive until the 1970s. By 1975 people could record videos at home. Video games also arrived in the 1970s with the arcade game, Pong. The proliferation of video games, and later computer games, attracted young people to spend long hours in front of a screen, and critics charge that some of the games are violent and lead to crime and cult behavior. Social psychologists have demonstrated that spending excessive time alone on video games may bring a breakdown in communication with friends or family.

1946-1981 • COMPUTERS ~ The computer industry began in the 1970s, almost without notice, though by the twenty-first century nothing came close to its power and influence. Early computers were room-sized machines weighing thousands of pounds. The first electronic computer, the Electronic Numerical Integrator and Calculator (ENIAC) was developed as early as 1946. It was 100 feet long and involved 30 tons of equipment including 18,000 vacuum tubes. In 1951 UNIVAC I was developed. These computers did little more than sort punch cards by categories, but they still could accomplish more in less time than people could. The development of transistors in the 1950s spurred the creation of ever-smaller computers, however.

In 1975 the Altair 8800 became the first official personal computer (PC). However, it was only a computer, without a screen or a keyboard. In 1977 Steven Jobs and Stephen Wozniak created the first Apple computers that truly began the computer age. (Apples are now called Macs.) They built the computer in a garage, and Steve Wozniak had to sell his car to finance the invention. In 1981 IBM entered the PC market and the competition between the two systems continues unabated. The computer industry seems to have grown exponentially. In 1961 there were 10,000 computers; in 1971, 100,000; and in 1991 there were 100 million data-processing computers. Millions of other computers were simple word processors. In 1981 computers were a $30 billion industry. By 1990 the worth was over $100 billion, more than triple in only ten years.

1970s • ALTERNATIVE RESOURCES

～ The 1970s also saw a pause in the rush to invent more and more labor-saving devices and ways to make life easier. The publication of Rachel Carson's *Silent Spring* in 1962, the influence of the peace and alternative living style movements of the 1960s, and the general social unrest created by the Civil Rights Movement and the anti-war demonstrations brought a search for alternate solutions to societal problems. The oil embargo of 1973 and the subsequent drastic rise in oil prices added impetus to the search for alternative sources of energy. Solar panels were promoted as cost efficient in many parts of the United States. In other parts, many people experimented with wind

Inventors have made out well in a continuing annual survey by the Lemelson-MIT Program in Cambridge, Massachusetts. The program, which encourages youngsters to think about becoming inventors, found almost half of all teens would choose the company of an inventor if stranded on an island. What's more, the 500 teen respondents ascribed noble reasons for becoming inventors. Forty-three percent said they would do it to help mankind; 34 percent to preserve the quality of life. On the down side, the respondents did not rate inventors highly among people they would like to meet: only 8 percent said so, versus the 30 percent who preferred musicians. The percentage of teen respondents who wanted somebody from the following fields as a companion on a deserted island: inventors 46 percent, musicians 19 percent, actors/actresses 13 percent, U.S. president 9 percent, and athletes 6 percent.

power. Some states offered tax incentives to those who used alternative fuels or energy sources. Recycling became a new industry. Environmental concerns sometimes took precedence over unchecked growth. The Green Revolution, which promoted new, safe ways to improve agricultural production, spread worldwide.

The 1970s also demonstrated that occasionally economic and social factors influence technology rather than the other way around. The conservation movement and the oil crisis promoted the move to smaller, lighter, more efficient cars, especially in Europe, which needed to import nearly all its oil and where old, narrow streets were congested with traffic.

1980-2000 THE COMMUNICATIONS REVOLUTION

The last twenty years of the century belong to the technological and communications revolution and their tremendous impact on change, not only in the United States, but in every corner of the world. As with so many inventions, there are positives and negatives. The impact on some individuals, groups, or nations may be positive; the impact on others may be negative. People may eventually experience a positive impact, but along the way, they must compromise certain values or traditions. Just as electricity brought immeasurable benefits and created tremendous positive direct and indirect impact on society, both economically and culturally, it also demanded changing traditional, simpler ways of living. The technological innovations of the communications revolution mean people can be in contact with each other almost instantly all the time. The Internet allows people to find information infinitely more easily and rapidly than printed information sources; researchers can easily find and share information instantly. People can be connected to others anywhere in the world.

This communications revolution also means that the sense of time has changed. Instant response, or instant gratification, is the mode in nearly all aspects of society. It also means that those who cannot participate in the new technology and the speed of change, for whatever economic or accessibility reasons, fall further behind ever more quickly. As Fareed Zakaria said in the *New York Times*, December 31, 2000, "globalization is sweeping old models aside, technology is bringing us together faster and more furiously than ever before, markets rule and governments follow. Protests to globalization have grown, but change is inevitable."

1980-2000 • ELECTRONICS ~ The 1980s saw great change in electronics. Development of digital products influenced many aspects of life. Digital tapes were invented in the early 1980s, and compact discs in 1983 in the U.S. (1982 in Japan and Europe). A cartoon from "Family Circus" in the 1980s summed up the speed of this change. The mother spent an entire day teaching the child to tell time with a traditional clock. The child hurried to open the gift his father brought him as a prize; it was a *digital* clock.

Video games moved from arcades to home computer systems. Games like "Pac Man," "Donkey Kong," and "Super Mario Brothers" were all the rage in the 1980s and vastly changed the way children spent their free time. By 1989, a handheld video game system, "Gameboy," was created. By 1994, nearly one-third of homes in the U.S. and Japan had one.

1980-2000

The continued development of wireless technology has also revolutionized communications through popularization of fax machines, first used by the U.S. Postal Service in 1959. Personal portable telephones became commercially produced in the mid-1980s and are now ubiquitous. People in remote areas or those without reliable telephone systems can be in communication anywhere, anytime through cellular phones.

To speed the growth of the communications revolution, computers have become ever faster and more complex; the microchip, ever smaller. A silicon chip that can control a computer is a microprocessor that can fit through the eye of a needle, yet includes millions of wireless transistors and circuits. In less than fifty years a computer that weighed 30 tons and could only sort information has transformed into a laptop computer weighing only a few pounds with the ability to perform multiple complex tasks simultaneously.

1970s • Fiber Optics ~ The laser was invented in 1960, but the field of fiber optics developed during the 1970s with the use of laser light instead of electric current. At the Corning Glass Works (now Corning Inc.), Robert Maurer, Donald Keck and Peter Schultz began the first development of what is like the fiber optics today except that the fiber optics were made with fused silica, a material that can be made extremely pure, but has a high melting point. Early single-mode fibers in the early 1970s bothered developers because they doubted it would be possible to achieve the tolerances needed to couple light efficiently into the tiny cores from light sources. Throughout the 1980s and into the next century, the use of lasers and fiber optics has expanded tremendously from the early days of single mode fibers. With the advancements of the 1980's fiber optics are now used from surgery to entertainment to communications. Optics networks reduce or eliminate the need for electrical regeneration signals. They use broadband networking which speeds up connections and communications tremendously. Some predict an explosion in the ability of fiber optic networks to keep up with demand for faster communication, especially in the business world.

Conclusion

Society is so vastly changed in 2000 that, though people might want to imagine otherwise, it would be very difficult for today's citizens to live in the world of 1900. Every invention led to other inventions and refinements and each depended on something created before it. One invention is often blended with other inventions. A simple example is the bar code, invented in 1974. It uses lasers, computers, and microchips to make both customer and supplier more exact and efficient. None of these was available 50 years earlier, but all depended on innovations developed even earlier. Inventions of war have been used for combat but also for improvement in the quality and convenience of life. The changes in every aspect of life are truly mind boggling—from electricity to sophisticated weapons of mass destruction, to appliances and labor-saving devices, to medicine and surgery, to transportation and communication, to entertainment, or even safety. There is no aspect of twentieth century society that has not been touched by innovation and invention.

Nevertheless, the innovation and invention of the twentieth century and the increasing speed of change merely signal greater changes to come. Perhaps the most significant innovation of the last decade of the twentieth century involves genetics and implications of the very recently acquired ability to map the human genome. The existence of DNA (deoxyribonucleic acid) was discovered in 1953 at Cambridge University in England. However, now society has the ability to create genetic changes deliberately and precisely. At the end of the twentieth century and the beginning of the twenty-first, people can only speculate on how such knowledge will affect American society and the world, positively or negatively.

Along with ethical issues, the twenty-first century will be faced with the need to find an environmentally positive solution to deal with the huge success of twentieth century inventions. Scientists are investigating all sorts of possibilities, including plants, which can draw toxic substances out of the ground, and bacteria that break down crude oil or decompose plastics. Possibilities for inventions seem limitless. But society must remember Edison's words that all inventions come by hard work.

BIBLIOGRAPHY

Abbott, David, ed. *Engineers and Inventors*. New York: Peter Bedrick Books, 1985.

American Inventions: a Chronicle of Achievements That Changed the World. New York: American Heritage, 1995.

Baker, John. *Food, Clothes and Shelter*. London: Kenneth Hudson, 1978.

Bilstein, Roger. *Flight in America: From the Wrights to the Astronauts*. Baltimore: The Johns Hopkins University Press, 2000.

Brown, Kenneth. *Inventors at Work: Interviews with Sixteen Notable American Inventors*. Redmond, WA: Microsoft Press, 1988.

Bunch, Bryan, and Alexander Hellemans, eds. *The Timetables of Technology*. New York: Simon & Schuster, 1993.

Burlingame, Roger. *Machines that Built America*. New York: Harcourt, Brace, & World, Inc, 1953.

Haber, Louis. *Black Pioneers of Science and Invention*. San Diego: Harcourt, Brace, Jovanovich, 1991.

Inventive Yankee, The: from Rockets to Roller Skates, 200 Years of Yankee Inventors and Inventions. Dublin, NH: Yankee Books, 1989.

James, Portia. *The Real McCoy: African American Invention and Innovation. 1619-1930*. Washington, D.C.: Smithsonian Institute Press, 1989.

Jennings, Peter and Todd Brewster. *The Century*. New York: Doubleday, 1998.

Larsen, Egon. *A History of Invention*. London: J.M. Dent & Sons, Ltd., 1969.

Lesley, Philip. *Everything and the Kitchen Sink*. New York: Farrar, Straus & Cudahy, Inc. 1955.

MacDonald, Anne. *Feminine Ingenuity; Women and Inventions in America*. New York: Balantine Books, 1992.

MacMillian *Encyclopedia of Science*. New York: MacMillian Publishing Company, 1991.

McDougall, Walter. *The Heavens and the Earth: a Political History of the Space Age*. New York: Basic Books, 1985.

Mollenhoff, Clark. *Atanasoff, Forgotten Father of the Computer*. Ames, IA: Iowa State University Press, 1988.

Mount, Ellis. *Milestones in Science and Technology: The Ready Reference Guide to Discoveries, Inventions, and Facts.* Phoenix: Oryx Press, 1994.

Newhouse, Elizabeth, ed. *Inventors and Discoverers Changing Our World.* Washington, D.C.: National Geographic Society, 1988

Platt, Richard. *Smithsonian Visual Timeline of Inventions.* London: Dorling Kindersley Ltd. 1994.

Ray, William. *The Art of Invention: Patent Models and Their Makers.* Princeton, NJ: Pyne Press, 1974.

Roland, Alex. *A Spacefaring People: Perspectives on Early Spaceflight.* Washington, D.C. 1985.

Smithsonian Book of Invention. New York: WW Norton and Co, 1978.

Webster, Raymond. *African American Firsts in Science and Technology.* Detroit: Gale Group, 1999.

Williams, Trevor. *History of Invention.* New York: Facts on File Publications, 1987.

———. *A Short History of Twentieth-Century Technology, c.1900-c.1950.* New York: Oxford University Press, 1982.

World Almanac Book of Inventions. New York: World Almanac Publications, 1985.

INTERNET RESOURCES

African-American Inventors
http://inventors.about.com/library/weekly/aa020600a.htm

INVENTORS & INVENTIONS
The inventions and their inventors that made America what it is today.
http://americanhistory.about.com/cs/inventors/index.htm (About American History)

GREAT INVENTORS AND INVENTIONS
History and information on famous inventors - when - where - how did they invent their now famous inventions.
http://inventors.about.com/library/bl/bl1_3t.htm (About Inventors)

INVENTORS
For the student - historical information on famous inventors and inventions and history timelines - For the professional - patents - new technology - manufacturing resources - interviews with successful independent and industrial inventor
http://inventors.about.com/mbody.htm (About Inventors)

INVENTIONS AND INVENTORS
Information on Inventions and nventors, strange gadgets, patents, facts, myths, machines and devices.
http://trivia.about.com/cs/inventions/index.htm (About Trivia)

HISTORICAL INVENTION AND INVENTORS INDEX
A listing of historical inventors and inventions which have been archived and indexed for historical and current research.
http://inventors.about.com/library/blindex.htm (About Inventors)

The Inventors Online Museum
http://www.inventorsmuseum.com/

Inventors Web Site
http://inventors.about.com

Inventor of the Week, Lemelson-M.I.T. Program's Invention Dimension website
http://web.mit.edu/invent/www/inventorweek.html

Invention Convention/National Congress of Inventor Organizations
http:/www.inventionconvention.com

NATIONAL COLLEGIATE INVENTORS AND INNOVATORS ALLIANCE
The NCIIA grants progam funds curriculum development and the work of teams of student inventors known as "E-Teams". The grants encourage interdisciplinary groups of students to work collaboratively to identify real-world problems, develop practical solutions, and commercialize their innovations.
http://www.nciia.org

Important Historical Inventions and Inventors
http://www.lib.lus.edu/sci/chem/patent/srs136_text.html

Medical Inventions
http://www.advanced.org/tqnew/library/21798.html

National Inventors Hall of Fame Index of Inventions
http://invent.org/book/book-index.html

Discovery Magazine
http://www.discoverymagazine.com

Odyssey Magazine
http://www.odysseymagazine.com

Ron Riley's Kids Inventors Resources
http://www.InventorEd.org/k-12/becameinv.html

Science Service Organization dedicated to advancing the understanding and appreciation of science through publications and educational programs.
http://www.sciserv.org

The Ultimate Science Fair Resource
http://www.scifair.org

United States Government Patents
http://www.uspto.gov

Diane N. Palmer

Law Enforcement

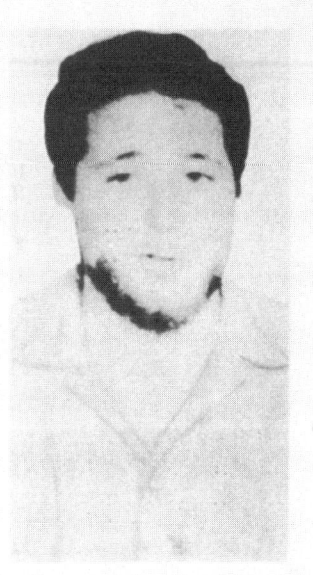

(1964) An FBI poster seeking information as to the whereabouts of Andrew Goodman, James Earl Chaney and Michael Henry Schwerner, Civil Rights campaigners who were missing in Mississippi.

TIMELINE

1789-1899 ~ Establishing Crime-Fighting Organizations

Congress authorizes recruitment of marshals to serve their warrants and subpoenas (1789) / New Orleans forms police force to control slavery (early 1800s) / Rioting in cities (1830s) / Boston (1838) and New York (1844) form police departments / Congress authorizes the Secret Service (1865) / Police exchange photos of criminals (1870s) / First federal prison opens (1891) / New York City conducts investigations into police corruption (1894) / Police training school established in New York (1897)

MILESTONES: Naturalization Law excludes non-whites from citizenship (1790) • Oliver Evans builds the first steam-powered motor vehicle in the U.S. (1805) • Beginning of Manifest Destiny doctrine of acquiring western territory (1845) • Fourteenth Amendment declares that all persons born or naturalized in America are citizens (1866) • Alexander Graham Bell with George Watson invent the telephone (1876)

1900-1929 ~ Crime Fighting Devices and Techniques

New York City introduces first law governing speed (1901) / Pennsylvania establishes a highway patrol (1905) / Oregon hires first policewoman (1905) / FBI created (1906) / Photos used to catch speeders (1909) / Boston police strike for better wages (1918) / Chicago Crime Commission formed in Chicago to oversee police (1919) / Taking a stolen car across state lines made a federal crime (1919) / Cleveland establishes first police radio band (1920s) / First modern lie detector invented (1921) / J. Edgar Hoover becomes director of the FBI (1924) / Wickersham Commission investigates police work and crime (1929) / Uniform classification of crimes issued by Chiefs of Police (1929)

MILESTONES: President McKinley assassinated (1901) • Indiana is the first state to pass a sterilization law; twenty-nine additional states pass sterilization legislation by 1935 (1907) • Mann Act prohibits transporting women across state lines for sexual activity (1910) • Kenyon Law prohibits sales of alcohol in dry states (1913) • Child labor abuse made a federal crime (1916) • Eighteenth Amendment prohibiting the sale of alcoholic beverages begins prohibition era (1919) • Hays Code restricts filmmakers from ridiculing the law (1920s) • Permanent immigration quotas imposed (1924)

1930-1949 ~ Prohibition Gangsters

FBI arrests famous gangsters and solidifies its public image (1930s) / Police establish fingerprint data banks (1930s) / Chicago establishes a police complaint bureau (1930s)

MILESTONES: Charities and churches are permitted to hold bingo games legally in Massachusetts (1931) and Rhode Island (1937) • Al Gross develops the two-way radio, or walkie-talkie, widely used in WWII (1938) • 54 percent of American adults gamble in one form or another (1940) • NBC, CBS and ABC television broadcast the House Un-American Activities Committee's investigation of communism in Hollywood (1947)

1950-1969 ~ Expanding and Containing Investigative Authority

Kefauver investigation of organized crime (1950s) / Special police squads saturate high-crime neighborhoods (1950s) / FBI's authority dramatically expanded (1960s) / Supreme Court rules that evidence seized in illegal searches cannot be used in state court trials (1961) / Model criminal code standardizes sentencing (1962) / Miranda decision forces police to read a suspect his rights (1966) / Supreme Court rules that police can stop and frisk suspects (1968)

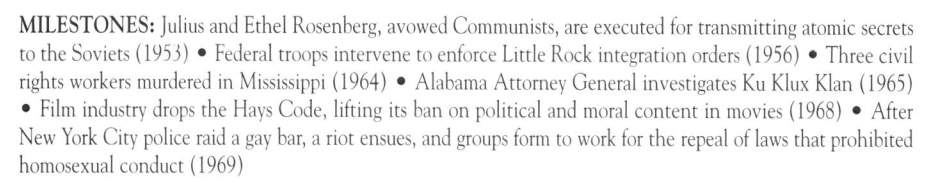

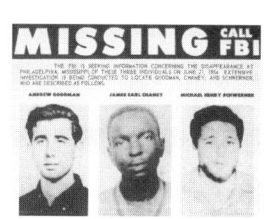

MILESTONES: Julius and Ethel Rosenberg, avowed Communists, are executed for transmitting atomic secrets to the Soviets (1953) • Federal troops intervene to enforce Little Rock integration orders (1956) • Three civil rights workers murdered in Mississippi (1964) • Alabama Attorney General investigates Ku Klux Klan (1965) • Film industry drops the Hays Code, lifting its ban on political and moral content in movies (1968) • After New York City police raid a gay bar, a riot ensues, and groups form to work for the repeal of laws that prohibited homosexual conduct (1969)

1970-2000 ~ Regulating Police Power

District court ruling limits police use of force (1975) / Supreme Court limits strip searches (1979) / Racial profiling adopted by police forces (1980s) / War on drugs targets minorities (1980s) / Rodney King incident forces police department reviews nationwide (1991)

MILESTONES: Homicide rate decreases by 33 percent (1990-1999) • U.S./Soviets agree to destroy some weapons (1987) • Dissolution of the Soviet Union ends the Cold War (1991) • O.J. Simpson is acquitted of charges of murdering his wife (1995)

INTRODUCTION

The nature of police work and policing changed dramatically through the twentieth century. At the beginning of the century, police lacked all the technical paraphernalia associated with modern policing. More significantly, the expectations of both the police and the policed moved away from nineteenth century assumptions that police officers would be the cop on the corner, involved in social welfare work and neighborhood politics. Through the twentieth century, police officers evolved from neighborhood political operatives to centrally controlled, trained professionals.

Despite all the changes wrought by the reformers, citizens continued to complain about their police. Disturbing reports of police brutality continued unabated. These complaints may have been exacerbated by the fact that, once reformed, police often seemed remote from the citizens they ostensibly served. By the end of the twentieth century, some critics had begun to complain that police should be involved in crime prevention and more responsive to local politicians. Some credited decentralized "community policing" with stemming the rise in the American murder rate. In a sense, then, policing came full circle, with something of a return to some nineteenth-century practices occurring by the close of the twentieth century.

1870-1915

1870-1915 • ORIGINS OF AMERICAN POLICING ~ New Orleans organized a police force early in the nineteenth century, chiefly to control urban slavery. Boston and New York City formed their police departments in 1838 and 1844, developing the new agencies out of the old night watch system. In the 1830s, cities experienced more rioting than had been the case in previous decades, an explosion of disorder that prompted urban leaders to call for the formation of police departments on the London model. Police worked long hours for low pay and only slowly adopted the notion of wearing a blue uniform. Partisan politics dominated these first police departments. Chosen chiefly for their political connections, police officers received no training. And because citizens saw them as agents of political machines, officers sometimes suffered disrespect and outright abuse.

By the end of the nineteenth century, reformers had begun to push for more professional law enforcement. In the 1870s, some police departments exchanged photographs of criminals from their "rogues galleries," suggesting the development of a professional collegiality across neighborhood lines. In addition, in the nineteenth century, police had begun to systematically identify criminals through a series of body measurements called the Bertillion system. As crime detection became more scientific, cities rationalized the hiring and promotion of officers. By 1915, most cities had placed their police departments under civil service.

At first, though, few departments provided any training for their officers. Training programs came in the twentieth century. New York established a training school in 1897 and Detroit did so in 1911. In 1908 August Vollmer began offering training lectures to members of the Berkeley, California police department. Vollmer advocated university training for police officers. Instead, by 1930, a dozen cities had set up training academies.

1900-1930 • REFORM AND CRIME COMMISSIONS ~ In the first decades of the twentieth century, reformers sought to centralize control of police on a military model. In highly politicized police departments, police captains worked closely with ward leaders and mayors, leaving police chiefs little real power. The reformers sought to empower the chiefs and organize special squads that operated out of headquarters rather than the precincts. Most importantly, reformers expected vice squads to really enforce liquor and morals laws rather than illegally "license" criminal activities by taking bribes. The reformers also sought to transfer health and welfare functions out of the police departments and into other municipal agencies.

Reformers achieved their goals through investigation, publicly exposing the corruption inherent in the old system. In 1894, the New York State senate appointed a special committee to investigate the New York Police Department. Chaired by Senator Clarence Lexow, this commission heard nearly 700 witnesses and collected 10,000 pages of testimony. The report charged that the police acted as agents of the Democratic party and licensed vice in return for bribes. Police officers sometimes abused rather than protected law-abiding citizens. The report was highly partisan but served as a model for police commissions to come.

In 1919, Chicago business interests formed the Chicago Crime Commission to watch over the local criminal justice sys-

(1919) Russians Raided. In 1919, Chicago business interests formed the Chicago Crime Commission to watch over the local criminal justice system. The Wickersham Commission published a fourteen volume investigation into police work and crime, the first national investigation of the American criminal justice system. The most famous element in the report was the commission's exposé of police third-degree tactics, the beating of prisoners to extract confessions. Seen here are some such tactics, a police raid to quash communist activities in an office belonging to the Union of Russians in Chicago.

1900-1920

tem. In Cleveland, city leaders organized the Cleveland Survey of Criminal Justice. Many more followed. By 1931, seven local, sixteen state and two national crime commissions had come into being. The most famous was the Wickersham Commission or the National Commission on Law Observance and Enforcement, established by President Herbert Hoover in 1929. The Wickersham Commission published a fourteen volume investigation into police work and crime, the first national investigation of the American criminal justice system. The most famous element in the report was the commission's exposé of police third-degree tactics, the beating of prisoners to extract confessions.

1900-1920 • STATE HIGHWAY PATROLS

The Texas Rangers got their start in 1835 and Massachusetts authorized a few state constables in 1865, but the real movement for state police did not come until the twentieth century. Pennsylvania started its Pennsylvania State Constabulary in 1905. Arizona and New Mexico started their own versions of the Texas Rangers in 1901 and 1905. Massachusetts started the Massachusetts District Police in 1920. Connecticut start-

---

Mississippi Highway Patrol

Mississippi did not start its highway patrol until 1938, when the state legislature enacted Senate Bill No. 161, creating the Mississippi Highway Safety Patrol and License Bureau under the Commissioner of Public Safety.

The 1938 law authorized a chief of patrol, a record clerk, a stenographer and 53 patrolmen. Governor Hugh White appointed Major T. B. Birdsong Commissioner of Public Safety. Birdsong organized a training school at Camp Shelby after consulting with state patrols in Texas, Arkansas and Louisiana, the FBI, and the American Red Cross. The department purchased 35 Harley-Davidson motorcycles, one Mercury and 19 Ford automobiles to patrol the state.

The first patrols in Mississippi had no radios. All the officers solicited contributions for a broadcasting station and receiving sets for the motorcycles and 18 of the cars. Lamar Life Insurance Company donated an obsolete broadcasting transmitter once used by radio station WJDX.

For many years after formation of the Mississippi Highway Patrol, county constables did most of the policing of state highways. In 1957, one motorist complained that he had been stopped by a constable and directed to a shabby looking house in the woods and fined $12.50 by a disreputable looking "judge" for "crossing the yellow line." Numerous complaints from out-of-state motorists reported citations by ill-kempt constables for technical, or imaginary, violations of traffic laws.

The highway patrol itself sometimes projected an image that fell short of professional. When Tom Scarbrough took over as Commissioner of Public Safety in the 1950s, he found he needed to tell his men to wear clean uniforms. He also instructed troopers to stop harassing out-of-state drivers.

Scarbrough also purchased equipment for a crime lab. In 1957, Mississippi finally purchased a polygraph, an ultraviolet light for identifying laundry marks, tape recorders and a "ballistic machine," essentially a camera attached to a microscope for the identification of bullets.

ed its state police unit in 1903, as did Michigan, Colorado and West Virginia in 1919. The Pennsylvania police followed a military model, assigning officers to "barracks" across the state. Pennsylvania political leaders expected their new police force to control labor unrest and settle strikes.

FEDERAL AGENCIES

1800s • THE SECRET SERVICE ~ In the 1789 Judiciary Act, Congress authorized recruitment of marshals, so federal judges would have officers available to serve their warrants and subpoenas. Their police function expanded, but marshals always act only in federal matters. At first, there was little federal policing to do, as the states had almost all the responsibility for keeping order. Marshals went after mail thieves and tried to solve murders that occurred on federal property. Westward expansion made the office of marshal more important; marshals policed the territories, turning over law enforcement responsibilities to state officials when their territory became a state. Political appointees, marshals earned no salary until 1896, subsisting on the fees they collected. In the last years of the twentieth century, the size of the marshals' service grew dramatically, from a staff of under a thousand to over four thousand by the end of the century.

The marshals did little investigating of crime. Congress resisted entrusting the executive branch with investigative powers. When asked to do so, Congress not only refused, but also passed a law limiting the Department of Justice's ability to launch investigations. Moreover, during the Civil War, federal law enforcement was anything but a smooth running machine. How modern day crime investigation came to be is an interesting story. Alan Pinkerton, a local barrel maker in Chicago, while out chopping wood for the barrels, discovered the operation of a counterfeit ring. Through his own invention he employed tactics unknown to local police to uncover and catch this ring of thieves. This was the beginning of the first financially successful private detective agency: The Pinkerton Detective Agency. Pinkerton and his agency became so notorious through their expert detective skills that it caught the ear of Abraham Lincoln. Lincoln in turn allowed Pinkerton to establish a government agency called the Secret Service. The Civil War Secret Service did not protect the president and no Secret Service agent was on duty when John Wilkes Booth assassinated Lincoln. Instead, the service carried out espionage missions against the South.

President Andrew Johnson briefly abolished the Secret Service, after he found out the service had placed spies in his own White House. Congress authorized the organization that became the modern Secret Service in 1865, charging the new agency with catching counterfeiters, not protecting the president. Under the leadership of director William P. Wood, the new Secret Service operated out of the Treasury Department rather than the War Department, as had been the case with the Civil War Secret Service. In 1867, Congress authorized the service to investigate the Ku Klux Klan as well as persons suspected of defrauding the government.

1898-1930 • GUARDING THE PRESIDENT ~ In 1869, Herman C. Whitley took over as director, transforming the service into a more efficient law enforcement unit. Within a year, Whitley stood at the head of eleven field offices throughout the country. After Whitley left, in 1874, Congress cut the service's budget and shrank its mission. The Secret Service ran into further trouble in 1898, when it became public knowledge that agents had been guarding the president's private home without Congressional sanction. Secret Service agents did accompany William McKinley in 1901, when he was assassinated, but they acted more as ushers than as bodyguards, guiding guests through a reception line rather than protecting the president.

The death of McKinley led the Secret Service to establish the first White House protective detail, with just two agents. Congress did not authorize protection of the president until 1906 in a bill called the Sundry Civil Expenses Act. In 1917, Congress made it a federal crime to threaten the president, but it did not become a federal crime to kill the president until after the 1963 assassination of President John F. Kennedy. In 1922, President Warren Harding created the White House Police Force, a unit separate from the metropolitan police. In 1930, the Secret Service incorporated the uniformed White House police into their ranks.

1906-1930 • THE FBI ~ The Federal Bureau of Investigation got its start later than the Secret Service. President Theodore Roosevelt established a Bureau of Investigation, later called the Federal Bureau of Investigation, by an executive order of July 26, 1906. Passage of the 1910 Mann Act, making it a federal crime to move women across state lines for prostitution or concubinage, gave the bureau something to do. The bureau also pursued alleged communists in the post-World War I Red scare, compiling dossiers and arresting thousands of suspected radicals, often without warrants. Under President Warren Harding, the bureau burglarized and wire-tapped its political opponents, searching through American citizens' private papers. Scandal tainted much of the bureau's early work and J. Edgar Hoover took over as director of the FBI in 1924, charged with cleaning up the agency. Hoover professionalized his bureau, improving training, establishing a merit system for promotion and firing unqualified agents.

The FBI's *Uniform Crime Reports*, today the yardstick of crime in America, had its origins at the end of the 1920s, when the International Association of Chiefs of Police formed a Committee on Uniform Crime Records. In 1929, the committee issued a report that proposed a uniform classification of crimes. The FBI adapted the system proposed by the chiefs.

1930s-1960s • FBI SURVEILLANCE ACTIVITIES ~ Franklin Roosevelt instructed the FBI to investigate communist and fascist groups. Hoover continued this mission after Roosevelt's death, focusing his attention on the Communist Party after World War II. In the 1960s, Hoover's men infiltrated antiwar, black and Ku Klux Klan organizations. Congressional investigations into the FBI's COINTELPRO operation revealed the use of surveillance, infiltration and provocation to disrupt these groups.

In the 1960s, Congress enlarged the FBI's authority dramatically, just as it had done under Franklin Roosevelt. Like Roosevelt, President Lyndon Johnson sought to expand the federal power and Congress passed a series of new crime control laws, including one against interstate bribery of sporting events, another that made draft card destruction a federal crime, and another that made illegal

Lindbergh Baby Kidnapping

On March 1, 1932, Charles A. Lindbergh called the New Jersey highway patrol to report that his baby had been kidnapped. New Jersey state troopers canvassed the Lindbergh estate, finding footprints, tire tracks and a homemade ladder the kidnapper had used to gain access to the nursery. Corporal Frank Kelly of the New Jersey highway patrol's Identification Bureau dusted the nursery, finding no prints. He dusted a ransom note the kidnapper left behind, but again, found no prints.

Police took the ladder to every contractor, carpenter and hardware store within a twenty-mile radius of Lindbergh's home. No one recognized it. At the time, police assumed epileptics to be crime prone, and a pair of detectives traveled to the state home for epileptics only to find that all of the inmates were accounted for. Police investigated Lindbergh's staff and every worker involved in constructing the house. New Jersey police sent a circular containing photographs of the ransom notes to hundreds of prisons and police agencies, asking if the handwriting matched that of any criminal in custody. Handwriting experts examined the documents in minute detail. Police sent pieces of the kidnap ladder to Arthur Koehler, a wood expert at the Department of Agriculture.

A World War I veteran and West Point graduate named H. Norman Schwarzkopf headed the New Jersey state police. He took charge of the investigation, but Lindbergh really made the key decisions. Lindbergh insisted on negotiating with the kidnapper without police involvement. He worked through an intermediary, John Condon. Lindbergh used Condon to deliver a fifty thousand dollar ransom to a man claiming to have the baby. Shortly after Lindbergh delivered the ransom money, two truck drivers discovered the Lindbergh baby, dead, not far from the Lindbergh house.

The discovery of the dead baby energized the search for the kidnappers. Koehler identified the type of wood used in the ladder and calculated that the lumber mill had planed the wood at a rate of 230 feet a minute, using a planer with six knives in its edge cutters and eight in its face cutters. Koehler found six mills with such a planer. Koehler matched the lumber from the ladder to a South Carolina mill and traced the wood to a Bronx lumberyard. Police placed every employee at the yard under surveillance and checked the handwriting of each worker against the ransom notes.

Police detectives and FBI agents showed Condon thousands of mug shots, hoping he could identify the man who took the ransom money.

Currency used to pay the ransom began turning up in various markets and banks. In 1934, a New York service station attendant wrote a customer's license number on a bill that came from the ransom. The customer turned out to be a German carpenter named Bruno Richard Hauptmann. Authorities arrested Hauptmann and searched his house and garage, finding $14,600 of the ransom money hidden in the walls. Hauptmann went on trial and a jury convicted him. New Jersey executed him April 3, 1936.

(1934) Bruno Hauptmann (right), in the back seat of a police car, leaving New York Police Headquarters for arraignment in a Bronx court, New York City. The German immigrant was booked on a charge of extortion in connection with the kidnapping and murder of the infant son of aviator Charles Lindbergh and his wife, Anne Morrow. He was convicted and executed in 1936 after many appeals.

1924-1950

false applications for loans insured by the Federal Housing Administration. It was also at this time that Congress finally made it a federal crime to kill the president or vice president.

Despite these new responsibilities, J. Edgar Hoover resisted efforts to make his bureau into a "national police force." Hoover refused to be drawn into national efforts to restrict drug abuse, leaving that mission to the Bureau of Narcotics and Dangerous Drugs and the Drug Enforcement Administration. The Post Office investigates crimes involving the mails. The Bureau of Customs looks into crime around the national borders while the Immigration and Naturalization Service enforces laws involving immigration. The Alcohol, Tobacco, and Firearms Bureau has law-enforcing responsibilities as well.

1924-PRESENT • FBI DIRECTORS ～ Hoover led the FBI from 1924 until his death in 1972. Some credited Hoover's long tenure to the secret files he allegedly kept in his office detailing the moral failings of leading American politicians. President Richard Nixon selected Louis Patrick Gray III to replace Hoover. Gray left in disgrace after the public learned he had destroyed documents related to Nixon's Watergate scandals. Clarence M. Kelley, former FBI agent and police chief, took charge in 1973. President Jimmy Carter appointed William Webster to head the FBI. When Webster left the FBI to head the Central Intelligence Agency, observers credited the former judge with turning the Bureau around, restoring morale, and effectively fighting terrorism. President Ronald Reagan chose William Sessions in 1987. Although Sessions joined the FBI with a reputation as a tough Texas lawman, he left in 1993 amid allegations that he used his office for personal benefit. President Bill Clinton chose Louis Freeh to direct the Bureau in 1993; Freeh resigned in 2001 and President Bush appointed Robert S. Mueller III to replace him.

Budget and of the Staff U.S. Marshals Service

	budget in millions	staff positions
1954	$6.6	963
1960	9.4	1003
1965	12.7	1078
1970	20.5	1248
1975	53.3	2049
1980	96.6	2772
1985	139.9	2579
1990	246.3	3250
1995	396.6	3854
1996	448.2	3990
1997	476.3	4162

SOURCE: U.S. Dept. of Justice, Bureau of Statistics. *Sourcebook of Criminal Justice Statistics*, 1998.

1930S-1950S • GANGBUSTERS ～ In the 1930s, the FBI led the federal government's "war" against organized crime. New laws made the war possible. Congress had made it a federal crime to transport stolen automobiles across state lines in 1919. The 1932 kidnapping of famed aviator Charles A. Lindbergh's son prompted Congress to enact a law against kidnapping. Shocking crimes by John Dillinger, Charles "Pretty Boy" Floyd, George "Machine Gun" Kelly, Lester "Baby Face Nelson" Gillis, Clyde Barrow and Bonnie Parker led President Franklin D. Roosevelt's attorney general to order federal action against organized crime. FBI agents shot and killed John Dillinger and Baby Face Nelson, and were responsible for tracking down Machine Gun Kelly. Hoover displayed a knack for

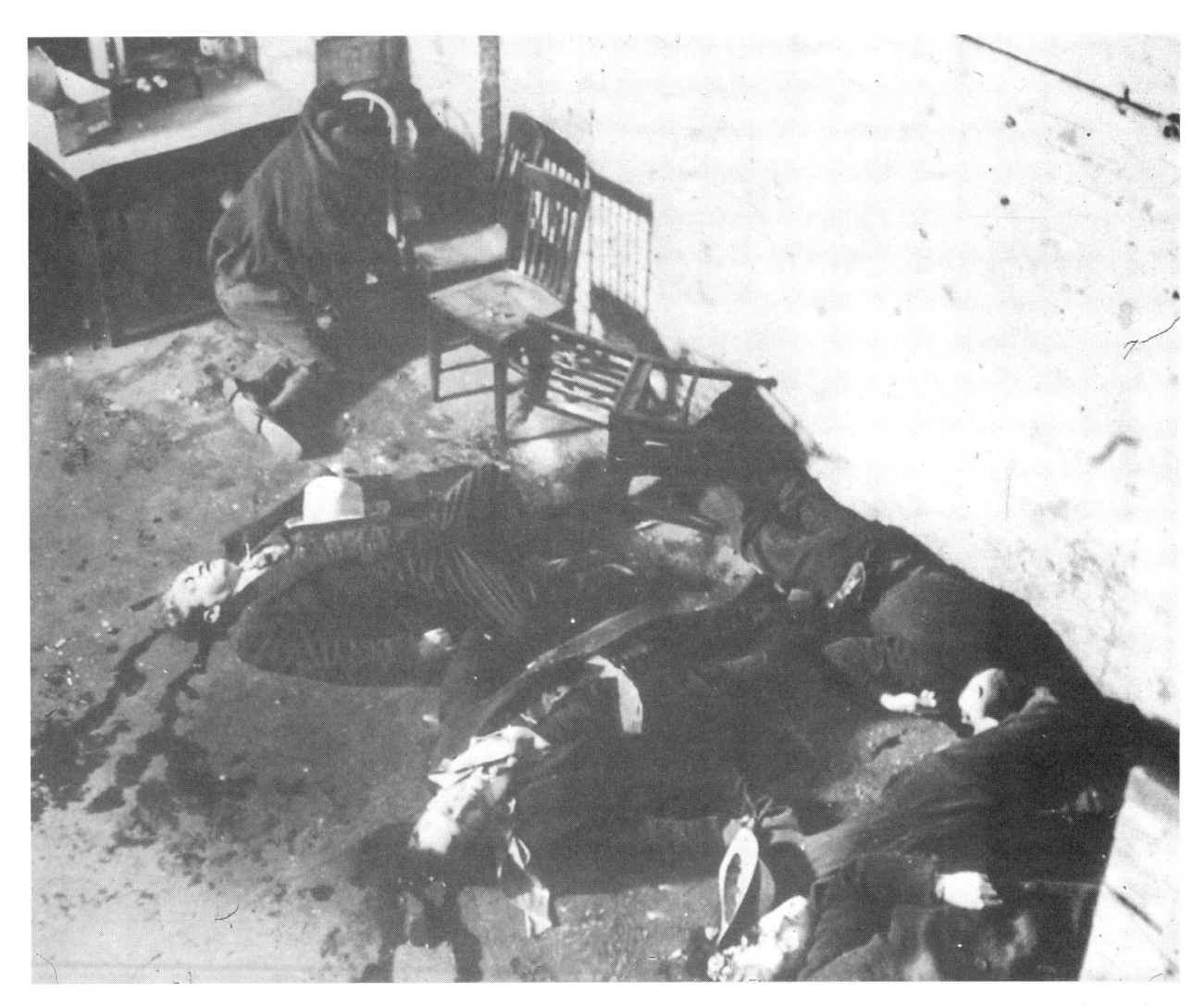

Valentine Massacre - 14th February 1929. Organized crime was completely out of control by 1929. Seen here are the dead bodies of gangsters, murdered in cold blood in Chicago by an unknown rival gang, in what was known as the 'St Valentine's Day Massacre'.

public relations and his men became known as "gangbusters." Congress expanded their federal responsibility to prosecute ordinary crimes, which had the effect of also enlarging the FBI's power. Television programs and movies further enhanced the FBI's image as the leader in the nation's fight against organized crime.

In the 1950s, Senator Estes Kefauver of Tennessee investigated organized crime, making headlines, and attracting the attention of television cameras. The publicity forced the FBI to renew its investigative efforts and inspired a host of television dramas and movies.

1905-PRESENT • POLICEWOMEN

Portland, Oregon hired the first policewoman in 1905, the city temporarily assigning Mrs. Lola Baldwin of the Traveler's Aid Society to the police department to help with the Lewis and Clark Exposition. Baldwin organized a Department of Public Safety for the Protection of Young Girls and Women. This experiment worked so well that the city permanently assigned Baldwin to the police department.

Other cities followed Portland's example. Mrs. Alice Stebbins Wells joined the Los Angeles police depart-

1950s

ment in 1910. Like Baldwin, Wells had a background in social work and worked with young women in trouble. More importantly, Wells traveled the nation urging women to join the police.

The first policewomen operated like social workers more than traditional police officers. Male police officers responded to calls that crimes had been committed. Women tried to prevent the crimes from happening through social work. Alice Stebbins Wells reassured her audiences that women would never take the place of male police officers. Women patrolled the places where youth gathered, searched for missing persons, and enforced laws at places of public recreation.

In the 1920s, the policewomen's movement nearly collapsed as reformers sought to strip police departments of their social functions. More emphasis on crime fighting made social work seem inappropriate. By the 1940s, many police departments employed no women at all.

Women returned to policing in the last quarter of the century. In 1972, the FBI announced that it would train its first two female agents, one a former nun and one a Marine Corps veteran. The FBI at first issued its women agents with smaller guns than it gave to its male agents, but then relented, issuing the same size weapon to both genders. FBI women carried special FBI purses, heavier to handle their guns.

By the end of the twentieth century, women made up ten percent of American police officers. Small town police departments were the least likely to hire women; only three percent of police officers in departments serving towns under 2,500 were women. In cities with a population of a million or more, women made up nearly sixteen percent of all police officers.

1920s-Present • Images of Policing in Television and Film ~ How Hollywood and the television industry chooses to depict crime and crime control plays an important role in many Americans' perceptions of their society. Polls show that persons who watch the most television have more exaggerated notions about crime and its pervasiveness than do persons who watch little television.

Some of the earliest movies depicted police officers as Keystone cops, bumbling fools. The national organization of police chiefs protested, fearing that the film industry was undermining societal values.

Beginning in the 1920s, Hollywood censored itself. To fend off government censors, the movie industry imposed the

(circa 1912) Mrs Alice Stebbins of the Los Angeles Police Department, one of the first policewomen in the world.

Hays Code, enforced by the Production Code Administration. In its Hays Code, the film industry set out rules and standards filmmakers had to follow or their movies would not be distributed. The Hays Code required that the law not be ridiculed. No sympathy could be expressed for law violators. This precept probably contributed to the generally favorable depiction of police and policing in many early films.

In 1968, Hollywood scrapped the Hays Code. Thereafter, film and television slowly began to take a more critical look at the criminal justice system. In the 1990s, African American moviemakers began making films about race and justice. These movies not only reflected directors' feelings of alienation, but came out at a time when polls showed that most Americans, regardless of race, had lost confidence in their law enforcement personnel. John Singleton's movie, *Boyz N the Hood* raised questions about the morality of imposing a single ethical standard on persons from different ethnic backgrounds. Should the law be applied to persons alienated from the prevailing legal culture? In Singleton's movies, and other films by black directors, white police officers appear as bigots, routinely and violently racist.

1918-1970 • POLICE UNIONISM

Before police unionism became established and accepted at the end of the 1960s, there were two earlier efforts to unionize police officers. The American Federation for Labor announced itself in favor of police unions in 1919. In two months 65 local organizations applied to the AFL for charters. When Cincinnati police struck for better wages in 1918, they won their fight. A different story unfolded in Boston where police had agitated for better wages for two years before going on strike in 1919. Boston patrolmen had as good a case for their demands as their Cincinnati colleagues, not having had a wage increase since 1898. Finally, after years of fruitless negotiation, 1,117 Boston police officers walked off the job on September 9. The strike proved a public relations disaster for the striking officers. Looters attacked stores, sounded false alarms and some citizens actually directed violence at the striking patrolmen. With public support turning against the strikers, Boston authorities suspended their striking officers and began recruiting a new police force. The city broke the union, but, to attract new recruits, raised wages to the levels sought by the strikers and, for the first time, provided free uniforms, another demand of the strikers.

A new round of efforts to unionize police departments met a similar fate in the 1940s. The American Federation of State, County, and Municipal Employees and its rival, the State, County, and Municipal Workers of America initiated this second campaign to union police officers. Many police in Los Angeles, St. Louis, Detroit, Portland, Miami and other cities joined AFSCME or SCMWA. Once again, city officials felt free to forcefully attack the union movement. The Los Angeles Police Commission banned the union and fired officers who did not renounce it. Authorities in other cities followed much the same procedure. The mayor of Jackson, Mississippi gave his officers a forty-eight hour ultimatum. The courts agreed that police officers had no right to unionize. While formal unions disappeared, city officials tolerated fraternal and benevolent organizations.

In the 1950s, municipal authorities gave garbage workers, teachers, firefighters and other city employees —but not police

—collective bargaining rights. This disparity may have helped prompt rank-and-file police to become more militant in their demands, staging slowdowns and other protests. By the early 1970s, police had won collective bargaining rights in major cities. Some states outlawed strikes by all public employees. Nonetheless, police in Detroit, Milwaukee, Baltimore and other cities did go on strike in the 1960s and 1970s. Fraternal orders of police and benevolent associations had become de facto unions.

At the end of the twentieth century, forty-six percent of American police departments permitted police unions. Smaller towns were least likely to allow unions. Only thirty percent of departments serving towns under 2,500 allowed police unions. Over eighty percent of departments serving urban areas with a population of a million or more allowed police unions.

1930s-Present • The Automobile and Policing

The automobile became widely available in the 1920s, transforming American culture. In 1930, 30,000 Americans died in automobile accidents. Car travel also seemed fatal to the family and traditional community life. Auto travel allowed family members to escape the supervision of neighbors and kin.

Widespread automotive travel changed policing in unexpected ways. The car quickly became associated with crime. The "get-away car" became a fixture in the popular imagination. Stealing cars became a major crime in the twentieth century. Thieves sometimes took stolen cars to "chop shops" where they could be disassembled for parts. Sometimes the thieves drove their stolen property to another state, "washed" the titles (using a forged title to get a valid title in another state is called "washing") and sold them to unsuspecting buyers. Thieves also exported stolen cars to foreign countries, at the rate of 200,000 a year. By 1984, car theft had become so widespread that Congress enacted the Motor Vehicle Enforcement Act. Despite the federal law, car stealing continued to expand, with 1,661,738 vehicle thefts in 1992. Many observers worried that car theft was out of control, and pointed out that the average car thief, even when convicted, did not go to jail, as the prisons could not accommodate so many convicted persons.

Sensational reports of violent assaults on drivers by car thieves galvanized public opinion in a way ordinary car theft never had. When car owners resisted the rising tide of car thefts with anti-theft devices, car thieves began to directly assault drivers, shoving them from cars at intersections and parking lots. Violently seizing a car from its driver came to be called carjacking, a term coined in Detroit, Michigan in 1992. The FBI reported 19,000 carjackings in 1991 and 21,000 in the first ten months of 1992. In one instance, a Maryland woman was shoved from her car by thieves, but got caught in her seatbelt. The thieves dragged her for two miles, sideswiping a fence in an attempt dislodge her. The thieves threw her baby from the car as they sped away. The woman died, but her baby, amazingly, lived.

1900-1950s • Catching Speeders

While the automobile generated new categories of crime for violent offenders, it also erased distinctions between the law violator and the law abiding. Most everyone who drives and parks breaks some law or ordinance some time. In 1901, New York introduced the first law on speed, making illegal any speed not "reasonable and proper." Soon the states inaugurated specific speed limits. Almost immediately, local governments began experiments with devices that would automatically identify speeders. Massachusetts used an apparatus that photographed automobiles from behind and then, exactly one second later, took another picture. The Supreme Judicial Court of Massachusetts decided a case arising from this procedure in 1909, finding that trial courts could admit such evidence in speeding cases.

Police began using radar to identify speeders after traffic engineers found it allowed them to study vehicle speeds when engineering highways. The first radar guns used by police had to be stationary; later, more advanced mechanisms could be used from a moving patrol car. In the 1950s, New York introduced the "phototraffic camera" which photographed speeders' license plates. Courts threw out citations based on such photographic evidence as the license plate merely identified the car's owner, not the driver. Although over seventy countries use cameras tripped by radar to catch speeders, cutting traffic deaths by as much as 84 percent, Americans have resisted the technology. When one police chief began using photo-radar devices, the local radio station accused him of Gestapo tactics and the state legislature outlawed the practice. Oakland, California had to suspend its photo-radar program after a judge refused to process the tickets. Proponents of improved traffic safety attribute American resistance to the nation's history of protecting individual rights, privacy and civil rights.

Cars also transformed the nature of police patrol. By 1910, many departments maintained an automobile flying squad to rush officers to crime scenes. In the 1920s, Detroit broadcast police calls over regular radio channels. Cleveland was the first city to use a special frequency for police communication. As police departments shifted from foot patrols to radio-dispatched cars, they found they lost contact with the citizenry. Foot patrols had been inefficient but they did enable officers to maintain positive contacts with citizens outside of adversary situations.

1990s • HIGH SPEED CHASES ~ At the end of the century, critics began to charge that high-speed auto pursuits of fleeing criminals by the police recklessly endangered the lives and property of innocent persons. Hollywood movies and television programming created film scenes where fictional suspects, followed by police

---

Ticketing the Mayor

~

Americans have effectively resisted increased police traffic surveillance because the violators are not people generally considered to be criminals. When police began enforcing traffic laws, officers found themselves citing prominent people, community leaders as criminals for the first time. Traffic control engendered tension between the police and the middle and upper classes. In some jurisdictions, the ability to "fix" a ticket distinguished upper class violators from the poorer classes.

1930s

Automobiles Sales and Total Registrations
(in thousands)

Year	Sales (thousands)	Registrations (thousands)
1910	181.0	458.3
1915	895.9	2,332.4
1920	1,905.5	8,131.5
1925	3,735.1	17,481.0
1930	2,787.4	23,034.7
1935	3,273.8	22,567.8
1940	3,717.3	27,465.8
1945	69.5	25,796.9
1950	6,665.8	40,339.0
1955	7,920.1	52,144.7
1960	6,674.7	61,682.3
1965	9,305.5	75,257.5
1970	6,546.8	89,279.8

SOURCE: *Historical Statistics of the United States: Colonial Times to 1970, Part 2*

cars, crashed through crowded intersections, careened around blind corners, and darted around pedestrians and other cars. As the film industry searched for ways to make its films more exciting, it escalated the recklessness of such pursuits. In real life, the police also seemed to more recklessly pursue fleeing suspects. Persons injured in high-speed chases filed more and more lawsuits against officers and their departments in efforts to recover damages as the century progressed. In court, judges and juries had to balance the damages suffered by individuals against the society's needs to arrest escaping felons.

In short, the car became closely associated with policing. Auto travel had the effect of antagonizing normally law-abiding citizens and replaced the cop on the beat with an officer in a car, remote from the citizens he served.

1930s • Expanding FBI Operations

~ Election of Franklin D. Roosevelt as president of the United States heralded greater government intervention in the lives of ordinary Americans. Hoover's FBI flourished under FDR. Under Roosevelt, Hoover launched a public relations effort that warned of a crime wave and highlighted the FBI's battle against crime. Professional criminologists doubted any national crime wave actually existed, pointing out that few kidnappings occurred, despite fears aroused by the murder of baby Lindbergh, and that most of the increase in criminal incidents grew out of increased automobile travel. Few Americans heeded the criminologists. Instead, everyone applauded the work of Hoover and his "G-Men." Congress passed new laws making kidnapping and travel across state lines to avoid prosecution federal crimes and established a National Police Academy.

While FDR served as president, the job of police officers came to be further focused on crime control more than social work, and crime fighting became a science. Reformers demanded meaningful statistics so they could measure the impact of crime prevention programs. Between 1930 and 1970 universities set up 200 associates, bachelors, masters and doctoral programs in police science, criminology and law enforcement. In Chicago, Northwestern University hosted the Scientific Crime Detection Laboratory, funded by businesses. The FBI established its crime lab two years later. Fingerprinting had been introduced early in the twentieth century, but had not immediately caught on. In the 1930s, police became obsessed with fingerprints and fingerprinting. Hoover reorganized the FBI's fingerprint filing system and greatly expanded it. In 1930, Congress

Fingerprints - circa 1930. Fingerprinting had been introduced early in the twentieth century but had not immediately caught on. In the 1930s, police became obsessed with fingerprints and fingerprinting. Shown here is a prisoner at Sing Sing prison, New York, having his fingerprints taken.

authorized a Division of Identification and Information within the FBI. Some fingerprint enthusiasts advocated mandatory universal fingerprinting for all Americans. President Franklin D. Roosevelt and other political leaders voluntarily submitted their fingerprints to the FBI in an effort to encourage everyone to turn in their prints.

1940S-1960S • SCANDAL AND REFORM ~ In the 1940s, one city after another experienced police scandals. A special investigator working for the San Francisco district attorney discovered that gamblers and liquor dealers paid a million dollars a year in protection to San Francisco police officers. A Los Angeles grand jury discovered that the local vice squad was paying a hundred dollars a night to prostitutes and running errands for organized crime figures. A Brooklyn newspaper revealed that a bookmaker in that city paid off local police. A Philadelphia grand jury found that local gamblers and prostitutes had paid off police in that city. A Federal grand jury caught the Kansas City Police Department intimidating and assaulting the mayor's political opponents.

A new generation of police chiefs extended the power of their offices. Thomas J. Gibbons served as commissioner of the Philadelphia police in the 1950s. William H. Parker ran the Los Angeles Police Department in the 1950s

1940s-1960s

and 1960s. Patrick V. Murphy ran the Syracuse, Detroit and New York City police departments. Reformers sought to protect these chiefs from political influence and several of them outlasted a number of city administrations.

Like earlier reformers, these new chiefs sought to centralize control of city policing. They did so by establishing special squads, just as had earlier reformers, and they consolidated precincts. Special intelligence squads inquired into organized crime and internal investigation squads examined corrupt police officers. Police departments also began offering better starting salaries and improved training for recruits.

As they focused on crime control, police departments moved away from the social work they had once pursued, shutting down athletic clubs and employment bureaus they had established earlier in the century. Police also launched campaigns to teach citizens to lock their doors and cars and avoid confidence artists. Police became more proactive, seeking to intercept criminals rather than merely respond to citizen complaints. San Francisco launched "Operation S" in the 1950s. A special "S" (for saturation) squad flooded into high-crime neighborhoods and stopped, questioned and frisked suspicious-looking persons. In one year the "S" squad stopped 20,000 people and filed 11,000 reports. Most of the thousand arrested were youth and blacks. Other cities followed similar procedures in a dramatic departure from previous, laissez-faire policing practices.

Reformers needed better statistics to measure the effectiveness of their innovations. San Francisco and St. Louis overhauled their records systems. Chicago established a central complaint bureau in the 1930s. New York moved record keeping from the precincts to headquarters. By the 1960s, most departments had improved their record keeping and provided more accurate statistics of crime in their cities.

1940s-1960s • CIVIL RIGHTS

Throughout much of the twentieth century the Ku Klux Klan and other racist groups infiltrated southern county sheriff departments, city police departments and state highway patrols. In Birmingham, Alabama, city leaders allowed a police officer to funnel the fruits of police wiretaps of civil rights organizations to the Ku Klux Klan. When civil rights demonstrators rode buses into town, the police allowed local hoodlums to attack and beat the bus riders without interference.

White southern police officers routinely brutalized African Americans even when the Ku Klux Klan was not present. In 1943, the sheriff of Baker County, Georgia, beat to death a young black man accused of stealing a tire. Federal authorities prosecuted Sheriff M. Claude Screws for violating his victim's civil rights. Though a federal case, the trial went before an all-white jury. Even so, prosecutors won a conviction. On appeal to the United States Supreme Court a year later, the government lost its case, and the conviction was overturned. Justice William O. Douglas wrote that federal prosecutors had to prove the racial intent of the officers they charged with violating citizens' civil rights. This proved an almost impossible standard to meet, and southern lawmen had little to fear from the Justice Department for years after 1944.

In 1956, FBI Director J. Edgar Hoover warned President Dwight Eisenhower and his cabinet that racial integration encouraged racial intermarriage and that communists sought to infiltrate the National

Association for the Advancement of Colored People. The Ku Klux Klan, Hoover continued, posed no threat. However, FBI agents did launch a few serious investigations of some incidents of racial violence, most notably the 1964 murders of three civil rights workers near Philadelphia, Mississippi, and the Bureau thoroughly infiltrated the Klan. More often, the FBI refused to intervene on behalf of civil rights workers caught in violent situations in the Deep South. FBI agents watched passively as southern police officers violated the rights of American citizens.

To break through this wall of indifference, the Civil Rights movement deliberately sent young men and women into the South to publicize many forms of racial oppression practiced there, including police-sanctioned brutalities. In 1964, the Neshoba County, Mississippi sheriff's department aided and abetted the murder of three young civil rights workers by Ku Klux Klansmen. The publicity over this and other incidents prompted a change of opinion in the South. White southerners, fearing anarchy, began to insist that order be maintained and laws enforced. Police departments and highway patrols across the South expelled Klansmen and other violent racists from their ranks in the mid-1960s. At least one Mississippi police chief ordered his officers to shoot to kill night-riding Klansmen. In 1965, Alabama Attorney General Richmond Flowers investigated the Ku Klux Klan in his state. Thereafter, Alabama officers seized Klan armaments and invaded Klan safe houses. When the governor of Florida heard of a Klan meeting in his state, he dispatched 140 highway patrol officers to break up the meeting. This brought to light (all over the South) racial vigilantism in the 1960s and a sincere effort was made to stop tolerating it.

1919-1968 • LONG HOT SUMMERS ~ Americans rioted throughout the twentieth century, often in response to police misconduct in racially tense situations. Rioting in Chicago started at segregated beaches in 1919. In 1943, 34 people died in a Detroit race riot. Harlem rioted in 1935 and 1943. When a white highway patrol officer stopped a motorist in 1965, rioting broke out in the Los Angeles neighborhood of Watts. Another police traffic stop prompted rioting in Newark two years later. Rumors of police brutality prompted a Detroit riot in 1967. When a white man assassinated Martin Luther King, Jr. in 1968, rioting erupted in 125 cities in 28 states, killing 46 people.

The Report of the National Advisory Commission on Civil Disorders, known as the Kerner Commission, stressed the importance of adroit police work. In a time of racial tension, any police action can attract a crowd and spark a riot. Commissioners worried that police tended not to know or understand the people they policed in ghettos. Further, the commission found incidents where the police rioted themselves.

1970S-PRESENT • BLACK POLICE OFFICERS ~ In the South cities hired few blacks as police officers until after World War II. Even then, cities restricted their black officers to black neighborhoods. As late as the 1960s, many southern cities did not allow black police officers to arrest white persons. Northern cities also limited black police officers to black areas and restricted their promotion possibilities.

Some cities, even in the North, refused to hire black officers at all for most of the century. In Boston, a 1973

1968-PRESENT

consent decree required the city to select recruits from a list that included one minority candidate for every white one. In 1983 the Justice Department filed a suit charging racial exclusion in hiring by the city of Cicero, Illinois, an all-white suburb of Chicago. Cicero and ten other communities settled the suit rather than go to trial. As a result of this suit, Cicero and other suburban communities hired black police officers for the first time.

At the end of the twentieth century racial and ethnic minorities made up 21 percent of all police officers. Some police commanders resisted efforts to end affirmative action on the theory that having African American, Latino and Vietnamese officers makes their departments more effective in the fight against crime. Minority officers can more comfortably interview nonwhite witnesses and suspects than can white officers. Some observers believe that the presence of minority police officers can also prevent such errors as the Boston Police Department's 1989 sweep through a black neighborhood, looking for the killer of a pregnant white woman. The killer, it turned out, was actually the woman's husband, not a black man, as he had claimed.

1968-PRESENT • POLICE BRUTALITY
∼ Under the common law, any felony could be punished with death and fugitive felons could be killed by pursuing officers or citizens. In the seventeenth century, courts began to insist that officers kill fleeing felons only as a "last resort." In the nineteenth and early twentieth centuries, American police followed the "last resort" rule. At the end of the nineteenth century, courts began to rule that only violent felons could be killed by pursuing officers. Improved policing convinced many judges that felons could be captured even when they eluded officers in an initial chase. This lessened reliance on the common law rule. In *Mattis v. Schnarr*, a 1975 case, a district court ruled that deadly force could be used by police only when life itself is endangered or great bodily harm is threatened. The American Law Institute favored this more enlightened rule, but some states still adhered to the old any-felony law.

In 1968, the Supreme Court encouraged police discretion when it ruled in *Terry v. Ohio* that police officers could stop and frisk people they think might be armed. The Court decided that these searches could be done without a warrant. Scholars have researched so-called "*Terry* searches," warrantless inspections carried out by the police under the *Terry v. Ohio* rule, and found that police tend to single out minority groups for such frisks.

In most police departments, an internal affairs division investigates citizen complaints of police brutality. Critics have complained that police investigations of fellow officers tend to be less than rigorous. Further, the insistence by police chiefs and police unions that such investigations be entirely confidential can also lead to abuses. Victims of police abuse sometimes fear turning in a complaint to the police. Police officers discourage complaining citizens, trying to persuade them not to push their concerns. Some cities have created independent citizen oversight committees.

Increased political power by blacks has discouraged some abuse by police officers. Detroit had a long history of poor relations between its black citizens and the police. After Detroit elected its first black mayor in 1973, Coleman A. Young, city officials restructured the police department. Young abolished

STRESS ("Stop Robberies, Enjoy Safe Streets"), an unpopular police decoy program. Young also launched an effort to hire and promote more black police officers. By 1983, police-community relations had improved.

Nonetheless, racism continues as a problem in American policing. In 1991, Los Angeles police brutally clubbed, stunned with electric stun guns, and kicked Rodney King. Caught on videotape, images of this incident shocked and sickened Americans across the country. Los Angeles set up a commission to investigate headed by Warren Christopher. The Christopher Commission documented the presence of overly violent officers in the Los Angeles Police Department and found police officers making racially offensive remarks on official police communications equipment. The commission, like previous reformers, called for better training and stricter supervision of the patrol force.

Police continue to rely on "racial profiling," a practice that assumes minority groups to be criminally inclined. In the 1980s, the Drug Enforcement Agency promoted racial profiling when it trained over 27,000 highway patrol officers from 48 states how to identify cars most likely to transport illegal drugs in Operation Pipeline. Police developed a strategy of stopping cars on minor traffic infractions as a pretext for searching for drugs without a warrant. One study of police stops on I-95 between January 1995 and September 1996 found that over seventy percent of the citizens halted were African American. Critics charge that few of the stopped cars actually contained drugs.

1920s • LIE DETECTORS ~ In 1921, John A. Larson constructed the first modern polygraph at the University of California. Polygraph machines measure a person's pulse, heart rate and blood pressure on the theory that an untruthful person will reveal himself or herself through changes in those physical functions. Just two years later the Court of Appeals of the District of Columbia threw out a murder conviction based on a lie detector test that had measured the suspect's blood pressure during interrogation. The judges decided that the science of lie detection had not yet been generally accepted in the scientific community and could not be admitted into court. For seventy years, courts generally followed this rule and disallowed lie detector evi-

Police Interrogations

~

The Constitution guards the rights of American citizens from unwarranted searches. The Fifth Amendment declares that "No person . . . shall be compelled in any criminal case to be a witness against himself . . . ." This means police cannot force a confession from an unwilling suspect. Nonetheless, American police have often forced suspects to testify against themselves. For much of the century, police used so-called third-degree techniques, beating or clubbing suspects to extract confessions. Police have also searched or examined the physical bodies of prisoners to extract evidence, making, in a sense, the person's body testify against them.

dence. Lie detector enthusiasts, like F. Lee Bailey, made little headway.

In 1993, the Supreme Court ruled that judges must treat lie detector evidence just as they treat all other expert testimony. This ruling had the effect of loosening the rule against polygraph evidence.

1965-1979 • STRIP SEARCHES ~ In many American cities, police routinely strip jailed suspects of their clothing and carefully inspect their naked bodies before admitting them to jail. Some jurisdictions strip search every person arrested for every crime, no matter how trivial the offense. Some police departments only strip search female detainees and not males.

The common law has long permitted searches of prisoners. Sixteenth-century English officers did not hesitate to strip naked and search members of the lower classes. Surviving texts depict officers exposing the bosoms and private parts of sometimes pregnant or ill female prisoners. Such practices continued in the American colonies. Nineteenth-century American prisons sometimes used strip searches to deliberately humiliate and degrade incoming prisoners.

Only with the civil rights movement in the mid-twentieth century did courts begin to look after the civil rights of imprisoned citizens. In 1965, after Congress passed the Civil Rights Act of 1964, the Supreme Court extended constitutional rights to prisoners. In a 1979 case entitled *Bell v. Wolfish*, the Supreme Court found that the Fourth Amendment to the Constitution limits strip searches. The Court decided, however, that just what constituted a "reasonable" strip search could not be spelled out. The Court ordered officers to balance person's privacy rights against the need for the search. The Court gave little or no guidance on how officers should do the required balancing. The Court promised generous deference to the officers to make the decision of whether to strip-search a citizen or not.

1966 • THE RIGHT TO REMAIN SILENT ~ In 1966 the Supreme Court tried to curb police intimidation of suspects. For many years police officers roughly interrogated suspects, sometimes torturing them into confessing. Police manuals instructed detectives on the art of intimidating suspects during interrogation. Prosecutors and police relied on suspects' confessions to "solve" cases. In *Miranda v. Arizona* (1966), the Court ordered police officers to tell suspects that they had a right to have an attorney present during questioning.

Miranda v. Arizona prompted a stiff wave of protest. Critics assailed the Court for "coddling" criminals, worrying that those guilty of murder and other criminals would escape justice. Congress passed a law intended to reverse the *Miranda v. Arizona* decision. In 1968, presidential candidate George Wallace blasted the Court in crude language, claiming that criminals laughed at police hamstrung by legalisms. Republican candidate Richard Nixon also criticized the justices, albeit in more measured language. The Democratic candidate, Hubert Humphrey, did not attack the Court, but he did not defend it either.

Over the years, police officers became less hostile to the Court's requirement that they alert suspects to their rights. Fictional detectives on television and in the movies began reading the required *Miranda* warning to their fictional suspects so routinely that the warning seemed a normal part of the arrest process. In court, police witnesses and prosecutors discovered that it was actually easier to get confessions accepted into evidence when the *Miranda* warning had been read than before 1966, when prosecutors had to prove that the defendant had voluntarily confessed. Judges assumed a confessing defendant had done so voluntarily when he or she did so after hearing his *Miranda* rights read by the interrogating officer.

1980s • GROWTH OF POLICING ~ Throughout the twentieth century cities devoted more and more money to increasingly high tech policing. The numbers of officers increased alongside increases in police department budgets.

1990s • DECLINE IN THE MURDER RATE ~ In the last decade of the twentieth century, the homicide rate declined sharply. Scholars could not definitively explain the drop, though many advanced competing theories, some based on changes in police practice.

Some attributed the decline in murder to a strategy called "community policing." In the 1990s, many police departments began asking citizens to identify problems for police attention. This approach made police more proactive and involved officers in matters once thought private. In the 1990s, over half of all police departments gave at least some, and forty percent gave all, their officers training in community policing. Two-thirds of departments serving larger cities had a full-time community policing unit. Other departments, without a full-time unit, still maintained a "community relations officer" or a "community resource officer" to coordinate policing with citizens' wants. Larger departments serving larger cities were more likely to initiate community policing than smaller departments.

Police departments also pursued an aggressive crime control strategy called "Broken Windows" designed to improve urbanites' quality of life. This approach to policing assumes that control of minor crimes—so-called "quality of life" misdemeanors—will prevent more serious felonies. Broken windows, panhandling, public drunkenness and graffiti create an environment where violent crime can take root and flourish. New York and Houston police sought to improve the quality of life in their cities as a way of controlling the most serious crimes. Chicago called its program CAPS, for Chicago Alternative Policing Strategy. Chicago sought to control gang violence by making it a crime for young males to loiter on streets. This proved unconstitutional, but some observer's claim that "hard" policing of "soft" crimes has contributed to the decline in murders.

Police Force Strength

	Per Capita Expenditures for Policing	Number of Police State and Local
1980	$66.73	658,188
1981	73.31	661,095
1982	82.11	668,001
1983	88.32	669,172
1984	96.20	681,801
1985	102.55	690,976
1986	109.34	705,182
1987	118.73	720,038
1988	126.63	725,903
1989	132.87	732,826
1990	144.04	747,809
1991	154.57	755,240
1992	162.05	769,977
1993	170.83	778,773
1994	176.71	806,336

SOURCE: U.S. Dept. of Justice, Bureau of Justice Statistics. *Sourcebook of Criminal Justice Statistics*, 1998

Both of these approaches to crime control represented a retreat from the reforms initiated in the Progressive era, and continued through the rest of the century. Reformers had sought to centralize control and divorce police officers from community politics. These new initiatives decentralized policing, giving more latitude to the officer on the street. They also immersed police officers in local politics and the social welfare missions once eschewed by the reformers.

CONCLUSION

Policing in the twentieth century became more centrally controlled, more professional and more unionized. The role of the Federal government increased, in no small measure due to the effectiveness of the FBI's publicity campaign begun under President Franklin D. Roosevelt. The FBI very successfully worked to present its agents as crime fighting, gang-busting "G-Men." Even conservatives leery of the increased government activity promoted by presidents Roosevelt and Johnson cheered the FBI's expanded mission.

By the end of the twentieth century, some observers called for a return to "community policing." The best way to curb crime, some said, was to decentralize control of the police, giving individual officers the opportunity to pick and choose likely suspects for police surveillance. But even as some promoted greater police latitude and decentralized control, others warned that police brutality and racial discrimination remained a problem. More lax supervision might lead to even more abuses of innocent minority citizens. At the end of the twentieth century, this tension between citizens' rights and crime control remained unresolved.

BIBLIOGRAPHY

Belknap, Michal R. *Federal Law and Southern Order: Racial Violence and Constitutional Conflict in the Post-Brown South*. Athens: University of Georgia Press, 1987.

Fisher, Jim. *The Lindbergh Case*. New Brunswick: Rutgers University Press, 1987.

Fogelson, Robert M. *Big-City Police*. Cambridge: Harvard University Press, 1977.

Friedman, Lawrence M. *Crime and Punishment in American History*. New York: Basic Books, 1993.

Harris, David A. "Driving While Black: Racial Profiling on our Nation's Highways." (1999): http://www.aclu.org/profiling/report/index.html

Joanes, Ana. "Does the New York City Police Department Deserve Credit for the Decline in New York City's Homicide Rates? A Cross-City Comparison of Policing Strategies and Homicide Rates," *Columbia Journal of Law and Social Problems* 33 (Spring 2000): 265.

Johnson, David R. *American Law Enforcement: A History*. St. Louis: Forum, 1981.

Melanson, Philip H. *The Politics of Protection: The U.S. Secret Service in the Terrorist Age*. New York: Praeger, 1984.

Monkkonen, Eric H. *Police in Urban America, 1860-1920*. Cambridge: Cambridge University Press, 1981.

Simon, Jonathan. "Driving Governmentality: Automobile Accidents, Insurance, and the Challenge to Social Order in the Inter-War Years, 1919-1941," *Connecticut Insurance Law Journal* 4 (1997/8): 521.

Ungar, Sanford J. *FBI*. Boston: Little, Brown, 1975.

Walker, Samuel. *A Critical History of Police Reform: The Emergence of Professionalism.* Lexington: D.C. Heath, 1977.

INTERNET RESOURCES

U.S. Department of Justice homepage
www.usdoj.gov

FBI homepage
www.fbi.gov

CIA homepage
www.cia.gov

Crime homepage links to 700 crime-related websites
http://lawenforcement.about.com/index.htm

ORGANIZED CRIME SITE
From the Godfather to the Sopranos, Meyer Lansky to Lucky Luciano.
http://organizedcrime.about.com/index.htm

Crime and Law Enforcement Mapping crime and crime statistics is a recent advancement in police technology.
http://geography.about.com/cs/crimeandlawenfo/index.htm

Crime Families - Fictional and Real Links to web sites focusing on North American crime families, both fictional and real.
http://organizedcrime.about.com/cs/crimefamilies1/index.htm

National Crime Prevention Council NCPC is a national nonprofit organization whose mission is to help America prevent crime and build safer, stronger communities.
http://mentalhealth.about.com/library/h/orgs/bl2939.htm

JUST FOR PARENTS
Crime links for parents
http://crime.about.com/cs/justforparents/index.htm

FOR KIDS AND PARENTS
Crime sites appropriate for children, and of interest to parents.
http://crime.about.com/cs/familylinks/index.htm

SAFE KIDS
Keeping your children safe
http://crime.about.com/library/blfiles/blsafekids.htm

Rape Prevention & Education What should you do if you've been raped? How can you avoid being raped? Advice about how to arm against rapist and other criminals.
http://littlerock.about.com/library/weekly/aa021201a.htm

CRIMINAL JUSTICE & LAW ENFORCEMENT
Articles, directories, statistics and all manner of commentary on criminal justice issues.
http://law.about.com/cs/criminaljustice/index.htm

JUSTNET - NATIONAL LAW ENFORCEMENT AND CORRECTIONS TECHNOLOGY CENTER
Online gateway to law enforcement and corrections technology information. Under the auspices of the National Institute of Justice
http://www.nlectc.org/

U.S. DEPARTMENT OF THE INTERIOR — BUREAU OF INDIAN AFFAIRS LAW Enforcement Bureau of Indian Affairs Law Enforcement Services
http://bialaw.fedworld.gov/

LAW ENFORCEMENT
Online Extensive list of (5,000) Law Enforcement Agencies
http://pimacc.pima.edu/dps/police.htm

POLICE JOBS
Employment, testing and interviewing guides for federal and state police jobs
http://www.policeemployment.com/

National Center for Rural Law Enforcement http://www.ncrle.net/

LAW ENFORCEMENT TECHNOLOGY
The leading source of information on technology available to law enforcement professionals. New products, technologies, and management innovations
http://www.letonline.com/

OFFICER.COM: LAW ENFORCEMENT
Resource Site Police, law enforcement and criminal justice links
http://www.officer.com/

Christopher Waldrep
San Francisco State University

LAWS AND THE U.S. LEGAL SYSTEM

(1970) Foot in Mouth Disease. A cartoon showing Vice President Spiro Agnew, famous for his own gaffes (1918-1996), teaching President Nixon (1913-1994) how to put his foot in his mouth after President Nixon's remarks about the guilt of Charles Manson before the trial was concluded.

TIMELINE

1900-1919 ~ Expanding Legal and Governmental Controls

Supreme Court upholds the right of employer and employee to contract for working hours free from government control in *Lochner v. New York* (1905) / Supreme Court upholds an Oregon law limiting maximum working hours of women in *Muller v. Oregon* (1908) / Income tax first levied on personal income (16th Amendment 1913) / Direct Election of Senators (17th Amendment 1913) / Clayton Anti-Trust Act is designed to strengthen the Sherman Anti-Trust Act by prohibiting corporate practices that were not specified as illegal, such as price fixing (1914) / Supreme Court rules that Congress has no authority to forbid the shipment of products made by children because the products themselves were not harmful in *Hammer v. Dagenhart* (1918) / Prohibition of Alcoholic Beverages (18th Amendment 1919) / Supreme Court sustains the Espionage Act of 1917 against a challenge that it violated the guarantee of freedom of speech and press in *Schenck v. U. S* (1919) / Supreme Court upholds the 1918 Sedition Law, which prohibits publishing data intended to undermine the U.S. government (1919)

MILESTONES: Pension plan for soldiers and federal employees consumes 30 percent of the federal budget (1900) • U.S. bans all Chinese immigration except for diplomats, students, and merchants (1900) • Margaret Sanger risks arrest by opening up birth control clinics and importing and distributing contraceptives illegally (1914) • Election of the first woman to Congress, Jeanette Rankin from Montana (1916) • President Wilson institutes the federal Mediation Commission to resolve labor disputes (1917) • Espionage Act prohibits open criticism of the U.S. government (1917) • Taking a stolen car across state lines is a federal crime (1919)

1920-1929 ~ Testing Court Decisions

Women's Suffrage gives women the right to vote (19th Amendment 1919) / Fordney-McCumber Tariff increases the duties on foreign manufactured goods by 25 percent in order to protect manufacturers from competition (1922) / *Moore v. Dempsey* establishes federal due process protections for defendants on trial in state courts (1923) / In *Olmstead v. U. S.* Supreme Court rules that wiretaps do not violate the Fourth Amendment's prohibition against unreasonable searches and seizures where no entry to private premises occurred (1925) / Supreme Court upholds a state law that makes it a crime to organize and participate in a group that advocates the overthrow by force of the established political system in *Whitney v. California* (1927) / Supreme Court rules that Virginia did not violate the Fourteenth Amendment's due process guarantee in *Buck v. Bell* by sterilizing a mentally defective mother (1927)

MILESTONES: Congress passes a law that allows civil service officials to receive retirement benefits at the age of 70; mechanics, letter carriers and clerks at 65; and railway clerks at 62 (1920) • Cable Act declares that an American woman married to an alien loses her citizenship (1922) • John T. Scopes, a school teacher in Tennessee, is arrested for teaching evolution to his students (1925) • Collective bargaining laws strengthened, giving unions more power (1928 and 1932) • Wickersham Commission investigates police work and crime (1929)

1930-1939 ~ Depression Era Measures

Hawley-Smoot Tariff increases taxes ranging from 31 to 49 percent on foreign imports, setting off a tariff war between trading countries (1930) / National Industrial Recovery Act is designed to revive industrial and business activity and to reduce unemployment (1933) / Repeal of Prohibition Amendment, legalizes alcohol again (21st Amendment 1933) / National Labor Relations Board is created to determine appropriate collective bargaining practices (1935) / Supreme Court invalidates the Agricultural Adjustment Act of 1933, which sought to regulate agriculture by paying benefits to farmers who reduced their production of certain commodities (1936) / Supreme Court finally abandons its earlier narrow view of the federal power to regulate interstate commerce (1937)

MILESTONES: Under pressure, the movie industry enacts the Production Code, regulating crime, sex, vulgarity, obscenity, profanity, costumes, dancing, and religion in films (1930) • Chicago establishes a police complaint bureau (1930s) • The Nobel Prize-winning geneticist, Hermann J. Muller, attacks the eugenics movement for "lending a false appearance of scientific basis to advocates of race and class prejudice" (1930s) • Economy Act stipulates that married women be discharged from their jobs (1932) • United Mine Workers of America (UMW), one of the nation's few interracial organizations, provides the organizational foundation for the emergence of industrial unionism (1935-1939)

1940-1949 ~ Wartime Court Decisions

Supreme Court upholds a state's right to require public school students to recite daily the national pledge of allegiance to the flag even if the restriction conflicts with their religious beliefs (1940) / Selective Service Act permits conscientious objectors to serve in non-combat positions (1940) / Executive Order 9066 forces Japanese Americans to relocate to internment camps (1942) / Repeal of the Chinese exclusion law permits Chinese immigration (1943) / Supreme Court reverses its 1940 decision by ruling that the state could not compel children to participate in a patriotic ceremony (Pledge of Allegiance) when it violated their religious beliefs (1944)

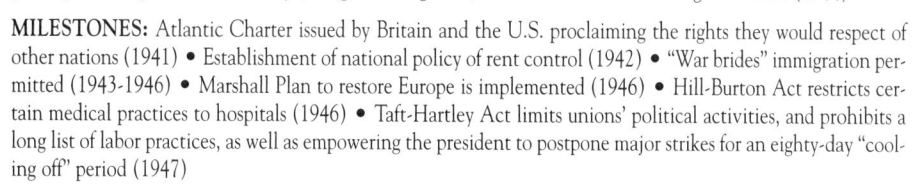

MILESTONES: Atlantic Charter issued by Britain and the U.S. proclaiming the rights they would respect of other nations (1941) • Establishment of national policy of rent control (1942) • "War brides" immigration permitted (1943-1946) • Marshall Plan to restore Europe is implemented (1946) • Hill-Burton Act restricts certain medical practices to hospitals (1946) • Taft-Hartley Act limits unions' political activities, and prohibits a long list of labor practices, as well as empowering the president to postpone major strikes for an eighty-day "cooling off" period (1947)

1950-1959 ~ Civil Rights

Supreme Court orders the University of Texas law school to admit an African American student because the state failed to fulfill the promise of equal protection under the Fourteenth Amendment (1950) / Limitation is set for U.S. presidents to two terms (22nd Amendment 1951) / Supreme Court upholds the Smith Act that made it unlawful to advocate or teach the violent overthrow of government in the United States or to belong to an organization dedicated to the accomplishment of these ends (1951) / McCarran-Walter Act permits Japanese to apply for citizenship (1952) / In *Brown v. the Board of Education of Topeka, Kansas*, Supreme Court rules that racial segregation in public schools is unconstitutional, and the concept of "separate but equal" is reversed (1954)

MILESTONES: United Auto Workers (UAW) signs a national union contract with General Motors that includes seniority provisions, a pension plan, cost-of-living allowances, and wage increases (1950) • Julius and Ethel Rosenberg, avowed Communists, are executed for transmitting atomic secrets to the Soviets (1953) • Arrest of Rosa Parks starts the Bus Boycott in Montgomery, Alabama (1955) • Federal troops intervene to enforce Little Rock integration orders (1956)

1960-1969 ~ Personal Rights

Presidential Electors granted for the District of Columbia (23rd Amendment 1961) / Supreme Court overturns a 1949 decision by stating that evidence obtained in violation of the Fourth Amendment that prohibits unreasonable search and seizure must be excluded from use at state and federal trials (1961) / Supreme Court rules that a non-denominational prayer written by the New York State Board of Regents to be said on an involuntary basis each school day is a direct violation of the First Amendment (1962) / Supreme Court overturns a 1942 case and requires states to provide legal counsel for indigent defendants in criminal cases (1963) / Civil Rights Act declares that American citizens cannot be segregated in public accommodations or discriminated against in employment (1964) / Civil Rights Voting Act enacted (1964) / Abolition of the Poll Tax (24th Amendment 1964) / In *Miranda v. Arizona* Supreme Court rules that suspects must be warned of their rights to protect themselves against self-incrimination before statements they make to the authorities can be used against them (1966) / Presidential Disability and Succession Act enacted (25th Amendment 1967)

MILESTONES: Civil Rights Act makes it a federal crime to transport explosives across state lines (1960) • Hazardous Substances Labeling Act requires warnings on dangerous household products (1960) • Attorney General Robert Kennedy leads war against organized crime (1960-1963) • Congress enacts the Sports Broadcasting Act, empowering the National Football League, as well as professional leagues in other sports, to negotiate as a single economic entity the sale of national broadcasting rights (1961) • Kennedy administration introduces Civil Rights legislation, which will not pass until 1964 (1962) • Federal Trade Commission requires cancer-warning labels on cigarette packages (1964) • New Hampshire is the first state to reinstate lotteries (1964) • Neshoba County, Mississippi sheriff's department aid and abet the murder of three young Civil Rights workers by Ku Klux Klansmen (1964) • Government indicts Muhammed Ali for evading the draft; the New York State Athletic Commission suspends his boxing license; and the World Boxing Association, noting that he could not defend the title, voids Ali's heavyweight championship (1967)

1970-1979 ～ Environmental Protection and Personal Freedoms

Clean Air Act requires automakers to reduce emissions of hydrocarbons, the major exhaust pollutant (1970) / Voting age reduced from 21 to 18 years (26th Amendment 1971) / Supreme Court rules that the state of Wisconsin cannot demand school attendance of Amish children if it infringes upon their free exercise of religion under the First and Fourteenth Amendments (1972) / Great Lakes Water Quality Act attempts to clean up the badly polluted waterways between the United States and Canada (1972) / Federal Water Pollution Control Act authorizes funds for sewage treatment plants (1972) / *Roe v. Wade* affirms a woman's right to privacy when deciding whether or not to terminate her pregnancy (1973) / Supreme Court rejects President Nixon's claim of executive privilege and orders him to turn over the Watergate tapes, leading to his resignation (1974) / Resource Conservation and Recovery Act addresses recycling and disposing of solid wastes (1976) / Clean Water Act makes it unlawful to discharge pollutants into navigable waters unless a permit is obtained (1977) / *Regents of the University of California v. Bakke* decrees that college admissions cannot be based on race alone (1978)

MILESTONES: Supreme Court vindicates Muhammed Ali, ruling that the government had violated his constitutional rights, clearing the way for his return to the ring (1970) • Comprehensive Drug Abuse Prevention and Control Act attempts to control illegal drugs and trafficking (1970) • Fair Packaging and Labeling Act sets standards for labeling additives to food (1975) • Occupational Safety and Health Act sets safety standards in the workplace (1970) • Age Discrimination and Employment Act rises the age for mandatory retirement from 65 to 70 (1978)

1980-2001 ～ International Law and U.S. Intervention Abroad

Gramm-Rudman-Hollings Balanced Budget Act attempts to eliminate deficit spending by the federal government (1985) / Immigration Reform Act makes it illegal for employers to hire undocumented workers (1987) / General Manuel Noriega is ousted by American forces in Panama (1989) / Americans With Disabilities Act enacted (1990) / Restraint placed on Congressional Salaries (27th Amendment 1992) / Federal regulations, many of which are arcane or obsolete, fill 130,000 pages (1995)

MILESTONES: President Carter imposes grain embargo and a U.S. boycott of Moscow Summer Olympics against the Soviet Union for invading Afghanistan (1980) • Establishment of state lotteries in Arizona, California, Colorado, Florida, Idaho, Indiana, Iowa, Kansas, Kentucky, Missouri, Montana, Oregon, South Dakota, Virginia, West Virginia and Wisconsin (1980s) • Congress passes the Economic Recovery Tax Act, decreasing personal income taxes by 25 percent and lowering the maximum tax rate from 70 to 50 percent (1981) • Congress considers but rejects most gun control legislation (1985-2000) • START Treaty between the U.S. and Russia reduces nuclear weapons (1990) • North American Free Trade Agreement opens trade borders to Mexico and Canada (1993) • Supreme Court rules that a child of an American mother, regardless of where it is born, automatically becomes a U.S. citizen while the child of a foreign mother by an American father must apply for citizenship (2001)

INTRODUCTION

Law has pervaded every aspect of society in the United States. Americans have looked to the principal varieties of law—constitutional, civil, and criminal—for the protection of their rights to life, liberty, and property. It has often been argued, especially in the twentieth century, that Americans have become overly dependent on the legal system to manage disputes about social, economic, and political problems rather than using other means available to them, such as private negotiations and participation in the political process. Many Americans had, and still have the "impulse to sue" and more than 10 million cases are filed in United States courts each year. An example of one such "frivolous " case was filed by a group of Washington Redskins' fans who went to federal court to try to reverse a referee's disputed call because it cost the Redskins a victory. Table 1 illustrates the types of cases brought before federal district courts in the 1990s. As the twentieth century progressed, civil lawsuits increasingly dealt with product liability, medical malpractice, and environmental issues.

Table 1. Types of Cases in Federal District Courts

Civil Cases	85.2%
Contract Actions	11.3%
Prisoner Petitions	21.6%
Civil Rights	13.3%
Personal Injury/Property Damage	10.1%
Product Liability	8.7%
Others (bankruptcy, tax suits, labor laws, and social security)	20%
Criminal Cases	14.8%
Drugs	3.8%
Fraud	2.4%
Immigration	1.7%
Drunk Driving and Traffic	1.6%
Weapons and Firearms	1.0%
Forgery/Counterfeiting/Embezzlement	0.7%
Others (larceny, theft, homicide, robbery, assault, and burglary)	3.6%

SOURCE: Administrative Office of the United States Court, 1992

The twentieth century evolved into an age of centralized, national power for the United States. During this time of world wars, a decade-long depression, social unrest, and worldwide political upheavals, the federal government's role grew while states' powers began to erode and slip away. Although playing key roles at times, the legisla-

(1877) Western Justice. In the "horse and buggy days" of the United States legal system, the public was the main regulator of legal issues. Seen here is the trial of a horse thief in a frontier town in America.

tive and judicial branches lost some of their power at the center to the executive branch during the twentieth century. Not only have five of the most powerful and influential presidents in U. S. history—Theodore and Franklin Roosevelt, Wilson, Truman, and Johnson—served in the twentieth century, but the number of executive agencies that now exist reflects a tenfold increase. The influence of the American legal system has also been felt worldwide as emerging democracies have modeled their constitutions on the U.S. constitution.

"If an individual enter into a state of society, the laws of that society must be the supreme regulator of their conduct."

Alexander Hamilton, 1788

As social conditions continually change, so must the law also change or become outdated. Every nation changes its laws in the manner that its political system prescribes. Democracies have developed four main methods of changing the law: (1) by court decision, (2) by legislation, (3) by administrative action, and (4) by direct action of the people.

By Court Decision. Judges change many laws by expanding or overruling precedents set in earlier cases. Especially in the United States during the twentieth century, judges often overruled precedents to bring the law into line with changing social conditions. In 1896, for example, the U.S. Supreme Court upheld a law that provided for "separate but equal" public facilities for blacks and whites. But in 1954, the Supreme Court ruled that racial segregation in public schools was unconstitutional, and the concept of "separate but equal" was reversed.

By Legislation. Legislatures may change laws as well as make them. A legislature can change a statute by amending it, by repealing it, or by passing a new law on the same subject. Franklin Delano Roosevelt's "New Deal" and Lyndon Baines Johnson's "Great Society" programs were two examples of the most active times in the history of the legislative change process. By late 1965, President Johnson had prodded Congress to enact nearly 90 different bills that supported Johnson's vision to eradicate the country's rampant urban poverty. This was the largest burst of legislative activity since FDR's first Hundred Days in 1933 when he sought ways to bring the country out of the Depression by creating massive government relief programs. Table 2 illustrates an example of the volume and number of bills introduced and passed in the House of Representatives and the Senate from 1981-2000 under normal circumstances.

Table 2. Bills Introduced, Passed, and Enacted by Congress 1980 – 2000

Congress	(Years)	Bills Introduced H	S	Bills Passed H	S	Bills Enacted
97th	(1981-82)	8,094	3,396	704	803	529
98th	(1983-84)	7,105	3,454	978	936	677
99th	(1985-86)	6,499	3,386	973	940	688
100th	(1987-88)	6,236	3,325	1061	1002	761
101th	(1989-90)	6,683	3,669	968	980	666
102th	(1991-1992)	7,771	4,245	932	947	610
103th	(1993-1994)	6,647	3,177	749	682	473
104th	(1995-1996)	4,542	2,266	611	518	337
105th	(1997-1998)	5,915	3,160	547	314	404
106th	(1999-2000)	5,681	3,287	NA	NA	580

SOURCE: *Congressional Quarterly Digest,* 2000

By Administrative Action. The president and government agencies have some autonomous authority to amend, repeal, or replace the regulations they make. In addition, they may be authorized to interpret an old regulation to meet changing conditions. The Environmental Protection Agency became a force during the twentieth century and is a good example of a government agency that can dictate administrative law. Table 3 illustrates some of the administrative action taken by the EPA during the 1970s.

Table 3. Important Environmental Legislation, 1970-1977

Year	Act/Agency/Agreement	Description
1970	Environmental Protection Agency	Combined existing government agencies concerned with pollution and environmental controls
1970	Clean Air Act	Required automakers to reduce emissions of hydrocarbons, the major exhaust pollutants
1972	Great Lakes Water Quality	Sought to clean up the badly polluted waterways between the United States and Canada
1972	Federal Water Pollution Control Act	Authorized funds for sewage treatment plants
1976	Resource Conservation and Concerned methods of recycling and disposing of Recovery Act	solid wastes
1977	Clean Water Act	Made it unlawful to discharge pollutants into navigable waters unless a permit is obtained.

SOURCE: Environmental Protection Agency

By Direct Action of the People. Some national and many local governments give the people direct power to change the law by referendum and by initiative. In a referendum, a law or a proposed law is submitted to the voters for their approval or rejection. In an initiative, a group of citizens proposes a law, which is then approved or rejected by the legislature or by referendum. The Progressive amendments, 16 through 19 and the failed Equal Rights Amendment are examples of this process. Table 4 lists the amendments that were added to the United States Constitution in the twentieth century.

Table 4. Twentieth Century Amendments

Amendment 16 (1913) Income Tax
Amendment 17 (1913) Direct Election of Senators
Amendment 18 (1919) Prohibition of Alcoholic Beverages
Amendment 19 (1920) Women's Suffrage
Amendment 20 (1933) "Lame Duck" Amendment
Amendment 21 (1933) Repeal of Prohibition Amendment
Amendment 22 (1951) Limit on Presidential Terms
Amendment 23 (1961) Presidential Electors for the District of Columbia
Amendment 24 (1964) Abolition of the Poll Tax
Amendment 25 (1967) Presidential Disability and Succession Act
Amendment 26 (1971) Eighteen Year Old Vote
Amendment 27 (1992) Restraint on Congressional Salaries

Progressive Thought and the Emergence of Modern America

"If the meanest man in the republic is deprived of his rights, then every man in the republic is deprived of his rights." — *Jane Addams, 1903*

Milestones

1904 *Northern Securities Company v. U. S.* (193 U. S. 197)
1905 *Lochner v. New York* (198 U. S. 45)
1908 *Muller v. Oregon* (208 U. S. 274)
1913 16th and 17th Amendments
1914 Federal Trade Commission and Clayton Antitrust Acts

1900 • Social Conditions and the Law at the Beginning of the Century ~ The twentieth century was to leave a legacy of legal milestones. In 1900, the United States was still a rural country and life was relatively simple during these "horse and buggy days." Urbanization, population growth, immigration, and the Industrial Revolution however, were beginning to reshape the American landscape and ultimately force legal change. As the United States became more urban in the twentieth century, laws related to housing, living conditions, green areas, restricted covenants (restricting use of property) and segregation were enacted. Population growth, especially the development of the suburbs, led to transportation and public highway laws. Although the United States is deemed a "Nation of Immigrants," laws and quotas restricting immigrants occurred throughout the twentieth century. The Industrial Revolution and its second coming in the twentieth century would lead to the passage of environmental, child labor, and minimum wage, and working conditions legislation as Americans attempted to improve the work place.

(1920) Members of the League of Nations looking over their shoulders during an assembly in Geneva, Switzerland.

1900-1914 • INTERNATIONAL LAW

At the beginning of the twentieth century, two United States presidents and their secretaries of states did a great deal to develop modern international law. President Theodore Roosevelt, who argued that arbitration and mediation should be used whenever possible in international affairs and his secretary of state Elihu Root, won Noble Peace Prizes for their efforts to improve the use of arbitration in settling international disputes. President Woodrow Wilson also won a Nobel Peace Prize for initiating the establishment of the League of Nations. His Secretary of State, Charles Evans Hughes, who worked to create new international rules through treaties, became the second American to sit on the Permanent Court of International Justice at The Hague, Netherlands. Two world wars, the Cold War, the threat of nuclear proliferation, a changing world order, environmental concerns, interdependent economies and world trade forced the United States from its isolationist policy of the nineteenth century into the role of an international world leader by the end of the twentieth century.

1900-1914 • THE FREE ENTERPRISE SYSTEM

By the early 1800s, Americans had begun to develop a flourishing economy based almost entirely on a system of free enterprise in which businesses regulated their dealings largely through contracts. The rapid growth of the U.S. economy in the 1800s therefore brought an enormous increase in contract law, which especially emphasized freedom of contract with no government interference. In 1905, in the case of *Lochner v. New York* (198 U. S. 45), the Supreme Court upheld the right of employer and employee to contract for working hours free from government control, thereby upholding the principle of free enterprise without government intervention. Since contracts were regarded strictly as private agreements, judges paid little attention to their social effects.

Complete freedom of contract had served the needs of America's rapidly expanding economy during the 1800s, but by 1900 many businesses in the United States were using this freedom to increase their profits at the expense of their employees, stockholders, and customers. For example, factory owners claimed that efforts to protect the rights of workers interfered with the owners' rights to contract freely with their employees. Employees often had to accept unfavorable contracts or lose their jobs.

During the 1800s, most Americans accepted the idea that the law should interfere with private business as little as possible. But the public's attitude toward the law changed greatly during the 1900s. The Progressive Era (1900-1919) forced legislators to face the problem of corporate responsibility. They did so by passing statutes such as the Federal Trade Commission Act of 1914 and the Clayton Anti-Trust Act of 1914 that reflected grants of and restrictions on Congressional and state power. The Federal Trade Commission Act was passed at President Wilson's recommendation as part of his trust regulation program. This act was designed to prevent unfair methods of competition in interstate commerce and subsequently began to single out such practices as trade boycotts, mislabeling and adulteration of commodities, and false claims to patents. The Clayton Anti-Trust Act was designed to strengthen the Sherman Anti-Trust Act (1890). It prohibited corporate practices that were not specified as illegal, such as price fixing.

1904-1930

These pieces of legislation influenced the shape of American life not only during the Progressive era but would impact rulings for the rest of the twentieth century.

1904-1908 • INDUSTRIALIZATION, TECHNOLOGY, AND URBANIZATION

~ Nowhere was this sociological jurisprudence more evident as when the courts were faced with a variety of new issues resulting from the transformations caused by industrialization, technology, and urbanization. Ground-breaking changes in business practices resulted from two court decisions. In the *Northern Securities Company v. U. S.* (1904) (193 U. S. 197), Northern Securities rejuvenated the Sherman Anti-Trust Act, which was invoked to uphold the government suit against the railroad holding company. A holding company is a corporation formed to buy up the stock of other companies in order to create a monopoly. In the Northern Securities case, the defendants argued that the act did not embrace the Constitutional power of Congress to regulate the mere transfer of property interest in any enterprise from one person to another. It was especially argued by the defendants that if the purchasing party was a corporation duly organized by a state and expressly authorized to make acquisitions here attained, the provision of the Sherman Act would invade powers constitutionally reserved to the sovereign states. This ruling represented a major modification of an earlier 1895 trust decision. The majority of the court now held that although the holding company itself was not engaged in interstate commerce, it sufficiently affected that commerce by restraining it and thus came within the scope of the federal anti-trust statute. *Muller v. Oregon* (1908) (208 U. S. 274) upheld an Oregon law limiting maximum working hours of women and denied that it impaired the liberty of contract guaranteed by the Fourteenth Amendment. For the first time, the courts ruled against business practices and established a precedent for government intervention to regulate business.

1913 • REVERSING CONSERVATIVE SUPREME COURT RULINGS

~ The Progressive Era transformed the conception of property in American legal thought through rulings by Justices Oliver Wendell Holmes, Louis Brandeis, and Charles Evans Hughes. The progressive court overturned the conservative 1890s decisions concerning the Sherman Anti-trust Act, a congressional act imposing the nation's first peacetime tax on personal income, and the use of federal judicial power to stop strikes. When new social and economic realities of the Great Depression and the New Deal occurred, the court continued on this path to bring a more liberal interpretation of the Constitution on Congressional legislation.

1919-1930 • PROGRESSIVE THOUGHT AND THE EMERGENCE OF MODERN AMERICA

~ The entrance of the United

Milestones

1919	*Shenck v. U. S.* (250 U. S. 616)/ *Abrams v. U. S.* (249 U. S. 47)
1920	Eighteenth Amendment
1921	Nineteenth Amendment
1923	1917-1930 (161 U. S. 525)
1924	Leopold Case
1925	Scopes Monkey and Billy Mitchell Trials
1927	Sacco-Vanzetti Case

States military into World War I in 1917 marked the transformation of the United States from a rural provincial country into a world leader, a role that was to greatly expand during the twentieth century. The United States entered into international markets forcing the expansion and emergence of international law. The war also led to important free speech decisions such as Oliver Wendell Holmes' "clear and present danger" ruling in Schenck v. U. S (249 U. S. 47), where the Court upheld the Espionage Act of 1917 against a challenge that it violated the guarantee of freedom of speech and press. In this case, the Court ruled that the First Amendment was not an absolute guarantee. Freedom of speech and press may be constrained if "words used are used in such circumstances and are of such a nature as to create a clear and present danger that they will bring about the substantive evils that Congress has a right to prevent." Holmes continued by saying: "Persecution for the expression of opinions seems to me perfectly logical…But when men have realized that time has upset many fighting faiths, they may come to believe even more than they believe the very foundation of their own conduct that the ultimate good desired is better reached by free trade in ideas…"

Holmes, however, dissented in Abrams v. U. S. (250 U. S 616) which upheld the 1918 Sedition Law. The Abrams case concerned the convictions of five Russian-born immigrants for writing, publishing, and distributing in New York City two allegedly seditious pamphlets criticizing the United States government for sending troops into Russia. Holmes' dissent stated "it is only the present danger of immediate evil or an intent to bring it about that warrants Congress in setting a limit to the expression of opinion…." He contended that the espionage and sedition acts must be construed to require conviction of a speaker only if it is proved that he intended his speech to have the criminal effect proscribed by the law.

The Roaring Twenties saw women finally gain the right to vote with the passage of the Nineteenth Amendment. Businesses prospered as the Jazz Age was in full swing. The 1920 census showed that more American citizens were living in urban areas than rural areas for the first time. The people of the United States had mixed feelings about the social, economic, and political changes taking place in the 1920s. While they applauded technological changes caused by Henry Ford's automobile, the development of the movies, and new household appliances, they also felt that the traditional values of small-town America were being threatened. The clash of these opposing ideas would bring about new laws and new court rulings.

Racism and anti-immigration feeling, for example, grew stronger in the 1920s as can be attested to by the race riots of 1919 in Chicago, the Brownsville Incident of 1906 in Texas, and the monumental trial of Sacco and Vanzetti in 1921. The Sacco-Vanzetti case typified the polarization that had occurred in America. Sacco and Vanzetti were militant radicals who associated with a group of anarcho-communists who advocated individual acts of terror against capitalism. After the Bolshevik Revolution in Russia (1917), anti-communist hysteria swept the country, and the two immigrants were arrested for attempted robbery of a factory payroll and murder of the paymaster. Despite disputed evidence, the men were convicted, primarily because of their radical views. Even though mass demonstrations in defense of the two were held in the United States, Latin America, and Europe, Sacco and Vanzetti were put to death in the electric chair in 1927.

Nativism was supported by legal immigration quota restrictions, such as the National Origins Act of 1921, 1924, and 1927 that were legislated by a xenophobic, national congress. The most extreme expression of nativism occurred with the resurgence of the Ku Klux Klan, which was reported to have five million members. For a brief time, the Klan achieved modest legal and political influence by forcing immigration restrictions and helping to elect nativist candidates to public office. They were able to elect a governor of Indiana, a mayor of Denver, and a variety of municipal and county office holders. The Klan also had enough power to disrupt the Democratic Presidential Convention of 1924 and prevented Al Smith from being nominated.

1924-1932 • Treaties and Pacts ～ Although President Woodrow Wilson chaired the commission which drafted the documents that formed the League of Nations, the United States Congress refused to join. It did, however, sign a series of treaties and pacts, the most notable being the Nine Power Treaty and the Kellogg-Briand Pact (1928). In theory, these agreements were to bring peace to the world, but in reality, they did not. Since the Republican presidents of the 1920s believed that pro-business policies brought prosperity at home, they also thought they could use diplomacy to advance American business interests with other nations. Supposedly a safeguard to this thinking was the passage of the Fordney-McCumber Tariff of 1922, which increased the duties on foreign manufactured goods by twenty-five percent in order to protect manufacturers from competition. From this time forward through the century, congress attempted to enact legislation that sheltered favored industries, such as steel and textiles, and resisted opening the country's trade borders. The twenty-five percent tariff measure proved successful in the short run but destructive in the long run. Another carry-over from World War I were the war debts and reparations issues: the Allies and Germany agreed to the Dawes Plan (1924) in which Germany agreed to pay reparations for their part in the war, but economic conditions became so bad in Germany that the Allies had to forgive most of the debt.

President Hoover took several late steps in an attempt to respond to the worldwide depression, and he made one of his worst mistakes when he signed into law the Hawley-Smoot Tariff in 1930, which increased taxes from thirty-one to forty-nine percent on foreign imports and set off a tariff war between trading countries. In 1931, Hoover proposed a debt moratorium on both Allied debts and reparations in hopes of helping to curb the deepening worldwide economic crisis. His efforts proved too little, too late because the Great Depression had already worsened in France, Great Britain, Germany, and Austria and continued worldwide.

Domestically, Hoover endorsed the creation of the Reconstruction Finance Corporation in 1932, a government-owned corporation that assisted faltering railroads, banks, life insurance companies, and other financial institutions, but this effort came too late to prevent the collapse of the economy and Hoover's defeat by Roosevelt in the 1932 election.

1920s • Supreme Court Rulings and Dissenting Opinions ～ The dominant social and political issues of the 1920s expressed sharp divisions in United States society. Urban modernists and rural fundamentalists fought at the Scopes Monkey Trials of 1925. Serious crime and gangsters accompanied the introduction of the Prohibition Amendment and the Volstead Act of 1919, which enforced the Eighteenth Amendment. Law and the disorder, created by prohibition and organized crime, pervaded American life until the Stock Market Crash of October 1929 interceded and brought all change to a screeching halt.

Many Americans were disturbed by the changes of the 1920s and felt that traditional values and Victorian standards of morality were being eroded away by rebelling youth and a more substantially diverse society. Legal scholars feel that some of the most important dissents occurred because of the temper of the times. Dissenting judges on the Supreme Court—that is, the minority of judges who do not agree with the court's decision—sometimes write opinions that powerfully persuade public opinion that later cause the court to reverse its decision. Holmes' dissent in *Abrams v. U.S* (250 U.S 616), 1919, as discussed above, set into legal thought the concept of "clear and present danger," which would be argued throughout the century. In *Whitney v. California* (274 U. S. 357) 1927, the Court upheld a state law that made it a crime to organize and participate in a group that advocated the overthrow by force of the established political system. Both Justices Holmes and Brandeis dissented saying that fear of danger is not enough to restrict the freedoms found in the First Amendment. The danger must be imminent and serious.

In *Olmstead v. U. S.* (279 U. S. 849), 1925, the Court ruled that wiretaps did not violate the Fourth Amendment's prohibition against unreasonable searches and seizures where no entry to private premises occurred. Brandeis and Holmes again dissented saying that "decency, security, and liberty alike demand that government officials shall be subject to the same rules of conduct that are commanded to the citizen. These dissents would become majority opinions during the Warren Court decisions of the 1960s. In 2001, the Supreme Court ruled that drug enforcement agencies could not use radiation surveillance of the exterior walls of a person's house to detect the possibility that marijuana was being grown inside, upholding the principle of illegal search and seizure.

On the other hand, legal scholars argue that some of the worst decisions ever made occurred in this period. In *Hammer v. Dagenhart* (247 U. S. 251), 1918, the Court ruled that Congress had no authority to forbid the shipment of products made illegally by children because the products themselves were not harmful. This ruling, which would be overturned in 1941, in effect declared that the Child Labor Act was unconstitutional. *Adkins v. Children's Hospital* (261 U. S. 525), 1923, invalidated an Act of Congress setting minimum wages for women and children as a price-fixing measure that violated the freedom of contract, prohibited by the Fifth Amendment. *Buck v. Bell*, 1927, upheld a law that sterilized a mentally defective mother and ruled that Virginia did not violate the Fourteenth Amendment's dues process guarantee. These issues would be revisited by later courts in post-World War II America and be debated again.

1929-1940 • ADMINISTRATIVE LAW AND THE NEW DEAL ~ "I often wonder whether we do not rest our hopes too much upon constitutions, upon laws and upon courts. These are false hopes, believe me, these are false hopes. Liberty lies in the hearts of men and women; when it dies, there, no constitution, no law, no court can save it."

Judge Learned Hand, 1941

(1934) Dr. New Deal. President Franklin Delano Roosevelt (1882 - 1945), seen as Dr. New Deal, trying several remedies for an ailing Uncle Sam; Congress is portrayed as a nurse following the doctor's orders.

1929-1940

Administrative law focuses on the operations of government agencies, and it ranks as one of the fastest-growing and most complicated branches of the law. Administrative law greatly expanded during the Depression of the 1930s with the development of such New Deal agencies as the Social Security Administration. National, state, and local governments set up many administrative agencies to do the work of government. Some agencies regulated such activities as banking, communications, trade, and transportation while others dealt with education, public health, and taxation. Still other agencies administered social welfare programs, such as old age and unemployment insurance. In most cases, the agencies were established in the executive branch of government under powers granted by the legislature. Administrative law consists chiefly of (1) the legal powers that are granted to administrative agencies by the legislature and (2) the rules that the agencies make to carry out their powers. Administrative law also includes court rulings in cases between the agencies and private citizens.

The Great Depression and the New Deal deserve careful attention for study of the development of law and the American legal system for four reasons. First, business planning and the role of law was to undergo tremendous changes during this time period while citizens of the United States in the 1930s endured

Milestones in Administrative Law

1931	*Near v. Minnesota* (283 U. S. 697)
1932	*Powell v. Alabama* (287 U. S. 45)
1933	Twentieth/Twenty-first Amendments
1933-37	New Deal Legislations and Court Cases
1935	*Schechter v. U. S.* (295 U. S. 495)
1936	*U. S. v. Butler* (297 U. S. 1)
1937	*Palko v. Connecticut* (302 U. S. 319)
1937	*NLRB v. Jones and Laughlin Steel Corporation* (301 U. S. 1)
1937-43	The Civil Liberty Cases
1943	*West Virginia State Board of Education v. Barnette* (319 U. S. 624)
1942	Executive Order 9066
1944	*Korematsu v. U. S.* (323 U. S. 214)

the greatest economic crisis in American history. Second, the Depression wrought deep changes in people's attitudes toward government's responsibilities and gave rise to a more powerful executive branch. Third, organized labor acquired new rights as labor organizations, law, and other social interests interacted. Fourth, the New Deal set in place legislation through which administrative law reshaped modern American capitalism.

The effect of the Depression on people's lives was one of the great shaping experiences of American history, ranking with the American Revolution, the Civil War, and the Industrial Revolution. More than Progressivism, the Depression enhanced the regulatory power of the federal government and the government's role in superimposing relief measures on the capitalist system, bringing the United States into a mild form of a welfare state, such as had appeared earlier in all of the industrial European nations. This era provides ample opportunities to assess Franklin Roosevelt's leadership, the many alternative formulas for ending the Depression, the ways in which the New Deal affected the Depression, and the ways in which the New Deal affected women, racial minorities, children, and other groups.

Since the early twentieth century, the executive branch of government has gained more and more lawmaking power in the United States. Table 6 illustrates the increase of executive authority over the legislative branch by the number of vetoes that some presidents issued in the twentieth century. In addition to this influence, hundreds of agencies have been formed in the executive branch. The rules and regulations issued by these agencies have brought about a huge increase in administrative law.

Table 6. Bills Vetoed by Each President (V), and Presidential Vetoes Overridden by Congress (o)

1932-2000	V	O	%
Clinton (2 terms)	30	2	6
Bush	24	1	5
Reagan (2 terms)	68	8	12
Carter	31	2	6
Ford	68	12	18
Nixon (1.5 terms)	43	5	12
L. Johnson (1.75 terms)	29	0	0
Kennedy	21	0	0
Eisenhower	18	2	1
Truman	250	12	5
F. Roosevelt (3 terms)	635	9	1

SOURCE: *Statistical Abstract of the United States.*

1933-1937 • SUPREME COURT RESTRICTIONS ON NEW DEAL PROGRAMS

~ Law and politics in the 1930s can best be demonstrated in Constitutional changes and statutes that reflect grants of and restrictions on Congressional and state power and of legislation. Important examples are the National Industrial Recovery Act (NIRA) of 1933, and the National Labor Relations Act (commonly known as the Wagner-Connery Act) of 1935. The NIRA, designed to revive industrial and business activity and to reduce unemployment, was based on the principle of industrial self-regulation that operated under government supervision through a system of fair codes. The Wagner Act created a new National Labor Relations Board that possessed the power to determine appropriate collective bargaining practices and was soon aided by state passed "Wagner Acts."

The New Deal brought about a myriad of "alphabet" laws and agencies and

1937-1945

the establishment of these agencies were to give rise to an increase in the number of administrative laws that were to become so prevalent throughout the rest of the twentieth century.

The period 1933-1937 is sometimes referred to as the "era of New Deal Laws and New Deal cases." Many of these alphabet acts resulted in important United States Supreme Court cases, such as *Schechter v. U. S.* (295 U. S. 495), *National Labor Relations Board v. Jones and Laughlin Steel Corporation* (301 U. S. 1) and *U. S. v. Butler* (297 U. S. 1) 1936, that raised critical economic and social questions of the times. Schechter or the "Sick Children Case" invalidated the NIRA on three grounds. Justice Hughes stated that the NIRA law gave excessive delegation of legislative power to the Executive branch of government, lacked constitutional authority, and regulated business wholly on an intrastate basis. In The National Relations Labor Board case, the court finally abandoned its earlier narrow view of the federal power to regulate interstate commerce. *U.S. v. Butler* invalidated the Agricultural Adjustment Act of 1933 which sought to regulate agricultural production by taxing processors of basic food commodities and then using the revenue to pay benefits to farmers who reduced their production of those commodities. The Court ruled that Congress could not combine the power to advocate for the common welfare with the power to tax in order to regulate a matter that was outside the scope of federal authority. The continued invalidation by the Supreme Court of major New Deal economic and social legislation led to the infamous "court packing" plan of President Franklin Delano Roosevelt of 1937 in which he wanted to add more justices to the Supreme Court who would be sympathetic to his programs.

1941-1945 • WORLD WAR II

With the U.S.'s entry into World War II in 1941, dramatic changes unfolded in the United States' laws and its legal system. The war caused massive population shifts as individuals drafted into the armed services reported to bases scattered around the country. Females often followed their dislocated soldiers. Women's lives were changed by long separations, new freedoms, and increased responsibilities. Women entered into the work force in significant numbers. Wartime conditions worsened a variety of social issues. Juvenile delinquency dramatically increased. Housing shortages provoked racial and ethnic conflict and led to riots in Detroit and Los Angeles. Every group in the United States population had to adjust to unique circumstances caused by the war. African Americans left the South and headed north. Mexican immigrants came in search of better jobs.

While African Americans made some headway by benefiting from A. Philip Randolph's work to get Executive Order 8802 passed, which forbad racial discrimination in job hiring, the Supreme Court in *Smith v. Allwright* (321 U. S. 649) allowed Texas to maintain its "white primary" by denying blacks membership in political parties as a way of excluding them from voting in primaries.

More than any other ethnic group, Japanese Americans suffered the humiliation of Executive Order 9066, which forced their relocation to prison camps. In *Hirabayashi v. U. S.* (320 U. S. 81) and *Korematsu v. U. S.* (323 U. S. 214) the Supreme Court declined to overturn the lower court rulings, assuring the internment of Japanese Americans for the duration of the war. The Court ruled in the Hirabayashi case that a curfew was within the boundaries of the War Powers Act but in Korematsu, the court declared for the first time that "all legal restrictions which curtail the civil rights of a single racial group are immediately suspect: the courts must subject them to the most rigid scrutiny." This ruling laid the foundation for later decisions that would expand personal liberty and individual rights by condoning the infringement of the rights of Japanese-Americans at this time.

The war in Europe and then in Asia encouraged a resurgence of American patriotism. In 1940, the court's emerging views of state power and religious freedom clashed in the case *Minersville School District v. Goitis* [310 U. S. 586]. The Court upheld a state's right to require public school students to recite daily the national pledge of allegiance to the flag even if the restriction conflicted with their religious beliefs. In *West Virginia Board of Education v. Barnett* [319 U. S. 624], however, the Court reversed itself in 1944 when it ruled that the state could not compel children to participate in a patriotic ceremony when it violated their religious beliefs. Issues from these cases would again be reviewed by the Court during the turbulence of 1960s America.

The war also greatly expanded the role of the Executive branch not only through President Roosevelt's numerous orders, letters, decrees, and directives but also through agencies such as the Office of Emergency Management and the Office of Price Administration. Many of the policies and the administrative laws of these organizations would lay the groundwork for the expansion of government's role, especially the Executive branch, in Post World War II America.

1945-1960s • THE AGE OF PROMISES, TURMOIL, AND CHANGE ~ "All persons shall be entitled to the full and equal enjoyment of the goods, services, facilities, privileges, advantages, and accommodations of any place of public accommodation, as defined in this section, without discrimination or segregation on the ground of race, color, religion, or national origin." *Civil Rights Act of 1964*.

Constitutional historian Herman Belz calls this time period the "Liberal Constitutionalism in a Bureaucratic Age: The Post-New Deal American Polity" and concludes that immediately after World War II, constitutional politics proceeded on assumptions laid down during the Depression. Questions of individual freedom came before the Court in increasing numbers during the post-World War II era. Cold War issues and the emerging Civil Rights Movement dominated the work of the Supreme Court during most of the 1950s. The intense concern over the threat of world communism produced a variety of laws and programs intended to prevent domestic subversion. Cold and hot war issues, such as Korea, Cuba, and Viet Nam gave rise to containment, brinksman-

(1964) Civil Rights Bill. U.S. President Lyndon B. Johnson looks over his shoulder and shakes the hand of Dr. Martin Luther King, Jr. (1929 - 1968) at the signing of the Civil Rights Act while officials look on, Washington D.C.

Milestones

1947	NATO
1948	Nuremberg/UN Declaration of Human Rights
1951	*Dennis et al. v. U. S.* (341 U. S. 494)/22nd Amendment
1954	*Brown v. Board of Education of Topeka* (347 U. S. 483)
1958	National Defense Education Act
1961	Twenty-third Amendment/*Mapp v. Ohio* (367 U. S. 643)
1962	*Engel v. Vitale* (370 U. S. 421)
1963	*Gideon v. Wainwright* (372 U. S. 335)
1964	Twenty-fourth Amendment/Civil Rights Act
1965	Civil Rights Voting Act
1966	*Miranda v. Arizona* (384 U. S. 436)
1967	Twenty-fifth Amendment
1967	Thurgood Marshall Becomes First African American Appointed to United States Supreme Court
1968	*Tinker v. De Moines* (393 U. S. 503)
1971	Twenty-sixth Amendment
1972	*Wisconsin v. Yoder* (406 U. S. 205)/*Furman v. Georgia* (408 U. S. 235)
1973	*Roe v. Wade* (410 U.S. 113)
1974	*Nixon v. United States* (418 U. S. 638)

ship, and détente. Trials and hearings such as the Alger Hiss case and McCarthyism laid the groundwork for later cases such as the Iran Contra hearings.

In 1951 the Court in *Dennis v. United States* [341 U. S. 394] upheld the Smith Act which made it unlawful to advocate or teach the violent overthrow of government in the United States or to belong to an organization dedicated to the accomplishment of these ends. The court upheld the conviction of eleven leaders of the Communist Party under this act.

The era also gave rise to the modern Presidency, a crisis of public authority in the 1960s, and a new wave of federal regulation in the 1970s. Truman, Eisenhower, Kennedy, Johnson, and Nixon were actors in the new Cold War era Presidency. None of the chief executives could dodge the changing world of politics either domestically or internationally as the Fair Deal, Moderate Republicanism, New Frontier, Great Society, and the Imperial Presidency administrations came into effect. Domestically each administration was marked by important legislation, such as the Taft-Hartley Act of 1947, the National Defense Education Act of 1958, the Alliance for Progress program, and Civil Rights Act of 1964 as the chief executives wrestled with labor problems, the space race, the economy, and social changes that were occurring.

1951-1964 • THE CIVIL RIGHTS MOVEMENT AND THE VOLATILE 60S

World War II unleashed a Human Rights Movement worldwide. In the United States, it originally took the form of the Civil Rights Movement. In 1951, the court announced two unanimous decisions that questioned the continuing validity of the 1895 *Plessy v. Ferguson's* "separate but equal doctrine." The first was *Sweatt v. Painter* [339 U. S. 629] in 1950 when the Court ordered the University of Texas law school to admit an African American student because the state failed to fulfill the promise of equal protection under the Fourteenth Amendment. The second was *McLaurin v. Oklahoma State Regents* [339 U. S. 637] in which the Court ordered the university to accept an African American student into all phases of campus life.

But it was *Brown v. the Board of Education of Topeka, Kansas* [347 U. S. 483] decision of May 17, 1954 that eventually would reverse Plessy. Using his tactics and thinking introduced in a 1930s case *Murray v. the University of Maryland Law School,* future Supreme Court Justice Thurgood Marshall argued the Brown case. Chief Justice Earl Warren opined "we conclude that in the field of public education, the doctrine of 'separate but equal' has no place. Separate educational facilities are inherently unequal." This case and the second Brown decision in 1955 were so fundamental and the public reaction so broad and deep that it tended to dominate all of the court's rulings of the 1950s. In case after case challenging various forms of segregation, the Court simply told lower courts to reconsider the facts of *Brown v. Board* decision.

The Civil Rights movement impacted the crisis of public authority of the 1960s. Probably the single most important law passed during this time period that influenced the shape of American life was the Civil Rights Act of 1964. Coupled with *Brown v. The Board of Education of Topeka* [347 US 483], 1954, the Civil Rights movement took the forefront of American legal action. The Warren Court was especially volatile in creating what some observers referred to as "judicial activism." During the 1960s, the Court moved into another area of state control, the application of due process requirements to state law enforcement and criminal procedures.

1960s • DUE PROCESS REVOLUTION IN CRIMINAL LAW

Due process of law is a basic principle in the American legal system that requires fairness in the government's dealing with persons. The term due process of law appears in the fifth and fourteenth amendments to the Constitution of the United States. These amendments forbid federal, state, and local governments from depriving a person of "life, liberty, or property, without due process of law." The Supreme Court of the United States has never clearly defined these words, and has applied them to a number of widely different situations.

Through law and custom, various safeguards have been developed in the United States to assure that persons accused of wrongdoing will be treated fairly. These

WARNING AS TO YOUR RIGHTS

You are under arrest. Before we ask you any questions, you must understand what your rights are.

You have the right to remain silent. You are not required to say anything to us at any time or to answer any questions. Anything you say can be used against you in court.

You have the right to talk to a lawyer for advice before we question you and to have him with you during questioning.

If you cannot afford a lawyer and want one, a lawyer will be provided for you.

If you want to answer questions now without a lawyer present you will still have the right to stop answering at any time. You also have the right to stop answering at any time until you talk to a lawyer.   P-4475

(1966) Miranda Warning. Since 1966 police have to advise a suspect that they have the right to remain silent and the right to counsel during interrogation. The 'Miranda Warning' is named for Ernesto Miranda, who was granted a retrial because he was not so advised.

safeguards are sometimes called procedural due process. Procedural due process includes the following requirements: (1) The law must be administered fairly. (2) People must be informed of the charges against them and must be given the opportunity for a fair hearing. (3) The person bringing the charges must not be allowed to judge the case. (4) Criminal laws must be clearly worded so that they give adequate warning of the action prohibited. Procedural due process concepts apply to civil and criminal cases.

Courts also have used the "due process" clauses of the Fifth and Fourteenth amendments to limit the content of laws, even though there was no procedural unfairness. For example, they have declared unconstitutional some laws restricting personal freedoms and business on the ground that the laws violate due process of law. One example the Supreme Court found to violate due process was a law limiting dwellings to single families, thereby depriving grandparents from living with their grandchildren. This practice involves the substance of public policy and is called substantive due process.

1960-1980 • THE LIBERAL SUPREME COURT ~ After the conclusion of War World II, the United States Supreme Court was divided between liberal (1960-1980) and conservative (1980-2000) benches. During the mid-1960s, the court, under the leadership of Chief Justice Earl Warren, became more active than it ever had been before. The court acted particularly in matters that it believed legislators had neglected and extended federal control into the social arena. The great majority of these matters were in the field of civil rights. During the 1950s and 1960s, the court used the power of judicial review to strike down a variety of state and local laws that supported racial segregation. The court based these decisions on the Fourteenth Amendment to the Constitution, which guarantees equal protection under the law.

In *Mapp v. Ohio* [367 U. S. 643], 1961, the Court overturned a 1949 decision by stating that evidence obtained in violation of the Fourth Amendment prohibiting unreasonable search and seizure, must be excluded from use at state and federal trials. The right to counsel appeared in both *Gideon v. Wainwright* [372 U. S. U. S. 335], 1963, and *Escobedo v. Illinois* [378 U. S. 478], 1964. The Gideon decision overturned a 1942 case and made states provide assistance of counsel for indigent defendants in criminal cases. The court expanded a suspect's right to counsel under the Sixth Amendment, holding that confessions obtained by police who had not advised the suspect of his right to counsel were inadmissible as evidence in court. In *Miranda v. Arizona* (384 U. S. 436), 1966, the Court ruled that suspects must be warned of their rights to protect themselves against self-incrimination before statements they make to the authorities can be used against them. These decisions revolutionized the legal rights of citizens and protected individuals against violations by police.

The court also used the Fourteenth Amendment in the 1970s to help ensure fair and equal treatment for women, aliens, poor people, and persons accused of crime. After the Watergate Scandal, however, the Burger Court shifted to a more conservative position on several issues, most notably criminal law and non-race-related equal protection matters.

The Civil Rights Movement of the 1960s and the ensuing Viet Nam war era of the 1970s gave rise to a plethora of other cases and controversies that also raised critical economic and social questions. Freedom of expression, speech, and the press, freedom of religion and the establishment clause, the rights of the accused, cruel and unusual punishment, search and seizure, privacy rights, the right to bear arms, and voting rights became the battleground issues for conservative and liberal forces.

Criticism of the Warren Court intensified with its rulings and interpretations of the First Amendment's "establishment" clause in the school prayer decision of *Engel v. Vitale* (370 U. S. 421), 1962. The Supreme Court ruled in Engel that a non-denominational prayer written by the New York State Board of Regents to be said on an involuntary basis each school day was a direct violation of the First Amendment. In *Wisconsin v. Yoder* (406 U. S. 205), 1972, which tested freedom of religion issues, the Court ruled that the state of Wisconsin's interest in demanding school attendance of Amish children to the age of 16 was not compelling enough to allow constitutional infringement upon their free exercise of religion under the First and Fourteenth Amendments.

There were other significant cases under the Warren court. *Tinker v. De Moines Independent School District* (393 U. S. 503) 1968 struck a victory for First Amendment protection of freedom of expression; *Furman v. Georgia* (408 U. S. 235) 1972 did not ban capital punishment altogether as a violation of the Eighth Amendment's "cruel and unusual punishment" clause but it did declare that existing capital punishment laws violated the Fourteenth Amendment's due process clause. *Nixon v. United States* (418 U. S. 638), 1974, is ironic because the Court that Nixon tried to shape failed him by denying his claims to executive privilege

(1973) Pro-Choice Demo. Pro-choice campaigners at a demonstration in favor of abortion in front of the American Hotel in mid-town New York, where the American Medical Association is holding its annual convention. The U.S. Supreme Court has ruled that it is a woman's right to have an abortion if she wishes it.

and ordered him to turn over the Watergate tapes that led to his resignation. This decision allowed the Court to reassert its power, claimed by John Marshall, to say what the law is and to maintain the principles of checks and balances and separations of powers.

Probably, the most controversial case of this era was *Roe v. Wade* (410 U.S. 113), 1973. The pro-abortion opinion, written by Harry Blackmun, a Nixon appointee, states the "right to privacy, whether it be founded in the Fourteenth Amendment's concept of personal liberty and restrictions upon state action...or...in the Ninth

1970-2000

Amendment's reservations of rights to the people, is broad enough to encompass a women's decision whether or not to terminate her pregnancy." This decision, which has led to violence between the two opposing camps, rests on the right to personal privacy that protects the individual from interference of the state and is still being debated today by pro-choice and pro-life advocates.

1970s • TECHNOLOGY AND THE LAW

∽ During the 1970s, many middle-class American citizens began to lose their faith in modern technology and industry and this lead Congress to establish a series of federal regulatory agencies to combat oil spills, nuclear power waste, and toxic dumps. Congress established the Environmental Protection Agency in 1970 to help regulate the protection of natural resources, and passed the Clean Air Act of 1970 and the Clean Water Act of 1977 (an amendment to the Federal Water Pollution Control Act of 1972).

American legal historians have noted that this era was marked with a variety of cases involving private action in defense of public rights, the response to judicial activism, and the new consumer movement.

1980-2000 • AGE OF CONSERVATISM

∽ "It is essential, if man is not to be compelled to have recourse, as a last resort, to rebellion against tyranny and oppression, that human rights should be protected by the rule of law." *United Nations Declaration of Human Rights, 1948.*

Some Individuals Who Have Had the Most Influence on the Law During the Twentieth Century

∽

6	Clarence Darrow
10	Earl Warren
18	Oliver Wendell Holmes
19	Louis Brandeis
27	Charles Evans Hughes
28	Hugo Black
29	William Douglass
30	Felix Frankfurter
39	Theodore Roosevelt
40	Woodrow Wilson
41	Franklin Delano Roosevelt
52	Martin Luther King
59	Thurgood Marshall
98	Sandra Day O'Connor

Numbers are the rankings of the author.

SOURCE: Darien A. McWhirter, *The Legal 100: A Ranking of the Individuals Who Have Most Influences on the Law*, Seacauaus, NJ: Citadel Press, 1998.

Milestones

1981	Sandra Day O'Connor first woman appointed to the United States Supreme Court
1985	*New Jersey v. TLO* (469 U. S. 325)
1995	O.J. Simpson Trial

The 1980s began the "Age of Conservatism" with the election of Ronald Reagan and a change in the Supreme Court's direction. The expansion of the importance of International Law and the proliferation of laws and regulations, whether they be created at the federal, state, or the local levels, characterize the court's shift.

The policies of presidents Nixon and Ford set the agenda for the development of a loose coalition of economic and political conservatives, religious fundamentalists, and Political Action Committees (PACs). These groups opposed forcing the presence of big government into people's daily lives and opposed issues they considered liberal: gun control, feminism, gay rights, and affirmative action. Supply-side economics, federal tax reduction, spending cuts, and deregulation of business were reflected in the Gramm-Rudman-Hollings Balanced Budget Act of 1985, which attempted to eliminate deficit spending by the federal government through the reduction of federally funded social programs.

Many of these issues began in the late 1970s with the taxpayer's revolt in California of Proposition 13 in 1978, the rise of moral revivalists such as Pat Robertson, Jerry Falwell, and Jim Bakker, and the Supreme Court ruling in *Regents of the University of California v. Bakker*, (1978) that decreed that college admissions could not be based on race alone.

1945-1992 • INTERNATIONAL LAW ∼ International law has a rich history dating back to antiquity. Modern international law is linked to the evaluation of the modern territorial state system that emerged in Western Europe in the sixteenth and seventeenth centuries. Because of its close ties to the Western state system, International Law is viewed as a product of Western values and tradition. Some of its rules have selectively come under increasing challenge from the non-Western world as well as from communist states. A major undertaking of the contemporary international system has been the creation and adoption of legal norms to which the global community subscribes.

International organizations such as the League of Nations and the United

(1955) Human Rights. A man looks at one of the first documents published by the United Nations, The Universal Declaration of Human Rights.

Nations epitomize the growth of international issues in the twentieth century. Prior to World War II, the United States widely deprecated international law and refused to participate in the League of Nations. Since 1945, international treaties related to the environment, labor, borders, and commerce have grown dramatically, and the United States has taken an active role in establishing them.

With the increase in the number of international laws have come the Permanent Court of Arbitration, the Permanent Court of International Justice, and the International Court of Justice, international protection of human rights through the Universal Declaration of Human Rights, and the Convention on the Prevention and Punishment of the Crime of Genocide.

1983-1992 • INTERNATIONAL UPHEAVAL ∼ President Ronald Reagan was determined to restore the United

1990s

States military might and superpower prestige in the world in 1980. Still reeling from the Iranian Hostage situation and the 1980 United States Olympic boycott, Reagan wanted to increase spending for defense and aid to anti-communist forces and began in Latin America. "Friendly" right-wing dictators in Nicaragua and El Salvador were given support while pro-Cuban forces were overthrown on the island of Grenada in 1983. Reagan's efforts to aid Nicaraguan contras, however, led to a serious scandal under his leadership. Mikhail Gorbachev's dynamic reforms called *glasnost* and *perestroika* helped to thaw the Cold War era, which eventually led to the fall of the Berlin Wall in 1989.

The Bush administration was dominated by spectacular changes in the Communist world beginning with the Tiananmen Square massacre in China, the overthrow of Communist governments in Eastern Europe, the formation of the Commonwealth of Independent States to replace the Soviet Union in 1991, and the START agreements in 1991 and 1992. Troubles brewed internationally, however, as General Manuel Noriega was ousted by American forces in Panama in 1989, the Persian Gulf War started in 1991, and civil war broke out in the Balkans in 1992, all of which resulted in U.S. military intervention.

1980S AND 1990S • DOMESTIC LAW ~ Domestic issues of the Reagan-Bush-Clinton administrations remained constant through the decades. The only difference was the approaches taken by the two parties towards legislating their outcomes. The major issues confronting lawmakers included the economy, health issues especially the AIDS epidemic, abortion, drug abuse, education and technology, crime and the crisis of urban America, immigration, and the environment.

Reaganomics and its deregulation policies of the economy shifted financial burdens from the federal level to state and local government. The Savings and Loan industry and the Environmental and Protection Agency, for example, were two areas largely affected by Reagan's administration policy of reducing big government's role in society. The eventual savings and loan disasters left American taxpayers with the brunt of the problem. Because EPA's budget was so dramatically reduced, a 75 percent drop in the number of anti-pollution cases referred to the justice Department for prosecution occurred. Although the Equal Rights Amendment was defeated in 1982, women, African Americans, Latinos, and Gays and Lesbians made some economic and social advances during these administrations.

Clinton's roller-coaster presidency created a program based on moderate reforms of domestic issues such as health care, welfare, budget deficit, and crime. Recycling, less automobile pollution, and exploring alternative energy sources also became major objectives for the environmentally concerned executive branch of government. Probably the single most important development of the 1990s, however, was the information superhighway and the advent of the Internet and email. In 1996, Congress passed the Telecommunications Act, a law which made it possible for local telephone, cable, and television companies to compete in providing telephone and cable service. Although the new technology enriched people's lives in the fields of health care, genetic engineering, entertainment, transportation, education, and space exploration, new legal test cases in the late 1990s involving Microsoft and Napster entered the judicial arena.

While the executive and legislative branches vied for control, the Supreme Court nominations of Sandra Day O'Connor, Antonin Scalia, Anthony M. Kennedy, David Souter, and Clarence Thomas, and the elevation of William Rehnquist to Chief Justice, shifted judicial power from the liberal left to the conservative right. The Court revisited domestic constitutional issues such as discrimination, abortion, and affirmative action. In 1989, the Court began to restrict a women's right to an abortion and imposed new restrictions on civil rights laws originally designed to protect the rights of women and minorities. The court also narrowed the rights of an arrested person. With the addition of Clinton's nomination of Ruth Bader Ginsburg, a liberal and the second woman to sit on the Court, test cases and decisions became closely contested. The Rehnquist Court evaluated racial gerrymandering, school desegregation, right to die, search and seizure, freedom of expression and association, and capital punishment. Many of these lingering issues will obviously become the focal point of legislation and legal opinions in the twenty-first century.

1990s • REFORMING THE LEGAL SYSTEM ~ Congress and the state legislatures pass thousands of laws each year, a problem that has worsened during the latter part of the twentieth century, and there are simply too many laws. New laws are added to the hundreds of volumes of federal and state statutes already in force. The regulations issued by federal and state agencies also accumulate at a rapid rate. By the mid-1990s, federal regulations alone filled about 130,000 pages.

As the number of laws has grown, the whole body of law has become more and more difficult to administer. In addition, the law has become so complex that people cannot possibly know how it affects them. A nation can make its laws simpler by organizing them into a uniform code. But common-law traditions are so strong in the United States that efforts to codify the nation's private laws have failed.

The enormous number of laws issued each year raises the question of whether society expects too much of the law. Many people believe that society can be governed by passing laws to anticipate every eventuality. This belief has led legislatures and the courts to make more and more laws to satisfy not only society's demands but also the demands of small, special-interest groups. But if the law tries to satisfy every demand, it can easily fail. People may then begin to doubt that the law can do anything at all. In addition, people tend to resent laws that interfere in their private affairs. As the number of laws grows, more and more aspects of life become regulated.

Many experts believe that questions of social importance should be settled by legislation rather than by decisions reached in courts. They point out that democratic government depends on the freedom of the legislature to reflect the will of the people. If the courts block this freedom, democracy is seriously weakened. Other experts believe that the courts must defend the constitutional rights of every American regardless of popular support.

As the law has grown more complex, the demand for professional legal services supporting the right to legal assistance has increased. As a result, even the most routine services, such as drawing up contracts and wills, have become more and more costly. Large corporations and wealthy people also complain about the exorbitant cost of litigation.

Since the early 1960s, the courts' decisions have ensured legal help for criminal defendants too poor to hire a lawyer. In addition, public and private legal aid services provide poor people with free counsel in private-law cases. However, many poor people do not know they have a right to these services, and so they do not benefit from them. Many middle-income Americans have also had difficulty affording professional legal help when they need it; they do not qualify for the free legal services available to the poor. To help remedy this problem, some lawyers in large cities have set up legal clinics that provide middle-income families with routine legal services at reduced rates.

CONCLUSION

"Separate educational facilities are inherently unequal.... [We] hold that the plaintiffs... [are] deprived of the equal protection of the laws guaranteed by the Fourteenth Amendment." *Earl Warren (1954)*

The concept of law is brought before every American's life everyday. Whether it comes from issues raised by the television series "Law and Order," discussing Judge Judy's most recent ruling, reading how your representative voted on a bill last week, watching C-SPAN, or participating in a referendum to repeal the tax cap in your local community, citizens of the United States are well aware of their legal system.

Today, most people believe that the private interests of some members of society should not deprive other members of their rights. Legislation and court decisions during the twentieth century have reflected this belief, especially by stressing the social aspects of such topics as contract law. For example, Congress and the state legislatures have passed many laws to help ensure the fairness of employment contracts. Some of these laws regulate working conditions and workers' wages and hours while other laws guarantee the right of workers to organize and to strike.

Legislation and court decisions have also changed many features of property, tort, and family law during the twentieth century. The social obligations of property owners have been enforced by zoning laws and by laws prohibiting environmental pollution. During the late nineteenth century, tort law held that a person could collect for an injury only if another person could be proved at fault. But the development of private and public insurance programs during the 1900s helped establish that a person should be paid for accidental injuries regardless of who was at fault. This "no fault" principle has made it unnecessary to sue for damages in certain cases. Changes in family law during the twentieth century reduced the legal rights of husbands over their wives and of fathers over their children. The law thus placed increased emphasis on women's and children's rights. To ensure equality for all Americans and to protect the economic and environmental interests of society, the law has had to limit some of the rights traditionally granted to individuals under private law. Property rights and freedom of contract, in particular, have been restricted—a matter of deep concern to many Americans.

The evolution of United States society during the twentieth century created a need for new laws, protections, rights and legal precedents. Changes in American culture created numerous conflicts in society. These conflicts led to new laws, interpretations, and issues. A century of progress in wrestling with these issues resulted in a legacy of legal milestones decreeing civil rights and personal freedoms to better mankind. This legacy has laid the foundation for the twenty-first century.

BIBLIOGRAPHY

Buergenthal, Thomas and Harold G. Maier. *Public International Law in a Nut Shell*. 2nd ed. Saint Paul, MN: West Publishing Co., 1990.

Fetner, Gerald L. *Ordered Liberty: Legal Reform in the Twentieth Century*. New York: Alfred Knopf, 1983.

Friedman, Lawrence M. *A History of American Law*. New York: Simon and Schuster, 1985.

Higgins, Rosalyn. *Problems and Process: International Law and How We Use It*. New York: Oxford University Press, 1994.

Horwitz, Morton J. *The Transformation of American Law, 1870-1960*. New York: Oxford University Press, 1992.

Johnson, Daniel. *The Consumer's Guide to Understanding and Using the Law*. Cincinnati: Betterway Books, 1984.

Johnson, Herbert A. *American Legal and Constitutional History: Cases and Materials*. San Francisco: Austin & Winfield, 1994.

Jones, Mark W. *An Introduction to International Law*. Boston: Little, Brown, 1988.

Lieberman, Jethro K. *The Litigious Society*. New York: Basic Books, 1981.

McWhirter, Darien A. *The Legal 100: A Ranking of the Individuals Who Have Most Influences on the Law*. Secaucus, NJ: Citadel Press, 1998.

Palmer, Kris E. *Constitutional Amendments 1789 to the Present*. Detroit: Gale Group, 2000.

Schwartz, Bernard. *A Book of Legal Lists: The Best and Worst in American Law*. New York: Oxford University Press, 1997.

Yogis, John. *Canadian Law Dictionary*. 2nd ed. New York: Barron's, 1990.

INTERNET RESOURCES

The two most comprehensive websites for researching topics related to laws and the legal system are:

http://www.llrx.com/

http://www.findlaw.com/

James F. Adomanis
Maryland Center for the Study of History

Leisure

~

(circa 1965) A Walt Disney 'Magic Castle' under construction at Disneyland in Orlando, Florida.

TIMELINE

1885-1919 ~ Simple Pleasures

Safety bicycle invented (1885) / Edison invents the motion picture (1889) / Proliferation of electric trolleys in cities (1890s) / Steeplechase Park built at Coney Island (1897) / Intercollegiate Athlete Association is formed and football rules are reformulated (1905) / Ford Model T built (1908) / Vaudeville peak of popularity (1910)

MILESTONES: Olympics staged at the World Exhibition in Paris (1900) • Significant segment of the American population consider gambling a sin (1900) • Physician William Osler argues that men should retire from work at the age of 60 (1905) • Alice Ramsey becomes the first woman to drive a car across the U.S., capturing Americans' imagination and interest in automobiles (summer 1909) • 17,000 weeklies, semi-weeklies, and tri-weeklies are published (1915)

1920-1929 ~ Fun in the Jazz Age

Formation of the Negro National League in baseball (1920) / "Flappers" frequent speakeasies, smoke cigarettes and engage in promiscuous sexual activity (1920s) / Harlem Renaissance produces renowned African American writers, artists, and musicians (1920s) / First commercial radio broadcast (1920) / First radio commercials (1922) / NBC radio network formed (1926) / Babe Ruth hits sixty home runs (1927) / *The Jazz Singer*, first talking picture, released (1927) / Walt Disney creates the first animated motion picture, *Steamboat Willie* (1929) / First national radio comedy show, *Amos 'n' Andy*, airs (1929)

MILESTONES: Helena Rubenstein and Elizabeth Arden start their cosmetic businesses (early 1920s) • Pig Stand in Dallas is the first drive-in restaurant (1921) • Founding of *Reader's Digest* for the "lowbrow" reader (1922) • First motel is built, in San Luis Obispo, California (1925) • Mail order catalogues and magazines bring fashion awareness to every household (1925-1929) • Coca Cola is sold in 66 countries (1929)

1930-1945 ~ Escape during Hard Times

Under pressure, the movie industry enacts the Production Code, addressing the use of crime, sex, vulgarity, obscenity, profanity, costumes, dancing, and religion in film (1930) / Women's golf becomes popular with the emergence of Mildred "Babe" Didrikson who was among the greatest athletes of the twentieth century (1930s) / Works Progress Administration launches the Federal Theater (1935) / Television displayed at New York World's Fair (1939) / Big Band era entertains war-time America (1941-1945) / Civilian consumer goods put on low priority for manufacture (1942) / Frank Sinatra draws thousands of "bobby-soxers" to concerts (1943) / First indoor shopping mall opens in Kansas City (1944)

MILESTONES: Nevada legalizes gambling, founding the economic basis for Las Vegas (1931) • Charities and churches are permitted to hold bingo games legally in Massachusetts (1931) and Rhode Island (1937) • Proliferation of radio soap operas, detective shows, and daytime programming (1930s) • Economy Act stipulates that married women be discharged from their jobs (1932) • Unemployment is 24.9 percent; 9,000 banks fail; 100,000 businesses fail (1932-1933) • Proliferation of African American newspapers (1930s) • Luxury liner, *Normandie* burns in New York City harbor as it is being converted to a U.S. troop carrier (1942)

1946-1959 ~ Rise of Popular Culture

First TV sets go on sale (1946) / Jackie Robinson integrates professional baseball (1947) / Comedian Milton Berle becomes TV's first superstar (1948) / First coast-to-coast television broadcast (1951) / *I Love Lucy* premieres (1951) / First McDonald's opens (1954) / Disneyland built (1955) / Elvis Presley releases first single (1956) / First indoor shopping mall opens (1956) / First TV remote control (1956) / Barbie doll created by Mattel (1959)

MILESTONES: *Lamp Unto My Feet*, a Sunday morning religious show originally aimed at children, is first broadcast; it runs for more than thirty years, making it one of TV's longest-running shows (1948) • U.S. liner *United States* commissioned, the fastest ocean liner ever built (1951) • Swanson introduces the TV dinner (1954) • Marlboro Man ad begins to enormous success (1954) • Supreme Court rules that a literary work containing explicit materials must be judged as a whole and not by its parts (1957)

1960-1969 ~ Cultural Revolution

Importance of television news programming emerges / The Beatles appear on *The Ed Sullivan Show* (1964) / NBC TV begins color programming (1964) / Marine theme park, Sea World, opens (1964) / Film industry drops the Hays Code, lifting its ban on political and "immoral" content in movies (1968) / Woodstock Music Festival attracts 400,000 young people to a 3-day outdoor "happening" (1969)

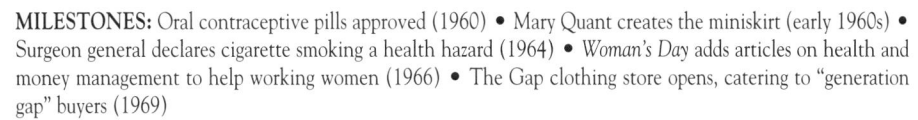

MILESTONES: Oral contraceptive pills approved (1960) • Mary Quant creates the miniskirt (early 1960s) • Surgeon general declares cigarette smoking a health hazard (1964) • *Woman's Day* adds articles on health and money management to help working women (1966) • The Gap clothing store opens, catering to "generation gap" buyers (1969)

1970-1999 ~ New Trends in Entertainment

Emergence of "relevance" television (1970s) / Title IX requires schools to provide for girls' sports (1972) / Watergate hearings become the top rated program on television (1973) / Home Box Office (HBO) becomes the first national cable network (1975) / VCRs marketed (1976) / MTV launched (1981) / High definition television invented (1986) / Channel One, targeted at children, inaugurated (1989) / Mosaic, first Internet browser, produced (1993)

MILESTONES: Billie Jean King defeats Bobby Riggs in the so-called Battle of the Sexes in straight sets 6-4, 6-3, and 6-3, before a record crowd at the Houston Astrodome and a television audience of some 50 million (September 20, 1973) • State lotteries are established in Arizona, California, Colorado, Florida, Idaho, Indiana, Iowa, Kansas, Kentucky, Missouri, Montana, Oregon, South Dakota, Virginia, West Virginia and Wisconsin (1980s) • Commercial advertising appears on religious networks (1980s) • With Larry Bird of the Celtics, Earvin "Magic" Johnson reinvigorates basketball's popularity, winning with the Los Angeles Lakers five NBA championships (1980, 1982, 1985, 1987, and 1988) • Country singer Willie Nelson hosts first Farm Aid benefit (1985) • Supermodels hide the fact that fashion is in a slump (1985-1987) • Public's insatiable desire for intimate details about celebrities gives rise to paparazzi journalists (1980s-1990s) • Mike Tyson is disqualified from the rematch with Evander Holyfield and his boxing license suspended when he bites off a piece of Holyfield's right ear (1997) • Serena Williams wins the U.S. Open, becoming the first black woman to win a Grand Slam title since Althea Gibson in 1958 (1999)

INTRODUCTION

In the nineteenth century, Americans had little time for leisure. Farming was a dawn-to-dusk occupation and factory workers typically worked twelve-hour days, six days a week. Leisure, such as it existed, was woven into the workday, a moment of rest caught here and there. The moral climate of the times discouraged leisure by marking it as wasteful and sinful. Free time was supposed to be spent in morally uplifting or educational activities like charity work or reading. For women, cultivating arts, such as singing and embroidery, were acceptable ways to spend leisure time. "Recreation," which implied a more active experience, particularly a physically active one, was acceptable to Americans, but "leisure," with its overtones of passivity and idleness, was not. The nation was still too close to its Puritan roots and still too much a religious society to regard leisure as something both desirable and necessary.

Yet, at the same time, recreational and leisure activities did exist and many established ideas about them shaped leisure in the twentieth century. Americans strongly believed that physical activity was good and that nature was a healthy and restorative place. Sports, such as boxing, already existed as a leisure activity, as did spas or places where the wealthy might take health cures. City parks became important around the time of the Civil War. The construction of Central Park in New York City, for example, brought millions of New Yorkers of all classes and nationalities close to nature. Trains facilitated travel, although vacationing, when it existed at all, generally meant staying at a hotel or spa rather than touring or touristing. Even before 1900, though, the honeymoon trip was a tradition and, the more Americans sprawled, the more common it became for people to travel to see kinfolk. Organized camping, including educational camps, also existed. The concept of paying for entertainment already existed in the nineteenth century, although often specifically under the guise of educating rather than entertaining. Barnum and Bailey's circus, for instance, pitched its sideshows as providing information about other cultures and customs. Expositions and fairs, like the Chicago World's Fair of 1893, both educated Americans about new products and instilled them with a sense of nationalism. Victorians, especially women, were collectors, and the hobby of collecting things was already, by the turn of the century, taking on commercial overtones thanks to the existence of trade cards and what at least one scholar has described as a male proclivity to be concerned with the monetary worth of collections.

By the end of the nineteenth century, the preconditions existed for a much more systematic desire for leisure. In factories, the workday began to shrink. Technology opened up all sorts of possibilities. The arrival of large numbers of Eastern and Southern European immigrants raised questions about what it meant to be an American, and products were marketed to fulfill the needs of specific groups. It is hardly surprising that purveyors of leisure activities would quickly follow suit.

1900 Conspicuous Consumption

At the turn of the century, class delineated very different access to leisure, both as a concept and as a set of experiences. After the Civil War, the nation's first visibly wealthy elite emerged in response to industrialization and, because of the increasingly national culture facilitated by the press and magazines, their lifestyle defined one end of a leisure spectrum. Although most of the early tycoons worked hard, so too did they feel certain social expectations about how they might spend their money. Someone like Andrew Carnegie, for instance, built public libraries in small communities across the country. Having contributed their good deeds to society, the wealthy felt free to spend their money for what social theorist Thorstein Veblen called "conspicuous consumption," a style of spending he associated with a wealthy, leisured class.

During the nineteenth century, the public display of wealth was regarded as vulgar, but as society became more obsessed with wealth, it became more acceptable, or at least more interesting to the masses who enjoyed watching how the rich lived. It was also the case that earlier, there simply weren't that many things for the wealthy to buy; their wealth was largely consumed by property and purchasing services. Technology made it possible for them to be the first large-scale consumers. The wealthy maintained mansions at the shore (Newport was a popular spot), lavish houses in the city, and hunting lodges in the mountains. They filled their houses with the latest gadgets and consumer

(circa 1955) The very wealthy at the turn of the century felt freer than previous generations to spend their money publicly. Here is one luxury item, a 1906 Cadillac touring car.

goods, electricity, elevators, artwork imported from Europe, victrolas, and bicycles. They traveled by ocean liner to Europe or by private railcar within the United States. They toured, relying on guides to educate them about the Scottish Highlands, Yellowstone Park, or whatever places struck their fancy. Their idea of roughing it by camping involved cooks and beds and fine wines. They employed French chefs to create elaborate meals and French and English nannies to educate their children. Most of their ideas about how to spend their leisure time were modeled on the European–especially British–upper class. They had few scruples about flaunting their wealth and their leisure.

Perhaps nothing so effectively conveyed their lifestyle as first-class travel on the new class of luxury liners that crossed the Atlantic. First-class passengers brought dozens of trunks with them, many of them filled with goods acquired on prolonged European vacations–Irish lace, Italian glass, French paintings. They brought many of the comforts of home with them when they traveled, including servants and, in some cases, cars that could be stashed in the cargo hold. On board ship, they mingled with one another, safely protected from second- and third-class passengers. They dined on the finest food, danced to orchestras provided for their pleasure, used gym facilities and masseuses, and enjoyed luxurious staterooms–some with private promenades–and the attentions of stewards. Their lives were privileged and insulated. When the Titanic sank in 1911, a higher percentage of first-class men survived than third-class children, despite the traditional notion that women and children should be the first to the lifeboats. Class distinctly shaped the leisure experience.

1890-1900 • Middle-class Leisure

~ Middle-class Americans, on the other hand, were more conflicted about leisure and spending. To the middle class, work was supposed to be a satisfying and socially useful activity that, therefore, did not require them to rest. Men had careers that kept them busy and their wives—in spite of technology that began to free them from the heavy work of the home— devoted their hours unselfishly to their families. Only during childhood did the middle class feel completely comfortable about indulging whims and interests. The middle class incorporated leisure only more cautiously into their lives, benefiting from the fruits of industrialization but also retaining a great deal of moral ambivalence about recreation.

Yet, ironically, members of the middle class were well-placed to enjoy leisure. Their houses, often built in early rings of "streetcar suburbs," contained modern conveniences that presupposed a more leisured lifestyle, with backyards, bathtubs, and telephones. Middle-class women learned to enjoy shopping as a leisure activity even before 1900. Large urban department stores like Marshall Field's in Chicago offered them the opportunity to spend the day in a luxurious world of beautiful things under the guise of obtaining necessary items for their families. Department stores were designed as a middle-class female experience, offering a safe space, including tea rooms where women could lunch, concierges to deal with packages, and lower-class shop girls to take their orders. The allure of shopping was so great that historians have noted that some middle-class women even resorted to shoplifting to satisfy their urges. Rural women denied access to nearby shopping primarily used catalogs to purchase items. More urban space opened up for women around 1900, not just department stores but also museums, bookstores, and cafes. While America's largest museums opened in the nineteenth century, smaller museums opened in the twentieth and those who frequented museums tended to be more female than male. Women not only visited museums; some began to devote their free time as volunteers who worked in them. Although women were hardly freed of traditional obligations and concerns, there was new public acceptance of unaccompanied women in public, shopping, browsing, walking in parks, visiting museums, and having tea. American middle-class women, many trained to play piano for the family's entertainment, were also big consumers of printed sheet music.

1900-1930 • TECHNOLOGY AND LEISURE ~ Technology altered the middle-class experience with leisure. Trolleys and subways made more of the city accessible to them. Automobiles increased their freedom even more. Bicycles, an enormous fad in the 1890s, provided yet another means of transport, one used by the middle class almost exclusively for leisure. By 1900, Americans owned over 10 million bicycles. Bicycles liberated middle-class women of some of

Year	Number of Phones per 1,000 People
1900	18
1910	82
1920	123
1930	163

SOURCE: *The American People: Creating a Nation and a Society* by Gary Nash et al.

their restrictive clothing. Telephones, first promoted for business, linked middle-class women to one another and facilitated recreational planning. Mass production techniques made more leisure goods more affordable and more available to middle-class children.

C.1900 • ENTERTAINMENT FOR CHILDREN ~ Until the second half of the nineteenth century, childhood meant hard work for most children, either in the fields, the factories, or helping mother. As childhood became clearly defined as a time of leisure, socialization, and future training, capitalists recognized the market and filled in the gap. Books and magazines aimed at children (such as *St. Nicholas Magazine*) appeared and toys, once handmade and improvised, became available to the middle class. For girls, very fancy, handmade German dolls were much prized, although generally not intended for play. Popular among boys were the machine-produced, metal wind-up toys with a circus or fanciful motif. President Teddy Roosevelt's love of animals sparked the creation of the first stuffed teddy bear in 1902. After the turn of the century, Milton Bradley and Parker Brothers began to manufacture board games for children too. Children were encouraged to enter fantasy worlds through such books as L. Frank Baum's *The Wizard of Oz* (1900).

1900s • MIDDLE-CLASS TOURING AND LEISURE ACTIVITIES ~ Although sometimes skeptical of leisure for the sake of leisure, middle-class Americans at the turn of the century were very much sold on nature as a concept, and Teddy Roosevelt's championing of the national park system was something they supported and embraced. Getting away to someplace restful and renewing, implicitly away from the bad air, disease, and noise of the city, was something middle-class Americans did when they could afford it. Few Americans had access to paid vacations, but the concept was most firmly established in workplaces that employed white, middle-class men. Touring was expensive and difficult, but there were many mountain and seaside establishments to cater to a host of vacationers. So popular were these that it was not unusual for a family to book one for a large portion of the summer so the mother and children could relax while the father commuted back and forth on weekends. Hotels, resorts, and inns were not only popular, but existed in such variety that nearly every vacationer could find what he/she wanted. Some were kosher establishments, for example, while a few, in places like Virginia, served only African Americans. Because there were always concerns about the unwholesomeness of certain establishments (which might include dancing or gambling), some resorts were affiliated with churches or youth groups. Despite these concerns, the middle class took it for granted that a vacation loosened certain social restrictions, including those on the mingling of the sexes. Camping was popular, although hardly as back-to-nature as modern-day backpacking. Mountains, lakes, and the seashore were popular summer vacation spots. Vacations provided middle-class people with an opportunity for freedom, for relaxation, and also to get away from the unhealthy city environment.

Physical activity was often one way the middle class justified leisure. Tennis, golf, biking, hiking, ice skating, and swimming were all regarded as healthy activities, even for females. A picnic in the park seemed a wholesome way to spend a day. The American game in 1900 was baseball, played by young boys and professional players alike. Attending a professional baseball game was a pricier endeavor than attending the vaudeville or similar amusements, but one that the middle class regarded as more wholesome. Football was less widely accepted as a sport, in part because of its brutality. In 1906, the college rules were rewritten to make the game less dangerous. College women participated in competitive sports as well, both at indoor games like basketball (in bloomers and, therefore, off limits to males) and outdoor, like tennis.

Paying money directly for entertainment made the middle class more nervous. A dinner out or a play were special occasion treats only the urban could manage. Circuses or other family activities were also special. Middle-class men sometimes belonged to clubs where they could converse with one another, eat, smoke, and handle business contacts, but the trend moved away from same-sex leisure after 1900. There were, of course, men's-only activities such as brothels, "peep" shows, and taverns. Middle-class morality remained fairly strict and religion exercised its power over women especially, directing them away from anything that seemed too indulgent or sinful. In general the middle class at the turn of the century was dubious of the urban entertainments available, especially vaudeville or saloons, the first amusement parks, dance halls, and nickel dumps (early movie houses). These became venues that attracted the poor and working-class Americans in their early days.

1900 • CHEAP AMUSEMENTS ~ The poor had less trouble with leisure as a concept because their work was physically hard, long, and not satisfying. As a result, they longed for free time to help them regain the sense of control lost in the stressful factory life where most made their living. Yet while they had the attitude for leisure, the working class had neither the time nor the money for much leisure activity. Working-class men, however, saw some leisure as their due and whenever possible budgeted for it, keeping part of their paycheck aside, even if only for cigarettes or beer. Their wives, on the other hand, had to weave leisure into their days and, unlike their husbands (who frequented saloons), took their leisure at home or in the streets.

Working-class budgets could hardly stretch to include vacations or bicycles. Working-class families socialized at home or through clubs and churches, relying on good company, stories, and music played by family members. Immigrants used leisure time to reinforce cultural bonds at religious activities. Churches became the cornerstone of immigrant culture in many urban areas, providing not just religious support, but a safe space for cultural activities like dances. Parents trusted that the churches would instill their children with good values, and were always comfortable sending their children to recreational activities sponsored by religious groups.

Public parks were very popular with the working class because they were free. Picnics or even just strolls on summer evenings made a nice change for people confined all day in a factory or cramped tenement. New York's Central Park was popular with people of all classes, but it was especially popular with the poor. They, like the middle class and the wealthy, believed that the urban environment was unhealthy, so any escape to green grass and open space was attractive to them. Because leisure for the working class was improvised and revolved around building community, leisure tended to make extra work for women, who were the ones who prepared ethnic feasts, packed picnic lunches, or organized church activities. Ethnicity and location played an enormous role in determining leisure. Italian Americans, for example, tended to be more home-centered and sheltering of women. Eastern European Jews, on the other hand, enjoyed a large community in New York City, particularly in the Lower East Side, which abounded with ethnic shops and entertainments. Women and children were generally free to circulate through this environment, finding their own entertainment. The rural poor, by contrast, had very few options.

Technology also left its mark on the working class in turn-of-the-century America, who were less ambivalent than the middle class about paying for entertainment. A trolley ride could take many immigrants to a large public park or the seashore for the day. With scrimping and saving, that excursion might also include a day at an amusement park, such as Coney Island. The middle class shunned Coney–at least until the park called Dreamland brought them more middle-class entertainments such as reenactments of the Boer War–but the working class loved the rides and spectacle. Working-class families also loved early movies, which were cheap (a nickel), safe, and in the neighborhood. Social researcher George Bevans, who wrote *How Workingmen Spend their Spare Time* (1913), found that workingmen spent the largest part of their free time at the movies. The "nickel dumps" also attracted many women, who attended matinees. Neighborhood movie theaters were cheaper and safer than vaudeville or legitimate theaters. As mass production techniques lowered the

(1946) Holidaymakers ride on the Ferris wheel at Coney Island, America's popular holiday resort, in Brooklyn, New York.

price of clothing, shopping, or at least window shopping, also became a pastime for poorer women who could pursue style. Dance halls were not as respectable as amusement parks or nickel theaters, but they were attractive to young people, who found them a good place to meet others. Historian Kathy Peiss has shown how such "cheap amusements" as the movies and the dance halls helped Americanize a generation of immigrants.

1900 • CHILDREN AND REFORMERS
~ Working-class children were often important parts of the family economy, although their labor was increasingly regulated in the early twentieth century. Although on a tight budget, they managed to find leisure too. Urban spaces were undeniably interesting to young people, who roamed the streets and frequented the playgrounds provided by urban reformers. The lure of an American culture was especially great. A 1910 study of 500 St. Louis newsboys found that 87 percent regularly attended movies. Although poor children longed for baseball mitts and roller skates, they made do with library books and stickball and public fire hydrants on hot summer days. Yet it was precisely the unsupervised roaming, interest in paid entertainment, and use of public facilities that worried reformers about so-called "street urchins." Middle-class educators and social workers, who wanted their own children to cherish childhood, regarded poor children with free time as potential delinquents and struggled to fill their time with more appropriate activities via settlement houses, public kindergartens and the Boy and Girl Scouts.

In fact, middle-class reformers devoted a lot of energy to trying to reform the leisure habits of the working class, especially the immigrant working class. Prohibition legislation, for instance, is commonly viewed as an attempt to impose middle-class values on the working class. The roughly 100 settlement houses founded in the early twentieth century by reformers like Jane Addams were intended to provide alternative leisure venues, particularly for women and children. These included nursery schools, cafes, art galleries, and lounges. Implicitly their aim was to teach immigrants how to make better choices about what they did when they weren't working.

1900 SMALL TOWN AND RURAL ENTERTAINMENT ~ Although leisure tended to be more of an urban phenomenon than a rural one, a majority of Americans still lived in small towns and rural areas in 1900. Their access to leisure was not so dependent on spending money to buy leisure activities. On farms leisure continued to be woven into the workday and at important times, like the harvest. Few Americans lived on raw frontiers any longer, though, and most rural areas got visiting speakers and traveling shows. Many small towns celebrated holidays with elaborate pageants, parades, or other festivities. Music and food were two important aspects of such celebrations and, inevitably, reflected regional tastes and history. Even when rural Americans left the countryside for the big cities, they tended to at least try to hold onto their traditions. Los Angeles's Iowa-born population, for instance, held an annual picnic. In general, rural leisure was less divided by gender or age.

Circuses were popular in America's smaller towns, often finding it increasingly hard to compete with the newer and fancier urban entertainments. These included not just the usual trained animals, clowns, and balancing acts, but sideshows as well. The sideshows tended to communicate differences between the United States and other, less "civilized" countries and to present individuals with unusual physical characteristics, like cojoined twins, Chang and Ang.

African-American sharecroppers, like their white counterparts, created their own celebrations for holidays and important personal occasions like birthdays and weddings. African-American churches provided the single best "safe" space for people otherwise denied access to public facilities. The culture that flourished there nurtured individuals and sometimes allowed for coded rebellion by such means as spirituals. Music, which was cheap and portable (in the form of instruments) was popular, as was dancing. Commercial amusements ignored African Americans, unless there were commercial possibilities to be exploited. African Americans also performed in minstrel shows, most of which played to white audiences.

For wealthier white farmers, the lure of being like urban Americans was strong, and technology had already begun to impose itself on their leisure. Cars, telephones and catalogs linked their families to the larger world. By the late nineteenth century, prosperous farmers were already part of a world-wide economy and relied on railroads, telegraphs, and telephones. It did not take too much prodding for them to think of the leisure possibilities of those tools.

1920s • MIDDLE-CLASS LEISURE ~ During the 1920s, the "cheap amusements" favored by the working class became more respectable, and in the process sometimes made them less affordable for the poor. One good example was the youth culture. Because middle-class youth courted in parlors under the watchful eyes of parents who looked for good mates (i.e. with good

LEISURE ~ 995

1920s

social standing and family background), there was little necessity for a dating culture. Dance halls were regarded as risqué and dating seemed akin to prostitution. However, as more acceptable urban spaces opened up to young people middle-class youths demanded the opportunity to indulge. Dance halls continued, but the more high-status venues for dances became high schools, colleges, and country clubs. Dances took on whole new dimensions with the introduction of formal wear, dance cards, and corsages, for example.

Young, urban, middle-class people increasingly dominated the world of public amusements because they had the free time, interest and the money to devote to leisure. Cars increased their mobility and gave them privacy. Young women, once encouraged to be selfless and moral, were under increasing pressure to look good and act flirtatious. An ever-larger amount of their leisure time was devoted to the beauty culture. They shopped, used make-up, and had their hair done at beauty parlors. They read magazines for style tips and modeled themselves after new movie stars like Clara Bow or Mary Pickford. Furthermore, the motion picture industry determined the standard of manly ideals with heroes such as Rudolph Valentino setting the high-water mark for looks and charm. By the 1920s, America's entertainment industry was shaping the tastes of middle-class youth through radio, advertising, and by capitalizing on new social freedoms. Flappers and their sheiks went to movie palaces equipped with fancy house organs, to proms, and to speakeasies to listen to jazz. They set the standards for style as well. Although the American woman obtained the right to vote in 1920, in the minds of a new generation, what was more important was the freedom from Victorian restraint, including the ability to move about publicly, to smoke, wear make-up, and short skirts. Young men were also influenced by this mixed-sex social arena. Like their dates, they needed to look good, but they also had to provide the cars, the corsages, and the admission fees to movies. Their contribution, in short, to the new public leisure subculture was money. As dating and dances became common activities in the 1920s for a broad segment of American youth, other, more traditional, youth activities suffered by comparison. Young people were not so interested anymore in lectures, church-organized activities, scouting, reading, or studying.

Older Americans were themselves caught up in this social whirl in the 1920s. Anecdotal information suggests that the rate of alcohol consumption in the U.S. might have increased during the 1920s because it was illegal. Certainly going to speakeasies and nightclubs, where alcohol was usually available, was a popular urban activity during the 1920s. Part of the allure was the exoticism of the scene. Thus, Harlem, the African-American neighborhood of New York City, attracted many white middle-class people interested in jazz, dancing, and nightclubs which often featured scantily-clad or exotically dressed black dancers.

Many Victorian strictures disappeared for wives and mothers as well as their daughters. A 1925 Clara Bow film, *Dancing Mothers*, for example, suggested that middle-aged women were entitled to fun too and that fun was defined as going to dances, on trips, and away for the weekend. New beauty standards that emphasized youthfulness and slenderness affected older women too. They also shopped, visited beauty parlors to obtain permanents, and practiced a new dance step, the Charleston.

Obviously small towns could not compete with big cities when it came to leisure-time entertainments. In many small towns, especially in the South, older values continued to prevail and leisure was filled with morally and spiritually uplifting activities connected with the churches. Well before the rest of the country, the South and rural Midwest were "dry" (no alcohol sales) and in some communities dancing was banned at public venues. Still, nearly every small town had a movie theater, and the Model T automobile (made by the Ford Motor Company) was affordable, reliable, and practical for farmers, who flocked to buy them. Those autos moved rural people longer distances, allowing them to visit relatives, seek out public and private entertainment, and feel connected with a world that was rapidly changing. In many small towns, the traditional arts consumed many people's free time. Women made quilts while men carved small wooden objects. Music was a very popular way to pass free time and many rural people knew how to play instruments as a result. Traditional folk songs or, for African Americans, blues, linked generations together and told stories to those who might not be literate, might not have access to books, and might never see a movie.

1920s • VAUDEVILLE, MOVIES, AND REVIVALS ~ Even if most Americans still lived in small towns, urban amusements of all kind dominated American leisure thinking in the Progressive Era and the 1920s. Despite reformers' attempts to promote more suitable activities, despite immigrant parents' attempts to hold onto cultural traditions, and despite prohibition morality, paying to have a good time was widely accepted. Vaudeville, which was initially regarded as too sexual for anyone but men, became more family oriented, cleaning up its acts and offering acrobats

(circa 1925) Religious revivalism was on the upswing in the 1920s.

and singers to attract women and children. Vaudeville was carefully calculated to offer something for everybody, interspersing comics, sentimental singers, and novelty acts to keep a diverse audience—especially one with perhaps only a moderate grasp on the English language—enchanted. Vaudeville performers typically performed on a circuit of theaters across the country. The more popular it became, the more markets it penetrated. By the 1920s, many middle-sized towns were on vaudeville circuits.

More important than vaudeville were movies, which removed any remaining stigma of decadence from public entertainment because of their far-reaching popularity with virtually every segment of the American population. Because they could be shown with little equipment, even small towns soon had theaters, and because entrepreneurs wanted to maximize their profits, the form was democratic. In southern cities, for example, theaters reserved particular evenings for African-American customers. Because movies were silent, they were a form of entertainment even immigrants with few English skills could enjoy. And because they were cheap, they became a form of family amusement.

Although early movie producers discouraged celebrity (lest they have to pay their entertainers more), figures like Mary Pickford, Charlie Chaplin, and Douglas Fairbanks emerged as early role models. Americans, particularly women, wanted to know about them and their personal lives, spawning a whole new industry: the movie magazine. A feminist, interviewing young women in the 1920s, was pleased to see that more young women wanted careers than to get married, but was dismayed when, in response to her query about what type of career, the largest number replied that they wanted to be in movies. The movies of the 1920s—many of them rather titillating—reinforced the emerging cultural emphasis on female beauty, youth, and sexuality.

Movies produced an entire range of leisure activities. Watching them could be a family experience, a date, or something married women did with one another during the afternoon. Couples who went to movies on dates needed restaurants and clubs to go to before and after the show. Even the music that accompanied the movies became a part of leisure. It could be purchased and played at home as sheet music, as records for the victrola, or, by the 1920s, heard on the radio. As more middle-class people flocked to movies, the theaters transformed themselves to cater to the fantasies of their customers. Some created whole worlds within their doors, with starry ceilings and mock cityscapes along the walls.

Through most of the 1920s, movies were silent, accompanied by piano music and narrated with simple subtitles. As the 1920s wore on, some urban movie palaces provided orchestras as accompaniment. In 1927, the movie industry began experimenting with sound, which forever changed the movie experience. By 1930, weekly attendance at the movies was 100 million (total population was 120 million), while weekly church attendance was 60 million.

Religious revivalism was on the upswing in the 1920s, however, fostered in part by the advent of the radio. Aimee Semple McPherson, a Los Angeles-based preacher, staged elaborate religious productions, but her empire collapsed when she ran off with a radio man. Billy Sunday, a former baseball player, was another popular radio evangelist. Father Divine (a.k.a. George Baker) built a large following among African Americans. These religious figures often preached against the corruption and temptations of modern life, suggesting that many Americans were still pretty uncomfortable with the growth of paid leisure activities.

1920s • Traveling ~ Cars, like movies, also drew the middle class into the world of commercial leisure. Cars moved people around the city, to theaters, to shops, to restaurants. While the middle class continued to use public transportation, they much preferred the automobile because it offered privacy and convenience. The middle class pioneered the idea of the Sunday drive, particularly out into the countryside—a trip, in its early

Motor Vehicle Registration & Car Sales

Year	Motor Vehicle Registration	Factory Sales
1900	8,000	4,100
1905	78,800	24,200
1910	468,500	181,000
1915	2,490,000	895,900
1920	9,239,100	1,905,500
1925	20,068,500	3,735,100
1930	23,034,753	2,787,400

SOURCE: *The American People: Creating a Nation and a Society* by Gary Nash et al.

days, that was often interrupted by flat tires or other automotive disasters. The middle class demand improved the system of roadways, paving many, and making it possible for people to get to natural places and vacation spots once only accessible by train. Tourist camps and roadside inns (eventually christened motels, short for motor hotels) sprung up along the roadways, providing places where people might stay. These were different from the old lodges and inns, catering to a population on the move. Nature beckoned Americans, although all too often they disturbed nature in the process, putting hotdog stands and souvenir shops near waterfalls, geysers, and panoramic vistas.

With more money, time, and interest in leisure, middle-class tastes predominated, although, increasingly, those tastes were influenced and shaped by commercial enterprises. Trips to Europe remained popular as ways of polishing or finishing young people, but more middle-class people were attracted to American spaces: Niagara Falls for honeymoons, Florida in the winter, Hollywood. The mid-1920s marked a huge boom in Florida real estate, intended as both investment and recreational land. Bad weather and many crooked deals took some of the attraction out of the Florida market thereafter, but the idea of going somewhere warm for the winter was certainly attractive to upper-middle-class people, who flocked to luxury hotels in Florida or Southern California.

One could travel to those places by car, but trains were more commonly the way to go. Trains provided a variety of accommodations, including compartments and sleeping berths. The food and service were renowned on many lines and offered one opportunity for middle-class people (who, by the 1920s, had more trouble finding and affording servants) to be served. For sheer luxury, however, there was travel by ocean liner, particularly on British lines like the Cunard or the White Star, which was known for its service. Although the Titanic disaster ended some of the worse class distinctions on ocean liners, the luxury remained.

1920s • TECHNOLOGY'S IMPACT ON LEISURE ~ Many things once reserved for the wealthy became accessible to larger numbers of Americans, thanks to mass production, mass markets, and a national transportation network. World War I marked an important turning point in the production of toys. Before World War I, the most desirable toys were hand-

1920s

made in Germany, but once that market was cut off, American toy manufacturers were forced to create toys of their own. The result was a booming doll industry, although other toys were also produced. By the 1920s, toys already began to have commercial tie-ins linking them to products, like the popular Campbell's Kids, who promoted soup.

Electricity reached about half of American homes by the 1920s, which brought gadgets for play as well as work, particularly phonographs and console radios. Electricity also transformed entertaining by making dozens of cooking-related items, such as electric chafing dishes, available to the homemaker. The American home had once been a haven against the outside world. By the 1920s, home entertainment, perhaps encouraged by a desire to display one's possessions, was more common. Installment buying in the 1920s encouraged people to acquire expensive radios, which were regarded as an investment for years of future home entertainment.

The emergence of mass communications also increased the variety of entertainments available to individuals. Radio began as wireless telegraphy, a hobby of interest mainly to young boys, who constructed their own crystal sets and listened for Morse code. But as an array of sounds began traveling on the waves and consumers no longer had to construct their own radios, listeners in the 1920s could hear music, sporting events, and, first, local programming and, by the latter 1920s, broadcasts on national networks. Radio helped popularize jazz and sports.

1920s • Sports ～ Reading about, watching, and listening to sports became an important leisure activity for men in the 1920s. College football and professional baseball were two very popular sports, and listeners could often hear them broadcast in the 1920s. Even before the 1920s, though, sports pages in newspapers reported on football, baseball, and a host of other sports, including boxing, tennis, and swimming. While young women admired movie stars, young men tended to spend some of their leisure time following the exploits of sports heroes. College football games were popular with college students, but baseball games in urban stadiums were the more popular father-son leisure bonding activities. George "Red" Grange, running back for the University of Illinois, was the most popular college football player of the 1920s. Other 1920s sports heroes (and heroines) included boxer Jack Dempsy, golfer Bobby Jones, and Gertrude Eberle, who swam the English Channel in 1926.

But baseball remained the American game of the 1920s. The American League formed in 1901 and the National League two years later. The World Series was one of the most popular sporting events broadcast by radio in the 1920s. The Series of 1919, marred by scandal, attracted a lot of attention. Eight players of the Chicago White Sox were accused of throwing the game to the Cincinnati Reds for money. While acquitted, the accusation suggests that baseball had, like much of leisure, become something to be bought and sold. Home-run king George Herman "Babe" Ruth had his likeness on everything from baseball cards to children's notebooks.

1920s • The Changing Philosophy of Leisure ～ During the 1910s, more Americans came to accept and welcome technology and along with that acceptance came a changed attitude toward leisure. While Americans once judged one another according to moral "inner" values, now people measured success by what one owned and how one spent one's free time. While the First World War briefly refocused American energies on productivity and usefulness, by its end, there was a kind of cynicism epitomized by the writer F. Scott Fitzgerald. Fitzgerald, like a lot of his generation, respected wealth, enjoyed leisure, and liked to consume.

By the end of the 1920s, a broad segment of Americans shared Fitzgerald's views. The idea of leisure was firmly entrenched in the American mind as a necessary antidote to the stresses of modern life. Leisure was a commodity, purchasable by various classes. For middle-class and upper-class Americans, privacy–or at least separation from the lower classes–was desirable and worth the extra cost. Leisure time remained, however, something one earned by hard work. Since married women did not earn money but worked at home, leisure for them was perhaps a more contested idea. As with the Victorian elite, the wife of a wealthy man, who did not have to engage in physical activity, had the opportunity to engage in such middle-class "female" leisures as playing bridge or mahjongg (a fad in the 1920s) or going to matinees. Leisure-time wives signified status for both the women and their husbands. Having removed many of the stigmas against leisure, leisure often became a way of expressing one's personality, tastes, talents, and class.

1930s • LEISURE DURING THE DEPRESSION ~ By the time of the Stock Market Crash of 1929, middle class people regarded leisure, like cars and radios, as a necessary part of life. As the jobless rate rose, more Americans had more free time than ever before, but

(circa 1935) During the depression people spent their money on less expensive items like musical equipment. Seen here is Louis Armstrong (1900-1971) in a promotional portrait for Selmer Trumpets.

few people had extra money to spend on leisure. Not surprisingly, the Depression limited leisure-related expenditures, but with some significant exceptions. Americans had long since embraced the notion that play was important to one's physical and mental health, an investment in one's happiness. This notion certainly did not disappear just because of hard times.

1930s • RADIO ~ Cheap, home-based leisure activities became more important during the Depression. Public library use rose as did the number of jigsaw puzzles Americans consumed. Stamp collecting (a

1930s

Radios in the United States

Year	Number of Households with Radios
1922	60,000
1925	2,750,000
1930	13,750,000
1935	21,456,000
1940	28,500,000

SOURCE: *Historical Statistics of the United States from Colonial Times to 1970.* U.S. Government Printing Office, 1975.

hobby pursued by Franklin Roosevelt), coin collecting, and other traditional hobbies, continued. Radio purchases climbed despite the economic downturn. As the cost of radios dropped, radio was regarded as a cheap amusement of its own, one that kept the family home and together. Families justified radio purchases by balancing their initial costs against the savings in going to the movies, buying newspapers or magazines, or going to sporting events or nightclubs. For many people out of work, radio was a link to the outside world. Recognizing the diversity of its Depression audience, the radio networks provided programs with appeal to many kinds of listeners, including dramas, music, serials, soap operas, quiz shows, public affairs programming, and foreign language programs for immigrants. During the Depression the audience for radio also expanded, thanks especially to Franklin Roosevelt's rural electrification program.

In the early 1930s, the staple of radio was music and the most common type of music played was dance music. Rudy Vallee, a popular 1920s singer, was but the first of a series of popular male vocalists. Bing Crosby, with a unique vocal style that was more jazz-oriented, was also popular during the 1930s as a radio and live performer. But with hundreds of AM radio stations across the country, individual stations could offer a variety of musical options. Although no single radio station catered solely to people of color, there were radio programs that

How Youth Spends Leisure

Already by the 1930s, there was social concern about the ways adolescents spent their free time. Movies and radio, the two mass entertainment media, triggered discussion familiar to parents today: how much time should teenagers be allowed to enjoy movies and radio and under what circumstances? Indeed, already by the 1930s, the average teenager devoted nearly 40 percent of his/her leisure time to listening to the radio and records and viewing movies.

With more forms of media available at the turn of the century, teens devote slightly more than half of their leisure time to media-generated entertainment like television, CDs, computers, and video games. Today's leisure, though, is also more structured than Depression-era leisure among youth, whose second favorite pastime was visiting with friends. Today organized sports, lessons, and clubs consume more time, although visiting with friends can take place in more formats, especially via e-mail or by cell phone. In both eras, though, the largest single chunk of teens' time was devoted to the same activity, sleep.

played jazz (often identified as "black" music), or country, or classical music. Because most music played on the radio was played live, small stations relied heavily on local talent, and local talent usually reflected local taste. Gospel music, old folksongs, and the blues were played on small Southern stations, for instance. While radio fostered a more national culture, music on the radio encouraged localism too.

1930s • MOVIES AND RESTAURANTS
~ Those who purchased radios to keep the family home, however, had to reckon with the popularity of the movies. Movies were just as much a necessity to most Americans as were radios. Movies, moreover, had the relatively new attraction of sound. Yet the movie studios recognized they were vulnerable because of the Depression. They worked hard to draw and keep an audience.

To make sure that their audiences saw movies as family fare, they instituted production codes that regulated the moral content. By the end of the 1930s, some movies experimented with color, including *The Wizard of Oz* and *Gone with the Wind*. And, to guarantee regular attendance, many movie houses offered incentives. Tuesday evening, traditionally a slow night, became "dish night" in thousands of movie theaters across the country, in which a dish was given to some members of the audience. Regular attendance on Tuesday evenings could, ultimately, yield one a new set of dishes. To make sure patrons perceived movie-going as a bargain, theaters offered double bills, newsreels, and cartoons.

Depression-era movies offered both frothy escapes from economic hard times and stories about those hard times. Popular stars included Mae West (before production codes), the Marx Brothers, W.C. Fields, Shirley Temple, Clark Gable, Katherine Hepburn, and Cary Grant. The movie musical, made possible because of sound, became a popular new genre, although Americans liked everything from screwball comedies (*Bringing Up Baby*) to gangster pictures (*Little Caesar*). One thing movies didn't offer was diversity. Although there were films made especially for African Americans and featuring African American casts, mainstream American films featured African Americans almost exclusively as cooks, maids, and butlers.

In the 1920s, prohibition had impacted America's fledgling restaurant industry and the Depression further reshaped it. Restaurants began as saloons, places where workingmen could get a meal and a beer at lunch. Some saloons continued to serve food, but restaurants broke away and became more upscale, catering to a middle-class dinner crowd during the Progressive Era. By the 1920s, though, prohibition reduced the lure of eating out. In the 1930s, few Americans had the extra cash to dine out in fancy restaurants. Chain restaurants, like Schrafft's, Child's and Stouffers, had trouble staying afloat during the 1930s and often resorted to gimmicks like all-you-can-eat days to survive. To compensate, some new restaurants tried fanciful designs, like Los Angeles's Brown Derby. White Castle, which made burgers, located its outlets near subway stops, hoping to attract customers on their way home.

Ethnic cuisine had little appeal to those outside the ethnic group, although "spaghetti houses" (Italian restaurants) existed in most cities and some adventurous diners sampled Chinese food in China towns. Greek American immigrants became perhaps the single most dominant ethnicity serving food, although rarely did they serve Greek food. Their success depended largely on their simplicity and cheapness.

Still, regional cuisine flourished not at restaurants, but at local festivals and events centered around food. During hard times, food and eating became symbolic of survival, and renewed interest in regionalism and tradition encouraged the growth of such events. These included barbecues in Texas, pig roasts in the Midwest, and fish fries in the Pacific Northwest. The fact that these were cheaper than commercial alternatives drew more people to them than during the "roaring" twenties.

1930s • READING ~ Reading was a common Depression activity because it could be done anywhere and at low cost. Fiction was popular, encouraged by the Book-of-the-Month Club, although there was obviously a limit on the number of people who could afford to buy books. More Americans than ever finished high school during the Depression, although with no promise of a job after graduation. As the educational level of Americans went up, so too did their consumption of reading materials. Popular magazines like *Time*, *Life*, and *Newsweek* reported on current events very much on the minds of Americans during the turbulent decade. Newspapers were also regarded as a necessity for many Americans who wanted to follow the news at home as well as in Europe and Asia. Immigrants, particularly, wanted news of current events at home and the foreign language press satisfied their demands for news.

1930s • POLITICAL INFLUENCES ON ENTERTAINMENT ~ The American Left, at its numeric peak during the 1930s, tried to construct a culture for its followers. The American Communist Party was the most successful. Drawing on the workingman's tradition, its culture was built around folksongs and similar amusements with a political edge. The Communist Party also helped organize book cooperatives and summer camps for children. It gave dances and musicals to raise money for political causes, such as the Loyalist fight against fascism in Spain. One noteworthy feature about the Communists' leisure culture was that it was integrated. The Communists also tried to encourage working people to participate in the arts, organizing the John Reed Clubs for writers and a similar organization for artists. Although Communists tried to influence the arts to build a socially realist art like in the Soviet Union, more commonly their interests lay with American folk arts and cultures. Perhaps the most familiar Communist artist during the period was singer Woody Guthrie, who performed folk and "hillbilly" music.

More successful at infusing politics into leisure were the Roosevelt administration's Work Progress Administration (WPA) projects. The Federal Arts Projects were intended to employ creative people while bringing culture to the masses. The Federal Theater, for example, brought productions of important plays, often in innovative presentations, to rural areas and to people of color. Living Newspapers likewise brought current events into the countryside and to places where people couldn't afford a daily paper or couldn't read. The Federal Writers Project produced guidebooks to each state, although tourism was one casualty of the Depression. Taken together, these programs further legitimized the idea that leisure was a valuable part of Americans' "pursuit of happiness."

For most Americans, though, leisure existed apart from political or social considerations during the 1930s. Christmas gift-giving, for example, actually intensified during the 1930s and consumers were exhorted by magazine ads with images of prosperous families exchanging much more expensive gifts than had been the case two decades earlier. The Roosevelt administration actually stimulated holiday shopping by moving Thanksgiving up a week to prolong the traditional season. Professional sports flourished, largely thanks to radio listeners. Although fewer Americans than ever could afford to travel, hotels and motels continued to exist and, alongside trains, commercial airlines offered their first flights to the wealthy.

Yet, by the end of the decade, politics cast their pall over the culture. War began in Europe in 1939, but even before that Americans had read about and listened to reports of Japanese atrocities in China, Hitler's dominance in Europe, the Spanish Civil War, and the Munich Crisis that brought Europe to the brink of war. American preparedness began to put people back to work again. People didn't have a lot of money, but some of what they did have went toward leisure activities they felt they'd deserved because of hard times.

1941-1945 • WORLD WAR II ~ If the Depression gave people free time and no money, the war gave Americans money but no time to spend it and nothing to spend it on. Manufacturing consumer goods had a low priority during World War II as rations and military production took precedence. This trend, in turn, limited peoples' leisure options. Still, Americans were an enterprising people and their need for leisure during wartime was significant.

Soldiers were in the military for the duration of the war, which meant the military had a long-term interest in keeping them happy. Psychological tests performed on all incoming soldiers suggested, though, that many were not emotionally healthy. The military became committed to providing for their off-hours. All U.S. military training facilities included recreational activities, although all these were segregated (like the military itself). For some northern African Americans, this was their first serious experience with legal segregation. USOs further provided leisure activities like canteens, movies, and dances, both at home and, whenever possible, abroad. Soldiers sent V (for victory) letters home, listened to special V records, and had their own armed forces radio stations. Victory girls served as hostesses at USO events.

Unlike World War I, when military authorities refused to concede that American soldiers might seek out sex in their free time, World War II commanders educated soldiers about the risks of sexually transmitted diseases and provided for regular prophylaxis. Female soldiers, however, were not included in this campaign and pregnancy was grounds for discharge.

The military worked especially hard to make sure that soldiers in combat zones could experience aspects of home during their leisure hours. Besides records and radio, soldiers got magazines and movies; many times, loved ones sent local papers so they could follow life on the home front. The military believed that food was a potent source of emotional support for soldiers and made sure, therefore, that what soldiers ate was strictly American in origin. Military cooks all used the same recipes and all food was shipped from the states. When the aircraft carrier *Lexington* was hit during the battle of the Coral Sea, the sailors ate their way through the ice cream supply. In places far away from home, thinking about familiar food was often a shorthand way of evoking feelings of comfort and security.

1941-1945

1941-1945 • LEISURE ON THE HOME FRONT ~ For people on the home front, leisure took on a divided quality. Most people had less time for leisure than before, but many incorporated leisure into their lives more systematically. Wartime production was the country's first priority. All raw materials were diverted to produce war materials. A whole host of leisure pleasures were impacted, from automobiles (not produced during the war, and gas, oil, and rubber for tires were rationed) to children's toys. As a result, things that by the end of the 1930s were regarded as leisure activities (gardening and sewing) were redefined as necessities. Many American women presided over Victory Gardens, growing produce they then canned.

Double and triple shifts and a workforce that drew, increasingly, on wives and mothers limited the number of hours workers had for leisure, but because many had money for the first time in a decade, many were prepared to make the most of the leisure they had. Movies drew Americans during the war, whether they told wartime stories or offered escape. Nightclubs, restaurants, and nightlife also flourished, despite the complications of rationing. Bowling attracted new converts, as did indoor roller rinks, miniature golf, and just about anything a soldier on leave and his date could do together. Travel options limited people, particularly those with limited time for leisure. Public transportation was crowded and—in Midwestern cities full of migrating southerners, both black and white–tense. Train travel was almost impossible because the military had first claim to all trains. But even if you could get somewhere by train, the odds are you wouldn't find anywhere to stay when you got

(1940) Dancing was a popular leisure activity during this time. Seen here is square dancing, which was more popular in the rural areas of the county.

there. In Washington D.C., for instance, virtually all hotel space was given over to new wartime workers. Purposeful travel increased during the war, but vacationing dropped off.

Automobiles During the Depression and World War II

Year	Number of Registered Automobiles
1930	23,034,753
1935	22,567,827
1940	27,465,826
1945	25,796,985
1950	40,339,077

SOURCE: U.S. Department of Transportation, Bureau of Highways

1941-1945 • NEW LEISURE ACTIVITIES FOR YOUNG PEOPLE ~ Radio remained a popular form of entertainment and leisure for young people. They could listen to radio in the privacy of their own homes and they could do other things while listening. At the same time, radio allowed people the luxury of leisure while keeping them linked to the larger world, providing security in an insecure world.

Youth became an important market during the war years, something often expressed in leisure venues. Increasing numbers of young people had jobs because of war's demands. With their own pocket money, they could spend as they pleased. At the same time, because of teacher shortages, many schools went to double and triple shifts, giving young people more free time and, because more of their mothers worked, less supervision. On both coasts, particularly among Latinos and African Americans, a dance hall culture known by its flamboyant zoot suits and swing dancing caught on. Decried by parents, the cause of a riot in Los Angeles (1943), and something "more respectable" teens shunned, the zoot suit culture captivated poor and working-class young men particularly and consumed their free time and free cash.

The idea of swing dancing extended beyond the zoot suiters, though. Swing, a form of jazz music, dominated the radio's musical offerings and record sales. Popular singers like Frank Sinatra also drew teens (especially female fans known as bobbysoxers) to their concerts, their radio performances, and their records. Big bands, including those led by Glen Miller and Artie Shaw, toured the country and played at large ballrooms such as Roseland in New York City. Some of the big bandleaders, such as Duke Ellington, were African American, and were as popular with white Americans as with black. The dancing connected with the music, jitterbugging, was a less extreme, less athletic version of the zoot suit culture, but it still spawned its own teen subculture, one that boasted its own jazz-inspired slang.

The youth culture of the war years scared parents, who worried that their children had too much leisure time and that they used it unproductively. Social concern about juvenile delinquency rose during the war years and was focused on how young people spent their leisure time

Zoot Suits

~

The Zoot Suit, for men, was characterized by fully-legged, tight-cuffed trousers and a long coat with wide lapels and wide, heavily padded shoulders.

1941-1945

in the absence of their working mothers. Curfew violations, for example, were established and enforced in many cities. Americans also worried about "Victory Girls," young women who devoted themselves to soldiers.

1941-1945 • PROFESSIONAL SPORTS ~ One aspect of leisure where the war had a big impact was on professional sports. It was difficult to field teams of athletes who were precisely of draft age and clearly good physical specimens. One solution was to create a professional women's baseball league, the All-American League, for the duration of the war. Created by chewing gum magnate P. K. Wrigley, the League had 550 players in its heyday, but quickly lost steam after the war as male players returned home. Occasional sport, like the neighborhood ball game, was limited by equipment shortages. Rubber was very scarce since nearly all of it came from Japanese-occupied territories. Rubber balls of all sorts were nearly impossible to get. Still, Americans continued to play basketball, football, and baseball everywhere, from schools to the internment camps that housed Japanese Americans.

1941-1945 • THE PSYCHOLOGY OF WAR AND LEISURE ~ War created a strong justification for leisure, intensifying Americans' belief that their hard work earned them pleasure and the chance to blow off steam. Soldiers, especially, had a live-for-today attitude that made them pursue their leisure activities with a vengeance. On-leave soldiers partied hard, drank copiously, and pursued women. Couples met, got engaged, and married in a hurry. Civilians behaved similarly, generally with less justification. Many were far from home or without loved ones and they wanted to have a good time. "Hillbilly music," the country western sound popular with white southerners, migrated to the west coast with shipyard workers and soon appeared on local radio stations and clubs. The same was true of the blues music played by African-American musicians as blacks moved into cities like Chicago and Detroit. Young people danced well into the night, even if they had to get up in the morning, for the sheer pleasure of dancing.

War created a live-for-today mentality that seemed to justify violating taboos. The black market, where Americans could buy scarce and rationed goods, flourished because people felt they were entitled to things they couldn't get, including car parts, clothes, liquor, and food. Young women, in some communities faced with a shortage of eligible men, pursued males more aggressively than was traditional. People whose families were torn apart by war or who had moved to wartime boom towns, escaped into theaters to watch movies with no references to war.

At war's end, Americans wanted to return to normal conditions, about which many had fantasized for a long time. Wistful nostalgia was a heavy theme in movies, popular songs, and radio dramas. But it was hard to achieve that dream because the world had been changed, millions of lives lost, and much of America's innocence had disappeared.

1950s • BABY BOOM, SUBURBS, AND DISNEYLAND ~ With lots of pent-up demand for consumer goods and the savings to buy them, the post-war economy boomed. As more Americans moved into the middle class (nearly 60 percent by 1960), the demand for new single-family houses skyrocketed, as well as demand for the labor-saving devices that would go in them, washers, dryers, home freezers, and the cars that would get their owners from

The Growth of Suburbs

Place of Residence	City	Suburb	Small Town
1940	31.6%	19.5%	48.9%
1950	32.3%	23.8%	43.9%
1960	32.6%	30.7%	36.7%

SOURCE: *The American People: Creating a Nation and a Society* by Gary Nash et al.

the new suburbs into the city or to the supermarket or the shopping mall.

Suburbanization greatly changed the idea of leisure. The new post-war suburbs consisted of little more than houses and the occasional store and church. Young families were removed from many familiar leisure activities, spending time with extended families, going to urban entertainments, dining out. Replacing these were suburban entertainments that took place within the neighborhoods themselves, daytime coffee klatches of young wives, weekend cocktail parties in rumpus rooms, drive-in movies with the kids nestled in the back of the station wagon.

Gender was very much a divide in the suburbs. There was a lot of social pressure on women to go back to their traditional, pre-war roles and this manifested itself in leisure activities. Despite gadget-filled new houses, women actually devoted more of their day to housework than before. Their leisure hours were often filled with extensions of these tasks, things their grandmothers defined as work, such as sewing, small crafts projects, paint-by-numbers sets, and baking. Masculinity was allegedly threatened in the 1950s, and not just because women were supposed to have too much power. Rather, it was the modern workplace, corporate and white collar, that kept men from being "real" men. Hobbies and leisure activities during the 1950s reflected an emphasis on masculinity. The popularity of do-it-yourself projects—wood working and home improvement—suggested that men wanted to work with their hands and, like their grandfathers, build things of practical use.

Yet for millions of Americans in the 1950s, more and more of their leisure time was consumed by television. Television decidedly changed leisure activities after World War II. Invented in the 1920s, but only successfully mass-marketed after the war, by the end of the 1950s the vast majority of American homes had a television. Television was perfectly suited for the army of suburbanites with large numbers of

(1955) Teens enjoyed spending their money and time on buying and playing records.

1950s

small children. It was home-based, cheap, and it promoted family togetherness. It offered something for everybody–cartoons for the kids, sports for dad, and drama for mom. TV quickly replaced radio as the home entertainment of choice for Americans and quickly consumed the lion's share of Americans' free time.

The Nielsen Top Ten Rated TV Shows of 1955-56

1. The $64,000 Question
2. I Love Lucy
3. The Ed Sullivan Show
4. Disneyland
5. The Jack Benny Show
6. December Bride
7. You Bet Your Life
8. Dragnet
9. I've Got a Secret
10. General Electric Theater

SOURCE: *Total Television* by Alex McNeil, 1984.

Television also steamrolled over regionalism. While local radio stations could promote local culture and provide an outlet for local musicians, television was dominated by national networks from the start. The introduction of immigration quotas in the 1920s had already weakened the diverse flavor of American culture. Suburbanization, which separated second and third generation members from their roots in urban enclaves, fostered homogenization and television provided a cultural picture of what "American" was supposed to look like. Although radio had its share of "ethnic" programs—*I Remember Mama* and *The Goldbergs*–TV tended to offer a blander, non-ethnic picture of American life. The leisure diversity between places like the Lower East Side of New York City and rural Kansas, shrank thanks to television and the flight from the cities and, especially the small towns, to the suburbs.

The Paint by Numbers Craze

In the 1950s, do-it-yourself became a virtual mania. Some ascribed it to men's need to assert their masculinity in an era when they no longer worked with their hands or even worked on their own. Others argued it reflected the lack of public entertainment in the suburbs. Critics read it as a sign that American culture was banal.

Whatever the reason, one kind of do-it-yourself that required very little skill and no power tools was the oil painting that could be filled in according to a color-coded series of numbers. Although children's coloring books were the first to employ the strategy, it was Max Klein, a former researcher for General Motors, who founded the Picture Craft Company that produced the "Craft Master" series of paint by number pictures, beginning in 1951. The company was immensely successful, selling $10 million worth of sets in the first two years of operation. Pets and landscapes were favorites with customers, although there was also a category of paintings called Old Masters, which featured the best-selling *Last Supper* ($11.50). It is still possible to purchase a paint by numbers picture, but the volume produced has dwindled, although there are collectors who cherish completed works purchased through collectibles markets.

1950s • TEENAGERS ~ Teenagers represented an increasingly important leisure market in the 1950s. Before the war, they had been called adolescents, an age designation, but the nickname teenager was more a marketing distinction. Teens had money and free time and, as more young people graduated from high school and went to college, a prolonged period of time before entering adulthood. Parents who lived through the Depression and World War II did not want their teenagers to miss out on anything, particularly anything material, and some parents lived out their fantasies by buying their sons and daughters cars, furniture, and expensive clothes.

In 1959, American Teens Owned

10,000,000 phonographs
1,000,000 television sets
25,000,000 Elvis Presley singles
2,000,000 electric razors
13,000,000 cameras

SOURCE: *Life Magazine*. August 31, 1959

Suburbs helped foster the teenage peer group. Although the stereotype of the 1950s home featured a stay-at-home mother, by 1960s, roughly a third of all mothers worked at least part time. Teenagers had less supervision than previous generations of young people. Separated from urban entertainments, too old to enjoy activities associated with childhood, teens spent time together, talking, eating, watching TV, listening to music, and dancing. The telephone was one way of keeping in touch. Many middle-class households added a second phone during the 1950s, often tucked somewhere where teens might have private conversations. The decline of party lines also assured privacy and meant that teens could stay on the phone longer. By the early 1960s, a line of phone, the more compact, pastel, Princess phone, was specifically marketed to teenage girls.

Teens were an important part of the commercial leisure culture of the 1950s. The attractions of the home appealed little to them. They could be lured to the movies, to cheap restaurants (including the first MacDonalds franchises), and to stores. Movies such as *Rebel without a Cause* (1955) and *Blackboard Jungle* (1955) were created specifically for teen audiences. Part of the appeal of the movie theater for teens was its relative privacy and darkness which, especially during thrillers, offered them the chance to embrace. The age when young people started dating lowered after World War II and more young couples "went steady." Sexual taboos began to fall. Teens wanted places where they could be alone and, most especially, beyond the watchful eye of parents, teachers, and other guidance figures. Churches tried to fight back with wholesome leisure activities like basketball leagues, but to little success.

The emergence of rock and roll in the 1950s also consumed a lot of teenagers' leisure time and leisure dollars. Rock and roll began as music played by African Americans that white teens picked up on their radios. Before long, white artists began playing the same kind of music, sometimes adapting songs performed by black artists. Rock and roll fueled record sales, the sale of transistor radios, and the popularity of movies like *Don't Knock the Rock* (1956) and *Jailhouse Rock* (1957). By the end of the 1950s, teens could also watch their favorite artists perform on shows like Dick Clark's "American Bandstand." Rock and roll formed the underpinning of teen leisure culture in

1950s

A Timeline of Toys & Games

1889 – Flexible Flyers (sleds)
1901 – Lionel Electric Trains
1902 – The Teddy Bear
1911 – Kewpie Dolls
1913 – Erector Sets
1915 – Tinker Toys
1916 – Lincoln Logs
1929 – Radio Flyer Wagons
1934 – Shirley Temple Dolls
1935 – Monopoly Games
1939 – View-Master
1943 – Chutes and Ladders
1945 – Slinky
1952 – Mr. Potato Head
1953 – Matchbox Cars
1955 – Play-Doh
1955 – Davy Crockett Caps
1957 – Frisbies
1958 – Hula Hoop
1959 – Barbie Dolls
1959 – Etch-a-Sketch
1962 – Easy Bake Oven
1962 – Slot Cars
1962 – Legos
1964 – G.I. Joe (1st action figure)
1966 – Twister
1968 – Hot Wheels Cars
1977 – Atari Video Games
1983 – Cabbage Patch Kids
1983 – Transformers
1985 – Teddy Ruxpin
1986 – American Girl Dolls
1988 – Nintendo

the 1950s. Parents were alarmed by rock's popularity, thinking it was too sexual and promoted too much racial interaction. Some tried to limit its influence and some high schools and colleges either banned it or school dances where rock music might be played. These efforts had little success and, in the end, one solution was to make rock and roll less outlaw in its presentation by promoting artists like Pat Boone or Fabian, clean-cut singers whose songs were softer and had a less prominent beat. Although both were popular, some teens found them too sweet. By the end of the 1950s there was a somewhat underground current of youth protest expressed in its leisure. The popularity of novels like *The Catcher in the Rye* (1951), Beat poetry, movies like *The Wild One* and folk music expressed the first rumblings of the youth protest culture of the 1960s.

1950s • CHILDREN ~ Children, too, became a market for leisure in the 1950s. Beginning in 1943, the birthrate rose, and it continued to skyrocket for about the next twenty years. One consequence was that whatever life stage these baby boomers were at, their needs and interests were important to the economy.

As the suburbs developed, the large number of children who lived in them shaped communities. Public swimming pools and recreational centers, clubs, and sports programs structured their afternoons, weekends, and summers, providing activities parents considered appropriate. In the 1950s, parents tried to fill their children's leisure with practical or educational activities. Sunday school programs offered secular fun as well as religious education. Dance, music, and horseback riding lessons taught skills. Little League and Pop Warner football gave little boys the opportunity to participate in sports rather than just watch them on TV. The Boy and Girl Scouts, and similar organizations, were led by adults and considered educational.

Part of the point of all this usefulness was to better situate children for their futures, but there was also a lot of parental fear of children "going wrong." The example of teenagers was never far from parents' minds; they did not want their children to grow up addicted to rock and roll, milk shakes, and fast cars. One popular form of children's entertainment—comic books—became a national obsession in the 1950s. There was even a congressional investigation in 1955 to determine whether or not comic books corrupted young people.

Although many parents experienced conflicting feelings about contributing to such pampered childhoods—far from the hard-work ethic in which they were raised—children's desires continued to be met by an abundance of consumer products. Children were at least as big a market as teenagers, something abundantly clear from the vast proliferation of toys in the 1950s. Not surprisingly, gender played a big role in toys in the 1950s too. Popular toys for boys included traditional building sets (Tinker Toys or the Erector Set), chemistry sets, and guns. Girls, on the other hand, were treated to increasingly sophisticated dolls, including Tiny Tears, Betsy Wetsy, and Chatty Cathy. Before 1959, most dolls were either babies or replicas of little girls (like the full-size Patty Playpal). In 1959, however, the Mattel Toy Company launched Barbie, a teenage fashion doll. Barbie offered little girls the opportunity to imagine adolescence, or at least an adolescence full of commodities that included a vast wardrobe, a dream house, and a consort named Ken (first marketed in 1961). Yet girls were not merely socialized to be homemakers as a vast industry of active toys like hula hoops, bicycles, and roller skates was pitched to both genders.

The large number of children in American households in the 1950s (by 1960, the average American woman had 3.61 children), meant that households were very child-centered, including leisure activities. The booming area of the restaurant industry in the 1950s, for example, was the family restaurant that offered cheap prices, kid-friendly foods

Barbie's Vital Stats

Barbie is sold in 140 countries at the rate of two each second. Barbie sales exceeded two billion dollars in 1997. She has so many outfits that Mattel, Inc., the company that produces Barbie, is also the fourth largest clothing manufacturer in the United States. Barbie has a boyfriend, Ken, and two younger sisters, Skipper and Kelly, and a host of friends, including Midge, Shani (her African American friend), and Becky, who is in a wheelchair. Although there has been some dispute about the exact dimensions of her body, the generally-accepted estimates of what she would look like if she were life-size are that she would stand 5 feet 10 inches tall and measure 35-20-32, although some argue her bust would be larger and her waist still smaller. Over the years, her careers have included fashion model, ballerina, flight attendant, medical doctor, Olympic athlete, TV news reporter, dentist, and, most recently, president. In 1993, the Barbie Liberation Organization kidnapped Teen Talk Barbies and Talking Duke G.I. Joe dolls from toy store shelves, switched their voice boxes, and then returned the dolls to the stores.

(1955) "Togetherness," a term coined by McCall's magazine in 1955, was supposed to summarize that interaction, yet few Americans quite knew what it meant. Besides home improvement projects and watching television, there was little that engaged both men and women around the house.

1950s

(like hamburgers), and fast service. A taste many G.I.s brought home from the war—pizza—proved to be very popular with children as well. Vacations also needed to be family-friendly. Camping increased in popularity, as did automobile trips (especially as the system of national highways improved). But for most American children, the dream vacation was to Disneyland, Walt Disney's theme park in Southern California. Unlike any previous amusement park, it proved a mecca for millions of visitors a year and children and adults alike enjoyed such rides as the Matterhorn (a roller coaster) and exhibits, some of which (like the speaking, moving model of Abraham Lincoln) harked back to the older leisure theme of education. Motels across the country began offering family rates and amenities (TVs and swimming pools) that would attract families to them.

1950s • GENDER

Family was important in 1950s America, the bulwark against Communism and the stability and normality that people sought after the Depression and the war. "Togetherness," a term coined by McCall's magazine in 1955, was supposed to summarize that interaction, yet few Americans quite knew what that meant. Besides home improvement projects and watching television, there was little that could engage both men and women together around the house, except maybe a Sunday afternoon barbecue. Gender roles in the 1950s were narrowly defined and, presumably, therefore, the leisure activities that interested men would not interest their wives. Leisure remained a gendered concept. Advertisements, for example, presented a picture of domesticity that provided for leisure for the breadwinner, often shown sitting in a lounge chair with a pipe and a book (or, later, a TV). Social assumptions about women's leisure, on the other hand, were less benign. Americans assumed housewives had more free time because they had more gadgets. The classic stereotype of housewives assumed that they sat around the house all day watching TV and eating bonbons. But with more work at home and more likelihood of a job outside the home, married women were often left out of the leisure picture. In fact, many leisure activities for the rest of the family made more work for mother, who packed for vacations, cleaned house before parties, or drove her children to basketball games and swimming lessons.

One popular leisure activity for women remained shopping, something that could still be justified as providing for the family. In 1956, the first indoor shopping mall, Southdale, was constructed in a Minneapolis suburb. Malls of all shapes and sizes followed, providing a somewhat different version of the earlier big-city shopping day in a large, luxurious department store. Malls were popular with women because they offered freedom, time away from families, and a safe space protected from the elements. Malls also became places where young people spent time because malls did not require an entrance fee and offered a wide variety of diversions including stores and places to eat.

1950s • SINGLES ~ While the country was more married than ever before in the 1950s and the social ideal of being young and married dominated the popular culture in some ways, manufacturers recognized that single people spent more of their income on leisure activities than any other segment of the population. This is why teens were so attractive a market, but young, single working people were even more attractive, for they had the most income of all. The 1950s marked the beginnings of a singles subculture that would flourish more significantly in the 1960s and beyond.

Playboy magazine, first published in 1953, promoted a bachelor lifestyle, consisting of dates with glamorous women. The far more chaste female version of this subculture was presented in Doris Day movies. Day was always a working girl who lived somewhere exciting, owned lots of glamorous clothes, went out to dinner and to nightclubs, had a cleaning woman to take care of her apartment, but who held out for Mr. Right on her own terms. Although only 9 percent of the population believed a single person could be happy, advertisers did their best to suggest that single status meant more self-indulgent things like stereos, sports cars, and furs. By contrast, mowing the lawn, washing diapers, and driving a station wagon looked unattractive.

Marital Status of the Population

Year	Married	Single	Divorced	Widowed
1940	60%	31%	2%	8%
1950	66%	23%	3%	8%
1960	68%	21%	3%	8%

SOURCE: U.S. Bureau of the Census

Urban nightlife continued to exist, although with the tax base flowing out to the suburbs many city centers lost their allure in the 1950s. Following World War II a small, very quiet gay subculture emerged in a few cities, particularly New York City and San Francisco. Bars that attracted a mostly gay and—less commonly—lesbian clientele, offered a relatively safe space for people heavily pressured to keep their sexual preferences quiet. As white, middle-class couples fled the cities, gays, people of color, recent immigrants, and other marginalized Americans claimed the cities for their own leisure activities. Even in the segregated south, African Americans in large cities constructed restaurants, cafes, nightclubs, and radio stations to cater to their communities.

1950s • LEISURE AS EXPRESSION OF AMERICANISM ~ In the 1950s, how Americans spent their leisure time was often seen as a symbolic statement about the superiority of the capitalist system over communism. Freedom of religion and freedom of the press, for instance, provided for leisure activities Russians could not have. At the same time, consumerism also represented capitalism at its most attractive. In 1959, vice president Richard Nixon brought an American dream house to Moscow to put on display, trumpeting the comfort, security, and con-

1960s

venience of the single family home. To some degree, however, Americans already suspected that their affluence was turning into decadence. The early success of the Russian space program, as evidenced by the launching of Sputnik, a satellite, in 1957, suggested to many Americans that their priorities were misspent and that the country ought to put more money and energy into science and technology rather than consumer goods.

A different kind of political statement about leisure was expressed in the Civil Rights movement. Leisure had been segregated in the South since the turn of the century. In part, the struggle for equal rights that emerged out of the bus boycott in Montgomery, Alabama in 1955 was about extending leisure activities to African Americans, including department stores, restaurants, and buses. Using the techniques of nonviolence, Southern blacks asked for full inclusion in American life, inclusion that was not only about economic equality, access to schools, and the right to vote, but also the opportunity to share fully in recreational facilities.

1960s • LEISURE FOR THE COUNTER CULTURE ~ In part because of the Civil Rights movement, leisure activities in the early 1960s became more purposeful. Young Americans, black and white, were eager to donate their free time to good causes and engage in struggle for a better quality of life. Under the leadership of John F. Kennedy, Americans renewed their enthusiasm for physical fitness, engaging in fifty-mile hikes and ski vacations. And, also under the influence of the Kennedys, Americans listened to more classical music, read more books, and attended more plays.

While family togetherness prevailed in the 1950s, the 1960s marked the emergence of a powerful singles sub-culture. The birth control pill (1961) freed American youth from concerns about pregnancy. The age at which young people first married reversed its downward trend. Helen Gurley Brown and her *Cosmopolitan* magazine promoted the single lifestyle for women the same way *Playboy* touted its advantages for men. Resorts, restaurants, and discotheques all catered to a single crowd, providing ample opportunities for the sexes to get together. Soon there were singles ski weekends, singles nights at bars and nightclubs, and even singles apartment complexes with recreation rooms and swimming pools to foster a different kind of togetherness than *McCall's* had in mind.

Rising Median Age of First Marriages

Year	Median Age for Males	Median Age for Females
1950	22.8	20.3
1960	22.8	20.3
1970	23.2	20.8
1980	24.7	22.0
1990	26.1	23.9
1998	26.7	25.0

SOURCE: U.S. Bureau of the Census

1960s • IMPROVING LEISURE ACTIVITIES WITH TECHNOLOGY AND AFFLUENCE ~ Technology and the general prosperity of the decade shaped 1960s leisure as much as the singles subculture did. Families began to purchase things like telephones and televisions for their teenagers, which solidified age-based cultures and broke down family bonds. The more developed suburbs became, the more places there were for teenagers to go without their parents: malls, bowling alleys, record shops, public pools, skating rinks. Increased teenage access to automobiles meant freedom to come and go as one pleased. In suburbs with high concentrations of children and relative safety, children roamed from house to house or biked. A children's subculture emerged just as clearly as a teenage one had earlier, shaped by Barbie dolls, Clue games, and the latest comic book. Housewives, otherwise deprived of adult companionship during the day, clustered together out of necessity. Their husbands, who might spend several hours a day commuting to and from work, also became close friends. The suburbs helped fragment the family and bound family members to same age and same sex cohorts.

Technology and affluence gave parents tools in response. They could fill their houses with material things that attracted young people: built-in swimming pools, ping pong tables, basketball hoops, stereos, and bicycles. The consequence was that leisure was almost never defined as "doing nothing" by the 1960s. More importantly, leisure almost did not exist, even for children, apart from expensive leisure "tools."

Vacations were another way of maintaining leisure togetherness in the face of forces pulling families apart. Although commercial airline travel existed before the 1960s, it was only in the 1960s that it became affordable for middle-class people. Yet the family car was the most common way to travel, sometimes towing a trailer or a family boat. Many parents set off in the hopes of teaching their children about America's history or natural wonders. Others went to resorts or family cabins. Often one of the goals of a family vacation in the 1960s was to spend free time with other family members. At the same time, singles travel boomed at resorts and, by the end of the decade, a trip to Europe was becoming common for middle-class teenagers.

1960s • COUNTERCULTURE LIFESTYLES ~ The turmoil of the 1960s raised new questions about the role of leisure in the minds of many young people. The hippie movement focused on lifestyle issues. It emphasized, among other things, living in the moment and valuing experiences over possessions. Hippies saw little reason to work; their lives were about leisure. Although few could actually live according to this ideal, many incorporated aspects of the hippie lifestyle. Life became

(1969) The Woodstock Music Festival in upstate New York attracted 400,000 young people who peacefully protested for "love not war" as they rejected some of the practices and values of their parents' generation.

LEISURE ~ 1017

more casual for the younger generation, who wore clothes once designated as leisure clothing (like trousers for women or sandals) all the time. Drugs, another part of the hippie lifestyle, also embedded themselves into the college leisure lifestyle in the 1960s. The so-called "generation gap" focused on the different leisure indulgences of two generations–parents' cocktail parties and martinis versus "sex, drugs, and rock and roll." The communalism of the countercultural lifestyle also appealed to young people who chose to live in shared houses, travel together, and move from experience to experience. The back-to-the-land movement spawned by the Counterculture also emphasized simplicity and nature, traditional themes in American history that had shaped, and continued to shape, vacations.

Although still a new phenomenon, the Counterculture and its values did have some impact on various leisure activities. In the middle 1960s, the Beatles kicked off a revolution in taste. Before long young people dressed differently, had different musical tastes, and longed to be "mod" and cosmopolitan. Yet in many ways, the Beatles industry settled into American culture in familiar ways, with Beatles bubblegum cards, lunchboxes, and a Saturday morning cartoon featuring the Fab Four. Until 1967-68, youth culture filtered down into the mainstream in similarly benign waves. The surfer style of 1964-65, for instance, produced the skateboard, a miniature surfboard on wheels for children and young teens. The spy mania, similarly, brought Americans *The Man from U.N.C.L.E.* TV program. But the Counterculture tended to impact leisure in somewhat more disconcerting ways, at least to parents. Movies like *The Graduate* (1967) and *Easy Rider* (1969) did not just portray adults as clueless, but as malign. And the Haight-Ashbury hippie scene in San Francisco attracted a lot of runaways prepared to jettison their suburban lives for something more exciting.

Still, serious interest in the hippie lifestyle was confined to a relatively small group of people at the end of the 1960s.

Collecting the Biggest, the Most, and the Oddest

Americans collect everything from Pez dispensers to antiques, but some Americans excel at collecting. On the Internet, sites reveal the full range of people's obsessions; there are over 31,000,000 Internet sites related to collecting and hobbies, including sites that allow collectors to trade and purchase records, books, china, stamps, coins, and toys. Nostalgia collections are big business with baby boomers, especially memorabilia from childhood or adolescence, like old lunch boxes, vintage Barbies, Beatles bubble gum cards, and Lionel trains. The Internet site eBay enables collectors to connect with one another across great distances, but many interest groups also maintain newsletters or hold annual conventions as well. It is difficult to predict what current collections will attain this kind of status, but Beanie Babies were popular toys to collect and exchange in the late 1990s and today's children enjoy trading Pokemon cards and Star Wars collectibles. Traditionally, the most popular items to collect in the United States include stamps, coins, antiques, books, and dolls.

Middle-class Americans' leisure was not all that different in the 1960s than in the 1950s. There were more gadgets, to be sure, and more toys aimed at the baby boomers (like skateboards and Hot Wheels cars), but the largest segment of Americans' free time was spent watching television. The 1960s were marked by a great deal of protest and change, but in leisure terms those changes didn't reach the population until the 1970s.

1960s • Expanding Leisure Opportunities ~ What did change was greater access to leisure for more people. For most of the 1960s, the nation enjoyed affluent times coming after an earlier decade of affluence. The result was that more Americans had the money to spend on leisure. Working-class people had access to paid vacations, to color TVs, and to skis. People of color had gained access to facilities once reserved for middle-class whites. Elderly Americans, once the poorest segment of the population, lived longer in the 1960s, but were better able to enjoy their free time thanks to pensions. Not until the 1960s could many people retire and still have the money to travel or indulge in hobbies. In the 1950s and 1960s, the American economy depended for a large part on consumerism, and consumerism was—to a certain extent—about leisure

Leisure was also elevated in the eyes of Americans to a more central spot in their lives. Televised sports, for instance, consumed more time on the weekly schedule. By 1970, professional football games were no longer just played (or televised) on Sundays, but also Monday nights. As the seasons for many sports lengthened, as leagues expanded, and as technology improved broadcast techniques, sports enthusiasts devoted more of their free time to watching games. By the 1960s, not only had sports expanded, so too had movies. Suburban malls added movie theaters to their offerings, simplifying options for people who, heretofore, had often had to travel into city centers to see first-run films. Fast food chains like Kentucky Fried Chicken, Taco Bell, Burger King, and McDonald's, enabled more people to eat out more frequently.

By the 1960s, few leisure taboos remained. Despite occasional expert commentary on the quality and nature of America's leisure activities (such as Newton Minnow's warning that the American television was a "vast wasteland"), few really concerned themselves with whether or not their leisure activities made them better people. While the Counterculture critiqued a lot of mainstream American culture for being bland, plastic, and conforming, certainly no one in the Counterculture disputed the value of leisure. Indeed, the Counterculture was about having more leisure and less work. Whatever one's class status, race, age, or region of the country, there was a general sense that the good life meant taking time to indulge one's desires, interests, and hobbies, and that time off was a good thing.

1970s • Self Indulgence ~ The hippie lifestyle and other social changes that began in the 1960s altered the American landscape. Young people waited longer to marry. Some lived with partners. The economic downturn of the 1970s meant that fewer children were able to recreate their parents' affluence. Many, though, were less interested in doing so than in finding fulfillment. This reflected the self-absorption of the decade and the hippie-inspired emphasis on self-improvement and personal

1970s Television Reflects a New Kind of Family

TV Show	"Pseudo" Family
The Mary Tyler Moore Show	Coworkers at a TV station
M*A*S*H	Military hospital during the Korean War
Three's Company	Roommates
Mork and Mindy	Human and space alien roommates
Alice	Widow, her son, and coworkers at a diner
WKRP in Cincinnati	Coworkers at a radio station
One Day at a Time	Divorced mother and daughters

growth. In leisure terms this meant more people devoted themselves to self-focused activities that helped them remake themselves.

Certainly the leisure subculture reflected this tendency. Television took a turn toward relevance in the early 1970s, replacing fantasy shows like *The Beverly Hillbillies* with programs like *The Mary Tyler Moore Show*, which featured a young, single woman negotiating her career and romantic life. The networks turned to relevancy in the 1970s precisely because their audiences were increasingly single and interested in seeing models of this singles lifestyle. Movies, too, moved away from family features and toward personal exploration and growth as a theme in films like *Last Tango in Paris* (1973).

For some people, personal growth meant participating in one of the many movements of the decade. Encounter groups of various kinds flourished, as did classes to teach yoga, meditation, and various eastern philosophies. Most of these existed outside the workplace and for the personal consumption of individuals on their own time. This kind of leisure activity had purpose; but it was self-focused. Families did not participate in self-actualization training; individuals did. At an extreme, cults existed, which not only occupied their adherents' leisure hours, but the whole of their lives. Some of these were religious; others were more political. Most involved communal living arrangements that took individuals away from the traditional family structure. For some Americans, most of their free time in the 1970s was about making themselves better, stronger, or more spiritual. Ironically, this was precisely the same goal of leisure activities for the middle class in earlier times, only in the 1970s society accepted it as self-indulgent, rather than social activity.

1970s • PHYSICAL FITNESS ~ The self-improvement aspect of the decade also had its physical dimension. Physical fitness in the 1970s was motivated mainly by health and beauty concerns. Doctors noted that the sedentary nature of many jobs plus the popularity of television made Americans overweight and unhealthy. They urged Americans to become physically active. Jogging, aerobics, cross-country skiing, and ten-speed bicycles offered leisure activities that got people moving. Backpacking, perhaps reflecting the Counterculture's back-to-nature emphasis, became a popular form of camping, and public hiking trails long maintained (like California's John Muir Trail) were sometimes as crowded as freeways during rush hour. Jogging became extremely popular in the 1970s. Across the country, malls, running clubs, and charities began organizing 5 kilometer (5K) races. Soon runners could subscribe to magazines like *Runner's World*, read books like *The Complete Runner*, and buy specially-designed jogging shorts and running shoes (like Nike's famed waffle trainer). The jogging shorts—short, tight, and made of nylon—became a symbol of the 1970s emphasis on physical fitness by showing off muscle and sexuality.

Until the 1970s, the world of sports was primarily masculine; but that changed thanks, in part, to the women's movement and related legislation. Title IX of the Educational Amendments (1972) opened up school sports to girls and, ultimately, had a profound impact on how girls spent their leisure time. In 1971, fewer than 300,000 girls nationwide participated in school sports, compared to 3.6 million boys. By 1998, 2.5 million girls and 3.7 million boys participated in school sports. In 1973, professional tennis player Billie Jean King defeated Bobby Riggs in a nationally televised match that reflected the growing feminist movement. King was *Sports Illustrated* magazine's first sportswoman of the year in 1971. Although professional sports for women had long existed, the 1970s marked the first decade of public visibility. The performance of Soviet gymnast Olga Korbet during the 1976 Olympics popularized gymnastics to a generation of pre-teen girls. New forms of physical activity also appeared in the 1970s and were aimed specifically at women. Actress Jane Fonda helped popularize aerobics with her workout studios and videotapes.

The Rise of Female Participation in NCAA Sports

Year	Number of Men Participating	Number of Women Participating
1981-82	167,055	64,390
1986-87	187,561	89,640
1991-92	183,672	94,920
1995-96	206,366	125,268
1998-99	207,592	145,832

SOURCE: *World Almanac and Book of Facts*, 2000

In the world of professional sports, hockey gained popularity, along with the continued popularity of football, baseball, and basketball. Also growing in popularity during the decade was soccer—not as a professional sport, but for boys and girls playing in local leagues. In general, sports programs diversified during the 1970s and athletes participated in a greater variety of sports than ever.

1970s • THE WILD LIFE ~ Values on the fringes in the 1960s spread to the more mainstream culture by the 1970s, which made the prevailing leisure culture more single-oriented and more influenced by the Counterculture than heretofore. One of those was relative tolerance for drug use, especially marijuana in the early 1970s and cocaine in the late 1970s. The 1970s also marked an era of remarkable sexual freedom. Singles bars became a place where people in search of what were known as "one night stands" (sexual liaisons with strangers) could link up with one another. Alcohol use, briefly scorned by the Counterculture, revived, and no college party was complete without a keg of beer. Americans had already rejected many of the moral and religious constraints once socially imposed on

(1968) Two holidaymakers on a water toboggan at Cypress Gardens, Florida.

1970s leisure. Once the family constraints were gone, a party lifestyle emerged that was particularly appealing to young single people squeezed by the worsening economy. Rock concerts became big business in the 1970s, moving to large venues (like stadiums), featuring sets and props, and selling t-shirts and related items along with tickets. Popular performers like the Rolling Stones, the Bee Gees, and Peter Frampton conveyed in their songs and presentations the decadence that was endemic in the era.

Part of the emerging leisure lifestyle was thrill-seeking. Things like sky diving challenged some young people. Others skied or sailed. Travels to places off-the-beaten track were also popular with young people, especially tropical places where singles congregated. Such activities were often expensive, suggesting that Americans, especially single Americans, pumped a larger percentage of their annual income into leisure activities than ever before.

1970s • MOVIE AND TV RENAISSANCE

The 1970s marked an era when American movies experimented with new themes, reflecting the freedom of the era as well as the willingness to push traditional boundaries. The blockbuster films, *Jaws* (1975) and *Star Wars* (1977), attracted large summer crowds. Films attempted to address political and social issues too, like *All the President's Men* (1976). A lot of movies made during the decade were designed to appeal to young people; the baby boom had reached college and beyond in the 1970s and, as young, single adults, had an especially large impact on the movie industry. Movies like *Animal House* (1978), *Blazing Saddles* (1974), and *The Rocky Horror Picture Show* (1975), which became a cult classic by the end of the 1970s, targeted the youth audience. Decadence was often a theme in 1970s movies. The popular film, *Cabaret* (1972), for instance, focused on café society in 1930s Berlin. *Rocky*

Nielsen's Top Ten Rated TV Shows for 1977-78

1. Laverne and Shirley
2. Happy Days
3. Three's Company
4. Charlie's Angels
5. All in the Family
6. Little House on the Prairie
7. 60 Minutes
8. M*A*S*H
9. One Day at a Time
10. Alice

SOURCE: *Total Television* by Alex McNeil, 1980

Horror contrasted the wholesome life with transvestites. And *Shampoo* (1975) told the story of a shallow, over-sexed male hairdresser.

Although the most important TV trend in the 1970s was the move toward more realistic programs, such as *All in the Family* and *Good Times*, excess was often present in television too. By mid-decade, the sexualization of American culture was evident in such programs as *Charlie's Angels* and *Three's Company*. In fact, it was so evident on television that it had a nickname: "jiggle TV." Hardly "relevant" in the way *All in the Family* might be, it nevertheless reflected back other aspects of 1970s culture, especially with its emphasis on young, single people, sexuality, and skimpy costumes.

1970s • Lifestyle and Leisure ~ Traditionally, career defined middle-class Americans' sense of themselves. In the 1970s, however, their lifestyle, and especially their leisure, better expressed who they were. This trend had several causes. One was the increasing amount of time young people spent unmarried, which gave them more time to develop individual tastes and hobbies. A second was the sluggish economy, which kept young people out of jobs they desired. A third was the Counterculture, which encouraged Americans to see the political, social, and environmental ramifications of their personal choices. Dress, hobbies, home decorations, and other lifestyle choices instantly communicated the status and philosophy of people in the 1970s. How one spent one's leisure was a large portion of this image.

High culture was not as valued in the 1970s as perhaps in other decades. There was less interest in reading, in symphonic music, or in art. Magazine sales declined and several (like *Look*) discontinued publication. Many people were entertained by the concept of *kitsch*, or deliberately lowbrow taste. Collectors, for example, went after colorful Depression-era Fiestaware dishes and 1950s chrome and formica tables. While upper class Americans used to collect antiques, now a broader segment of the population went after what were known as "collectibles" (objects less than 75 years old), many of them reflecting the popular culture. Lunchboxes with television stars from the 1950s, for example, became popular. The Pet Rock (a rock in a box) was a fad in the mid-1970s.

Beginning in the middle 1970s, the disco phenomenon focused American attention once again on youth, only this time on working-class youth. Disco was in some ways the antithesis of the hippie movement, but it was also a leisure activity that was more important to many of its supporters than their jobs. Clubs across the country opened their doors to young people. Disco did not involve live music, but recorded disco music with a driving beat played by disc jockeys. Clubs became meeting spots for disco enthusiasts. The dress was sexy and form fitting, clearly more formal than the loose-fitting hippie look. Disco was a way of life, one that revolved around clubs like New York's Studio 54, and involved drugs, alcohol, and sex as well as dancing. The lifestyle was captured in the movie *Saturday Night Fever* (1977). Disco fascinated many Americans, and its focus on dance affected even many who scorned the movement itself.

1970s • Subcultures ~ At the end of the decade another youth trend emerged: punk. Drawing on currents from New York City and London, punks

(1971) Dancers demonstrating a home disco at the Ideal Home Exhibition.

1970s were young people who rebelled against the culture. They were somewhat nihilistic in their attitudes. Punk, like disco, was a way of life that included a subculture focused around clubs, music, drugs, and dancing. Unlike the disco subculture, punks deliberately rejected middle-class American culture, including its leisure activities. The quintessential American punk band was the Ramones, who specialized in short-but-loud three-chord songs. British punks tended to be working class in background and an expression of frustration, but in the United States the punk subculture appealed more to middle-class teenagers.

Black pride movements that grew out of the Civil Rights movement helped focus leisure for African-American young people. Funk, a kind of black disco, emerged around the same time as disco. A fascination with things African also influenced dress, food, and décor. Yet as more African Americans moved into the American mainstream, their children often enjoyed the same leisure activities as whites, including sports and movies. Poorer blacks, however, were unable to afford the increasing number of tools necessary to enjoy the middle class's version of leisure–powerboats and skis and Club Med vacations. Their recreations tended to be more family- or community-based. In the 1970s, many black churches, like other fundamentalist churches, grew in size and strength. Religion offered urban blacks a community focus, a place to pray, sing, meet, and work for the community. Because of gains from the Civil Rights Movement, many African Americans who were successful felt obligated to give back to their communities in their leisure hours, organizing sports programs in the inner cities, tutoring teenagers, or renovating houses.

The gay liberation movement (beginning in 1969) generated a flamboyant gay subculture distinctly focused around leisure. Its center was the Castro neighborhood of San Francisco. There, and in similar clusters in other large cities, gays existed in sufficient numbers to dominate the local culture, including clubs, movie theaters, and parks. Gay men had a lot of disposable income, which made them attractive to entrepreneurs. The emphasis was on having fun and meeting others, often strictly for sex. Because gay men had lived in the shadows for so long, many particularly enjoyed being visible. Thus, gay pride parades, drawing on a tradition of parades in American society, became one way of making the culture very visible to others.

1970s • SUBURBAN MIDDLE CLASS
~ Even amongst the suburban middle class, leisure changed in the 1970s. Although the decade was not as affluent as the 1960s or the 1950s, the middle class still had the leisure to spend on itself and the general ethos of the times meant that many indulged in things they wanted–European vacations, hot tubs, antiques. In many families, leisure became more gender-divided with men spending more time in sports-related activities and women spending more time shopping. The middle class also absorbed the young's tendency to express themselves in leisure terms and to regard their hobbies as statements of who they were. Thus, hobbyists saw nothing wrong with devoting time and money to their hobbies, be they model railroads, knitting, or raising orchids.

By the end of the decade, there were signs that Americans were tiring of the decadence of the 1970s. Young people might have enjoyed leisure centered around disco or one represented by the party-hardy lifestyle, but as the boomers aged, many were finally ready to settle down, find permanent jobs, and consider families of their own. The leisure excesses of the 1970s disappeared almost as quickly as they appeared.

1980s • BEYOND THE "ME" DECADE
~ As disco died out and the Reagan years began, Americans became more sober about their work ethic and, consequently, the public fascination with some aspects of the 1970s lifestyle declined. While the fitness boom remained, Nancy Reagan's "just say no" to drugs campaign had its impact. The economy improved, but not for the poorest Americans. In fact, many middle-class Americans needed two incomes to hang onto middle-class status. During the Reagan era the public's fascination shifted to the lifestyles of the very wealthy, like Donald Trump or Lee Iaccoca, but few Americans could actually aspire to their lifestyles. Most Americans found themselves working harder than ever and with less time for leisure.

Even though many Americans do not read books, the art of reading revived somewhat after the 1970s. Several factors contributed to this rediscovery of a very old-fashioned form of leisure. One was the emergence of specialty reading series, like

---

Gender and Reading Preferences

~

Gender stereotypes are alive and well, if recent polls are accurate. They suggest that men's and women's choices when selecting books, magazines, or television programs conform to traditional assumptions about the genders. Men's top choices were sports (41%), government and politics (29%), finance and investment (21%), and technology and the Internet (19%). Women's top choices, on the other hand, were personal health issues (34%), entertainment and celebrities (32%), and government and politics (23%). Romance novels and mysteries remain popular leisure reading forms for women, while men tend to be more attracted to spy, crime, and suspense books. Both men and women enjoy biography, although more women than men read biography. Both also read self-help books, although the kinds of self-help books they read also vary by gender.

romance novels and mysteries. Such niche literature had always existed, but was easier for consumers to obtain thanks to mall bookstore chains like B. Dalton or, later, Barnes and Noble superstores. The talk show host, Oprah Winfrey, encouraged reading by showcasing particular books. Books on tape also attracted new readers. The overlap between books and movies also drew new readers to bestsellers. By the 1980s, supermarkets routinely sold romance novels and self-help books, but many Americans got their books at public libraries. In 1993, there were 9,050 public libraries in the United States. With the new baby boom of the 1980s (when boomers had children), parents were eager to inculcate their children with a love of reading, and this brought many Americans back to the library.

Yuppies (young, urban professionals) emerged mid-decade and while they actually constituted but a small percentage of the country, the yuppie mentality took hold and redefined leisure. Yuppies worked hard and found little time for pleasure, but in their free time they played very hard. Yuppie leisure included fitness, but more for show than for the joy of the act itself. Yuppies tended to frequent gyms and classes rather than exercise outside on their own. Fitness, for them, was about self-discipline and self-esteem. Aerobics classes were marketed to attractive, upscale working women who wanted to look good and become competitive. That image was popularized by the movie *Flashdance* (1983) in which a pretty, feisty and ambitious young woman evolves from a welder by day to achieve her dream of becoming a dancer through the discipline of physical fitness.

Yuppies were also interested in a kind of competitive eating. Different food fads came and went in the 1980s—jumbo muffins, frozen yogurt, Cajun cuisine, croissants, and pasta to name a few. Yuppie eating occurred in restaurants and was a way of demonstrating that one knew all the latest places and trends. Yuppie vacationing was very high energy. It was not tourism in the sense of going places to see things, but involved lots of physical activities at resorts where Americans were actually sheltered from the local lifestyle in places like Cancun or Jamaica. So-called extreme sports of the 1990s had their roots in the yuppie penchant for things like para-sailing and bungee jumping. Yuppies had little interest in cultural activities like reading or symphonic music. Some cultural commentators explained yuppie tastes in compensatory terms, arguing that since they could not afford the finer things in life their parents could at their ages (like single-family homes), yuppies indulged themselves in smaller ways, buying fresh-roasted coffee beans they ground themselves, designer sneakers, and health club memberships.

Yuppies were urban-based and leisure life to some extent swung back into the cities in the 1980s. Some of this was facilitated by subway systems in places like the Washington D.C. area and the San Francisco Bay Area that made it possible for suburbanites to also venture into the city for an evening or on a weekend. City centers revitalized, offering expanded urban malls (like Water Tower Place in Chicago) with movie theaters, nightclubs, and restaurants. Although suburbs continued to expand, most Americans regarded their cultural possibilities as negligible and their recreational options as family oriented rather than hip.

1980s • HOME ENTERTAINMENT

Family entertainment made a comeback in the mid-to-late 1980s. As job stress

American Film Institute's List of the Top Ten Movies of All Time

1. Citizen Kane (1941)
2. Casablanca (1942)
3. The Godfather (1972)
4. Gone with the Wind (1939)
5. Lawrence of Arabia (1962)
6. The Wizard of Oz (1939)
7. The Graduate (1967)
8. On the Waterfront (1954)
9. Schindler's List (1993)
10. Singin' in the Rain (1952)

SOURCE: *World Almanac and Book of Facts*, 2000

---

increased, fewer and fewer people were interested in going out in the evening. As houses grew larger and more commodious, more people wanted to stay home and relax. As boomers settled down, married, and had children of their own, going out became more complicated. In fact, by the late 1980s, a term described the staying-home phenomenon, "cocooning." Technology also made the home a comfortable leisure space. VCRs enabled people to watch rented movies at home. Cable TV expanded their viewing options still further. CD players provided excellent sound quality for those interested in music. Answering machines could record calls, so those who did not want to be bothered by interruptions did not have to be. And, microwave ovens could cook meals or popcorn in a manner of minutes. For those without microwaves or the time to grocery shop, food could be delivered or picked up on the way home. In the 1980s in a few large cities, entrepreneurs experimented with drive-thru grocery stores where people could collect their groceries without leaving their cars. By the late 1990s, on-line grocery stores enabled at least a few people to order food on-line and have it delivered.

1980s • MALLS ~ Home could even offer shopping in the 1980s and shopping continued to dominate Americans' free time. Catalog stores like Eddie Bauer and L.L. Bean enabled middle-class people to shop from the privacy of their homes. On-line shopping surged in 1998-99, pioneered by Amazon.com, which sold books, videos, and CDs. In 2001, Americans spent $235 billion on-line. Still, while catalogs could be read in the evening and the Internet made it possible to—as one e-business advertised—shop in your underwear, going out to shop had its own kind of allure. Mini malls and strip malls, located near residential areas,

(1941) With the advent of VCRs people could rent movies. What a luxury to stay at home to watch what is widely considered the best movie of all time "Citizen Kane."

1990s

were convenient, safe, and quick places to get cash, rent a video, or buy a dozen bagels. Full-sized malls got bigger and more elaborate in the 1980s and 1990s, suggesting that shopping wasn't just about convenience, but also luxury. The culmination of this trend was the 1992 construction of the Mall of America in Bloomington, Minnesota. The Mall of America offered not only a traditional mall, but an amusement park in its center, a college, an aquarium, and a tier of nightclubs and theaters. People from all over the world flew to the Mall of America to "power shop" and leave, some never even venturing outside.

Beginning in the 1970s, but becoming more significant in the 1980s and 1990s, suburban malls became a center of teen activity. Teens frequented malls because they required little money and their parents found them acceptable places to congregate. As more teens flowed into the malls, mall owners introduced amenities that appealed to them, like video arcades, fast food outlets, and multi-plex theaters. Teens not only shopped at the malls; they also constituted a fair percentage of the workforce at malls. The presence of teens on both sides of the cash register sometimes alarmed other customers and some of the larger malls instituted control mechanisms, including curfews, by the late 1990s. A distinctive mall culture existed, especially in the 1990s, represented by popular teenage singers like Tiffany and Debbie Gibson, or, less flattering, by the song, "Valley Girl." The movie, *Fast Times at Ridgemont High* (1982), displayed the sub-culture most completely.

1980s-1990s • CARS ~ One reason for the existence of a mall culture for teenagers was the likelihood that many members of any teenage group had their own cars or regular access to the family car. By the 1990s especially, more Americans spent more time in cars than ever. Cars helped blur the line between leisure and work because, thanks to fast food drive-thru windows, they could serve as private restaurants. With tape decks and CD players and car phones, it was possible to "multi-task," a 1990s term for doing multiple things at once. Cars had long been popular with teenagers both for the mobility they offered and their privacy. By the 1980s, cars offered American workers their own private moments of leisure snatched in the middle of the workday. Despite environmental concerns, cars became larger in the 1990s, especially as more consumers sought out 4-wheel drive SUVs (Sports Utility Vehicles). Regularly promoted with images of nature that suggested their drivers used them for camping, skiing, or wilderness ventures, most were merely ways of providing a larger, comfortable, and safer driving experience. The notion that cars were perceived by Americans as part of leisure rather than work was perhaps best symbolized by that increasingly ubiquitous piece of equipment, the cup-holder.

Number of Automobiles Registered in the United States

Year	Number of Cars Registered
1980	121,600,843
1985	127,885,193
1990	133,700,497
1995	128,386,775
1998	131,838,538

SOURCE: U.S. Department of Transportation, Bureau of Highways

1980s-1990s • Sports ~ Fitness remained an American leisure time passion in the 1980s and 1990s, even as Americans were more out of shape by the end of the century. Malls, for instance, invited shoppers to "mall walk" their perimeters, hoping that, thereafter, they would stop to shop or eat a snack. Americans loved sports, but they loved watching them more than participating themselves. Indeed, technology made it possible to watch sports at virtually any hour of the day or night. Cable TV networks like ESPN catered specifically to sports enthusiasts and showed a variety of sports, including women's sports. In 2000, fully 21 percent of all adults surveyed regularly watched *Monday Night Football*. New sports challenged the ascendancy of the traditional big three (baseball, basketball, and football), including golf, wrestling and ice-skating, the latter popular with female viewers as well as male. "Extreme sports," that challenged participants to challenge limits by going faster and higher, proved popular with the new generation of sports enthusiasts. Sports is no longer a male pursuit; fully a third of all TV viewers of professional football are female. With so many girls engaged in sports in high school, interest remains high with women, both as spectators and participants. Women today cheer for and are involved in women's professional soccer, basketball, and hockey. The soccer mom, who drives her children to team sports and watches and sometimes coaches them, has become so ubiquitous that politicians even courted her in the 1990s. And, men and women discovered cross country skiing and rollerblading in large numbers in the 1980s and rediscovered skateboards and experimented with snowboards in the 1990s.

1980s-1990s • Computers ~ Beginning in the 1980s, the home computer became a source of leisure for growing numbers of Americans. In the 1970s a few enthusiasts began to build computers in their garages, much as young boys built crystal radio sets nearly a century before. In the 1980s, the first home computers went on the market. At first their uses were limited, but modems, the Internet, and the World Wide Web changed all that in the 1990s. By the end of the century more American homes than not had computers in them and some 80 million Americans surfed the 'net. The expense and technological expertise necessary to buy and install a computer have limited computer-related hobbies' popularity. Poorer Americans and older Americans are more likely to be excluded from this increasingly popular form of leisure entertainment. Sociologists predicted that the use of home computers would isolate Americans and occupy all their free time. In fact, many Internet users compensated for time spent on the computer by cutting back on other leisure activities, particularly TV watching. And, e-mail and personal webpages made it possible for families and friends to stay in communication with one another on a day-to-day basis. Grandparents, for example, viewed pictures of grandchildren born far away. The Internet also facilitated connections between hobbyists, collectors, and sports enthusiasts. Runners could check their race results on-line; on-line auctions allowed collectors to swap goods; chat rooms facilitated discussions about rare stamps or sports memorabilia.

1980s-1990s • Video Games ~ Video games got their start in the 1970s with Pong, a clumsy version of electronic ping pong. By the 1980s, these games

1980s–1990s

were housed in large arcades where, for a quarter, you could play such popular games as Pac-Man, Ms. Pac-Man, and Frogger. Also beginning in the 1970s, home video games existed, but it was not until the late 1980s, with the refinement of the Nintendo system, that these games achieved large popularity. Nintendo games hooked into TVs, could be played by one or two players, and offered variety in the form of game cartridges. Further refinements continued into the 1990s as computer technology improved. Video games drew many critics concerned with the violence, sometimes sexual images, and the absence of games appealing to girls. Hand-held video games, particularly the Game Boy system, were popular with younger boys beginning in the middle 1990s. In the mid-1990s, there was a brief flurry of interest in virtual reality games, but the set-up proved to be too costly for most entrepreneurs and most venues closed rather quickly.

1990s • Structuring Leisure Time ~ In general, in the 1980s and 1990s, entertainment-related gadgets became more costly and more complicated, creating a two-tiered system of leisure that is not only divided by class but also, sometimes by age and gender. CD players, DVD players, video cameras, and treadmills cost money but also required some expertise and tended to intimidate some potential users. Each was intended to give the individual more control over his or her leisure, a quality that became a status symbol for middle-class people as their lives became more complex. The two-income couple became a way of life in these decades, putting increasing stress on families and, at the same time, making couples busier. Treadmills and VCRs allowed people to pursue leisure when they could fit it in, all in the privacy of their own homes. But gadgets have also made it possible to blur the line between leisure and work. Cell phones, for instance, ostensibly offer freedom, but mean that even during leisure time people are still tied to their jobs. The same is true of modems, pagers, and fax machines, all of which allow middle-class jobs to intrude on free time.

Yuppies taught Americans to structure their leisure time more purposefully and this remains a common strategy within the middle class. Middle-class children, for instance, are often scheduled into activities, including play dates and games. Magazines advise busy women to schedule their visits to the gym, make dates with their husbands, and even plan sex in advance. The manufacturers of games urge Americans to plan a family game night once a week. Marketers recognize the commercial possibilities of training Americans to regularize their leisure activities. This structuring of leisure time occurs primarily because the middle class has more free money than free time. Working-class families have been more resistant to this trend and more inclined to conceive of leisure in terms of the freedom to do what they want when they want it. Leisure remains a concept affected by class status and money.

Top Five U.S. Theme Parks

1. Walt Disney World (Orlando, Florida)
2. Disneyland (Anaheim, California)
3. Epcot Center (Orlando, Florida)
4. Universal Studios (Orlando, Florida)
5. Seaworld (Orlando, Florida)

SOURCE: *Amusement Business*. September 2000

1980s-1990s • TRAVEL ~ Because of two-income families, Americans—whatever their class—have more money for travel, but less time. The mini-vacation, which often extends a three-day weekend, became a trend in the 1980s and 1990s. Fewer families rough it on vacation any longer. Camping and backpacking, very popular in the 1960s and 1970s, have given way to family vacations at resorts like Walt Disney World. And when families camp these days, they more often do it in large recreational vehicles than in traditional tents. International travel is also popular, especially during years when the dollar is strong internationally. And many of those who ventured abroad chose less-well-traveled paths. Although many international travelers were bound for Europe, increasing numbers sought out Asian destinations or Australia. Far more commercialized resorts existed in the 1990s than ever before, including casinos on Indian reservations, theme parks, the concert stages in Branson, Missouri, and fantasy camps for sports enthusiasts.

As the American population aged, increasing attention was paid to the leisure activities of America's senior citizens. Currently the wealthiest segment of the population, retired people have the most leisure time. Travel is a popular activity for older people, encouraged in part by the availability in many places of senior discounts. Senior traveling has been facilitated by the recreational vehicle, which has become the primary home for some retired persons. Seniors are very popular with those in the travel business because they tend to stay on vacation longer and opt for more luxurious accommodations than families with young children. Since seniors often travel year round and seek out popular destinations on the off season, they provide income when other travelers do not. Although some retired Americans travel for recreation, in search of particular sports activities, or to link up with friends, others want learning experiences. One very popular, albeit expensive, program for seniors has been the Elder Hostels, which offer educational tours of many kinds. Such travelers, for example, can learn about the tulip industry in the Netherlands, cooking in France, or the rain forest in Brazil.

Traveler Spending in the United States

Year	Billions of Dollars Spent by U.S. Domestic Travelers	Billions of Dollars Spent by U.S. International Travelers
1990	291	43
1992	306	55
1994	340	58
1996	386	70
1998	446	74

SOURCE: *World Almanac and Book of Facts, 2000*

1980s-1990s • COLLECTORS ~ Collections increased in numbers and variety in the 1980s and 1990s. One of the reasons why was the increased visibility of various kinds of collecting, in part facilitated by the Internet. At the same time, commercial enterprises have entered the collectible market, manufacturing commemorative coins, plates, and figurines along with the means to display them. Yet the collection mania has also been fed by baby boomers eager to reconnect with childhood memorabilia. Today one can collect anything from Barbie dolls to Flintstone glasses. Beanie babies, small stuffed toys, were

(1970) Russian-born writer Vladimir Nabokov (1899 - 1977) was almost as renowned for collecting butterflies as for writing novels. Here, he is in a forest near Montreux, Switzerland.

1990s an exception to the notion that boomers wanted items from their pasts. While millions of children collected Beanies because they were cute and cuddly, their mothers were more likely to consider their market value, a style of collecting that historians suggest was traditionally "male." About one in three Americans today collects something, whether it is coins, stamps or baseball cards. Television commercials routinely pitch collectibles. Despite the seeming modernity of collecting in the 1980s and 1990s, it represents a hobby with deep roots in American leisure culture.

1990s • TELEVISION ~ Although there existed, at century's end, a vast number of leisure activities, the number one leisure activity in 1999 remained television watching. Despite all the attacks on television as banal, the unflattering description of the "couch potato," and doctors' warnings about the increasing obesity of the population, people find TV soothing and mindless. Yet it is also true that television is no longer just a form of leisure, but also a source of information about leisure. Cable stations like the Golf Channel or Home and Garden TV teach people to improve their swing or to make a torte. The popularity of television symbolizes many leisure trends. Television watching takes place in private; like much of American leisure today it does not occur in a public space. TV can, today, be controlled so that people can watch what they want when they want to. TV is also expensive; there is a gap between what a poor viewer can watch and what a richer viewer linked to satellite TV or premium cable options can see. TV is technological; it comes in enhanced versions, big-screens, and other choices. TV is commercial; it is consumed and viewers make choices, just as Americans buy other leisure forms and make choices about them based on information given them from enterprises with vested interests in those choices. And,

A Snapshot of some Aspects of American Leisure in 1997

Leisure Object	Total Number in the U.S.	In Use per 1,000 Population
Radio	570,000,000	2,116
Television	217,000,000	805
Newspaper	103,000,000	391
Telephone	133,577,000	518
Automobile	136,000,000	500

SOURCE: *World Almanac and Book of Facts, 2000*

because its viewers can "multi-task," watching TV while paying bills, doing homework, or folding laundry, people feel less guilty about spending time frivolously when they watch it.

CONCLUSION

Although leisure has changed in its many dimensions, many debates remain. In 1900, middle-class tastes defined what was appropriate and what was not in terms of leisure. That definition was based on moral, religious, and practical beliefs. By the end of the twentieth century, marketing decisions, more than any other single factor, shape American leisure. Because leisure is a multi-billion dollar industry, focus groups, surveys, polls, and ratings systems determine what will or will not be available. Certainly individual Americans have freedom of choice, but their choices are affected by advertising, marketing decisions, and the like. There has been a long debate in American history about whether advertising shapes demand or reflects it. Leisure spending, more flexible than spending on housing, transportation, or food, is a relatively unpredictable area of the economy, but one entrepreneurs would very much like to control.

Technology has had an immense impact on leisure habits. Two of the most common reasons why Americans seek out new technology are to free up time for leisure and to fill leisure time. Electricity, transistors, plastics, computers, and satellites have all affected leisure choices. Americans, on the whole, are attracted to gadgets and technology and this has been especially true of gadgets and technology freely chosen out of interest (as opposed to required at work). Part of the allure of technology seems to be the sense of modernity something new offers as well as the feeling of being part of a trend.

Across the span of the twentieth century, technology freed up more time for Americans. During the late twentieth century different commentators reached different conclusions about how hard Americans worked. Some argued they worked fewer hours than ever and indulged in much leisure during the actual work day while others suggested that technology so blurred the line between working and not working that Americans logged in more hours on their jobs. Whichever is true, the average worker in 2000 worked fewer hours than the average worker in 1900 and could look forward to more paid vacation time and retirement at the end of his/her lifespan. The physical nature of work changed too, because of technology. Even factory work is different and many blue-collar workers assemble small electronic items rather than automobiles. The end result is that the average worker is not so physically tired at the end of his/her working day and, often, seeks some kind of physical experience after a long workday spent sitting. Perhaps for this reason, some employers provide on-site gym facilities or mid-day classes.

Ideology has also changed. In the nineteenth century, many American families still functioned as economic units and the desires of any one member were less important than the needs of the collectivity. This unselfishness extended to leisure. The middle class pioneered the idea of family as a launching ground for the individual; but for much of the twentieth century, family leisure unity prevailed. By the last few decades of the century, however, individualism predominated. The more individual leisure became, the more it expressed personal tastes, talents, and interests. Today leisure is not just relaxing, recharging, or winding down; it is a personal statement.

Despite all this, Americans still often feel guilty about indulging in leisure, especially when that leisure is truly about doing nothing productive. Perhaps that is why so many race to fill up their leisure hours with activities. It is just as hard to do nothing in 2000 as 1900. Although in many of its dimensions, American leisure looked very different at the end of the century than at the beginning, many commonalities remained. Americans still liked to read, walk, travel, play sports, collect things, and be with one another in their free time. Leisure was still partly differentiated by age, race, class status, and location. However much Americans worry about leisure, in 2000 they were more committed to it, in terms of hours and money devoted to leisure activities, and sheer numbers, than they had been a century before. The pursuit of leisure dominated not just the American economy, but Americans' lives, thoughts, and values.

BIBLIOGRAPHY

Aron, Cindy. *Working at Play: A History of Vacations in the United States*. New York: Oxford, 1999.

Bailey, Beth. *From Front Porch to Back Seat: Courtship in Twentieth Century America*. Baltimore: Johns Hopkins University Press, 1989.

Baritz, Loren. *The Good Life: The Meaning of Success for the American Middle Class*. New York: Harper and Row, 1982, 1990.

Barnow, Erik. *Tube of Plenty*. Rev. ed. New York: Oxford University Press, 1982.

Bergman, Andrew. *We're in the Money: Depression America and Its Films*. Chicago: Ivan Dee, 1971.

Cross, Gary. *Kids' Stuff: Toys and the Changing World of American Childhood*. Cambridge: Harvard University Press, 1997.

Denning, Michael. *The Cultural Front: The Laboring of American Culture in the Twentieth Century*. New York: Verso, 1996.

Douglas, Susan. *Listening In: Radio and the American Imagination from Amos 'N' Andy and Edward R. Murrow to Wolfman Jack and Howard Stern*. New York: Random House, 1999.

Gelber, Steven M. *Hobbies: Leisure and the Culture of Work in America*. New York: Columbia University Press, 1999.

Grover, Kathryn, ed. *Hard at Play: Leisure in America, 1840-1940*. Amherst: University of Massachusetts Press, 1992.

Guttman, Allen. *Women's Sports: A History*. New York: Columbia University Press, 1991.

Marling, Karal Ann. *As Seen on TV: The Visual Culture of Everyday Life in the 1950s*. Cambridge: Harvard University Press, 1994.

McNeil, Alex. *Total Television*. New York: Penguin, 1980. Reprint 1984.

Nasaw, David. *Going Out: The Rise and Fall of Public Amusements*. New York: Basic Books, 1993.

Peiss, Kathy. *Cheap Amusements: Working Women and Leisure in Turn-of-the-Century New York*. Philadelphia: Temple University Press, 1986.

Perrett, Geoffrey. *Days of Sadness, Years of Triumph: The American People, 1939-1945*. Madison: University of Wisconsin Press, 1985.

Sklar, Robert. *Movie-made America: A Social History of American Movies*. New York; Random House, 1975.

Smulyan, Susan. *Selling Radio: The Commercialization of American Broadcasting, 1920-1934*. Washington, D.C.: Smithsonian Institution Press, 1994.

INTERNET RESOURCES

TRAVEL-RELATED
www.travelandleisure.com is American Express's site.

www.recreation.gov is a guide to recreation on government lands.

www.gorp.com/dow is the National Forest Service's campground guide.

SPORTS
http://sportsillustrated.cnn.com.

COLLECTING
www.collectingnation.com offers links to various more specialized sites.

http://toycollecting.about.com/m.body.html or www.barbie.com on toys.

www.stamplink.com focuses on stamp collecting.

www.ebay.com is the place for swapping and selling collectibles.

CRAFTS
www.leisurearts.com links to needlework, cooking, and home and garden sites.

www.foodtv.com is TV's Food network's site.

SHOPPING
Most stores have on-line catalogs, as in www.eddiebauer.com or www.gap.com.

www.mallofamerica.com is Minnesota's Mall of America's official web site.

MOVIES, TV, RADIO, MUSIC, BOOKS
www.afionline.org is the American Film Institute's official web site.

www.mtr.org is the Museum of Television and Radio's web site.

www.old-time.com features information about radio's golden age.

www.amazon.com sells books, movies, and music on-line.

MUSEUMS
www.si.edu is the link to the Smithsonian Institution.

www.metmuseum.org is the link to New York City's Metropolitan Museum.

Judy Kutulas
St. Olaf College